CAS PROFESSIONAL STANDARDS
FOR HIGHER EDUCATION

Seventh Edition
2009

Laura A. Dean, Ph.D.
CAS Publications Editor
Assistant Professor, College Student Affairs Administration
University of Georgia

Council for the Advancement of Standards
in Higher Education

Washington, DC

CAS Professional Standards for Higher Education
7th Edition

© Copyright 2009 by the Council for the Advancement of Standards in Higher Education

Library of Congress Cataloging-in-Publication Data
Dean, Laura A.
CAS Professional Standards for Higher Education
Includes bibliographic references.

ISBN-13: 978-1-58328-026-3
1. Student Affairs, 2. Student Services, 3. Professional Standards, 4. Advising,
5. Counseling, 6. Higher Education, 7. Learning Assistance

This book is a revision of *CAS Professional Standards* previously published in 1986, 1997, 1999, 2001, 2003, and 2006.

Council for the Advancement of Standards in Higher Education

CAS Professional Standards for Higher Education (7th ed.)

Table of Contents

Table of Contents, *continued*

New or revised since 2006 edition

Appendices

CAS

CAS President's Letter to the Profession

As President of the Council for the Advancement of Standards in Higher Education, I am thrilled and honored to introduce the 7th edition of the CAS Professional Standards for Higher Education. This 7th edition is released on the 30th anniversary of CAS! This edition honors the work of CAS since its founding in 1979 to advance standards for quality programs and services for students that promote student learning and development and promote the critical role of self-assessment in professional practice.

CAS is comprised of 36 member associations. The directors from those associations engage in a thoughtful and detailed consensus process to develop and approve new CAS standards or revise existing standards. The 40 CAS standards in this 7th edition were developed with expert feedback from a broad range of associations and professionals across the United States and Canada. Thirty years of this unique consensus model of advancing standards and assessment were honored by a number of associations with their contributions to higher education award in 2009 (for example, ACPA: College Student Educators International, National Council for Student Development of the American Community College Association).

The emphasis in recent years on accountability for student outcomes further emphasizes the importance of standards-based practice intentionally designed for comprehensive student learning and developmental outcomes. To support the importance of the assessment of these outcomes, this edition includes a critical revision of the CAS taxonomy of student outcomes. Building on the CAS outcomes in the 6th edition, the work of *Learning Reconsidered* (NASPA/ACPA, 2004), and other scholarship on outcomes, CAS revised the student learning and development outcomes into six broad categories (called domains): knowledge acquisition, construction, integration and application; cognitive complexity; intrapersonal development; interpersonal competence; humanitarianism and civic engagement; and practical competence. CAS asserts that all professional practice should be designed to achieve specific outcomes for students.

The CAS process is built on a commitment that all professionals are motivated to do self-assessment of their programs and services for continuous improvement. This self- assessment process is a tenet of professional practice, guided by the CAS standards and self-assessment guides.

My sincere thanks and admiration to the many CAS Directors, expert reviewers, and editors who worked diligently on behalf of our profession to advance the student experience in our colleges and universities through these standards and campus self-assessment practices. These colleagues epitomize the professionalism we all value through their full time work at their institutions, in their professional associations, and on behalf of CAS. We invite and welcome your suggestions for new standards and for advancing the work of CAS through your own associations and functional areas. It is worth the effort to examine your own practice through the CAS framework–your students will benefit!

Best Wishes,

Susan R. Komives

Susan R. Komives
CAS President
Professor, University of Maryland

References

NASPA/ACPA (2004). *Learning reconsidered: A campus-wide focus on the student experience.* Washington, DC: National Association of Student Personnel Administrators and the American College Personnel Association

Editor's Note

As I write this, at the conclusion of the process of assembling, editing, and finalizing this seventh edition of the *CAS Professional Standards for Higher Education*, I continue to be amazed at the number of voices and perspectives that have come together, found consensus, and joined to articulate these standards and related information. We often talk about the importance of collaboration in CAS and the significance of the consortium structure of the group, but as the editor, I have a unique perspective on the number of people involved in creating, revising, discussing (and discussing, and discussing), approving, proofreading, and then disseminating and educating others about the standards and the other work of the Council. I am grateful to each and every one of them.

In his remarks accepting the 2009 ACPA Contribution to Higher Education award on behalf of CAS, Ted K. Milller, one of the founders and the former president and editor for CAS, reflected on our work:

> Some contend that history is biography, in which recognition is gained through charismatic figures and not the organizations to which they belong and for which they toil. But with CAS there has been no central charismatic figure. Rather there has been a multi-organizational dedication to a central purpose, a cause that lights our way to enhancing the education and development of the students we serve. . . Small, but significant incremental progress, over time, has been the CAS mantra. And, consequently, subtle increments will continue to obtain until one day in the future, practitioners may look up and realize that higher education has changed as if struck by lightning. However, even if those differences look and feel like a bolt out of the blue, we know better. And we celebrate the increments by which we advance, one standard at a time. The *CAS Initiative* is bigger than any one person and longer than any one lifetime. . .

I was struck by Ted's remarks because they captured so well one of the things I've grown to appreciate most about CAS — the way that so many come together around a central purpose and commitment and stay dedicated to making the small changes that can make a big difference in the lives of practitioners and the students that we all serve.

As we publish this seventh edition of CAS Professional Standards in Higher Education, I do want to pause to celebrate the increments. Everyone who has touched this work throughout the process — committee members, external experts, Executive Committee members, Board members, contextual statement contributors — has influenced and enriched the final product. This book also still owes a debt to Ted Miller, whose sure hand and clear voice guided so many previous editions and laid a strong foundation for this one.

On a personal note, I am grateful to the members of the CAS Executive Committee, for their support, assistance, encouragement, and trust in me. I am also grateful to the American College Counseling Association (ACCA) for their continued support of my role as the ACCA representative to the Board; by maintaining me as their Director for over ten years, they have allowed me to accept an increasing role in the work of CAS. The University of Georgia has supported my involvement in CAS and my work as editor, and I extend my appreciation especially to the CSAA program faculty, to the Counseling and Human Development Services Department, to the College of Education, and to the students who assisted in the process. Special thanks goes to Jen Wells, whose unfailing willingness to assist, problem-solve, follow up, and take on the technical aspects of production with precision and an eye for detail have made this process much more sane and more enjoyable. Finally, thanks to the CAS Board, present and past, the amazing group of people that I am proud to call my colleagues and friends. While Ted may be right that CAS has no central charismatic figure, it is full of wonderful professionals whose voices have blended to create this book. My thanks go to them, and to all of you who work with us to be of service to our students and our institutions.

Laura A. Dean
CAS Publications Editor
Assistant Professor, College Student Affairs Administration
University of Georgia

PROLOGUE
CAS Professional Standards for Higher Education

Overview of this Edition

This 2009 edition of *CAS Professional Standards for Higher Education,* often referred to as the *CAS Blue Book* or the *CAS Book of Standards*, is the seventh iteration of professional standards generated and promulgated by the Council for the Advancement of Standards in Higher Education (CAS). This edition contains 26 previously published functional area standards, along with 9 standards that have recently undergone major revision and 5 new standards that appear for the first time in this edition. This brings the total number of functional area standards to 40, including the standard for Masters-Level Student Affairs Professional Preparation Programs. CAS continues to attract interest from professionals across higher education, whether they are seeking to use existing professional standards or to develop new ones.

As institutions of higher learning face new challenges, faculty and staff members often find it necessary to implement their responsibilities in new and different ways. Approaches and strategies that were previously successful may need to be amended as institutions and programs evolve and student populations and characteristics change. As institutions and their constituents change, so too must the vehicles that guide practice within the shifting culture. As new developments occur that result in previously unrecognized or newly identified student needs, programs and services must change as well. In light of these factors, each CAS standard must be viewed as a living document that will shift over time as it reflects an evolving function.

The standards that have been revised since the 2006 edition include those focused on Assessment Services, Campus Activities, College Unions, International Students, Learning Assistance Programs, Recreational Sports, Registrars, Student Leadership, and TRIO and Other Educational Opportunity Programs. As the field changes, so does our language, and several of these have been renamed to reflect more current philosophy and practice. Additionally, new standards have been developed in the areas of Adult Learners, Auxiliary Services, Dining Services, Graduate and Professional Students, and Undergraduate Research. Again, the development of new standards reflects the evolving nature of our work in higher education. As has been increasingly true in previous editions, the breadth of CAS standards focuses attention not only on functions that comprise the traditional student affairs areas and directly support student learning and development, but also on other educational functions essential to institutional effectiveness that may be less focused on direct work with students. This expanded CAS vision reflects an increased emphasis on developing standards to guide professional practice throughout the whole of higher education.

In addition to the inclusion of new standards and revision of existing ones, every set of standards has been embedded with the updated General Standards, which were revised in 2008. The General Standards appear within nearly every other set of standards and represent areas of practice that are essential regardless of functional area. CAS periodically reviews and updates the General Standards to ensure their currency. This revision has expanded the number of parts that comprise each set of standards to 14, adding a separate section to address the growing area of Technology. It also includes the revision of the CAS Learning and Development Outcomes, a major change in the structure of the outcome domains which is described later in this book. Finally, it aligns the General Standards with the essentials of professional practice today.

Also included in this edition are two documents that were published for the first time in the previous edition, the *CAS Characteristics of Individual Excellence* and the *CAS Statement of Shared Ethical Principles*. Both the result of extended work within CAS, these materials expand the work of CAS to the consideration of the hallmarks of high quality professional practice and of the ethical values that we hold in common across functional areas.

Rationale and Evolution

As appears obvious in retrospect, CAS was created as a direct response to the emerging profession's need to establish standards to guide both practice and preparation. By the 1960s, the felt need for a profession-wide entity to speak as one voice for all was very apparent. An initial attempt to establish such a group, the Council of Student Personnel Associations in Higher Education (COSPA), was mounted in the late 1960s by 10 student affairs associations. This consortium is best remembered for its promotion of an enlightened approach to student affairs practice reflected in a statement published in 1972 by its Commission of Professional Development entitled "Student Development Services in Post-Secondary Education"

(Rentz, 1994). Unfortunately, COSPA was dissolved in 1976, largely as a result of member disillusionment resulting from unresolved political issues.

CAS was established as a consortium comparable to COSPA for an equally important, though less ambitious, purpose. Whereas COSPA was intended to function on a full range of professional issues, CAS from the outset sought to avoid politicization and to be driven by shared values rather than special interests. Consequently, the purposes and objectives of CAS are highly focused, which tends to protect the Council from internal strife resulting from member disagreement about its designated purpose and the processes used to accomplish its mission.

Although some professional associations or inter-association collectives may work to establish standards of good practice for specific student support services, their products and models are unlikely to become part of the educational culture unless they are viewed as an enhancement to the broad educational interests of students and institutions. In other words, credibility within the whole of higher education is more effectively gained through collective action than through narrowly defined initiatives of individuals or associations. For standards of professional practice to be truly viable, they must reflect the interests and values of multiple professional organizations and the functional areas they champion. CAS strives to provide this collaborative avenue to establishing thoughtful, balanced, and achievable standards upon which all can rely.

A Legacy of Collaboration

CAS was established over thirty years ago for purposes of developing and promulgating standards of professional practice to guide higher education practitioners and their institutions, especially in regard to work with college students. The Council for the Advancement of Standards in Higher Education, a name adopted in 1992 to reflect the expanded context of the Council's higher education focus, was originally established in 1979 as a not-for-profit corporation called the Council for the Advancement of Standards for Student Services/Development Programs. Impetus for its existence was encouraged by a movement on the part of several national associations to develop accreditation standards for academic programs that prepare counselors and counselor educators. This movement, which culminated in the establishment of the Council for the Accreditation of Counseling and Related Educational Programs (CACREP) in 1980, provided the American College Personnel Association (ACPA) with impetus to

create a set of preparation standards for use in master's level college student affairs administration programs. Rather than promulgating these standards as its own, ACPA sought out other professional associations interested in the development of standards for student affairs preparation and practice. The National Association of Student Personnel Administrators (NASPA) indicated an interest in the project, and the two associations jointly issued invitations to a meeting of interested professional associations. Seven student affairs- oriented organizations sent representatives to the exploratory meeting held in Alexandria, Virginia in June 1979. This meeting resulted in the creation of an inter-association consortium for purposes of developing and promulgating professional standards to guide both student affairs practice and academic preparation of those who administer student support programs and services. A subsequent organizational meeting in September 1979 resulted in the establishment of CAS as a not-for-profit corporate consortium of 11 charter member associations (see Appendix A).

Today, after nearly three decades of collaboration and a name change to reflect its expanded interests, the Council for the Advancement of Standards in Higher Education is composed of 36 member associations from the U.S. and Canada, and has generated and promulgated 39 sets of functional area standards and guidelines, one set of master's level academic preparation program standards for college student affairs administration, statements regarding characteristics of individual excellence for professionals in higher education and the ethical principles that are held in common across the many areas of professional practice represented at CAS, and a learning and development outcomes model that reflects the most current thought on the intended results of quality practice.

Considering the history of CAS, it now seems certain that without CAS working collaboratively and speaking collectively on behalf of practitioners and their functional area specialties, there would be no profession-wide criteria of good practice such as the CAS standards. In effect, CAS desires to represent every college and university educator and functional area specialist who believes the learning and development of all students to be the essence of higher education.

A Mission of Quality Enhancement

CAS was founded to implement several profession-wide initiatives, with emphasis on the development and promulgation of professional standards. As CAS has evolved, its *raison d'être* has shifted as well. The following reflects the contemporary CAS mission, as revised in 2008:

> The mission of the Council for the Advancement of Standards in Higher Education (CAS) is to promote the improvement of programs and services to enhance the quality of student learning and development. CAS is a consortium of professional associations who work collaboratively to develop and promulgate standards and guidelines and to encourage self-assessment.

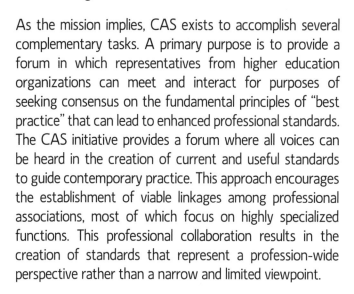

As the mission implies, CAS exists to accomplish several complementary tasks. A primary purpose is to provide a forum in which representatives from higher education organizations can meet and interact for purposes of seeking consensus on the fundamental principles of "best practice" that can lead to enhanced professional standards. The CAS initiative provides a forum where all voices can be heard in the creation of current and useful standards to guide contemporary practice. This approach encourages the establishment of viable linkages among professional associations, most of which focus on highly specialized functions. This professional collaboration results in the creation of standards that represent a profession-wide perspective rather than a narrow and limited viewpoint.

Not only does the CAS initiative provide a vehicle for the development of functional area and academic preparation standards, but it also provides a well recognized and credible profession-wide entity to publish and promulgate standards and related materials and to encourage and educate practitioners to apply the standards effectively in their work with students. Further, and of special significance, the CAS consortium speaks with a single voice that bridges numerous specialty areas and can represent the profession-at-large on matters concerning professional standards and quality assurance.

Foundations for Standards and Guidelines
The initial full CAS publication, *CAS Standards and Guidelines* (CAS, 1986), was based on the premise that practitioners needed access to a comprehensive and valid set of criteria by which to judge program quality and effectiveness. Further, it was viewed as essential that those standards represent quality practices that any college or university program could reasonably achieve.

From the CAS perspective, virtually all functional areas of practice, no matter how specialized, have identifiable commonalties with other functions. For example, an institution's admission, academic advising, campus activities, and career services programs, although established to accomplish clearly different purposes, will each benefit from establishing a written mission statement that is compatible with the mission of the institution. Likewise, the same is true for human, fiscal, physical, and technological resources; legal responsibilities; campus and community relations; ethical considerations; and assessment, among others. Consequently, CAS developed and has incorporated a number of common criteria that have relevance for each and every functional area, no matter what its primary focus. These common criteria are referred to as "general standards" and are embedded in all functional area standards. These general standards are designed to overcome the "silo effect" so common throughout higher education in which autonomous administrative units, programs, and services function independently and sometimes inconsistently. In effect, the general standards make the CAS standards highly utilitarian and promote inter-departmental, inter-program, and inter-service cooperation and collaboration. Users are encouraged to view the CAS standards and guidelines as vehicles that interconnect administrative units. Because what these various functional units have in common (e.g., educational purpose, student learning and development) often exceeds their differences, the effective practitioner will find that collaboration between and among units will enhance the educational environment in many important ways.

Another use of the general standards is in those offices or areas for which no CAS standards have been developed. While the general standards do not offer the specialty standards designed to address specifically the particular functional area, they do offer essential standards of practice that are applicable to all areas and so can be used where no other standards exist. The general standards are also useful in conducting an assessment of an office that has multiple functional responsibilities (e.g., activities, leadership, and orientation). By identifying the general standards that are the same in each of the relevant sets of standards, practitioners can recognize the parts of the standards that overlap and the parts that speak to the various functions, thereby creating one non-repetitive set of standards that reflects the complex nature of the office.

The CAS standards and guidelines are written using similar language to clearly reflect the intent of the statements. All CAS standards use the auxiliary verbs "**must**" and "**shall**" and appear in **bold print** so that users can quickly identify them. As previously noted, all functional areas have specialty standards in addition to the general standards. Specialty standards are essential to accomplishing a support program's purpose and appear in **bold print** as do the general standards.

CAS standards are constructed to represent criteria that every higher education institution and its student support programs should be expected and able to meet with the application of reasonable effort and diligence. Although the standards are carefully worded, it is sometimes helpful to amplify them by providing additional information to facilitate the user's ability to interpret them accurately. Also, when programs are organizationally mature, there is need to provide users with additional criteria that may be used to make good programs even better. Consequently, as a supplement to its standards, CAS has established "guidelines" designed to clarify and amplify the standards. Guidelines may be used to guide enhanced practice when a program has previously achieved high levels of effectiveness. Guidelines use the auxiliary verbs "should" and "may" and are printed in lightface type to distinguish them from the standards.

In summary, CAS functional area standards and guidelines are basic statements that should be achievable by any program in any higher education institution when adequate and appropriate effort, energy, and resources are applied. Further, standards reflect a level of good practice generally agreed upon by the profession-at-large. In addition to the standards, guidelines are incorporated into each functional area to amplify and explain the standards and to guide enhanced practice. This dual presentation is helpful because functional area programs in both early and advanced stages of development can use the CAS standards effectively. Most important is the fact that the CAS standards have been conceived and developed via a profession-wide process that can ensure continuity and consistency of practice among all higher education institutions. In addition, each set of standards is reviewed regularly to assess currency and determine need for revision.

In considering the CAS standards and guidelines, it is important to note and understand that they are not value-neutral. As discussed further in the next section (see CAS Context), there is a clear set of values that serves as the underpinning for the standards. They are derived from the theories and models that inform our work and from the historical documents that have guided the development of our field; they serve today as important touchstones for the ideas that shape our approaches and that have shaped these standards. While these ideas have been consistently incorporated in the development of the standards to date, there has been some criticism that they are too reflective of the democratic culture of U.S. higher education and therefore not inclusive enough for application to a global higher education environment. As users of CAS standards broaden to an international arena, so does the geo-political environment that increasingly connects us. These new situations and voices may inform future development of the standards, but they remain grounded in American ideals.

Influence of CAS on Practice

The CAS standards and guidelines were established for institutions' student support programs and services to use for program development, program self-study, and staff development purposes. Although the standards have utility for institutional and program accreditation purposes, CAS has not sought to establish its own accrediting process. Rather, CAS takes the position that individualized institutional and program "self-regulation" is the preferred route to program quality and effectiveness. CAS views its profession-wide role as that of developing and promulgating professional standards to guide practice and of educating practitioners in the appropriate use of those standards.

The professional role of the Council for the Advancement of Standards in Higher Education has become increasingly important during the past three decades. The first order of business for CAS was to develop and promulgate professional standards of practice and preparation for student affairs and student support programs and services. However, CAS is now viewed by many as an important professional development vehicle as well. Results of CAS user surveys designed to determine how CAS influences professional practice and how CAS materials are used have been revealing.

Many practitioners indicated that CAS standards are important because they speak to issues of institutional change as practitioners struggle to meet the needs of ever-changing student bodies, not only in numbers but in age, gender, race, ethnicity, ability, sexual orientation, and long-term goals as well. One respondent shared the perspective that

> ". . . as each campus has examined its own situation, and looked to its peers for ideas, the CAS standards have guided not only implementation but review and evaluation. Most of this work was done in expansionary times. Now as we regroup, downsize,

retrench, whatever institutions name it, we need to have some means by which to measure what we do. The CAS standards, in all of the functional areas, serve as an excellent tool to begin that process. They are flexible without being vague, broad without being limitless, and ideal for what we constantly face in higher education, change."

This comment reflected the value of the CAS initiative for entry-level professionals:

"I can easily imagine that the standards would provide indispensable guidance for some of our younger or less experienced colleagues in graduate education. ✓ It must be like having a consultant's report at your finger tips that attests, 'Do at least this much well, and you will find success in your program'."

The CAS enterprise has led to a number of spin-offs in that some professional groups have expanded on the standards to meet sometimes highly specific professional needs. One example is in the area of learning assistance. As one respondent noted,

"No sooner than the first *Learning Assistance Program Standards* were published, we were already talking about how to build upon that work. Whereas the CAS standards addressed broad basic elements that are essential to a comprehensive learning assistance program, practitioners in the field expressed interest in obtaining similar statements that addressed pedagogical components as well."

Consequently, the National Association for Developmental Education [NADE] responded to the challenge by creating "NADE Guides." These documents emulated the CAS standards assessment model and addressed the specific functions of tutoring services, adjunct instructional programs, developmental coursework, and the teaching/learning process. This developmental activity led to inter-association cooperation among learning assistance and developmental education organizations and paved a path for communication and collaboration in subsequent revisions of the *CAS Learning Assistance Program Standards* that follow in Part 2 of this volume. A related comment was made by a close observer of CAS initiatives.

"I have two general observations. First, CAS has filled a void that no other organization could accomplish. A network has been established to mutually equip the student affairs profession with standards of performance. Second, the CAS effort has attracted increased attention and offered increased value over the years. A genuine service has been provided to the academy by helping and guiding all students toward achieving holistic development."

Another CAS-sponsored survey was initiated in Spring 2000 and directed by Jan L. Arminio at Shippensburg University (Arminio & Gochenaur, 2004). CAS surveyed over 5,000 individual members from 22 CAS member associations. Of those responding, 62.5% had heard of CAS (i.e., 85 percent of responding vice presidents; 67% of functional area directors, 66% of new professionals, and 31% of faculty members). Of those who stated that CAS has positively influenced their programs, 27% believed CAS positively influenced programs through assessing current programs, 22% in expanding current programs, 13% through clarifying mission and goals, 10% by justifying current programs, 8% by emphasizing student and staff training, 5% as a guide for new programs, and 4% to influence budget programs. Eighty-two percent of vice presidents and associate vice presidents for student affairs stated that CAS standards were positively associated with learning outcomes. A member of NACA noted, "CAS has closed the loop in student activities advising to see if student leaders learn or do not."

Additional research is needed to answer other important questions about the influence of CAS and its initiatives. In an article published in the *College Student Affairs Journal* (2003), Don G. Creamer, a past president of CAS, offers several CAS-related research questions that need to be addressed:

1. What is the level of use of CAS Standards by functional area and geographic area?
2. What is the type and frequency of use of CAS Standards and Guidelines?
3. How do CAS Standards shape professional practice?
4. What is the role of CAS in shaping educational programs and services?
5. Do practitioners perceive that the use of CAS Standards and Guidelines improves their performance?
6. Does CAS benefit professionals' learning and development?
7. Are programs and services that meet CAS Standards and Guidelines more effective in meeting learning goals than those that do not?
8. How does professional practice that is influenced by CAS in turn influence student learning?

The recently created CAS research grant program is intended to provide support for researchers interested in pursuing these and related questions.

There can be little doubt that the CAS initiative has been fruitful during its nearly thirty year existence. Although there is much work yet to do, the Council for the Advancement of Standards in Higher Education has made a professional difference and is prepared to continue its important efforts toward professionalizing programs and services in higher education.

Recent Developments

While continuing to develop and revise functional area standards, CAS has also continued to explore ways to improve and enhance its work. One of the most significant and potentially influential CAS initiatives was the 2003 revision of the CAS general standards, along with the subsequent 2008 revision. The 2003 revision included a new, major emphasis on student learning and development, which is evident primarily in the Program component (Part Two of each functional area standard). This section included a table of 16 student learning and development outcome domains designed to guide practitioners in their attempts to both emphasize and assess student learning and development.

The 2008 revision builds on this work, maintaining the focus on student learning and development, but reconceptualizing the structure and expression of the outcome domains. Rather than the previous 16 areas, the new revision is comprised of 6 broad categories which are then further defined into narrower dimensions to assist practitioners in implementing them. As described more fully in the contextual statement that introduces the General Standards later in this book, the revision resulted from CAS's observation that the many sets of outcomes existing in the field were confusing for practitioners and the subsequent decision to convene a "think tank" of experts to consider how best to integrate and build on the previous approaches. The result, later amended and approved by the CAS Board of Directors, is the CAS Learning and Development Outcomes statement and chart, which also appears later in this volume. This process and its outcome are good examples of CAS's role in higher education, that of creating collaborative strategies to address challenges to good practice and then disseminating the results with the intention of helping practitioners and bringing coherence to the field.

In 2006, in conjunction with the previous edition of this book, CAS published a companion book to the Standards. The Frameworks for Assessing Learning and Development Outcomes (FALDOs) were created to assist practitioners

in developing sound and effective strategies for assessing outcomes. Because they were based on the previous 16 student learning and development outcome domains, the FALDOs have not been reprinted with this edition; however, they still provide useful insight into the process of understanding and designing ways to assess intended learning and development outcomes.

CAS has also used its collective voice and inter-association collaboration to develop two statements related to the work of individual professionals in higher education. The first, the CAS Characteristics of Individual Excellence for Professional Practice in Higher Education, is designed to define a list of necessary attributes for professionals in higher education that is broader than competencies and includes other markers of professionalism. While CAS has historically focused on quality assurance with regard to programs and services, the Characteristics were created to suggest the hallmarks of quality on an individual basis. The second statement, the CAS Statement of Shared Ethical Principles, articulates those values which underlie the ethics statements of CAS member associations. By identifying the themes, the statement is designed to highlight the beliefs shared by professionals working across the range of functional areas in higher education. Like the standards themselves, the Characteristics of Individual Excellence and the Statement of Shared Ethical Principles seek to identify, articulate, and promulgate quality practices in the work that we do.

Finally, since it is part of the CAS mission to promote improvement of programs and services and to encourage self-assessment, CAS has also begun to educate practitioners in a more direct way. While individual member associations typically offer CAS-related training and workshops at conferences and other professional development venues, CAS now offers a national symposium, timed to coincide with the publication of new editions of CAS Professional Standards for Higher Education. This opportunity to learn from experts in the field and network with others engaged in the process of using CAS on their campuses is the latest initiative designed to further the work of the Council, with the intention of enhancing student learning and development across our campuses. From the earliest conversations thirty years ago, that is the thread that has been constant throughout the development, discussions, and initiatives of the Council for the Advancement of Standards, and that is the goal that will continue to inform our work into the future.

References

Arminio, J. & Gochenaur, P. (2004). After 16 years of publishing standards, do CAS standards make a difference? *College Student Affairs Journal, 23,* 51-65.

Council for the Advancement of Standards (CAS). (1986). *CAS standards and guidelines for student service/ development programs.* Iowa City: American College Testing Program.

Council of Student Personnel Associations in Higher Education. (1994; 1972). Student development services in post-secondary education (pp. 428-447). In A. L. Rentz (Ed.), *Student affairs: A profession's heritage.* Washington, DC: American College Personnel Association.

Creamer, D. G. (2003). Research needed on the use of CAS standards and guidelines. *College Student Affairs Journal, 22*(2), 109-124.

CAS Context
CAS Professional Standards for Higher Education

A standard to guide practice is an essential characteristic of any established profession. It is vital during the evolution of a mature profession that a relevant set of standards be developed and promulgated by and for those working in that arena. The Council for the Advancement of Standards in Higher Education (CAS) was founded in 1979 as a profession-wide entity to establish standards to guide practice by student affairs, student development, and student support service providers employed by institutions of higher learning. Currently, 36 professional associations hold membership in CAS, representing nearly 100,000 higher education service providers. This book provides 40 functional area standards for use by the profession at large, as well as statements related to individual characteristics of excellence and to ethical principles. This edition of CAS Professional Standards represents the seventh major iteration of CAS standards, the first having been published under the auspices of the American College Testing Program (CAS, 1986).

During the twentieth century, college and university student support programs evolved from a few faculty members being assigned part-time to attend to students' needs beyond the classroom to the establishment of institutional divisions designed to complement the educational goals of academic affairs. Further, contemporary student support programs employ many full-time, well-qualified staff members, most with highly specialized knowledge and skills and with advanced degrees. There is little doubt that the complexity of the student support services enterprise has increased as organizational structures have expanded. It is largely in response to the increased complexity of role, function, and purpose that the CAS standards were developed. As the field matured and the responsibilities of its practitioners expanded, a complementary need for accountability increased. It is no longer feasible, let alone desirable, for practitioners to function on the basis of best guesses or intuition when creating environments conducive to student learning and development. Likewise, practitioners have demanded that standards be developed to guide the quality of practice. The CAS functional area standards and guidelines have been developed to meet these important professional needs. CAS was created as a bellwether for the profession at large. To ensure cross-fertilization of theories, research, and application strategies from the field as a whole, knowledgeable representatives

from its member associations bring to the table the most current thinking in the functional areas they represent and champion. This commitment to collaboration among functional area specialties ensures that no single component will dominate the foundations that underlie the generation, revision, and presentation of each CAS standard. Although the standards reflect a broad range of interests, they are clearly values- driven. Underlying them is a set of fundamental principles upon which CAS was founded and by which it is guided.

CAS Guiding Principles

The fundamental principles that undergird the work of CAS and guide its initiatives are organized into five categories. They were derived from theories and conceptual models implicit within human development, group dynamics, student learning, organizational management, and higher education administration that inform the work of student affairs administrators, student development educators, and student support service providers.

Students and Their Institutions

These initial eight principles are concerned with how students learn and the environmental conditions that institutions need to emphasize for learning and development to occur. The first four principles were derived from the 1938 and 1949 editions of the Student Personnel Point of View (Miller & Prince, 1976, p.4) and reflect fundamental "truths" upon which the CAS standards and guidelines are based. Principles five through eight reflect institutional perspectives that complement the student-focused viewpoint. When combined, these principles represent the presuppositions upon which student support programs and services are founded.

- The student must be considered as a whole person.
- Each student is a unique person and must be treated as such.
- The student's total environment is educational and must be used to achieve full development.
- Students seek higher education in responsible ways and will, when encouraged to do so, access appropriate educational resources when they are provided, made known, and relevant to students' felt educational and developmental needs.
- Institutions of higher learning are purposeful and function as social and cultural resources to provide

opportunities for students to learn and develop in holistic ways.

- The primary responsibility for learning and development rests with the student.
- Institutions of higher learning reflect the diversity of the societies and cultures in which they exist.
- Institutions are responsible for creating learning environments that provide a choice of educational opportunities and challenge students to learn and develop while providing support to nurture their development.

Each CAS functional area standard was created to inform practitioners about the criteria that represent fundamental levels of programmatic and organizational quality that must be met if institutions are to be effective in facilitating student learning and development.

In effect, when a college or university provides programs and services that meet or exceed the CAS criteria, the institution will have effectively implemented an intentional educational environment conducive to the learning and development of its students. It is important to note that the CAS standards do not dictate that students, individually or collectively, must conform to a prescribed standard of involvement or behavior. Rather, they call for institutions and student support programs to meet a standard of programmatic and organizational efficiency and effectiveness sufficient to provide opportunity and encouragement for students to grow, develop, and achieve individual potentials. They further call upon institutions and their programs and services to identify the outcomes that they intend students to achieve and to assess those outcomes to determine the extent to which they have been accomplished. The institution and its educational programs are social resources that provide citizens opportunities to expand their horizons and capacities to serve society. The CAS standards have been developed and promulgated from a profession-wide point of view to provide institutions with a relevant, reasonable, and achievable set of voluntary professional standards.

Diversity and Multiculturalism

Issues of diversity in institutions of higher education can be fraught with dissension and discord. The CAS standards assert the importance of affirming the existence of diversity and considering its influence when creating and implementing educational and developmental initiatives. In an increasingly complex and shrinking global environment, it is essential that students learn to function effectively and

justly when exposed to ideas, beliefs, values, physical and mental abilities, sexual orientations, gender expressions, and cultures that differ from their own. Two principles in this regard are embedded in the CAS standards.

- Recognizing the ubiquitous nature of human diversity, institutions are committed to eliminating barriers that impede student learning and development, attending especially to establishing and maintaining diverse human relationships essential to survival in a global society.
- Justice and respect for differences bond individuals to community; thus education for multicultural awareness and positive regard for differences is essential to the development and maintenance of a health engendering society.

The CAS standards call for institutions and their student support programs to recognize the increasingly diverse societies to be served and the importance of enhancing students' capacities to function effectively within the context of constantly shifting environments and opinions. CAS recognizes that the spirit of affirmative action is inherent in the delivery of effective student support services and that discrimination against any student population or employment category is antithetical to belief in the dignity of the individual. This proposition is fundamental to student development theory and its applications to practice. The CAS standards reinforce the fact that those responsible for creating educational environments need to be open to and accepting of differences, and that they must recognize that such environments are important for enhancing the quality of the education provided and the learning achieved. Further, the standards consistently call for staffing with personnel whose demographic characteristics reflect those of the institution's constituencies. In addition, all students must have access to the educational and co-curricular resources available to the academic community at large; no student, for any reason, should be denied access to them.

Organization, Leadership, and Human Resources

The CAS standards reflect the belief that form follows function; consequently, the structure of an organization should mirror the purposes for which it was established. It is essential that institutions, programs, and services be based on a mutually determined, clearly and publicly stated, and well-understood purpose. Without a clearly defined mission, an institution and its programs are virtually rudderless and will ultimately founder. Unmistakably defined lines of authority must be drawn, detailed duties and job responsibilities described, and policies and procedures established to guide the desired processes. Those who lead and administer programs of student support must remember that because theory without practice is empty, and practice without theory is blind, it is essential that the theory embraced be connected to the purposes sought in pursuit of quality practice. Three basic principles concerned with these factors also underlie the CAS standards.

- Capable, credible, knowledgeable, and experienced leadership is essential for institutional success; organizational units are most successful when their missions and outcome expectations are effectively documented and understood by all concerned.
- Effective programs and services require well-qualified staff members who understand and support the student learning and development outcomes the programs are intended to promote.
- Student learning and personal development will be enhanced when staff members at all levels of responsibility possess appropriate, relevant, and adequate educational preparation and practical experience.

CAS standards do not prescribe organizational or administrative structures to which institutions and programs are expected to adhere. CAS is guided by the belief that every institution is unique and must establish the frame of administrative reference most appropriate to its particular mission. Consequently, the standards do not prescribe specific requirements, but rather provide fundamental criteria that practitioners can use to judge the effectiveness of their current or projected structures. For example, certain elements clearly are essential to functional success, including employing leaders who possess viable visions of how and what is to be achieved and are suitably positioned for access to the highest administrative levels. Leaders and staff members alike must possess effective managerial skills, be properly titled, and be well qualified by both education and experience. Under-educated and under-experienced staff members, good intentions notwithstanding, will virtually always fail to accomplish the program's objectives over the long term.

Health Engendering Environments

Institutional environments of quality combine educational philosophies and values in conjunction with adequate physical facilities, human resources, and fiscal support to create positive input on the education and development of students. The establishment of effective, health-generating environments is an important aspect of the CAS standards.

- Student support and developmental programs and services prosper in benevolent environments that provide students with appropriate levels of challenge and support.

The primary purpose of education has always been to promote change, both in individuals and in society. College and university student support programs are primarily educational enterprises. Clearly, the Student Learning Imperative (ACPA, 1996) prevails throughout each CAS functional area standard because an important purpose of the standards is to provide criteria that can be used to judge a program's capacity and effectiveness in creating learning and development opportunities. The establishment of educational environments conducive to student learning and development is essential if an institution of higher learning is to achieve its educational purposes.

Ethical Considerations

A major component in each CAS standard incorporates the fundamental ethical expectations to which all student support practitioners must adhere to ensure fair and equitable practice. Just as a mission statement is essential to provide programs with direction, ethical standards are essential to guide the behavior of staff members in ways that enhance the overall integrity of both the program and its host institution.

- Because special mentoring relationships exist between students and those who facilitate their learning and development, support service providers must exemplify impeccable ethical behavior in both their professional relationships and their personal lives.

As an essential task of every profession's emergence, it establishes and codifies ethical standards to guide the behavior of its members. The CAS standards provide the essential ethical foundations upon which to build humane, ethical practice. Without a clearly defined code of ethics, support service staff members would have little or no guidance for establishing and maintaining a reasonable level of effective moral and ethical behavior. The best of intentions are insufficient if they are not founded on a solid ethical base that can be understood and acknowledged by all concerned. Practitioners can be informed by their own association's ethical codes, the relevant criteria in the CAS standards, and the CAS Statement of Shared Ethical Principles.

Putting CAS Standards to Work

CAS standards and guidelines are conceived and crafted

with care to be instructive and useful to practitioners and educational leaders. Based upon professional judgment and societal expectations, they include principles that are fundamental to student learning and development and guidelines for practice for particular functional areas.

Because CAS believes in the importance of self-assessment, the standards and guidelines, as well as other CAS-related materials, are offered as criteria that can be used in multiple ways toward the goal of assuring and enhancing quality practice. As noted in the CAS Preamble (below), they can be used for design of new programs and services, for determining the efficacy of programs, for staff development, or for programmatic assessment as part of an institutional self-study. CAS does not prescribe or proscribe ways of using the standards; rather, they are intended to be tools for practitioners to use to improve practice.

The development of an assessment process is a task that many practitioners are facing today. While CAS can be an important tool for part of the plan, it is important to think about the larger picture. Upcraft and Schuh (1996, pp. 27-30), in describing a comprehensive assessment model, assert that it should include the following:

- Keeping track of who uses student services, programs, and facilities
- Assessing of student and other clientele needs
- Assessing clientele satisfaction
- Assessing campus environments and student cultures
- Assessing outcomes
- Conducting comparable institutions assessment (i.e., benchmarking)
- Using nationally accepted standards to assess

An institution, division, program, or service with an assessment plan that incorporates all of these elements will have abundant documentation with which to complete a CAS self-study. Assessing the separate elements of the program or service supplies the evidence with which to support ratings in the self-study process.

Self-Study Process

The most thorough and, perhaps, productive use of the standards involves a self-study process for program evaluation. This process involves others at the institution in examining evidence to determine collectively whether the program is in compliance with the standards. Involvement of others serves several purposes; it ensures a broader and more objective perspective, increases knowledge and awareness of the program across the institution,

and develops support for implementation of identified improvements.

For each set of standards and guidelines, CAS provides a Self-Assessment Guide (SAG) that includes a recommended comprehensive self-study process for program evaluation. Seven basic steps to using a SAG are suggested for implementing a functional area self-study. The following, in summary form, is the recommended self-study process.

1. Establish and Prepare the Self-Assessment Team

Division and functional area leaders need first to determine the functional area or areas to be evaluated and the reason for the project. This may be dictated by institutional program review cycles or planning for accreditation processes, or it may result from internal divisional goals and needs.

It is desirable to involve the full functional area staff in the initial planning stage of the self-study process, including support staff members and knowledgeable students and faculty members when feasible. This approach provides opportunity for shared ownership in the evaluation. For a self-study of a single functional area, a representative group of three to five members, including one or more knowledgeable individuals from outside the area under review, should be selected to compose the primary self-study team.

Initially, the team should familiarize itself with the relevant CAS functional area standard by examining it carefully before making individual or group judgments. It is important that all members come to understand and interpret the standard in similar fashion. Team training should be conducted to ensure that members' interpretive differences are resolved before initiating the study. Likewise, ground rules for the study should be established and agreed upon. Team members should realize and accept that disagreement is natural, healthy, and probably inevitable, but the resulting debates will usually strengthen the team's understanding and ultimate consensus on the matter. Finally, the team should discuss whether any of the guidelines (included with the standards to indicate areas where practice can be enhanced beyond the minimum expectations) should be treated as a standard for self-study purposes. For example, a functional area guideline might include the statement "facilities should include a private office where individual consultations can be held." The study team may decide that this guideline statement, which is not a CAS standard compliance requirement, is imperative at their institution and should therefore be treated as a standard for purposes of their self-study. If so decided, a criterion measure statement such as "private office space is available for staff members to use for consultation purposes" would be inserted as a criterion measure to be rated along with the other criterion measures included in the SAG and evaluated accordingly.

It is helpful to have relevant documents and evidence collected prior to initiating the self-study. While the team may identify additional information that is needed to complete the review, having basic documents from the functional area available at the outset will assist them in making progress in their work (see further detail in 3. below).

2. Beginning the Self-Study

It is suggested that team members use the CAS Functional Area Self-Assessment Guide (SAG) to implement the self-study. When used, the initial steps are for members to review available documentation, to rate the criterion measures individually and then collectively to make judgments about how well the program meets the criteria. The SAG provides a 4-point scale from Not Met to Fully Met for rating the criterion measures, which reflect the essence of the standards.

3. Identify and Summarize Evaluative Evidence

Judging the program by rating it against the standard's criterion measures and identifying program strengths and weaknesses does not represent a completed self-study. Rather, the process requires documentation of the evidence that supports each criterion measure rating. The nature of such documentary evidence may be quantitative, qualitative, or, most typically, a combination of the two. For example, quantitative measures might include the staff-to-student ratio for a given activity, an analysis of the cost-effectiveness of a given activity, or the results of a developmental task assessment of student learning and development outcome achievement. Qualitative documentation, on the other hand, might include notes on the process used to develop the program's mission or outcome objectives or structured interviews with students. Essential documentation includes relevant publications (e.g., student and staff handbooks), program descriptions (e.g., career decision-making workshop outlines), program evaluation data (e.g., program assessment results), institutional data (e.g., student profiles), and self-study initiated research (e.g., student survey or focus group results). No self-study can be considered complete without relevant data and related documentation to support and

validate the team's judgments. These data can be collected over time and stored in a database for self-study purposes. Such data also have utility for preparing annual reports.

The Program section of the CAS standards for every functional area includes learning and development outcome domains for which programs must demonstrate outcomes. It is particularly important that outcomes assessment information be available for review, since assessing the results of our work is a crucial part of determining the effectiveness of the program or service.

Following the rating and review procedure, it is desirable for the study team to invite the full staff to review and discuss the team's interim assessment of program compliance with the standards. This approach provides opportunity to inform all staff members of the team's evaluation and permits all staff members to explore together how well the program appears to be accomplishing its stated purpose. Through this process, team members may be exposed to alternative interpretations of the study results-to-date and obtain additional insight into the program from the perspective of others.

4. Identify Discrepancies

Study team members should compare their ratings and interpretations of program characteristics, accomplishments, strengths, and shortcomings against the criteria expressed in the standard. Further, the study team should carefully review each criterion measure and related practice that study team members rated as Not Done, Unsatisfactory, or where rated discrepancies of two or more were noted. A specific rationale should be prepared for each shortcoming identified.

When discrepancies are noted between the assessment criteria and actual practice, it is possible to identify existing operational problems that need resolution. For example, each standard calls for the existence of a program mission statement consistent with the nature and goals of the institution. If the program has no written mission statement or an outdated one, then the discrepancy between the standard and actual program practice clearly calls for the creation of a current, relevant program mission statement that is consistent with the institution's mission.

5. Determine Appropriate Corrective Action

The self-study team should describe in detail the adjustments that need to be implemented for the program to achieve the quality and effectiveness to which it aspires. For example, returning to the example of the program mission, the action required would call for program staff members to draft a statement delineating the elements they believe are agreed upon, circulate them for review and comment, and then prepare and disseminate a final program mission statement to guide the program and its services.

An important point to note in regard to corrective action is the importance of subdividing the overall task into manageable parts that can be accomplished in step-by-step fashion. Trying to revise a total functional area in one step is neither a desirable nor an effective approach to program development. It is important that the study team list specific actions identified in the self-study that require implementation. It is also desirable to set priorities on the list by order of importance, need, feasibility, and achievability of the desired change.

6. Recommend Steps for Program Enhancement
Even excellent programs can be further refined to provide more desirable and effective outcomes. Action in this regard is particularly relevant for programs in which self-study team members identified selected guidelines calling for enhanced functioning to be rated as standards for their setting. Unless staff members are satisfied with meeting basic standards only, additional initiatives can be implemented to enhance program quality and effectiveness. This can be accomplished by listing each specific action identified in the self-study that would enhance and strengthen services and setting priorities among them for follow-up purposes.

7. Prepare an Action Plan
As the self-study process comes to closure, it is important for staff members to identify and establish priorities to influence the program's future directions. This represents a process of comparing past performance with desired outcomes and can best be accomplished by carefully reviewing the actual self-study process that was conducted to ensure that all relevant program issues are addressed. The post-self-assessment action plan should acknowledge the program's strengths as well as its shortcomings as it moves toward establishing a strategic approach for correcting deficiencies and initiating enhancements. The primary goal of this final step is to identify and set priorities for future actions and directions, after comparing the results of the self-study with the outcomes to which the program aspires.

The process for preparing a final program action plan consists of preparing a comprehensive action plan for implementing program changes, identifying resources (i.e., human, fiscal, physical) that are essential to program enhancement, establishing dates by which specific actions are to be completed, identifying responsible parties to complete the action steps, and setting a tentative start-up date for initiating a subsequent self-study.

For those interested in obtaining additional information and training on the self-assessment process described above, CAS has produced an e-learning program that is incorporated into the CAS Self-Assessment Guides CD ROM; information is available on the CAS website, www.cas.edu.

Other Uses of the CAS Standards
In addition to the model presented for full program self-study, the CAS standards are a resource that can be used for a number of other purposes. The uses outlined below are representative; since the standards and guidelines are tools to be used by practitioners, there are not really "wrong" ways to use them, as long as the values and spirit underlying them are honored.

Design of New Programs and Services
As student and institutional needs change, the opportunity may arise to develop a new program or service on campus, or to expand or restructure existing areas. In doing so, it is helpful to have criteria to serve as an outline to guide and ground planning. The functional area standards and guidelines can serve as a helpful resource when such planning is needed. The mission and program sections are particularly helpful in specifying important goals and components relevant to the functional area being developed.

Staff Development
Staff members can study the various criteria to determine how well they and their colleagues are implementing the standards in their daily work with students. The relevant functional area standards can be used as an orientation device to assist new professionals in understanding and reviewing their areas, as a point of discussion for supervisors and staff to discuss program strengths and weaknesses, as a resource for educating others at the institution about what is involved in a sound program, or as the format by which annual program reports are prepared. The more the CAS standards are used within a division or institution, the more it will lead to a common language and shared perception of the elements of good practice.

The most comprehensive staff development program, using one of the functional area standards and guidelines, or the General Standards, as a training device, may require from several hours to a full day of meeting time during which staff members share responsibility for leading discussions about the standard's various components. This approach is particularly valuable when a program or division self-study is in the offing. In such an instance, staff members can both learn how CAS standards can be used to guide and influence good practice and how they can provide a vehicle for implementing a self-study. Training staff members before conducting a self-study typically produces a more comprehensive and valuable program evaluation.

Academic Preparation

The CAS standards have another valuable educational function when used as a resource in formal academic preparation programs, especially in an introductory course concerned with student support functions common to institutions of higher learning. The 40 CAS functional area standards and their accompanying contextual statements, as well as the statements regarding individual characteristics, shared ethical principles, and learning and development outcomes, all presented in Part 2 of this book, provide an excellent primer for those entering the fields of student affairs and higher education administration. The contextual statements summarize the roles and functions of key program and service units, their primary purposes, historical perspectives, and relevant resources available to explore the areas in greater detail. These succinct summary statements provide an introduction for those unfamiliar with the areas under study. The CAS standards provide an in-depth description of the characteristics common to and expected of the various functional areas.

For students who desire to examine a given functional area in greater detail or participate in a practicum, internship, or other field-based experience, the CAS Self-Assessment Guide (SAG) provides a unique resource for obtaining a comprehensive understanding. Each functional area SAG includes the standards, guidelines, and criterion measures that can be used to judge the level of compliance a program exhibits in regard to the standards. Using a SAG, students can readily identify a program's strengths and shortcomings. Further, the SAG has utility as a vehicle for both students and supervisors to use for examining together and discussing the various components of the area under study. For learning the basics of student support functions, there is no better information available than that provided by the CAS standards and the complementary Self-Assessment Guides that operationalize the various standards.

Credibility and Accountability

Any profession, along with its practitioners, must exhibit a reasonable level of credibility if it is to survive. Professional entities lacking user confidence will be at best underutilized and may ultimately disappear. In effect, credibility is essential to the existence of all service agencies, including those associated with higher education. Through publication of and adherence to standards of professional practice, institutions seek to assure potential student users and the general public of their competence and credibility. Both laypersons and professionals alike attribute credibility to programs, professions, and institutions that meet stringent standards; compliance with such standards demonstrates that quality is present.

Various means have been established to ensure accountability and quality assurance. Institutional and academic program credibility is typically established through accreditation, a voluntary process by which agencies encourage and assist institutions and their sub-units (e.g., colleges, schools, departments, and programs) to evaluate and improve their programs and services (Eaton, 2001). Information about the institutions and programs that voluntarily meet or exceed acceptable standards of quality and effectiveness is made public by the accrediting body. It is not uncommon for institutions not possessing accreditation status to be denied federal aid or other resources available to accredited institutions. Graduates of non-accredited institutions may be denied admission to graduate schools or certain employment opportunities. Accreditation is intended to assure the public that an institution and its programs do indeed provide quality education.

However, the general public cannot be assured that individuals who have diplomas, certificates, or degrees from accredited institutions and programs are, in fact, effective practitioners. Consequently, various structures have been established by professional and governmental oversight agencies to judge the professional qualifications of service providers in education, health, and social service areas.

Three primary methods have been established to enable individuals to document their professional qualifications: registry, certification, and licensure. CAS, which is a consortium of higher education professional associations, focuses minimal attention on these credentialing options, although some have encouraged CAS to expand its focus into registry or certification, which are often initiated by non-governmental professional bodies. Licensure, on the other hand, is largely the province of governments. For instance, licenses based on generally comparable criteria are required of physicians, psychologists, and lawyers in all states; counselors and engineers, on the other hand, are judged by diverse criteria from state to state.

As demand for accountability in higher education increases, so too does demand for practitioner accountability. CAS endorses self-regulation as the most viable approach to program accountability, calling for each institution to initiate a program of self-assessment for its student support programs, services, and personnel. Whether student support units are administratively assigned to student affairs, academic affairs, business affairs, or elsewhere in the organizational hierarchy, CAS encourages program review and evaluation on a continuing basis using the CAS standards. From this perspective, self-regulation becomes a preferred strategy to establish and maintain credibility.

When deemed appropriate and desirable, the various functional areas could invite representatives from peer institutions, or professionals with particular expertise in the areas being studied, to review their self-assessment reports as part of the validation process. Self-regulation requires institutions and their leaders to establish their own policies and procedures for institutional assessment and evaluation and to adhere to them when evaluating quality and effectiveness. Thus, through continuing assessment, institutions can compile and maintain in databases the internal documentation required by regional accrediting bodies and governmental oversight agencies. Self-regulation provides institutions and their student support programs with tools to achieve and evidence quality assurance. In effect, if institutions accept responsibility for initiating meaningful and well considered assessment processes and procedures, there is less likelihood that external oversight agencies, governmental or otherwise, will seek to do so.

Example Applications

The following is a summary of examples of how CAS standards have been applied in practice and for purposes of professional staff development.

Institutional Program Review

From an institutional perspective, many practitioners view the CAS standards as a staple for conducting comprehensive program reviews. One institution's policy requires that a standard external to the institution be used to implement periodic comprehensive program reviews. Because CAS standards are readily available, easily understood, consistent across functional areas, and simple to use, they are often the standard of choice for administrative unit reviews. The fact that operational versions of the standards in the form of CAS Self-Assessment Guides (SAGs) are also available

has increased the ease with which the standards can be used for program review purposes. In addition, the existence of the CAS standards typically informs practitioners that professional practice is not based simply on instinct or history. Rather, it consists of the application of the collective wisdom of the profession and is subject to assessment and regulation.

Program Development and Advocacy

From a programmatic perspective, the CAS standards have special utility for emerging student support areas. For example, educators responsible for guiding programs of learning assistance and developmental education tend to exhibit strong commitment to promoting the use of professional standards in their ranks. Many leaders in this arena literally "invented" their programs and learned from each other what worked best to produce quality outcomes. During the past two decades, the CAS Learning Assistance Programs Standards and Guidelines has become a shared document among learning assistance practitioners. Leaders in this arena have indicated that the CAS standards provided a common ground to unite those responsible for ensuring that students receive the special attention and support they need to be successful.

Two important uses of the standards in addition to the self-assessment function were identified from another program-specific perspective: one as a guide for initiating new programs and the other for advocacy. The National Clearinghouse for Commuter Programs (NCCP) frequently receives requests from institutions desiring to establish on-campus commuter programs. Most practitioners interested in such initiatives fail initially to comprehend the scope of the functions essential to a comprehensive program. Often, the initiator is interested in establishing a particular type of program (e.g., peer mentoring or orientation for commuters) or service (e.g., off-campus housing referral, commuter newsletter). When such requests are made, the CAS standards are readily available as a professionally sanctioned tool that provides guidance to those interested in providing support for such populations.

Advocacy was a second use noted, because it is often helpful when consulting with colleagues about student support programs to make a case for broadening the administrators' understanding of what is required to meet the basic essentials. All too often, campus administrators tend to limit their initial thinking about a new program to relatively basic issues such as access, and not to think in terms of how a new program could help students become better integrated into the campus community or enhance their learning and development. The CAS standards have great utility for opening institutional leaders' eyes to the importance of comprehensive programming and helping them to grasp a broader view.

From another professional association perspective, the Association of Fraternity/Sorority Advisors [AFA] discovered that standards can be extremely beneficial in relating association purpose to the broader mission of higher education and those of various institutions. Association leaders determined that when colleagues utilized the CAS standards to establish or reorganize various student support services, those program changes were typically not challenged because the standards provided a recognized level of credibility that did not exist prior to the availability of the CAS standards.

Professional Preparation

From the vantage point of graduate education, many student affairs preparation programs have integrated the CAS standards into their curricula. Often, the concept of quality assurance is quite vague to graduate students, especially at the master's level. However, the idea of applying standards to practice is more concrete and students can quickly come to understand the role, function, and utility of professional standards. Thus, students from the outset can begin to internalize the professional interests of self-regulation and improvement. Many college student affairs academic programs have incorporated the CAS standards into their practicum and internship experiential components. Students may complete a "mini-self-study" of the functional areas to which they are assigned as part of their practical field-work experiences. This not only ensures that future practitioners know about the existence of the CAS standards, but also provides them with direct experience that enhances their ability to put the standards into practice as they move into entry level positions.

CAS Initiatives

The Council for the Advancement of Standards in Higher Education was established as a profession-wide collaborative body to develop and promulgate professional standards and to inform those responsible for providing higher education with information about how to use standards effectively. CAS functional area standards were created as living, evolving documents. The Council established a periodic review program to ensure that each standard undergoes

regular review and updating. Protocols to guide the development of new and the revision of existing standards are in place and appear in Appendix B. These protocols identify the processes, participants, and procedures used by CAS to create and review its standards. Completion of a typical standard review takes approximately one year from initiation to Board adoption. It may take slightly longer to complete a new standard because an initial draft must be written before the CAS review process can be initiated. Historically, by the time a functional area standard has undergone the long and arduous development and review, the CAS Board of Directors has nearly always been unanimous in its decision to adopt a new or revised standard, and in fact, the Board review process is designed to lead to consensus.

In the rich discussions that emerge around the Board table, other issues or needs are sometimes identified. When ideas emerge that are found to be within the scope and purpose of CAS, projects to support and enhance the work of CAS are undertaken. This is the genesis of the projects that have developed into the SAGs, the FALDOs, the Characteristics of Individual Excellence, the Statement of Shared Ethical Principles, and the CAS National Symposium.

In addition to its primary purpose to develop and promulgate professional standards, CAS takes seriously its responsibility to inform and educate the higher education community and the public about the importance of professional standards and their utility for institutional and program self-assessment. Over the years, CAS Board members have represented the Council in numerous conferences, workshops, and instructional activities designed to inform members of the higher education community about CAS initiatives and instruct practitioners in using the standards. Most of the CAS member associations have periodically included CAS-related presentations and training workshops in their conference programs. On several occasions, CAS representatives have made presentations at the annual American Association of Higher Education Assessment Forum, and CAS has been represented internationally at the European Association of Institutional Research in Prague and through an invited series of seminars in South Africa. Likewise, CAS has sponsored a series of assessment workshops designed to instruct higher education personnel in the use of CAS standards in combination with regional accrediting criteria when implementing institutional accreditation self-studies. In 2006, CAS initiated the first CAS National Symposium to further educate participants on the implementation of the CAS approach and materials;

the second is being held in 2009 in conjunction with the publication of this edition of the *CAS Professional Standards* and the newly revised CAS Learning and Development Outcomes.

The CAS standards provide an important tool that expresses to students, faculty, and administrators alike the complex and vital nature of student support programs and services and their relationship to student learning and development. There are ample indications within higher education that there is a lack of understanding about the importance of creating supportive, health engendering environments for students as an important condition that enhances the higher education experiences. Over the years, those providing students with basic educational support services have often been viewed as secondary or supplemental participants in achieving the academic mission, rather than integral to it. The creation of clearly articulated professional standards has gone far to deepen the understanding of faculty and administrative colleagues and to increase their confidence in the valuable educational and developmental role that student support service providers offer students.

Note: The preceding section was adapted from previous editions and was originally authored by Ted K. Miller.

References

American College Personnel Association (ACPA). (March/April 1996). Special issue: The student learning imperative. *Journal of College Student Development, 37*(2).

Council for the Advancement of Standards (CAS). (1986). *CAS standards and guidelines for student service/development programs.* Iowa City: American College Testing Program.

Eaton, J. S. (March/April 2001). Regional accreditation reform: Who is served? *Change Magazine*, 39-45.

Miller, T. K., & Prince, J. S. (1976). *The future of student affairs: A guide to student development for tomorrow's higher education.* San Francisco: Jossey-Bass.

Upcraft, M.L., & Schuh, J.H. (1996). *Assessment in student affairs: A guide for practitioners..* San Francisco: Jossey-Bass.

CAS Preamble

Approved by CAS Board of Directors
November 18, 1994
Washington, DC

Let us raise a standard to which the wise and honest can repair.

- George Washington, 1787

The CAS Purpose

The Council for the Advancement of Standards in Higher Education (CAS) develops and promulgates standards that enhance the quality of a student's total learning experience in higher education. CAS is a consortium of associations in higher education whose representatives achieve consensus on the nature and application of standards that guide the work of practitioners. CAS derives its authority from the prestige and traditional influence of its member associations and from the consensus of those members in establishing requirements for high-quality practice.

The CAS philosophy is grounded in beliefs about excellence in higher education, collaboration between teacher and learner, ethics in educational practice, student development as a major goal of higher education, and student responsibility for learning. Taken together, these beliefs about practice shape the vision for all CAS endeavors.

- The beliefs about excellence require that all programs and services in institutions of higher education function at optimum level.

- The beliefs about collaboration require that learning be accomplished in concert by students and educators.

- The beliefs about ethics require that all programs and services be carried out in an environment of integrity and high ideals.

- The beliefs about student development require that the student be considered as a whole person in the context of a diverse population and a diversity of institutions, that outcomes of education be comprehensive, and that the total environment be structured to create opportunities for student involvement and learning.

- The beliefs about responsibility require that the institution recognize the rights and responsibilities of students as its citizens and that it provide an array of resources and learning opportunities that enable students to exercise their responsibility to take full advantage of them.

CAS collectively develops, examines, and endorses standards and guidelines for program and service areas in higher education. The CAS approach to ensuring quality educational experiences is anchored in the assumption that its standards and guidelines can be used in a variety of ways to enhance institutional quality. They can, for example, be used for design of programs and services, for determination of the efficacy of programs, for staff development designed to enhance the skills of those providing professional services, for programmatic self-assessment to assure institutional effectiveness, and for self-regulation purposes.

Background

The Council for the Advancement of Standards in Higher Education was established in 1979 as the Council for the Advancement of Standards for Student Services/Development Programs, a consortium of professional associations representing student affairs practitioners committed to assuring quality programs and services for students. Members of nearly 32 established professional associations have directed their interests, talents, and resources to develop and promulgate professional standards and guidelines based on state-of-the-art thinking about educational programs and services. From the beginning, CAS has employed an open process of consensus-building among the representatives of member associations as the primary tool for producing its standards and guidelines.

The Council published the original set of 16 functional area standards and the academic preparation standards in 1986, with a grant from American College Testing (ACT). In 1988, CAS developed a Self-Assessment Guide (SAG) for each set of functional area standards to facilitate program assessment and evaluation. Each SAG is an operational version of a functional area standard designed to provide practitioners with a detailed instrument for self-assessment.

education, including those serving undergraduate, graduate, traditional, and nontraditional students. CAS now oversees the development of standards for new service areas and the systematic review and periodic revision of existing standards and guidelines.

The CAS Approach to Self-Regulation and Self-Assessment

Self-regulation is an internally motivated and directed institutional process devoted to the creation, maintenance, and enhancement of high-quality programs and services. CAS believes this approach is preferable to externally motivated regulation, because those within an institution generally have the clearest perceptions of its mission, goals, resources, and capabilities. The essential elements of self-regulation include:

- Institutional culture that values involvement of all its members in decision making,
- Quality indicators that are determined by the institution,
- Use of standards and guidelines in quality assurance,
- Collection and analysis of data on institutional performance, and
- Commitment to continuing improvement that presupposes freedom to explore and develop alternative directions for the future.

The success of self-regulation depends on mutual respect between an institution and its members. Within the self-regulated institution, individual accomplishments are valued, goals are based on shared vision, systems are open and interactive, processes are carried out in a climate of mutual trust and caring, conflicts are mediated in the best interests of the entire community, and achievements are recognized and rewarded. Such an environment stimulates individual and group initiatives and fosters self-determination of goals. In a self-regulating environment, members identify quality indicators in consultation with a variety of internal and external constituencies and stakeholders, including professional associations.

These indicators may include professionally derived standards, such as those of CAS, which comprise the views of many professional practitioners and professional associations. Self-regulation relies on the willingness and capacity of the organization to examine itself meticulously, faithfully, and reliably, and then to assemble the pertinent results of that examination into coherent reports that constituents can comprehend and use. Such reports are essential for recording the evidence assembled in self-study, for displaying synthesis and analysis of information, for fostering the broad participation of members in the self-regulation process, and for registering benchmark results and conclusions for future reference.

Finally, the self-regulation process relies on the institution's capacity to modify its own practices as needed. A culture that supports self-regulation must operate in a climate that permits members to make independent choices among reasonable alternatives. These choices constitute a commitment to constant improvement of educational practices and of the health of the organization.

CAS Characteristics of Individual Excellence for Professional Practice in Higher Education

CAS Contextual Statement

Defining competencies of student affairs and other professionals in higher education who plan, implement, and offer programs and services is the mark of a maturing profession. A number of authors and organizations have framed competencies in several broad areas. For example, Pope, Reynolds, and Mueller (2004) identified competencies in the areas of 1) administration and management, 2) multicultural awareness, knowledge, and skills, 3) helping and advising, 4) assessment and research, 5) teaching and training, 6) ethics and professional standards, and 7) translation and use of theory to guide practice. This document seeks to define a list of necessary attributes for professionals in higher education that is broader than competencies and includes other markers of professionalism. These characteristics of excellence can be used in an evaluative format, both self evaluation and in the context of "360 degree" (Tornow, London, & Associates, 1998) or supervisory format.

There are numerous purposes for the creation and use of this document. One purpose is to move the student affairs profession and other professionals within the higher education context to more concrete, concise, and agreed upon characteristics that are expected of professionals who provide, implement, and facilitate programs and services in higher education. Another purpose is to assist in the enculturation of new professionals into the profession by defining what it means to be a professional in higher education. This document also seeks to clarify the context within which people are choosing to work. In response to the literature on supervision that indicates that supervision in higher education is often irregular and when it does occur stresses operational tasks rather than professional development (Arminio & Creamer, 2001; Saunders, Cooper, Winston, & Chernow, 2000; Winston & Creamer, 1997), this document was created to provide aspirational expectations for higher education professionals (Carpenter, 2003).

Because it is the intent of this document to honor individual differences that people bring to their practice, when perceived differences from the expected characteristics are identified these differences need to be discussed. It is through these discussions with supervisors and colleagues that such differences can be acknowledged and their implications explored.

This document offers direction for professional development whether prompted by self evaluation or from supervisory evaluation. In either case, this document is intended to be used in collaboration and discussion with a supervisor, supervisees, students, and/or colleagues. From these discussions an individual professional development plan can be created and then movement toward accomplishing that plan be evaluated.

References

Arminio, J. & Creamer, D. G. (2001). What quality supervisors say about quality supervision. *College Student Affairs Journal, 21,* 35-44.

Carpenter, D. S. (2003). Professionalism. In S. R. Komives & D. Woodard Jr (Eds.). *Student services: A handbook for the profession* (4th edition; pp. 573-592). San Francisco: Jossey-Bass.

Pope, R. L., Reynolds, A. L., & Mueller, J. A. (2004). *Multicultural competence in student affairs.* San Francisco: Jossey-Bass.

Saunders, S. A., Cooper, D. L. Winston, R. B. Jr., & Chernow, E. (2000). Supervising staff in student affairs: Exploration of the synergistic approach. *Journal of College Student Development, 41,* 1281-191.

Tornow, W. W., London, M., & Associates (1998). *Maximizing the value of 360-degree feedback.* San Francisco: Jossey-Bass.

Winston, R. B., Jr., & Creamer, D. G. (1997). *Improving staffing practices in student affairs.* San Francisco: Jossey-Bass.

CAS Characteristics of Individual Excellence for Professional Practice in Higher Education

Evaluating individual professional practice in higher education requires the identification of ideal performance characteristics that describe excellence in professional practice. This document has evolved from multi-faceted professional competencies that are inherent in the purpose, development, and application of the CAS Standards and Guidelines. It assumes a philosophy and practice of life-long learning and professional development shared by individual practitioners and their institutions. Characteristics are grouped into **General Knowledge and Skills**, **Interactive Competencies**, and **Self Mastery**.

General Knowledge and Skills
General Knowledge
1. Understands and supports the broad responsibility of the institution for enhancing the collegiate experience for all students
2. Possesses appropriate knowledge of relevant theories, literature, and philosophies on which to base informed professional practice
3. Knows values, historical context, and current issues of one's profession
4. Has developed, can articulate, and acts consistently with a sound educational philosophy consistent with the institution's mission
5. Understands and respects similarities and differences of people in the institutional environment
6. Understands relevant legal issues

General Skills
7. Manages and influences campus environments that promote student success
8. Works to create campus and related educational environments that are safe and secure
9. Effectively utilizes language through speaking, writing, and other means of communication
10. Engages disparate audiences effectively
11. Teaches effectively directly or through example
12. Thinks critically about complex issues
13. Works collaboratively
14. Is trustworthy and maintains confidentiality
15. Exercises responsible stewardship of resources
16. Engages in evaluation and assessment to determine outcomes and identify areas for improvement
17. Uses technology effectively for educational and institutional purposes
18. Bases decisions on appropriate data
19. Models effective leadership

Interactive Competencies
With students:
20. Counsels, advises, supervises, and leads individuals and groups effectively
21. Knows the developmental effects of college on students
22. Knows characteristics of students attending institutions of higher education
23. Knows students who attend the institution, use services, and participants in programs
24. Interacts effectively with a diverse range of students
25. Provides fair treatment to all students and works to change aspects of the environment that do not promote fair treatment
26. Values differences among groups of students and between individuals; helps students understand the interdependence among people both locally and globally
27. Actively and continually pursues insight into the cultural heritage of students
28. Encourages student learning through successful experiences as well as failures

With Colleagues and the Institution
29. Supervises others effectively
30. Manages fiscal, physical, and human resources responsibly and effectively
31. Judges the performance of self and others fairly
32. Contributes productively in partnerships and team efforts
33. Demonstrates loyalty and support of the institution where employed
34. Behaves in ways that reflect integrity, responsibility, honesty, and with accurate representation of self, others, and program
35. Creates and maintains campus relationships characterized by integrity and responsibility
36. Effectively creates and maintains networks among colleagues locally, regionally, nationally, and internationally
37. Contributes to campus life and supports activities that promote campus community

Self Mastery
38. Commits to excellence in all work
39. Intentionally employs self reflection to improve practice and gain insight
40. Responds to the duties of one's role and also to the spirit of one's responsibilities
41. Views his or her professional life as an important element of personal identity
42. Strives to maintain personal wellness and a healthy lifestyle
43. Maintains position-appropriate appearance
44. Stays professionally current by reading literature, building skills, attending conferences, enhancing technological literacy, and engaging in other professional development activities
45. Manages personal life so that overall professional effectiveness is maintained
46. Belongs to and contributes to activities of relevant professional associations
47. Assumes proper accountability for individual and organizational mistakes
48. Espouses and follows a written code of professional ethical standards
49. Abides by laws and institutional policies and works to change policies that are incongruent with personal and professional principles
50. Re-evaluates continued employment when personal, professional, and institutional goals and values are incompatible and inhibit the pursuit of excellence

CAS Statement of Shared Ethical Principles

The Council for the Advancement of Standards in Higher Education (CAS) has served as a voice for quality assurance and promulgation of standards in higher education for thirty years. CAS was established to promote inter-association efforts to address quality assurance, student learning, and professional integrity. It was believed that a single voice would have greater impact on the evaluation and improvement of services and programs than would many voices speaking for special interests by individual practitioners or by single-interest organizations.

CAS includes membership of over 35 active professional associations and has established standards in 40 functional areas. It has succeeded in providing a platform through which representatives from across higher education can jointly develop and promulgate standards of good practice that are endorsed not just by those working in a particular area, but by representatives of higher education association.

CAS often cites George Washington, who said, "Let us raise a standard to which the wise and honest can repair." CAS has raised standards; it is now time to focus on the attributes, such as wisdom and honesty, of those professionals who would use the standards. Professionals working to provide services in higher education share more than a commitment to quality assurance and standards of practice. A review of the ethical statements of member associations demonstrates clearly that there are elements of ethical principles and values that are shared across the professions in higher education.

Most of the member associations represented in CAS are guided by ethical codes of professional practice enforced through the prescribed channels of its association. CAS acknowledges and respects the individual codes and standards of ethical conduct of their organizations. From these codes, CAS has created a statement of shared ethical principles that focuses on seven basic principles that form the foundation for CAS member association codes: autonomy, non-malfeasance, beneficence, justice, fidelity, veracity, and affiliation. This statement is not intended to replace or supplant the code of ethics of any professional association; rather, it is intended to articulate those shared ethical principles. It is our hope that by articulating those shared beliefs, CAS can promulgate a better understanding of the professions of those in service to students and higher education.

Principle I - Autonomy
We take responsibility for our actions and both support and empower an individual's and group's freedom of choice.
- We strive for quality and excellence in the work that we do
- We respect one's freedom of choice
- We believe that individuals, ourselves and others, are responsible for their own behavior and learning
- We promote positive change in individuals and in society through education
- We foster an environment where people feel empowered to make decisions
- We hold ourselves and others accountable
- We study, discuss, investigate, teach, conduct research, and publish freely within the academic community
- We engage in continuing education and professional development

Principle II — Non-Malfeasance
We pledge to do no harm.
- We collaborate with others for the good of those whom we serve
- We interact in ways that promote positive outcomes
- We create environments that are educational and supportive of the growth and development of the whole person
- We exercise role responsibilities in a manner that respects the rights and property of others without exploiting or abusing power

Principle III - Beneficence
We engage in altruistic attitudes and actions that promote goodness and contribute to the health and welfare of others.
- We treat others courteously
- We consider the thoughts and feelings of others
- We work toward positive and beneficial outcomes

Principle IV - Justice

We actively promote human dignity and endorse equality and fairness for everyone.

- We treat others with respect and fairness, preserving their dignity, honoring their differences, promoting their welfare
- We recognize diversity and embrace a cross-cultural approach in support of the worth, dignity, potential, and uniqueness of people within their social and cultural contexts
- We eliminate barriers that impede student learning and development or discriminate against full participation by all students
- We extend fundamental fairness to all persons
- We operate within the framework of laws and policies
- We respect the rights of individuals and groups to express their opinions
- We assess students in a valid, open, and fair manner and one consistent with learning objectives
- We examine the influence of power on the experience of diversity to reduce marginalization and foster community

Principle V - Fidelity

We are faithful to an obligation, trust, or duty.

- We maintain confidentiality of interactions, student records, and information related to legal and private matters
- We avoid conflicts of interest or the appearance thereof
- We honor commitments made within the guidelines of established policies and procedures
- We demonstrate loyalty and commitment to institutions that employ us
- We exercise good stewardship of resources

Principle VI - Veracity

We seek and convey the truth in our words and actions.

- We act with integrity and honesty in all endeavors and interactions
- We relay information accurately
- We communicate all relevant facts and information while respecting privacy and confidentiality

Principle VII — Affiliation

We actively promote connected relationships among all people and foster community.

- We create environments that promote connectivity
- We promote authenticity, mutual empathy, and engagement within human interactions

When professionals act in accordance with ethical principles, program quality and excellence are enhanced and ultimately students are better served.   As professionals providing services in higher education, we are committed to upholding these shared ethical principles, for the benefit of our students, our professions, and higher education.

Some concepts for this code were adopted from:
Kitchner, K. (1985). Ethical principles and ethical decisions in student affairs. In H. Canon & R. Brown (Eds.), *Applied ethics in student services* (New Directions in Student Services, No. 30, pp. 17-30). San Francisco: Jossey-Bass.

CAS Learning and Development Outcomes
Contextual Statement

six categories

The Council for the Advancement of Standards in Higher Education (CAS) promotes standards to enhance opportunities for student learning and development from higher education programs and services. Responding to the increased shift in attention being paid by educators and their stakeholders from higher education inputs (i.e., standards and benchmarks) to the outcomes of students attending higher education, in 2003 CAS articulated sixteen domains of learning outcomes. However, in 2008 after the publication of *Learning Reconsidered 2* (2006), CAS reviewed the learning outcomes it had promoted and decided an integration of both learning outcome documents would enhance the profession's efforts in promoting student learning and development. Consequently, CAS hosted a "think tank" involving writers of *Learning Considered 2*, CAS directors, and prominent practitioners and faculty members in student affairs to make recommendations for a revised learning outcomes document.

Upon recommendations of the think tank, CAS revised the student learning and development outcomes into six broad categories (called domains): knowledge acquisition, construction, integration and application; cognitive complexity; intrapersonal development; interpersonal competence; humanitarianism and civic engagement; and practical competence. To comply with CAS standards, institutional programs and services must identify relevant and desirable learning from these domains, assess relevant and desirable learning, and articulate how their programs and services contribute to domains not specifically assessed. For each of the domains, CAS offers examples illustrating achievement of the student learning outcomes.

This learning outcomes model further defines or clarifies each of the six domains by identifying learning outcome dimensions. Offering dimensions of learning within corresponding domains allows for a more focused assessment approach based on institutional mission and priorities. The revised CAS learning outcomes document heightens the differentiation of interpersonal competence and interpersonal development (though certainly the two influence each other), highlights the integration of humanitarianism and civic engagement, and adds the dimensions of global perspective and technological competence to important learning outcomes.

The CAS Board of Directors reviewed and approved the six domains, learning outcome dimensions, and examples of learning and development outcomes at its October 2008 meeting. The domains and learning outcome dimensions will be embedded in each functional area standard. The examples will be referenced in each functional area standard and appear in the chart that follows.

Reference

Keeling, R. (Ed.). (2006). *Learning reconsidered 2: Implementing a campus-wide focus on the student experience.* American College Personnel Association, Association of College and University Housing Officers-International, Association of College Unions-International, National Academic Advising Association, National Association for Campus Activities, National Association of Student Personnel Administrators, National Intramural-Recreational Sports Association.

Contributor: Jan Arminio, Shippensburg University, NACA

CAS Learning and Development Outcomes[1]

Student Outcome Domain[2]	Dimensions of Outcome Domains	Examples of Learning and Development Outcomes
Knowledge acquisition, construction, integration, and application	Understanding knowledge from a range of disciplines	Possesses knowledge of human cultures and the physical world; possesses knowledge of [a specific] one or more subjects
	Connecting knowledge to other knowledge, ideas, and experiences	Uses multiple sources of information and their synthesis to solve problems; knows how to access diverse sources of information such as the internet, text observations, and data bases
	Constructing knowledge	Personalizes learning; makes meaning from text, instruction, and experience; uses experience and other sources of information to create new insights; generates new problem-solving approaches based on new insights; recognizes one's own capacity to create new understandings from learning activities and dialogue with others
	Relating knowledge to daily life	Seeks new information to solve problems; relates knowledge to major and career decisions; makes connections between classroom and out-of-classroom learning; articulates career choices based on assessment of interests, values, skills, and abilities; provides evidence of knowledge, skills, and accomplishments resulting from formal education, work experience, community service, and volunteer experiences, for example in resumes and portfolios
Cognitive complexity	Critical thinking	Identifies important problems, questions, and issues; analyzes, interprets, and makes judgments of the relevance and quality of information; assesses assumptions and considers alternative perspectives and solutions[3]
	Reflective thinking	Applies previously understood information, concepts, and experiences to a new situation or setting; rethinks previous assumptions
	Effective reasoning	Uses complex information from a variety of sources including personal experience and observation to form a decision or opinion; is open to new ideas and perspectives
	Creativity	Integrates mental, emotional, and creative processes for increased insight; formulates a new approach to a particular problem
Intrapersonal development	Realistic self-appraisal, self-understanding, and self-respect	Assesses, articulates, and acknowledges personal skills, abilities, and growth areas; uses self-knowledge to make decisions such as those related to career choices; articulates rationale for personal behavior; seeks and considers feedback from others; critiques and subsequently learns from past experiences; employs self-reflection to gain insight; functions without need for constant reassurance from others; balances needs of self with needs of others
	Identity development	Integrates multiple aspects of identity into a coherent whole; recognizes and exhibits interdependence in accordance with environmental, cultural, and personal values; identifies and commits to important aspects of self

	Commitment to ethics and integrity	Incorporates ethical reasoning into action; explores and articulates the values and principles involved in personal decision-making; acts in congruence with personal values and beliefs; exemplifies dependability, honesty, and trustworthiness; accepts personal accountability
	Spiritual awareness	Develops and articulates personal belief system; understands roles of spirituality in personal and group values and behaviors; critiques, compares, and contrasts various belief systems; explores issues of purpose, meaning, and faith
Interpersonal competence	**Meaningful relationships**	Establishes healthy, mutually beneficial relationships with others; treats others with respect; manages interpersonal conflicts effectively; demonstrates appropriately assertive behavior
	Interdependence	Seeks help from others when needed and offers assistance to others; shares a group or organizational goal and works with others to achieve it; learns from the contributions and involvement of others; accepts supervision and direction as needed
	Collaboration	Works cooperatively with others, including people different from self and/or with different points of view; seeks and values the involvement of others; listens to and considers others' points of view
	Effective leadership	Demonstrates skill in guiding and assisting a group, organization, or community in meeting its goals; identifies and understands the dynamics of a group; exhibits democratic principles as a leader or group member; communicates a vision, mission, or purpose that encourages commitment and action in others
Humanitarianism and Civic Engagement	**Understanding and appreciation of cultural and human differences**	Understands one's own identity and culture; seeks involvement with people different from oneself; articulates the advantages and impact of a diverse society; identifies systematic barriers to equality and inclusiveness, then advocates and justifies means for dismantling them; in interactions with others, exhibits respect and preserves the dignity of others
	Global perspective	Understands and analyzes the interconnectedness of societies worldwide; demonstrates effective stewardship of human, economic, and environmental resources
	Social responsibility	Recognizes social systems and their influence on people; appropriately challenges the unfair, unjust, or uncivil behavior of other individuals or groups; participates in service/volunteer activities that are characterized by reciprocity; articulates the values and principles involved in personal decision-making; affirms and values the worth of individuals and communities
	Sense of civic responsibility	Demonstrates consideration of the welfare of others in decision-making; engages in critical reflection and principled dissent; understands and participates in relevant governance systems; educates and facilitates the civic engagement of others
Practical competence	**Pursuing goals**	Sets and pursues individual goals; articulates rationale for personal and educational goals and objectives; articulates and makes plans to achieve long-term goals and objectives; identifies and works to overcome obstacles that hamper goal achievement

	Communicating effectively	Conveys meaning in a way that others understand by writing and speaking coherently and effectively; writes and speaks after reflection; influences others through writing, speaking or artistic expression; effectively articulates abstract ideas; uses appropriate syntax and grammar; makes and evaluates presentations or performances; listens attentively to others and responds appropriately
	Technological competence	Demonstrates technological literacy and skills; demonstrates the ethical application of intellectual property and privacy; uses technology ethically and effectively to communicate, solve problems, and complete tasks; stays current with technological innovations
	Managing personal affairs	Exhibits self-reliant behaviors; manages time effectively; develops strategies for managing finances
	Managing career development	Takes steps to initiate a job search or seek advanced education; constructs a resume based on clear job objectives and with evidence of knowledge, skills, and abilities; recognizes the importance of transferrable skills
	Demonstrating professionalism	Accepts supervision and direction as needed; values the contributions of others; holds self accountable for obligations; shows initiative; assesses, critiques, and then improves the quality of one's work and one's work environment
	Maintaining health and wellness	Engages in behaviors and contributes to environments that promote health and reduce risk; articulates the relationship between health and wellness in accomplishing goals; exhibits behaviors that advance the health of communities
	Living a purposeful and satisfying life	Makes purposeful decisions regarding balance among education, work, and leisure time; acts in congruence with personal identity, ethical, spiritual, and moral values

[1] This document is an adaptation of *Learning Reconsidered* and the CAS Learning Outcomes
[2] Categories adapted from *Learning Reconsidered (2004)* and Kuh, Douglas, Lund, & Ramin Gyurmek (1994)
[3] These examples are adopted from the George Mason University *Critical Thinking Assessment Report* (2006)

References

Council for the Advancement of Standards in Higher Education. (2006). *CAS professional standards for higher education* (6th ed.). Washington, DC: Author.

George Mason University (2006). *Critical Thinking Assessment Report*. Retrieved September 8, 2008 from https:assessment.gmu.edu/StudentLearningCompetencies/Critical/AssessProposal.html

Keeling, R. P. (2006). *Learning reconsidered 2: Implementing a campus-wide focus on the student experience*. American College Personnel Association (ACPA), Association of College and University Housing Officers-International (ACUHO-I), Association of College Unions-International (ACUI), National Academic Advising Association (NACADA), National Association for Campus Activities (NACA), National Association of Student Personnel Administrators (NASPA), and National Intramural-Recreational Sports Association (NIRSA).

Kuh, G. D., Douglas, K. B., Lund, J. P., & Ramin Gyurmek, J. (1994). *Student learning outside the classroom: Transcending artificial boundaries. (*ASHE-ERIC Higher Education Report No. 8.). Washington, D.C.: The George Washington University, Graduate School of Education and Human Development.

NASPA/ACPA (2004). *Learning reconsidered: A campus-wide focus on the student experience*. Washington, DC: National Association of Student Personnel Administrators and the American College Personnel Association.

The Role of the CAS General Standards
CAS Standards Contextual Statement

The Council for the Advancement of Standards in Higher Education (CAS) was established in 1979 as a consortium of professional associations whose members championed student learning and development in a variety of functional areas. From the outset, CAS identified its primary mission as the development and promulgation of professional standards that higher education practitioners could use to guide, develop, and assess programs and services. By 1986, with a repayable grant from the American College Testing Program (ACT), CAS had created 16 sets of functional area standards and published them in the first CAS "Blue Book." It was clear by the time of the initial publication that there were a number of characteristics common to all functional areas, commonalties that demanded inclusion in all current and future CAS standards. As a result, a set of *General Standards* (sometimes referred to as "boilerplate") were devised that CAS Board members unanimously agreed were relevant to all the student learning and development programs championed by CAS member associations. As the CAS General Standards evolved over the years, the Council consistently held to the principle that the fundamental commonalities underlying student learning and development are of the essence and must be maintained within the context of all CAS standards.

The 2002 revision of the General Standards is notable for its increased emphasis on achievable, observable, and assessable outcomes associated with student learning and development. Earlier versions of the CAS General Standards included a list of developmental domains (e.g., intellectual growth, effective communication, realistic self-appraisal, clarified values, career choices, leadership, and meaningful interpersonal relationships among others) for functional area programs to consider in their educational efforts. The 2002 revision, however, reaffirmed and reinforced the importance of the specified outcome domains by building into the General Standards a stated expectation that all functional area programs must place emphasis on identifying relevant learning outcomes and assessing their achievement by students.

To underscore the importance of the various outcome domains for all functional areas and to facilitate assessment of outcome domains by the functional areas, the 2002 revision of the General Standards included a table listing the 16 domains (intellectual growth, effective communication, enhanced self-esteem, realistic self-appraisal, clarified values, career choices, leadership development, healthy behavior, meaningful interpersonal relationships, independence, collaboration, social responsibility, satisfying and productive lifestyles, appreciating

diversity, spiritual awareness, and personal and educational goals), along with examples of achievement indicators that could be used to guide the assessment process. The indicators represented examples of observable student behaviors that practitioners could use to judge learning and development achievement. CAS published the *Frameworks for Assessing Learning and Development Outcomes* (2006) to further assist practitioners in implementing outcomes assessment activities. In effect, the 2002 revision of the General Standards recognized the potential educational impact that functional area programs can have upon student learning and development and reflected the need for them to emphasize and influence that learning as a significant part of their missions.

With the publication of *Learning Reconsidered 2* (2006), CAS decided that an integration of the learning outcomes from the General Standards and from Learning Reconsidered would enhance the profession's efforts in promoting student learning and development. Consequently, CAS hosted a "think tank" involving writers of *Learning Considered 2*, CAS directors, and prominent practitioners and faculty members in student affairs to recommend revisions to the CAS student learning and development domains. Simultaneously, CAS commenced the review and revision of the whole General Standards.

In 2008 the CAS Board of Directors adopted the revisions to the student learning and development outcomes and the General Standards that require institutional programs and services to identify relevant and desirable learning from six broad categories (called domains), assess relevant and desirable learning, and articulate how their programs and services contribute to domains not specifically assessed. The six domains are knowledge acquisition, construction, integration and application; cognitive complexity; intrapersonal development; interpersonal competence; humanitarianism and civic engagement; and practical competence. Each domain is further defined or clarified by learning outcome dimensions, which allow for a more focused assessment approach based on institutional mission and priorities. The domains and learning outcome dimensions are embedded in each functional area standard. Examples illustrating achievement of the student learning outcomes for each of the domains appear in the CAS Learning and Development Outcomes Chart and are referenced in each functional area standard.

Other significant features of the 2008 revision of the CAS General Standards include recognition of the pervasive use of technologies in programs and services with the creation of a new section on Technology; the reordering of the now 14 sections; and new standards and guidelines addressing sustainability practices, emergency and crisis response, and prevention efforts.

Those who use CAS standards for program evaluation, development, and enhancement will note the importance of the six learning outcome domains and the fact that all functional areas will be required to identify and assess the relevant and desirable learning from among the six domains and to articulate how their programs and services contribute to those domains not specifically assessed. It is anticipated that over time the student learning and development emphases among student support programs and services will increase and that ultimately these programs that currently complement formal academic learning will become coordinate in status as a recognized vehicle for student learning and development.

Although the CAS General Standards were not designed to stand alone, they are presented here to remind and inform educators about the commonalities that exist among the many student support programs and services throughout higher education. There can be little doubt that if those who lead and practice in such programs combine their collective powers to make an educational difference in the lives of the students they serve, the resulting educational trust will carry student support programs and services to new heights of achievement for all concerned.

References

Keeling, R. (Ed.). (2006). *Learning reconsidered 2: Implementing a campus-wide focus on the student experience.* American College Personnel Association, Association of College and University Housing Officers-International, Association of College Unions-International, National Academic Advising Association, National Association for Campus Activities, National Association of Student Personnel Administrators, National Intramural-Recreational Sports Association.

Strayhorn, T. (2006). *Frameworks for assessing learning and development outcomes.* Washington, DC: Council for the Advancement of Standards in Higher Education.

Contributors:

Current edition:
Patricia Carretta, George Mason University, NACE
Jan Arminio, Shippensburg University, NACA

Previous editions:
Laura A. Dean, University of Georgia, ACCA
Ted K. Miller, University of Georgia, ACPA/CAS

CAS General Standards
CAS Standards and Guidelines

Part 1. MISSION

Programs and services must develop, disseminate, implement, and regularly review their mission. Mission statements must be consistent with the mission of the institution and with professional standards. Programs and services in higher education must enhance overall educational experiences by incorporating student learning and development outcomes in their mission.

Part 2. PROGRAM

The formal education of students, consisting of the curriculum and the co-curriculum, must promote student learning and development outcomes that are purposeful and holistic and that prepare students for satisfying and productive lifestyles, work, and civic participation. The student learning and development outcome domains and their related dimensions are:

- knowledge acquisition, integration, construction, and application
    o Dimensions: understanding knowledge from a range of disciplines; connecting knowledge to other knowledge, ideas, and experiences; constructing knowledge; and relating knowledge to daily life

- cognitive complexity
    o Dimensions: critical thinking; reflective thinking; effective reasoning; and creativity

- intrapersonal development
    o Dimensions: realistic self-appraisal, self-understanding, and self-respect; identity development; commitment to ethics and integrity; and spiritual awareness

- interpersonal competence
    o Dimensions: meaningful relationships; interdependence; collaboration; and effective leadership

- humanitarianism and civic engagement
    o Dimensions: understanding and appreciation of cultural and human differences; social responsibility; global perspective; and sense of civic responsibility

- practical competence
    o Dimensions: pursuing goals; communicating effectively; technical competence; managing personal affairs; managing career development; demonstrating professionalism; maintaining health and wellness; and living a purposeful and satisfying life

[See *The Council for the Advancement of Standards Learning and Developmental Outcomes* statement for examples of outcomes related to these domains and dimensions.]

Consistent with the institutional mission, programs and services must identify relevant and desirable student learning and development outcomes from among the six domains and related dimensions. When creating opportunities for student learning and development, programs and services must explore possibilities for collaboration with faculty members and other colleagues.

Programs and services must assess relevant and desirable student learning and development outcomes and provide evidence of their impact on student learning and development. Programs and services must articulate how they contribute to or support students' learning and development in the domains not specifically assessed.

Programs and services must be:
- integrated into the life of the institution
- intentional and coherent
- guided by theories and knowledge of learning and development
- reflective of developmental and demographic profiles of the student population
- responsive to needs of individuals, diverse and special populations, and relevant constituencies

Part 3. LEADERSHIP

Because effective and ethical leadership is essential to the success of all organizations, leaders with organizational authority for the programs and services must:
- articulate a vision and mission for their programs and services
- set goals and objectives based on the needs of the population served and desired student learning and development outcomes
- advocate for their programs and services
- promote campus environments that provide meaningful opportunities for student learning, development, and integration
- identify and find means to address individual, organizational, or environmental conditions that foster or inhibit mission achievement
- advocate for representation in strategic planning initiatives at appropriate divisional and institutional levels
- initiate collaborative interactions with stakeholders who have legitimate concerns and interests in the functional area
- apply effective practices to educational and administrative processes
- prescribe and model ethical behavior
- communicate effectively
- manage financial resources, including planning, allocation, monitoring, and analysis

- incorporate sustainability practices in the management and design of programs, services, and facilities
- manage human resource processes including recruitment, selection, development, supervision, performance planning, and evaluation
- empower professional, support, and student staff to accept leadership opportunities
- encourage and support scholarly contribution to the profession
- be informed about and integrate appropriate technologies into programs and services
- be knowledgeable about federal, state/provincial, and local laws relevant to the programs and services and ensure that staff members understand their responsibilities by receiving appropriate training
- develop and continuously improve programs and services in response to the changing needs of students and other populations served and the evolving institutional priorities
- recognize environmental conditions that may negatively influence the safety of staff and students and propose interventions that mitigate such conditions.

Part 4. HUMAN RESOURCES

Programs and services must be staffed adequately by individuals qualified to accomplish the mission and goals. Within institutional guidelines, programs and services must establish procedures for staff selection, training, and evaluation; set expectations for supervision; and provide appropriate professional development opportunities to improve the leadership ability, competence, and skills of all employees.

Professional staff members must hold an earned graduate or professional degree in a field relevant to the position they hold or must possess an appropriate combination of educational credentials and related work experience.

Degree- or credential-seeking interns must be qualified by enrollment in an appropriate field of study and by relevant experience. These individuals must be trained and supervised adequately by professional staff members holding educational credentials and related work experience appropriate for supervision.

Student employees and volunteers must be carefully selected, trained, supervised, and evaluated. They must be educated on how and when to refer those in need of additional assistance to qualified staff members and must have access to a supervisor for assistance in making these judgments. Student employees and volunteers must be provided clear and precise job descriptions, pre-service training based on assessed needs, and continuing staff development.

Employees and volunteers must receive specific training on institutional policies and privacy laws regarding their access to student records and other sensitive institutional information (e.g., in the USA, Family Educational Rights and Privacy Act, FERPA, or equivalent privacy laws in other states/provinces or countries).

Programs and services must have technical and support staff members adequate to accomplish their mission. All members of the staff must be technologically proficient and qualified to perform their job functions, be knowledgeable about ethical and legal uses of technology, and have access to training and resources to support the performance of their assigned responsibilities.

All members of the staff must receive training on policies and procedures related to the use of technology to store or access student records and institutional data.

Programs and services must ensure that staff members are knowledgeable about and trained in emergency procedures, crisis response, and prevention efforts. Prevention efforts must address identification of threatening conduct or behavior of students, faculty members, staff, and others and must incorporate a system or procedures for responding, including but not limited to reporting them to the appropriate campus officials.

Salary levels and benefits for all staff members must be commensurate with those for comparable positions within the institution, in similar institutions, and in the relevant geographic area.

Programs and services must maintain position descriptions for all staff members.

To create a diverse staff, programs and services must institute hiring and promotion practices that are fair, inclusive, proactive, and non-discriminatory.

Programs and services must conduct regular performance planning and evaluation of staff members. Programs and services must provide access to continuing and advanced education and professional development opportunities.

Part 5. ETHICS

Persons involved in the delivery of programs and services must adhere to the highest principles of ethical behavior. Programs and services must review relevant professional ethical standards and develop or adopt and implement appropriate statements of ethical practice. Programs and services must publish these statements and ensure their periodic review by relevant constituencies.

Programs and services must orient new staff members to relevant ethical standards and statements of ethical practice.

Staff members must ensure that privacy and confidentiality are maintained with respect to all communications and records to the extent that such records are protected under the law and appropriate statements of ethical practice. Information contained in students' education records must not be disclosed except as allowed by relevant laws and institutional policies. Staff members must disclose to appropriate authorities information judged to be of an emergency nature, especially when the safety of the individual or others is involved, or when otherwise required by institutional policy or relevant law.

Staff members must be aware of and comply with the provisions contained in the institution's policies pertaining to human subjects research and student rights and responsibilities, as well as those in other relevant institutional policies addressing ethical practices and confidentiality of research data concerning individuals.

Staff members must recognize and avoid personal conflicts of interest or appearance thereof in the performance of their work.

Staff members must strive to insure the fair, objective, and impartial treatment of all persons with whom they interact.

When handling institutional funds, staff members must ensure that such funds are managed in accordance with established and responsible accounting procedures and the fiscal policies or processes of the institution.

Promotional and descriptive information must be accurate and free of deception.

Staff members must perform their duties within the limits of their training, expertise, and competence. When these limits are exceeded, individuals in need of further assistance must be referred to persons possessing appropriate qualifications.

Staff members must use suitable means to confront and otherwise hold accountable other staff members who exhibit unethical behavior.

Staff members must be knowledgeable about and practice ethical behavior in the use of technology.

Part 6. LEGAL RESPONSIBILITIES

Staff members must be knowledgeable about and responsive to laws and regulations that relate to their respective responsibilities and that may pose legal obligations, limitations, or ramifications for the institution as a whole. As appropriate, staff members must inform users of programs and services, as well as officials, of legal obligations and limitations including constitutional, statutory, regulatory, and case law; mandatory laws and orders emanating from federal, state/provincial, and local governments; and the institution's policies.

Programs and services must have written policies on all relevant operations, transactions, or tasks that may have legal implications.

Staff members must neither participate in nor condone any form of harassment or activity that demeans persons or creates an intimidating, hostile, or offensive campus environment.

Staff members must use reasonable and informed practices to limit the liability exposure of the institution and its officers, employees, and agents. Staff members must be informed about institutional policies regarding risk management, personal liability, and related insurance coverage options and must be referred to external sources if coverage is not provided by the institution.

The institution must provide access to legal advice for staff members as needed to carry out assigned responsibilities.

The institution must inform staff and students in a timely and systematic fashion about extraordinary or changing legal obligations and potential liabilities.

Part 7. EQUITY and ACCESS

Programs and services must be provided on a fair, equitable, and non-discriminatory basis in accordance with institutional policies and with all applicable state/provincial and federal statutes and regulations. Programs and services must maintain an educational and work environment free from discrimination in accordance with law and institutional policy.

Discrimination must be avoided on the basis of age; cultural heritage; disability; ethnicity; gender identity and expression; nationality; political affiliation; race; religious affiliation; sex; sexual orientation; economic, marital, social, or veteran status; and any other bases included in local, state/provincial, or federal laws.

Consistent with the mission and goals, programs and services must take action to remedy significant imbalances in student participation and staffing patterns.

Programs and services must ensure physical and program access for persons with disabilities. Programs and services must be responsive to the needs of all students and other populations served when establishing hours of operation and developing methods of delivering programs and services.

Programs and services must recognize the needs of distance learning students by providing appropriate and accessible services and assisting them in identifying and gaining access to other appropriate services in their geographic region.

Part 8. DIVERSITY

Within the context of each institution's unique mission, diversity enriches the community and enhances the collegiate experience for all; therefore, programs and services must create and nurture environments that are welcoming to and bring together persons of diverse backgrounds.

Programs and services must promote environments that

are characterized by open and continuous communication that deepens understanding of one's own identity, culture, and heritage, as well as that of others. Programs and services must recognize, honor, educate, and promote respect about commonalties and differences among people within their historical and cultural contexts.

Programs and services must address the characteristics and needs of a diverse population when establishing and implementing policies and procedures.

Part 9. ORGANIZATION and MANAGEMENT

To promote student learning and development outcomes, programs and services must be structured purposefully and managed effectively to achieve stated goals. Evidence of appropriate structure must include current and accessible policies and procedures, written performance expectations for all employees, functional workflow graphics or organizational charts, and clearly stated program and service delivery expectations.

Programs and services must monitor websites used for distributing information to ensure that the sites are current, accurate, appropriately referenced, and accessible.

Evidence of effective management must include use of comprehensive and accurate information for decisions, clear sources and channels of authority, effective communication practices, procedures for decision-making and conflict resolution, responses to changing conditions, systems of accountability and evaluation, and processes for recognition and reward. Programs and services must align policies and procedures with those of the institution and provide channels within the organization for their regular review.

Part 10. CAMPUS and EXTERNAL RELATIONS

Programs and services must reach out to relevant individuals, campus offices, and external agencies to:
- establish, maintain, and promote effective relations
- disseminate information about their own and other related programs and services
- coordinate and collaborate, where appropriate, in offering programs and services to meet the needs of students and promote their achievement of student learning and development outcomes

Programs and services must have procedures and guidelines consistent with institutional policy for responding to threats, emergencies, and crisis situations.
Systems and procedures must be in place to disseminate timely and accurate information to students and other members of the campus community during emergency situations.

Programs and services must have procedures and guidelines consistent with institutional policy for communicating

with the media.

Part 11. FINANCIAL RESOURCES

Programs and services must have adequate funding to accomplish their mission and goals. In establishing funding priorities and making significant changes, a comprehensive analysis, which includes relevant expenditures, external and internal resources, and impact on the campus community, must be conducted.

Programs and services must demonstrate fiscal responsibility and cost effectiveness consistent with institutional protocols.

Part 12. TECHNOLOGY

Programs and services must have adequate technology to support their mission. The technology and its use must comply with institutional policies and procedures and be evaluated for compliance with relevant federal, state/provincial, and local requirements.

Programs and services must maintain policies and procedures that address the security and back up of data.

When technology is used to facilitate student learning and development, programs and services must select technology that reflects current best pedagogical practices.

Technology, as well as any workstations or computer labs maintained by the programs and services for student use, must be accessible and must meet established technology standards for delivery to persons with disabilities.

When programs and services provide student access to technology, they must provide:
- access to policies that are clear, easy to understand, and available to all students
- access to instruction or training on how to use the technology
- access to information on the legal and ethical implications of misuse as it pertains to intellectual property, harassment, privacy, and social networks.

Student violations of technology policies must follow established institutional student disciplinary procedures.

Students who experience negative emotional or psychological consequences from the use of technology must be referred to support services provided by the institution.

Part 13. FACILITIES and EQUIPMENT

Programs and services must have adequate, accessible, suitably located facilities and equipment to support their mission and goals. If acquiring capital equipment as defined by the institution, programs and services must take into account expenses related to regular maintenance and life cycle costs. Facilities and equipment must be evaluated regularly, including consideration of sustainability, and be in compliance with relevant federal, state/provincial, and local requirements to provide for access, health, safety, and security.

Staff members must have work space that is well-equipped, adequate in size, and designed to support their work and responsibilities. For conversations requiring privacy, staff members must have access to a private space.

Staff members who share work space must have the ability to secure their work adequately.

The design of the facilities must guarantee the security of records and ensure the confidentiality of sensitive information.

The location and layout of the facilities must be sensitive to the special needs of persons with disabilities as well as the needs of constituencies served.

Programs and services must ensure that staff members are knowledgeable of and trained in safety and emergency procedures for securing and vacating the facilities.

Part 14. ASSESSMENT and EVALUATION

Programs and services must establish systematic plans and processes to meet internal and external accountability expectations with regard to program as well as student learning and development outcomes. Programs and services must conduct regular assessment and evaluations. Assessments must include qualitative and quantitative methodologies as appropriate, to determine whether and to what degree the stated mission, goals, and student learning and development outcomes are being met. The process must employ sufficient and sound measures to ensure comprehensiveness. Data collected must include responses from students and other affected constituencies.

Programs and services must evaluate regularly how well they complement and enhance the institution's stated mission and educational effectiveness.

Results of these evaluations must be used in revising and improving programs and services, identifying needs and interests in shaping directions of program and service design, and recognizing staff performance.

Revision approved October 2008

The Role of Academic Advising Programs
CAS Standards Contextual Statement

Academic advising is an essential element of a student's collegiate experience. Advising evolves from the institution's culture, values, and practices and is delivered in accordance with these factors. Advising practice draws from various theories and strategies in the social sciences, humanities, and education (e.g., teaching and counseling, the psychology of learning, communication studies, theories of decision making and information transfer, and story telling as a mechanism for understanding human experiences). "In recent years, increasing political, social and economic demands, along with newly developed technologies, have spurred changes in educational delivery systems, student access, and faculty roles. As a result of these changes, more specialized student support opportunities have emerged, including adaptations in academic advising. And as White (2000) noted with a growing 'number of majors available on college campuses, an increasingly complex and rapidly shifting work environment. . ., and a dizzyingly extensive array of out-of-class educational experiences to choose from, college students are demanding more and better advising'"(NACADA, 2005).

Academic advising is one of the very few institutional functions that connect all students to the institution. As higher educational curricula become increasingly complex and as educational options expand, pressure to make the academic experience as meaningful as possible for students has increased as well. Higher education, in turn, has responded with renewed attention to the need for quality academic advising.

"Once almost exclusively a faculty function, today academic advising has come forward as a specialization within the higher education community. While remaining a role that faculty members play, academic advising has emerged as an area of expertise in and of itself" (NACADA, 2005). Habley (2005) expounds the notion that "advising bears the distinction of being the only structured activity on campus in which all students have the opportunity for on-going, one-to-one interaction with a concerned representative of the institution, and this fact is a source of its tremendous potential today" (NACADA, 2005). This, coupled with increasing educational options, has brought pressure to make the student educational experiences as meaningful as possible.

The establishment of the National Academic Advising Association (NACADA) following the first national conference on advising in 1977 was a significant turning point in according recognition to those within higher education who consider their work in academic advising as purposeful and unique. Today, NACADA flourishes with membership numbering more than 9100 and national and regional meetings that attract more than 6000 participants annually. The NACADA Statement of Core Values, last revised in 2004, meets the need for ethical principles to guide advising practice and provides a professional framework for all academic advisors to examine their behaviors.

Academic advising became a significant category within professional literature during the 1980s, and this trend continues today. NACADA publishes the *NACADA Journal*, a juried research journal, along with books, monographs, videos and CDs that examine various aspects of advising. Some of the most referenced resources in the field include *Academic Advising: A comprehensive handbook, The Status of Academic Advising: The Findings from the ACT Sixth National Survey*, the *Guide to Assessment in Academic Advising*, and the resources found on the Web from the *NACADA Clearinghouse of Academic Advising Resources*. Information about NACADA's publications, as well as a link to the *Clearinghouse*, can be located electronically via the NACADA web site on the World Wide Web at www.nacada.ksu.edu. The NACADA Executive Office is an excellent source of general information.

Academic advising is a crucial component of all students' experiences in higher education. Within this context, students can find meaning in their lives, make significant decisions about the future, be supported to achieve to their maximum potential, and access all that higher education has to offer. When practiced with competence and dedication, academic advising can enhance retention rates. In an age often characterized by impersonality and detachment, academic advising provides a vital personal connection that students need.

References, Readings, and Resources

Campbell, S., Nutt, C., Robbins, R. Kirk-Kuwaye, M. and Higa, L. (2005). *Guide to Assessment in Academic Advising*. Manhattan, KS: National Academic Advising Association.

Gordon, V.M., & Habley, W. R. (Eds.). (2000). *Academic advising: A comprehensive handbook*. San Francisco: Jossey-Bass.

Habley, W. R. (2004). *The Status of Academic Advising: Findings from the ACT Sixth National Survey*. Manhattan, KS: National Academic Advising Association.

Habley, W.R. (August, 2005). Foundations of academic advising. Presentation. 2005 NACADA Summer Institute.

NACADA. (2004). Statement of Core Values. Retrieved January 24, 2006 from http://www.nacada.ksu.edu/Clearinghouse/AdvisingIssues/Core-Values.htm

NACADA. (2005). The History and Definitions of Academic Advising. In *What is Academic Advising: Foundation of Academic Advising CD Series.* Manhattan, KS: National Academic Advising Association.

NACADA. (2006). Clearinghouse of Academic Advising Resources. Retrieved January 24, 2005 from http://www.nacada.ksu.edu/Resources/index.htm.

White, E. R. (2000). Developing Mission, Goals, and Objectives for the Advising Program. In V.N. Gordon & W.R. Habley (Eds.), *Academic advising: A comprehensive handbook* (pp. 180-191). San Francisco: Jossey-Bass.

Contributors:

Current edition:
Eric R. White, The Pennsylvania State University
Charlie Nutt, NACADA, with input from Marsha Miller, NACADA

Previous editions:
Linda C. Higginson, The Pennsylvania State University

Academic Advising Programs
CAS Standards and Guidelines

Part 1. MISSION

The primary purpose of Academic Advising Programs (AAP) is to assist students in the development of meaningful educational plans.

AAP must develop, disseminate, implement, and regularly review their mission. Mission statements must be consistent with the mission of the institution and with professional standards. AAP in higher education must enhance overall educational experiences by incorporating student learning and development outcomes in their mission.

The institution must have a clearly written mission statement pertaining to academic advising that must include program goals and expectations of advisors and advisees.

Part 2. PROGRAM

The formal education of students, consisting of the curriculum and the co-curriculum, must promote student learning and development outcomes that are purposeful and holistic and that prepare students for satisfying and productive lifestyles, work, and civic participation. The student learning and development outcome domains and their related dimensions are:

• knowledge acquisition, integration, construction, and application
   o Dimensions: understanding knowledge from a range of disciplines; connecting knowledge to other knowledge, ideas, and experiences; constructing knowledge; and relating knowledge to daily life

• cognitive complexity
   o Dimensions: critical thinking; reflective thinking; effective reasoning; and creativity

• intrapersonal development
   o Dimensions: realistic self-appraisal, self-understanding, and self-respect; identity development; commitment to ethics and integrity; and spiritual awareness

• interpersonal competence
   o Dimensions: meaningful relationships; interdependence; collaboration; and effective leadership

• humanitarianism and civic engagement
   o Dimensions: understanding and appreciation of cultural and human differences; social responsibility; global perspective; and sense of civic responsibility

• practical competence
   o Dimensions: pursuing goals; communicating effectively; technical competence; managing personal affairs; managing career development; demonstrating professionalism; maintaining health and wellness; and

living a purposeful and satisfying life

[See *The Council for the Advancement of Standards Learning and Developmental Outcomes* statement for examples of outcomes related to these domains and dimensions.]

Consistent with the institutional mission, Academic Advising Programs (AAP) must identify relevant and desirable student learning and development outcomes from among the six domains and related dimensions. When creating opportunities for student learning and development, AAP must explore possibilities for collaboration with faculty members and other colleagues.

AAP must assess relevant and desirable student learning and development outcomes and provide evidence of their impact on student learning and development. Programs and services must articulate how they contribute to or support students' learning and development in the domains not specifically assessed.

AAP must be:
- integrated into the life of the institution
- intentional and coherent
- guided by theories and knowledge of learning and development
- reflective to needs of individuals, diverse and special populations, and relevant constituencies

Both students and advisors must assume shared responsibility in the advising process. AAP must assist students to make the best academic decisions possible by encouraging identification and assessment of alternatives and consideration of the consequences of their decisions.

The ultimate responsibility for making decisions about educational plans and life goals should rest with the individual student.

AAP must be guided by a set of written goals and objectives that are directly related to its stated mission.

AAP must:
- promote student growth and development
- assist students in assessing their interests and abilities, examining their educational goals, making decisions and developing short-term and long-term plans to meet their objectives
- discuss and clarify educational, career, and life goals
- provide accurate and timely information and interpret institutional, general education, and major requirements
- assist students to understand the educational context within which they are enrolled
- advise on the selection of appropriate courses and other educational experiences
- clarify institutional policies and procedures
- evaluate and monitor student academic progress and

- the impact on achievement of goals
  - reinforce student self-direction and self-sufficiency
  - direct students with educational, career, or personal concerns, or skill/learning deficiencies, to other resources and programs on the campus when necessary
  - make students aware of and refer to educational, institutional, and community resources and services (e.g., internship, study abroad, honors, service-learning, research opportunities)
  - collect and distribute relevant data about student needs, preferences, and performance for use in institutional decisions and policy

AAP should provide information about student experiences and concerns regarding their academic program to appropriate decision makers.

AAP should make available to academic advisors all pertinent research (e.g., about students, the academic advising program, and perceptions of the institution).

The academic advisor must review and use available data about students' academic and educational needs, performance, and aspirations.

AAP must identify environmental conditions that may positively or negatively influence student academic achievement and propose interventions that may neutralize negative conditions.

AAP must provide current and accurate advising information to students and academic advisors.

AAP should employ the latest technologies for delivery of advising information.

Academic advising conferences must be available to students each academic term.

Academic advisors should offer conferences in a format that is convenient to the student, i.e., in person, by telephone, or on-line. Advising conferences may be carried out individually or in groups.

Academic advising caseloads must be consistent with the time required for the effective performance of this activity.

The academic status of the student being advised should be taken into consideration when determining caseloads. For example, first year, undecided, under-prepared, and honors students may require more advising time than upper-division students who have declared their majors.

Academic advisors should allow an appropriate amount of time for students to discuss plans, programs, courses, academic progress, and other subjects related to their educational programs.

When determining workloads it should be recognized that advisors may work with students not officially assigned to them and that contacts regarding advising may extend beyond direct contact with the student.

Part 3. LEADERSHIP

Because effective and ethical leadership is essential to the success of all organizations, Academic Advising Programs (AAP) leaders with organizational authority for the programs and services must:

- articulate a vision and mission for their programs and services
- set goals and objectives based on the needs of the population served and desired student learning and development outcomes
- advocate for their programs and services
- promote campus environments that provide meaningful opportunities for student learning, development, and integration
- identify and find means to address individual, organizational, or environmental conditions that foster or inhibit mission achievement
- advocate for representation in strategic planning initiatives at appropriate divisional and institutional levels
- initiate collaborative interactions with stakeholders who have legitimate concerns and interests in the functional area
- apply effective practices to educational and administrative processes
- prescribe and model ethical behavior
- communicate effectively
- manage financial resources, including planning, allocation, monitoring, and analysis
- incorporate sustainability practices in the management and design of programs, services, and facilities
- manage human resource processes including recruitment, selection, development, supervision, performance planning, and evaluation
- empower professional, support, and student staff to accept leadership opportunities
- encourage and support scholarly contribution to the profession
- be informed about and integrate appropriate technologies into programs and services
- be knowledgeable about federal, state/provincial, and local laws relevant to the programs and services and ensure that staff members understand their responsibilities by receiving appropriate training
- develop and continuously improve programs and services in response to the changing needs of students and other populations served and the evolving institutional priorities
- recognize environmental conditions that may negatively influence the safety of staff and students and propose interventions that mitigate such conditions

Part 4. HUMAN RESOURCES

Academic Advising Programs (AAP) must be staffed adequately by individuals qualified to accomplish the mission

and goals. Within institutional guidelines, AAP must establish procedures for staff selection, training, and evaluation; set expectations for supervision; and provide appropriate professional development opportunities to improve the leadership ability, competence, and skills of all employees.

Academic advising personnel may be full-time or part-time professionals who have advising as their primary function or may be faculty whose responsibilities include academic advising. Paraprofessionals (e.g., graduate students, interns, or assistants) or peer advisors may also assist advisors.

AAP professional staff members must hold an earned graduate or professional degree in a field relevant to the position they hold or must possess an appropriate combination of educational credentials and related work experience.

Academic advisors should have an understanding of student development, student learning, career development, and other relevant theories in education, social sciences, and humanities.

Academic advisors should have a comprehensive knowledge of the institution's programs, academic requirements, policies and procedures, majors, minors, and support services.

Academic advisors should demonstrate an interest and effectiveness in working with and assisting students and a willingness to participate in professional activities.

Sufficient personnel must be available to address students' advising needs without unreasonable delay.

Degree- or credential-seeking interns must be qualified by enrollment in an appropriate field of study and by relevant experience. These individuals must be trained and supervised adequately by professional staff members holding educational credentials and related work experience appropriate for supervision.

Student employees and volunteers must be carefully selected, trained, supervised, and evaluated. They must be educated on how and when to refer those in need of additional assistance to qualified staff members and must have access to a supervisor for assistance in making these judgments. Student employees and volunteers must be provided clear and precise job descriptions, pre-service training based on assessed needs, and continuing staff development.

Employees and volunteers must receive specific training on institutional policies and privacy laws regarding their access to student records and other sensitive institutional information (e.g., in the USA, Family Educational Rights and Privacy Act, FERPA, or equivalent privacy laws in other states/provinces or countries).

AAP must have technical and support staff members adequate to accomplish their mission. All members of the staff must be technologically proficient and qualified to perform their job functions, be knowledgeable about ethical and legal uses of technology, and have access to training

and resources to support the performance of their assigned responsibilities.

Support personnel should maintain student records, organize resource materials, receive students, make appointments, and handle correspondence and other operational needs. Technical staff may be used in research, data collection, systems development, and special projects.

All members of the staff must receive training on policies and procedures related to the use of technology to store or access student records and institutional data.

AAP must ensure that staff members are knowledgeable about and trained in emergency procedures, crisis response, and prevention efforts. Prevention efforts must address identification of threatening conduct or behavior of students, faculty members, staff, and others and must incorporate a system or procedures for responding, including but not limited to reporting them to the appropriate campus officials.

Salary levels and benefits for all staff members must be commensurate with those for comparable positions within the institution, in similar institutions, and in the relevant geographic area.

AAP must maintain position descriptions for all staff members.

To create a diverse staff, AAP must institute hiring and promotion practices that are fair, inclusive, proactive, and non-discriminatory.

AAP must conduct regular performance planning and evaluation of staff members. AAP must provide access to continuing and advanced education and professional development opportunities.

AAP must strive to improve the professional competence and skills of all personnel it employs.

Continued professional development should include areas such as the following and how they relate to academic advising:
- theories of student development, student learning, career development, and other relevant theories in education, social sciences, and humanities
- academic policies and procedures, including institutional transfer policies and curricular changes
- legal issues including U.S. Family Education and Records Privacy Act (FERPA)/Canadian Freedom Of Information and Protection of Privacy (FOIPP) and other privacy laws and policies
- technology and software training (e.g., degree audit, web registration)
- institutional resources (e.g., research opportunities, career services, internship opportunities, counseling and health services, tutorial services)
- ADA (disability-related accommodations) compliance issues

Part 5. ETHICS

Persons involved in the delivery of Academic Advising

Programs (AAP) must adhere to the highest principles of ethical behavior. AAP must review relevant professional ethical standards and develop or adopt and implement appropriate statements of ethical practice. AAP must publish these statements and ensure their periodic review by relevant constituencies.

Advisors must uphold policies, procedures, and values of their departments and institutions.

Advisors should consider ethical standards or other statements from relevant professional associations.

AAP must orient new staff members to relevant ethical standards and statements of ethical practice.

AAP staff members must ensure that privacy and confidentiality are maintained with respect to all communications and records to the extent that such records are protected under the law and appropriate statements of ethical practice. Information contained in students' education records must not be disclosed except as allowed by relevant laws and institutional policies. AAP staff members must disclose to appropriate authorities information judged to be of an emergency nature, especially when the safety of the individual or others is involved, or when otherwise required by institutional policy or relevant law.

When emergency disclosure is required, AAP should inform the student that it has taken place, to whom, and why.

AAP staff members must be aware of and comply with the provisions contained in the institution's policies pertaining to human subjects research and student rights and responsibilities, as well as those in other relevant institutional policies addressing ethical practices and confidentiality of research data concerning individuals.

AAP staff members must recognize and avoid personal conflicts of interest or appearance thereof in the performance of their work.

AAP staff members must strive to insure the fair, objective, and impartial treatment of all persons with whom they interact.

When handling institutional funds, AAP staff members must ensure that such funds are managed in accordance with established and responsible accounting procedures and the fiscal policies or processes of the institution.

Promotional and descriptive information must be accurate and free of deception.

AAP staff members must perform their duties within the limits of their training, expertise, and competence. When these limits are exceeded, individuals in need of further assistance must be referred to persons possessing appropriate qualifications.

AAP staff members must use suitable means to confront and otherwise hold accountable other staff members who exhibit unethical behavior.

AAP staff members must be knowledgeable about and practice ethical behavior in the use of technology.

Part 6. LEGAL RESPONSIBILITIES

Academic Advising Programs (AAP) staff members must be knowledgeable about and responsive to laws and regulations that relate to their respective responsibilities and that may pose legal obligations, limitations, or ramifications for the institution as a whole. As appropriate, staff members must inform users of programs and services, as well as officials, of legal obligations and limitations including constitutional, statutory, regulatory, and case law; mandatory laws and orders emanating from federal, state/provincial, and local governments; and the institution's policies.

AAP must have written policies on all relevant operations, transactions, or tasks that may have legal implications.

AAP staff members must neither participate in nor condone any form of harassment or activity that demeans persons or creates an intimidating, hostile, or offensive campus environment.

AAP staff members must use reasonable and informed practices to limit the liability exposure of the institution and its officers, employees, and agents. AAP staff members must be informed about institutional policies regarding risk management, personal liability, and related insurance coverage options and must be referred to external sources if coverage is not provided by the institution.

The institution must provide access to legal advice for AAP staff members as needed to carry out assigned responsibilities.

The institution must inform AAP staff and students in a timely and systematic fashion about extraordinary or changing legal obligations and potential liabilities.

Part 7. EQUITY and ACCESS

Academic Advising Programs (AAP) must be provided on a fair, equitable, and non-discriminatory basis in accordance with institutional policies and with all applicable state/provincial and federal statutes and regulations. AAP must maintain an educational and work environment free from discrimination in accordance with law and institutional policy.

Discrimination must be avoided on the basis of age; cultural heritage; disability; ethnicity; gender identity and expression; nationality; political affiliation; race; religious affiliation; sex; sexual orientation; economic, marital, social, or veteran status; and any other bases included in local, state/provincial, or federal laws.

Consistent with the mission and goals, AAP must take action to remedy significant imbalances in student participation and staffing patterns.

AAP must ensure physical and program access for persons with disabilities. AAP must be responsive to the needs of all students and other populations served when establishing hours of operation and developing methods of delivering programs and services.

AAP must recognize the needs of distance learning students by providing appropriate and accessible services and assisting them in identifying and gaining access to other appropriate services in their geographic region.

Part 8. DIVERSITY

Within the context of each institution's unique mission, diversity enriches the community and enhances the collegiate experience for all; therefore, Academic Advising Programs (AAP) must create and nurture environments that are welcoming to and bring together persons of diverse backgrounds.

AAP must promote environments that are characterized by open and continuous communication that deepens understanding of one's own identity, culture, and heritage, as well as that of others. AAP must recognize, honor, educate, and promote respect about commonalties and differences among people within their historical and cultural contexts.

AAP must address the characteristics and needs of a diverse population when establishing and implementing policies and procedures.

Part 9. ORGANIZATION and MANAGEMENT

To promote student learning and development outcomes, Academic Advising Programs (AAP) must be structured purposefully and managed effectively to achieve stated goals. Evidence of appropriate structure must include current and accessible policies and procedures, written performance expectations for all employees, functional workflow graphics or organizational charts, and clearly stated program and service delivery expectations.

AAP must monitor websites used for distributing information to ensure that the sites are current, accurate, appropriately referenced, and accessible.

Evidence of effective management must include use of comprehensive and accurate information for decisions, clear sources and channels of authority, effective communication practices, procedures for decision-making and conflict resolution, responses to changing conditions, systems of accountability and evaluation, and processes for recognition and reward. AAP must align policies and procedures with those of the institution and provide channels within the organization for their regular review.

The design of AAP must be compatible with the institution's organizational structure and its students' needs. Specific advisor responsibilities must be clearly delineated, published, and disseminated to both advisors and advisees.

Students, faculty advisors, and professional staff must be informed of their respective advising responsibilities.

AAP may be a centralized or decentralized function within an institution, with a variety of people throughout the institution assuming responsibilities.

AAP must provide the same services to distance learners as it does to students on campus. The distance education advising must provide for appropriate real time or delayed interaction between advisors and students.

Part 10. CAMPUS and EXTERNAL RELATIONS

Academic Advising Programs (AAP) must reach out to relevant individuals, campus offices, and external agencies to:
- establish, maintain, and promote effective relations
- disseminate information about their own and other related programs and services
- coordinate and collaborate, where appropriate, in offering programs and services to meet the needs of students and promote their achievement of student learning and development outcomes

AAP must have procedures and guidelines consistent with institutional policy for responding to threats, emergencies, and crisis situations. Systems and procedures must be in place to disseminate timely and accurate information to students and other members of the campus community during emergency situations.

AAP must have procedures and guidelines consistent with institutional policy for communicating with the media.

Academic advising is integral to the educational process and depends upon close working relationships with other institutional agencies and the administration. AAP should be fully integrated into other processes of the institution. Academic advisors should be consulted when there are modifications to or closures of academic programs.

For referral purposes, AAP should provide academic advisors a comprehensive list of relevant external agencies, campus offices, and opportunities.

Part 11. FINANCIAL RESOURCES

Academic Advising Programs (AAP) must have adequate funding to accomplish their mission and goals. In establishing funding priorities and making significant changes, a comprehensive analysis, which includes relevant expenditures, external and internal resources, and impact on the campus community, must be conducted.

AAP must demonstrate fiscal responsibility and cost effectiveness consistent with institutional protocols.

Special consideration should be given to providing funding for the professional development of advisors.

Financial resources should be sufficient to provide high-quality print and web-based information for students and training materials for advisors. Sufficient financial resources should be provided to promote the academic advising program.

Part 12. TECHNOLOGY

Academic Advising Programs (AAP) must have adequate technology to support their mission. The technology and its use must comply with institutional policies and procedures and be evaluated for compliance with relevant federal, state/provincial, and local requirements.

AAP must maintain policies and procedures that address the security and back up of data.

When technology is used to facilitate student learning and development, AAP must select technology that reflects current best pedagogical practices.

Academic advisors must have access to computing equipment, local networks, student data bases, and the Internet.

Technology, as well as any workstations or computer labs maintained by the AAP for student use, must be accessible and must meet established technology standards for delivery to persons with disabilities.

When AAP provide student access to technology, they must provide:
- access to policies that are clear, easy to understand, and available to all students
- access to instruction or training on how to use the technology
- access to information on the legal and ethical implications of misuse as it pertains to intellectual property, harassment, privacy, and social networks.

Student violations of technology policies must follow established institutional student disciplinary procedures.

Students who experience negative emotional or psychological consequences from the use of technology must be referred to support services provided by the institution.

AAP must ensure that on-line and technology-assisted advising includes appropriate mechanisms for obtaining approvals, consultations, and referrals.

Part 13. FACILITIES and EQUIPMENT

Academic Advising Programs (AAP) must have adequate, accessible, suitably located facilities and equipment to support their mission and goals. If acquiring capital equipment as defined by the institution, AAP must take into account expenses related to regular maintenance and life cycle costs. Facilities and equipment must be evaluated regularly, including consideration of sustainability, and be in compliance with relevant federal, state/provincial, and local requirements to provide for access, health, safety, and security.

AAP staff members must have work space that is well-equipped, adequate in size, and designed to support their work and responsibilities. For conversations requiring privacy, staff members must have access to a private space.

AAP staff members who share work space must have the ability to secure their work adequately.

The design of the facilities must guarantee the security of records and ensure the confidentiality of sensitive information.

The location and layout of the facilities must be sensitive to the special needs of persons with disabilities as well as the needs of constituencies served.

AAP must ensure that staff members are knowledgeable of and trained in safety and emergency procedures for securing and vacating the facilities.

Privacy and freedom from visual and auditory distractions must be considered in designing appropriate facilities.

Part 14. ASSESSMENT and EVALUATION

Academic Advising Programs (AAP) must establish systematic plans and processes to meet internal and external accountability expectations with regard to program as well as student learning and development outcomes. AAP must conduct regular assessment and evaluations. Assessments must include qualitative and quantitative methodologies as appropriate, to determine whether and to what degree the stated mission, goals, and student learning and development outcomes are being met. The process must employ sufficient and sound measures to ensure comprehensiveness. Data collected must include responses from students and other affected constituencies.

AAP must evaluate regularly how well they complement and enhance the institution's stated mission and educational effectiveness.

Results of these evaluations must be used in revising and improving programs and services, identifying needs and interests in shaping directions of program and service design, and recognizing staff performance.

General Standards revised in 2008;
AAP content developed/revised in 1986, 1997, & 2005

The Role of Admission Programs
CAS Standards Contextual Statement

When colonial colleges were founded, their primary mission was similar to the English tradition of providing liberal education and professional study for young men of intellectual and financial ability. Admission programs focused on identifying and admitting young men for the ministry. However, as other colleges were subsequently founded, chartered, and funded, their missions changed to address changes in student needs, ages, religions, social class, identities, and proximity to campus.

The role of admissions professionals and the process of admissions today might best be understood by considering two competing forces: service to the institution and service to prospective students. In general, the overall responsibility of admissions professionals is to help students understand the process of transition to college, admission criteria, and the competitiveness of their credentials. These tasks are typically accomplished through personal interactions, group presentations, publications, and other recruitment and counseling strategies.

The admissions professional must also have a firm understanding of the institution's mission, enrollment goals, fiscal priorities, and student and departmental needs. When performing well, the successful admissions professional serves a vital role establishing good matches between students and institutions. Just as changes in demographics, finances, laws, and shifts in the competitiveness of their credentials have affected prospective college students, the role of the admissions officer has also changed over time, from the functions suggested by titles such as registrar, counselor, dean and director, marketer, and recruiter to that of enrollment manager.

In general, admission professionals . . .
- provide information and assistance to prospective students (first time students as well as potential transfer students), families, and secondary school and community college counselors on the academic, financial, curricular, and co-curricular offerings of their institutions
- evaluate the qualifications of applicants
- develop, implement, and coordinate the institution's strategic marketing or recruitment plans
- work with the college faculty and administration to develop, implement, and evaluate enrollment policies and goals for the institution
- establish cooperative relationships with secondary school and community college counselors and other relevant constituencies

- work in concert with other campus offices to ensure that students are not only recruited but retained and eventually graduate

The admissions professional today is faced with many challenges: diverse students and student needs, high college costs, limited financial aid, and intense competition for students. They must also apply new technologies to deliver messages about the institution. Today, admission policies range from being "open-admission," or access institutions, to being highly competitive and selective. Similarly, the hundreds of thousands of applicants present varying ability levels, financial concerns, personal challenges, and academic interests, and admission officers must be prepared to serve them all. Admissions offices must have appropriate and adequate staff, policies, and skills in human relations to manage their important roles.

In recent years, admissions professionals have increasingly recognized the benefits of cooperating with other student affairs professionals to enhance students' educational experiences. During the past decade, enrollment management models have been developed to bring greater sophistication in efforts to recruit, retain, educate, and graduate students. On today's campuses, models for admissions offices may include such areas as admissions, recruitment or outreach, financial assistance, orientation, housing, transfer counseling, and academic advising—all reporting to a central administrator. Enrollment management assumes the establishment of activities based on an understanding of market research, student impact research, and organizational theory. Enrollment management paradigms are viewed as on-going processes that can enable college and university administrators to exert greater influence over factors that shape their enrollments. Clearly, today's admissions professionals must continue to respect students and their need for quality counseling and support throughout the whole admission process, while they also address institutional expectations. The *Admission Program Standards and Guidelines* that follow have been designed to facilitate the admission professional's response to these increasingly complex demands.

References, Readings, and Resources

American Association of Collegiate Registrars and Admissions Officers. (1997). *The college admission handbook.* Washington, DC: Author.

American Association of Collegiate Registrars and Admissions Officers (AACRAO), The College Entrance Examination

Board (CEEB), The Educational Testing Services (ETS), and the National Association of College Admission Counselors (NACAC). (1995). *Challenges in college admissions: A report of a survey of undergraduate admissions policies, practices, and procedures.* Washington, DC: Authors.

Fetter, J. (1995) *Questions and admissions: Reflections on 100,000 admissions decisions at Stanford.* Stanford, CA: Stanford University Press.

Goodchild, L. F., & Wechsler, H. W. (eds.) (1989). The statutes of Harvard, 1646. *ASHE Reader on The History of Higher Education.* pp. 89-90. Needham Heights, MA: Ginn Press.

Hossler, E. & Litten, L. (1993). *Mapping the higher education landscape.* New York: The   College Entrance Examination Board.

Loeb, J. (1992). *Academic standards in higher education.* New York: The College Entrance Examination Board.

National Association for College Admission Counseling. (1993). *Achieving diversity: Strategies for the recruitment and retention of traditionally underrepresented students.* Alexandria, VA: Author.

Steinberg, J. (2002). *The gatekeepers: Inside the admissions process of a premier college.* London: Penguin Books.

American Association of Collegiate Registrars and Admission Officers (AACRAO)
One Dupont Circle, NW, Suite 330, Washington, DC 20036-1171
202-293-9161; 202-872-8857 (fax);
http://www.reg.uci.edu/aacrao
Publisher of *College and University.*

The College Board
45 Columbus Avenue, New York, NY 10023
212-713-8000; http://www.collegeboard.org
Publisher of *The College Review*

The National Association for College Admission Counseling (NACAC)
1631 Prince Street, Alexandria, Virginia 22314-2818
703-836-2222; 703-836-8015 (fax);
http://www.nacac.com
Publisher of the *Journal of College Admission*

The National Association of Graduate Admissions Professionals (NAGAP)
www.nagap.org
Publisher of the *NAGAP Journal*

Contributors:
Current edition:
Jan Arminio, Shippensburg University

Previous editions:
Joyce Smith, National Association for College Admission Counseling

Admission Programs
CAS Standards and Guidelines

Part 1. MISSION

Admission Programs (AP) must develop, disseminate, implement, and regularly review their mission. Mission statements must be consistent with the mission of the institution and with professional standards. AP in higher education must enhance overall educational experiences by incorporating student learning and development outcomes in their mission.

AP must:
- address the abilities, needs, and expectations of prospective students as they move from secondary to postsecondary education, from one postsecondary institution to another, or as they return from a period of non-enrollment to formal learning
- establish, promulgate, and implement admission criteria that accurately represent the mission, goals, and purposes of the institution and that accommodate the abilities, needs, and interests of potential students
- reflect the mission, goals, policies, procedures, facilities, and characteristics of the parent institution and must be compatible with the ability of the institution to bring adequate resources to bear upon the relevant needs and aspirations of all students accepted for enrollment
- develop and regularly review institutional goals for admission with appropriate individuals within the institution; such goals must be consistent with good admission practices and with the nature and mission of the institution

Generally, in higher education, the terms "admission," "admission program," and "admission counselor" refer respectively to the processes, the agencies, and the institutional agents involved in the many activities that are related to the formal entry of students into postsecondary institutions. These generally include recruitment, counseling, selection, enrollment, orientation, advisement, and retention of students. In practice, institutions may establish separate agencies to provide these programs and services.

AP should provide or ensure personalized counseling that is responsive to the needs and expectations of each prospective student and his or her family, with particular attention given to the transition process.

Admission criteria should also reflect a variable approach which includes the student's academic record (e.g., grade point average, test scores, class rank), personal characteristics, and extracurricular involvement.

Part 2. PROGRAM

The formal education of students, consisting of the curriculum and the co-curriculum, must promote student learning and development outcomes that are purposeful and holistic and that prepare students for satisfying and productive lifestyles, work, and civic participation. The student learning and development outcome domains and their related dimensions are:

- knowledge acquisition, integration, construction, and application
  - Dimensions: understanding knowledge from a range of disciplines; connecting knowledge to other knowledge, ideas, and experiences; constructing knowledge; and relating knowledge to daily life

- cognitive complexity
  - Dimensions: critical thinking; reflective thinking; effective reasoning; and creativity

- intrapersonal development
  - Dimensions: realistic self-appraisal, self-understanding, and self-respect; identity development; commitment to ethics and integrity; and spiritual awareness

- interpersonal competence
  - Dimensions: meaningful relationships; interdependence; collaboration; and effective leadership

- humanitarianism and civic engagement
  - Dimensions: understanding and appreciation of cultural and human differences; social responsibility; global perspective; and sense of civic responsibility

- practical competence
  - Dimensions: pursuing goals; communicating effectively; technical competence; managing personal affairs; managing career development; demonstrating professionalism; maintaining health and wellness; and living a purposeful and satisfying life

[See *The Council for the Advancement of Standards Learning and Developmental Outcomes* statement for examples of outcomes related to these domains and dimensions.]

Consistent with the institutional mission, Admission Programs (AP) must identify relevant and desirable student learning and development outcomes from among the six domains and related dimensions. When creating opportunities for student learning and development, AP must explore possibilities for collaboration with faculty members and other colleagues.

AP must assess relevant and desirable student learning and development outcomes and provide evidence of their impact on student learning and development. AP must articulate how they contribute to or support students' learning and development in the domains not specifically assessed.

AP must be:
- integrated into the life of the institution

- intentional and coherent
- guided by theories and knowledge of learning and development
- reflective of developmental and demographic profiles of the student population
- responsive to needs of individuals, diverse and special populations, and relevant constituencies

AP must:

- provide programs and services designed to establish, meet, and maintain desired enrollment
- promote and maintain integrity, timeliness, and accuracy in program delivery
- promote deliberate educational planning opportunities for all relevant constituencies
- provide oral and written information for all relevant constituencies
- promote and provide equal access to all eligible prospective students interested in and capable of pursuing an education at the institution

Admission priorities, preferences, and objectives must be stated clearly in the formal admission policies and procedures of the institution. This statement must be easily obtainable by individuals seeking admission.

Not every student is suited for a particular postsecondary institution. Proper student-institutional matches are a major factor in the persistence of students toward graduation.

The distribution of current and complete information is an important priority for admission offices. Students and parents require comprehensive information on admission policies, requirements and procedures, as well as on institutional program offerings, selection criteria, acceptance decisions and financial aid opportunities. All admission personnel should be well informed and able to share such information in a variety of contexts in the interest of deliberate planning.

All AP professional staff members should be expected to perform the admission counseling function.

This includes the following activities and interventions:

- assistance and direction of students engaged in the admission process to encourage an appropriate match between student interests and available postsecondary opportunities
- acquisition and dissemination of timely, accurate, and relevant information regarding postsecondary opportunities, curriculum choices, and future educational plans
- promotion and development of individual problem-solving practices by students
- referral of students to appropriate institutional or other resources in response to particular needs
- encouragement of students toward deliberate choices and realistic expectations regarding institutional and personal standards of performance
- effective work with students of different levels of ability
- acknowledgment and positive use of proper interest in the student on the part of high school counselors, faculty, administrators, and students' families
- facilitation of proper exchange of non-restricted information among high schools, postsecondary institutions, families, students, and others involved in the admission process
- encouragement of students to engage in effective life planning
- provision of opportunities for a personal interview to students who are being considered for enrollment, where appropriate
- making available to prospective students information regarding financial aid opportunities and deadlines; standard financial aid forms should be available through the admission office as well as through any financial aid office
- providing to students who are offered admission information about academic advising and counseling, and student orientation programs and activities

The AP may be accomplished through practices which may include but are not limited to:

- recruitment, marketing and public relations activities (e.g., high school visits, college fairs, direct mail campaigns, publications, alumni relations and assistance, dissemination of admission and financial aid information)
- admission counseling (e.g., evaluation of student credentials, selection, and notification)
- pre-enrollment counseling (e.g., academic advisement and orientation)
- establishment of institutional policies regarding advanced placement, prior college level credit, or credit for equivalent experience

Part 3. LEADERSHIP

Because effective and ethical leadership is essential to the success of all organizations, Admission Program (AP) leaders with organizational authority for the programs and services must:

- articulate a vision and mission for their programs and services
- set goals and objectives based on the needs of the population served and desired student learning and development outcomes
- advocate for their programs and services
- promote campus environments that provide meaningful opportunities for student learning, development, and integration
- identify and find means to address individual, organizational, or environmental conditions that foster or inhibit mission achievement
- advocate for representation in strategic planning initiatives at appropriate divisional and institutional

levels

- initiate collaborative interactions with stakeholders who have legitimate concerns and interests in the functional area
- apply effective practices to educational and administrative processes
- prescribe and model ethical behavior
- communicate effectively
- manage financial resources, including planning, allocation, monitoring, and analysis
- incorporate sustainability practices in the management and design of programs, services, and facilities
- manage human resource processes including recruitment, selection, development, supervision, performance planning, and evaluation
- empower professional, support, and student staff to accept leadership opportunities
- encourage and support scholarly contribution to the profession
- be informed about and integrate appropriate technologies into programs and services
- be knowledgeable about federal, state/provincial, and local laws relevant to the programs and services and ensure that staff members understand their responsibilities by receiving appropriate training
- develop and continuously improve programs and services in response to the changing needs of students and other populations served and the evolving institutional priorities
- recognize environmental conditions that may negatively influence the safety of staff and students and propose interventions that mitigate such conditions

Part 4. HUMAN RESOURCES

Admission Programs (AP) must be staffed adequately by individuals qualified to accomplish the mission and goals. Within institutional guidelines, AP must establish procedures for staff selection, training, and evaluation; set expectations for supervision; and provide appropriate professional development opportunities to improve the leadership ability, competence, and skills of all employees.

AP professional staff members must hold an earned graduate or professional degree in a field relevant to the position they hold or must possess an appropriate combination of educational credentials and related work experience.

Degree- or credential-seeking interns must be qualified by enrollment in an appropriate field of study and by relevant experience. These individuals must be trained and supervised adequately by professional staff members holding educational credentials and related work experience appropriate for supervision.

Student employees and volunteers must be carefully selected, trained, supervised, and evaluated. They must be educated on how and when to refer those in need of additional assistance to qualified staff members and must have access to a supervisor for assistance in making these judgments. Student employees and volunteers must be provided clear and precise job descriptions, pre-service training based on assessed needs, and continuing staff development.

Employees and volunteers must receive specific training on institutional policies and privacy laws regarding their access to student records and other sensitive institutional information (e.g., in the USA, Family Educational Rights and Privacy Act, FERPA, or equivalent privacy laws in other states/provinces or countries).

AP must have technical and support staff members adequate to accomplish their mission. All members of the staff must be technologically proficient and qualified to perform their job functions, be knowledgeable about ethical and legal uses of technology, and have access to training and resources to support the performance of their assigned responsibilities.

All members of the staff must receive training on policies and procedures related to the use of technology to store or access student records and institutional data.

AP must ensure that staff members are knowledgeable about and trained in emergency procedures, crisis response, and prevention efforts. Prevention efforts must address identification of threatening conduct or behavior of students, faculty members, staff, and others and must incorporate a system or procedures for responding, including but not limited to reporting them to the appropriate campus officials.

Salary levels and benefits for all staff members must be commensurate with those for comparable positions within the institution, in similar institutions, and in the relevant geographic area.

AP must maintain position descriptions for all staff members.

To create a diverse staff, AP must institute hiring and promotion practices that are fair, inclusive, proactive, and non-discriminatory.

AP must conduct regular performance planning and evaluation of staff members. AP must provide access to continuing and advanced education and professional development opportunities.

The chief admission officer should be an experienced and effective manager and have substantial work experience in admission-related employment.

AP professional staff members should be competent to provide assistance to the prospective student and to work effectively to assist each student with his or her educational goals. This assistance may include, but should not be limited to, the following:

- ethical and objective presentation of the institution's programs and opportunities; careful and concerned analysis of each student's goals
- establishment of a clear understanding of likely student-

institution compatibility

- responsible decision-making in the selection of an institution
- knowledgeable guidance and counseling on all admission issues and concerns; interpretation of tasks and statistical data
- explanation of and placing in a proper context any relevant governmental policy or practice on education

The AP professional staff should be knowledgeable in the areas of marketing, financial aid, and testing and should demonstrate knowledge and sensitivity to the needs of traditionally under-represented students and students with a special talent. Activities in these special areas of concern should contribute positively to the reputation of the institution and its position in the higher education marketplace.

Each AP staff member should be specifically trained to articulate the institution's unique and essential aspects. This training should be supplemental to formal outside training. While no specific timeline is prescribed, a minimum of two weeks' specialized training is recommended. Included in this training should be:
- a thorough tour of the campus
- familiarization with the college catalog, all academic programs, freshman and transfer admission policies, and all service and social aspects of the institution
- systematic orientation to relevant other facets of the institution
- familiarization with clerical and financial aid operations

Institutions should provide ongoing opportunities for career-related information and professional growth to the entire AP staff. This process will promote effective admission services and encourage the continued involvement of admission personnel in the field. Numerous avenues promote professional growth. These include in-service workshops, membership and participation in professional organizations, and the development of an admission library. A library should include current scholarly literature, research findings, trade journals, and newspapers.

Continuing education is essential for all admission officers. It is important to be alert to changes within the field and to be able to integrate changes into daily practice when appropriate. Every admission officer should be:
- willing to seek out and implement new ideas
- able to translate new ideas into practical methods for improving the overall operation of the admission function
- willing to seek out and use new conceptual frameworks and equipment that bring information to students more clearly and effectively
- aware of relevant developments in the broad context of formal education and able to incorporate these developments in his or her work

For formal training in preparation for professional admission work, suggested areas for graduate work include student services administration and higher education management. Additional course work may include computer literacy, research and statistical methods, counseling, enrollment management, legal issues relating to admission and higher education, leadership skills, transcript evaluation, and public relations.

AP support staff members such as administrative assistants, transcript evaluators, and office assistants should possess the academic background, experience, personal interest, and competence necessary for effective performance of their responsibilities. Support staff should be skilled in interpersonal communications, public relations, referral techniques, and dissemination of information.

Training in procedures, policies, and good office practices should be included in the employment orientation for clerical and support staff. Such training will promote a consistent presentation of the institution and dependable performance of staff.

An annual AP staff workshop to plan and review admission programs is recommended. Topics and components of the workshop may include current issues in college admission, team development, marketing, computer operations, and financial aid issues and status.

Part 5. ETHICS

Persons involved in the delivery of Admission Programs (AP) must adhere to the highest principles of ethical behavior. AP must review relevant professional ethical standards and develop or adopt and implement appropriate statements of ethical practice. AP must publish these statements and ensure their periodic review by relevant constituencies.

AP must orient new staff members to relevant ethical standards and statements of ethical practice.

AP staff members must ensure that privacy and confidentiality are maintained with respect to all communications and records to the extent that such records are protected under the law and appropriate statements of ethical practice. Information contained in students' education records must not be disclosed except as allowed by relevant laws and institutional policies. AP staff members must disclose to appropriate authorities information judged to be of an emergency nature, especially when the safety of the individual or others is involved, or when otherwise required by institutional policy or relevant law.

AP staff members must be aware of and comply with the provisions contained in the institution's policies pertaining to human subjects research and student rights and responsibilities, as well as those in other relevant institutional policies addressing ethical practices and confidentiality of research data concerning individuals.

AP staff members must recognize and avoid personal conflicts of interest or appearance thereof in the performance of their work.

AP staff members must strive to insure the fair, objective, and impartial treatment of all persons with whom they interact.

When handling institutional funds, AP staff members must ensure that such funds are managed in accordance with established and responsible accounting procedures and the fiscal policies or processes of the institution.

Promotional and descriptive information must be accurate and free of deception.

All printed material including application forms, financial aid information, and promotional literature must accurately represent the institution's goals, services, programs, and policies.

AP staff members must perform their duties within the limits of their training, expertise, and competence. When these limits are exceeded, individuals in need of further assistance must be referred to persons possessing appropriate qualifications.

AP staff members must use suitable means to confront and otherwise hold accountable other staff members who exhibit unethical behavior.

AP staff members must be knowledgeable about and practice ethical behavior in the use of technology.

As professional members of the institution's staff, AP personnel must receive compensation in the form of a fixed salary, rather than commissions or bonuses on the number of students recruited or enrolled.

Admission officers must insure timely and fair administration of policies regarding: admission decisions; proper notification; wait-listing; evaluating student competencies, credentials, and prior credits; and confidentiality in keeping with federal and state laws.

Promotional publications, written communications, and presentations must:
- state entrance requirements clearly and precisely
- include a current and accurate admission calendar
- provide precise information on opportunities for financial aid
- offer accurate and detailed information regarding special programs
- include realistic descriptions, illustrations, and photographs of the campus and community.

Development of admission criteria must be centered around the probability of academic success. When evaluating applicants, particularly those with special talents, admission officers must be guided by their best judgment and should make exception to established admission policies only after a thorough and prudent evaluation of all relevant circumstances including, where appropriate, consultation with relevant other agencies.

In some cases applicants may possess outstanding talent in drama, music, athletics, art, or other areas. These students might not meet all established criteria for academic success. However, in some cases a special talent can motivate a student to perform well in a secondary school program. Where this is possible, admission officers are encouraged to acknowledge the special talent when evaluating the applicant.

In some cases, the applicants may possess special needs. For instance, students with learning disabilities or those from academically disadvantaged backgrounds might be admitted. Ethical practices would insist that the appropriate support services be available for these students if they are admitted.

Any comparisons made between or among institutions must be based on accurate and appropriate data. General comments of a disparaging nature about other institutions must be avoided.

Part 8. LEGAL RESPONSIBILITIES

Admission Program (AP) staff members must be knowledgeable about and responsive to laws and regulations that relate to their respective responsibilities and that may pose legal obligations, limitations, or ramifications for the institution as a whole. As appropriate, staff members must inform users of programs and services, as well as officials, of legal obligations and limitations including constitutional, statutory, regulatory, and case law; mandatory laws and orders emanating from federal, state/provincial, and local governments; and the institution's policies.

AP must have written policies on all relevant operations, transactions, or tasks that may have legal implications.

AP staff members must neither participate in nor condone any form of harassment or activity that demeans persons or creates an intimidating, hostile, or offensive campus environment.

AP staff members must use reasonable and informed practices to limit the liability exposure of the institution and its officers, employees, and agents. AP staff members must be informed about institutional policies regarding risk management, personal liability, and related insurance coverage options and must be referred to external sources if coverage is not provided by the institution.

The institution must provide access to legal advice for AP staff members as needed to carry out assigned responsibilities.

The institution must inform AP staff and students in a timely and systematic fashion about extraordinary or changing legal obligations and potential liabilities.

Admission counselors must be aware of the legal and ethical limits and standards relevant to their professional roles, and perform any counseling or guidance functions accordingly.

Part 7. EQUITY and ACCESS

Admission Programs (AP) must be provided on a fair, equitable, and non-discriminatory basis in accordance with institutional policies and with all applicable state/provincial and federal statutes and regulations. AP must maintain an educational and work environment free from discrimination in accordance with law and institutional policy.

Discrimination must be avoided on the basis of age; cultural heritage; disability; ethnicity; gender identity and expression; nationality; political affiliation; race; religious affiliation; sex;

sexual orientation; economic, marital, social, or veteran status; and any other bases included in local, state/provincial, or federal laws.

Consistent with the mission and goals, AP must take action to remedy significant imbalances in student participation and staffing patterns.

AP must ensure physical and program access for persons with disabilities. AP must be responsive to the needs of all students and other populations served when establishing hours of operation and developing methods of delivering programs and services.

AP must recognize the needs of distance learning students by providing appropriate and accessible services and assisting them in identifying and gaining access to other appropriate services in their geographic region.

All admission publications and forms must clearly state students' rights and responsibilities in the admission process. Admission practices must be congruent with the institution's policies on Equal Opportunity, Access, and Affirmative Action. Admission publications must reflect relevant institutional policies.

Part 8. DIVERSITY

Within the context of each institution's unique mission, diversity enriches the community and enhances the collegiate experience for all; therefore, Admission Programs (AP) must create and nurture environments that are welcoming to and bring together persons of diverse backgrounds.

AP must promote environments that are characterized by open and continuous communication that deepens understanding of one's own identity, culture, and heritage, as well as that of others. AP must recognize, honor, educate, and promote respect about commonalties and differences among people within their historical and cultural contexts.

AP must address the characteristics and needs of a diverse population when establishing and implementing policies and procedures.

Part 9: ORGANIZATION and MANAGEMENT

To promote student learning and development outcomes, Admission Programs (AP) must be structured purposefully and managed effectively to achieve stated goals. Evidence of appropriate structure must include current and accessible policies and procedures, written performance expectations for all employees, functional workflow graphics or organizational charts, and clearly stated program and service delivery expectations.

AP must monitor websites used for distributing information to ensure that the sites are current, accurate, appropriately referenced, and accessible.

Evidence of effective management must include use of comprehensive and accurate information for decisions, clear sources and channels of authority, effective communication practices, procedures for decision-making and conflict resolution, responses to changing conditions, systems of accountability and evaluation, and processes for recognition and reward. AP must align policies and procedures with those of the institution and provide channels within the organization for their regular review.

The institution must appoint or designate a chief admission officer. This officer must be positioned in the institutional organization so that the needs of students and the operations of admission are both well-represented and advocated at the highest levels of administration.

The specific title and lines of accountability may vary among institutions in light of particular settings and institutional needs. Selection of the chief admission officer should be based on personal characteristics as well as formal training.

The chief admission officer should be able to develop, advocate, and implement a statement of the mission goals and objectives for the admission program on campus.

The chief admission officer should create an effective system to manage the programs, services, and personnel of the admission office. He or she should plan, organize, staff, lead, and regularly assess programs. The leader should also be able to coordinate the admission program with other institutional services and with institutional development activities.

The chief admission officer should attract and select qualified staff members who are capable of making informed decisions about policies, procedures, personnel, budgets, facilities, and equipment. He or she should assume responsibility for program and staff development, assessment, and improvement.

Administrative policies and organization structures should be written, properly disseminated and posted, and modified when necessary.

AP programs, policies, and procedures should minimally include:
- an organizational chart which depicts areas of accountability and reporting relationships for units and personnel as appropriate
- job descriptions that accurately reflect the duties and responsibilities for all admission program personnel
- clearly stated criteria used in the decision making process for admission to the institution and the source of authority for the criteria employed
- steps for appealing, evaluating, or revising policies and procedures

Part 10. CAMPUS and COMMUNITY RELATIONS

Admission Programs (AP) must reach out to relevant individuals, campus offices, and external agencies to:
- establish, maintain, and promote effective relations
- disseminate information about their own and other

related programs and services
- coordinate and collaborate, where appropriate, in offering programs and services to meet the needs of students and promote their achievement of student learning and development outcomes

AP must have procedures and guidelines consistent with institutional policy for responding to threats, emergencies, and crisis situations. Systems and procedures must be in place to disseminate timely and accurate information to students and other members of the campus community during emergency situations.

AP must have procedures and guidelines consistent with institutional policy for communicating with the media.

AP documents used by academic advising and counseling, orientation, housing, counseling, testing, the office of records, and international student services must be accurate and handled with confidentiality.

Institutional organizational functions and constituencies linked to admission typically include financial aid, student development, student activities, athletics, student accounts, academic support, counseling, career planning and placement, the registrar, records, the faculty, the alumni, and institutional advancement. Residents of the larger community in which the institution is located may also have special interests regarding institutional admission practices.

Students with special needs should be identified and referral made to the appropriate office. Special needs may include those with learning disabilities, physical handicaps, deficiencies in certain academic skills, and those who come from educationally disadvantaged backgrounds. Financial aid and admission decisions should be made independently. However, the financial aid office should have access to appropriate information in the student's admission file. After financial aid has been allocated, the admission office should have access to information regarding the amount and characteristics of the financial aid award. Admission decisions should be based on the establishment of a match between the student's needs and the characteristics of the institution. A student's apparent ability to pay for the services of the institution should not affect the admission decision.

Part 11. FINANCIAL RESOURCES

Admission Programs (AP) must have adequate funding to accomplish their mission and goals. In establishing funding priorities and making significant changes, a comprehensive analysis, which includes relevant expenditures, external and internal resources, and impact on the campus community, must be conducted.

AP must demonstrate fiscal responsibility and cost effectiveness consistent with institutional protocols.

The institution must prescribe policies governing:
- in-kind consideration in lieu of cash payment, reimbursement, or remuneration for approved admission-related activity or participation

- any necessary external contractual agreements (e.g., professional consultation fees, special mailings)
- travel, accommodations, and all expenditures authorized for recruitment purposes; reimbursements for out-of-pocket expenses

Institutions should provide support for an admission program that offers prospective students ample opportunities to:
- inquire about the entrance requirements and nature of the institution
- inquire about and receive counseling regarding the institution's admission process and apply for admission
- receive financial aid information and forms
- be interviewed as applicants for admission
- receive assistance in orientation and academic advisement

Institutional admission offices should be able to respond in a timely manner to requests for information, literature, programs, and services upon the request of prospective students.

Part 12. TECHNOLOGY

Admission Programs (AP) must have adequate technology to support their mission. The technology and its use must comply with institutional policies and procedures and be evaluated for compliance with relevant federal, state/ provincial, and local requirements.

AP must maintain policies and procedures that address the security and back up of data.

When technology is used to facilitate student learning and development, AP must select technology that reflects current best pedagogical practices.

Technology, as well as any workstations or computer labs maintained by the AP for student use, must be accessible and must meet established technology standards for delivery to persons with disabilities.

When AP provide student access to technology, they must provide:
- access to policies that are clear, easy to understand, and available to all students
- access to instruction or training on how to use the technology
- access to information on the legal and ethical implications of misuse as it pertains to intellectual property, harassment, privacy, and social networks.

Student violations of technology policies must follow established institutional student disciplinary procedures.

Students who experience negative emotional or psychological consequences from the use of technology must be referred to support services provided by the institution.

Part 13. FACILITIES and EQUIPMENT

Admission Programs (AP) must have adequate, accessible, suitably located facilities and equipment to support their mission and goals. If acquiring capital equipment as defined by the institution, AP must take into account expenses related to regular maintenance and life cycle costs. Facilities and equipment must be evaluated regularly, including consideration of sustainability, and be in compliance with relevant federal, state/provincial, and local requirements to provide for access, health, safety, and security.

AP staff members must have work space that is well-equipped, adequate in size, and designed to support their work and responsibilities. For conversations requiring privacy, staff members must have access to a private space.

AP staff members who share work space must have the ability to secure their work adequately.

The design of the facilities must guarantee the security of records and ensure the confidentiality of sensitive information.

The location and layout of the facilities must be sensitive to the special needs of persons with disabilities as well as the needs of constituencies served.

AP must ensure that staff members are knowledgeable of and trained in safety and emergency procedures for securing and vacating the facilities.

Sufficient office space should be allocated for confidential interviews and counseling, processing of all relevant documents, files, and staff supervision.

Security measures, facilities, and equipment appropriate for handling cash or negotiable paper should be provided when necessary.

The admission office should be readily accessible to prospective students, parents and others who have need for admission services or personnel.

Special concern for providing readily accessible and nearby parking, or the availability of convenient public transportation, is strongly recommended.

Campus maps and highly visible signage that will assist visitors and prospective students to locate the admission office are strongly recommended.

Part 14. ASSESSMENT and EVALUATION

Admission Programs (AP) must establish systematic plans and processes to meet internal and external accountability expectations with regard to program as well as student learning and development outcomes. AP must conduct regular assessment and evaluations. Assessments must include qualitative and quantitative methodologies as appropriate, to determine whether and to what degree the stated mission, goals, and student learning and development outcomes are being met. The process must employ sufficient and sound measures to ensure comprehensiveness. Data collected must include responses from students and other affected constituencies.

AP must evaluate regularly how well they complement and enhance the institution's stated mission and educational effectiveness.

Results of these evaluations must be used in revising and improving programs and services, identifying needs and interests in shaping directions of program and service design, and recognizing staff performance.

Each institution should require that its admission offices, programs, and staff be evaluated regularly. This evaluation should determine the effectiveness of services to students and their families, achievement of departmental and institutional goals, and direction toward more efficient cost-effective operations. The periodic study of needs, interests, and expectations of prospective and current students and others served by the program may be conducted in conjunction with these evaluations. Data collected from the study should be used to determine the effectiveness of institutional admission policies and programs. Marketing and recruitment techniques used by the admission office should be regularly reviewed.

General Standards revised in 2008;
AP content developed/revised in 1987, & 1997

The Role of Adult Learner Programs and Services
CAS Standards Contextual Statement

Over the last twenty-five years, there has been an influx of adult learners seeking higher education, along with the heightened perception of the importance of higher education in "developing knowledgeable, literate citizens for a postmodern global society" (Kasworm, Sandmann, & Sissel, 2000, p. 449). According to the Lumina Foundation, more than 40 percent of today's college students are adult learners. Community colleges are often the most accessible and popular for adult learners, because of convenient locations, cost, remedial course offerings, and practical programs designed for the adult workforce (Lumina Foundation, n.d.). Furthermore, in institutions whose admissions criteria and practices are highly tailored to traditional-age applicants, adult learners may be disproportionately represented in the non-degree seeking and provisionally admitted ranks of students.

Although institutional definitions of an adult learner vary, the adult learner is typically under forty, has a high school education at minimum, works full time, is married and with children, and is most likely to be found living a suburb (Merriam & Brockett, 2007). Included within the ranks of adult learners are full- and part-time employees, recently discharged veterans, unemployed workers, single parents, career changers, and retirees. They may live on campus, in local communities, commute some distance, or study at a distance. They turn to higher education for many reasons such as earning degrees, certificates, or other credentials; taking courses for work-enhancement purposes; positioning themselves for new opportunities in order to increase earning power; and for enrichment.   However, there is "strong evidence that participation in formal adult education is most often tied to career or job motives" (Merriam & Brockett, p. 132). Despite the diversity of the adult learner and their motivations for enrollment, they seek from higher education an understanding of both their needs and their attributes. They also seek an institution that has a desire to be responsive and interested in enrolling them in academic programs they want and when they are available to take them.

Adult learners bring various life experiences and motivations to the classroom.   Their participation challenges current structures and processes (Kaswom, Sandmann, & Sissel, 2000). However, there are many obstacles which prevent adult learners from participated in higher education. Lack of time and money are the two most often cited reasons for their nonparticipation (Merriam & Brockett, 2007; Merriam, Cafarella, & Baumgartner, 2006). Furthermore, socio-economic status and race have a large impact on one's ability to enter and succeed in adult education (Merriam & Brockett) and must therefore be considered when structure adult learning programs.

Given higher education's long-standing focus on traditional-age and residential students, adult learners often have been seen as the purview of ancillary units such as continuing and distance education units in land-grant universities, evening and weekend colleges in urban universities, and community colleges. Faculty in student personnel preparation programs have conducted much of their research on and written about the young, residential students who have been easier to access than adult learners. As a consequence, new professionals may think of college student development solely from the perspective of 17- to 23-year olds. When the numbers of traditional-age high school graduates have fallen periodically, some institutions including private colleges have changed their practices and policies to serve the adult learner more effectively.

In the meantime, the dislocation of the nation's manufacturing economy has called for the re-education of thousands of furloughed workers. The knowledge economy has called for adults with high school diplomas, some college, or associate degrees to earn bachelors and advanced degrees. Divorce, separation, and the death of a spouse have triggered a return to learning by many eager to increase their earning power to improve not only their own standard of living and that of their children. Longer life spans have caused persons to turn to higher education for second careers and for intellectual stimulation in their retirement. As these social and economic changes have occurred, adults have sought access to and responsiveness from colleges, academic departments, and support services beyond the units that had served them previously.

As adults encountered and became concerned about difficulties with gaining admission to "mainstream" academic programs and access to financial aid, with faculty unwilling to consider awarding credit for prior college-level learning, and with a college environment that they sometimes characterized as lonely, if not hostile, Adult Learner Programs and Services (ALPS) units finally began to appear on college campuses in the 1970's. Other ALPS units were created because college and university faculty and staff realized the social and economic trends as well as the attributes that adult learners brought to higher education and wanted to increase their enrollment; or they learned that adult graduation rates were less than the overall institution's graduation rate and wanted to increase adult learner success. Focusing on providing support systems for adult learners is important not only for the initial transition to formal education, but also for persistence (Kasworm, Sandmann, & Sissel, 2000).

Many factors, including institutional type, structure, and history as well as the rationale for founding Adult Learner Programs and Services units, have influenced the placement of ALPS in the institutional structure, the mission of ALPS, and the activities and expertise of ALPS staff. For example, ALPS units have been placed in student affairs, continuing and distance education, affirmative action, and academic support divisions. In turn, the ALPS mission may focus more on student access, on supporting enrolled student success, and on select populations of adult learners or the focus may be more comprehensive. The CAS standards and guidelines provide a basis for program self-assessment and program development as institutional leaders seek to respond to projected increases in the number and diversity of adult learners and as they seek to provide a standard of program and service excellence to those whom they currently recruit and enroll.

References, Readings, and Resources

Adult learners in higher education: Barriers to success and strategies to improve results. (March 2007). Report prepared for the U.S. Department of Labor, Employment and Training Administration, Office of Policy Development and Research by Jobs for the Future. http://www.doleta.gov/reports/searcheta/occ/

Aslanian, C. B. (2001). Adult students today. New York: The College Board.

Aslanian, C. B., & Brickell, H. M. (1988). How Americans in transition study for college credit. New York: The College Board.

Aslanian, C. B., & Brickell, H. M. (1980). Americans in transition: Life changes as reasons for adult learning. New York: The College Entrance Examination Board.

Bash, L. (2003). Adult learners: Why they are important to the 21st century college or university. The Journal of Continuing Higher Education, 51 (3), 18-26.

Donaldson, J.F. & Townsend, B. K. (2007). Higher education journals' discourse about adult undergraduate students. The Journal of Higher Education, 78 (1), 27-50.

Harrison, C. H. (May 2000). The adult learner: Not a student yet. A thesis in Adult Education, The Pennsylvania State University.

Kasworm, C. (2003). What is collegiate involvement for adult undergraduates? Paper presented at the Annual Meeting of the American Educational Research Association, Chicago, IL. (ERIC Document Reproduction Service No. ED 481 228).

Kasworm, C. E., & Blowers, S. S. (1994). Adult undergraduate students: Patterns of learning involvement. Final Research Report, University of Tennessee, Knoxville, TN. Washington, DC: Office of Educational Research and Improvement. (ERIC Document Reproduction Service No. ED 376 321).

Kasworm, C. E., Polson, C. J., & Fishback, S. J. (2002). Responding to adult learners in higher education. Malabar, FL: Krieger Publishing Company.

Kasworm, C.E., Sandmann, L.R., & Sissel, P.A. (2000). Adult learners in higher education. In E. Hayes & A. Wilson (Eds.), Handbook of Adult and Continuing Education (pp. 33-49). San Francisco: Jossey-Bass.

Kilgore, D., & Rice, P.J. (2003). New directions for student services: Meeting the special needs of adult students. San Francisco: Jossey-Bass.

Lumina Foundation for Education. (n.d.). Adult Learners. Retrieved June 15, 2009, from http://www.luminafoundation.org/our_work/student_success/adult_learners.html

Merriam, S. & Brockett, R. (2007). The profession and practice of adult education: An introduction. San Francisco: Jossey-Bass.

Pusser, B., Breneman, D. W., Gansneder, B. M., Kohl, K. J., Levin, J. S., Milam, J. H., & Turner, S. E. (March 2007). Returning to learning: Adults' success in college is key to America's future. Report of the Lumina Foundation for Education, Indianapolis, IN.

Schlossberg, N. K., Lynch, A. Q., & Chickering, A. W. (1989). Improving higher education environments for adults. San Francisco: Jossey Bass Publishers.

Sissel, P. A., Hansman, C. A., & Kasworm, C. E. (2001). The politics of neglect: Adult learners in higher education. New Directions for Adult and Continuing Education, 91, 17-27.

Contributor:
Charlene H. Harrison, The Pennsylvania State University

Adult Learner Programs and Services
CAS Standards and Guidelines

Part 1. MISSION

The mission of Adult Learner Programs and Services (ALPS) is to ensure that adult learners gain equitable access to all relevant curricular and co-curricular opportunities of the institution. ALPS must ensure that programs and services support adult learner success and advocate for adult learners to ensure that they are treated fairly and justly.

Equitable access may be differentiated based upon degree status, course load, fee payment status, or other criteria.

ALPS must develop, disseminate, implement, and regularly review their mission. Mission statements must be consistent with the mission of the institution and with professional standards. ALPS in higher education must enhance overall educational experiences by incorporating student learning and development outcomes in their mission.

Part 2. PROGRAM

Adult Learner Programs and Services (ALPS) must provide direct delivery of programs and services and work collaboratively with other essential institutional units to ensure that adult learners gain full access to and support from all curricular and co-curricular opportunities offered by the institution.

Institutions must clarify the availability of programs and services based upon the student's status.

ALPS must help adult learners gain access to the institution and its academic and financial aid programs.

To assist adult learners in gaining access to the institution and its enrollment, academic, and financial aid programs, ALPS staff members should:
- be available to meet and/or communicate one-on-one with prospective adult learners
- articulate admissions, transfer enrollment, re-enrollment, non-degree registration, and financial aid procedures and provide information about topics such as academic refresher resources, child and elder care, and application deadlines
- conduct programs for prospective adult learners on applying for admission, re-enrollment, and financial aid, and on relating careers to academic programs
- monitor the progress of adult learner applicants, re-enrollees, and registrants through the application, acceptance, and registration process and through the financial aid application process
- ensure that recruitment literature, websites, list serves, and other outreach efforts are created that target adult learners and contain messages relevant to their needs and concerns
- represent the institution in the community at workplaces and community centers to help bring prospective adults to the institution
- ensure that institutional resources are available at convenient hours for adult learners

ALPS must provide programs and services that assist in increasing the retention of adult learners.

To increase the success of adult learners, the ALPS staff members should:
- plan, deliver, and evaluate (either independently or in collaboration with others) orientation and other programs that acquaint adult learners and their families/support networks with the institution's academic and out-of-class resources that enhance their likelihood of success, and with others like themselves
- inform adult learners of the availability of emergency funds, short-term loans, and scholarships
- initiate and advise adult learner honor societies and student organizations
- initiate and conduct recognition programs for adult learners that bring together both the learners and those who support them

ALPS staff members must collect data and conduct research on the institution's adult learners and on policies and practices that disproportionately impact them.

ALPS staff members may engage in these efforts either independently or in collaboration with others.

ALPS staff members must educate others about the characteristics, needs, and contributions of adult learners.

For ALPS staff members to educate others in the institution to adult learners' needs and attributes, they should:
- be familiar with literature and research about adult learners
- establish relationships with faculty in adult education and other relevant academic disciplines and with staff members in the institutional research office
- meet with academic advisors, admissions, financial aid and student affairs staff members, and other staff and faculty members
- collaborate and network with colleagues to offer training, provide data, and share research in order to inform decision making and practice
- write articles and reports and deliver programs to campus and community audiences

ALPS staff members must advocate for curricular and co-curricular policies, procedures, and programs that are responsive to the needs and concerns of adult learners.

To advocate for adult learners, ALPS staff members should:
- assess and monitor adult learners' needs and the degree to which the institution is meeting them

- understand and be able to articulate the diverse nature of the institution's adult learners
- support individual adult learners and adult student organizations in their self-advocacy
- promote life experiences as criteria for membership in student organizations, including honor societies and for major awards

ALPS staff members must create affirming environments where prospective and enrolled adult learners may interact with one another.

The formal education of students, consisting of the curriculum and the co-curriculum, must promote student learning and development outcomes that are purposeful and holistic and that prepare students for satisfying and productive lifestyles, work, and civic participation. The student learning and development outcome domains and their related dimensions are:

- **knowledge acquisition, integration, construction, and application**
  - o **Dimensions: understanding knowledge from a range of disciplines; connecting knowledge to other knowledge, ideas, and experiences; constructing knowledge; and relating knowledge to daily life**

- **cognitive complexity**
  - o **Dimensions: critical thinking; reflective thinking; effective reasoning; and creativity**

- **intrapersonal development**
  - o **Dimensions: realistic self-appraisal, self-understanding, and self-respect; identity development; commitment to ethics and integrity; and spiritual awareness**

- **interpersonal competence**
  - o **Dimensions: meaningful relationships; interdependence; collaboration; and effective leadership**

- **humanitarianism and civic engagement**
  - o **Dimensions: understanding and appreciation of cultural and human differences; social responsibility; global perspective; and sense of civic responsibility**

- **practical competence**
  - o **Dimensions: pursuing goals; communicating effectively; technical competence; managing personal affairs; managing career development; demonstrating professionalism; maintaining health and wellness; and living a purposeful and satisfying life**

[See *The Council for the Advancement of Standards Learning and Developmental Outcomes* statement for examples of outcomes related to these domains and dimensions.]

Consistent with the institutional mission, ALPS must identify relevant and desirable student learning and development outcomes from among the six domains and related dimensions. When creating opportunities for student learning and development, ALPS must explore possibilities for collaboration with faculty members and other colleagues.

ALPS must assess relevant and desirable student learning and development outcomes and provide evidence of their impact on student learning and development. ALPS must articulate how they contribute to or support students' learning and development in the domains not specifically assessed.

ALPS must be:
- **integrated into the life of the institution**
- **intentional and coherent**
- **guided by theories and knowledge of learning and development**
- **reflective of developmental and demographic profiles of the student population**
- **responsive to needs of individuals, diverse and special populations, and relevant constituencies**

ALPS staff members should be familiar with the CAS Standards and Guidelines for Distance Education Programs and with the CAS Commuter and Off-Campus Living Programs Standards and Guidelines.

Part 3. LEADERSHIP

Because effective and ethical leadership is essential to the success of all organizations, Adult Learner Programs and Services (ALPS) leaders with organizational authority for the programs and services must:

- **articulate a vision and mission for their programs and services**
- **set goals and objectives based on the needs of the population served and desired student learning and development outcomes**
- **advocate for their programs and services**
- **promote campus environments that provide meaningful opportunities for student learning, development, and integration**
- **identify and find means to address individual, organizational, or environmental conditions that foster or inhibit mission achievement**
- **advocate for representation in strategic planning initiatives at appropriate divisional and institutional levels**
- **initiate collaborative interactions with stakeholders who have legitimate concerns and interests in the functional area**
- **apply effective practices to educational and administrative processes**
- **prescribe and model ethical behavior**
- **communicate effectively**
- **manage financial resources, including planning, allocation, monitoring, and analysis**
- **incorporate sustainability practices in the management and design of programs, services, and facilities**
- **manage human resource processes including recruitment, selection, development, supervision, performance planning, and evaluation**
- **empower professional, support, and student staff to**

accept leadership opportunities
- encourage and support scholarly contribution to the profession
- be informed about and integrate appropriate technologies into programs and services
- be knowledgeable about federal, state/provincial, and local laws relevant to the programs and services and ensure that staff members understand their responsibilities by receiving appropriate training
- develop and continuously improve programs and services in response to the changing needs of students and other populations served and the evolving institutional priorities
- recognize environmental conditions that may negatively influence the safety of staff and students and propose interventions that mitigate such conditions.

ALPS leaders must understand and adhere to institutional policies and procedures for research.

ALPS leaders must inform themselves about program and service approaches that are successful in other higher education or professional settings and establish working relationships with a network of colleagues who are dedicated to serving adult learners optimally.

Part 4. HUMAN RESOURCES

Adult Learner Programs and Services (ALPS) must be staffed adequately by individuals qualified to accomplish the mission and goals. Within institutional guidelines, ALPS must establish procedures for staff selection, training, and evaluation; set expectations for supervision; and provide appropriate professional development opportunities to improve the leadership ability, competence, and skills of all employees.

ALPS professional staff members must hold an earned graduate or professional degree in a field relevant to the position they hold or must possess an appropriate combination of educational credentials and related work experience.

Degree- or credential-seeking interns must be qualified by enrollment in an appropriate field of study and by relevant experience. These individuals must be trained and supervised adequately by professional staff members holding educational credentials and related work experience appropriate for supervision.

Student employees and volunteers must be carefully selected, trained, supervised, and evaluated. They must be educated on how and when to refer those in need of additional assistance to qualified staff members and must have access to a supervisor for assistance in making these judgments. Student employees and volunteers must be provided clear and precise job descriptions, pre-service training based on assessed needs, and continuing staff development.

Employees and volunteers must receive specific training on institutional policies and privacy laws regarding their access to student records and other sensitive institutional information (e.g., in the USA, Family Educational Rights and Privacy Act, FERPA, or equivalent privacy laws in other states/provinces or countries).

ALPS must have technical and support staff members adequate to accomplish their mission. All members of the staff must be technologically proficient and qualified to perform their job functions, be knowledgeable about ethical and legal uses of technology, and have access to training and resources to support the performance of their assigned responsibilities.

All members of the staff must receive training on policies and procedures related to the use of technology to store or access student records and institutional data.

ALPS must ensure that staff members are knowledgeable about and trained in emergency procedures, crisis response, and prevention efforts. Prevention efforts must address identification of threatening conduct or behavior of students, faculty members, staff, and others and must incorporate a system or procedures for responding, including but not limited to reporting them to the appropriate campus officials.

Salary levels and benefits for all staff members must be commensurate with those for comparable positions within the institution, in similar institutions, and in the relevant geographic area.

ALPS must maintain position descriptions for all staff members.

To create a diverse staff, ALPS must institute hiring and promotion practices that are fair, inclusive, proactive, and non-discriminatory.

ALPS must conduct regular performance planning and evaluation of staff members. ALPS must provide access to continuing and advanced education and professional development opportunities.

Part 5. ETHICS

Persons involved in the delivery of Adult Learner Programs and Services (ALPS) must adhere to the highest principles of ethical behavior. ALPS must review relevant professional ethical standards and develop or adopt and implement appropriate statements of ethical practice. ALPS must publish these statements and ensure their periodic review by relevant constituencies.

ALPS must orient new staff members to relevant ethical standards and statements of ethical practice.

ALPS staff members must ensure that privacy and

confidentiality are maintained with respect to all communications and records to the extent that such records are protected under the law and appropriate statements of ethical practice. Information contained in students' education records must not be disclosed except as allowed by relevant laws and institutional policies. ALPS staff members must disclose to appropriate authorities information judged to be of an emergency nature, especially when the safety of the individual or others is involved, or when otherwise required by institutional policy or relevant law.

ALPS staff members must be aware of and comply with the provisions contained in the institution's policies pertaining to human subjects research and student rights and responsibilities, as well as those in other relevant institutional policies addressing ethical practices and confidentiality of research data concerning individuals.

ALPS staff members must recognize and avoid personal conflicts of interest or appearance thereof in the performance of their work.

ALPS staff members must strive to insure the fair, objective, and impartial treatment of all persons with whom they interact.

When handling institutional funds, ALPS staff members must ensure that such funds are managed in accordance with established and responsible accounting procedures and the fiscal policies or processes of the institution.

Promotional and descriptive information must be accurate and free of deception.

ALPS staff members must perform their duties within the limits of their training, expertise, and competence. When these limits are exceeded, individuals in need of further assistance must be referred to persons possessing appropriate qualifications.

ALPS staff members must use suitable means to confront and otherwise hold accountable other staff members who exhibit unethical behavior.

ALPS staff members must be knowledgeable about and practice ethical behavior in the use of technology.

Part 6. LEGAL RESPONSIBILITIES

Adult Learner Programs and Services (ALPS) staff members must be knowledgeable about and responsive to laws and regulations that relate to their respective responsibilities and that may pose legal obligations, limitations, or ramifications for the institution as a whole. As appropriate, staff members must inform users of programs and services, as well as officials, of legal obligations and limitations including constitutional, statutory, regulatory, and case law; mandatory laws and orders emanating from federal, state/provincial, and local governments; and the institution's policies.

ALPS must have written policies on all relevant operations, transactions, or tasks that may have legal implications.

ALPS staff members must neither participate in nor condone any form of harassment or activity that demeans persons or creates an intimidating, hostile, or offensive campus environment.

ALPS staff members must use reasonable and informed practices to limit the liability exposure of the institution and its officers, employees, and agents. ALPS staff members must be informed about institutional policies regarding risk management, personal liability, and related insurance coverage options and must be referred to external sources if coverage is not provided by the institution.

The institution must provide access to legal advice for ALPS staff members as needed to carry out assigned responsibilities.

The institution must inform ALPS staff and students in a timely and systematic fashion about extraordinary or changing legal obligations and potential liabilities.

Part 7. EQUITY and ACCESS

Adult Learner Programs and Services (ALPS) must be provided on a fair, equitable, and non-discriminatory basis in accordance with institutional policies and with all applicable state/provincial and federal statutes and regulations. ALPS must maintain an educational and work environment free from discrimination in accordance with law and institutional policy.

Discrimination must be avoided on the basis of age; cultural heritage; disability; ethnicity; gender identity and expression; nationality; political affiliation; race; religious affiliation; sex; sexual orientation; economic, marital, social, or veteran status; and any other bases included in local, state/provincial, or federal laws.

Consistent with the mission and goals, ALPS must take action to remedy significant imbalances in student participation and staffing patterns.

ALPS must ensure physical and program access for persons with disabilities. ALPS must be responsive to the needs of all students and other populations served when establishing hours of operation and developing methods of delivering programs and services.

ALPS must recognize the needs of distance learning students by providing appropriate and accessible services and assisting them in identifying and gaining access to other appropriate services in their geographic region.

Part 8. DIVERSITY

Within the context of each institution's unique mission,

diversity enriches the community and enhances the collegiate experience for all; therefore, Adult Learner Programs and Services (ALPS) must create and nurture environments that are welcoming to and bring together persons of diverse backgrounds.

ALPS must promote environments that are characterized by open and continuous communication that deepens understanding of one's own identity, culture, and heritage, as well as that of others. ALPS must recognize, honor, educate, and promote respect about commonalties and differences among people within their historical and cultural contexts.

ALPS must address the characteristics and needs of a diverse population when establishing and implementing policies and procedures.

On campuses where adult learners constitute a distinct minority and under-served population, they should be considered an under-represented population. Means for serving this under-represented population could include a task force on adult learner recruitment and retention and/or an adult learner commission with faculty, staff, and student membership.

Part 9. ORGANIZATION and MANAGEMENT

To promote student learning and development outcomes, Adult Learner Programs and Services (ALPS) must be structured purposefully and managed effectively to achieve stated goals. Evidence of appropriate structure must include current and accessible policies and procedures, written performance expectations for all employees, functional workflow graphics or organizational charts, and clearly stated program and service delivery expectations.

ALPS must monitor websites used for distributing information to ensure that the sites are current, accurate, appropriately referenced, and accessible.

Evidence of effective management must include use of comprehensive and accurate information for decisions, clear sources and channels of authority, effective communication practices, procedures for decision-making and conflict resolution, responses to changing conditions, systems of accountability and evaluation, and processes for recognition and reward. ALPS must align policies and procedures with those of the institution and provide channels within the organization for their regular review.

ALPS must inform institutional leaders of its role in creating, reviewing, and implementing institutional policies and procedures that are responsive to the assessed needs of adult learners.

Part 10. CAMPUS and EXTERNAL RELATIONS

Adult Learner Programs and Services (ALPS) must reach out to relevant individuals, campus offices, and external agencies to:
- establish, maintain, and promote effective relations

- disseminate information about their own and other related programs and services
- coordinate and collaborate, where appropriate, in offering programs and services to meet the needs of students and promote their achievement of student learning and development outcomes

ALPS staff members should serve on committees that address policies and procedures that affect adult learners.

If there is more than one campus unit whose clientele are principally adult learners, ALPS should share information and collaborate with those offices. Examples of on-campus units with which ALPS staff members should collaborate include continuing and distance education, commuter and off-campus living programs, campus information and visitor services programs, graduate and professional student services, veterans' programs, child care center(s), and critical access and service-providing units such as admissions, financial aid, the registrar's office, the library, career services, and learning and advising centers. This collaboration also should ensure that students enrolled at off-site locations are provided with equitable access to institutional resources.

The community agencies with which ALPS staff members should have a working relationship include local community education and literacy programs, TRIO and other equal opportunity programs, community libraries, retiree programs, veterans' programs, vocational rehabilitation offices, and social service agencies.

ALPS must have procedures and guidelines consistent with institutional policy for responding to threats, emergencies, and crisis situations. Systems and procedures must be in place to disseminate timely and accurate information to students and other members of the campus community during emergency situations.

ALPS must have procedures and guidelines consistent with institutional policy for communicating with the media.

Part 11. FINANCIAL RESOURCES

Adult Learner Programs and Services (ALPS) must have adequate funding to accomplish their mission and goals. In establishing funding priorities and making significant changes, a comprehensive analysis, which includes relevant expenditures, external and internal resources, and impact on the campus community, must be conducted.

ALPS must demonstrate fiscal responsibility and cost effectiveness consistent with institutional protocols.

Adult learners should benefit equitably from fee-supported programs and services, including the establishment of programs and services that address their unique needs.

Part 12. TECHNOLOGY

Adult Learner Programs and Services (ALPS) must have adequate technology to support their mission. The technology and its use must comply with institutional policies and procedures and be evaluated for compliance with relevant federal, state/provincial, and local requirements.

ALPS must maintain policies and procedures that address the security and back up of data.

When technology is used to facilitate student learning and development, ALPS must select technology that reflects current best pedagogical practices.

Technology, as well as any workstations or computer labs maintained by the ALPS for student use, must be accessible and must meet established technology standards for delivery to persons with disabilities.

When ALPS provide student access to technology, they must provide:
- access to policies that are clear, easy to understand, and available to all students
- access to instruction or training on how to use the technology
- access to information on the legal and ethical implications of misuse as it pertains to intellectual property, harassment, privacy, and social networks

ALPS should be responsive to adult learner differences in competencies, knowledge, and comfort levels with technology.

Student violations of technology policies must follow established institutional student disciplinary procedures.

Students who experience negative emotional or psychological consequences from the use of technology must be referred to support services provided by the institution.

Part 13. FACILITIES and EQUIPMENT

Adult Learner Programs and Services (ALPS) must have adequate, accessible, suitably located facilities and equipment to support their mission and goals. If acquiring capital equipment as defined by the institution, ALPS must take into account expenses related to regular maintenance and life cycle costs. Facilities and equipment must be evaluated regularly, including consideration of sustainability, and be in compliance with relevant federal, state/provincial, and local requirements to provide for access, health, safety, and security.

ALPS staff should advocate for access to facilities that are physically close to campus programs to enable adult learners to engage with staff and faculty members and to interact with prospective and enrolled students.

To create an affirming environment in which prospective and enrolled adult learners may interact with one another and the ALPS staff members, ALPS should advocate for access to facilities that include:
- lounge and reception areas that are welcoming and comfortable
- kitchenette space to prepare and store meals
- locker facilities
- study area which permits the consumption of food and beverages
- computers and printers
- use of traditional and electronic means of communication, including display racks, bulletin boards, websites, and on-line portals
- traditional and/or electronic library of books, articles, videos, and other resources about adult learners and on topics useful to them such as study skills, financing one's education, and managing multiple roles
- toys, games, and other items for the use of children who accompany their parents/guardians to campus

ALPS staff members should work with other units such as commuter and off-campus living programs, continuing and distance education, and child care programs to assure the availability of facilities that meet adult learners' needs.

Adult learner student organizations should have access to facilities that support successful operations.

ALPS staff members must have work space that is well-equipped, adequate in size, and designed to support their work and responsibilities. For conversations requiring privacy, staff members must have access to a private space.

ALPS staff members who share work space must have the ability to secure their work adequately.

The design of the facilities must guarantee the security of records and ensure the confidentiality of sensitive information.

The location and layout of the facilities must be sensitive to the special needs of persons with disabilities as well as the needs of constituencies served.

ALPS must ensure that staff members are knowledgeable of and trained in safety and emergency procedures for securing and vacating the facilities.

Part 14. ASSESSMENT and EVALUATION

Adult Learner Programs and Services (ALPS) must establish systematic plans and processes to meet internal and external accountability expectations with regard to program as well as student learning and development outcomes. ALPS must conduct regular assessment and evaluations. Assessments must include qualitative and quantitative methodologies as appropriate, to determine whether and to what degree the stated mission, goals, and student learning and development outcomes are being met. The process must employ sufficient and sound measures to ensure comprehensiveness. Data collected must include responses from students and other affected constituencies.

ALPS must evaluate regularly how well they complement and enhance the institution's stated mission and educational effectiveness.

Results of these evaluations must be used in revising and

improving programs and services, identifying needs and interests in shaping directions of program and service design, and recognizing staff performance.

ALPS assessment activities should include a focus on demographics of adult applicants and enrollees, academic performance variables, retention studies, use of and satisfaction with campus programs and services, the impact on adult learners of institutional policies and practices, access to and receipt of financial aid, and student use of the institution's prior learning assessment options, e.g., College Level Examination Program (CLEP).

General Standards revised in 2008;
ALPS content developed in 2008

The Role of Alcohol, Tobacco, and Other Drug Programs

CAS Standards Contextual Statement

Abuse of alcohol, tobacco, and other drugs has historically been a major concern for institutions of higher education. Many colleges and universities have employed a variety of approaches over the years to address alcohol, tobacco, and other drug (ATOD) abuse and associated problems. During the mid-twentieth century serious research started to document the prevalence of alcohol and other drug use on America's college campuses. This newfound interest in an age-old problem may have been precipitated by the death of two students during drinking parties in 1949 and a third incident that year in which a student almost died while being initiated into a drinking club (Strauss & Bacon, 1953). Unfortunately, it seems that such needless and senseless tragedies are still the primary impetus for action in the early part of the twenty-first century.

A little over 50 years ago, a landmark study conducted at Yale University was arguably the first formal research-based indication of substance use on college campuses in the United States. By analyzing the responses to a self-administered questionnaire completed by more than 15,000 students at 27 colleges, researchers identified specific rates of alcohol use by college students and their rationale for drinking (Strauss & Bacon, 1953). Yale researchers conducted their survey concentrating on two key pieces of information: how frequently students drank and how much alcohol they consumed. This was an area that generated further research studies and shaped ATOD programs, both in the areas of prevention and intervention, for the next twenty or more years.

In 1975, the Monitoring the Future project was established to study changes in the attitudes and behaviors of America's youth (Johnston, O'Malley, Bachman, & Schulenberg, 2004). From these studies, trends began to emerge that documented the prevalence of alcohol and other drug abuse among college students and the negative consequences that students experienced as a result of their substance use (Lucey, 2006). Research in the 1990s identified not only how much alcohol and other drugs that college students were using, but also why they used various substances and the negative consequences suffered as a result of such use (Core Institute, 2000). This broadening of scope in research brought much needed attention to the consequences of use, abuse, and high-risk behavior.

As the field continued to become more organized and scientific in its approach to understanding the scope of the

problem, a majority of the national research on college-based alcohol and other drug abuse began to originate from one of two places: the Core Institute, located at Southern Illinois University at Carbondale, and the Harvard School of Public Health. While these remain two of the major tools for data collection, a number of other survey instruments are also used to varying degrees by colleges and universities. These include surveys developed by the American College Health Association (i.e., National College Health Assessment) and the Cooperative Institutional Research Program (i.e., College Student Survey), each of which goes beyond looking solely at substance abuse issues by examining broader health-related and campus life issues. (Lucey, 2006).

In 1999, the National Institute on Alcohol Abuse and Alcoholism (NIAAA) convened a blue-ribbon panel of leading researchers, college and university presidents, and students to review research and engage in a series of discussions to address the serious problem of college student alcohol use. Over the course of three years, this task force developed a ground-breaking report outlining the extent of the problem and its many manifestations and providing a guiding framework upon which to develop sound and effective campus alcohol programs. The 2002 report, "A Call to Action: Changing the Culture of Drinking at U.S. Colleges" was landmark because for the first time, the troubling dimensions of the college alcohol problem were outlined in terms so stark, no college administrator, alumnus, or student could deny its deadly and damaging ramifications. However compelling the information, many prevention practitioners would argue the most important contribution of the report was its recommendations for effective alcohol prevention in the college population. This included the call for an overarching comprehensive program framework and the delineation of four tiers of effectiveness. This information changed how we look at and choose programs for our campuses, and has helped to emphasize the importance of program evaluation and assessment.

With the continued scientific focus on prevention work, we see more clearly that alcohol remains the primary substance of abuse, and we continue to see a rise in the abuse of other substances, most notably marijuana and prescription and over-the-counter medications. According to one large study, the nonmedical use of prescription medications is second only to marijuana as the most common form of illicit drug use; in addition, the percentage of students reporting the abuse of prescription stimulants can be as high as 25% on some campuses (McCabe, Knight, Teter, & Wechsler, 2005). These drugs are being abused not only in isolation but in combination with each other and with alcohol as well as other drugs. With the rise of these prescription drugs in circulation and the ease of access through internet pharmacies, this is a fast growing challenge facing the prevention field and ATOD programs. Not only has there been a rise in the abuse of prescription medication but a rise in the abuse of over-the-counter medications such as cold and cough medications containing DMX (e.g., Robitussin, Alka-Seltzer), which is used for its dissociative and psychedelic properties. There is a belief held by students that there is no real danger or abuse potential in using these drugs as they are, after all, medications. As this behavior increases, the field is faced with the task of looking for new strategies and modifying existing programs to focus on this emerging epidemic.

The rise in abuse of these substances combined with the continued heavy use of alcohol, tobacco, marijuana, and other drugs continues to stretch ATOD prevention and intervention program resources. Adding to the stress of existing resources is the tightening of campus prevention budgets and the limited availability of local, state/provincial, and federal funding. Along with this trend the field continues to see the challenge of inadequate staffing to fully address the expanding range of ATOD program issues.

While there is more for the field of prevention and ATOD programs to address and resources seem to be drying up, there has been progress in the practice of prevention as the field continues to look to evidenced-based programming with a heavy focus on comprehensive strategies and environmental management practices. Elements of many of these approaches have been highlighted and deconstructed in "Experiences in Effective Prevention: The U.S. Department of Education's Alcohol and Other Drug Prevention Models on College Campuses Grants" published in 2007 by the U.S. Department of Education's Higher Education Center for Alcohol and Other Drug Abuse and Violence Prevention.

There are also a growing number of campus and community stakeholders getting involved in the work of prevention, including law enforcement and campus security, faculty, parents, community and professional agencies/associations. Evidence of this growth can be seen in NASPA's Alcohol and Other Drug Knowledge Community and the 2006 reorganization of The Network Addressing Collegiate Alcohol and Other Drug Issues-- both allowing for a broad range of student affairs professionals to become involved in prevention and programming efforts and gain access to a wealth of knowledge through regional trainings and technical assistance from other professionals.

One area of the field that has received a great deal of attention in recent years is assessment, whether that be in the assessment of student behavior as we saw grow in the 1990s or the assessment of the effectiveness of ATOD education, prevention, and intervention programs that has grown in the last decade. Programming now being offered and assessed on many campuses includes motivational interviewing, policies restricting access, individual counseling, support groups, recovery houses, social norms marketing, campus-community task forces, peer education, brief interventions, curriculum infusion, educational sanctions, policy promotion, medical amnesty policies, and the list goes on. Not every program is right for each campus, but through intentional programming and thorough assessment, ineffective programs can be discarded, effective ones retained, and new programs added. The CAS standards offer guidance for ATOD program development and evaluation, necessary components in the pursuit of effective practice.

References, Readings, and Resources

AMA Office of Alcohol & Other Drug Abuse: www.ama-assn.org/ama/pub/category/3337.html

American College Health Associations ATOD Coalition: http://www.acha.org/about_acha/ctfs/coalition_atd.cfm

Amethyst Initiative (2008). *Initiative description.* Retrieved on September 27, 2008 from the World Wide Web: http://www.amethystinitiative.org

Anderson, D.S., & Milgram, G.G. (1996). *Promising practices: Campus alcohol strategies sourcebook.* Fairfax, VA: George Mason University.

BACCHUS and GAMMA Peer Education Network: www.bacchusgamma.org

Califano, Jr., J.A. (2007) *Accompanying statement.* Retrieved on September 29, 2008 National Center on Addiction and Substance Abuse at Columbia University (CASA). *You've Got Drugs: IV: Prescription Drug Pushers on the Internet* (New York, 2007).

Coombs, R.H., & Ziedonis, D. (1995). *Handbook on drug abuse prevention: A Comprehensive strategy to prevent the abuse of alcohol and other drugs.* Boston: Allyn & Bacon.

Core Institute (2000). *1999 statistics on alcohol and other drug use on American campuses, Carbondale:* Core Institute. Retrieved September 12, 2000, from http:.siu.edu/departments/coreinst/public_html/recent.html

Johnston, L.D., O'Malley, P.M., Bachman, J.G., & Schulenberg, J.E. (2004). *National survey results on drug use for the monitoring the future study, 1975-2003.* Rockville: National Institute on Drug Abuse

Lucey, R. (2006). Substance abuse on campus: A brief history. In R. Chapman (Ed.), *When they drink: Practitioner views and lessons learned.* Glassboro, NJ: Rowan University Press.

Journal of Drug Education.   Amityville, NY: Baywood Publishing Co.

McCabe, S. E., Knight, J. R., Teter, C. J., & Wechsler, H. (2005). Nonmedical use of prescription stimulants among U.S. college students: Prevalence and correlates from a national survey. *Addiction, 99,* 96—106.

NIAAA Report (2005). *Call to action information.* Retrieved on October 3, 2008 from   http://www.campushealthandsafety.org/niaaa/

National Clearinghouse for Alcohol and Drug Information (NCADI): www.health.org

National Institute of Drug Abuse (NIDA): www.drugabuse.gov

National Institute on Alcohol Abuse and Alcoholism (NIAAA): www.collegedrinkingprevention.gov

Strauss, R., & Bacon, S.D. (1953). *Dinking in college.* New Haven: Yale University Press.

U.S. Department of Education's Higher Education Center publications: www.edc.org/hec

The Network — Addressing Collegiate Alcohol and Other Drug Issues: http://www.thenetwork.ws/

Wechsler, H., Dowdall, G., Davenport, A., & Castillo, S. (1995). Correlates of college student binge drinking. *American Journal of Public Health, 85, 7.*

Contributor:
Current edition:
John Watson, Drexel University, The Network

Previous editions:
Carole Middlebrooks, University of Georgia, The Network

Alcohol, Tobacco, and Other Drug Programs
CAS Standards and Guidelines

For the purpose of this document, the term "alcohol, tobacco, and other drug use or abuse" includes: (1) the illegal use of alcohol, tobacco, prescription medications, and other drugs, and (2) the high-risk use and/or abuse of alcohol, tobacco, prescription medications, over-the-counter medications, and nutritional supplements.

Part 1. MISSION

Alcohol, Tobacco, and Other Drug Programs (ATODP) must develop, disseminate, implement, and regularly review their mission. Mission statements must be consistent with the mission of the institution and with professional standards. ATODP in higher education must enhance overall educational experiences by incorporating student learning and development outcomes in their mission.

The goals of ATODP must:
- acknowledge and mitigate the inherent risks to the total community associated with alcohol, tobacco, and other drug use
- develop, disseminate, interpret, and support the enforcement of campus regulations that are consistent with institutional policies and local, state/provincial, and federal law
- promote healthy choices concerning the use of alcohol, tobacco, and other drugs, emphasizing the elimination of illegal use, high-risk behavior, harmful use, and related violence
- promote a safe, healthy, and learning-conducive environment
- define ATODP policies and practices for prevention, education, training, intervention, evaluation, referral, and treatment
- develop shared ownership of the issue by involving all entities of the campus community including governing boards, administrators, faculty and staff members, students, and community leaders
- protect the legal rights of students

Part 2. PROGRAM

The formal education of students, consisting of the curriculum and the co-curriculum, must promote student learning and development outcomes that are purposeful and holistic and that prepare students for satisfying and productive lifestyles, work, and civic participation. The student learning and development outcome domains and their related dimensions are:

- knowledge acquisition, integration, construction, and application
  - Dimensions: understanding knowledge from a range of disciplines; connecting knowledge to other knowledge, ideas, and experiences; constructing knowledge; and relating knowledge to daily life

- cognitive complexity
  - Dimensions: critical thinking; reflective thinking; effective reasoning; and creativity

- intrapersonal development
  - Dimensions: realistic self-appraisal, self-understanding, and self-respect; identity development; commitment to ethics and integrity; and spiritual awareness

- interpersonal competence
  - Dimensions: meaningful relationships; interdependence; collaboration; and effective leadership

- humanitarianism and civic engagement
  - Dimensions: understanding and appreciation of cultural and human differences; social responsibility; global perspective; and sense of civic responsibility

- practical competence
  - Dimensions: pursuing goals; communicating effectively; technical competence; managing personal affairs; managing career development; demonstrating professionalism; maintaining health and wellness; and living a purposeful and satisfying life

[See *The Council for the Advancement of Standards Learning and Developmental Outcomes* statement for examples of outcomes related to these domains and dimensions.]

Consistent with the institutional mission, Alcohol, Tobacco, and Other Drug Programs (ATODP) must identify relevant and desirable student learning and development outcomes from among the six domains and related dimensions. When creating opportunities for student learning and development, ATODP must explore possibilities for collaboration with faculty members and other colleagues.

ATODP must assess relevant and desirable student learning and development outcomes and provide evidence of their impact on student learning and development. ATODP must articulate how they contribute to or support students' learning and development in the domains not specifically assessed.

ATODP must be:
- integrated into the life of the institution
- intentional and coherent
- guided by theories and knowledge of learning and development
- reflective of developmental and demographic profiles of the student population
- responsive to needs of individuals, diverse and special populations, and relevant constituencies

ATODP must involve students, faculty members, staff, and community constituents to reduce heavy and high-risk use of alcohol, tobacco, prescription medication, and other drugs.

ATODP must include:

- environmental management strategies
- institutional policies
- enforcement strategies
- bi-annual review
- community collaboration
- training and education
- assistance and referral
- student leadership

ATODP staff must serve as positive role models for ethical and healthy behaviors.

Because faculty and staff members' behaviors often serve as models for students, resources should be available on-campus to assist supervisors in dealing with employees who exhibit high-risk behavior related to alcohol, tobacco, and other drugs.

ATODP must develop and provide education on policies, laws, prevention, intervention and treatment resources, and training for students, including student organizations.

ATODP education and training programs should address the cultural and economic context in which society promotes and condones alcohol, tobacco, and other drug use, including traditions and rituals conducive to high-risk drinking. Other topics may include: legal, physiological, psychological, and social aspects and effects of alcohol, tobacco, and other drug use, abuse, and dependency; high-risk uses of alcohol; risk factors for groups, including risk factors for groups as identified through assessment; differences between actual student use and perceptions of student use; and the impact of alcohol, tobacco, and other drug use related to physiological and behavioral differences linked with gender. Techniques and protocols for identifying and referring students with problems to appropriate campus entities should also be included.

ATODP should develop, provide, and advocate strategies that model practical applications of prevention theories and research results, including environmental approaches, risk reduction approaches, social norms approaches, student assistance programs, curricular infusion projects, development of on-campus task forces, and the development of campus and community coalitions.

ATODP should provide training for faculty and staff members in identifying, intervening, and referring students with alcohol, tobacco, and other drug problems.

ATODP should use public health prevention strategies that are evidenced-based and have demonstrated effectiveness in reducing heavy and high-risk drinking and other drug use in college populations.

ATODP should advocate for incorporating alcohol, tobacco, and other drugs information within relevant courses and expanding campus library holdings.

ATODP must provide access to support services for students with alcohol or other drug-related concerns.

Student involvement in assistance services may be voluntary upon self-initiation or referral, or mandatory upon referral by judicial authorities or other entities.

The student assistance services program should include confidential individual assessment for students to explore and evaluate their attitudes, perceptions, and behaviors; explore and evaluate the consequences, risk factors, and relationship to alcohol or other drugs; and make decisions based on the student's individual situation.

Student assistance services should provide, with peer involvement, a coordinated system across the campus for intervention and referral services for students. This system should include training programs on alcohol abuse and other drug use and on referral skills.

Student assistance services should identify and maintain contacts with campus and community entities that offer effective treatment, education, and support to students, family members, and friends. Such services may include structured education and counseling sessions for individuals and groups; community service work; disability support services; self-help groups such as Alcoholics Anonymous, Narcotics Anonymous, Al-Anon and Adult Children of Alcoholics; support groups; and detoxification and in-patient therapy.

Part 3. LEADERSHIP

Because effective and ethical leadership is essential to the success of all organizations, Alcohol, Tobacco, and Other Drug Program (ATODP) leaders with organizational authority for the programs and services must:

- **articulate a vision and mission for their programs and services**
- **set goals and objectives based on the needs of the population served and desired student learning and development outcomes**
- **advocate for their programs and services**
- **promote campus environments that provide meaningful opportunities for student learning, development, and integration**
- **identify and find means to address individual, organizational, or environmental conditions that foster or inhibit mission achievement**
- **advocate for representation in strategic planning initiatives at appropriate divisional and institutional levels**
- **initiate collaborative interactions with stakeholders who have legitimate concerns and interests in the functional area**
- **apply effective practices to educational and administrative processes**
- **prescribe and model ethical behavior**
- **communicate effectively**
- **manage financial resources, including planning, allocation, monitoring, and analysis**
- **incorporate sustainability practices in the management and design of programs, services, and facilities**
- **manage human resource processes including recruitment, selection, development, supervision, performance planning, and evaluation**

- empower professional, support, and student staff to accept leadership opportunities
- encourage and support scholarly contribution to the profession
- be informed about and integrate appropriate technologies into programs and services
- be knowledgeable about federal, state/provincial, and local laws relevant to the programs and services and ensure that staff members understand their responsibilities by receiving appropriate training
- develop and continuously improve programs and services in response to the changing needs of students and other populations served and the evolving institutional priorities
- recognize environmental conditions that may negatively influence the safety of staff and students and propose interventions that mitigate such conditions

ATODP leaders should provide institutional leaders with information on ATODP issues on their campus to engender support.

Part 4. HUMAN RESOURCES

Alcohol, Tobacco, and Other Drug Programs (ATODP) must be staffed adequately by individuals qualified to accomplish the mission and goals. Within institutional guidelines, ATODP must establish procedures for staff selection, training, and evaluation; set expectations for supervision; and provide appropriate professional development opportunities to improve the leadership ability, competence, and skills of all employees.

ATODP professional staff members must hold an earned graduate or professional degree in a field relevant to the position they hold or must possess an appropriate combination of educational credentials and related work experience.

ATODP should be supervised by professional staff members who have earned a master's degree from an accredited institution in fields of study such as health education, student services/development, psychology, social work, counseling, education, public health, or other appropriate health-related area, and who have relevant training and experience. Such training and experience should include prevention and intervention, assessment and treatment issues and strategies, and supervised work with older adolescents and adults of all ages.

ATODP prevention specialists must hold a minimum of a bachelor's degree in a related field and have relevant training and experience.

Training and experience should include an understanding of prevention and intervention strategies as well as work experience with college students.

Degree- or credential-seeking interns must be qualified by enrollment in an appropriate field of study and by relevant experience. These individuals must be trained and supervised adequately by professional staff members holding educational credentials and related work experience appropriate for supervision.

Student employees and volunteers must be carefully selected, trained, supervised, and evaluated. They must be educated on how and when to refer those in need of additional assistance to qualified staff members and must have access to a supervisor for assistance in making these judgments. Student employees and volunteers must be provided clear and precise job descriptions, pre-service training based on assessed needs, and continuing staff development.

Employees and volunteers must receive specific training on institutional policies and privacy laws regarding their access to student records and other sensitive institutional information (e.g., in the USA, Family Educational Rights and Privacy Act, FERPA, or equivalent privacy laws in other states/provinces or countries).

ATODP must have technical and support staff members adequate to accomplish their mission. All members of the staff must be technologically proficient and qualified to perform their job functions, be knowledgeable about ethical and legal uses of technology, and have access to training and resources to support the performance of their assigned responsibilities.

All members of the staff must receive training on policies and procedures related to the use of technology to store or access student records and institutional data.

ATODP must ensure that staff members are knowledgeable about and trained in emergency procedures, crisis response, and prevention efforts. Prevention efforts must address identification of threatening conduct or behavior of students, faculty members, staff, and others and must incorporate a system or procedures for responding, including but not limited to reporting them to the appropriate campus officials.

Salary levels and benefits for all staff members must be commensurate with those for comparable positions within the institution, in similar institutions, and in the relevant geographic area.

ATODP must maintain position descriptions for all staff members.

To create a diverse staff, ATODP must institute hiring and promotion practices that are fair, inclusive, proactive, and non-discriminatory.

ATODP must conduct regular performance planning and evaluation of staff members. ATODP must provide access to continuing and advanced education and professional development opportunities.

ATODP should provide training on problem recognition and referral procedures for professional and support staff, pre-professionals, and paraprofessionals.

Part 5. ETHICS

Persons involved in the delivery of Alcohol, Tobacco, and Other Drug Programs (ATODP) must adhere to the highest principles of ethical behavior. ATODP must review relevant professional ethical standards and develop or adopt and implement appropriate statements of ethical practice. ATODP must publish these statements and ensure their periodic review by relevant constituencies.

ATODP must orient new staff members to relevant ethical standards and statements of ethical practice.

ATODP staff members must ensure that privacy and confidentiality are maintained with respect to all communications and records to the extent that such records are protected under the law and appropriate statements of ethical practice. Information contained in students' education records must not be disclosed except as allowed by relevant laws and institutional policies. ATODP staff members must disclose to appropriate authorities information judged to be of an emergency nature, especially when the safety of the individual or others is involved, or when otherwise required by institutional policy or relevant law.

ATODP staff members must be aware of and comply with the provisions contained in the institution's policies pertaining to human subjects research and student rights and responsibilities, as well as those in other relevant institutional policies addressing ethical practices and confidentiality of research data concerning individuals.

ATODP staff members must recognize and avoid personal conflicts of interest or appearance thereof in the performance of their work.

ATODP staff members must strive to insure the fair, objective, and impartial treatment of all persons with whom they interact.

When handling institutional funds, ATODP staff members must ensure that such funds are managed in accordance with established and responsible accounting procedures and the fiscal policies or processes of the institution.

Promotional and descriptive information must be accurate and free of deception.

ATODP staff members must perform their duties within the limits of their training, expertise, and competence. When these limits are exceeded, individuals in need of further assistance must be referred to persons possessing appropriate qualifications.

ATODP staff members must use suitable means to confront and otherwise hold accountable other staff members who exhibit unethical behavior.

ATODP staff members must be knowledgeable about and practice ethical behavior in the use of technology.

Part 6. LEGAL RESPONSIBILITIES

Alcohol, Tobacco, and Other Drug Programs (ATODP) staff members must be knowledgeable about and responsive to laws and regulations that relate to their respective responsibilities and that may pose legal obligations, limitations, or ramifications for the institution as a whole. As appropriate, staff members must inform users of programs and services, as well as officials, of legal obligations and limitations including constitutional, statutory, regulatory, and case law; mandatory laws and orders emanating from federal, state/provincial, and local governments; and the institution's policies.

ATODP must have written policies on all relevant operations, transactions, or tasks that may have legal implications.

ATODP staff members must neither participate in nor condone any form of harassment or activity that demeans persons or creates an intimidating, hostile, or offensive campus environment.

ATODP staff members must use reasonable and informed practices to limit the liability exposure of the institution and its officers, employees, and agents. ATODP staff members must be informed about institutional policies regarding risk management, personal liability, and related insurance coverage options and must be referred to external sources if coverage is not provided by the institution.

The institution must provide access to legal advice for ATODP staff members as needed to carry out assigned responsibilities.

ATODP staff members must be aware of and seek advice from the institution's legal counsel on privacy and disclosure of student information and parental notification.

The institution must inform ATODP staff and students in a timely and systematic fashion about extraordinary or changing legal obligations and potential liabilities.

Part 7. EQUITY and ACCESS

Alcohol, Tobacco, and Other Drug Programs (ATODP) must be provided on a fair, equitable, and non-discriminatory basis in accordance with institutional policies and with all applicable state/provincial and federal statutes and regulations. ATODP must maintain an educational and work environment free from discrimination in accordance with law and institutional policy.

Discrimination must be avoided on the basis of age; cultural heritage; disability; ethnicity; gender identity and expression; nationality; political affiliation; race; religious affiliation; sex; sexual orientation; economic, marital, social, or veteran status; and any other bases included in local, state/provincial, or federal laws.

Consistent with the mission and goals, ATODP must take action to remedy significant imbalances in student participation and staffing patterns.

ATODP must ensure physical and program access for persons with disabilities. ATODP must be responsive to the needs of all students and other populations served when establishing hours of operation and developing methods of delivering programs and services.

ATODP must recognize the needs of distance learning students by providing appropriate and accessible services and assisting them in identifying and gaining access to other appropriate services in their geographic region.

Part 8. DIVERSITY

Within the context of each institution's unique mission, diversity enriches the community and enhances the collegiate experience for all; therefore, Alcohol, Tobacco, and Other Drug Programs (ATODP) must create and nurture environments that are welcoming to and bring together persons of diverse backgrounds.

ATODP must promote environments that are characterized by open and continuous communication that deepens understanding of one's own identity, culture, and heritage, as well as that of others. ATODP must recognize, honor, educate, and promote respect about commonalties and differences among people within their historical and cultural contexts.

ATODP must address the characteristics and needs of a diverse population when establishing and implementing policies and procedures.

Part 9. ORGANIZATION and MANAGEMENT

To promote student learning and development outcomes, Alcohol, Tobacco, and Other Drug Programs (ATODP) must be structured purposefully and managed effectively to achieve stated goals. Evidence of appropriate structure must include current and accessible policies and procedures, written performance expectations for all employees, functional workflow graphics or organizational charts, and clearly stated program and service delivery expectations.

ATODP must monitor websites used for distributing information to ensure that the sites are current, accurate, appropriately referenced, and accessible.

Evidence of effective management must include use of comprehensive and accurate information for decisions, clear sources and channels of authority, effective communication practices, procedures for decision-making and conflict resolution, responses to changing conditions, systems of accountability and evaluation, and processes for recognition and reward. ATODP must align policies and procedures with those of the institution and provide channels within the organization for their regular review.

The ATODP director or coordinator must be placed within the institution's organizational structures so as to be able to promote cooperative interaction with appropriate campus and community entities and to develop the support of high-level administrators.

The scope and structure of ATODP should be defined by the size, nature, complexity, and philosophy of the institution.

ATODP should maintain an advisory board, preferably appointed by the executive officer, comprised of knowledgeable members of the campus and community, for advice and support on polices and programs.

ATODP must collaborate in the development of policies to:
- maintain consistency with federal, state/provincial, and local laws and regulations
- promote an educational, social, and living environment free from the abuse of alcohol, tobacco, and legal drugs, and the use of illegal drugs
- define geographic jurisdictions and demographic characteristics of populations to whom policies pertain
- define individual and group behaviors and group activities that are prohibited both on campus property and at off-campus events controlled by the institution
- specify the potential consequences for using or possessing, distributing, or manufacturing different amounts and/or categories of alcohol, tobacco, and other drugs
- establish protocols and procedures for the involvement of campus law enforcement, campus judicial programs, and other campus entities
- establish protocols and procedures for referring individuals with alcohol, tobacco, or other drug problems to appropriate sources for assistance
- define campus procedures on the availability and marketing of alcoholic beverages, if permitted
- define appropriate procedures for any permitted use of alcohol or tobacco

Part 10. CAMPUS and EXTERNAL RELATIONS

Alcohol, Tobacco, and other Drug Programs (ATODP) must reach out to relevant individuals, campus offices, and external agencies to:
- establish, maintain, and promote effective relations
- disseminate information about their own and other related programs and services
- coordinate and collaborate, where appropriate, in offering programs and services to meet the needs of students and promote their achievement of student learning and development outcomes

ATODP must have procedures and guidelines consistent with institutional policy for responding to threats, emergencies, and crisis situations. Systems and procedures must be in place to disseminate timely and accurate information to students and other members of the campus community during emergency situations.

ATODP must have procedures and guidelines consistent with institutional policy for communicating with the media.

ATODP must gather and disseminate information to the campus community, including students, their parents, staff, and faculty members on alcohol, tobacco, and other drug problems, risk reduction strategies, resources, and related topics.

ATODP must maintain effective working relationships with various campus offices and community groups and agencies to promote a healthy environment in which the use or abuse of alcohol and use of other drugs does not interfere with the learning, performance, or social aspects of college life,

These campus offices may include senior administrators; medical services; health promotion and prevention services; counseling; law enforcement and safety; judicial programs; residential life; campus information and visitor services; fraternity and sorority life; athletics; student and other campus media; disability support services, student activities offices and student organizations; academic departments; personnel services; and community relations and public affairs. Community agencies may include relevant local, state/provincial, and federal agencies and authorities such as the state liquor store control authority, state alcohol agency, the office of highway traffic safety, mayor and council, neighborhood associations, faith community, family, parents or guardians, school systems, area health care and treatment providers, support groups, as well as representatives from the local chamber of commerce and the hospitality industry.

ATODP should engage the campus and community in the issues of access and availability of alcohol, tobacco, and other drugs, and in the enforcement of the law.

ATODP must work with campus and community resources to encourage staff members to utilize appropriate screening protocols.

Part 11. FINANCIAL RESOURCES

Alcohol, Tobacco, and Other Drug Programs (ATODP) must have adequate funding to accomplish their mission and goals. In establishing funding priorities and making significant changes, a comprehensive analysis, which includes relevant expenditures, external and internal resources, and impact on the campus community, must be conducted.

ATODP must demonstrate fiscal responsibility and cost effectiveness consistent with institutional protocols.

The institution should provide sufficient baseline funding for ATODP so that staff members may spend the majority of their time on planning, programming, providing services, and evaluation rather than on seeking new or continuing funding sources.

Part 12. TECHNOLOGY

Alcohol, Tobacco, and Other Drug Programs (ATODP) must have adequate technology to support their mission.

The technology and its use must comply with institutional policies and procedures and be evaluated for compliance with relevant federal, state/provincial, and local requirements.

ATODP must maintain policies and procedures that address the security and back up of data.

When technology is used to facilitate student learning and development, ATODP must select technology that reflects current best pedagogical practices.

Technology, as well as any workstations or computer labs maintained by the programs ATODP for student use, must be accessible and must meet established technology standards for delivery to persons with disabilities.

When ATODP provide student access to technology, they must provide:
- access to policies that are clear, easy to understand, and available to all students
- access to instruction or training on how to use the technology
- access to information on the legal and ethical implications of misuse as it pertains to intellectual property, harassment, privacy, and social networks

Student violations of technology policies must follow established institutional student disciplinary procedures.

Students who experience negative emotional or psychological consequences from the use of technology must be referred to support services provided by the institution.

ATODP should possess, or have access to, equipment and services such as audio-visual equipment and services, printing services, campus and community media resources, and computers.

Part 13. FACILITIES and EQUIPMENT

Alcohol, Tobacco, and Other Drug Programs (ATODP) must have adequate, accessible, suitably located facilities and equipment to support their mission and goals. If acquiring capital equipment as defined by the institution, ATODP must take into account expenses related to regular maintenance and life cycle costs. Facilities and equipment must be evaluated regularly, including consideration of sustainability, and be in compliance with relevant federal, state/provincial, and local requirements to provide for access, health, safety, and security.

ATODP staff members must have work space that is well-equipped, adequate in size, and designed to support their work and responsibilities. For conversations requiring privacy, staff members must have access to a private space.

ATODP staff members who share work space must have the ability to secure their work adequately.

The design of the facilities must guarantee the security of records and ensure the confidentiality of sensitive information.

The location and layout of the facilities must be sensitive to the special needs of persons with disabilities as well as the needs of constituencies served.

ATODP must ensure that staff members are knowledgeable of and trained in safety and emergency procedures for securing and vacating the facilities.

Facilities for ATODP should support a range of services, including prevention, education, assessment, intervention, programming, and a resource center.

Office space should be physically separate from human resources, campus security, and judicial programs.

ATODP should be provided facilities that ensure confidentiality and a location in which students, faculty members, and staff might access and read information on alcohol, tobacco, and other drugs.

Part 14. ASSESSMENT and EVALUATION

Alcohol, Tobacco, and Other Drug Programs (ATODP) must establish systematic plans and processes to meet internal and external accountability expectations with regard to program as well as student learning and development outcomes. ATODP must conduct regular assessment and evaluations. Assessments must include qualitative and quantitative methodologies as appropriate, to determine whether and to what degree the stated mission, goals, and student learning and development outcomes are being met. The process must employ sufficient and sound measures to ensure comprehensiveness. Data collected must include responses from students and other affected constituencies.

ATODP must evaluate regularly how well they complement and enhance the institution's stated mission and educational effectiveness.

Results of these evaluations must be used in revising and improving programs and services, identifying needs and interests in shaping directions of program and service design, and recognizing staff performance.

ATODP must assess systematically the following campus factors:
- attitudes, beliefs, and behaviors regarding alcohol, tobacco, and other drug use, abuse, and dependency
- consequences of alcohol, tobacco, or other drug use or abuse upon social skills; academic and work performance; property damage; policy violations; health, counseling, and disciplinary caseloads; and other indicators of problems
- perceptions of campus alcohol, tobacco, and other drug use norms
- features of the environment that abet high-risk alcohol use, tobacco, and other drug use; marketing and promotion that promotes heavy or underage consumption of alcohol; inconsistent enforcement of campus policy and community law; lack of availability of alcohol-free social and recreational options on campus

and in the surrounding community

ATODP should assess the norms, behaviors, and behavioral consequences of specific focus populations.

ATODP and other campus entities must exchange general and non-confidential assessment results of mutual application and benefit.

General Standards revised in 2008;
ATODP content developed/revised in 1990, 1997, & 2003

The Role of Assessment Services
CAS Standards Contextual Statement

Though the need for assessment and program evaluation in higher education has long been acknowledged by the field, it remains a pressing need today. In fact, the concerns raised in *A Test of Leadership* (2006), a report of the commission appointed by Secretary of Education Margaret Spellings, about the "less inspiring realities of postsecondary education" in the U.S., make an effective and comprehensive assessment program imperative (p. ix).

Early proponents of outcomes assessment included William Rainey Harper, President of the University of Chicago, who in 1889 called on colleges and universities to adopt a program of research with the college student as the subject "in order that the student may receive the assistance so essential to his [sic] highest success, another step in the onward evolution will take place. This step will be the scientific study of the student" (as cited in Rentz, 1996, p. 28).

Responding to Harper's vision, the *Student Personnel Point of View* in 1937 challenged the field of student services to employ "studies designed to improve these functions and services" (p. 42). Later in the document, four specific kinds of studies were called for: student out of class life and its connection to the educational mission, faculty and student out of class relationships, financial aid to students, and after college studies to ascertain the effects of college on careers and personal adjustment (American Council of Education, 1937).

The 1949 revision of the *Student Personnel Point of View* (American Council of Education, 1949) stated the "principal responsibility of personnel workers lies in the area of progressive program development...this means that each worker must devote a large part of time to the formulation of new plans and to the continuous evaluation and improvement of current programs (p. 34). This document also stressed the importance of personnel workers being "thoroughly trained in research methods as a part of their professional preparation" (p. 35). Ultimately, the standard for student affairs programs, according to the 1949 document is in "the difference it makes in the development of individual students" (p. 34).

These historical and foundational documents in the field give clear evidence that the role of assessment and program evaluation in higher education and student affairs is important in the education of the "whole" student. While most agree about the importance of conducting research on students and programs, few student affairs divisions have considered it a vital part of their operations. However, the field is paying increased attention to the need for assessment, due in part to increasing emphasis on accountability from accreditation agencies and institutions themselves.

In the past decade, student affairs documents have continued the call for assessment and accountability of program effectiveness as it relates to student learning and development. *The Student Learning Imperative* (1996) charged student affairs staff to "participate in efforts to assess student learning...and periodically audit institutional environments to reinforce those factors that enhance, and eliminate those that inhibit, student involvement in educationally-purposeful activities" (p. 6). The *Principles of Good Practice for Student Affairs* (1996) asserted the need to use systematic inquiry to improve student and institutional performance. Specifically, "student affairs educators who are skilled in using assessment methods acquire high-quality information; effective application of this information to practice results in programs and change strategies which improve student achievement" (p. 3). In *Learning Reconsidered* (2004) the language of assessment and student learning is more comprehensive. "Student Affairs must lead broad, collaborative institutional efforts to assess overall student learning and to track, document, and evaluate the role of diverse learning experiences...assessment should be a way of life–part of the institutional culture" (p.26).

More recently, student affairs literature has focused on enabling practitioners to implement assessment. These "how-to" guides provide information about writing outcomes, designing instruments, and performing qualitative as well as quantitative assessments (Bresciani, Zelna, & Anderson, 2004). These resources include *Learning Reconsidered 2* (2006), published to meet the need for practical assistance in assessing the implementation of the principles in *Learning Reconsidered*; Strayhorn's (2006) *Frameworks for Assessing Learning and Development Outcomes*; and the self-assessment guides published by CAS. In addition, professional associations have begun to provide their members with assessment tools, as have numerous for-profit companies. Campuses today should have a comprehensive assessment plan that includes consideration of learning outcomes, student needs and inputs, campus environments, student motivation, student use and satisfaction, and cost effectiveness (Schuh & Upcraft, 2001).

Bresciani, Zelna, & Anderson (2004) offered uses and reasons for conducting assessment in student affairs, based on a compilation of other works, including those by the

American Association for Higher Education (1994), Bresciani (2003), Ewell (1997a), Maki (2004), Palomba and Banta (1999), and Upcraft and Schuh (1996). These sources noted the multiple reasons for carrying out assessment: reinforcing or emphasizing unit missions; improving a program's quality or performance; comparing a program's quality or value to the program's previously defined principles; informing planning, decision-making, and policy discussions at the local, state, regional, and national levels; evaluating programs and personnel; assisting in the request for additional funds from the college or university and external community; assisting in the reallocation of resources; assisting in meeting accreditation requirements; identifying models of best practices and national benchmarks; celebrating successes while reflecting on the attitudes and approaches taken in improving learning and development; and creating a culture of continuous improvement—a culture of accountability, learning, and improvement.

Assessment efforts may take many forms. Assessment is most commonly known as "any effort to gather, analyze, and interpret evidence which describes institutional, divisional or agency effectiveness" (Upcraft & Schuh, 1996). Assessment can employ both qualitative and quantitative data collection methods such as interviews, focus groups, observations, rubrics, portfolios, surveys, and questionnaires. On-line survey software is used frequently in creating personalized assessments. The terms assessment, research, and evaluation are often used interchangeably, but there are distinctions. According to Jones, Torres, & Arminio (2006),

> Briefly, research concerns theory: forming it, confirming it, and disconfirming it. Research assumes broader implications than one institution or program. Assessment, on the other hand, is more focused on the outcomes of participant programs, though this can be very broad to include an entire institution. It does not infer individual student outcomes. The purpose of assessment is to guide practice rather than to relate practice to theory. Evaluation is even more particular to a specific program and is concerned with the satisfaction, organization, and attendance of a program. (p. 30)

Assessment is a process that can be used to discover an institution's best practices and to bring about continual improvement within the unique context of each institution. Student affairs divisions undertaking assessment efforts should not be discouraged by the seeming enormity of the task. The important consideration is to be purposeful, systematic, and to use sound research methods that improve operations incrementally.

Assessment Services (AS) is sometimes organized as a single unit, while at other institutions AS is a collective of institutional or department assessment bodies. In any case, collaboration and consultation between and with AS and various individuals and departments as well as institutional leadership is imperative. For a discussion of specific skills necessary to work in AS in addition to those discussed in the attached CAS standards, the ACPA Assessment Skills and Knowledge (ASK) standards may be informative. The standards articulated here offer principles for assessment that are valuable for those working in or directing an assessment office, as well as those conducting assessments as a part of their position responsibilities in another functional area.

References, Readings, and Resources

American Association of Higher Education (1994). *Nine principles of good practice for assessing student learning* [On-line]. Retrieved from http://www.iuk.edu/%7Ekoctla/assessment/9principles.shtml

American College Personnel Association (1996). *The student learning imperative: Implications for student affairs* [On-line]. Retrieved from http://www.acpa.nche.edu/sli/sli.htm

American College Personnel Association. (2006). *ASK standards: Assessment skills and knowledge content standards for student affairs practitioners and scholars.* Washington, DC: Author.

American Council of Education. (1937). *The student personnel point of view: A report of a conference on the philosophy and development of student personnel work in colleges and universities* [On-line]. Retrieved from http://www.myacpa.org/pub/documents/1937.pdf

American Council of Education. (1949). *The student personnel point of view: A report of a conference on the philosophy and development of student personnel work in colleges and universities* [On-line]. Retrieved from http://www.myacpa.org/pub/documents/1949.pdf

Banta, T. W. & Kuh, G. D. (1998). A missing link in assessment: Collaboration between academic and student affairs professionals. *Change,* (March/April), 40-48.

Blimling, G. S. & Whitt, E. J. (1999). *Good practices in student affairs: Principles to foster student learning.* San Francisco: Jossey-Bass.

Bresciani, M. J. (2003). An updated outline for assessment plans. NetResults [On-line]. Retrieved from http://www.naspa.org/

Bresciani, M. J., Zelna, C. L., & Anderson, J. A. (2004). *Assessing student learning and development.* Washington, DC: NASPA.

Ewell, P. T. (1997a). From the states: Putting it all on the line—South Carolina's performance funding initiative. *Assessment Update, 9*(1), 9-11.

Jones, S. R., Torres, V. & Arminio, J. (2006). *Negotiating the complexities of qualitative research.* New York: Routledge.

Keeling, R. P. (2006). *Learning reconsidered 2: Implementing a campus-wide focus on the student experience.* American College Personnel Association, Association of College and University Housing Officers-International, Association of College Unions-International, National Academic Advising Association, National Association for Campus Activities, National Association of Student Personnel Administrators, National Intramural-Recreational Sports Association.

Maki, P. (2004). *Assessing for learning.* Sterling, VA: Stylus.

National Association of Student Personnel Administrators & American College Personnel Association. (2004) *Learning reconsidered: A campus-wide focus on the student experience.* Washington, DC: NASPA & ACPA. Retrieved from http://www.myacpa.org/pub/documents/LearningReconsidered.doc

Palomba, C. A., & Banta, T. W. (1999). *Assessment essentials: Planning, implementing and improving assessment in higher education.* San Francisco: Jossey-Bass.

Rentz, A. L. (1996). A history of student affairs. In A. L. Rentz (Ed.), Student affairs practice in higher education (p.28-55). Springfield, IL: Thomas.

Schuh, J., & Upcraft, M. L. (1998). Facts and myths about assessment in student affairs. *About Campus,* (Nov/Dec), 2-8.

Schuh, J. H., Upcraft, M. L., & Associates, (2001). *Assessment practice in student affairs: An application manual.* San Francisco: Jossey-Bass.

Suskie, L. (2004). *Assessing student learning: A common sense guide.* Bolton, MA: Anker.

Strayhorn, T.L. (2006). *Frameworks for assessing learning development outcomes.* Washington, DC: Council for the Advancement of Standards in Higher Education.

US Department of Education. (2006). *A test of leadership: Charting the future of U.S. Higher Education.* Jessup, MD: Ed Pubs.

Upcraft, M.L., & Schuh, J.H. (1996). *Assessment in student affairs: A guide for practitioners.* San Fancisco: Jossey-Bass.

Williamson, E.G., & Biggs, D.A. (1975). *Student personnel work: A program of development relationships.* New York: John Wiley & Sons.

Contributors:
Current edition:
Jan Arminio, Shippensburg University

Previous editions:
Joel H. Scott, University of Georgia (Baylor University) (2006)
Cara Skeat, Gainesville State College/University of Georgia (2006)
Roger B. Winston, Jr., University of Georgia

Assessment Services
CAS Standards and Guidelines

Part 1. MISSION

The mission of Assessment Services (AS) is to develop a comprehensive assessment program to increase the institution's knowledge about students, the educational environment, and institutional effectiveness to continuously improve student programs and services and to enhance student learning.

AS must develop, disseminate, implement, and regularly review their mission. Mission statements must be consistent with the mission of the institution and with professional standards. AS in higher education must enhance overall educational experiences by incorporating student learning and development outcomes in their mission.

Part 2. PROGRAM

The formal education of students, consisting of the curriculum and the co-curriculum, must promote student learning and development outcomes that are purposeful and holistic and that prepare students for satisfying and productive lifestyles, work, and civic participation. The student learning and development outcome domains and their related dimensions are:

• knowledge acquisition, integration, construction, and application
   o Dimensions: understanding knowledge from a range of disciplines; connecting knowledge to other knowledge, ideas, and experiences; constructing knowledge; and relating knowledge to daily life

• cognitive complexity
   o Dimensions: critical thinking; reflective thinking; effective reasoning; and creativity

• intrapersonal development
   o Dimensions: realistic self-appraisal, self-understanding, and self-respect; identity development; commitment to ethics and integrity; and spiritual awareness

• interpersonal competence
   o Dimensions: meaningful relationships; interdependence; collaboration; and effective leadership

• humanitarianism and civic engagement
   o Dimensions: understanding and appreciation of cultural and human differences; social responsibility; global perspective; and sense of civic responsibility

• practical competence
   o Dimensions: pursuing goals; communicating effectively; technical competence; managing personal affairs; managing career development; demonstrating

professionalism; maintaining health and wellness; and living a purposeful and satisfying life

[See *The Council for the Advancement of Standards Learning and Developmental Outcomes* statement for examples of outcomes related to these domains and dimensions.]

Consistent with the institutional mission, Assessment Services (AS) must identify relevant and desirable student learning and development outcomes from among the six domains and related dimensions. When creating opportunities for student learning and development, AS must explore possibilities for collaboration with faculty members and other colleagues.

AS must assess relevant and desirable student learning and development outcomes and provide evidence of their impact on student learning and development. AS must articulate how they contribute to or support students' learning and development in the domains not specifically assessed.

AS must be:
  ▪ integrated into the life of the institution
  ▪ intentional and coherent
  ▪ guided by theories and knowledge of learning and development
  ▪ reflective of developmental and demographic profiles of the student population
  ▪ responsive to needs of individuals, diverse and special populations, and relevant constituencies

Regardless of its structure, AS must collaborate and consult with institutional research or various departments to ensure that assessment efforts address institutional needs.

AS may be organized as a functional area or be a collective body of assessment initiatives across an institution.

Whenever there are both AS and an institutional research function in an institution, there should be clear delineation of responsibilities.

In institutions that do not have AS, a senior officer must be an advocate for assessment and program evaluation and must collaborate and consult with, and otherwise provide support to, institutional assessment efforts.

AS must include activities that assess student needs and student learning and development outcomes, assess whether goals are being achieved, describe student characteristics, determine whether professional standards are being met, and determine effectiveness of programs and services for students. Results of these studies must be disseminated to appropriate personnel and students in the institution.

AS must:
  ▪ describe the demographics, personal characteristics, and behaviors of students
  ▪ conduct regular assessments of student needs

- review and use available literature about the characteristics and developmental changes of post-secondary students
- assess whether the work of AS is consistent with and achieves stated objectives
- use appropriate professional standards, tools, and instruments for assessment
- study the extent to which students, programs, departments, and institutions meet their overall educational goals and determine conditions that enhance or hamper goal achievement
- study the impact of the college experience on students and alumni
- examine retention and graduation rates
- compare institutional practices against professional standards
- investigate the impact of campus culture
- assist others in the effective use of assessment to inform decisions and guide the development and improvement of services, programs, and policies

AS should examine cost effectiveness and the level of student satisfaction with programs and services.

AS practices must be conducted in the context of existing and developing strategic initiatives.

AS should provide assessment and evaluation support for other institutional offices and institutional decision makers.

AS should:
- collect and analyze student data beginning with pre-enrollment characteristics and continuing through follow-up studies of graduates and other former students
- plan, coordinate, or conduct regular studies of various programs, facilities, services, classes, and student sub-groups
- describe students' intellectual, emotional, social, moral, spiritual, vocational, and physical development and behavior; such data should be regularly collected, updated, and disseminated
- analyze data to identify trends in student behavior and attitudes to consider the implications for institutional policies and practices
- analyze data to identify retention trends to consider the implications for institutional policies and practices
- collect and analyze data, including cost effectiveness data, to be used for making decisions about the continuation, modification, or termination of programs and services
- compare institutional practices against benchmarks
- coordinate assessment plans across units and act as a resource to faculty and staff regarding assessment and evaluation efforts
- disseminate information about assessment and evaluation findings to members of the campus community
- guide and evaluate research and assessment efforts conducted by students
- track campus studies, for example in theses and dissertations, in which campus students are participants

Part 3. LEADERSHIP

Because effective and ethical leadership is essential to the success of all organizations, Assessment Services (AS) leaders with organizational authority for the programs and services must:
- articulate a vision and mission for their programs and services
- set goals and objectives based on the needs of the population served and desired student learning and development outcomes
- advocate for their programs and services
- promote campus environments that provide meaningful opportunities for student learning, development, and integration
- identify and find means to address individual, organizational, or environmental conditions that foster or inhibit mission achievement
- advocate for representation in strategic planning initiatives at appropriate divisional and institutional levels
- initiate collaborative interactions with stakeholders who have legitimate concerns and interests in the functional area
- apply effective practices to educational and administrative processes
- prescribe and model ethical behavior
- communicate effectively
- manage financial resources, including planning, allocation, monitoring, and analysis
- incorporate sustainability practices in the management and design of programs, services, and facilities
- manage human resource processes including recruitment, selection, development, supervision, performance planning, and evaluation
- empower professional, support, and student staff to accept leadership opportunities
- encourage and support scholarly contribution to the profession
- be informed about and integrate appropriate technologies into programs and services
- be knowledgeable about federal, state/provincial, and local laws relevant to the programs and services and ensure that staff members understand their responsibilities by receiving appropriate training
- develop and continuously improve programs and services in response to the changing needs of students and other populations served and the evolving institutional priorities
- recognize environmental conditions that may negatively influence the safety of staff and students and propose interventions that mitigate such conditions.

AS leaders must:
- understand the foundations of higher education
- understand the educational value and objectives of

programs and services
- interpret assessment results to guide educational practice
- advocate for institutional response to assessment findings
- serve as an expert in administering effective and efficient assessment programs
- stay current about trends in assessment
- work to ensure that students are not over-assessed
- understand and be able to use various research and assessment methodologies and methods

Part 4. HUMAN RESOURCES

Assessment Services (AS) must be staffed adequately by individuals qualified to accomplish the mission and goals. Within institutional guidelines, AS must establish procedures for staff selection, training, and evaluation; set expectations for supervision; and provide appropriate professional development opportunities to improve the leadership ability, competence, and skills of all employees.

AS professional staff members must hold an earned graduate or professional degree in a field relevant to the position they hold or must possess an appropriate combination of educational credentials and related work experience.

Degree- or credential-seeking interns must be qualified by enrollment in an appropriate field of study and by relevant experience. These individuals must be trained and supervised adequately by professional staff members holding educational credentials and related work experience appropriate for supervision.

Student employees and volunteers must be carefully selected, trained, supervised, and evaluated. They must be educated on how and when to refer those in need of additional assistance to qualified staff members and must have access to a supervisor for assistance in making these judgments. Student employees and volunteers must be provided clear and precise job descriptions, pre-service training based on assessed needs, and continuing staff development.

Employees and volunteers must receive specific training on institutional policies and privacy laws regarding their access to student records and other sensitive institutional information (e.g., in the USA, Family Educational Rights and Privacy Act, FERPA, or equivalent privacy laws in other states/provinces or countries).

AS must have technical and support staff members adequate to accomplish their mission. All members of the staff must be technologically proficient and qualified to perform their job functions, be knowledgeable about ethical and legal uses of technology, and have access to training and resources to support the performance of their assigned responsibilities.

All members of the staff must receive training on policies and procedures related to the use of technology to store or access student records and institutional data.

AS must ensure that staff members are knowledgeable about and trained in emergency procedures, crisis response, and prevention efforts. Prevention efforts must address identification of threatening conduct or behavior of students, faculty members, staff, and others and must incorporate a system or procedures for responding, including but not limited to reporting them to the appropriate campus officials.

Salary levels and benefits for all staff members must be commensurate with those for comparable positions within the institution, in similar institutions, and in the relevant geographic area.

AS must maintain position descriptions for all staff members.

To create a diverse staff, AS must institute hiring and promotion practices that are fair, inclusive, proactive, and non-discriminatory.

AS must conduct regular performance planning and evaluation of staff members. AS must provide access to continuing and advanced education and professional development opportunities.

Within the institution, a qualified professional AS staff member must be designated to coordinate the assessment efforts and must work closely with or be responsive to leaders of programs and services.

The number of staff members assigned to assessment efforts should be a function of the size, complexity, and purpose of the institution. Institutions unable to assign a full-time professional staff member should devote a portion of their institutional research program's resources to this effort.

Staff assigned responsibility for assessment should possess effective communication and consultation skills and have an appropriate combination of coursework, training, and experience in the following areas: research methodology, design, and analysis; computer literacy; program planning implementation and evaluation; and human development theory, including the study of student sub-group cultures. When staff members lack adequate knowledge in any of these critical areas, they should seek expertise from appropriate resources.

Part 5. ETHICS

Persons involved in the delivery of Assessment Services (AS) must adhere to the highest principles of ethical behavior. AS must review relevant professional ethical standards and develop or adopt and implement appropriate statements of ethical practice. AS must publish these statements and ensure their periodic review by relevant constituencies.

AS must orient new staff members to relevant ethical standards and statements of ethical practice.

AS staff members must ensure that privacy and confidentiality are maintained with respect to all communications and records to the extent that such records are protected under the law and appropriate statements of ethical practice. Information contained in students' education records must not be disclosed except as allowed by relevant laws and institutional policies. AS staff members must disclose to appropriate authorities information judged to be of an emergency nature, especially when the safety of the individual or others is involved, or when otherwise required by institutional policy or relevant law.

AS staff members must be aware of and comply with the provisions contained in the institution's policies pertaining to human subjects research and student rights and responsibilities, as well as those in other relevant institutional policies addressing ethical practices and confidentiality of research data concerning individuals.

AS must seek from the institutional review board approval to study human subjects for studies whose findings will be published beyond internal review of the institution. AS must know and adhere to the human subjects policies and procedures of the institution.

AS should seek approval to conduct assessment studies through the institution's human subjects review process.

AS staff members must recognize and avoid personal conflicts of interest or appearance thereof in the performance of their work.

AS staff members must strive to insure the fair, objective, and impartial treatment of all persons with whom they interact.

When handling institutional funds, AS staff members must ensure that such funds are managed in accordance with established and responsible accounting procedures and the fiscal policies or processes of the institution.

Promotional and descriptive information must be accurate and free of deception.

AS staff members must perform their duties within the limits of their training, expertise, and competence. When these limits are exceeded, individuals in need of further assistance must be referred to persons possessing appropriate qualifications.

AS staff members must use suitable means to confront and otherwise hold accountable other staff members who exhibit unethical behavior.

AS staff members must be knowledgeable about and practice ethical behavior in the use of technology.

AS must ensure that the privacy or anonymity of study participants and the confidential nature of data are not breached.

AS must regularly purge identifiable information collected about students and other participants to protect their privacy, consistent with institutional policies and federal guidelines.

AS should maintain raw data for a number of years, based on applicable policy, after the study's written report is completed to respond to subsequent questions. Instances involving research on sensitive topics may require protections such as a Certificate of Confidentiality.

AS must acknowledge methodological limitations of assessment studies.

These limitations could include unrepresentative samples, low response rate, or errors in trying to make decisions from ungeneralizable qualitative findings.

Part 6. LEGAL RESPONSIBILITIES

Assessment Services (AS) staff members must be knowledgeable about and responsive to laws and regulations that relate to their respective responsibilities and that may pose legal obligations, limitations, or ramifications for the institution as a whole. As appropriate, staff members must inform users of programs and services, as well as officials, of legal obligations and limitations including constitutional, statutory, regulatory, and case law; mandatory laws and orders emanating from federal, state/provincial, and local governments; and the institution's policies.

AS must have written policies on all relevant operations, transactions, or tasks that may have legal implications.

AS staff members must neither participate in nor condone any form of harassment or activity that demeans persons or creates an intimidating, hostile, or offensive campus environment.

AS staff members must use reasonable and informed practices to limit the liability exposure of the institution and its officers, employees, and agents. AS staff members must be informed about institutional policies regarding risk management, personal liability, and related insurance coverage options and must be referred to external sources if coverage is not provided by the institution.

The institution must provide access to legal advice for AS staff members as needed to carry out assigned responsibilities.

The institution must inform AS staff and students in a timely and systematic fashion about extraordinary or changing legal obligations and potential liabilities.

Part 7. EQUITY and ACCESS

Assessment Services (AS) must be provided on a fair, equitable, and non-discriminatory basis in accordance with institutional policies and with all applicable state/provincial and federal statutes and regulations. AS must maintain an educational and work environment free from discrimination in accordance with law and institutional policy.

Discrimination must be avoided on the basis of age; cultural heritage; disability; ethnicity; gender identity and expression; nationality; political affiliation; race; religious affiliation; sex; sexual orientation; economic, marital, social, or veteran status; and any other bases included in local, state/provincial, or federal laws.

Consistent with the mission and goals, AS must take action to remedy significant imbalances in student participation and staffing patterns.

AS must ensure physical and program access for persons with disabilities. AS must be responsive to the needs of all students and other populations served when establishing hours of operation and developing methods of delivering programs and services.

AS must ensure inclusion of persons with disabilities in data collection efforts in compliance with local, state/provincial, and federal guidelines.

AS must recognize the needs of distance learning students by providing appropriate and accessible services and assisting them in identifying and gaining access to other appropriate services in their geographic region.

Part 8. DIVERSITY

Within the context of each institution's unique mission, diversity enriches the community and enhances the collegiate experience for all; therefore, Assessment Services (AS) must create and nurture environments that are welcoming to and bring together persons of diverse backgrounds.

AS must promote environments that are characterized by open and continuous communication that deepens understanding of one's own identity, culture, and heritage, as well as that of others. AS must recognize, honor, educate, and promote respect about commonalties and differences among people within their historical and cultural contexts.

AS must address the characteristics and needs of a diverse population when establishing and implementing policies and procedures.

AS must design studies and collect data so that potential differential outcomes based on diversity among sub-groups can be explored.

Part 9. ORGANIZATION and MANAGEMENT

To promote student learning and development outcomes, Assessment Services (AS) must be structured purposefully and managed effectively to achieve stated goals. Evidence of appropriate structure must include current and accessible policies and procedures, written performance expectations for all employees, functional workflow graphics or organizational charts, and clearly stated program and service delivery expectations.

AS must monitor websites used for distributing information to ensure that the sites are current, accurate, appropriately referenced, and accessible.

Evidence of effective management must include use of comprehensive and accurate information for decisions, clear sources and channels of authority, effective communication practices, procedures for decision-making and conflict resolution, responses to changing conditions, systems of accountability and evaluation, and processes for recognition and reward. AS must align policies and procedures with those of the institution and provide channels within the organization for their regular review.

Because outcomes assessment and program evaluation efforts are conducted on most campuses in cooperation with other institutional research and evaluation efforts, a staff member must be designated to manage specific assessment activities, priorities, and timelines.

Assessment goals should result from a collaborative effort between leaders of AS, those responsible for the various programs and services being assessed, and others responsible for institutional research efforts.

Part 10. CAMPUS and EXTERNAL RELATIONS

Assessment Services (AS) must reach out to relevant individuals, campus offices, and external agencies to:
- establish, maintain, and promote effective relations
- disseminate information about their own and other related programs and services
- coordinate and collaborate, where appropriate, in offering programs and services to meet the needs of students and promote their achievement of student learning and development outcomes

AS must adhere to all institutional policies with respect to the communication of student data.

Regular and effective communication systems for the dissemination of results must be established and maintained with academic and administrative offices, institutional governance bodies, and other appropriate constituencies.

AS must have procedures and guidelines consistent with institutional policy for responding to threats, emergencies, and crisis situations. Systems and procedures must be in place to disseminate timely and accurate information to students and other members of the campus community during emergency situations.

AS must have procedures and guidelines consistent with institutional policy for communicating with the media.

Part 11. FINANCIAL RESOURCES

Assessment Services (AS) must have adequate funding to accomplish their mission and goals. In establishing funding priorities and making significant changes, a comprehensive analysis, which includes relevant expenditures, external and internal resources, and impact on the campus community, must be conducted.

AS must demonstrate fiscal responsibility and cost effectiveness consistent with institutional protocols.

Financial resources should be sufficient to support study conceptualization, data collection, data entry and analysis, and the dissemination of assessment and research findings, as well as methodological training for staff.

Part 12. TECHNOLOGY

Assessment Services (AS) must have adequate technology to support their mission. The technology and its use must comply with institutional policies and procedures and be evaluated for compliance with relevant federal, state/provincial, and local requirements.

AS must maintain policies and procedures that address the security and back up of data.

When technology is used to facilitate student learning and development, AS must select technology that reflects current best pedagogical practices.

Technology, as well as any workstations or computer labs maintained by the AS for student use, must be accessible and must meet established technology standards for delivery to persons with disabilities.

When AS provide student access to technology, they must provide:
- access to policies that are clear, easy to understand, and available to all students
- access to instruction or training on how to use the technology
- access to information on the legal and ethical implications of misuse as it pertains to intellectual property, harassment, privacy, and social networks.

Student violations of technology policies must follow established institutional student disciplinary procedures.

Students who experience negative emotional or psychological consequences from the use of technology must be referred to support services provided by the institution.

AS must have access to sufficient data analysis software for

efficient data collection, storage, retrieval, and analysis.

Both statistical analysis software and qualitative analysis software should be available.

AS must have timely access to appropriate institutional records.

AS should advocate for integration of institutional databases.

Part 13. FACILITIES and EQUIPMENT

Assessment Services (AS) must have adequate, accessible, suitably located facilities and equipment to support their mission and goals. If acquiring capital equipment as defined by the institution, AS must take into account expenses related to regular maintenance and life cycle costs. Facilities and equipment must be evaluated regularly, including consideration of sustainability, and be in compliance with relevant federal, state/provincial, and local requirements to provide for access, health, safety, and security.

AS staff members must have work space that is well-equipped, adequate in size, and designed to support their work and responsibilities. For conversations requiring privacy, staff members must have access to a private space.

AS staff members who share work space must have the ability to secure their work adequately.

The design of the facilities must guarantee the security of records and ensure the confidentiality of sensitive information.

The location and layout of the facilities must be sensitive to the special needs of persons with disabilities as well as the needs of constituencies served.

AS must have sufficient secure storage facilities to maintain materials related to studies.

AS must ensure that staff members are knowledgeable of and trained in safety and emergency procedures for securing and vacating the facilities.

Part 14. ASSESSMENT and EVALUATION

Assessment Services (AS) must establish systematic plans and processes to meet internal and external accountability expectations with regard to program as well as student learning and development outcomes. AS must conduct regular assessment and evaluations. Assessments must include qualitative and quantitative methodologies as appropriate, to determine whether and to what degree the stated mission, goals, and student learning and development outcomes are being met. The process must employ sufficient and sound measures to ensure comprehensiveness. Data collected must include responses from students and other affected

constituencies.

AS should model good assessment practices related to its own operations as well as when assisting other entities within the institution.

AS must evaluate regularly how well they complement and enhance the institution's stated mission and educational effectiveness.

Results of these evaluations must be used in revising and improving programs and services, identifying needs and interests in shaping directions of program and service design, and recognizing staff performance.

General Standards revised in 2008;
AS (formerly Outcomes Assessment and Program Evaluation) content developed/revised in 1986, 1997, & 2008

The Role of Auxiliary Services Functional Areas
CAS Standards Contextual Statement

Both "student affairs" and "auxiliary services" are names used to describe multi-functional umbrella organizations that, through a variety of means, address the out-of-classroom needs of students, faculty, staff, and visitors on college and university campuses. Auxiliary services typically encompass functional areas that follow business practices and principles in their service design and provision. Student affairs functional areas are more likely to focus upon student life, personal development, student learning, and well being. This distinction will vary from campus to campus, and each campus determines the heading under which each student service functional area will exist.

Over the past thirty years, several business processes and structures have been introduced to the provision of auxiliary services at colleges and universities and, in describing an Auxiliary Services Functional Area (ASFA), the following terms are among those currently used:

Vendor: A service provider that has permission to deliver a service, using its own resources, consistent with conditions and parameters set forth by the institution. Examples may include ice cream/hot dog trucks, dry cleaning services, and pizza deliverers.

Outsourced Provider: A service provider that is hired by the institution to fill a specific need. Examples may include transportation services, travel offices, and copy services.

Contracted provider: An entity contractually assigned to provide a continuous service, usually over multiple years, within detailed specifications, on the premises of the institution. Examples may include bookstores, food services and laundry services.

Licensor: A branded provider of services who contractually sells rights to the institution for use of its name, products, and/or processes, consistent with the institution following the licensor's guidelines and standards for providing the service. Examples may include fast food outlets and mail packaging/service shops.

Auxiliary (Ancillary) Service: A service wholly owned by the institution, either directly or through a subsidiary, which exists solely to serve the institution's students, faculty, staff, and visitors. Examples may include institutionally operated stores and dining programs.

Self-supporting Service: An institutional service that functions net-neutral, under normal circumstances, but may be called upon from time to time to fill an institutional funding need. Examples may be found within any of the aforementioned classifications of service.

Auxiliary services may include, but are not limited to housing, student unions, bookstores, dining services, food courts with nationally recognized brands, conference services, health services, campus card programs, parking/transportation services, mail services, telecommunications, cable and internet services, student athletics, campus recreation centers, retail outlets, convenience stores, banking services, computer kiosks, other retail outlets, and contracted services. ASFA, through their quality, reliability, and ease of use, are expected to positively impact student recruitment and retention and to enhance the student life experience. ASFA may be expected to provide additional funds to the institution. Organizationally, although many campuses include ASFA within student life, ASFA may report through administrative affairs or be structured as a separate division of the institution. ASFA may also be structured as independent not-for-profit educational corporations (in the U.S., designated as 501(c)(3) corporations by the Internal Revenue Service) with affiliation to an institution. When services are provided by outsourced companies, the auxiliary services role may be one of intermediary between private service providers and the institution.

Today's institutions face decreasing public support, as well as pressure to minimize tuition increases, hence there is the need to find alternative sources of revenue. Within this context are students and parents who want sophisticated and varied campus services. ASFA face declining institutional funding and at the same time, expectations to generate revenue, offer new services, provide excellent customer service, give exceptional value, and use the best technology in delivering their services. In addition to following general standards of practice germane to all functional areas in higher education, it is necessary that ASFA also follow the best business enterprise standards and guidelines to accomplish their mission.

While ASFA professionals are concerned with providing quality campus services, and funding those services, they are equally concerned with supporting the academic mission of their institution. Among their many roles, ASFA give students places to live, eat, buy textbooks and supplies, recreate, meet, study, attend campus events, socialize, and work on campus. As a major source of on-campus student employment, auxiliary services play an important role in promoting individual student success.

The CAS Standards and Guidelines for ASFA may be used to assess a multi-functional auxiliary service organization. They may also be used to augment the CAS General Standards in development and revision of standards and guidelines for individual functional areas that are structured as auxiliary services.

References, Readings, and Resources

Indiana University Center for Postsecondary Research. (1999). *National Survey of Student Engagement*. Bloomington, IN: Author.

Myers, R. (2006, June). A great auxiliary service: 13 steps to get from good to great. *College Services, The Journal of the National Association of College Auxiliary Services,* 51-56.

Pittman, J. (2005, October). Understanding campus culture: A key to operating successful auxiliary services. *The Journal of the National Association of College Auxiliary Services,* 20-23.

Terrana, M., & Grills, C. (2001, February). Wanted: Successful higher education managers. *National Association of College and University Business Officers,* 40-43.

Towle, M., Rinehart, J., & Olsen, D. (2006, September 27). Student employees: Creating meaningful educational experiences. *University of Minnesota, NACAS/NASPA Webcast, www.NASPA.org*

Contributor:

Dr. Jeffrey Pittman, Regent University

Auxiliary Services Functional Areas
CAS Standards and Guidelines

Part 1. MISSION

Auxiliary Services Functional Areas (ASFA) are multi-functional organizations that address many of the out-of-classroom needs of students, faculty, staff, and visitors on college and university campuses. Typical ASFA follow business practices and principles in their service design, and they operate enterprises that provide goods and services on campus.

ASFA must adhere to ethical, effective, efficient, and sustainable business practices in the provision of relevant, quality, on-campus services that support and enhance the campus environment for students, faculty, staff, and visitors, and provide opportunities for student development.

ASFA must develop, disseminate, implement, and regularly review their mission. Mission statements must be consistent with the mission of the institution and with professional standards. ASFA in higher education must enhance overall educational experiences by incorporating student learning and development outcomes in their mission.

Part 2. PROGRAM

Auxiliary Services Functional Areas (ASFA) are expected to provide programs that target specific needs; facilities; items for sale that the ASFA and institution consider appropriate to the campus community; support services for students, faculty members, staff, and visitors; administration; information; clearly stated schedules and hours of operation; value; efficiency; and a fair cost structure.

The formal education of students, consisting of the curriculum and the co-curriculum, must promote student learning and development outcomes that are purposeful and holistic and that prepare students for satisfying and productive lifestyles, work, and civic participation. The student learning and development outcome domains and their related dimensions are:

- knowledge acquisition, integration, construction, and application
    o Dimensions: understanding knowledge from a range of disciplines; connecting knowledge to other knowledge, ideas, and experiences; constructing knowledge; and relating knowledge to daily life

- cognitive complexity
    o Dimensions: critical thinking; reflective thinking; effective reasoning; and creativity

- intrapersonal development
    o Dimensions: realistic self-appraisal, self-understanding, and self-respect; identity development; commitment to ethics and integrity; and spiritual awareness

- interpersonal competence
    o Dimensions: meaningful relationships; interdependence; collaboration; and effective leadership

- humanitarianism and civic engagement
    o Dimensions: understanding and appreciation of cultural and human differences; social responsibility; global perspective; and sense of civic responsibility

- practical competence
    o Dimensions: pursuing goals; communicating effectively; technical competence; managing personal affairs; managing career development; demonstrating professionalism; maintaining health and wellness; and living a purposeful and satisfying life

[See *The Council for the Advancement of Standards Learning and Developmental Outcomes* statement for examples of outcomes related to these domains and dimensions.]

Consistent with the institutional mission, ASFA must identify relevant and desirable student learning and development outcomes from among the six domains and related dimensions. When creating opportunities for student learning and development, ASFA must explore possibilities for collaboration with faculty members and other colleagues.

ASFA must assess relevant and desirable student learning and development outcomes and provide evidence of their impact on student learning and development. ASFA must articulate how they contribute to or support students' learning and development in the domains not specifically assessed.

ASFA must be:
- integrated into the life of the institution
- intentional and coherent
- guided by theories and knowledge of learning and development
- reflective of developmental and demographic profiles of the student population
- responsive to needs of individuals, diverse and special populations, and relevant constituencies

ASFA, in conjunction with appropriate partners, must:
- introduce and orient students to facilities, services, staff members, and functions
- educate students on relevant safety, security, and emergency concerns
- clearly explain policies, procedures, and expectations
- develop an atmosphere conducive to educational pursuits, community, and interpersonal growth, in a safe and non-threatening environment
- provide a balanced variety of social, cultural, and

intellectual options that is reflective of the diversity of the campus
- **remain transparent and open to dialogue with customers and stakeholders**

ASFA, in conjunction with appropriate partners, may be expected to:
- establish formal relationships and agreements with other campus service units
- collaborate with specific academic and campus units in design and provision of ASFA services
- provide opportunities for student employment, management training, and leadership development
- contribute to the socialization of students
- be self-funding (self-supporting) and contribute financially to the institution
- adhere to generally accepted practices of accounting, audit, and business records management
- function as an ancillary enterprise (separate but in concert with the academic enterprise)
- supervise contract-managed functional areas and services

Part 3. LEADERSHIP

Because effective and ethical leadership is essential to the success of all organizations, Auxiliary Services Functional Areas (ASFA) leaders with organizational authority for the programs and services must:
- **articulate a vision and mission for their programs and services**
- **set goals and objectives based on the needs of the population served and desired student learning and development outcomes**
- **promote campus environments that provide meaningful opportunities for student learning, development, and integration**
- **identify and find means to address individual, organizational, or environmental conditions that foster or inhibit mission achievement**
- **advocate for representation in strategic planning initiatives at appropriate divisional and institutional levels**
- **initiate collaborative interactions with stakeholders who have legitimate concerns and interests in the functional area**
- **apply effective practices to educational and administrative processes**
- **prescribe and model ethical behavior**
- **communicate effectively**
- **manage financial resources, including planning, allocation, monitoring, and analysis**
- **incorporate sustainability practices in the management and design of programs, services, and facilities**
- **manage human resource processes including recruitment, selection, development, supervision, performance planning, and evaluation**
- **empower professional, support, and student staff to**

accept leadership opportunities
- **encourage and support scholarly contribution to the profession**
- **be informed about and integrate appropriate technologies into programs and services**
- **be knowledgeable about federal, state/provincial, and local laws relevant to the programs and services and ensure that staff members understand their responsibilities by receiving appropriate training**
- **develop and continuously improve programs and services in response to the changing needs of students and other populations served and the evolving institutional priorities**
- **recognize environmental conditions that may negatively influence the safety of staff and students and propose interventions that mitigate such conditions**
- **advocate for their programs and services**

ASFA leaders should provide all employees with guidance on:
- using effective and appropriate strategies for communicating with customers and stakeholders
- staying current with student needs, issues, perspectives, and desires
- cultivating and perpetuating relations with all campus departments
- working with student, campus, and academic leaders and organizations
- exercising safety and the safe provision of ASFA programs, goods, and services
- facility maintenance and efficient use of campus facilities, equipment, and financial and human resources
- employing standards, best practices, and processes for budgeting, contracting, purchasing, accounting, reporting, auditing, personnel administration, and record keeping
- establishing and maintaining effective relations with community and business agencies and offices
- promoting equal access to services, programs, and facilities for all students, faculty members, staff, and other customers
- implementing effective practices and responses to trends in the respective ASFA functional area community or industry

Part 4. HUMAN RESOURCES

Auxiliary Services Functional Areas (ASFA) must be staffed adequately by individuals qualified to accomplish the mission and goals. Within institutional guidelines, ASFA must establish procedures for staff selection, training, and evaluation; set expectations for supervision; and provide appropriate professional development opportunities to improve the leadership ability, competence, and skills of all employees.

ASFA professional staff members must hold an earned graduate or professional degree in a field relevant to the position they hold or must possess an appropriate combination of educational credentials and related work experience.

Degree- or credential-seeking interns must be qualified by enrollment in an appropriate field of study and by relevant experience. These individuals must be trained and supervised adequately by professional staff members holding educational credentials and related work experience appropriate for supervision.

Student employees and volunteers must be carefully selected, trained, supervised, and evaluated. They must be educated on how and when to refer those in need of additional assistance to qualified staff members and must have access to a supervisor for assistance in making these judgments. Student employees and volunteers must be provided clear and precise job descriptions, pre-service training based on assessed needs, and continuing staff development.

Employees and volunteers must receive specific training on institutional policies and privacy laws regarding their access to student records and other sensitive institutional information (e.g., in the USA, Family Educational Rights and Privacy Act, FERPA, or equivalent privacy laws in other states/provinces or countries).

ASFA must have technical and support staff members adequate to accomplish their mission. All members of the staff must be technologically proficient and qualified to perform their job functions, be knowledgeable about ethical and legal uses of technology, and have access to training and resources to support the performance of their assigned responsibilities.

All members of the staff must receive training on policies and procedures related to the use of technology to store or access student records and institutional data.

ASFA must ensure that staff members are knowledgeable about and trained in emergency procedures, crisis response, and prevention efforts. Prevention efforts must address identification of threatening conduct or behavior of students, faculty members, staff, and others and must incorporate a system or procedures for responding, including but not limited to reporting them to the appropriate campus officials.

Salary levels and benefits for all staff members must be commensurate with those for comparable positions within the institution, in similar institutions, and in the relevant geographic area.

ASFA must maintain position descriptions for all staff members.

To create a diverse staff, ASFA must institute hiring and promotion practices that are fair, inclusive, proactive, and non-discriminatory.

ASFA must conduct regular performance planning and evaluation of staff members. ASFA must provide access to continuing and advanced education and professional development opportunities.

Staff must include persons reasonably capable of providing temporary oversight for entire units as well as their specialty, should the need require it.

Staff members must have technical skills, training, and experience pertinent to their work.

All ASFA staff members must understand and comply with financial, legal, personnel, and safety laws, regulations, and policies, as they relate to the core function of their unit.

Administrators in charge of ASFA and facilities must have appropriate education, experience, and credentials to adequately and safely provide a level of management consistent with industry standards and institutional expectations.

ASFA staff members must be knowledgeable about programs, goods, and services offered directly.

ASFA staff members should be familiar with related services offered by other campus agencies.

In addition to providing fair wages, ASFA should treat student employment as an important part of a student's education and intentionally incorporate career-related skills, training, and professional responsibilities into the employment experience.

ASFA should provide living wages to all employees.

A thorough job training program should be provided for all employees and volunteers and should include leadership and personal development opportunities.

ASFA staff members should strive to develop and maintain staff relations in a climate of mutual respect, support, trust, and interdependence. Recognizing the strengths and limitations of each professional staff member, professional development opportunities should be regularly made available, consistent with needs and budgets.

Relationships between ASFA and their shareholders will depend heavily on the effectiveness, cooperation, support, and behavior of front line service personnel. Training should be closely supervised and monitored, and current industry practices should be evident in service processes, standards, and evaluation.

Desirable qualities of ASFA staff members should include:

- knowledge of and ability to use management and leadership principles
- ability to train, influence, supervise, and evaluate student employees and volunteers, particularly at entry levels
- experience in assessment and planning
- interpersonal skills applicable to a variety of cultures
- ability to explain the ASFA mission and articulate the program's relationship to the mission of the institution
- knowledge of and ability to apply student development and learning theories

Desirable qualities of staff members may include:

- technical proficiency certification
- knowledge of environmental and industry trends
- effective professional communication and presentation skills

- attributes necessary to meet job-related physical requirements

Part 5. ETHICS

Persons involved in the delivery of Auxiliary Services Functional Areas (ASFA) must adhere to the highest principles of ethical behavior. ASFA must review relevant professional ethical standards and develop or adopt and implement appropriate statements of ethical practice. ASFA must publish these statements and ensure their periodic review by relevant constituencies.

ASFA must orient new staff members to relevant ethical standards and statements of ethical practice.

ASFA staff members must ensure that privacy and confidentiality are maintained with respect to all communications and records to the extent that such records are protected under the law and appropriate statements of ethical practice. Information contained in students' education records must not be disclosed except as allowed by relevant laws and institutional policies. ASFA staff members must disclose to appropriate authorities information judged to be of an emergency nature, especially when the safety of the individual or others is involved, or when otherwise required by institutional policy or relevant law.

ASFA staff members must be aware of and comply with the provisions contained in the institution's policies pertaining to human subjects research and student rights and responsibilities, as well as those in other relevant institutional policies addressing ethical practices and confidentiality of research data concerning individuals.

ASFA staff members must recognize and avoid personal conflicts of interest or appearance thereof in the performance of their work.

ASFA staff members must strive to insure the fair, objective, and impartial treatment of all persons with whom they interact.

When handling institutional funds, ASFA staff members must ensure that such funds are managed in accordance with established and responsible accounting procedures and the fiscal policies or processes of the institution.

Promotional and descriptive information must be accurate and free of deception.

ASFA staff members must perform their duties within the limits of their training, expertise, and competence. When these limits are exceeded, individuals in need of further assistance must be referred to persons possessing appropriate qualifications.

ASFA staff members must use suitable means to confront and otherwise hold accountable other staff members who exhibit unethical behavior.

ASFA staff members must be knowledgeable about and practice ethical behavior in the use of technology.

Marketing and advertising, when conducted, must be informative, accurate, respectful, non-deceptive, and useful to students, faculty members, staff, and visitors.

Private information disclosed by clients, students, faculty members, staff, and visitors in the course of conducting business (e.g., credit card information, medical conditions) must be treated as confidential unless clearly indicated otherwise by the person providing it.

ASFA representatives must not accept gifts from those who seek to do business or who intend to bid on contracts.

They should avoid activities that give the appearance of favoritism or advantage to any entity seeking to do business with ASFA.

Ethical standards of relevant professional associations should be considered.

ASFA should consider the ethical standards and expectations of suppliers and contractors with whom they do business.

Each ASFA staff member should respect students as individuals, each with rights and responsibilities, each with goals and needs, and with this in mind, should seek to create and maintain environments that enhance learning and personal development.

ASFA should exercise professionalism, expertise, and care in the development and handling of requests for proposals, bids, and contracts related to purchases, lease agreements, contractual service agreements, and any agreement that affects students and/or the institution.

Part 6. LEGAL RESPONSIBILITIES

Auxiliary Services Functional Areas (ASFA) staff members must be knowledgeable about and responsive to laws and regulations that relate to their respective responsibilities and that may pose legal obligations, limitations, or ramifications for the institution as a whole. As appropriate, staff members must inform users of programs and services, as well as officials, of legal obligations and limitations including constitutional, statutory, regulatory, and case law; mandatory laws and orders emanating from federal, state/provincial, and local governments; and the institution's policies.

ASFA must have written policies on all relevant operations, transactions, or tasks that may have legal implications.

ASFA staff members must neither participate in nor condone any form of harassment or activity that demeans persons or creates an intimidating, hostile, or offensive campus environment.

ASFA staff members must use reasonable and informed practices to limit the liability exposure of the institution and its officers, employees, and agents. ASFA staff members must be informed about institutional policies regarding risk management, personal liability, and related insurance coverage options and must be referred to external sources if coverage is not provided by the institution.

The institution must provide access to legal advice for ASFA staff members as needed to carry out assigned responsibilities.

The institution must inform ASFA staff and students in a timely and systematic fashion about extraordinary or changing legal obligations and potential liabilities.

ASFA leaders must have specific knowledge of legal issues and requirements that apply to functional areas under their control.

ASFA must continually monitor liability for potentially harmful, wrongful, or negligent activities and situations.

ASFA professionals must be aware of and understand due process, employment procedures, equal opportunity, civil rights, and liberties.

ASFA may be required to carry insurance if not sufficiently covered under the institution's policy.

Part 7. EQUITY and ACCESS

Auxiliary Services Functional Areas (ASFA) must be provided on a fair, equitable, and non-discriminatory basis in accordance with institutional policies and with all applicable state/provincial and federal statutes and regulations. ASFA must maintain an educational and work environment free from discrimination in accordance with law and institutional policy.

Discrimination must be avoided on the basis of age; cultural heritage; disability; ethnicity; gender identity and expression; nationality; political affiliation; race; religious affiliation; sex; sexual orientation; economic, marital, social, or veteran status; and any other bases included in local, state/provincial, or federal laws.

Consistent with the mission and goals, ASFA must take action to remedy significant imbalances in student participation and staffing patterns.

ASFA must ensure physical and program access for persons with disabilities. ASFA must be responsive to the needs of all students and other populations served when establishing hours of operation and developing methods of delivering programs and services.

ASFA should provide services and information through a variety of appropriate formats including web sites; e-mail; walk-ins during office hours; telephone; individual appointments; and customer service systems.

ASFA should ensure that services provided through third parties are offered on a fair and equitable basis and in a manner consistent with the mission of the institution.

ASFA may provide manuals, instructions, policies, signs, and training, in one or more languages in addition to English for predominant groups of employees who speak a language other than English.

ASFA must recognize the needs of distance learning students by providing appropriate and accessible services and assisting them in identifying and gaining access to other appropriate services in their geographic region.

Part 8. DIVERSITY

Within the context of each institution's unique mission, diversity enriches the community and enhances the collegiate experience for all; therefore, Auxiliary Services Functional Areas (ASFA) must create and nurture environments that are welcoming to and bring together persons of diverse backgrounds.

ASFA must promote environments that are characterized by open and continuous communication that deepens understanding of one's own identity, culture, and heritage, as well as that of others. ASFA must recognize, honor, educate, and promote respect about commonalties and differences among people within their historical and cultural contexts.

ASFA must address the characteristics and needs of a diverse population when establishing and implementing policies and procedures.

All institutional units and contractors that provide services to students must share responsibility for meeting the needs of the wide variety of students on campus. Coordinated efforts to promote multicultural sensitivity and the elimination of prejudicial behaviors in all functional areas on campus must be encouraged.

ASFA should make reasonable effort to address and educate the campus community concerning cultural, religious, racial, socioeconomic, and other aspects of identity that are unique to ASFA services, such as food, holiday recognition, and products offered for sale.

Outsourced programs and services are accountable to the institution. As such, a diversity liaison should exist within each outsourced ASFA to help ensure that a diverse workplace and environment exist, consistent with the goals of the institution.

Part 9. ORGANIZATION and MANAGEMENT

To promote student learning and development outcomes, Auxiliary Services Functional Areas (ASFA) must be structured purposefully and managed effectively to achieve stated goals. Evidence of appropriate structure must include current and accessible policies and procedures, written performance expectations for all employees, functional workflow graphics or organizational charts, and clearly stated program and service delivery expectations.

ASFA must monitor websites used for distributing information to ensure that the sites are current, accurate, appropriately referenced, and accessible.

Evidence of effective management must include use of

comprehensive and accurate information for decisions, clear sources and channels of authority, effective communication practices, procedures for decision-making and conflict resolution, responses to changing conditions, systems of accountability and evaluation, and processes for recognition and reward. ASFA must align policies and procedures with those of the institution and provide channels within the organization for their regular review.

ASFA must maintain accurate and current documentation on:
- operational policies and procedures
- agreements (e.g., contracts, leases) with outsourced service providers and vendors including good faith agreements and amendments
- memoranda of understanding with campus service providers
- standards of performance and other expectations of service providers
- access provisions for clients and employees with disabilities
- day-to-day operations such as fiscal controls, maintenance of physical plant and equipment, provision of services, supervision of personnel, and customer relations

ASFA must consult with members of the campus community regarding its operations, governance, and programming structure, and the formulation of ASFA policies and procedures.

ASFA, in consultation with students, faculty members, staff, administration, and other constituents, must determine and document facility operating polices, budgets, allocations of funds, employment policies, space allocation, products and services to be offered, and hours of operation.

When these areas of consideration are part of a contractual agreement, it may be necessary to address them within pre-determined review or renewal time frames.

ASFA should be organized to:
- deliver successful programs, goods, and services that are supportive of the institution's mission
- operate its business enterprises effectively and efficiently
- conduct satisfaction surveys, learning outcomes evaluations, and other assessment
- meet or exceed fiscal expectations, consistent with its organizational structure
- maintain its physical plant resources
- exercise enterprising and entrepreneurial leadership in a manner that does not detract from the core mission of the institution

Involvement of the campus community may include students, faculty members, staff, visitors, alumni, and other constituents and stakeholders, as appropriate. Typically such involvement is through advisory, governing, and program boards, committees, or through feedback via surveys and focus groups.

Additional areas for consideration in determining structure and management of the ASFA may include:
- availability and characteristics of facilities
- size, nature, and mission of the institution
- size, scope, proximity, and availability of services in the surrounding community
- ratio of residential to commuter/off-campus student populations
- budget and finance expectations
- institutional philosophy, policies, and preferences concerning outsourcing and privatization
- variety of delivery methods being employed or available to the institution
- degree of integration with academic disciplines and academic service units
- goals of ASFA and its partners

Part 10. CAMPUS and EXTERNAL RELATIONS

Auxiliary Services Functional Areas (ASFA) must reach out to relevant individuals, campus offices, and external agencies to:
- establish, maintain, and promote effective relations
- disseminate information about their own and other related programs and services
- coordinate and collaborate, where appropriate, in offering programs and services to meet the needs of students and promote their achievement of student learning and development outcomes

ASFA must have procedures and guidelines consistent with institutional policy for responding to threats, emergencies, and crisis situations. Systems and procedures must be in place to disseminate timely and accurate information to students and other members of the campus community during emergency situations.

ASFA must have procedures and guidelines consistent with institutional policy for communicating with the media.

When services are managed by outside contractors, processes must be in place to ensure that administration of the services remains the responsibility of the institution.

ASFA should share information, initiate and promote program opportunities, encourage staff development, and enhance ASFA program visibility by:
- establishing cooperative relationships with procurement, student affairs, and academic departments, and direct service providers such as campus programs, alumni, parking, visitor services, libraries, bookstore, enrollment management, athletics, institutional advancement, campus information, and visitor services
- encouraging staff participation in civic and community organizations such as Rotary, Kiwanis, and Chamber of Commerce as well as involvement in ASFA professional associations
- nurturing cooperative relationships with local, state/provincial, and federal governmental entities

ASFA should adhere to institution-wide processes that systematically involve academic affairs, student affairs, and administrative units such as police, physical plant, and business offices.

ASFA should collaborate with campus agencies, as appropriate, and meet regularly with other service providers to coordinate schedules and facility use and to review services and activities under development.

ASFA should serve as a resource to the campus and community by providing professional advice on market demand, development of new auxiliary services, related business issues, and current industry activities.

ASFA should value marketing as a core function for education about, and promotion of, equal access to ASFA products and services by all constituent groups.

ASFA should provide quality customer service to all constituents and ensure they are fairly represented on ASFA governing and advisory boards.

Students should be the principal beneficiaries of ASFA, although outreach should include all constituents, including faculty members, staff, alumni, visitors, members of the community, and others.

Student government and similar groups should have ongoing involvement with ASFA and their operations.

Student publications and electronic media should be used for communicating information about ASFA.

Relationships among campus administrative staff and employees/representatives of outside contractors should be cultivated and supervised carefully.

Relations with contract service providers should receive close and frequent attention and review. Assessment of these services should be collaborative and continuous.

ASFA should foster partnerships that engage and involve campus and contract service providers in all segments of the campus community.

ASFA should foster initiatives that ensure all service providers become stakeholders in advancing the mission of the institution.

Part 11. FINANCIAL RESOURCES

Auxiliary Services Functional Areas (ASFA) must have adequate funding to accomplish their mission and goals. In establishing funding priorities and making significant changes, a comprehensive analysis, which includes relevant expenditures, external and internal resources, and impact on the campus community, must be conducted.

ASFA must demonstrate fiscal responsibility and cost effectiveness consistent with institutional protocols.

Funds to support the ASFA, insofar as it is possible and desirable, should be generated from pricing set at fair market rates.

For self-support programs:

- when net operating income is achieved, ASFA should establish operating reserve funds as a buffer against future shortfalls and capital reserve funds for facilities renewal
- when lower than expected revenue in any one-year results in a deficit, ASFA should access reserve funds to offset the deficit

Financial planning and projections should include budget data for both current and long-term expenditures, including capital expenditures and deferred maintenance costs.

A program of asset management should be in place so that resources are adequate for meeting future repair and replacement requirements for key equipment and facilities.

ASFA should underwrite a fair proportion of overhead costs associated with shared services that support the entire campus.

The institution's budget commitment to ASFA should be sufficient to achieve its mission and to provide appropriate services, facilities, and programs deemed necessary to maintain standards and diversity of programs, goods, and services, commensurate with the organizational structure, aspirations, image, and the reputation of the institution.

ASFA should maintain adequate financial resources to ensure reasonable pricing of services, adequate programming, staffing, proper maintenance, and professional development.

ASFA may be expected to fund specific campus needs and contribute to the general fund.

Part 12. TECHNOLOGY

Auxiliary Services Functional Areas (ASFA) must have adequate technology to support their mission. The technology and its use must comply with institutional policies and procedures and be evaluated for compliance with relevant federal, state/provincial, and local requirements.

ASFA should use current and appropriate technology to facilitate, improve, assess, and extend access to its programs, products, services, and facilities.

ASFA must maintain policies and procedures that address the security and back up of data.

When technology is used to facilitate student learning and development, ASFA must select technology that reflects current best pedagogical practices.

Technology, as well as any workstations or computer labs maintained by the ASFA for student use, must be accessible and must meet established technology standards for delivery to persons with disabilities.

When ASFA provide student access to technology, they must provide:

- **access to policies that are clear, easy to understand, and available to all students**
- **access to instruction or training on how to use the technology**
- **access to information on the legal and ethical**

implications of misuse as it pertains to intellectual property, harassment, privacy, and social networks.

Student violations of technology policies must follow established institutional student disciplinary procedures.

Students who experience negative emotional or psychological consequences from the use of technology must be referred to support services provided by the institution.

Part 13. FACILITIES and EQUIPMENT

Auxiliary Services Functional Areas (ASFA) must have adequate, accessible, suitably located facilities and equipment to support their mission and goals. If acquiring capital equipment as defined by the institution, ASFA must take into account expenses related to regular maintenance and life cycle costs. Facilities and equipment must be evaluated regularly, including consideration of sustainability, and be in compliance with relevant federal, state/provincial, and local requirements to provide for access, health, safety, and security.

ASFA staff members must have work space that is well-equipped, adequate in size, and designed to support their work and responsibilities. For conversations requiring privacy, staff members must have access to a private space.

ASFA staff members who share work space must have the ability to secure their work adequately.

The design of the facilities must guarantee the security of records and ensure the confidentiality of sensitive information.

The location and layout of the facilities must be sensitive to the special needs of persons with disabilities as well as the needs of constituencies served.

ASFA must ensure that staff members are knowledgeable of and trained in safety and emergency procedures for securing and vacating the facilities.

ASFA must periodically review and evaluate equipment and facilities to assess current and future needs.

Regularly scheduled cleaning of public areas must be provided, and grounds associated with ASFA facilities, which may include streets, paved walks, and parking lots, must be clean and well maintained.

Recycling, energy conservation, and sustainability efforts must be implemented throughout the ASFA and be compliant with institutional guidelines, government regulations, and contractual agreements.

ASFA facilities may include retail outlets; dining centers; vending operations; restaurants; residences; recreation and athletic facilities; event venues; office buildings; parking lots and transportation structures; manufacturing and production operations; maintenance shops; and shipping, receiving, and storage centers.

ASFA facilities should be sufficient to meet the needs of the program, consistent with agreements among institutional and community agencies and with students.

Size of facilities should comply with minimum effective service standards established by appropriate professional organizations for each functional area.

Facilities should be accessible, clean, reasonably priced, appropriately designed, well maintained, and have adequate safety and security features.

Facilities with multi-use capability, such as dining rooms and lounges, should be available for campus events and programs at times when they are not needed to support ASFA functions.

New construction projects should be responsive to the current and future needs of the campus community. Decisions about new construction should be based upon clearly defined needs and consistent with the mission of the institution, which may include adherence to institutional standards for sustainability.

Maintenance and renovation programs should be implemented in all operations and should include:
- preventive maintenance and audit procedures to ensure physical safety
- replacement reserves
- timely repair of equipment, vehicles, facilities, and building systems
- modifications to facilities and systems to keep them attractive, effective, efficient, and safe
- sustainable designs and practices whenever feasible

Systematically planned replacement cycles should exist for furnishings, mechanical and electrical systems, maintenance equipment, floor/wall/window treatments, and serving/point of service equipment.

The institution should be reimbursed for campus services, facilities, technology, and equipment that are used to support ASFA.
ASFA should monitor their impact on the community surrounding the campus and should work to maintain amicable relationships with affected non-university entities.

Part 14. ASSESSMENT and EVALUATION

Auxiliary Services Functional Areas (ASFA) must establish systematic plans and processes to meet internal and external accountability expectations with regard to program as well as student learning and development outcomes. ASFA must conduct regular assessment and evaluations. Assessments must include qualitative and quantitative methodologies as appropriate, to determine whether and to what degree the stated mission, goals, and student learning and development outcomes are being met. The process must employ sufficient and sound measures to ensure comprehensiveness. Data collected must include responses from students and other affected constituencies.

ASFA must evaluate regularly how well they complement

and enhance the institution's stated mission and educational effectiveness.

Results of these evaluations must be used in revising and improving programs and services, identifying needs and interests in shaping directions of program and service design, and recognizing staff performance.

Cost analysis and market research must be conducted at least annually when setting fees for goods and services to be offered to students, faculty members, and staff.

ASFA must maintain accurate and current documentation on program data such as usage rates, peak times of usage, learning outcomes, sales and revenue, student satisfaction, and value-contribution.

Both internal and external evaluations and assessments should be encouraged.

Periodic reports, statistically valid research, outside reviews, and other tools measuring student needs and opinions should be utilized.

ASFA should collaborate with institutional research units to generate data that could be useful, such as in projecting contributions to the local economy, increasing student enrollment, or stimulating research.

A representative cross-section of qualified people from campus communities should be involved in reviewing ASFA.

ASFA should generate and disseminate an annual report identifying overall goals, program data, changes in services provided, financial contributions, regular feedback from participants, and opportunities that contribute to the overall effectiveness and quality of the institution.

General Standards revised in 2008;
ASFA content developed in 2007

The Role of Campus Activities Programs
CAS Standards Contextual Statement

One of the first noted formal campus organizations established for the purpose of bringing students together (primarily for debating important issues of the day) was the Oxford Union founded in 1823. The Union's clubs also provided educational opportunities beyond the classroom, through such group activities as discussions of literature and poetry and involvement in hobbies and recreational activities. Today, numerous clubs and organizations (hundreds on some campuses) offer students opportunities to learn through their involvement in campus life. There is little debate now that the collegiate experience involves what occurs outside the classroom and that a college education includes more than what goes on in the classroom.

Campus activities describes in part the combined efforts of clubs and organizations established for and/or by students, including, but not limited to, governance, leadership, service, cultural, social, diversity, recreational, artistic, political and religious activities. Many of these efforts focus on programs that serve to educate, develop, or entertain club, organization, or group members, their guests, and the campus community.

Theory of involvement contends that the amount of energy—both physical and psychological—that students expend at their institution positively affects their development during college. Studies indicate that students who are involved in campus life devote considerable energy to their academic programs, spend considerable time on campus, participate actively in student organizations, and interact frequently with other students (Astin, 1996; Kuh, Douglas, Lund, Ramin-Gyurmek, 1994). Campus activities is one of the vehicles for involving students with the institution.

Though students' efforts are the backbone of campus activities, campus activity advisors serve as the catalysts for these efforts. They plan and implement training for student leaders and group members to assist them in attaining their goals, primarily regarding working with others; provide continuity for student clubs and organizations from year to year; educate students about institution policy, related legal matters, and fiscal responsibility; mediate conflicts between individuals and groups; encourage innovation and responsibility in program implementation; provide opportunities to practice leadership and organizational skills; integrate knowledge gained in the classroom with actual practice; and instruct about ethics, diversity, and other critical values.

The role of campus activity advisors is certainly linked to the quality of a student's involvement experience and thus a student's development. The CAS Standards and Guidelines that follow offer direction for campus activity advisors to create quality campus activity programs that are engaging, developmental, and experiential.

References, Readings, and Resources

Astin, A. W. (1996a). Involvement in learning revisited: Lessons we have learned. *Journal of College Student Development, 37*, 123-134.

Boatman, S. (1997). Leadership programs in campus activities. *The management of campus activities.* Columbia, SC: National Association of Campus Activities Education Foundation.

Cuyjet, M. J. (1996). Program development and group advising. In S. R. Komives & D. B. Woodward, Jr. (Eds.), *Student services: A handbook for the profession* (3rd ed., pp. 397-414). San Francisco: Jossey-Bass.

Julian, F. (1997). Law and campus life. *The management of student activities.* Columbia, SC: National Association for Campus Activities.

Kuh, G. D., Douglas, K. B., Lund, J. P., & Ramin-Gyurmek, J. (1994). *Student learning outside the classroom: Transcending artificial boundaries.* ASHE-ERIC Higher Education Report No. 8, Washington, DC: The George Washington University, Graduate School of Education and Human Development.

Meabon, D., Krehbiel, L., & Suddick, D. (1996). Financing campus activities. *The management of student activities.* Columbia, SC: National Association for Campus Activities.

Metz, N. D. (1996). *Student development in college unions and student activities.* Bloomington, IN: Association of College Unions International.

Nejman, M. R. (1995). *Diversity, student activities, and their roles in community colleges: Developing an effective program to achieve unity through diversity.* Columbia, SC: National Association for Campus Activities.

Roberts, D. C. (2003). Community Building and Programming. In S. R. Komives & D. B. Woodard (Eds.), *Student Services: A handbook for the profession* (4th ed.) (pp. 539-554). San Francisco: Jossey Bass.

Skipper, T. L. & Argo, R. (Eds.). (2003). *Involvement in campus activities and the retention of first-year college students.* Columbia, SC: National Resource Center for the First-Year Experience & Students in Transition and National Association of Campus Activities.

American College Personnel Association, Commission for Students, Their Activities and Their Community. One Dupont Circle, N.W., Suite 300, Washington, DC 20036-1110. (202) 835-2272; Webpage: http://www.myacpa.org

Association of College Unions International (ACUI), One City
Center. 120 W. Seventh Street, Suite 200, Bloomington, IN
47404-3925; Webpage: www.acui.org

National Association for College Activities. 13 Harbison Way,
Columbia, SC 29212-3401. (803) 732-6222; Web Page:
www.naca.org

Contributor:

Jan Arminio, Shippensburg University, NACA

Campus Activities Programs
CAS Standards and Guidelines

Part 1. MISSION

The purpose of Campus Activities Programs (CAP) must be to enhance the overall educational experience of students through development of, exposure to, and participation in programs and activities that improve student cooperation and leadership while preparing students to be responsible advocates and citizens and complementing the institution's academic programs.

These activities could be intellectual, social, recreational, cultural, multicultural, and spiritual in nature. Programs could pertain to leadership, governance, community service, healthy lifestyles, and organizational development.

CAP must develop, disseminate, implement, and regularly review their mission. Mission statements must be consistent with the mission of the institution and with professional standards. CAP in higher education must enhance overall educational experiences by incorporating student learning and development outcomes in their mission.

CAP must provide opportunities for students to:
- participate in co-curricular activities
- participate in campus governance
- advocate for their organizations and interests
- develop leadership abilities
- develop healthy interpersonal relationships
- use leisure time purposefully
- develop ethical decision-making skills
- advocate for student organizations and interests

Part 2. PROGRAM

The formal education of students, consisting of the curriculum and the co-curriculum, must promote student learning and development outcomes that are purposeful and holistic and that prepare students for satisfying and productive lifestyles, work, and civic participation. The student learning and development outcome domains and their related dimensions are:

- knowledge acquisition, integration, construction, and application
  - Dimensions: understanding knowledge from a range of disciplines; connecting knowledge to other knowledge, ideas, and experiences; constructing knowledge; and relating knowledge to daily life

- cognitive complexity
  - Dimensions: critical thinking; reflective thinking; effective reasoning; and creativity

- intrapersonal development
  - Dimensions: realistic self-appraisal, self-understanding, and self-respect; identity development; commitment to ethics and integrity; and spiritual awareness

- interpersonal competence
  - Dimensions: meaningful relationships; interdependence; collaboration; and effective leadership

- humanitarianism and civic engagement
  - Dimensions: understanding and appreciation of cultural and human differences; social responsibility; global perspective; and sense of civic responsibility

- practical competence
  - Dimensions: pursuing goals; communicating effectively; technical competence; managing personal affairs; managing career development; demonstrating professionalism; maintaining health and wellness; and living a purposeful and satisfying life

[See *The Council for the Advancement of Standards Learning and Developmental Outcomes* statement for examples of outcomes related to these domains and dimensions.]

Consistent with the institutional mission, Campus Activities Programs (CAP) must identify relevant and desirable student learning and development outcomes from among the six domains and related dimensions. When creating opportunities for student learning and development, CAP must explore possibilities for collaboration with faculty members and other colleagues.

CAP must assess relevant and desirable student learning and development outcomes and provide evidence of their impact on student learning and development. CAP must articulate how they contribute to or support students' learning and development in the domains not specifically assessed.

CAP must be:
- integrated into the life of the institution
- intentional and coherent
- guided by theories and knowledge of learning and development
- reflective of developmental and demographic profiles of the student population
- responsive to needs of individuals, diverse and special populations, and relevant constituencies

CAP must be comprehensive and reflect and promote the diversity of student interests and needs, allowing especially for the achievement of a sense of self-esteem and community pride.

A comprehensive CAP program should include offerings that vary in type, size, scheduling, and cost.

CAP must be of broad scope, inclusive of all educational domains for student learning and development.

Programs should include activities that:

- complement classroom instruction and academic learning
- offer instruction and experience in leadership and working in groups
- promote physical and psychosocial well-being
- promote understanding of and interaction with people of one's own culture and other cultures
- foster meaningful interactions between students and members of the faculty, staff, and administration
- build specific group communities and identity with the campus community

CAP must offer and encourage student participation in student-led campus activities.

Additional encouragement can come from club advisors, faculty members, staff, parents, peers, administrators, and others.

CAP should create environments in which students can:

- explore activities in individual and group settings for self-understanding and growth
- learn about diverse cultures and experiences
- explore ideas and issues through the arts
- design and implement programs to enhance social, cultural, multicultural, social justice, intellectual, recreational, service, and campus governance involvement
- comprehend institutional policies and procedures and their relationship to individual and group interests and activities
- learn of and use campus facilities and other resources
- plan, market, implement, and assess programs

CAP should enhance the retention and graduation of students and strengthen campus and community relations. Programs and events should be planned and implemented collaboratively by students, professional staff, and faculty members.

CAP must ensure that the institution has a policy for the registration and recognition of student organizations.

CAP must include these fundamental functions: implementing campus programs that add vibrancy to the campus, advising student organizations that implement programs or services, advising student governing organizations, ensuring the proper and efficient stewardship of funds including the student activity fee and institutional allocation, and implementing training, development, and educational opportunities.

Programs may evolve from CAP office or from student organizations and student governing bodies and should add richness to the institution and its integral functions. The CAP should strive to build student institutional loyalty and allegiance while promoting citizenship and civility.

Student and student organizations' awards programs should be based on fair and equitable criteria.

These functions may be achieved directly or in collaboration or consultation with other campus entities.

Programs sponsored by CAP must be produced and promoted according to professional and institutional practices and

protocols.

Promotion methods CAP may use include the creation and dissemination, either in print or on-line, of activities calendars, organizational directories, student handbooks, and programming and financial management guides.

Entertainment programs should:

- reflect the values stated in the institution and CAP mission statements
- maintain admission fees at levels that encourage widespread student attendance
- implement hospitality requirements that prohibit the provision of alcohol to entertainers where appropriate
- include a constituency-based advisory system for activities planning, implementation, and evaluation, to ensure coordination within the larger campus academic calendar

Contracts must be signed by an appropriate authority identified by institutional policies and procedures.

CAP should provide guidance and training that enables students to recruit, negotiate with, and select performers.

Advising
CAP must provide effective administrative support for student organizations. Every student organization must have an advisor. The criteria for who may serve as an advisor and the role and responsibilities of advisors must be defined by the institution.

Responsibilities of advisors can include attending organization meetings, meeting with organization officers as a group or individually, overseeing budget and financial transactions, serving as an advocate for the organization, serving as a liaison between the institution and students, assisting the organization in problem-solving, and overseeing the election and/or appointment of new officers. Advising can take place through face-to-face meetings or via telephone, email, instant messaging, or other communication methods.

Advisors should be institutional faculty members, staff, or graduate student employees.

Advisors must be knowledgeable of legal issues and institutional policies, especially regarding risk management.

CAP must provide information and training opportunities for advisors.

CAP staff should be available to provide oversight and to consult and problem-solve with advisors. Advisors who volunteer their time should be recognized by the institution for their contributions.

Advisors should:

- be knowledgeable of student development theory and philosophy to appropriately support students and also to encourage learning and development.
- have adaptive advising styles in order to be able to work with students with a variety of skill and knowledge levels
- have interest in the students involved in the organization

- have expertise in the topic for which the student group is engaged
- understand organizational development processes and team building .

Student Governance

Student governance groups must have a written mission, purpose, and process for continuity of leadership that is regularly reviewed. Criteria for student involvement must be clear, widely publicized, easily accessible, and consistently followed. Budgeting and fiscal procedures must be clearly defined and must follow all applicable laws. Clearly defined grievance procedures must exist to settle disagreements regarding continuity of leadership, budgeting procedures, and ethics violations by student leaders.

Student governance groups could include undergraduate and graduate student government associations, residence hall associations, campus center governing boards, sports club councils, fraternity and sorority governance councils, media boards, and college councils.

Student governance groups must be encouraged to operate in accordance with institutional values, mission, and policies, and be informed of possible consequences for failure to do so.

Student governance groups may conduct a wide variety of activities and services, including executive, judicial, legislative, business or service functions, and educational or entertainment programming.

Institutions must have policies and procedures for providing an advisor to student governance organizations.

Training, Education, and Development

CAP must ensure that there are training, education, and development opportunities for students involved in student organizations.

Many CAP are responsible for the training, education, and development of students who are involved in student organizations. As outlined in the CAS Standards for Student Leadership Programs, training involves those activities designed to prepare students to assume leadership positions, improve performance of the individual in the role presently occupied, and enhance participants' knowledge and understanding of specific leadership theories, concepts, models, and institutional policies and procedures needed to work effectively. Successful developmental opportunities often occur in an environment that empowers students to mature and develop toward greater levels of leadership complexity.

CAP training, education, and development activities must be delivered by a diverse range of faculty members, students, and staff, using diverse pedagogies, and take place in a variety of ways.

Training, education, and development activities may take the form of retreats; one-on-one conversations; manuals, handbooks, and other publications; workshops and conferences; seminars; mentoring; and for-credit courses.

CAP training, education, and development opportunities must take into account differing student developmental levels.

Students should be trained in leadership concepts and skills, organizational development, ethical behavior, and other skills particular to distinctive programming requirements, such as contracting for entertainment.

Additional information on leadership programs for students can be found in the CAS Student Leadership Programs standards and guidelines.

Part 3. LEADERSHIP

Because effective and ethical leadership is essential to the success of all organizations, leaders with organizational authority for the Campus Activities Programs (CAP) must:
- **articulate a vision and mission for their programs and services**
- **set goals and objectives based on the needs of the population served and desired student learning and development outcomes**
- **advocate for their programs and services**
- **promote campus environments that provide meaningful opportunities for student learning, development, and integration**
- **identify and find means to address individual, organizational, or environmental conditions that foster or inhibit mission achievement**
- **advocate for representation in strategic planning initiatives at appropriate divisional and institutional levels**
- **initiate collaborative interactions with stakeholders who have legitimate concerns and interests in the functional area**
- **apply effective practices to educational and administrative processes**
- **prescribe and model ethical behavior**
- **communicate effectively**
- **manage financial resources, including planning, allocation, monitoring, and analysis**
- **incorporate sustainability practices in the management and design of programs, services, and facilities**
- **manage human resource processes including recruitment, selection, development, supervision, performance planning, and evaluation**
- **empower professional, support, and student staff to accept leadership opportunities**
- **encourage and support scholarly contribution to the profession**
- **be informed about and integrate appropriate technologies into programs and services**
- **be knowledgeable about federal, state/provincial, and local laws relevant to the programs and services and ensure that staff members understand their responsibilities by receiving appropriate training**
- **develop and continuously improve programs and services**

- in response to the changing needs of students and other populations served and the evolving institutional priorities
- **recognize environmental conditions that may negatively influence the safety of staff and students and propose interventions that mitigate such conditions.**

Opportunities for student learning and development could include activities boards; student governance bodies; academic, performance, cultural, arts, religious, recreational, and special interest organizations; program boards; theatrical productions; and media boards.

The CAP should be aware of the institutional strategic plan and be ready to respond to contemporary conditions and emergency preparedness. These conditions could include response to natural disasters, celebrations of notable achievements, and the changing nature of the student population.

Part 4. HUMAN RESOURCES

Campus Activities Programs (CAP) must be staffed adequately by individuals qualified to accomplish the mission and goals. Within institutional guidelines, CAP must establish procedures for staff selection, training, and evaluation; set expectations for supervision; and provide appropriate professional development opportunities to improve the leadership ability, competence, and skills of all employees.

Appropriate continuous training opportunities should be offered for all CAP staff members. This can include training in leadership, organizational planning, diversity, ethical decision making, and communication skills. Staff members should seek to enhance their resourcefulness, empathy, creativity, and openness to serving diverse student populations. Staff members should also seek to increase their knowledge of current issues. Training and development opportunities could be achieved through participation with professional organizations.

Depending upon the scope of campus activities programs, the staff may include an activities director, a program coordinator, organization and program advisors, orientation and leadership specialists, a technology specialist, and a bookkeeper/financial officer.

CAP professional staff members must hold an earned graduate or professional degree in a field relevant to the position they hold or must possess an appropriate combination of educational credentials and related work experience.

Relevant fields may include college student affairs, higher education administration, organizational development, or other related programs. Graduate studies should include courses in the behavioral sciences, management, recreation, student affairs, student development, and research techniques. The CAP may require particular training and experience appropriate to serving distinct campus populations and specialized campus or community needs.

The primary functions of full-time professional staff members may include the administration and coordination of campus activities programs; assessment of student interests and needs; planning, implementing, and evaluating programs with students; assisting student organizations in planning and implementing their programs; advising student groups; advising student governance organizations; and providing training, education, and development opportunities for students and advisors involved in student organizations.

Additional qualifications of campus activities staff members should include:

- ability to collaborate with faculty members, administrators, staff colleagues, students, and all other constituencies
- capacity to interpret or advocate student concerns and interests to the campus community
- expertise in the development of students
- ability to create and deliver programs, activities, and services to students and to student groups
- experience in promoting student leadership
- capability of serving as a role model for ethical behavior
- commitment to professional and personal development
- knowledge of group dynamics and ability to work effectively with groups
- ability to supervise a variety of staff including students, support staff, and professional staff
- knowledge of contracting procedures and contract negotiations
- skills in working with agents and performers
- experience in effectively managing budgets
- appropriate expertise in the use of technology
- ability to supervise student staff members
- ability to balance the role of student advocate and the interest of the institution

At least one professional staff member should be assigned responsibility for campus activities programs.

Degree- or credential-seeking interns must be qualified by enrollment in an appropriate field of study and by relevant experience. These individuals must be trained and supervised adequately by professional staff members holding educational credentials and related work experience appropriate for supervision.

Student employees and volunteers must be carefully selected, trained, supervised, and evaluated. They must be educated on how and when to refer those in need of additional assistance to qualified staff members and must have access to a supervisor for assistance in making these judgments. Student employees and volunteers must be provided clear and precise job descriptions, pre-service training based on assessed needs, and continuing staff development.

Thorough training should be provided for student employees and volunteers to enable them to carry out their duties and responsibilities and to enhance their personal experiences with campus activities programs.

Employees and volunteers must receive specific training on institutional policies and privacy laws regarding their

access to student records and other sensitive institutional information (e.g., in the USA, Family Educational Rights and Privacy Act, FERPA, or equivalent privacy laws in other states/provinces or countries).

CAP must have technical and support staff members adequate to accomplish their mission. All members of the staff must be technologically proficient and qualified to perform their job functions, be knowledgeable about ethical and legal uses of technology, and have access to training and resources to support the performance of their assigned responsibilities.

All members of the staff must receive training on policies and procedures related to the use of technology to store or access student records and institutional data.

CAP must ensure that staff members are knowledgeable about and trained in emergency procedures, crisis response, and prevention efforts. Prevention efforts must address identification of threatening conduct or behavior of students, faculty members, staff, and others and must incorporate a system or procedures for responding, including but not limited to reporting them to the appropriate campus officials.

Salary levels and benefits for all staff members must be commensurate with those for comparable positions within the institution, in similar institutions, and in the relevant geographic area.

CAP must maintain position descriptions for all staff members.

To create a diverse staff, programs and services must institute hiring and promotion practices that are fair, inclusive, proactive, and non-discriminatory.

CAP must conduct regular performance planning and evaluation of staff members. CAP must provide access to continuing and advanced education and professional development opportunities.

Joint staff development efforts should be encouraged with colleagues in allied programs such as recreational sports, residence hall programming, and special programs for international students and students from traditionally under-represented groups.

Identification of staff with authority to enter into binding contracts must be made by the institution and clearly disseminated and explained to students and advisors.

Part 5. ETHICS

Persons involved in the delivery of Campus Activities Programs (CAP) must adhere to the highest principles of ethical behavior. CAP must review relevant professional ethical standards and develop or adopt and implement appropriate statements of ethical practice. CAP must publish these statements and ensure their periodic review by relevant constituencies.

Applicable statements may include principles and standards

pertaining to:

- civil and ethical conduct
- accuracy of information (i.e., accurate presentation of institutional goals, services, and policies to the public and the college or university community, and fair and accurate representation in publicity and promotions)
- conflict of interest
- role conflicts
- fiscal accountability
- fair and equitable administration of institutional policies
- student involvement in relevant institutional decisions
- free and open exchange of ideas through campus activities programs
- fulfillment of contractual arrangements and agreements
- role modeling of ethical leadership practices

CAP must orient new staff members to relevant ethical standards and statements of ethical practice.

CAP staff members must ensure that privacy and confidentiality are maintained with respect to all communications and records to the extent that such records are protected under the law and appropriate statements of ethical practice. Information contained in students' education records must not be disclosed except as allowed by relevant laws and institutional policies. CAP staff members must disclose to appropriate authorities information judged to be of an emergency nature, especially when the safety of the individual or others is involved, or when otherwise required by institutional policy or relevant law.

CAP staff members must be aware of and comply with the provisions contained in the institution's policies pertaining to human subjects research and student rights and responsibilities, as well as those in other relevant institutional policies addressing ethical practices and confidentiality of research data concerning individuals.

CAP staff members must recognize and avoid personal conflicts of interest or appearance thereof in the performance of their work.

CAP staff members must strive to insure the fair, objective, and impartial treatment of all persons with whom they interact.

When handling institutional funds, CAP staff members must ensure that such funds are managed in accordance with established and responsible accounting procedures and the fiscal policies or processes of the institution.

Promotional and descriptive information must be accurate and free of deception.

CAP staff members must perform their duties within the limits of their training, expertise, and competence. When these limits are exceeded, individuals in need of further assistance must be referred to persons possessing appropriate qualifications.

CAP staff members must use suitable means to confront and

otherwise hold accountable other staff members who exhibit unethical behavior.

CAP staff members must be knowledgeable about and practice ethical behavior in the use of technology.

Part 6. LEGAL RESPONSIBILITIES

Campus Activities Programs (CAP) staff members must be knowledgeable about and responsive to laws and regulations that relate to their respective responsibilities and that may pose legal obligations, limitations, or ramifications for the institution as a whole. As appropriate, staff members must inform users of programs and services, as well as officials, of legal obligations and limitations including constitutional, statutory, regulatory, and case law; mandatory laws and orders emanating from federal, state/provincial, and local governments; and the institution's policies.

CAP must have written policies on all relevant operations, transactions, or tasks that may have legal implications.

CAP staff members must neither participate in nor condone any form of harassment or activity that demeans persons or creates an intimidating, hostile, or offensive campus environment.

CAP staff members must use reasonable and informed practices to limit the liability exposure of the institution and its officers, employees, and agents. Staff members must be informed about institutional policies regarding risk management, personal liability, and related insurance coverage options and must be referred to external sources if coverage is not provided by the institution.

The institution must provide access to legal advice for CAP staff members as needed to carry out assigned responsibilities.

The institution must inform CAP staff and students in a timely and systematic fashion about extraordinary or changing legal obligations and potential liabilities.

CAP staff members should be well informed about current campus and student legal issues, including risk management, free speech, organization recognition and registration procedures, contractual issues, and student fees.

Part 7. EQUITY and ACCESS

Campus Activities Programs (CAP) must be provided on a fair, equitable, and non-discriminatory basis in accordance with institutional policies and with all applicable state/provincial and federal statutes and regulations. CAP must maintain an educational and work environment free from discrimination in accordance with law and institutional policy.

Discrimination must be avoided on the basis of age; cultural heritage; disability; ethnicity; gender identity and expression; nationality; political affiliation; race; religious affiliation; sex; sexual orientation; economic, marital, social, or veteran status; and any other bases included in local, state/provincial, or federal laws.

Consistent with the mission and goals, CAP must take action to remedy significant imbalances in student participation and staffing patterns.

CAP must ensure physical and program access for persons with disabilities. CAP must be responsive to the needs of all students and other populations served when establishing hours of operation and developing methods of delivering programs and services.

CAP must recognize the needs of distance learning students by providing appropriate and accessible services and assisting them in identifying and gaining access to other appropriate services in their geographic region.

Outreach efforts could include electronic voting for student elections and student fee assessments and online communities.

Part 8. DIVERSITY

Within the context of each institution's unique mission, diversity enriches the community and enhances the collegiate experience for all; therefore, Campus Activities Programs (CAP) must create and nurture environments that are welcoming to and bring together persons of diverse backgrounds.

CAP must promote environments that are characterized by open and continuous communication that deepens understanding of one's own identity, culture, and heritage, as well as that of others. CAP must recognize, honor, educate, and promote respect about commonalties and differences among people within their historical and cultural contexts.

CAP must address the characteristics and needs of a diverse population when establishing and implementing policies and procedures.

CAP staff must design and implement strategies for involving and engaging diverse student populations.

CAP must provide educational programs that emphasize self-assessment and personal responsibility for creating and improving relationships across differences.

CAP must support and participate in creating a welcoming and nurturing educational environment for all students.

Part 9. ORGANIZATION and MANAGEMENT

To promote student learning and development outcomes, Campus Activities Programs (CAP) must be structured purposefully and managed effectively to achieve stated goals. Evidence of appropriate structure must include current and accessible policies and procedures, written performance expectations for all employees, functional workflow graphics or organizational charts, and clearly stated program and service delivery expectations.

CAP must monitor websites used for distributing information to ensure that the sites are current, accurate, appropriately referenced, and accessible.

Evidence of effective management must include use of comprehensive and accurate information for decisions, clear sources and channels of authority, effective communication practices, procedures for decision-making and conflict resolution, responses to changing conditions, systems of accountability and evaluation, and processes for recognition and reward. CAP must align policies and procedures with those of the institution and provide channels within the organization for their regular review.

CAP may be organized as an autonomous unit or may be organized in the same unit as the campus union or other programming units.

Part 10. CAMPUS and EXTERNAL RELATIONS

Campus Activities Programs (CAP) must reach out to relevant individuals, campus offices, and external agencies to:
- establish, maintain, and promote effective relations
- disseminate information about their own and other related programs and services
- coordinate and collaborate, where appropriate, in offering programs and services to meet the needs of students and promote their achievement of student learning and development outcomes

CAP must have procedures and guidelines consistent with institutional policy for responding to threats, emergencies, and crisis situations. Systems and procedures must be in place to disseminate timely and accurate information to students and other members of the campus community during emergency situations.

CAP must have procedures and guidelines consistent with institutional policy for communicating with the media.

CAP should encourage faculty and staff members throughout the campus community to be involved in campus activities. Faculty members should serve as valuable resources related to their academic disciplines, especially as lecturers, performers, artists, and workshop facilitators. Faculty and staff members who serve as advisors should work directly with organizations in program and leadership development and should be supported by CAP staff. Faculty and staff members, administrators, and students may serve together on advisory boards to provide leadership for important initiatives.

CAP is a highly visible operation both on and off campus and may be influential in forming public opinion about the institution and creating a positive environment for the entire community. In that regard, to build bridges and connections, CAP staff may volunteer for campus-wide or community-based committees, initiatives, and programs beyond the traditional student affairs areas.

Part 11. FINANCIAL RESOURCES

Campus Activities Programs (CAP) must have adequate funding to accomplish their mission and goals. In establishing funding priorities and making significant changes, a comprehensive analysis, which includes relevant expenditures, external and internal resources, and impact on the campus community, must be conducted.

CAP must demonstrate fiscal responsibility and cost effectiveness consistent with institutional protocols.

Methods for establishing, collecting, and allocating student and user fees must be clear and equitable. The authority and processes for decisions relevant to campus activities fees must be clearly established and funds must be spent consistent with established priorities.

Authority for decisions relevant to campus activities fees should rest in large part with students and are typically initiated by a vote of the student body. The fees, once approved through institutional processes, may be managed and allocations distributed by representative student governing bodies or by other allocation boards or committees.

Finance committees of student organizations or student governments should work collaboratively with staff members to establish campus activities fees and priorities. Students and staff members should share responsibility for budget development and implementation according to mutually established program priorities.

Students who have fiscal responsibility must be provided with information and training regarding institutional regulations and policies that govern accounting and the appropriate handling of funds.

CAP should provide educational programs and training to students about the basics of financial management.

Due to the large amounts of money generated by campus activities and the transience of the student population, good business practice dictates that reasonable safeguards be established to ensure responsible management of and accounting for the funds involved. Student organizations may be required to maintain their funds with the institution's business office in which an account for each group is established and where bookkeeping and auditing services are provided. When possible, it is recommended that processes be established to permit individual student organizations to manage their own business transactions. Within this framework, CAP works collaboratively with student organizations on matters of bookkeeping, budgeting, and other matters of fiscal accountability, including contract negotiations, consistent with institutional practices.

Funds for CAP may be provided through state/provincial appropriations, institutional budgets, activities fees, user fees, membership and other specialized fees, revenues from programming or fund-raising projects, grants, and foundation resources. Funds may be supplemented by income from ticket sales, sales of promotional items, and individual or group gifts consistent with institutional policies.

In conjunction with students, CAP must establish clear policies and procedures for funding and managing major campus events and entertainment programs necessitating large financial commitments, including concerts, athletic rivalries, homecoming, alumni days, campus traditions, and family weekend.

Part 12. TECHNOLOGY

Campus Activities Programs (CAP) must have adequate technology to support their mission. The technology and its use must comply with institutional policies and procedures and be evaluated for compliance with relevant federal, state/provincial, and local requirements.

Technological capabilities should accommodate all common communication systems including email, on-line calendars, electronic portfolios, pod casts, instant messaging, web browsing, telephone and video conferencing, and other emerging technologies.

CAP must maintain policies and procedures that address the security and back up of data.

When technology is used to facilitate student learning and development, CAP must select technology that reflects current best pedagogical practices.

Technology, as well as any workstations or computer labs maintained by the CAP for student use, must be accessible and must meet established technology standards for delivery to persons with disabilities.

When CAP provide student access to technology, they must provide:
- access to policies that are clear, easy to understand, and available to all students
- access to instruction or training on how to use the technology
- access to information on the legal and ethical implications of misuse as it pertains to intellectual property, harassment, privacy, and social networks.

Student violations of technology policies must follow established institutional student disciplinary procedures.

Students who experience negative emotional or psychological consequences from the use of technology must be referred to support services provided by the institution.

Part 13. FACILITIES and EQUIPMENT

Campus Activities Programs (CAP) must have adequate, accessible, suitably located facilities and equipment to support their mission and goals. If acquiring capital equipment as defined by the institution, CAP must take into account expenses related to regular maintenance and life cycle costs. Facilities and equipment must be evaluated regularly, including consideration of sustainability, and be in compliance with

relevant federal, state/provincial, and local requirements to provide for access, health, safety, and security.

CAP staff members must have work space that is well-equipped, adequate in size, and designed to support their work and responsibilities. For conversations requiring privacy, staff members must have access to a private space.

CAP staff members who share work space must have the ability to secure their work adequately.

The design of the facilities must guarantee the security of records and ensure the confidentiality of sensitive information.

The location and layout of the facilities must be sensitive to the special needs of persons with disabilities as well as the needs of constituencies served.

CAP must ensure that staff members are knowledgeable of and trained in safety and emergency procedures for securing and vacating the facilities.

Facilities should be located conveniently and designed with flexibility to serve the wide variety of functions associated with campus activities. Appropriate facilities, accessible to all members of the college community, should be provided, including student organization offices and adequately sized and equipped public performance spaces.

The CAP may be located in the college union. [See CAS Standards and Guidelines for College Unions.] In addition to their traditional programming, social, and service facilities, unions typically house campus activities programs, student organization offices, and related meeting, work, and storage rooms. Campus activities may also take place in residence halls, recreation centers, fraternity and sorority houses, sports facilities, worship centers, and other locations. CAP space should be designed to encourage maximum interaction among students and between staff members and students.

Part 14. ASSESSMENT and EVALUATION

Campus Activities Programs (CAP) must establish systematic plans and processes to meet internal and external accountability expectations with regard to program as well as student learning and development outcomes. CAP must conduct regular assessment and evaluations. Assessments must include qualitative and quantitative methodologies as appropriate, to determine whether and to what degree the stated mission, goals, and student learning and development outcomes are being met. The process must employ sufficient and sound measures to ensure comprehensiveness. Data collected must include responses from students and other affected constituencies.

Assessment instrumentation and methods should be scientifically designed and implemented, and when possible, staff should seek advice and guidance and work collaboratively with institutional research offices.

CAP must evaluate regularly how well they complement

and enhance the institution's stated mission and educational effectiveness.

Results of these evaluations must be used in revising and improving programs and services, identifying needs and interests in shaping directions of program and service design, and recognizing staff performance.

The CAP should be evaluated regularly and the findings should be disseminated to appropriate campus agencies and constituencies including appropriate student organizations. Evaluation procedures should yield evidence relative to the achievement of program goals, student learning outcomes, quality and scope of program offerings, responsiveness to expressed interests, program attendance and effectiveness, cost effectiveness, quality and appearance of facilities, student success and retention, and equipment use and maintenance. Data sources should include students, staff, alumni, faculty members, administrators, community members, and relevant documents and records. Student self-assessment should be encouraged through the use of such techniques as electronic portfolios.

Records of program evaluations should be maintained in the office of the administrative leader of the CAP and should be accessible to planners of subsequent programs.

General Standards revised in 2008;
Campus Activities content developed/revised in 1986, 1997, & 2006

The Role of Campus Information and Visitor Services
CAS Standards Contextual Statement

The development of the campus information and visitor services field was a direct result of the increasing diversity, size, complexity, and specialization of institutions of higher learning during the 20th century. This pattern was particularly seen on campuses in the United States and necessitated the development of information centers to address the many informational needs of large and complex campus communities. Often these centers evolved into, or were combined with, visitor services to become comprehensive campus gateway operations providing entry points to institutions for all visitors, including prospective students, alumni, and others. The common objective of campus information and visitor services (CIVS) is to bring people, programs, and campus services and resources together through increased accessibility to information.

Some of the earliest examples of visitor services and centers include the establishment in 1951 of the Visitor Center at the U.S. Military Academy at West Point and the creation of the Visitor Information Center at the University of California at Berkeley in 1965. Historically, these programs originated as extensions of institutional recruitment activities and efforts. One of the earliest examples of specialized information and referral services can be traced to the 1970 establishment of the Campus Assistance Center at the University of Wisconsin-Madison. Specialized information and referral programs were often established as information and rumor control efforts responding to the rapid expansion of campuses and increasing lack of trust in traditional institutional communication methods. By providing inquirers with the information and services they needed, or referring them to the appropriate resources when necessary, these programs were quickly judged to be highly useful in providing improved communication opportunities and increasing the quality of campus life. These early campus information and visitor service programs quickly became permanent campus operations with philosophies focused on access and individualized service. Additionally, many of the programs established clear guidelines for assisting inquirers in a friendly, sensitive manner and assuring appropriate confidentiality. CIVS programs have had a profound impact on campus communities through commitment to the principle of providing inquirers with clear, concise, thorough, and nonjudgmental information and referrals in the most welcoming environment possible.

By the late 1980s, the increasing institutional pressure for better accountability, outreach, and service to the broader campus community resulted in an increase in the number of campus information and visitor services operations. Easy accessibility to appropriate and timely information is a critical component for institutions in reaching instructional, research, and outreach goals. For many constituents, especially during downtimes—evenings, weekends, and breaks—campus information and visitor services programs become the physical embodiment of an institution. Increasing emphasis on quality improvement and service within the higher education community has been another driving force in the growing number of campus information and visitor services programs. The importance of the Internet, mass communication (e.g., radio and cable television), and new media (e.g., streaming video, podcasts) in the provision of information, and the need for support services that can assure the accuracy and relevance of this information, have also served to increase the importance of campus information and visitor services programs. By having access to an easily available and credible information and visitor services program, inquirers are assisted in making well-informed choices, planning wise courses of action, and taking advantage of the available and/or unique resources of the institution and the surrounding community.

These standards and guidelines provide a framework for excellence in the provision of campus information and visitor services. CIVS is the process of linking people who have campus-related questions to the appropriate resources and services. Also, CIVS provides feedback to service providers and discovers gaps and duplication in campus programs and services that should be addressed. This feedback loop can lead to quality service improvements that make campus operations more efficient. Inquiries can comprise anything related to the campus community, such as directions to a campus building or event; how to contact a department, faculty or staff member; or whom to contact or where to go for issues of a personal nature, to resolve a problem, or to apply for admission. Inquirers may be current students, staff, faculty, alumni, prospective students and their families, other visitors, or anyone needing information about the institution. CIVS programs serve as a gateway to the institution, providing one-on-one information to inquirers. When a direct answer is not possible, then the goal is to make a referral, paying careful attention to the needs of the inquirer, assessment of appropriate resources and response modes, identification of programs and services capable of meeting those needs, provision of sufficient information about each program and service to help inquirers make informed choices, location of alternative resources when services are unavailable, and active linking of the inquirer to needed services when necessary.

The standards and guidelines that follow are intended to assist in the development of CIVS programs that make such high quality service possible.

References, Readings, and Resources

Hefferlin, J.B. L. (1971). *Information Services for Academic Administration.* San Francisco: Jossey-Bass

Alliance of Information and Referral Systems. (undated). *Out of the shadows: Information and referral bringing people and services together.* Seattle, Washington: Author.

Alliance of Information and Referral Systems. (undated). *The ABC's of I & R: A self-study guide for information and referral staff.* Seattle, Washington: Author.

Collegiate Information and Visitor Services Association (CIVSA), Rutgers - The State University of New Jersey Campus Information Services, 542 George Street New Brunswick, New Jersey. 08901. (732) 932-9342; (732) 932-9359 (fax); Publisher of *The Welcomer.* Web Site: www.civsa.org

Contributor:
Matthew J. Weismantel, Rutgers University, CIVS

Campus Information and Visitor Services
CAS Standards and Guidelines

Part 1. MISSION

The overall mission of Campus Information and Visitor Services (CIVS) is to facilitate access to the institution by providing accurate information and appropriate referrals. CIVS is a primary point of access to the institution. By providing comprehensive contact information and general descriptions for many aspects of the institution, CIVS must meet the introductory informational needs of the campus community: students, faculty members, staff, prospective students and their family members, alumni, and general visitors.

To accomplish this mission, CIVS must:

- provide accurate information and referrals
- provide a welcoming environment
- be readily accessible
- emphasize personal communication and interaction

CIVS must have a strong commitment to student learning and development, contributing generally to institutional and other agency missions, and because students are an integral part of mission delivery. This commitment must be reflected in its mission statement and demonstrated through quality supervision, staff development, and performance appraisals.

CIVS must develop, disseminate, implement, and regularly review their mission. Mission statements must be consistent with the mission of the institution and with professional standards. CIVS in higher education must enhance overall educational experiences by incorporating student learning and development outcomes in their mission.

Part 2. PROGRAM

Campus Information and Visitor Services (CIVS) must be responsive to the needs and interests of students, faculty members, staff, alumni, prospective students, and other inquirers.

A broad array of information and services must be available to ensure that accurate resources are provided in a timely manner that accommodates the needs of inquirers.

These services may include telephone or other electronic means of contact, or a walk-in facility, such as a visitor or information center, in which the inquirer has one-to-one, human contact and easy access to information resources such as catalogs, calendars, booklets, schedules, fliers, maps, books, and brochures.

Multiple media approaches must be used to provide information.

Such approaches may include signage, maps, 24-hour recorded telephone information, emergency assistance, and up-to-date web-site listings and e-mail.

The formal education of students, consisting of the curriculum and the co-curriculum, must promote student learning and development outcomes that are purposeful and holistic and that prepare students for satisfying and productive lifestyles, work, and civic participation. The student learning and development outcome domains and their related dimensions are:

- knowledge acquisition, integration, construction, and application
  - Dimensions: understanding knowledge from a range of disciplines; connecting knowledge to other knowledge, ideas, and experiences; constructing knowledge; and relating knowledge to daily life

- cognitive complexity
  - Dimensions: critical thinking; reflective thinking; effective reasoning; and creativity

- intrapersonal development
  - Dimensions: realistic self-appraisal, self-understanding, and self-respect; identity development; commitment to ethics and integrity; and spiritual awareness

- interpersonal competence
  - Dimensions: meaningful relationships; interdependence; collaboration; and effective leadership

- humanitarianism and civic engagement
  - Dimensions: understanding and appreciation of cultural and human differences; social responsibility; global perspective; and sense of civic responsibility

- practical competence
  - Dimensions: pursuing goals; communicating effectively; technical competence; managing personal affairs; managing career development; demonstrating professionalism; maintaining health and wellness; and living a purposeful and satisfying life

[See *The Council for the Advancement of Standards Learning and Developmental Outcomes* statement for examples of outcomes related to these domains and dimensions.]

Consistent with the institutional mission, CIVS must identify relevant and desirable student learning and development outcomes from among the six domains and related dimensions. When creating opportunities for student learning and development, CIVS must explore possibilities for collaboration with faculty members and other colleagues.

CIVS must assess relevant and desirable student learning and development outcomes and provide evidence of their impact on student learning and development. CIVS must articulate how they contribute to or support students' learning and development in the domains not specifically assessed.

CIVS must be:
- integrated into the life of the institution
- intentional and coherent
- guided by theories and knowledge of learning and development
- reflective of developmental and demographic profiles of the student population
- responsive to needs of individuals, diverse and special populations, and relevant constituencies

CIVS must provide specific information and referral to existing campus programs or, when such programs do not exist, actively link inquirers to alternative community and other programs that can meet their specific needs.

CIVS programs must be easily accessible to assist inquirers in making well-informed choices, planning wise courses of action, and taking advantage of available institutional resources.

CIVS must develop and maintain an accurate information retrieval and delivery system of available campus and community resources. This system must be updated regularly to ensure timeliness, accuracy, and comprehensiveness of information.

CIVS must be available at locations and times that meet the needs of the inquirers.

CIVS must provide feedback to appropriate campus officials regarding conditions that may negatively influence an inquirer's interaction with the institution and propose interventions to remedy such conditions.

Feedback topics may include statistics, data analysis, relevant documentation of service use (identifying unmet needs, gaps, and services duplication), and inquirer characteristics.

CIVS must strive to assist inquirers in a friendly, caring, sensitive, and non-judgmental manner and provide clear, concise information. CIVS must protect the privacy of individuals within the campus community from inappropriate inquiry.

CIVS must establish and maintain a planned program of activities to increase campus and community awareness of its services, mission, goals, and objectives.

Campus information and visitor services may include a campus visitor center, a campus information center, a campus tour program, broadcast services, campus outreach, and student recruitment programs. Information and services may include:
- campus orientation and tour programs
- display and presentation space
- broadcast and electronic informational resources and support
- visitor reception space including appropriate support services and facilities adequate in size and scope to meet the volume of inquirers to be assisted

CIVS should be a principal provider of structure and content to the institution's on-line information systems.

A range of information should be provided to inquirers, including brief responses, such as names or phone numbers, as well as details about an organization's policies and procedures.

Program activities may include:
- participation in training programs of other offices and departments
- provision of printed materials such as brochures, posters, directional information and exhibits
- public service announcements
- hosting orientation tours
- information-based web site
- role as a resource for other campus and community support services

Part 3. LEADERSHIP

Because effective and ethical leadership is essential to the success of all organizations, Campus Information and Visitor Services (CIVS) leaders with organizational authority for the programs and services must:
- articulate a vision and mission for their programs and services
- set goals and objectives based on the needs of the population served and desired student learning and development outcomes
- advocate for their programs and services
- promote campus environments that provide meaningful opportunities for student learning, development, and integration
- identify and find means to address individual, organizational, or environmental conditions that foster or inhibit mission achievement
- advocate for representation in strategic planning initiatives at appropriate divisional and institutional levels
- initiate collaborative interactions with stakeholders who have legitimate concerns and interests in the functional area
- apply effective practices to educational and administrative processes
- prescribe and model ethical behavior
- communicate effectively
- manage financial resources, including planning, allocation, monitoring, and analysis
- incorporate sustainability practices in the management and design of programs, services, and facilities
- manage human resource processes including recruitment, selection, development, supervision, performance planning, and evaluation
- empower professional, support, and student staff to accept leadership opportunities
- encourage and support scholarly contribution to the profession
- be informed about and integrate appropriate technologies into programs and services

- be knowledgeable about federal, state/provincial, and local laws relevant to the programs and services and ensure that staff members understand their responsibilities by receiving appropriate training
- develop and continuously improve programs and services in response to the changing needs of students and other populations served and the evolving institutional priorities
- recognize environmental conditions that may negatively influence the safety of staff and students and propose interventions that mitigate such conditions

Part 4. HUMAN RESOURCES

Campus Information and Visitor Services (CIVS) must be staffed adequately by individuals qualified to accomplish the mission and goals. Within institutional guidelines, CIVS must establish procedures for staff selection, training, and evaluation; set expectations for supervision; and provide appropriate professional development opportunities to improve the leadership ability, competence, and skills of all employees.

Continuing staff development experiences should include in-service training programs, professional conferences, workshops, and other continuing education activities.

CIVS staff positions must be filled based on a defined set of qualifications such as level of education, work experience, and personal characteristics (e.g., integrity, communication skills, leadership ability).

CIVS professional staff members must hold an earned graduate or professional degree in a field relevant to the position they hold or must possess an appropriate combination of educational credentials and related work experience.

Degree- or credential-seeking interns must be qualified by enrollment in an appropriate field of study and by relevant experience. These individuals must be trained and supervised adequately by professional staff members holding educational credentials and related work experience appropriate for supervision.

Student employees and volunteers must be carefully selected, trained, supervised, and evaluated. They must be educated on how and when to refer those in need of additional assistance to qualified staff members and must have access to a supervisor for assistance in making these judgments. Student employees and volunteers must be provided clear and precise job descriptions, pre-service training based on assessed needs, and continuing staff development.

Employees and volunteers must receive specific training on institutional policies and privacy laws regarding their access to student records and other sensitive institutional information (e.g., in the USA, Family Educational Rights and Privacy Act, FERPA, or equivalent privacy laws in other states/provinces or countries).

CIVS must have technical and support staff members adequate to accomplish their mission. All members of the staff must be technologically proficient and qualified to perform their job functions, be knowledgeable about ethical and legal uses of technology, and have access to training and resources to support the performance of their assigned responsibilities.

All members of the staff must receive training on policies and procedures related to the use of technology to store or access student records and institutional data.

CIVS must ensure that staff members are knowledgeable about and trained in emergency procedures, crisis response, and prevention efforts. Prevention efforts must address identification of threatening conduct or behavior of students, faculty members, staff, and others and must incorporate a system or procedures for responding, including but not limited to reporting them to the appropriate campus officials.

A formal training program must be required for all staff, especially those who will be providing direct service.

Training programs should include experiences for initial employee orientations as well as on-the-job training, in-service group training, and individualized training based on employee needs.

Staff-training programs should include:
- strategies for understanding campus and community resources
- information retrieval, delivery and data collection
- overview of mission, vision, role, purpose, function, structure, policies, and procedures
- student development theory and practice
- customer service and basic communication skills such as interviewing, listening, empathy, clarification and problem-solving; overcoming communication barriers (e.g., hearing impaired, speakers of English as a second language)

Salary levels and benefits for all staff members must be commensurate with those for comparable positions within the institution, in similar institutions, and in the relevant geographic area.

Every CIVS staff member must be expected to show respect for all inquirers.

CIVS must maintain position descriptions for all staff members.

To create a diverse staff, CIVS must institute hiring and promotion practices that are fair, inclusive, proactive, and non-discriminatory.

CIVS must conduct regular performance planning and evaluation of staff members. CIVS must provide access to continuing and advanced education and professional development opportunities.

Periodic formal written evaluations of CIVS staff must be

Periodic formal written evaluations of CIVS staff must be conducted and kept on record.

Part 5. ETHICS

Persons involved in the delivery of Campus Information and Visitor Services (CIVS) must adhere to the highest principles of ethical behavior. CIVS must review relevant professional ethical standards and develop or adopt and implement appropriate statements of ethical practice. CIVS must publish these statements and ensure their periodic review by relevant constituencies.

Ethical standards or other statements from relevant professional associations should be considered.

CIVS must orient new staff members to relevant ethical standards and statements of ethical practice.

CIVS staff members must ensure that privacy and confidentiality are maintained with respect to all communications and records to the extent that such records are protected under the law and appropriate statements of ethical practice. Information contained in students' education records must not be disclosed except as allowed by relevant laws and institutional policies. CIVS staff members must disclose to appropriate authorities information judged to be of an emergency nature, especially when the safety of the individual or others is involved, or when otherwise required by institutional policy or relevant law.

CIVS staff members must be aware of and comply with the provisions contained in the institution's policies pertaining to human subjects research and student rights and responsibilities, as well as those in other relevant institutional policies addressing ethical practices and confidentiality of research data concerning individuals.

CIVS staff members must recognize and avoid personal conflicts of interest or appearance thereof in the performance of their work.

CIVS staff members must strive to insure the fair, objective, and impartial treatment of all persons with whom they interact.

When handling institutional funds, CIVS staff members must ensure that such funds are managed in accordance with established and responsible accounting procedures and the fiscal policies or processes of the institution.

Promotional and descriptive information must be accurate and free of deception.

CIVS staff members must perform their duties within the limits of their training, expertise, and competence. When these limits are exceeded, individuals in need of further assistance must be referred to persons possessing appropriate qualifications.

CIVS staff members must use suitable means to confront and otherwise hold accountable other staff members who exhibit unethical behavior.

CIVS staff members must be knowledgeable about and practice ethical behavior in the use of technology.

Part 6. LEGAL RESPONSIBILITIES

Campus Information and Visitor Services (CIVS) staff members must be knowledgeable about and responsive to laws and regulations that relate to their respective responsibilities and that may pose legal obligations, limitations, or ramifications for the institution as a whole. As appropriate, staff members must inform users of programs and services, as well as officials, of legal obligations and limitations including constitutional, statutory, regulatory, and case law; mandatory laws and orders emanating from federal, state/provincial, and local governments; and the institution's policies.

CIVS must have written policies on all relevant operations, transactions, or tasks that may have legal implications.

CIVS staff members must neither participate in nor condone any form of harassment or activity that demeans persons or creates an intimidating, hostile, or offensive campus environment.

CIVS staff members must use reasonable and informed practices to limit the liability exposure of the institution and its officers, employees, and agents. CIVS staff members must be informed about institutional policies regarding risk management, personal liability, and related insurance coverage options and must be referred to external sources if coverage is not provided by the institution.

The institution must provide access to legal advice for CIVS staff members as needed to carry out assigned responsibilities.

The institution must inform CIVS staff and students in a timely and systematic fashion about extraordinary or changing legal obligations and potential liabilities.

Part 7. EQUITY and ACCESS

Campus Information and Visitor Services (CIVS) must be provided on a fair, equitable, and non-discriminatory basis in accordance with institutional policies and with all applicable state/provincial and federal statutes and regulations. CIVS must maintain an educational and work environment free from discrimination in accordance with law and institutional policy.

Discrimination must be avoided on the basis of age; cultural heritage; disability; ethnicity; gender identity and expression; nationality; political affiliation; race; religious affiliation; sex; sexual orientation; economic, marital, social, or veteran status; and any other bases included in local, state/provincial, or federal laws.

Consistent with the mission and goals, CIVS must take action to remedy significant imbalances in student participation and staffing patterns.

CIVS must ensure physical and program access for persons with disabilities. CIVS must be responsive to the needs of all students and other populations served when establishing hours of operation and developing methods of delivering programs and services.

CIVS must recognize the needs of distance learning students by providing appropriate and accessible services and assisting them in identifying and gaining access to other appropriate services in their geographic region.

Part 8. DIVERSITY

Within the context of each institution's unique mission, diversity enriches the community and enhances the collegiate experience for all; therefore, Campus Information and Visitor Services (CIVS) must create and nurture environments that are welcoming to and bring together persons of diverse backgrounds.

CIVS must promote environments that are characterized by open and continuous communication that deepens understanding of one's own identity, culture, and heritage, as well as that of others. CIVS must recognize, honor, educate, and promote respect about commonalties and differences among people within their historical and cultural contexts.

CIVS must address the characteristics and needs of a diverse population when establishing and implementing policies and procedures.

Part 9. ORGANIZATION and MANAGEMENT

Campus Information and Visitor Services (CIVS) is most effective in an atmosphere of staff teamwork and continuous improvement.

To promote student learning and development outcomes, CIVS must be structured purposefully and managed effectively to achieve stated goals. Evidence of appropriate structure must include current and accessible policies and procedures, written performance expectations for all employees, functional workflow graphics or organizational charts, and clearly stated program and service delivery expectations.

CIVS must monitor websites used for distributing information to ensure that the sites are current, accurate, appropriately referenced, and accessible.

Evidence of effective management must include use of comprehensive and accurate information for decisions, clear sources and channels of authority, effective communication practices, procedures for decision-making and conflict resolution, responses to changing conditions, systems of accountability and evaluation, and processes for recognition

and reward. CIVS must align policies and procedures with those of the institution and provide channels within the organization for their regular review.

CIVS must have well developed policies regarding the type, breadth, and currency of information contained in the information retrieval and delivery system. The information retrieval and delivery system used by campus information and visitor services must be organized according to a standardized search system. The information system must have the capacity to accept changes in a very short time frame for information that may change in between regularly scheduled updates.

Policies for the information retrieval and delivery system should include, but not be limited to, responsiveness to inquirers and proximity of the resource to the campus.

CIVS must develop and maintain accurate, up-to-date resource files that include information on available campus resources and procedures for verifying accuracy.

Informational resources should be profiled to include:
- legal name, common name, and acronym address (i.e., room, building name, street, city, zip code)
- email address
- telephone number, fax number, hours and days of service
- type and description of service(s) provided
- population(s) served
- date of last update
- internet address
- eligibility guidelines
- intake procedures
- required documents
- cost
- waiting period for service
- contact person
- auspices (i.e., city, state/province, private, social service, campus)

CIVS must establish and use a system of collecting and organizing inquirer data for appropriate referral and feedback to the campus community.

Campus information and visitor services should pursue meaningful research to review and improve programs and services. Members of the campus community should be involved in the review of these findings, as well as in the design and governance of campus information and visitor services. Students, faculty members, staff, and appropriate external agencies should be involved through committees, councils, and boards.

Part 10. CAMPUS and EXTERNAL RELATIONS

Campus Information and Visitor Services (CIVS) must reach out to relevant individuals, campus offices, and external agencies to:
- establish, maintain, and promote effective relations
- disseminate information about their own and other

related programs and services
- coordinate and collaborate, where appropriate, in offering programs and services to meet the needs of students and promote their achievement of student learning and development outcomes

CIVS must have procedures and guidelines consistent with institutional policy for responding to threats, emergencies, and crisis situations. Systems and procedures must be in place to disseminate timely and accurate information to students and other members of the campus community during emergency situations.

CIVS must have procedures and guidelines consistent with institutional policy for communicating with the media.

CIVS should collaborate closely with campus offices and external agencies to ensure accuracy, timeliness, and reliability of information being provided to inquirers.

When appropriate, inquirers should be referred to other resources, and staff may actively participate in this linking process. This referral process is often integrated with information dissemination, intervention, and advocacy. Inquirers should be encouraged to re-contact the campus information and visitor service if additional information or assistance is needed.

Within institutional guidelines, CIVS should intervene and advocate for inquirers when information is inaccurate or misleading and/or inquirer needs have not been addressed satisfactorily. Follow-up on more complex problem situations should occur to determine the extent to which inquirer needs have been met.

Part 11. FINANCIAL RESOURCES

Campus Information and Visitor Services (CIVS) must have adequate funding to accomplish their mission and goals. In establishing funding priorities and making significant changes, a comprehensive analysis, which includes relevant expenditures, external and internal resources, and impact on the campus community, must be conducted.

CIVS must demonstrate fiscal responsibility and cost effectiveness consistent with institutional protocols.

Institutional funds for campus information and visitor services should be allocated on a permanent basis.

In addition to institutional commitment of general funds, other funding sources may be considered including state/provincial appropriations, federal resources, fees and generated revenue, local community funding, donations, and contributions.

Financial resources should be sufficient to provide high quality print and electronic information.

Part 12. TECHNOLOGY

Campus Information and Visitor Services (CIVS) must have adequate technology to support their mission. The technology and its use must comply with institutional policies and

procedures and be evaluated for compliance with relevant federal, state/provincial, and local requirements.

CIVS must maintain policies and procedures that address the security and back up of data.

When technology is used to facilitate student learning and development, CIVS must select technology that reflects current best pedagogical practices.

Technology, as well as any workstations or computer labs maintained by the CIVS for student use, must be accessible and must meet established technology standards for delivery to persons with disabilities.

When CIVS provide student access to technology, they must provide:
- access to policies that are clear, easy to understand, and available to all students
- access to instruction or training on how to use the technology
- access to information on the legal and ethical implications of misuse as it pertains to intellectual property, harassment, privacy, and social networks

Student violations of technology policies must follow established institutional student disciplinary procedures.

Students who experience negative emotional or psychological consequences from the use of technology must be referred to support services provided by the institution.

Part 13. FACILITIES and EQUIPMENT

Campus Information and Visitor Services (CIVS) must have adequate, accessible, suitably located facilities and equipment to support their mission and goals. If acquiring capital equipment as defined by the institution, CIVS must take into account expenses related to regular maintenance and life cycle costs. Facilities and equipment must be evaluated regularly, including consideration of sustainability, and be in compliance with relevant federal, state/provincial, and local requirements to provide for access, health, safety, and security.

CIVS staff members must have work space that is well-equipped, adequate in size, and designed to support their work and responsibilities. For conversations requiring privacy, staff members must have access to a private space.

CIVS staff members who share work space must have the ability to secure their work adequately.

The design of the facilities must guarantee the security of records and ensure the confidentiality of sensitive information.

The location and layout of the facilities must be sensitive to the special needs of persons with disabilities as well as the needs of constituencies served.

CIVS must ensure that staff members are knowledgeable of

and trained in safety and emergency procedures for securing and vacating the facilities.

CIVS must play an active role in the design and decision-making process for campus signage.

The CIVS facility should include space for confidential interviewing, display for materials, visitor reception, and information and referral operations. State-of-the-art telephone and computer capability should also be included.

The CIVS facility should be accessible to and by public transportation and be at a location that can best represent the "front door" of the institution.

Part 14. ASSESSMENT and EVALUATION

Campus Information and Visitor Services (CIVS) must establish systematic plans and processes to meet internal and external accountability expectations with regard to program as well as student learning and development outcomes. CIVS must conduct regular assessment and evaluations. Assessments must include qualitative and quantitative methodologies as appropriate, to determine whether and to what degree the stated mission, goals, and student learning and development outcomes are being met. The process must employ sufficient and sound measures to ensure comprehensiveness. Data collected must include responses from students and other affected constituencies.

CIVS must evaluate regularly how well they complement and enhance the institution's stated mission and educational effectiveness.

Results of these evaluations must be used in revising and improving programs and services, identifying needs and interests in shaping directions of program and service design, and recognizing staff performance.

CIVS must maintain an on-going process to collect inquirer use and inquirer satisfaction information.

General Standards revised in 2008;
CIVS content developed/revised in 2000

Campus Religious and/or Spiritual Programs
CAS Standards and Guidelines

The origins of religious programs at colleges and universities can be traced to their earliest beginnings in Colonial America. The first institutions of higher education were based on Protestant Christian values and had the education of clergy as one of their primary purposes. Religious and moral instruction served as the foundation of the curriculum and formed the cornerstone of a college life whose primary goal was to educate a new elite class of leaders and professionals for the young American nation (Cawthon & Jones, 2004; Hartley, 2004; Temkin & Evans, 1998).

During the 19th century, the purpose of higher education shifted away from religion toward scholarship and research, leading to a more secular culture on college campuses, where religion became marginalized (Hartley, 2004). The Morrill Land-Grant Act of 1862 and Morrill Act of 1890 made public education more available and led to the increased enrollment of students from a variety of religious and spiritual backgrounds (Butler, 1989). The creation of this new "modern" university, the weakening between institutions and their founding religious denominations, and increases in the number of non-Protestant students on college campuses, caused religious denominations to establish a variety of student organizations (e.g., Baptist Student Union, Catholic Newman Club, Jewish Hillel, Presbyterian Student Association, United Methodist Wesley Foundation) during a period from the early 1900s to 1950s. A number of independent ecumenical organizations (e.g., Campus Crusade for Christ, Fellowship of Christian Athletes, InterVarsity Fellowship) not associated with specific denominations originated during this period (Cawthon & Jones, 2004).

In defining terms such as spirituality and religion, individuals construct meanings that are as varied as the ways institutions structure programs related to this area. This standard can be used as a guide to help both assess the needs of students and to structure student religious programs to serve these needs. As students look toward more diverse options to fulfill their spiritual and religious development, institutions should continue to equip staff with knowledge of issues that surround these programs.

For the purposes of these standards, religion is defined by function, rather than substance. Spirituality, more nebulous but present and relevant as a concept and practice on college campuses, is not synonymous with religion. Spiritually-related activities are defined as outward signs of internal meaning making processes (Love, 2001).

A clear distinction should be made between two separate but related functions of an educational institution: providing for the academic study of religions, and for programs that promote the spiritual and moral development of its students. A distinction should also be made between accommodation and promotion of religions and faiths by public institutions. The courts have mandated an even-handed accommodation of religious beliefs, but prohibited the promotion of a particular religious belief. According to the courts, any public institution's program must meet the following conditions to avoid violating the "establishment" clause of the US Constitution: It must have a secular purpose; its principal or primary effect must be one that neither advances nor inhibits religion; and it must not foster an excessive entanglement of the public institution with religion.

Recently there has been a noticeable increase of interest in religious and spiritual matters on college campuses (Love, 2001). Manning contends that the factors impacting this increase include: (1) Generation X's shift from materialism, (2) Baby Boomers becoming more reflective as they age, or (3) a desire for concrete meaning in a post modern world (2001). The diversification of American higher education has led to an environment where various religious and spiritual faiths and practices are more accepted (Hartley, 2004). As college campuses have become more diverse ethnically and culturally, particularly with the increased enrollment of international students at American colleges and universities, there has been an increase in the presence of non-Judeo-Christian religious groups and organizations (e.g., Muslim Student Association, Pagan Student Association, Unitarian Universalist Association) (Temkin & Evans, 1998).

While people may argue the impetus for the increase in interest, the importance of it must not be missed. Love points out that spirituality exists in everyday life and not just religious practices and that spiritually-related activities are outward signs of meaning making processes (2001). Fowler believed this to be true when he set out to "operationalize a rich concept of faith and to begin to look more systematically at faith in a constructive-developmental perspective" (2001). Involvement with religiously-affiliated student organizations or clubs can also provide an avenue for students to develop leadership and interpersonal skills. Religious programs and services often provide significant out-of-classroom developmental opportunities for college students.

Campus Religious/Spiritual Programs may be structured differently on individual campuses according to the needs and limitations of each institution. There is no preferred organizational or programming structure. Organization structures range from coordinating committees to individual staff members that work directly with these programs. Institution type, size, goals and mission are just a few of the factors that impact the workings of religious/spiritual programs on a campus. One major difference among institutions is between public and private secular colleges and universities and private religiously affiliated colleges and universities. The later type of institution may expect staff to sign creeds, have specific religious training, and may have a religiously-oriented mission statement that states its preference towards a particular faith or denomination, while the former may have legal constraints or preferences that prevent them from engaging in the same expectations. In general the courts have held that the First Amendment provides protection to religious believers and non-believers, and that the state shall be neutral in its relations with persons who profess a belief or disbelief in any religion, *Everson v. Board of Education*, 330 US 1(1977). This is particularly applicable to public institutions. However, the legal standards related to dealing with religious/spiritual programs across higher education are in a constant state of change and evolution. Therefore, those who administer Campus Religious and Spiritual Programs (CRSP) must work to maintain familiarity with current relevant case law.

References, Readings, and Resources

Butler, J. (1989). An overview of religion on campus. In Butler, J. (Ed.). Religion on campus. *New Directions for Student Services*, No. 46. San Francisco: Jossey-Bass.

Cawthon, T. W., & Jones, C. (2004). A description of traditional and contemporary campus ministries. *College Student Affairs Journal, 23*(2), p. 158-172.

Fowler, J.W. (2001). Faith development theory and the postmodern challenges. *The International Journal for the Psychology of Religion, 11*, 159-172.

Hartley, H. V. III (2004). How college affects students' religious faith and practice: A review of the research. *College Student Affairs Journal, 23*(2), p. 111-129.

Love, P.G. (2001). Spirituality and student development: Theoretical connections. *New Directions for Student Services, 95*, 7-16.

Manning, K. (2001). Infusing soul into student affairs: Organizational theory and models. *New Directions for Student Services, 95*, 27-35.

Temkin, L., & Evans, N. J. (1998). Religion on campus: Suggestions for cooperation between student affairs and campus-based religious organizations. *NASPA Journal, 36*(1), p. 61- 69.

Association of College and University Religious Affairs — http://www.acuraonline.org

National Association of College and University Chaplains — http://www.nacuc.net

National Campus Ministry Association — http://www.campusministry.net

Contributors:
Current edition:
Diane L. Cooper, University of Georgia
Merrily Dunn, University of Georgia
S. Bryan Rush, University of Georgia/Erskine College
J.D. White, University of Georgia/Student Voice
Previous editions:
Diane L. Cooper, University of Georgia

Campus Religious and/or Spiritual Programs
CAS Standards and Guidelines

Part 1. MISSION

The purpose of Campus Religious and/or Spiritual Programs (CRSP) is to provide access to programs that enable interested students to pursue full spiritual growth and development and to foster a campus atmosphere in which interested members of the college community may freely express their religion, spirituality, and faith.

A private or religiously affiliated institution may state its preference for a particular faith or spiritual tradition and may directly use its own resources for this purpose.

CRSP must develop, disseminate, implement, and regularly review their mission. Mission statements must be consistent with the mission of the institution and with professional standards. CRSP in higher education must enhance overall educational experiences by incorporating student learning and development outcomes in their mission.

Public institutions without formal religious and/or spiritual programs should make provisions for religious and spiritual programs indirectly, that is, through cooperation with off-campus agencies that provide religious services and programs.

The goals of CRSP should provide opportunities for interested students to:
- receive the religious and/or spiritual support they seek
- articulate a personal philosophy
- acquire skills and knowledge to address issues of values, ethics, and morality
- examine the interaction of faith, intellectual inquiry, and social responsibility as bases for finding and affirming meaning and satisfaction in life
- participate in dialogue between and among representatives of the religious and/or spiritual and the secular
- participate with others in the expression of their faith(s)

Part 2. PROGRAM

The formal education of students, consisting of the curriculum and the co-curriculum, must promote student learning and development outcomes that are purposeful and holistic and that prepare students for satisfying and productive lifestyles, work, and civic participation. The student learning and development outcome domains and their related dimensions are:

- **knowledge acquisition, integration, construction, and application**
    - o **Dimensions: understanding knowledge from a range of disciplines; connecting knowledge to other knowledge, ideas, and experiences; constructing knowledge; and relating knowledge to daily life**

- **cognitive complexity**
    - o **Dimensions: critical thinking; reflective thinking; effective reasoning; and creativity**

- **intrapersonal development**
    - o **Dimensions: realistic self-appraisal, self-understanding, and self-respect; identity development; commitment to ethics and integrity; and spiritual awareness**

- **interpersonal competence**
    - o **Dimensions: meaningful relationships; interdependence; collaboration; and effective leadership**

- **humanitarianism and civic engagement**
    - o **Dimensions: understanding and appreciation of cultural and human differences; social responsibility; global perspective; and sense of civic responsibility**

- **practical competence**
    - o **Dimensions: pursuing goals; communicating effectively; technical competence; managing personal affairs; managing career development; demonstrating professionalism; maintaining health and wellness; and living a purposeful and satisfying life**

[See *The Council for the Advancement of Standards Learning and Developmental Outcomes* statement for examples of outcomes related to these domains and dimensions.]

Consistent with the institutional mission, Campus Religious and/or Spiritual Programs (CRSP) must identify relevant and desirable student learning and development outcomes from among the six domains and related dimensions. When creating opportunities for student learning and development, CRSP must explore possibilities for collaboration with faculty members and other colleagues.

CRSP must assess relevant and desirable student learning and development outcomes and provide evidence of their impact on student learning and development. CRSP must articulate how they contribute to or support students' learning and development in the domains not specifically assessed.

CRSP must be:
- integrated into the life of the institution
- intentional and coherent
- guided by theories and knowledge of learning and development
- reflective of developmental and demographic profiles of the student population
- responsive to needs of individuals, diverse and special populations, and relevant constituencies

CRSP will vary depending on the requirements and beliefs of specific denominations and faiths, as well as the needs and traditions of the particular institution.

To the extent either required or prohibited by constitutional, statutory, or regulatory provisions, institutions must provide reasonable opportunities for students to:

- **question, explore, understand, affiliate with or avoid, and express or reject various religious faiths and/or spiritual beliefs and practices**
- **seek individual counseling or group associations for the examination and application of religious and/or spiritual values and beliefs**
- **worship communally and individually**
- **pray and meditate**

In public institutions, staff members may coordinate programs, while personnel associated with religious groups provide direct service to campus community.

In religiously affiliated and private secular colleges, religious programs and direct service may be provided by staff members of the institution.

The types of religious programs and activities offered may include:
- co-curricular religious studies
- opportunities for religious and/or spiritual nurturance
- service opportunities
- where appropriate by law, regulation, or policy, opportunity to propagate religions or faiths
- where appropriate by law, regulation, or policy, opportunity to practice rituals of religion or faith
- advocacy for particular ethical or moral policies in public life
- opportunities to relate religious and spiritual beliefs to academic and professional programs
- programs that mark significant events or experiences in the life of the community, e.g., death, tragedy, memorials, or celebrations

In addition, institutions may provide guidance services to promote spiritual or religious growth. Co-curricular programs (e.g., lectures, discussions, service projects) that are designed to help students understand their faiths and the faiths of others may also be offered.

Part 3. LEADERSHIP

Because effective and ethical leadership is essential to the success of all organizations, Campus Religious and/or Spiritual Programs (CRSP) leaders with organizational authority for the programs and services must:

- **articulate a vision and mission for their programs and services**
- **set goals and objectives based on the needs of the population served and desired student learning and development outcomes**
- **advocate for their programs and services**
- **promote campus environments that provide meaningful opportunities for student learning, development, and integration**
- **identify and find means to address individual, organizational, or environmental conditions that foster or inhibit mission achievement**

- **advocate for representation in strategic planning initiatives at appropriate divisional and institutional levels**
- **initiate collaborative interactions with stakeholders who have legitimate concerns and interests in the functional area**
- **apply effective practices to educational and administrative processes**
- **prescribe and model ethical behavior**
- **communicate effectively**
- **manage financial resources, including planning, allocation, monitoring, and analysis**
- **incorporate sustainability practices in the management and design of programs, services, and facilities**
- **manage human resource processes including recruitment, selection, development, supervision, performance planning, and evaluation**
- **empower professional, support, and student staff to accept leadership opportunities**
- **encourage and support scholarly contribution to the profession**
- **be informed about and integrate appropriate technologies into programs and services**
- **be knowledgeable about federal, state/provincial, and local laws relevant to the programs and services and ensure that staff members understand their responsibilities by receiving appropriate training**
- **develop and continuously improve programs and services in response to the changing needs of students and other populations served and the evolving institutional priorities**
- **recognize environmental conditions that may negatively influence the safety of staff and students and propose interventions that mitigate such conditions**

Part 4. HUMAN RESOURCES

Campus Religious and/or Spiritual Programs (CRSP) must be staffed adequately by individuals qualified to accomplish the mission and goals. Within institutional guidelines, CRSP must establish procedures for staff selection, training, and evaluation; set expectations for supervision; and provide appropriate professional development opportunities to improve the leadership ability, competence, and skills of all employees.

At public institutions, religious programs may be coordinated by a professional individual and/or a committee. Professional or volunteer persons named (and paid) by the religious and spiritual groups represented on the campus may carry out their respective activities. The title "director" or "coordinator" of religious programs is more appropriate because of the predominantly educational and liaison functions of the position.

At private institutions, campus religious programs are typically coordinated by a professional in an appropriate field or a committee. Additional staff members may be employed by the institution. Religious groups may also provide additional staff for the institution.

Religiously related institutions should permit on-campus programs of religions or spiritual beliefs other than those espoused by the institution. Titles for the director or coordinator at private institutions include chaplain, director of religious life or spiritual development, or other title specific to a religious or spiritual tradition.

CRSP professional staff members must hold an earned graduate or professional degree in a field relevant to the position they hold or must possess an appropriate combination of educational credentials and related work experience.

When the coordinator of religious and/or spiritual programs represents a particular religious and/or spiritual body, that person should possess qualifications consistent with the particular body represented and appropriate for a higher education setting.

Any director or coordinator should have:
- an understanding of and a commitment to spiritual and religious development as a part of a student's human growth
- the ability to treat fairly all varieties of campus religious experience and personal faith
- awareness and understanding of the beliefs of religious and spiritual groups affiliated with that campus

Depending upon the legal constraints of the institution, the responsibilities of the director or coordinator for religious and/or spiritual programs may include:
- the development and communication of policies relating to religious and spiritual programs that are educationally sound and legally acceptable
- the development of procedures whereby students may organize for religious, spiritual, or moral purposes and participate in programs and activities aimed at their spiritual and/or religious growth
- the provision of access to campus facilities for those responsible for religious or spiritual programs
- the provision of opportunities for guidance in relation to students' religious or spiritual needs
- coordination with other campus decision makers on matters related to religious and/or spiritual activities such as scheduling and examinations

Degree- or credential-seeking interns must be qualified by enrollment in an appropriate field of study and by relevant experience. These individuals must be trained and supervised adequately by professional staff members holding educational credentials and related work experience appropriate for supervision.

Student employees and volunteers must be carefully selected, trained, supervised, and evaluated. They must be educated on how and when to refer those in need of additional assistance to qualified staff members and must have access to a supervisor for assistance in making these judgments. Student employees and volunteers must be provided clear and precise job descriptions, pre-service training based on assessed needs, and continuing staff development.

Employees and volunteers must receive specific training on institutional policies and privacy laws regarding their access to student records and other sensitive institutional information (e.g., in the USA, Family Educational Rights and Privacy Act, FERPA, or equivalent privacy laws in other states/provinces or countries).

CRSP must have technical and support staff members adequate to accomplish their mission. All members of the staff must be technologically proficient and qualified to perform their job functions, be knowledgeable about ethical and legal uses of technology, and have access to training and resources to support the performance of their assigned responsibilities.

All members of the staff must receive training on policies and procedures related to the use of technology to store or access student records and institutional data.

CRSP must ensure that staff members are knowledgeable about and trained in emergency procedures, crisis response, and prevention efforts. Prevention efforts must address identification of threatening conduct or behavior of students, faculty members, staff, and others and must incorporate a system or procedures for responding, including but not limited to reporting them to the appropriate campus officials.

Salary levels and benefits for all staff members must be commensurate with those for comparable positions within the institution, in similar institutions, and in the relevant geographic area.

Officials should be fair and equitable in relationships with all agencies participating in the program.

CRSP must maintain position descriptions for all staff members.

To create a diverse staff, CRSP must institute hiring and promotion practices that are fair, inclusive, proactive, and non-discriminatory.

CRSP must conduct regular performance planning and evaluation of staff members. CRSP must provide access to continuing and advanced education and professional development opportunities.

Affiliation with appropriate professional organizations is encrouaged.

When a staff member represents a particular religious and/or spiritual body, that person should possess qualifications consistent with the particular body they represent and appropriate for a higher education setting.

Part 5. ETHICS

Persons involved in the delivery of Campus Religious and/or Spiritual Programs (CRSP) must adhere to the highest principles of ethical behavior. Programs CRSP must review relevant professional ethical standards and develop or adopt

and implement appropriate statements of ethical practice. CRSP must publish these statements and ensure their periodic review by relevant constituencies.

CRSP must orient new staff members to relevant ethical standards and statements of ethical practice.

CRSP staff members must ensure that privacy and confidentiality are maintained with respect to all communications and records to the extent that such records are protected under the law and appropriate statements of ethical practice. Information contained in students' education records must not be disclosed except as allowed by relevant laws and institutional policies. CRSP staff members must disclose to appropriate authorities information judged to be of an emergency nature, especially when the safety of the individual or others is involved, or when otherwise required by institutional policy or relevant law.

CRSP staff members must be aware of and comply with the provisions contained in the institution's policies pertaining to human subjects research and student rights and responsibilities, as well as those in other relevant institutional policies addressing ethical practices and confidentiality of research data concerning individuals.

CRSP staff members must recognize and avoid personal conflicts of interest or appearance thereof in the performance of their work.

CRSP staff members must strive to insure the fair, objective, and impartial treatment of all persons with whom they interact.

Accommodation must be made so that students, faculty members, and staff from various religions and faiths may carry out the essential practices of their belief systems.

When handling institutional funds, CRSP staff members must ensure that such funds are managed in accordance with established and responsible accounting procedures and the fiscal policies or processes of the institution.

Promotional and descriptive information must be accurate and free of deception.

CRSP staff members must perform their duties within the limits of their training, expertise, and competence. When these limits are exceeded, individuals in need of further assistance must be referred to persons possessing appropriate qualifications.

CRSP staff members must use suitable means to confront and otherwise hold accountable other staff members who exhibit unethical behavior.

CRSP staff members must be knowledgeable about and practice ethical behavior in the use of technology.

CRSP staff members must avoid any actions that favor one particular faith over another.

As the institution carries out its academic program, fair and reasonable consideration should be given to the need of campus members to participate in the basic activities of their faiths. Institutional policies and practices should be reviewed regularly so as to avoid undue interference with the exercise of religious and/or spiritual traditions.

Private institutions that sponsor or require particular religious activities must clearly state so in their pre-admission literature, thus permitting a potential student to exercise choice in this regard before admission.

CRSP staff members must work to provide reasonable access for all groups and points of view to any public forums sponsored by the institution.

Membership requirements for on-campus religious organizations at public institutions must be consistent with the group's stated purposes. All religious and/or spiritual organizations must be accorded the same rights and privileges and be held accountable in the same manner as any other campus organization.

CRSP staff members must attempt to protect students, through policy and practice, from undue influence or harassment from persons advocating particular religious positions or activities.

Part 6. LEGAL RESPONSIBILITIES

Campus Religious and/or Spiritual Programs (CRSP) staff members must be knowledgeable about and responsive to laws and regulations that relate to their respective responsibilities and that may pose legal obligations, limitations, or ramifications for the institution as a whole. As appropriate, staff members must inform users of programs and services, as well as officials, of legal obligations and limitations including constitutional, statutory, regulatory, and case law; mandatory laws and orders emanating from federal, state/provincial, and local governments; and the institution's policies.

CRSP must have written policies on all relevant operations, transactions, or tasks that may have legal implications.

CRSP staff members must neither participate in nor condone any form of harassment or activity that demeans persons or creates an intimidating, hostile, or offensive campus environment.

CRSP staff members must use reasonable and informed practices to limit the liability exposure of the institution and its officers, employees, and agents. CRSP staff members must be informed about institutional policies regarding risk management, personal liability, and related insurance coverage options and must be referred to external sources if coverage is not provided by the institution.

The institution must provide access to legal advice for CRSP staff members as needed to carry out assigned responsibilities.

The institution must inform CRSP staff and students in a timely and systematic fashion about extraordinary or changing legal obligations and potential liabilities.

Part 7. EQUITY and ACCESS

Campus Religious and/or Spiritual Programs (CRSP) must be provided on a fair, equitable, and non-discriminatory basis in accordance with institutional policies and with all applicable state/provincial and federal statutes and regulations. CRSP must maintain an educational and work environment free from discrimination in accordance with law and institutional policy.

Discrimination must be avoided on the basis of age; cultural heritage; disability; ethnicity; gender identity and expression; nationality; political affiliation; race; religious affiliation; sex; sexual orientation; economic, marital, social, or veteran status; and any other bases included in local, state/provincial, or federal laws.

Consistent with the mission and goals, CRSP must take action to remedy significant imbalances in student participation and staffing patterns.

CRSP must ensure physical and program access for persons with disabilities. CRSP must be responsive to the needs of all students and other populations served when establishing hours of operation and developing methods of delivering programs and services.

CRSP must recognize the needs of distance learning students by providing appropriate and accessible services and assisting them in identifying and gaining access to other appropriate services in their geographic region.

Part 8. DIVERSITY

Within the context of each institution's unique mission, diversity enriches the community and enhances the collegiate experience for all; therefore, Campus Religious and/or Spiritual Programs (CRSP) must create and nurture environments that are welcoming to and bring together persons of diverse backgrounds.

CRSP must promote environments that are characterized by open and continuous communication that deepens understanding of one's own identity, culture, and heritage, as well as that of others. CRSP must recognize, honor, educate, and promote respect about commonalties and differences among people within their historical and cultural contexts.

CRSP must address the characteristics and needs of a diverse population when establishing and implementing policies and procedures.

Part 9. ORGANIZATION and MANAGEMENT

To promote student learning and development outcomes,

Campus Religious and/or Spiritual Programs (CRSP) must be structured purposefully and managed effectively to achieve stated goals. Evidence of appropriate structure must include current and accessible policies and procedures, written performance expectations for all employees, functional workflow graphics or organizational charts, and clearly stated program and service delivery expectations.

CRSP must monitor websites used for distributing information to ensure that the sites are current, accurate, appropriately referenced, and accessible.

Evidence of effective management must include use of comprehensive and accurate information for decisions, clear sources and channels of authority, effective communication practices, procedures for decision-making and conflict resolution, responses to changing conditions, systems of accountability and evaluation, and processes for recognition and reward. CRSP must align policies and procedures with those of the institution and provide channels within the organization for their regular review.

CRSP activities, policies, and procedures should be scrutinized regularly in light of the growing body of law in the area of religion and higher education.

Part 10. CAMPUS and EXTERNAL RELATIONS

Campus Religious and/or Spiritual Programs (CRSP) must reach out to relevant individuals, campus offices, and external agencies to:
- establish, maintain, and promote effective relations
- disseminate information about their own and other related programs and services
- coordinate and collaborate, where appropriate, in offering programs and services to meet the needs of students and promote their achievement of student learning and development outcomes

CRSP must have procedures and guidelines consistent with institutional policy for responding to threats, emergencies, and crisis situations. Systems and procedures must be in place to disseminate timely and accurate information to students and other members of the campus community during emergency situations.

CRSP must have procedures and guidelines consistent with institutional policy for communicating with the media.

Because religion and/or spirituality may be a concern of many academic disciplines and may have an important impact on student development, staff assigned to religious programs should consult with and coordinate their programs with interested colleagues.

The CRSP director or coordinator may interact with faculty and staff formally through advisory councils or through informal contacts.

Continuing attention should be given to developing and improving relationships with both on-campus and off-campus constituencies. Specific religious and/or spiritual programs and action projects may arise from many sources (e.g., academic departments, on-campus functional areas such as residence halls and campus centers, and off-campus organizations, whether local, regional, national, and/or international).

The coordinator, faculty, staff, and administrators of the institution should meet with personnel from religious and/or spiritual groups on a periodic basis.

Part 11. FINANCIAL RESOURCES

Campus Religious and/or Spiritual Programs (CRSP) must have adequate funding to accomplish their mission and goals. In establishing funding priorities and making significant changes, a comprehensive analysis, which includes relevant expenditures, external and internal resources, and impact on the campus community, must be conducted.

All institutions must provide sufficient funding for any institutional staff member(s) and the operational costs related to religious and/or spiritual programs.

If this assignment accounts for only a part of an individual staff member's work load, the budget should clearly indicate the portion that is available for religious and spiritual programs.

CRSP must demonstrate fiscal responsibility and cost effectiveness consistent with institutional protocols.

Funding for personnel and programs of adjunct agencies (i.e., not directly provided by the institution) must be assumed by the sponsors of the adjunct agency.

Part 12. TECHNOLOGY

Campus Religious and/or Spiritual Programs (CRSP) must have adequate technology to support their mission. The technology and its use must comply with institutional policies and procedures and be evaluated for compliance with relevant federal, state/provincial, and local requirements.

CRSP must maintain policies and procedures that address the security and back up of data.

When technology is used to facilitate student learning and development, CRSP must select technology that reflects current best pedagogical practices.

Technology, as well as any workstations or computer labs maintained by the CRSP for student use, must be accessible and must meet established technology standards for delivery to persons with disabilities.

When CRSP provide student access to technology, they must provide:
- access to policies that are clear, easy to understand, and available to all students
- access to instruction or training on how to use the technology
- access to information on the legal and ethical implications of misuse as it pertains to intellectual

property, harassment, privacy, and social networks

Student violations of technology policies must follow established institutional student disciplinary procedures.

Students who experience negative emotional or psychological consequences from the use of technology must be referred to support services provided by the institution.

Part 13. FACILITIES and EQUIPMENT

Campus Religious and/or Spiritual Programs (CRSP) must have adequate, accessible, suitably located facilities and equipment to support their mission and goals. If acquiring capital equipment as defined by the institution, CRSP must take into account expenses related to regular maintenance and life cycle costs. Facilities and equipment must be evaluated regularly, including consideration of sustainability, and be in compliance with relevant federal, state/provincial, and local requirements to provide for access, health, safety, and security.

CRSP staff members must have work space that is well-equipped, adequate in size, and designed to support their work and responsibilities. For conversations requiring privacy, staff members must have access to a private space.

CRSP staff members who share work space must have the ability to secure their work adequately.

The design of the facilities must guarantee the security of records and ensure the confidentiality of sensitive information.

The location and layout of the facilities must be sensitive to the special needs of persons with disabilities as well as the needs of constituencies served.

CRSP must ensure that staff members are knowledgeable of and trained in safety and emergency procedures for securing and vacating the facilities.

Opportunity must be provided for all student religious and/or spiritual organizations to utilize campus facilities on the same basis as other student organizations.

In public institutions, whenever space is made permanently or exclusively available for specific staff of affiliated agencies, arrangements should be made whereby the institution is appropriately reimbursed for expenses.

Private institutions may provide facilities designed to suit the purpose(s) of a specific religious group(s).

Institutions should provide fair and equitable arrangements and facilities (including in campus centers, academic buildings, or residential units) for specific religious and/or spiritual groups' programming and practices.

Suitable areas should be provided for individual meditation and small group spiritual interaction.

The institution should provide for or coordinate student religious and/or spiritual dietary differences.

Part 14. ASSESSMENT and EVALUATION

Campus Religious and/or Spiritual Programs (CRSP) must establish systematic plans and processes to meet internal and external accountability expectations with regard to program as well as student learning and development outcomes. CRSP must conduct regular assessment and evaluations. Assessments must include qualitative and quantitative methodologies as appropriate, to determine whether and to what degree the stated mission, goals, and student learning and development outcomes are being met. The process must employ sufficient and sound measures to ensure comprehensiveness. Data collected must include responses from students and other affected constituencies.

Each institution should require evaluation of its religious program to determine the achievement of goals, the constituencies reached, and its overall effectiveness.

This evaluation may be made in concert with the periodic examination of the diverse needs and interests of students and other members of the campus community.

CRSP must evaluate regularly how well they complement and enhance the institution's stated mission and educational effectiveness.

Data should be collected from officers and advisors of campus religious and spiritual organizations to determine the effectiveness of policies affecting religious activity.

Results of these evaluations must be used in revising and improving programs and services, identifying needs and interests in shaping directions of program and service design, and recognizing staff performance.

General Standards revised in 2008;
CRSP (formerly Religious Programs) content developed/revised in 1986, 1997, & 2006

The Role of Career Services
CAS Standards Contextual Statement

The first evidence of assistance in career services dates back to the 19th century, when commercial employment agencies began to place graduates of the nation's teacher training programs into jobs. More than 200 such agencies existed by the late 1800s. By the turn of the century, an increasing number of institutions had begun to realize their responsibility to help graduates find jobs. When the first institutional appointment and placement services were established, faculty members typically took responsibility for them on a part-time basis. Soon many institutions established programs staffed by full-time "appointment secretaries." By 1920, approximately 75 percent of the nation's normal schools had established placement services; as a direct result of the increasing number of college-sponsored placement services, the number of external agencies decreased.

Both of the first professional associations focusing on job placement for college graduates, the National Institutional Teacher Placement Association and the National Association of Appointment Secretaries, were established in 1924. In 1927, the former organization evolved into the American Association for Employment in Education (AAEE), while the latter became the American College Personnel Association (ACPA) in 1931. In addition, others concerned with business and industrial placement established the Eastern College Placement Association, and by the 1940s seven other regional associations had been formed.

Following World War II, the economy exploded and employers sought to hire the nation's college graduates to meet expanding needs. By the mid-1950s, on-campus recruiting of college graduates had reached its apex, with more than 65 percent of the current career services centers having been established between 1947 and 1960. Over the years, the function of these offices shifted from solely providing placement activities to providing a broad range of career activities. Accordingly, this shift is reflected by office name changes from "placement office" to "career planning and placement office" to the currently preferred title, "career services center."

A forerunner to a comprehensive national association, the Association of School and College Placement, was formed in 1940. This group published the *School and College Placement* magazine, now known as the *NACE Journal*. In 1956, the national association was incorporated as the College Placement Publications Council and its name was shortened in 1957 to the College Placement Council. In

1995, the association became the National Association of Colleges and Employers (NACE). Today, the core purpose of NACE is to facilitate the employment of the college educated; it works to meet this mission in a variety of ways, including by providing an important connection between college career services centers and HR/staffing offices focused on recruiting and hiring new college graduates.

Two other professional organizations in the field include the National Career Development Association (NCDA) and the American Association for Employment in Education (AAEE). In 1913, the National Vocational Guidance Association was founded. In 1985 it became the National Career Development Association (NCDA) and is a founding division of the American Counseling Association (ACA). Its aim is to promote the career development of all people throughout the life span. The American Association for Employment in Education (AAEE) was founded in 1934 to connect K-12 school recruiters with career services administrators and education faculty from higher education institutions that prepare educators. AAEE provides information, resources, and networking opportunities to assist schools, colleges and universities in the employment of educators for staffing excellence in education.

Today, the majority of colleges and universities have career centers. Their services often include career counseling; programming such as job-search workshops and networking events; career and job fairs; assistance with co-op, internship, and externship programs; on-campus recruiting; and job posting and resume referral services. In the typical center, many of these services are available electronically through the career center's web site.

In the 21st century, career services is tasked to meet increasingly complex and sophisticated challenges that include more diversity, globalization, and technology. Career services professionals need to be both culturally sensitive in working with students and knowledgeable about career options both in the United States and internationally. Today's traditional-age students, characterized by their high comfort level with and expectation of technology, and "virtual" students, created through distance learning options, require that career services professionals have an increasingly high level of technical competence. Today's career services professional must balance high-tech and high-touch service and delivery in serving students and employers. Career changers, including alumni, veterans, and others who are working on second, third, and fourth careers, are turning to career services to provide assistance through traditional and nontraditional means.

An increasing focus in higher education on assessment and accountability necessitates career services professionals to find meaningful measures by which to demonstrate their value to students, faculty, administrators, parents, and employers. Developing productive relationships not only with employers but also with faculty and other campus constituencies has never been more important. Increased emphasis on the part of employers on internships/co-ops, electronic recruiting, and diversity recruiting require a corresponding emphasis on the part of career services professionals.

The 21st century career services leader requires a broader range of skills and competencies beyond those once considered traditional for professionals involved in the career planning and development field. These include leadership, managerial, technical, financial, marketing, assessment, and analytical skills.

References, Readings, and Resources

Bryant, B.J. (Ed.). (2008). *The job search handbook for educators.* Columbus, OH: American Association for Employment in Education.

Bryant, B.J. (Ed.). (2008). *The job hunter's guide: services and career fairs for educators.* Columbus, OH: American Association for Employment in Education.

Bryant, B.J. (Ed.). (2008). *Educator supply and demand research report.* Columbus, OH: American Association for Employment in Education.

Celebrating 50 years of excellence: organization history. National Association of Colleges and Employers. www.naceweb.org/50thanniversary/history.htm

NACE Attracting New Professionals Task Force (2004). *Career services in higher education* (PowerPoint presentation). www.naceweb.org/committee/whitepapers/CS_Professionals.ppt. Bethlehem, PA: National Association of Colleges and Employers.

NACE Future Trends Task Force (2005). *The future of college recruiting and hiring: Executive summary.* Bethlehem, PA: National Association of Colleges and Employers

Ratcliffe, R. S. (2004). Use of the CAS Standards by Career Services Directors at Four- Year Public Colleges and Universities (Doctoral Dissertation, Virginia Polytechnic Institute and State University, 2004). Available at http://scholar.lib.vt.edu/theses/available/etd-07262004-150008/

State of the Profession: 2006-07 NACE Career Services Benchmark Survey (2006-07). Bethlehem, PA: National Association of Colleges and Employers.

The Professional Standards for College and University Career Services (2006). National Association of Colleges and Employers. www.naceweb.org/standards/default.htm

The Professional Standards Evaluation Workbook (2006). National Association of Colleges and Employers. www.naceweb.org/standards/default.htm

ACPA, Commission on Career Development. One DuPont Circle, Suite 300, Washington, DC 20036-1188. Phone: 202/835-2272. FAX: 202/296-3286. Web site: www.acpa.nche.edu.

American Association for Employment in Education (AAEE). 3040 Riverside Drive, Suite 125, Columbus, OH 43221. Phone: 614/485-1111. FAX: 614/485-9609. Web site: www.aaee.org

National Association of Colleges and Employers (NACE). 62 Highland Avenue, Bethlehem, PA 18017. Phone: 800/544-5272. FAX: 610/868-0208. Web site: www.naceweb.org.

National Career Development Association. 305 N. Beech Circle, Broken Arrow, OK 74012. Phone: 918-663-7060. Fax: 918-663-7058. Website: www.ncda.org.

Contributors:

Alison Angell, Lesley University, AAEE
Patricia Carretta, George Mason University, NACE
Mimi Collins, NACE
R. Samuel Ratcliffe, Virginia Military Institute, NACE

Career Services
CAS Standards and Guidelines

Part 1. MISSION

The primary mission of Career Services (CS) is to assist students and other designated clients through all phases of their career development.

In addition, the mission of CS is:
- **to provide leadership to the institution on career development concerns**
- **to develop positive relationships with employers and external constituencies**
- **to support institutional outcomes assessment and relevant research endeavors**

CS must develop, disseminate, implement, and regularly review their mission. Mission statements must be consistent with the mission of the institution and with professional standards. CS in higher education must enhance overall educational experiences by incorporating student learning and development outcomes in their mission.

The stated mission should include helping students and other designated clients:
- to develop self-knowledge related to career choice and work performance by identifying, assessing, and understanding their competencies, interests, values, and personal characteristics
- to obtain educational and occupational information to aid career and educational planning and to develop an understanding of the world of work
- to select personally suitable academic programs and experiential opportunities that enhance future educational and employment options
- to take personal responsibility for developing job-search competencies, future educational and employment plans, and career decisions
- to gain experience through student activities, community service, student employment, research or creative projects, cooperative education, internships, and other opportunities
- to link with alumni, employers, professional organizations, and others who can provide opportunities to develop professional interests and competencies, integrate academic learning with work, and explore future career possibilities
- to prepare for finding suitable employment by developing job-search skills, effective candidate presentation skills, and an understanding of the fit between their competencies and both occupational and job requirements
- to seek desired employment opportunities or entry into appropriate educational, graduate, or professional programs

CS must promote a greater awareness within the institution of the world of work and the need for and nature of career development over the life span.

Because of the expertise and knowledge on career-related matters, CS should be involved in key administrative decisions related to student services, institutional development, curriculum planning, and external relations.

Part 2. PROGRAM

The formal education of students, consisting of the curriculum and the co-curriculum, must promote student learning and development outcomes that are purposeful and holistic and that prepare students for satisfying and productive lifestyles, work, and civic participation. The student learning and development outcome domains and their related dimensions are:

- **knowledge acquisition, integration, construction, and application**
  - o **Dimensions: understanding knowledge from a range of disciplines; connecting knowledge to other knowledge, ideas, and experiences; constructing knowledge; and relating knowledge to daily life**

- **cognitive complexity**
  - o **Dimensions: critical thinking; reflective thinking; effective reasoning; and creativity**

- **intrapersonal development**
  - o **Dimensions: realistic self-appraisal, self-understanding, and self-respect; identity development; commitment to ethics and integrity; and spiritual awareness**

- **interpersonal competence**
  - o **Dimensions: meaningful relationships; interdependence; collaboration; and effective leadership**

- **humanitarianism and civic engagement**
  - o **Dimensions: understanding and appreciation of cultural and human differences; social responsibility; global perspective; and sense of civic responsibility**

- **practical competence**
  - o **Dimensions: pursuing goals; communicating effectively; technical competence; managing personal affairs; managing career development; demonstrating professionalism; maintaining health and wellness; and living a purposeful and satisfying life**

[See *The Council for the Advancement of Standards Learning and Developmental Outcomes* statement for examples of outcomes related to these domains and dimensions.]

Consistent with the institutional mission, Career Services (CS) must identify relevant and desirable student learning and development outcomes from among the six domains and related dimensions. When creating opportunities for student learning and development, CS must explore possibilities for collaboration with faculty members and other colleagues.

CS must assess relevant and desirable student learning and

development outcomes and provide evidence of their impact on student learning and development. CS must articulate how they contribute to or support students' learning and development in the domains not specifically assessed.

CS must be:
- integrated into the life of the institution
- intentional and coherent
- guided by theories and knowledge of learning and development
- reflective of developmental and demographic profiles of the student population
- responsive to needs of individuals, diverse and special populations, and relevant constituencies

CS must be based on an educational philosophy of teaching career development and related processes. CS must assist students and other designated clients to develop the skills necessary to compete in a rapidly changing, competency-based, global workplace.

Components of the CS must be clearly defined and articulated. To effectively accomplish its purpose, the program must include:
- career counseling
- information and resources on careers and further education
- opportunities for career exploration through experiential learning
- job search services
- services to employers
- consultation and outcomes assessment

CS must be delivered in a variety of formats in recognition of institutional settings, different learning styles, cultural differences, and special needs.

Program components of CS must be designed for and reflective of the career development needs and interests of students and other designated clients; current research, theories, and knowledge of career development and learning; contemporary career services practices and national standards of practice; economic trends, opportunities, and/ or constraints; the varying needs and employment practices among small businesses, large corporations, government, and nonprofit organizations; and the priorities and resources of the institution.

CS must work collaboratively with academic divisions, departments, individual faculty members, student services, and other relevant constituencies of the institution to enhance students' career development.

CS must develop and implement intentional marketing strategies and outreach programming to promote awareness and encourage use of the services.

Program goals must be reviewed and updated regularly, and communicated, as appropriate, to students, administrators, faculty members, staff, and employers and other constituencies.

CS should disseminate information on the availability, scope, and use of career services through institutional publications, campus media, presentations, outreach, and orientation programs.

Career Counseling
The institution must offer career counseling that assists students and other designated clients at any stage of their career development to:
- understand the relationship between self-knowledge and career choice through assessment of interests, competencies, values, experience, personal characteristics, and desired lifestyles
- obtain and research occupational, educational, and employment information
- establish short-term and long-term career goals
- explore a full range of career and work possibilities
- make reasoned, informed career choices based on accurate self-knowledge and accurate information about the world of work

Career counseling should:
- be available to students throughout their academic experience
- encourage students to take advantage of timely involvement in self-assessment, career decision-making, and career planning activities
- assist students to assess their skills, values, and interests by reflecting on past experiences
- assist students to integrate self-knowledge into their career planning
- recognize that students' career decision making is inextricably linked to additional psycho-social, personal, developmental, and cultural issues and beliefs
- encourage and facilitate students' exploration of career interests through field visits, student employment, cooperative education, internships, shadowing experiences, research or creative projects, and informational interviews with working professionals
- be provided through a variety of formats, such as scheduled appointments, drop-in periods, group programs, career planning courses, outreach programs, and information technology

Career counseling should be offered through career services in order to link students' career exploration and decision-making process with access to employers and employment information.

Information and Resources on Careers and Further Study
CS must help students and other designated clients to identify and access valid career information for their educational and career planning.

CS should provide information and resources:
- to help students assess and relate their interests, competencies, needs and expectations, education, experience, personal background, and desired lifestyle to the employment market
- for constituent groups on career and employment topics and

the ethical obligations of students, employers, and others involved in the employment process

- on current employment opportunities and on employers to ensure that candidates have the widest possible choices of employment
- to help students identify and pursue future educational objectives

Information and resources must be:

- **comprehensive, enabling students and other designated clients to explore the widest range of information**
- **current and reflective of economic, occupational, and workplace trends**
- **accessible to clients**
- **organized in a system that is user-friendly, flexible, and adaptable to change**

The scope of information and resources available to clients should include:

- self-assessment and career planning
- occupational and job market information
- options for further study (e.g., community college articulation; graduate and professional school information)
- job search information
- experiential learning, internship, and job listings
- employer information

CS must provide access to information and resources on the internet.

Career information, resources, and means of delivery must be compatible with the size and nature of the student population, the career and geographic interests of the students, and the scope of academic programs.

CS must provide information for students and other designated clients to identify and pursue future educational objectives in the context of lifelong learning.

Opportunities for Career Exploration through Experiential Learning

Experiential learning programs enable students to integrate their academic studies with work experiences and career exploration.   The institution must provide experiential learning opportunities.

Experiential learning includes cooperative education, work-based learning, apprenticeships, student teaching, internships, work-study jobs, and other campus employment, volunteer experiences, service-learning, undergraduate research, and shadowing experiences.

Experiential learning programs administered through CS must:

- **provide students with opportunities to define both learning and career objectives and to reflect upon learning and other developmental aspects of their experience**
- **help students to identify employers for career development and potential employment**
- **teach students appropriate search and application**

techniques

- **support institutional efforts to provide students with additional financial resources for attending college and/ or opportunities for obtaining academic credit**
- **ensure adequate site supervision**

Experiential learning programs administered through CS should promote mentor/mentee relationships. When experiential learning opportunities are provided by other departments, CS should work closely with those departments.

Job Search Services

Job search services must assist students and other designated clients to:

- **develop job-search competencies**
- **present themselves effectively as candidates for employment**
- **obtain information on employment opportunities, trends, and prospective employers**
- **connect with employers through campus recruitment programs, job listings, referrals, direct application, networking, publications, and information technology**
- **identify relevant career management issues (e.g., gender, age, sexual orientation, dual career, disability, cultural, mental health)**
- **access and effectively use career and employer resources on the internet**

Job search services may include offering site visits; campus recruiting; resume referrals; credential file services; information sessions; meetings with faculty members; pre-recruiting activities; student access to employer information; posting job openings; and career and job fairs. Job search service should help students and other designated clients develop skills to uncover hidden job markets germane to their career interests.

CS must develop and implement marketing strategies that cultivate employment opportunities for students.

Services to Employers

Employers are both vital partners in the educational process and primary customers of career services. CS must offer services to employers that reflect student interests and employer needs.

Employer services may include: providing employers with information on academic departments and students within legal and policy guidelines; assisting in recruiting student populations; arranging experiential learning options such as shadowing experiences, internships, student teaching, or cooperative education; providing video conference interviewing; creating advertising and promotional vehicles; seeking input through career center advisory board membership; and organizing individual employer recruiting and college relations consultations.

CS must identify the range of employers it will serve (e.g., for profit, government, contract agencies, not-for-profit) and articulate policies that guide its working relationships with each of these constituencies.

CS must:

- develop strategic objectives for employer services and job development that yield maximum opportunities for the institution's students and graduates
- inform, educate, and consult with employers on the nature of services provided and student candidates available
- encourage employer participation in programs that meet career and employment needs of students and other designated clients (e.g., career conferences, career and alumni fairs, cooperative education and internships, career planning courses, classroom presentations)
- develop and maintain relationships with employers who may provide career development and employment opportunities for students
- facilitate employer involvement and communication with faculty members, students, and administrators concerning career and employment issues
- promote adherence to professional and ethical standards that model professional and ethical conduct for students
- enhance customer service and continuous improvement by using feedback from employers on key performance indicators and measures of services

CS must provide timely, pertinent information to employers regarding:

- the institutional student profile, academic programs and curricula, enrollments, and academic calendar
- class profile according to majors
- recruiting options available to reach targeted students
- policies, procedures, and instructions for using the services
- institutional non-discrimination policies with which employers must comply

CS must treat employers fairly and equitably.

CS must develop policies for working with third-party recruiters and vendors.

Consultation and Outcomes Assessment

CS must provide consultative services to employers, faculty members, staff, administrators, students, and designated clients that are timely, knowledgeable, ethical, and responsive to constituent needs.

To develop effective long-term relationships with employers, CS must provide guidance to employers on how to develop effective college relations and recruiting strategies.

CS should provide guidance on:

- effective and appropriate strategies for reaching and attracting students
- student needs, issues, and developmental perspectives
- cultivating relations with academic departments
- working with student leaders and student clubs and organizations
- timely corporate/organizational presence and participation in

on-campus recruiting, fairs, and pre-recruiting
- using appropriate campus resources for visibility
- internship, co-op, and full-time hiring guidelines, processes, and programs
- promoting equal access for all students to all employment opportunities

To support the institution's mission and goals, CS must provide faculty and staff and administrative units with information, guidance, and support on career development and employment issues and linkages with the broader community.

CS should support faculty and staff and administrative units by:

- identifying and disseminating information on employment trends, top employing organizations, and co-op and internship sponsors
- provide employer feedback on the preparation of students for jobs, the curriculum, and the hiring process
- raising awareness of appropriate ethical and legal guidelines for student referrals
- increasing awareness of career development issues and available resources
- providing and interpreting aggregate data on student learning and career-related outcomes for purposes such as accreditation, marketing, institutional development, and curriculum development

CS must consult with students and student groups regarding policy interpretation, program development, and relationships with employers.

Part 3. LEADERSHIP

Because effective and ethical leadership is essential to the success of all organizations, Career Services (CS) leaders with organizational authority for the programs and services must:

- articulate a vision and mission for their programs and services
- set goals and objectives based on the needs of the population served and desired student learning and development outcomes
- advocate for their programs and services
- promote campus environments that provide meaningful opportunities for student learning, development, and integration
- identify and find means to address individual, organizational, or environmental conditions that foster or inhibit mission achievement
- advocate for representation in strategic planning initiatives at appropriate divisional and institutional levels
- initiate collaborative interactions with stakeholders who have legitimate concerns and interests in the functional area
- apply effective practices to educational and administrative processes

- prescribe and model ethical behavior
- communicate effectively
- manage financial resources, including planning, allocation, monitoring, and analysis
- incorporate sustainability practices in the management and design of programs, services, and facilities
- manage human resource processes including recruitment, selection, development, supervision, performance planning, and evaluation
- empower professional, support, and student staff to accept leadership opportunities
- encourage and support scholarly contribution to the profession
- be informed about and integrate appropriate technologies into programs and services
- be knowledgeable about federal, state/provincial, and local laws relevant to the programs and services and ensure that staff members understand their responsibilities by receiving appropriate training
- develop and continuously improve programs and services in response to the changing needs of students and other populations served and the evolving institutional priorities
- recognize environmental conditions that may negatively influence the safety of staff and students and propose interventions that mitigate such conditions

If career components are offered through multiple units, the institution must designate a leader or leadership team to provide strategic direction and align career services with the mission of the institution and the needs of the constituencies served.

CS leaders should coordinate efforts with other units in the institution providing career components to integrate career services into the broader educational mission. Key constituencies served by each unit should be clearly identified and reflected in the mission and goals of the unit.

CS leaders must be advocates for the advancement of career services within the institution.

CS leaders should participate in institutional decisions about career services objectives and policies. CS leaders should participate in institutional decisions related to the identification and designation of clients served. Clients may include students, alumni, community members, and employers. Decisions about clients served should include type and scope of services offered and the fees, if any, that are charged.

Part 4. HUMAN RESOURCES

Career Services (CS) must be staffed adequately by individuals qualified to accomplish the mission and goals. Within institutional guidelines, CS must establish procedures for staff selection, training, and evaluation; set expectations for supervision; and provide appropriate professional development opportunities to improve the leadership ability, competence, and skills of all employees.

CS staff must, in combination, have the competencies necessary to effectively perform the primary functions. Primary functions are program management and administration; program and event administration; career counseling and consultation; teaching/training/educating; marketing/promoting/outreach; brokering/connecting/linking; and information management.

The primary functions should include the following core competencies and knowledge domains.

Management and administration
Core Competencies
> Needs assessment; program design, implementation and evaluation; strategic & operational planning; program integration and integrity; staffing; staff development and supervision; budget planning and administration; political sensitivity and negotiation skills; ability to synthesize, interpret and report information.

Knowledge Domains
> Systems theory; organizational development; research design; statistics; accounting and budgeting procedures; revenue generation; principles; purchasing; staff selection; supervision; performance appraisals; management of information systems; customer service; marketing.

Program and event administration
Core Competencies
> Needs assessment; goal setting; program planning, implementation, and evaluation; budget allocation; time management; problem solving; attention to detail.

Knowledge Domains
> Systems, logistics, and procedures; project management; customer service.

Career counseling and consultation
Core Competencies
> Needs assessment and diagnosis; intervention design and implementation; test administration and interpretation; counseling; feedback; evaluation; advising; empathy and interpersonal sensitivity; work with individuals and groups; use of career, occupational, and employment information.

Knowledge Domains
> Career development theories; adult development theory and unique issues for special populations; statistics; counseling processes; evaluation of person-job fit; job analysis; career decision-making; behavior management; job search, interviews, and resumes.

Teaching/training/educating
Core Competencies
> Needs assessment; program/workshop design; researching, evaluating, and integrating information; effective teaching strategies; coaching; work with individuals and groups; use of technology for delivery of content.

Knowledge Domains
> Setting learning objectives; designing curricula and learning resources for specific content areas; experiential learning; career development and job search process; learning styles.

Marketing/ promoting/ outreach

Core Competencies

Needs assessment and goal setting; written and interpersonal communication; public speaking; job development; effective use of print, web, personal presentation methods.

Knowledge Domains

Customer service; knowledge of institution and its academic programs; career services; employer and faculty needs and expectations; recruiting and staffing methods, trends.

Brokering/ connecting/ linking

Core Competencies

Organize information, logistics, people, and processes toward a desired outcome; consulting; interpersonal skills.

Knowledge Domains

Systems and procedures; candidate/resume referral; recruiting and experiential learning operations; human resource selection practices.

Information management

Core Competencies

Organization and dissemination; storage and retrieval; computing systems and applications; data entry and analysis; acquisition of appropriate career resources; web design.

Knowledge Domains

Library/resources center organization; computer systems and applications; specific electronic management information systems.

CS professional staff members must hold an earned graduate or professional degree in a field relevant to the position they hold or must possess an appropriate combination of educational credentials and related work experience.

Degree- or credential-seeking interns must be qualified by enrollment in an appropriate field of study and by relevant experience. These individuals must be trained and supervised adequately by professional staff members holding educational credentials and related work experience appropriate for supervision.

Student employees and volunteers must be carefully selected, trained, supervised, and evaluated. They must be educated on how and when to refer those in need of additional assistance to qualified staff members and must have access to a supervisor for assistance in making these judgments. Student employees and volunteers must be provided clear and precise job descriptions, pre-service training based on assessed needs, and continuing staff development.

Employees and volunteers must receive specific training on institutional policies and privacy laws regarding their access to student records and other sensitive institutional information (e.g., in the USA, Family Educational Rights and Privacy Act, FERPA, or equivalent privacy laws in other states/provinces or countries).

Training should include customer service, program procedures, and information and resource utilization.

CS must have technical and support staff members adequate to accomplish their mission. All members of the staff must be technologically proficient and qualified to perform their job functions, be knowledgeable about ethical and legal uses of technology, and have access to training and resources to support the performance of their assigned responsibilities.

All members of the staff must receive training on policies and procedures related to the use of technology to store or access student records and institutional data.

CS must ensure that staff members are knowledgeable about and trained in emergency procedures, crisis response, and prevention efforts. Prevention efforts must address identification of threatening conduct or behavior of students, faculty members, staff, and others and must incorporate a system or procedures for responding, including but not limited to reporting them to the appropriate campus officials.

Career information facilities should be staffed with persons who have the appropriate competencies to assist students and other designated clients in accessing and effectively using career information and resources. A technical support person or support service should be available to maintain computer and information technology systems for career services.

Salary levels and benefits for all staff members must be commensurate with those for comparable positions within the institution, in similar institutions, and in the relevant geographic area.

CS must maintain position descriptions for all staff members.

To create a diverse staff, CS must institute hiring and promotion practices that are fair, inclusive, proactive, and non-discriminatory.

CS must conduct regular performance planning and evaluation of staff members. CS must provide access to continuing and advanced education and professional development opportunities.

CS professional staff members must engage in continuing professional development activities to keep abreast of the research, theories, legislation, policies and developments that affect career services.

Staff training and development should be ongoing and promote knowledge and skill development across program components.

All staff must be trained in legal, confidential, and ethical issues related to career services.

Part 5. ETHICS

Persons involved in the delivery of Career Services (CS) must adhere to the highest principles of ethical behavior. CS must review relevant professional ethical standards and develop or adopt and implement appropriate statements of ethical practice. CS must publish these statements and ensure their periodic review by relevant constituencies.

Ethical standards or other statements from relevant professional associations should be considered.

CS must orient new staff members to relevant ethical standards and statements of ethical practice.

CS must ensure that privacy and confidentiality are maintained with respect to all communications and records to the extent that such records are protected under the law and appropriate statements of ethical practice. Information contained in students' education records must not be disclosed except as allowed by relevant laws and institutional policies. CS staff members must disclose to appropriate authorities information judged to be of an emergency nature, especially when the safety of the individual or others is involved, or when otherwise required by institutional policy or relevant law.

CS staff members must be aware of and comply with the provisions contained in the institution's policies pertaining to human subjects research and student rights and responsibilities, as well as those in other relevant institutional policies addressing ethical practices and confidentiality of research data concerning individuals.

CS staff members must recognize and avoid personal conflicts of interest or appearance thereof in the performance of their work.

CS staff members must strive to insure the fair, objective, and impartial treatment of all persons with whom they interact.

When handling institutional funds, CS staff members must ensure that such funds are managed in accordance with established and responsible accounting procedures and the fiscal policies or processes of the institution.

Promotional and descriptive information must be accurate and free of deception.

CS staff members must perform their duties within the limits of their training, expertise, and competence. When these limits are exceeded, individuals in need of further assistance must be referred to persons possessing appropriate qualifications.

CS staff members must use suitable means to confront and otherwise hold accountable other staff members who exhibit unethical behavior.

CS staff members must be knowledgeable about and practice ethical behavior in the use of technology.

CS leaders/managers should provide guidance and education on these standards to all persons involved in providing career services, including, but not limited to, entry-level professionals, support staff, student staff, interns, graduate assistants, faculty and staff, employers, service providers, and other administrators.

Part 6. LEGAL RESPONSIBILITIES

Career Services (CS) staff members must be knowledgeable about and responsive to laws and regulations that relate to their respective responsibilities and that may pose legal obligations, limitations, or ramifications for the institution as a whole. As appropriate, staff members must inform users of programs and services, as well as officials, of legal obligations and limitations including constitutional, statutory, regulatory, and case law; mandatory laws and orders emanating from federal, state/provincial, and local governments; and the institution's policies.

CS must have written policies on all relevant operations, transactions, or tasks that may have legal implications.

CS staff members must neither participate in nor condone any form of harassment or activity that demeans persons or creates an intimidating, hostile, or offensive campus environment.

CS staff members must use reasonable and informed practices to limit the liability exposure of the institution and its officers, employees, and agents. CS staff members must be informed about institutional policies regarding risk management, personal liability, and related insurance coverage options and must be referred to external sources if coverage is not provided by the institution.

The institution must provide access to legal advice for CS staff members as needed to carry out assigned responsibilities.

The institution must inform CS staff and students in a timely and systematic fashion about extraordinary or changing legal obligations and potential liabilities.

Career services staff members must be aware of and seek advice from the institution's legal counsel on: privacy and disclosure of student information contained in education records; defamation law regarding references and recommendations on the behalf of students and other designated clients; laws regarding employment referral practices of the career services office and others employed by the institution that refer students for employment; affirmative action regulations and laws regarding programs for special populations; liability issues pertaining to experiential learning programs; laws regarding eligibility to work; laws regarding contracts governing service provided by outside vendors; and laws regarding grant administration.

Career services must maintain appropriate records for future work with students and other designated clients.

Part 7. EQUITY and ACCESS

Career Services (CS) must be provided on a fair, equitable, and non-discriminatory basis in accordance with institutional policies and with all applicable state/provincial and federal statutes and regulations. CS must maintain an educational and work environment free from discrimination in accordance

with law and institutional policy.

CS should ensure that employers who use career services adhere to the word and spirit of equal employment opportunity and affirmative action. CS staff should make every effort to inform or educate faculty members about issues relevant to discriminatory practices related to their referral of students directly to employers.

Discrimination must be avoided on the basis of age; cultural heritage; disability; ethnicity; gender identity and expression; nationality; political affiliation; race; religious affiliation; sex; sexual orientation; economic, marital, social, or veteran status; and any other bases included in local, state/provincial, or federal laws.

Consistent with the mission and goals, CS must take action to remedy significant imbalances in student participation and staffing patterns.

These groups may include traditionally under-represented, evening, part-time, commuter, and international students, and students with disabilities.

CS must ensure physical and program access for persons with disabilities. CS must be responsive to the needs of all students and other populations served when establishing hours of operation and developing methods of delivering programs and services.

To respond to the needs of students and other designated clients, career services should provide services in-person, on-line, via telephone, e-mail, or other formats. CS should be responsive to the needs of all its constituencies through the establishment of office hours, customer service systems, and on-line operations.

CS must recognize the needs of distance learning students by providing appropriate and accessible services and assisting them in identifying and gaining access to other appropriate services in their geographic region.

Part 8. DIVERSITY

Within the context of each institution's unique mission, diversity enriches the community and enhances the collegiate experience for all; therefore, Career Services (CS) must create and nurture environments that are welcoming to and bring together persons of diverse backgrounds.

CS must promote environments that are characterized by open and continuous communication that deepens understanding of one's own identity, culture, and heritage, as well as that of others. CS must recognize, honor, educate, and promote respect about commonalties and differences among people within their historical and cultural contexts.

CS must address the characteristics and needs of a diverse population when establishing and implementing policies and procedures.

CS should work in conjunction with the institution's special services and minority organizations to enhance students' awareness and appreciation of cultural and ethnic differences. Collaborating departments and organizations should provide educational programs that help under-represented students, multicultural students, and individuals with disabilities to identify and address their unique needs related to career development and employment. CS should initiate partnerships and collaborative programming with other offices representing specific populations to ensure appropriate service delivery.

Part 9. ORGANIZATION and MANAGEMENT

To promote student learning and development outcomes, Career Services (CS) must be structured purposefully and managed effectively to achieve stated goals. Evidence of appropriate structure must include current and accessible policies and procedures, written performance expectations for all employees, functional workflow graphics or organizational charts, and clearly stated program and service delivery expectations.

CS must monitor websites used for distributing information to ensure that the sites are current, accurate, appropriately referenced, and accessible.

Evidence of effective management must include use of comprehensive and accurate information for decisions, clear sources and channels of authority, effective communication practices, procedures for decision-making and conflict resolution, responses to changing conditions, systems of accountability and evaluation, and processes for recognition and reward. CS must align policies and procedures with those of the institution and provide channels within the organization for their regular review.

Other areas for consideration in determining structure and management of career services should include:
- size, nature, and mission of the institution
- number and scope of academic-related services
- scope and intent of recruiting services
- philosophy and delivery system for services
- varied delivery methods (e.g., direct contact, technology)

CS should be integrated with, and complementary to, employment-related services.

Part 10. CAMPUS and EXTERNAL RELATIONS

Career Services (CS) must reach out to relevant individuals, campus offices, and external agencies to:
- **establish, maintain, and promote effective relations**
- **disseminate information about their own and other related programs and services**
- **coordinate and collaborate, where appropriate, in offering programs and services to meet the needs of students and promote their achievement of student learning and development outcomes**

As an integral function within the institution, CS must develop and maintain effective relationships with relevant

stakeholders at the institution and in the community.

To achieve this, CS should develop institutional support for career development and employment programs by:
- participating fully in campus activities such as faculty organizations, committees, student orientation programs, classroom presentations, academic courses in career planning, and student organization programs
- arranging appropriate programs that use alumni experience and expertise
- establishing cooperative relationships with other offices and services to support the practice of mutual referrals, information exchange, resource sharing, and other program functions
- providing information and reports to the academic administration, faculty, and key offices of the institution regarding career services for students, employers, and alumni
- developing informal or formal student, faculty, or employer advisory groups
- encouraging dialogues among employers, faculty members, and administrators concerning career issues and trends for students and graduates

In addition, CS should:
- encourage staff participation in and through professional associations and community activities related to career and employment issues (e.g., chambers of commerce, workforce development functions, employer open houses, workshops, federally mandated one stop centers, school-to-work efforts)
- raise issues and concerns with the legal counsel of the institution regarding compliance with laws as they pertain to employment, recruitment, supervision (e.g., interns)

CS must have procedures and guidelines consistent with institutional policy for responding to threats, emergencies, and crisis situations. Systems and procedures must be in place to disseminate timely and accurate information to students and other members of the campus community during emergency situations.

CS must have procedures and guidelines consistent with institutional policy for communicating with the media.

Part 11. FINANCIAL RESOURCES

Career Services (CS) must have adequate funding to accomplish their mission and goals. In establishing funding priorities and making significant changes, a comprehensive analysis, which includes relevant expenditures, external and internal resources, and impact on the campus community, must be conducted.

CS must demonstrate fiscal responsibility and cost effectiveness consistent with institutional protocols.

CS should cultivate employer support of the institution, which may include scholarships and other forms of financial support, in coordination with development office efforts. While outside revenue may be generated to supplement the services it should not replace institutional funding. Revenue generated from employers,

vendors, students, and other designated clients should be limited and reasonable to carry out stated objectives.

Part 12. TECHNOLOGY

Career Services (CS) must have adequate technology to support their mission. The technology and its use must comply with institutional policies and procedures and be evaluated for compliance with relevant federal, state/provincial, and local requirements.

CS must maintain policies and procedures that address the security and back up of data.

When technology is used to facilitate student learning and development, CS must select technology that reflects current best pedagogical practices.

Technology, as well as any workstations or computer labs maintained by the CS for student use, must be accessible and must meet established technology standards for delivery to persons with disabilities.

When CS provide student access to technology, they must provide:
- **access to policies that are clear, easy to understand, and available to all students**
- **access to instruction or training on how to use the technology**
- **access to information on the legal and ethical implications of misuse as it pertains to intellectual property, harassment, privacy, and social networks**

Student violations of technology policies must follow established institutional student disciplinary procedures.

Students who experience negative emotional or psychological consequences from the use of technology must be referred to support services provided by the institution.

Part 13. FACILITIES and EQUIPMENT

Career Services (CS) must have adequate, accessible, suitably located facilities and equipment to support their mission and goals. If acquiring capital equipment as defined by the institution, CS must take into account expenses related to regular maintenance and life cycle costs. Facilities and equipment must be evaluated regularly, including consideration of sustainability, and be in compliance with relevant federal, state/provincial, and local requirements to provide for access, health, safety, and security.

CS staff members must have work space that is well-equipped, adequate in size, and designed to support their work and responsibilities. For conversations requiring privacy, staff members must have access to a private space.

CS must provide: private offices for professional staff in order to perform counseling or other confidential work; support staff work areas; reception and student registration area; career resource center; storage space sufficient to

accommodate resources, supplies and equipment; technology resources for students and staff sufficient to support career services functions; access to conference rooms, computer labs and large group meeting rooms; private interview facilities for employers and students to accommodate the scope of the recruiting program; and reception spaces adequate to accommodate on-campus recruiting and career counseling services.

CS should be in a convenient location for students and employers and project a welcoming, professional atmosphere for its users. A private employer workspace should be available. Parking for visitors should be adequate and convenient.

CS staff members who share work space must have the ability to secure their work adequately.

The design of the facilities must guarantee the security of records and ensure the confidentiality of sensitive information.

Contracts with outside vendors must include adherence to ethics, confidentiality, security, institutional policies, as well as reflect support of career services programs, goals, and standards.

The location and layout of the facilities must be sensitive to the special needs of persons with disabilities as well as the needs of constituencies served.

CS must ensure that staff members are knowledgeable of and trained in safety and emergency procedures for securing and vacating the facilities.

Part 14. ASSESSMENT and EVALUATION

Career Services (CS) must establish systematic plans and processes to meet internal and external accountability expectations with regard to program as well as student learning and development outcomes. CS must conduct regular assessment and evaluations. Assessments must include qualitative and quantitative methodologies as appropriate, to determine whether and to what degree the stated mission, goals, and student learning and development outcomes are being met. The process must employ sufficient and sound measures to ensure comprehensiveness. Data collected must include responses from students and other affected constituencies.

CS must evaluate regularly how well they complement and enhance the institution's stated mission and educational effectiveness.

Career services must conduct regular evaluations to improve programs and services, to adjust to changing client needs, and to respond to environmental threats and opportunities.

In order for institutions to employ comparable methods for evaluation, resources from recognized peers and professional associations should be consulted. CS should collaborate with institutional research units, state agencies, accrediting bodies, and other evaluative groups that generate and assess evaluation information. CS should promote institutional efforts to conduct relevant research on career development, institutional issues such as academic success and retention, student learning outcomes, employment trends, and career interests.

Evaluations should include:

- review of the strategic plan, mission, human resources needs, diversity efforts, and other areas covered in this document
- regular feedback from participants on events, programs, and services
- systematic needs assessment to guide program development
- first destination surveys at or following graduation
- employer and student feedback regarding experiential learning programs
- alumni follow-up surveys administered at specific times after graduation
- reports and satisfaction surveys from students and other constituencies interacting with career services such as employers, faculty members, and other post-secondary institutions

Results of these evaluations must be used in revising and improving programs and services, identifying needs and interests in shaping directions of program and service design, and recognizing staff performance.

CS should prepare and disseminate annual and special reports, including career services philosophy, goals and objectives, current programs and services, service delivery information, first destination information, and graduate follow-up information.

General Standards revised in 2008;
CS content developed/revised in 1986, 1997, & 2000

The Role of Clinical Health Services

CAS Standards Contextual Statement

Clinical health services have a unique position within institutions of higher education (IHEs). Despite the absence of universal access to health care in our society, we recognize the need for it — and we struggle to achieve it. IHEs can play a role in ensuring access to medical care for college students, some of whom do not have health insurance, by advocating for institutions of higher education to provide access to quality health care insurance and mandating coverage. Institutions of higher education can also play a role in ensuring access to medical care for college students, by providing non-duplicative treatment of illness and injury with convenient clinical health services. These clinical health services also work with campus or community prevention programs to manage communicable diseases and to address, with local public health departments, other public health and safety needs on a college campus. Access to quality medical and nursing care as well as management of public health and safety needs are important aspects of creating a campus community.

The complexity and comprehensiveness of health-related programs and services provided by an IHE varies extensively by student demographics, institutional mission, and the availability of community resources. There are often constellations of services that may or may not be administratively connected with the clinical health service, all focused on the same mission of enhancing health as it advances student learning. These various services and policies are non-clinical methodologies, such as a policy of mandatory health care insurance, fitness and recreation opportunities, tutoring services, health promotion services, personal and group counseling, campus master planning, public health policy, and public safety efforts.

In 1860, Edward Hitchcock Jr., physician and Professor of Hygiene at Amherst College, was charged by the president of the college to develop methods to advance the health of students (Packwood, 1989). "Student," as the focus of these efforts, implies a commitment to enhancing the capacity to learn. These students are individuals who are not members of just any population, but a population engaged in a specific purpose, learning. In response to this charge, Dr. Hitchcock used physical fitness and hygiene education. During the early part of the twentieth century, in response to outbreaks and epidemics of communicable diseases and a lack of community resources, campus infirmaries were created to isolate students with infectious diseases. In the 1950s, as veterans returned and took advantage of the GI Bill, physicals and immunizations were added, as was customary in the military.

Societal and behavioral risk factors moved to the forefront in the 1960s and 1970s, and recognition of the impact of developmental and psychosocial concerns on students' ability to achieve their academic potential brought new institutional investments in counseling services as an element of health services provided.

Some of the historical reasons for providing clinical health services on campus remain pertinent today. However, financing the delivery of health care has changed. The majority of students are insured and therefore covered for primary care and other medical services off campus or near their parents, thus creating a level of double coverage. However, students who are uninsured and enrolled at institutions without a policy of mandatory health insurance can access only the services provided through a student health fee or the general fund, both of which are paid by all enrolled students. These uninsured students may also access care through community resources for the uninsured. It is important to remember that because all institutions do not require or provide health care insurance, nationally upwards of thirty percent of the student population (ACHA, 2004) is uninsured for any type of access to community medical services. This situation of double coverage for most and very limited coverage for some students can be remedied by a policy of mandatory health care insurance coverage and tailored campus health fee supported services that complement, not duplicate, insurance reimbursable services.

Regardless of the access to health care insurance issue, the issues that pose a threat to the student's academic success are now more often psychosocial, behavioral, or environmental rather than risks from infection or other diseases. Although data collected by the American College Health Association National College Health Assessment (ACHA-NCHA) show that colds, flu, sore throats, and sinus infections still often rank as frequent in the student population, they do not pose a threat to academic success. The great majorities of health-related reasons for academic problems are not medical, but rather environmental or cultural, such as intra- or interpersonal difficulties, stress, lack of routine exercise or balanced nutrition, excessive computer use, and sleep hygiene.

Our perception of the factors and influences that contribute to the health and well-being of an individual and affect the quality of student learning and campus life has changed in the past four decades; the nature and character of all the campus health-related services should change in parallel. The criterion against which to assess the continued value of any health-related service is its relationship to supporting student learning and the academic environment. Clinical health services are rightly compared to other primary care ambulatory medical services in the community. However, medical or nursing care is just one aspect of a vast array of possible programs and services financed by institutional appropriations or a "health fee." Depending upon the needs and capacities of the campus and the surrounding community, some other possible functional areas for coordinated efforts are counseling services, health promotion or wellness services, residence life programs, recreation services, and services for students with disabilities. To be effective, these areas should not necessarily report to the same director or campus administrator, as various theoretical models (student development, ecological, public health or medical) apply.

Using a student development model or an ecological model with an emphasis on primary prevention, societal intervention, and community environment creates strong foundation from which to provide appropriate student-centered programs and services. The model, however, is not as important as the assessment and decision process through which leaders responsible for the connection of health and student learning come to a conscious choice and an intentional design for the variety of services offered. The most important aspect of any clinical health service will be its ability to create and maintain necessary, non-duplicate, responsive services, as well as collaborative relationships with the larger community, the faculty, and the student affairs staff. These relationships are essential in maintaining an emphasis on assisting in a student's academic success and a focus on the population's needs for a healthy and safe campus community (Jackson & Weinstein, 1997).

Clinical health services can be one of a variety of methods used to advance the health of students to the extent that such efforts enhance the learning environment at that institution of higher education. Clinical health services must make it a priority to first address health risks and problems contextually appropriate to a student's capacity to learn. These may include prevention of, or a response to wide-spread viral or bacterial infections and the health consequences of violence, racism, sexism, and heterosexist behaviors. Services must also meet the special needs of the physically and mentally challenged. A comprehensive ambulatory health care facility is not as important as coordinated relevant and cost-effective initiatives. Campuses must maintain a focus on services that support learning and effectively set priorities within this academic context.

Although institutions differ in size, scope and setting, there

are universal concepts that affect the level of provision of medical and nursing care to college students. These standards and guidelines are offered to serve in this process.

References, Readings, and Resources

American College Health Association. (2004). American College Health Association - National College Health Assessment (ACHA-NCHA) Web Summary. Updated June 2004. Available at http://www.acha.org .

American College Health Association. (2008). Guidelines and White Papers Baltimore, MD: Author.

Centers for Disease Control and Prevention. (1997). Youth risk behavior surveillance: National college health risk behavior survey-United States. *MMWR, 46*(6), 1-56.

Jackson, M., & Weinstein, H. (1997). The importance of healthy communities of higher education. *Journal of American College Health, 45*, 237-241.

Keeling, R.P. (2000). Beyond the campus clinic: A holistic approach to student health. *AAC&U Peer Review, 2*(3), 13-18.

Neinstein, L.S. (2002). *Adolescent health care: A practical guide.* Philadelphia: Lippincott Williams & Wilkins.

Packwood, W. (1989). *College student personnel services.* Springfield, IL: Charles C. Thomas.

Patrick, K. (1988). Student health: Medical care within institutions of higher education. *Journal of the American Medical Association, 260*, 3301-3305.

Silverman, D., Underhile, R., & Keeling, R. (2008). Student health reconsidered: A radical proposal for thinking differently about health-related programs and services for students. *Student Health Spectrum*, June 2008, 4-11

Swinford, P. (2002). Advancing the health of students: A viewpoint. *Journal of American College Health,* May 2002.

United States Department of Human Services. (2000). *Healthy people 2010: National health promotion and disease prevention objectives.* DHHS (PHS) Pub. No. 91-50212. Washington, DC: U.S. Department of Health and Human Services.

American College Health Association [ACHA]. ACHA National Office, P.O. Box 28937. Baltimore, MD 21240-8937. (410) 859-1500; Fax (410) 859-1510. http://www.acha.org

Contributors:

Paula Swinford, University of Southern California, ACHA
Kristen Buzzbee, CAS ACHA Alternate
Richard P. Keeling, MD, K&A, NYC, CAS Public Director
Mary Hoban and Victor Lieno, ACHA Staff

Clinical Health Services
CAS Standards and Guidelines

Part 1. MISSION

The purpose of Clinical Health Services (CHS) is to provide, promote, support, and integrate individual healthcare, clinical preventive services, clinical treatment for illness, patient education, and public health responsibilities. Such services must take into consideration the health status of the student population and the learning environment. These services must be consistent with the educational mission of the institution and must comply with relevant legal requirements, state/provincial regulations, and professional standards. The mission must reflect the fundamental assumption that health and social justice are inextricably interconnected. CHS must serve as a method of advancing the health of the students, thereby enhancing the learning environment at the institution of higher education it serves.

The following characteristics exemplify CHS that are consistent with the environment of healthcare delivery and the environment of higher education:

- access to multiple data sources on the characteristics and health status of the population
- a spectrum of services that supports the learning mission of the campus community and health in its broadest sense
- easy and equal access to services by all students
- advocacy for a healthy campus community by providing leadership on policy issues regarding health risks of the population in the context of the learning environment
- evidence of measures of quality, such as accreditation of services, the use of recognized standards, and data on service delivery and effectiveness
- significant student involvement in advising the program's mission, goals, services, funding, and evaluation
- providing leadership during a health-related crises
- collaboration with other campus health-related programs and services

CHS must develop, disseminate, implement, and regularly review their mission. Mission statements must be consistent with the mission of the institution and with professional standards. CHS in higher education must enhance overall educational experiences by incorporating student learning and development outcomes in their mission.

Part 2. PROGRAM

The formal education of students, consisting of the curriculum and the co-curriculum, must promote student learning and development outcomes that are purposeful and holistic and that prepare students for satisfying and productive lifestyles, work, and civic participation. The student learning and development outcome domains and their related dimensions are:

- knowledge acquisition, integration, construction, and application
    - o Dimensions: understanding knowledge from a range of disciplines; connecting knowledge to other knowledge, ideas, and experiences; constructing knowledge; and relating knowledge to daily life
- cognitive complexity
    - o Dimensions: critical thinking; reflective thinking; effective reasoning; and creativity
- intrapersonal development
    - o Dimensions: realistic self-appraisal, self-understanding, and self-respect; identity development; commitment to ethics and integrity; and spiritual awareness
- interpersonal competence
    - o Dimensions: meaningful relationships; interdependence; collaboration; and effective leadership
- humanitarianism and civic engagement
    - o Dimensions: understanding and appreciation of cultural and human differences; social responsibility; global perspective; and sense of civic responsibility
- practical competence
    - o Dimensions: pursuing goals; communicating effectively; technical competence; managing personal affairs; managing career development; demonstrating professionalism; maintaining health and wellness; and living a purposeful and satisfying life

[See *The Council for the Advancement of Standards Learning and Developmental Outcomes* statement for examples of outcomes related to these domains and dimensions.]

Consistent with the institutional mission, Clinical Health Services (CHS) must identify relevant and desirable student learning and development outcomes from among the six domains and related dimensions. When creating opportunities for student learning and development, CHS must explore possibilities for collaboration with faculty members and other colleagues.

CHS must assess relevant and desirable student learning and development outcomes and provide evidence of their impact on student learning and development. CHS must articulate how they contribute to or support students' learning and development in the domains not specifically assessed.

CHS must be:

- integrated into the life of the institution
- intentional and coherent
- guided by theories and knowledge of learning and development
- reflective of developmental and demographic profiles of the student population

- **responsive to needs of individuals, diverse and special populations, and relevant constituencies**

CHS must acknowledge that health and social justice are inextricably interconnected.

CHS must establish appropriate policies and procedures for responding to emergency situations, especially where CHS facilities, personnel, and resources are not equipped to handle emergencies and/or when services are closed.

CHS must provide an infrastructure to support its services. The program must also create and maintain a network of services throughout the campus and surrounding communities.

Regardless of the size or scope of the institution, CHS must conform to a general level of acceptable practice that is theory-based and data-driven, and compliant with pertinent statutes, regulations, and professional standards.

In determining the scope of services to be offered, the following guidelines should apply:
- data on the affordability and accessibility of local healthcare resources, the insurance coverage of individual students, and the health status of the population should be collected and used to set priorities and tailor the CHS to the specific campus context
- CHS should contribute to the general education of students in the areas of behaviors and environments that promote physical, psychological, spiritual, and social health
- the scope and objectives of the services should be planned and outlined according to standards of practice utilizing data, goals and objectives, focus populations, assessment strategies and evaluative methodologies
- the educational goals of CHS should be consistent with nationally and internationally developed healthcare objectives
- documented evidence of organized strategic planning and implementation should be available
- CHS should create opportunities to address documented health issues and medical services needs within the student community it serves
- appropriate interdisciplinary and interagency collaboration should occur regularly

In determining the quality of services provided, the following guidelines should apply:
- access for all students to essential medical, nursing, and counseling services
- provision of services in accordance with standards of professional practice and ethical conduct and concern for the costs versus benefits to the health status of the population
- maintenance of accreditation, staff certification, and licensure where appropriate
- cost-effective and relevant services designed to address unique campus configurations
- coordination of services to ensure coverage with no duplication
- identification of less expensive alternative resources for

individual healthcare when appropriate
- provision of appropriate referrals for additional or alternative treatments or assessments

Part 3. LEADERSHIP

Because effective and ethical leadership is essential to the success of all organizations, Clinical Health Services (CHS) leaders with organizational authority for the programs and services must:
- **articulate a vision and mission for their programs and services**
- **set goals and objectives based on the needs of the population served and desired student learning and development outcomes**
- **advocate for their programs and services**
- **promote campus environments that provide meaningful opportunities for student learning, development, and integration**
- **identify and find means to address individual, organizational, or environmental conditions that foster or inhibit mission achievement**
- **advocate for representation in strategic planning initiatives at appropriate divisional and institutional levels**
- **initiate collaborative interactions with stakeholders who have legitimate concerns and interests in the functional area**
- **apply effective practices to educational and administrative processes**
- **prescribe and model ethical behavior**
- **communicate effectively**
- **manage financial resources, including planning, allocation, monitoring, and analysis**
- **incorporate sustainability practices in the management and design of programs, services, and facilities**
- **manage human resource processes including recruitment, selection, development, supervision, performance planning, and evaluation**
- **empower professional, support, and student staff to accept leadership opportunities**
- **encourage and support scholarly contribution to the profession**
- **be informed about and integrate appropriate technologies into programs and services**
- **be knowledgeable about federal, state/provincial, and local laws relevant to the programs and services and ensure that staff members understand their responsibilities by receiving appropriate training**
- **develop and continuously improve programs and services in response to the changing needs of students and other populations served and the evolving institutional priorities**
- **recognize environmental conditions that may negatively influence the safety of staff and students and propose interventions that mitigate such conditions**

CHS leaders should continuously strive to eliminate duplicate coverage for care and contribute to a campus culture that supports health.

As the institution is legally constituted, the institution must have a defined governance structure that sets policy and is ultimately responsible for the CHS and its operations.

Part 4. HUMAN RESOURCES

Clinical Health Services (CHS) must be staffed adequately by individuals qualified to accomplish the mission and goals. Within institutional guidelines, CHS must establish procedures for staff selection, training, and evaluation; set expectations for supervision; and provide appropriate professional development opportunities to improve the leadership ability, competence, and skills of all employees.

CHS should:
- strive to improve the professional competence and skill, as well as the quality of performance of all personnel it employs
- provide personnel with convenient access to on-line library resources that include materials pertinent to operational, administrative, institutional, and research services
- encourage participation of personnel in seminars, workshops, and other educational activities pertinent to its mission, goals, objectives, and the professional role
- verify participation in relevant external professional development programs, when attendance at such activities is required of professional personnel
- monitor the use of resources available to its personnel to identify that activities are relevant to the mission, goals, and objectives, and to maintain the licensure and/or certification of professional personnel
- identify continuing education activities based on quality improvement findings and the education criteria established by recognized professional authorities

CHS professional staff members must hold an earned graduate or professional degree in a field relevant to the position they hold or must possess an appropriate combination of educational credentials and related work experience.

CHS must establish criteria and implement a procedure to review and verify credentials of staff.

Degree- or credential-seeking interns must be qualified by enrollment in an appropriate field of study and by relevant experience. These individuals must be trained and supervised adequately by professional staff members holding educational credentials and related work experience appropriate for supervision.

Student employees and volunteers must be carefully selected, trained, supervised, and evaluated. They must be educated on how and when to refer those in need of additional assistance to qualified staff members and must have access to a supervisor for assistance in making these judgments. Student employees and volunteers must be provided clear and precise job descriptions, pre-service training based on assessed needs, and continuing staff development.

Student employees and volunteers must never have access to the personal health information of other students.

Employees and volunteers must receive specific training on institutional policies and privacy laws regarding their access to student records and other sensitive institutional information (e.g., in the USA, Family Educational Rights and Privacy Act, FERPA, or equivalent privacy laws in other states/provinces or countries).

CHS must have technical and support staff members adequate to accomplish their mission. All members of the staff must be technologically proficient and qualified to perform their job functions, be knowledgeable about ethical and legal uses of technology, and have access to training and resources to support the performance of their assigned responsibilities.

All members of the staff must receive training on policies and procedures related to the use of technology to store or access student records and institutional data.

CHS must ensure that staff members are knowledgeable about and trained in emergency procedures, crisis response, and prevention efforts. Prevention efforts must address identification of threatening conduct or behavior of students, faculty members, staff, and others and must incorporate a system or procedures for responding, including but not limited to reporting them to the appropriate campus officials.

Salary levels and benefits for all staff members must be commensurate with those for comparable positions within the institution, in similar institutions, and in the relevant geographic area.

CHS must maintain position descriptions for all staff members.

To create a diverse staff, CHS must institute hiring and promotion practices that are fair, inclusive, proactive, and non-discriminatory.

Staff members must take part in training sessions about gender, sexual orientation, racial, cultural, religious and/or spiritual, and ethnic sensitivity and should be aware of and involved in campus and community matters.

CHS must conduct regular performance planning and evaluation of staff members. CHS must provide access to continuing and advanced education and professional development opportunities.

Specific aspects of the CHS for which staff should be assigned include business and financial management, community relations, and assessment.

Leaders should involve staff members in designing the organizational structure and in creating and reviewing policies and procedures that reinforce and foster health-engendering behaviors.

When CHS staff is involved in formal teaching or supervision, policies governing those activities must be consistent with the mission, goals, policies, and objectives of the institution.

When CHS staff is involved in research and publishing, policies governing those activities must be consistent with mission, goals, priorities, and objectives of the institution and capabilities of the program.

All CHS staff must be informed of the research policies of the institution and CHS.

Part 5. ETHICS

Persons involved in the delivery of Clinical Health Services (CHS) must adhere to the highest principles of ethical behavior. CHS must review relevant professional ethical standards and develop or adopt and implement appropriate statements of ethical practice. CHS must publish these statements and ensure their periodic review by relevant constituencies.

CHS must orient new staff members to relevant ethical standards and statements of ethical practice.

CHS staff members must ensure that privacy and confidentiality are maintained with respect to all communications and records to the extent that such records are protected under the law and appropriate statements of ethical practice. Information contained in students' education records must not be disclosed except as allowed by relevant laws and institutional policies. CHS staff members must disclose to appropriate authorities information judged to be of an emergency nature, especially when the safety of the individual or others is involved, or when otherwise required by institutional policy or relevant law.

The task of media relations involving individual health status should be assigned to staff members who are knowledgeable about information that can be released.

Staff members should prevent visitors from entering the facility in any manner that would compromise confidentiality.

CHS staff members must be aware of and comply with the provisions contained in the institution's policies pertaining to human subjects research and student rights and responsibilities, as well as those in other relevant institutional policies addressing ethical practices and confidentiality of research data concerning individuals.

CHS staff members must recognize and avoid personal conflicts of interest or appearance thereof in the performance of their work.

Products and services should not be promoted for any other reason than the individual's or the community's benefit.

CHS staff members must strive to insure the fair, objective, and impartial treatment of all persons with whom they interact.

When handling institutional funds, CHS staff members must ensure that such funds are managed in accordance with established and responsible accounting procedures and the fiscal policies or processes of the institution.

Promotional and descriptive information must be accurate and free of deception.

CHS staff members must perform their duties within the limits of their training, expertise, and competence. When these limits are exceeded, individuals in need of further assistance must be referred to persons possessing appropriate qualifications.

CHS staff members must use suitable means to confront and otherwise hold accountable other staff members who exhibit unethical behavior.

CHS staff members must be knowledgeable about and practice ethical behavior in the use of technology.

All marketing and advertising concerning the clinical health services must communicate the scope and range of services provided without deception.

Clinical health services should inform individuals of their basic rights and responsibilities regarding service. Such rights and responsibilities should include:

- service that is competent, considerate, and compassionate; recognizes basic human rights; safeguards personal dignity; and respects values and preferences
- provision of appropriate privacy, including protection from access to confidential information by faculty members, staff, student workers, and others
- ability to receive services from the staff member of choice
- accurate information regarding competencies and credentials of the clinical health services staff
- use of identified methods to express grievances and make suggestions
- information concerning individual health status and available services
- individual disclosure of complete and full information on health status that will be treated confidentially and for which the individual gives authority to approve or refuse release in compliance with applicable federal and state/provincial laws
- an explicit process to share necessary personal health information with mental health/counseling/psychotherapy services and other higher education faculty and staff on a need-to-know basis
- an explicit process for consent to share necessary personal health information with off-campus entities

Part 6. LEGAL RESPONSIBILITIES

Clinical Health Services (CHS) staff members must be knowledgeable about and responsive to laws and regulations that relate to their respective responsibilities and that may pose legal obligations, limitations, or ramifications for the institution as a whole. As appropriate, staff members must inform users of programs and services, as well as officials, of legal obligations and limitations including constitutional, statutory, regulatory, and case law; mandatory laws and orders emanating from federal, state/provincial, and local governments; and the institution's policies.

CHS must have written policies on all relevant operations, transactions, or tasks that may have legal implications.

CHS staff members must neither participate in nor condone any form of harassment or activity that demeans persons or creates an intimidating, hostile, or offensive campus environment.

CHS staff members must use reasonable and informed practices to limit the liability exposure of the institution and its officers, employees, and agents. CHS staff members must be informed about institutional policies regarding risk management, personal liability, and related insurance coverage options and must be referred to external sources if coverage is not provided by the institution.

The institution must provide access to legal advice for CHS staff members as needed to carry out assigned responsibilities.

The institution must inform CHS staff and students in a timely and systematic fashion about extraordinary or changing legal obligations and potential liabilities.

CHS must inform the institutional community of its policies and procedures addressing:

- individual rights and responsibilities
- balancing protection of individual health and safety with individual rights to confidentiality and privacy
- risk management
- medical access insurance coverage
- informed consent
- access, release content, and maintenance of individual records in accordance with legal obligations and limitations
- research
- medical dismissal of students

CHS must develop and maintain a systematic risk management program appropriate for the organization.

Risk management programs should focus on:
- methods by which individuals may be dismissed from or refused services
- methods of collecting unpaid accounts
- review of litigation related to the institution's CHS
- review of all deaths, trauma, or adverse events where there is health risk
- communication with the liability insurance carrier
- methods of dealing with inquiries from government agencies, attorneys, consumer advocate groups, reporters, and the media
- methods of managing a situation with an impaired staff member
- methods for complying with governmental regulations and

contractual agreements
- methods of transporting students with medical emergencies
- maintenance of confidential records

Part 7. EQUITY and ACCESS

Clinical Health Services (CHS) must be provided on a fair, equitable, and non-discriminatory basis in accordance with institutional policies and with all applicable state/provincial and federal statutes and regulations. CHS must maintain an educational and work environment free from discrimination in accordance with law and institutional policy.

CHS should accommodate the unique needs of individuals with disabilities and should encourage faculty, staff, and other students to develop awareness of and sensitivity to individuals with disabilities. Students with disabilities should be encouraged to self-identify individual needs as soon as possible following admission (pre-matriculation) so that accommodations can be made.

For students with physical disabilities, CHS staff should advocate that the institution meet special needs through clinical health services, housing, food services, and counseling services. Whenever possible, the institution should eliminate architectural barriers that create difficulties for students with physical disabilities.

Discrimination must be avoided on the basis of age; cultural heritage; disability; ethnicity; gender identity and expression; nationality; political affiliation; race; religious affiliation; sex; sexual orientation; economic, marital, social, or veteran status; and any other bases included in local, state/provincial, or federal laws.

Students with special health risks may be identified by information provided on health history or behavioral assessment forms, or through screening, surveillance, and education services.

Students with chronic health conditions may be identified and informed of support services.

CHS may provide services directly or identify appropriate resources in the community to meet the special needs of these students.

Consistent with the mission and goals, CHS must take action to remedy significant imbalances in student participation and staffing patterns.

CHS must ensure physical and program access for persons with disabilities. CHS must be responsive to the needs of all students and other populations served when establishing hours of operation and developing methods of delivering programs and services.

CHS must recognize the needs of distance learning students by providing appropriate and accessible services and assisting them in identifying and gaining access to other appropriate services in their geographic region.

CHS must ensure that students are informed about the importance of medical and dental access insurance and how to make an informed decision based on their needs.

As a condition of enrollment, students may be required to provide evidence that they have adequate medical access through healthcare insurance coverage.

Medical access through insurance coverage should be available to all eligible students.

Part 8. DIVERSITY

Within the context of each institution's unique mission, diversity enriches the community and enhances the collegiate experience for all; therefore, Clinical Health Services (CHS) must create and nurture environments that are welcoming to and bring together persons of diverse backgrounds.

CHS must promote environments that are characterized by open and continuous communication that deepens understanding of one's own identity, culture, and heritage, as well as that of others. CHS must recognize, honor, educate, and promote respect about commonalties and differences among people within their historical and cultural contexts.

CHS must address the characteristics and needs of a diverse population when establishing and implementing policies and procedures.

Every contact should be viewed as an opportunity to recognize and honor diversity to address specific concerns that might impact health and quality of life for the individual and community.

Students should be provided an environment of caring with an inclusive approach, which is essential for establishing levels of confidentiality, trust, and comfort.

CHS should establish procedures for students to discuss with staff their comfort or discomfort with various approaches in delivery of services.

Individuals should be accepted in a free and open manner and in an atmosphere of mutual respect to encourage candid discussion of sensitive personal issues. Staff members should demonstrate sensitivity and understanding to students from diverse backgrounds and cultures to provide satisfactory services.

Part 9. ORGANIZATION and MANAGEMENT

To promote student learning and development outcomes, Clinical Health Services (CHS) must be structured purposefully and managed effectively to achieve stated goals. Evidence of appropriate structure must include current and accessible policies and procedures, written performance expectations for all employees, functional workflow graphics or organizational charts, and clearly stated program and service delivery expectations.

CHS should be defined by the size, nature, complexity, and mission of the institution and by the documented needs and capabilities of the population it serves, as well as the availability of local community resources.

CHS should establish and maintain an advisory board with broad constituent representation, with specific duties and responsibilities for policy, budget, services, facilities, and resources.

CHS should make initial staff appointments, reappointments, and assignment or curtailment of clinical privileges based upon a professional review of credentials and as directed by institutional policy and state/provincial regulations and statutes.

CHS must monitor websites used for distributing information to ensure that the sites are current, accurate, appropriately referenced, and accessible.

Evidence of effective management must include use of comprehensive and accurate information for decisions, clear sources and channels of authority, effective communication practices, procedures for decision-making and conflict resolution, responses to changing conditions, systems of accountability and evaluation, and processes for recognition and reward. CHS must align policies and procedures with those of the institution and provide channels within the organization for their regular review.

CHS should establish criteria and institute procedures for assessment and evaluation of medical access insurance policies.

The CHS director or coordinator must be placed within the institution's organizational structure to be able to promote cooperative interactions with appropriate campus and community entities.

Part 10. CAMPUS and EXTERNAL RELATIONS

Clinical Health Services (CHS) must reach out to relevant individuals, campus offices, and external agencies to:
- **establish, maintain, and promote effective relations**
- **disseminate information about their own and other related programs and services**
- **coordinate and collaborate, where appropriate, in offering programs and services to meet the needs of students and promote their achievement of student learning and development outcomes**

CHS must have procedures and guidelines consistent with institutional policy for responding to threats, emergencies, and crisis situations. Systems and procedures must be in place to disseminate timely and accurate information to students and other members of the campus community during emergency situations.

CHS must have procedures and guidelines consistent with institutional policy for communicating with the media.

To ensure success, CHS must maintain good relations with students, faculty members, staff, alumni, the local community, contractors, and support agencies.

CHS must comply with these standards even when contracted for or outsourced by the Institution.

CHS staff should participate actively with their institution in designing policies and practices and developing further resources and services that have direct impact on the health status of the campus population.

CHS should review and assess health aspects of relevant institutional policies and practices. These issues may include but are not limited to drug use policies and treatment, blood-borne diseases, sexual harassment/assault, suicide and homicide threats, and discrimination of all types.

Policies on requirements for immunization prior to and during matriculation should be implemented and maintained to assure compliance, protect community health, and meet the needs of students at risk.

CHS should collaborate to minimize duplication of services with campus and community partners.

CHS should address the level and the priorities of campus services as determined by institution-specific population health status surveys, available community resources, user data and institutional context. CHS should review potential health hazards or problems related to academic activities.

CHS should identify and utilize community services, whenever appropriate, to build resource/service networks and create awareness within the community about special needs populations.

Part 11. FINANCIAL RESOURCES

Clinical Health Services (CHS) must have adequate funding to accomplish their mission and goals. In establishing funding priorities and making significant changes, a comprehensive analysis, which includes relevant expenditures, external and internal resources, and impact on the campus community, must be conducted.

CHS must demonstrate fiscal responsibility and cost effectiveness consistent with institutional protocols.

Financial planning and projections should include budget data for both current and long-term expenditures that include capital expenditures and deferred maintenance costs.

Part 12. TECHNOLOGY

Clinical Health Services (CHS) must have adequate technology to support their mission. The technology and its use must comply with institutional policies and procedures and be evaluated for compliance with relevant federal, state/provincial, and local requirements.

CHS must maintain policies and procedures that address the security and back up of data.

When technology is used to facilitate student learning and development, CHS must select technology that reflects current best pedagogical practices.

Technology, as well as any workstations or computer labs maintained by the CHS for student use, must be accessible and must meet established technology standards for delivery

to persons with disabilities.

When CHS provide student access to technology, they must provide:
- access to policies that are clear, easy to understand, and available to all students
- access to instruction or training on how to use the technology
- access to information on the legal and ethical implications of misuse as it pertains to intellectual property, harassment, privacy, and social networks

Student violations of technology policies must follow established institutional student disciplinary procedures.

Students who experience negative emotional or psychological consequences from the use of technology must be referred to support services provided by the institution.

Part 13. FACILITIES and EQUIPMENT

Clinical Health Services (CHS) must have adequate, accessible, suitably located facilities and equipment to support their mission and goals. If acquiring capital equipment as defined by the institution, CHS must take into account expenses related to regular maintenance and life cycle costs. Facilities and equipment must be evaluated regularly, including consideration of sustainability, and be in compliance with relevant federal, state/provincial, and local requirements to provide for access, health, safety, and security.

CHS staff members must have work space that is well-equipped, adequate in size, and designed to support their work and responsibilities. For conversations requiring privacy, staff members must have access to a private space.

CHS staff members who share work space must have the ability to secure their work adequately.

The design of the facilities must guarantee the security of records and ensure the confidentiality of sensitive information.

The location and layout of the facilities must be sensitive to the special needs of persons with disabilities as well as the needs of constituencies served.

CHS must ensure that staff members are knowledgeable of and trained in safety and emergency procedures for securing and vacating the facilities.

CHS facilities should support a range of activities including clinical treatment, intervention and consultation, patient education, and policy development. A safe, functional, and efficient environment is crucial to providing appropriate services and achieving desired outcomes.

Depending upon services offered, environmental conditions should include:
- necessary facilities, technology, and equipment to handle individual or campus emergencies

- regulations prohibiting smoking
- elimination of hazards that might lead to slipping, falling, electrical shock, burns, poisoning, or other trauma
- adequate reception areas, toilets, and telephones
- parking for guests, patients, and people with disabilities
- accommodations for persons with physical disabilities
- adequate lighting and ventilation
- clean and properly maintained facilities
- facilities that provide for confidentiality and privacy of services and records
- testing and proper maintenance of equipment
- a system for the proper identification, management, handling, transport, treatment, and disposition of hazardous materials and wastes whether solid, liquid, or gas
- appropriate alternative power sources in case of emergency
- technology to support services and facilities

Part 14. ASSESSMENT and EVALUATION

Clinical Health Services (CHS) must establish systematic plans and processes to meet internal and external accountability expectations with regard to program as well as student learning and development outcomes. CHS must conduct regular assessment and evaluations. Assessments must include qualitative and quantitative methodologies as appropriate, to determine whether and to what degree the stated mission, goals, and student learning and development outcomes are being met. The process must employ sufficient and sound measures to ensure comprehensiveness. Data collected must include responses from students and other affected constituencies.

CHS should maintain an active, organized, peer-based, quality management and improvement program that links peer review, quality improvement activities, and risk management in an organized, systematic way.

Periodically, the organization should assess user and non-user satisfaction with services and facilities provided by the clinical health services and incorporate findings into quality improvement.

To develop criteria used to evaluate services, staff members should understand, support, and participate in programs of quality management and improvement. Data should be collected in an on-going manner to identify unacceptable or unexpected trends or occurrences.

The quality improvement program should address administrative and cost issues and service outcomes.

CHS must evaluate regularly how well they complement and enhance the institution's stated mission and educational effectiveness.

Results of these evaluations must be used in revising and improving programs and services, identifying needs and interests in shaping directions of program and service design, and recognizing staff performance.

General Standards revised in 2008;

CHS (formerly College Health Programs) developed/revised in 2001 & 2006

The Role of College Honor Societies
CAS Standards Contextual Statement

The purposes of honor societies in colleges and universities are threefold. First, they exist primarily to recognize the attainment of scholarship of a superior quality. Second, a few societies recognize the development of leadership qualities and of commitment to service and excellence in research, in addition to a strong scholarship record. Third, to the degree that this recognition is coveted, they encourage the production of superior scholarship and leadership. To accomplish these objectives, it is clear that an honor society must define and maintain a truly high standard of eligibility for membership and achieve sufficient status by so doing that membership becomes something to be highly valued.

The honor society has followed the expansion and specialization of higher education in America. When Phi Beta Kappa was organized in 1776, there was no thought given to its field because all colleges then in existence were for the training of men for the service of the church and the state. With the expansion of education into new fields a choice had to be made, and Phi Beta Kappa elected to operate in the field of liberal arts and sciences. Although this was not finally decided until 1898, the trend was evident earlier; the 1880s saw the establishment of Tau Beta Pi in the field of engineering and Sigma Xi in scientific research.

Early in the 20th century, other honor societies came into being. Phi Kappa Phi was organized to accept membership from all academic fields in the university. A few others of this nature had origins in Black, Catholic, or Jesuit colleges and universities. These honor societies became known as general honor societies. Other variations have developed since that time. Leadership honor societies recognized meritorious attainments in all-around leadership and campus citizenship. Numerous societies drew membership from the various departments of study, recognizing good work in the student's special field of study. These societies are generally known as specialized honor societies. Another variation recognized scholastic achievement during the freshman or sophomore year. Yet another variation recognized achievement in associate degree programs.

The national organization of each honor society sets standards for establishing collegiate chapters and requirements for administering them. Chapters are chartered to institutions and have a dual relationship: maintain national honor society standards and requirements and abide by institutional policies and procedures.

The Association of College Honor Societies (ACHS) was founded in 1925 to join forces for the establishment and maintenance of useful functions and desirable standards, including criteria for membership, for governance of each member society, and for chapter operation. In addition to defining honor societies, similar student organizations with more liberal membership requirements were named Recognition Societies. Baird's Manual*, for many years the definitive reference of college organizations, adopted the ACHS definitions for classification of Honor Societies and Recognition Societies.

The standards and functions originally named in the early history of ACHS still have relevance today as ACHS fulfills a certifying function in assuring candidates for membership as well as institutions that member societies have met the high standards. The standards also serve a role for judging credibility of non-member societies.

The challenge in the 21st century is the same as when ACHS was founded: to use academic and operational standards to allay the confusion prevailing on campuses and among the public regarding the credibility and legitimacy of newly emerging honor societies. A plethora of Internet societies, for-profit societies, and an increasingly narrow focus of specialized societies gives rise to the need for the CAS standards to guide colleges and universities in setting regulations for official recognition of campus honor societies. Students, parents, and the public can use the standards as criteria for judging quality.

References, Readings, and Resources

Association of College Honor Societies. (2002). *ACHS Handbook, 2002-2005.* 4990 Northwind Dr., Ste. 140, East Lansing, MI 48823-5031. Web site: www.achsnatl.org.

Warren, J. W. (2000). *Prelude to the new millennium: Promoting honor for seventy-five years.* East Lansing, MI: Association of College Honor Societies. www.achsnatl.org/history.asp.

Note: *Baird's Manual of American College Fraternities*, last published in 1991 by Baird's Manual Foundation, was the authoritative reference work on college Greek-letter societies since first published in 1879.

Contributor:
Dorothy I. Mitstifer, ACHS

College Honor Societies

CAS Standards and Guidelines

Part 1. MISSION

The mission of College Honor Societies (CHS) is to confer distinction for high achievement in undergraduate, graduate, and professional studies; in student leadership; in service; and in research.

CHS must develop, disseminate, implement, and regularly review their mission. Mission statements must be consistent with the mission of the institution and with professional standards. Programs and services in higher education must enhance overall educational experiences by incorporating student learning and development outcomes in their mission.

The following historical functions are properly served by CHS:

- foster a spirit of liberal education
- stimulate and encourage intellectual development
- stand for freedom of mind and spirit and for democracy of learning
- provide spiritual and intellectual leadership
- preserve valuable traditions and customs
- provide opportunities for members to associate in mutual understanding for the purpose of advancing society in the art of democratic living
- stimulate worthy attitudes for the improvement of the general welfare of the institution
- impose upon members high citizenship responsibilities and emphasize deeper study and discussion of the political-moral tradition—its characteristics, ideals, and possibilities

Part 2. PROGRAM

The formal education of students, consisting of the curriculum and the co-curriculum, must promote student learning and development outcomes that are purposeful and holistic and that prepare students for satisfying and productive lifestyles, work, and civic participation. The student learning and development outcome domains and their related dimensions are:

- knowledge acquisition, integration, construction, and application
    o Dimensions: understanding knowledge from a range of disciplines; connecting knowledge to other knowledge, ideas, and experiences; constructing knowledge; and relating knowledge to daily life

- cognitive complexity
    o Dimensions: critical thinking; reflective thinking; effective reasoning; and creativity

- intrapersonal development
    o Dimensions: realistic self-appraisal, self-understanding, and self-respect; identity development; commitment

to ethics and integrity; and spiritual awareness

- interpersonal competence
    o Dimensions: meaningful relationships; interdependence; collaboration; and effective leadership

- humanitarianism and civic engagement
    o Dimensions: understanding and appreciation of cultural and human differences; social responsibility; global perspective; and sense of civic responsibility

- practical competence
    o Dimensions: pursuing goals; communicating effectively; technical competence; managing personal affairs; managing career development; demonstrating professionalism; maintaining health and wellness; and living a purposeful and satisfying life

[See *The Council for the Advancement of Standards Learning and Developmental Outcomes* statement for examples of outcomes related to these domains and dimensions.]

Consistent with the institutional mission, College Honor Societies (CHS) must identify relevant and desirable student learning and development outcomes from among the six domains and related dimensions. When creating opportunities for student learning and development, CHS must explore possibilities for collaboration with faculty members and other colleagues.

CHS must assess relevant and desirable student learning and development outcomes and provide evidence of their impact on student learning and development. CHS must articulate how they contribute to or support students' learning and development in the domains not specifically assessed.

CHS must be:

- integrated into the life of the institution
- intentional and coherent
- guided by theories and knowledge of learning and development
- reflective of developmental and demographic profiles of the student population
- responsive to needs of individuals, diverse and special populations, and relevant constituencies

Programs of CHS must include the following elements:

- educational programming that complements the academic curriculum
- opportunities for recognition by the institution
- faculty, staff, and administrator involvement and interaction with students

The process for establishment of collegiate chapters of CHS must include:

- formal chartering of each chapter by institution and college/department petition
- approval by official action of the governing body of the national organization
- jointly defined relationship between the institution and the college honor society that must be formalized, documented, and disseminated
- candidate selection by the campus chapter
- membership invitation by the campus chapter

In order to maintain good standing with the national organization, CHS chapters must comply with the national organization's policies.

The national organization of a college honor society must be governed by its membership and must include:

- officers/board members elected by the national membership
- chapter representation in the governing body
- national membership participation in approving and revising by-laws
- independent financial review and full financial disclosure

Classifications of CHS include general scholarship, general leadership, specialized scholarship, and freshman and sophomore and two year honor societies. Minimum scholastic qualifications in each classification of CHS should include:

- general scholarship — top 20%, not earlier than 5th semester
- general leadership — top 35%, not earlier than 5th semester
- specialized scholarship — top 35%, not earlier than 4th semester
- freshman and sophomore and two-year (associate degree) honor societies — adherence to the same high standards with the exception of semesters completed

"Recognition Societies" are those organizations with lower scholastic criteria.

Part 3. LEADERSHIP

Advisers (faculty or staff member) must represent the institution in advising chapters of College Honor Societies (CHS). The adviser must model leadership principles, establish a climate and structure that facilitates leadership development, determine expectations of accountability, and fairly assess student performance.

Chapter governance documents and the names of officers and advisers must be filed annually both with the institution and the national organization.

Institutions should maintain a centralized registry of CHS organizations.

Because effective and ethical leadership is essential to the success of all organizations, advisers must ensure that CHS leaders with organizational authority for the programs and services:

- articulate a vision and mission for their programs and services

- set goals and objectives based on the needs of the population served and desired student learning and development outcomes
- advocate for their programs and services
- promote campus environments that provide meaningful opportunities for student learning, development, and integration
- identify and find means to address individual, organizational, or environmental conditions that foster or inhibit mission achievement
- advocate for representation in strategic planning initiatives at appropriate divisional and institutional levels
- initiate collaborative interactions with stakeholders who have legitimate concerns and interests in the functional area
- apply effective practices to educational and administrative processes
- prescribe and model ethical behavior
- communicate effectively
- manage financial resources, including planning, allocation, monitoring, and analysis
- incorporate sustainability practices in the management and design of programs, services, and facilities
- manage human resource processes including recruitment, selection, development, supervision, performance planning, and evaluation
- empower professional, support, and student staff to accept leadership opportunities
- encourage and support scholarly contribution to the profession
- be informed about and integrate appropriate technologies into programs and services
- be knowledgeable about federal, state/provincial, and local laws relevant to the programs and services and ensure that staff members understand their responsibilities by receiving appropriate training
- develop and continuously improve programs and services in response to the changing needs of students and other populations served and the evolving institutional priorities
- recognize environmental conditions that may negatively influence the safety of staff and students and propose interventions that mitigate such conditions

Leaders of CHS are elected by their peers to organize chapter activities.

Leaders of CHS should be students.

Part 4. HUMAN RESOURCES

College Honor Societies (CHS) must be staffed adequately by honor society advisers, qualified to accomplish the mission and goals. Within institutional guidelines, CHS must establish procedures for adviser selection, training, and evaluation; set expectations for supervision; and provide appropriate professional development opportunities to improve the leadership ability, competence, and skills of advisers.

Advisers of CHS must be employed by the institution as faculty or staff members and hold an earned graduate or professional degree in a field relevant to the position they hold or must possess an appropriate combination of educational credentials and related work experience.

With very few exceptions, faculty and staff are not employed as CHS advisers; most are volunteers.

Degree- or credential-seeking interns must be qualified by enrollment in an appropriate field of study and by relevant experience. These individuals must be trained and supervised adequately by professional staff members holding educational credentials and related work experience appropriate for supervision.

Graduate student advisers of CHS must be qualified by enrollment in an appropriate field of study and by relevant experience. These individuals must be trained and supervised adequately by professional staff members holding educational credentials and related work experience appropriate for supervision.

Leaders and advisers must be carefully trained, supervised, and evaluated. They must be educated on how and when to refer those in need of additional assistance to qualified staff members and must have access to a supervisor for assistance in making these judgments. Student leaders must be provided clear and precise job descriptions, pre-service training based on assessed needs, and continuing leadership development.

Student employees and volunteers must be carefully selected, trained, supervised, and evaluated. They must be educated on how and when to refer those in need of additional assistance to qualified staff members and must have access to a supervisor for assistance in making these judgments. Student employees and volunteers must be provided clear and precise job descriptions, pre-service training based on assessed needs, and continuing staff development.

Employees and volunteers must receive specific training on institutional policies and privacy laws regarding their access to student records and other sensitive institutional information (e.g., in the USA, Family Educational Rights and Privacy Act, FERPA, or equivalent privacy laws in other states/provinces or countries.)

CHS must have technical and support staff members adequate to accomplish their mission. All members of the staff must be technologically proficient and qualified to perform their job functions, be knowledgeable about ethical and legal uses of technology, and have access to training and resources to support the performance of their assigned responsibilities.

All members of the staff must receive training on policies and procedures related to the use of technology to store or access student records and institutional data.

CHS must ensure that staff members are knowledgeable

about and trained in emergency procedures, crisis response, and prevention efforts. Prevention efforts must address identification of threatening conduct or behavior of students, faculty members, staff, and others and must incorporate a system or procedures for responding, including but not limited to reporting them to the appropriate campus officials.

Salary levels and benefits for CHS advisers must be commensurate with those for comparable positions within the institution, in similar institutions, and in the relevant geographic area.

CHS must maintain position descriptions for advisers and leaders.

To create a diverse staff, CHS must institute hiring and promotion practices that are fair, inclusive, proactive, and non-discriminatory.

CHS must conduct regular performance planning and evaluation of staff members, advisers, and leaders. CHS must provide access to continuing and advanced education and professional development opportunities.

Part 5. ETHICS

Persons involved in the activities of College Honor Societies (CHS) must adhere to the highest principles of ethical behavior. CHS must review relevant professional ethical standards and develop or adopt and implement appropriate statements of ethical practice. CHS must publish these statements and ensure their periodic review by relevant constituencies.

CHS must orient new advisers and staff members to relevant ethical standards and statements of ethical practice.

Advisers of CHS must ensure that privacy and confidentiality are maintained with respect to all communications and records to the extent that such records are protected under the law and appropriate statements of ethical practice. Information contained in students' education records must not be disclosed except as allowed by relevant laws and institutional policies. Advisers of CHS must disclose to appropriate authorities information judged to be of an emergency nature, especially when the safety of the individual or others is involved, or when otherwise required by institutional policy or relevant law.

Advisers of CHS must be aware of and comply with the provisions contained in the institution's policies pertaining to human subjects research and student rights and responsibilities, as well as those in other relevant institutional policies addressing ethical practices and confidentiality of research data concerning individuals.

Advisers of CHS must recognize and avoid personal conflicts of interest or appearance thereof in the performance of their work.

Advisers of CHS must strive to insure the fair, objective, and impartial treatment of all persons with whom they interact.

When handling institutional funds, advisers of CHS must ensure that such funds are managed in accordance with established and responsible accounting procedures and the fiscal policies or processes of the institution.

Promotional and descriptive information must be accurate and free of deception.

Advisers of CHS must perform their duties within the limits of their training, expertise, and competence. When these limits are exceeded, individuals in need of further assistance must be referred to persons possessing appropriate qualifications.

Advisers of CHS must use suitable means to confront and otherwise hold accountable other staff members who exhibit unethical behavior.

Advisers of CHS must be knowledgeable about and practice ethical behavior in the use of technology.

Part 6. LEGAL RESPONSIBILITIES

Advisers of College Honor Societies (CHS) must be knowledgeable about and responsive to laws and regulations that relate to their respective responsibilities and that may pose legal obligations, limitations, or ramifications for the institution as a whole. As appropriate, advisers must inform users of programs and services, as well as officials, of legal obligations and limitations including constitutional, statutory, regulatory, and case law; mandatory laws and orders emanating from federal, state/provincial, and local governments; and the institution's policies.

CHS must have written policies on all relevant operations, transactions, or tasks that may have legal implications.

Advisers of CHS must neither participate in nor condone any form of harassment or activity that demeans persons or creates an intimidating, hostile, or offensive campus environment.

Advisers of CHS must use reasonable and informed practices to limit the liability exposure of the institution and its officers, employees, and agents. Advisers of CHS must be informed about institutional policies regarding risk management, personal liability, and related insurance coverage options and must be referred to external sources if coverage is not provided by the institution.

The institution must provide access to legal advice for advisers of CHS as needed to carry out assigned responsibilities.

The institution must inform advisers and members of CHS in a timely and systematic fashion about extraordinary or changing legal obligations and potential liabilities.

Part 7. EQUITY and ACCESS

Advisers of College Honor Societies (CHS) must ensure that programs and services are provided on a fair, equitable, and non-discriminatory basis in accordance with institutional policies and with all applicable state/provincial and federal statutes and regulations. CHS must maintain an educational and work environment free from discrimination in accordance with law and institutional policy. Advisers must ensure that invitations to membership in CHS are distributed on a fair and equitable basis.

Policies and practices of CHS must not discriminate on the basis of age; cultural heritage; disability; ethnicity; gender identity and expression; nationality; political affiliation; race; religious affiliation; sex; sexual orientation; economic, marital, social, or veteran status; and any other bases included in local, state/provincial, or federal laws.

Consistent with the mission and goals, CHS must take action to remedy significant imbalances in student participation and staffing patterns.

CHS must ensure physical and program access for persons with disabilities. CHS must be responsive to the needs of all students and other populations served when establishing hours of operation and developing methods of delivering programs and services.

CHS must recognize the needs of distance learning students by providing appropriate and accessible services and assisting them in identifying and gaining access to other appropriate services in their geographic region.

CHS must include outreach to underrepresented populations in membership recruitment activities.

Part 8. DIVERSITY

Within the context of each institution's unique mission, diversity enriches the community and enhances the collegiate experience for all; therefore, College Honor Societies (CHS) must create and nurture environments that are welcoming to and bring together persons of diverse backgrounds.

CHS must promote environments that are characterized by open and continuous communication that deepens understanding of one's own identity, culture, and heritage, as well as that of others. Programs and services must recognize, honor, educate, and promote respect about commonalties and differences among people within their historical and cultural contexts.

CHS must address the characteristics and needs of a diverse population when establishing and implementing policies and procedures.

Part 9. ORGANIZATION and MANAGEMENT

To promote student learning and development outcomes, College Honor Societies (CHS) must be structured purposefully and managed effectively to achieve stated goals. Evidence of appropriate structure must include current and accessible policies and procedures, written performance expectations for all employees, functional workflow graphics or organizational charts, and clearly stated program and service delivery expectations.

CHS must monitor websites used for distributing information to ensure that the sites are current, accurate, appropriately referenced, and accessible.

Evidence of effective management must include use of comprehensive and accurate information for decisions, clear sources and channels of authority, effective communication practices, procedures for decision-making and conflict resolution, responses to changing conditions, systems of accountability and evaluation, and processes for recognition and reward. CHS must align policies and procedures with those of the institution and provide channels within the organization for their regular review.

Part 10. CAMPUS and EXTERNAL RELATIONS

College Honor Societies (CHS) must reach out to relevant individuals, campus offices, and external agencies to:
- establish, maintain, and promote effective relations
- disseminate information about their own and other related programs and services
- coordinate and collaborate, where appropriate, in offering programs and services to meet the needs of students and promote achievement of student learning and development outcomes

CHS must have procedures and guidelines consistent with institutional policy for responding to threats, emergencies, and crisis situations. Systems and procedures must be in place to disseminate timely and accurate information to students and other members of the campus community during emergency situations.

CHS must have procedures and guidelines consistent with institutional policy for communicating with the media.

Part 11. FINANCIAL RESOURCES

College Honor Societies (CHS) must have adequate funding to accomplish their mission and goals. In establishing funding priorities and making significant changes, a comprehensive analysis, which includes relevant expenditures, external and internal resources, and impact on the campus community, must be conducted.

CHS must demonstrate fiscal responsibility and cost effectiveness consistent with institutional protocols.

Part 12. TECHNOLOGY

College Honor Societies (CHS) must have adequate technology to support their mission. The technology and its use must comply with institutional policies and procedures and be evaluated for compliance with relevant federal, state/provincial, and local requirements.

CHS must maintain policies and procedures that address the security and back up of data.

When technology is used to facilitate student learning and development, CHS must select technology that reflects current best pedagogical practices.

Technology, as well as any workstations or computer labs maintained by the CHS for student use, must be accessible and must meet established technology standards for delivery to persons with disabilities.

When CHS provide student access to technology, they must provide:
- access to policies that are clear, easy to understand, and available to all students
- access to instruction or training on how to use the technology
- access to information on the legal and ethical implications of misuse as it pertains to intellectual property, harassment, privacy, and social networks

Student violations of technology policies must follow established institutional student disciplinary procedures.

Students who experience negative emotional or psychological consequences from the use of technology must be referred to support services provided by the institution.

Part 13. FACILITIES and EQUIPMENT

College Honor Societies (CHS) must have adequate, accessible, suitably located facilities and equipment to support their mission and goals. If acquiring capital equipment as defined by the institution, CHS must take into account expenses related to regular maintenance and life cycle costs. Facilities and equipment must be evaluated regularly, including consideration of sustainability, and be in compliance with relevant federal, state/provincial, and local requirements to provide for access, health, safety, and security.

Meeting space for chapter activities and storage space for chapter materials (memorabilia, documents, files) should be available. Chapter files should be stored electronically and securely. Storage space for other chapter property should be available.

Advisers of CHS must have work space that is well-equipped, adequate in size, and designed to support their work and responsibilities. For conversations requiring privacy, staff members must have access to a private space.

Advisers of CHS who share work space must have the ability to secure their work adequately.

The design of the facilities must guarantee the security of records and ensure the confidentiality of sensitive information.

The location and layout of the facilities must be sensitive to the special needs of persons with disabilities as well as the needs of constituencies served.

CHS must ensure that staff members are knowledgeable of

and trained in safety and emergency procedures for securing and vacating the facilities.

Part 14. ASSESSMENT and EVALUATION

College Honor Societies (CHS) must establish systematic plans and processes to meet internal and external accountability expectations with regard to program as well as student learning and development outcomes. CHS must conduct regular assessment and evaluations. Assessments must include qualitative and quantitative methodologies as appropriate, to determine whether and to what degree the stated mission, goals, and student learning and development outcomes are being met. The process must employ sufficient and sound measures to ensure comprehensiveness. Data collected must include responses from students and other affected constituencies.

CHS must evaluate regularly how well they complement and enhance the institution's stated mission and educational effectiveness.

Results of these evaluations must be used in revising and improving programs and services, identifying needs and interests in shaping directions of program and service design, and recognizing adviser and leader performance.

General Standards revised in 2008;
CHS content developed in 2005

The Role of College Unions
CAS Standards Contextual Statement

Today's college union is a unifying force that brings together students, faculty, administrators, staff, alumni, and guests. It provides a forum for divergent viewpoints and creates an environment where all feel welcome. Optimally the union is a centrally-located building where members of the campus community come together, formally and informally, yet the union idea is broader than bricks and mortar.

The college union primarily refers to an organization or program which evolved from the debating tradition of British Universities. The earliest college union, founded at Cambridge University in 1815, was literally a "union" of three debating societies. The first U.S. college union was organized at Harvard in 1832; like its British predecessors, it existed primarily for debating purposes. By the late 1800s, the Harvard Union had embraced the concept of being a general club. The first building erected explicitly for union purposes was Houston Hall at the University of Pennsylvania. Built in 1896, it housed lounges, dining rooms, reading and writing rooms, an auditorium, game rooms, and student offices; it was given to the university by the Houston family as a "place where all may meet on common ground."

In the 1930s, the success of civic recreational and cultural centers influenced college union leaders to view the union as the campus counterpart of the "community center," with an educational and recreational mission to perform. The first extensive period of union building construction took place following World War II, as enrollments surged and colleges and universities sought to better fulfill the needs of students and faculty. A second building boom occurred in the 1990s and 2000s as the original facilities have been renovated or replaced, and other institutions built their first unions.

Traditionally, the union was described as the "hearthstone" or "living room" of the campus. Today's union is the gathering place of the campus. As the 21st century begins, the college union movement has concentrated on building community, emphasizing its educational mission, and promoting student development and leadership. During this time, the names of facilities that embody the union idea have expanded to include college union, memorial union, student union, college center, student center, and campus center, among others. Funding and institutional preferences have led to the variety of names. Regardless of the name of the facility on a specific campus, the fundamental principle of college unions remains to bring together and unify its campus.

The contemporary college union offers many services used by all members of the campus community. College unions often include banks, post offices, child care, dining facilities, study lounges, computer labs, bookstores, and other services the campus community, and especially students, rely on during the course of the day while they are on campus. In providing these services, the college union supports the community focus on academic and personal achievement. College unions vary by institutional size, scope, and purpose. No student formula identifies the optimum size of a college union. However, the Association of College Unions International (ACUI) has a benchmarking mechanism, ACUInfo, which allows for institutional comparison in size and facilities.

In 2005, ACUI announced a set of eleven core competencies for the college union and student activities profession. Developed over six years, the core competencies are a composite set of knowledge and behaviors that provide the basis and foundation for professional practice in college union and student activities work. Subsequently, ACUI initiated a project to develop a list of skills associated with each competency. The ACUI website has more information about these efforts which could be used to complement the CAS standards.

The college union provides numerous educationally purposeful activities outside the classroom, which are "key to enhancing learning and personal development," according to *The Student Learning Imperative* (ACPA, 1994). The union contributes to the education of the student body at large through its cultural, educational, social, and recreational programs; the union also educates the students involved in its governance and program boards and those it employs. The role statement defines the union as "a student centered organization that values participatory decision making. Through volunteerism, its boards, committees, and student employment, the union offers firsthand experience in citizenship and educates students in leadership, social responsibility, and values." These models of college union governance foster student/staff partnerships that form the foundation for student development and leadership training.

The modern college union is a complex entity, offering a wide array of programs and services to the campus community. The standards and guidelines that follow outline the characteristics of a college union that offers high quality experiences and uses informed practice to reach out to a diverse range of constituents.

References, Readings, and Resources

American College Personnel Association [ACPA]. (1994). *The student learning imperative.* Washington, DC: Author.

Butts, P. F. (1971). *The college union idea.* Bloomington, IN: Association of College Unions International.

McMillan, A., & Davis, N. T. (Eds.) (1989). *College unions: Seventy-five years.* Bloomington, IN: Association of College Unions International.

Metz, N. D. (Ed.) (1996). *Student development in college unions and student activities.* Bloomington, IN: Association of College Unions International.

Metz, N., & Sievers, C. S. (2002). *Student leadership in college unions and student activities.* Bloomington, IN: Association of College Unions International.

Mitchell, R. L. (1997). *Metaphors, semaphores and two-by-fours: Reflections on a personal profession.* Bloomington, IN: Association of College Unions International..

Maul, S. Y. (1994). *Building community on campus.* Bloomington, IN: Association of College Unions International..

Association of College Unions International (ACUI) Central Office, One City Centre, Suite 200, 120 W. Seventh St., Bloomington, IN 47404-3925. (812) 855-8550; www.acui.org

The Bulletin, ACUI publication, published bimonthly; available from the ACUI Central Office.

Contributors:
Current edition:
Bob Rodda, College of Wooster, ACUI
Previous editions:
Nancy Davis Metz, ACUI

College Unions
CAS Standards and Guidelines

Part 1. MISSION

The primary goals of the College Union (CU) must be to bring campus constituents together, build campus community, support and initiate programs, provide services, and maintain facilities that promote student learning and development.

The CU must develop, disseminate, implement, and regularly review their mission. Mission statements must be consistent with the mission of the institution and with professional standards. The CU in higher education must enhance overall educational experiences by incorporating student learning and development outcomes in their mission.

The CU should provide educational, social, cultural, and recreational programs, services, and facilities that enhance the quality of campus life.

Students must be the principal constituents of the CU.

The CU should provide opportunities for students to learn and practice leadership, program planning, organizational management, social and civic responsibility, and interpersonal skills.

The vitality, variety, and spontaneity of the CU's activities should stem primarily from student boards, committees, and student-directed initiatives.

The CU must be an inclusive environment where interaction and understanding among individuals from diverse backgrounds occurs.

Part 2. PROGRAM

The formal education of students, consisting of the curriculum and the co-curriculum, must promote student learning and development outcomes that are purposeful and holistic and that prepare students for satisfying and productive lifestyles, work, and civic participation. The student learning and development outcome domains and their related dimensions are:

- **knowledge acquisition, integration, construction, and application**
  - o Dimensions: understanding knowledge from a range of disciplines; connecting knowledge to other knowledge, ideas, and experiences; constructing knowledge; and relating knowledge to daily life
- **cognitive complexity**
  - o Dimensions: critical thinking; reflective thinking; effective reasoning; and creativity
- **intrapersonal development**
  - o Dimensions: realistic self-appraisal, self-understanding, and self-respect; identity development; commitment to ethics and integrity; and spiritual awareness

- **interpersonal competence**
  - o Dimensions: meaningful relationships; interdependence; collaboration; and effective leadership
- **humanitarianism and civic engagement**
  - o Dimensions: understanding and appreciation of cultural and human differences; social responsibility; global perspective; and sense of civic responsibility
- **practical competence**
  - o Dimensions: pursuing goals; communicating effectively; technical competence; managing personal affairs; managing career development; demonstrating professionalism; maintaining health and wellness; and living a purposeful and satisfying life

[See *The Council for the Advancement of Standards Learning and Developmental Outcomes* statement for examples of outcomes related to these domains and dimensions.]

Consistent with the institutional mission, the College Union (CU) must identify relevant and desirable student learning and development outcomes from among the six domains and related dimensions. When creating opportunities for student learning and development, the CU must explore possibilities for collaboration with faculty members and other colleagues.

The CU must assess relevant and desirable student learning and development outcomes and provide evidence of their impact on student learning and development. The CU must articulate how they contribute to or support students' learning and development in the domains not specifically assessed.

The CU must be:
- **integrated into the life of the institution**
- **intentional and coherent**
- **guided by theories and knowledge of learning and development**
- **reflective of developmental and demographic profiles of the student population**
- **responsive to needs of individuals, diverse and special populations, and relevant constituencies**

The CU must include programs, activities and events, services, and facilities that address campus, community, and student needs.

CU programs, activities, and events could include:
- student development programs
- social, cultural, intellectual, and diversity programs
- leisure activities and recreational opportunities
- student leadership development programs and opportunities
- service-learning and community service programs
- performances

- entertainment
- tournaments
- outdoor recreation and travel
- social events
- educational programs
- crafts and hobbies
- leisure activities
- continuing education opportunities

CU services could include:
- food services
- retail stores and services
- communication technology
- mailing and duplication services
- information center
- campus and community information

CU facilities could include:
- commuter accommodations
- rooms of various sizes and configurations for meetings, banquets, conferences, and programs
- office space for student organization including storage
- office space for relevant administrative functions
- recreational facilities
- rest rooms that meet all constituents' needs
- technological capabilities including connectivity to campus intranets, the Internet, and emerging technologies
- exhibit spaces
- art galleries
- quiet rooms, lounges, and study spaces
- conference facilities
- studios

The CU must provide opportunities for student, staff, and faculty involvement in program planning, policy development, and facility operation.

The CU should also provide appropriate opportunities for involvement, participation, and collaboration with alumni and other institutional stakeholders.

Spaces in the CU should be comfortable, inviting, and attractive, and appropriate space should be consistently available for informal and spontaneous interactions.

The CU should create and support programs that instill an enduring affinity for the institution, including the history, legacy, traditions, and culture of the institution.

Part 3. LEADERSHIP

Because effective and ethical leadership is essential to the success of all organizations, College Union (CU) leaders with organizational authority for the programs and services must:
- **articulate a vision and mission for their programs and services**
- **set goals and objectives based on the needs of the population served and desired student learning and development outcomes**
- **advocate for their programs and services**
- **promote campus environments that provide meaningful opportunities for student learning, development, and integration**
- **identify and find means to address individual, organizational, or environmental conditions that foster or inhibit mission achievement**
- **advocate for representation in strategic planning initiatives at appropriate divisional and institutional levels**
- **initiate collaborative interactions with stakeholders who have legitimate concerns and interests in the functional area**
- **apply effective practices to educational and administrative processes**
- **prescribe and model ethical behavior**
- **communicate effectively**
- **manage financial resources, including planning, allocation, monitoring, and analysis**
- **incorporate sustainability practices in the management and design of programs, services, and facilities**
- **manage human resource processes including recruitment, selection, development, supervision, performance planning, and evaluation**
- **empower professional, support, and student staff to accept leadership opportunities**
- **encourage and support scholarly contribution to the profession**
- **be informed about and integrate appropriate technologies into programs and services**
- **be knowledgeable about federal, state/provincial, and local laws relevant to the programs and services and ensure that staff members understand their responsibilities by receiving appropriate training**
- **develop and continuously improve programs and services in response to the changing needs of students and other populations served and the evolving institutional priorities**
- **recognize environmental conditions that may negatively influence the safety of staff and students and propose interventions that mitigate such conditions.**

In addition CU leaders must:
- **promote efforts to build community**
- **use principles of good organizational management**
- **facilitate good planning processes and philosophies**
- **use leadership skills to effectively manage facilities**
- **demonstrate intercultural competencies**
- **conduct outreach and marketing that describes and promotes the programs and services of the CU**
- **ensure excellent customer services**
- **utilize developmental and learning theories to design and implement learning initiatives and experiences for students**
- **engage in professional development activities to stay current with research and best practices**

Part 4. HUMAN RESOURCES

The College Union (CU) must be staffed adequately by individuals qualified to accomplish the mission and goals. Within institutional guidelines, the CU must establish procedures for staff selection, training, and evaluation; set expectations for supervision; and provide appropriate professional development opportunities to improve the leadership ability, competence, and skills of all employees.

The CU professional staff members must hold an earned graduate or professional degree in a field relevant to the position they hold or must possess an appropriate combination of educational credentials and related work experience.

Graduate degrees should be earned in fields relevant to the CU including, but not limited to, college student affairs; student development; public, business, or higher education administration; and recreation studies.

CU staff responsible for programs, services, and facilities must have appropriate combinations of education, experience, and credentials to adequately and safely provide a level of management and leadership consistent with relevant industry standards and institutional expectations.

Cross training should be made available to enable appropriate staff to assume critical operations and responsibilities during unforeseen situations.

Staff members should possess: (a) knowledge of and ability to use management principles, including the effective management of volunteers; (b) understanding of and the ability to apply student development theory; (c) skills in assessment, planning, training, and evaluation; (d) interpersonal skills; (e) technical skills; (f) understanding of CU philosophy; (g) commitment to institutional mission; and (h) safety and emergency management skills.

Degree- or credential-seeking interns must be qualified by enrollment in an appropriate field of study and by relevant experience. These individuals must be trained and supervised adequately by professional staff members holding educational credentials and related work experience appropriate for supervision.

The CU should offer internships or practica to graduate students pursuing advanced degrees in college student affairs; student development; public, business, or higher educational administration; and recreation studies. These students should be utilized in a manner consistent with the missions of the CU and graduate programs.

Student employees and volunteers must be carefully selected, trained, supervised, and evaluated. They must be educated on how and when to refer those in need of additional assistance to qualified staff members and must have access to a supervisor for assistance in making these judgments. Student employees and volunteers must be provided clear and precise job descriptions, pre-service training based on assessed needs, and continuing staff development.

Employees and volunteers must receive specific training on institutional policies and privacy laws regarding their access to student records and other sensitive institutional information (e.g., in the USA, Family Educational Rights and Privacy Act, FERPA, or equivalent privacy laws in other states/provinces or countries).

Student employees and volunteers should be an integral part of the CU's operation. Their work experience should be an important part of their educational experience and contribute to increased engagement in the campus community. A thorough training program should be provided for part-time student employees and volunteers and, depending on their assigned duties, might include leadership training, group facilitation skills, communication skills, CU policies, and emergency procedures.

The CU must have technical and support staff members adequate to accomplish their mission. All members of the staff must be technologically proficient and qualified to perform their job functions, be knowledgeable about ethical and legal uses of technology, and have access to training and resources to support the performance of their assigned responsibilities.

Staff members may include food service personnel, audio visual technicians, stage hands, information technology staff, maintenance personnel, support staff, attendants, housekeepers, reservationists, sales clerks, and cashiers.

All members of the CU staff must receive training on policies and procedures related to the use of technology to store or access student records and institutional data.

The CU must ensure that staff members are knowledgeable about and trained in emergency procedures, crisis response, and prevention efforts. Prevention efforts must address identification of threatening conduct or behavior of students, faculty members, staff, and others and must incorporate a system or procedures for responding, including but not limited to reporting them to the appropriate campus officials.

Salary levels and benefits for all staff members must be commensurate with those for comparable positions within the institution, in similar institutions, and in the relevant geographic area.

The CU must maintain position descriptions for all staff members.

To create a diverse staff, the CU must institute hiring and promotion practices that are fair, inclusive, proactive, and non-discriminatory.

The CU must conduct regular performance planning and evaluation of staff members. The CU must provide access to continuing and advanced education and professional development opportunities.

Part 5. ETHICS

Persons involved in the delivery of the College Union (CU) must adhere to the highest principles of ethical behavior. The CU must review relevant professional ethical standards and develop or adopt and implement appropriate statements of ethical practice. The CU must publish these statements and ensure their periodic review by relevant constituencies.

The CU must orient new staff members to relevant ethical standards and statements of ethical practice.

CU staff members must ensure that privacy and confidentiality are maintained with respect to all communications and records to the extent that such records are protected under the law and appropriate statements of ethical practice. Information contained in students' education records must not be disclosed except as allowed by relevant laws and institutional policies. CU staff members must disclose to appropriate authorities information judged to be of an emergency nature, especially when the safety of the individual or others is involved, or when otherwise required by institutional policy or relevant law.

CU staff members must be aware of and comply with the provisions contained in the institution's policies pertaining to human subjects research and student rights and responsibilities, as well as those in other relevant institutional policies addressing ethical practices and confidentiality of research data concerning individuals.

CU staff members must recognize and avoid personal conflicts of interest or appearance thereof in the performance of their work.

CU staff members must strive to insure the fair, objective, and impartial treatment of all persons with whom they interact.

When handling institutional funds, CU staff members must ensure that such funds are managed in accordance with established and responsible accounting procedures and the fiscal policies or processes of the institution.

Promotional and descriptive information must be accurate and free of deception.

CU staff members must perform their duties within the limits of their training, expertise, and competence. When these limits are exceeded, individuals in need of further assistance must be referred to persons possessing appropriate qualifications.

CU staff members must use suitable means to confront and otherwise hold accountable other staff members who exhibit unethical behavior.

CU staff members must be knowledgeable about and practice ethical behavior in the use of technology.

Part 6. LEGAL RESPONSIBILITIES

College Union (CU) staff members must be knowledgeable about and responsive to laws and regulations that relate to their respective responsibilities and that may pose legal obligations, limitations, or ramifications for the institution as a whole. As appropriate, staff members must inform users of programs and services, as well as officials, of legal obligations and limitations including constitutional, statutory, regulatory, and case law; mandatory laws and orders emanating from federal, state/provincial, and local governments; and the institution's policies.

The CU must have written policies on all relevant operations, transactions, or tasks that may have legal implications.

CU staff members must neither participate in nor condone any form of harassment or activity that demeans persons or creates an intimidating, hostile, or offensive campus environment.

CU staff members must use reasonable and informed practices to limit the liability exposure of the institution and its officers, employees, and agents. Staff members must be informed about institutional policies regarding risk management, personal liability, and related insurance coverage options and must be referred to external sources if coverage is not provided by the institution.

The institution must provide access to legal advice for CU staff members as needed to carry out assigned responsibilities.

The institution must inform CU staff and students in a timely and systematic fashion about extraordinary or changing legal obligations and potential liabilities.

Part 7. EQUITY and ACCESS

College Union (CU) programs and services must be provided on a fair, equitable, and non-discriminatory basis in accordance with institutional policies and with all applicable state/provincial and federal statutes and regulations. The CU must maintain an educational and work environment free from discrimination in accordance with law and institutional policy.

Discrimination must be avoided on the basis of age; cultural heritage; disability; ethnicity; gender identity and expression; nationality; political affiliation; race; religious affiliation; sex; sexual orientation; economic, marital, social, or veteran status; and any other bases included in local, state/provincial, or federal laws.

Consistent with the mission and goals, the CU must take action to remedy significant imbalances in student participation and staffing patterns.

The CU must ensure physical and program access for persons with disabilities. The CU must be responsive to the needs of all students and other populations served when establishing hours of operation and developing methods of delivering programs and services.

The CU must recognize the needs of distance learning students by providing appropriate and accessible services and assisting them in identifying and gaining access to other appropriate services in their geographic region.

Part 8. DIVERSITY

Within the context of each institution's unique mission, diversity enriches the community and enhances the collegiate experience for all; therefore, the College Union (CU) must create and nurture environments that are welcoming to and bring together persons of diverse backgrounds.

The CU must promote environments that are characterized by open and continuous communication that deepens understanding of one's own identity, culture, and heritage, as well as that of others. The CU must recognize, honor, educate, and promote respect about commonalties and differences among people within their historical and cultural contexts.

The CU must address the characteristics and needs of a diverse population when establishing and implementing policies and procedures.

CU governing and programming boards should represent campus diversity and institutional goals for inclusion.

The CU should conduct outreach to include and engage all populations in the life of the Union.

Outsourced programs and services are accountable to the institution. Therefore, the CU should encourage providers of outsourced programs and services to offer a diverse workforce and inclusive environment.

Part 9. ORGANIZATION and MANAGEMENT

To promote student learning and development outcomes, College Union (CU) programs and services must be structured purposefully and managed effectively to achieve stated goals. Evidence of appropriate structure must include current and accessible policies and procedures, written performance expectations for all employees, functional workflow graphics or organizational charts, and clearly stated program and service delivery expectations.

The CU must monitor websites used for distributing information to ensure that the sites are current, accurate, appropriately referenced, and accessible.

Evidence of effective management must include use of comprehensive and accurate information for decisions, clear sources and channels of authority, effective communication practices, procedures for decision-making and conflict resolution, responses to changing conditions, systems of accountability and evaluation, and processes for recognition and reward. The CU must align policies and procedures with those of the institution and provide channels within the organization for their regular review.

The CU must be organized to provide effective social, cultural, intellectual, and recreational programming; offer appropriate

business enterprises and services; and maintain its physical plant.

The CU must involve members of the campus community in its governance and programming structure and in the formulation of CU policies.

Involvement of the campus community should include students, faculty and staff members, and alumni. Involvement could include parents and local community members. Typically such involvement is through advisory, governing, and program boards. These boards should address issues such as (a) facility operating policies related to the use and/or rental of CU facilities by campus and non-campus groups, (b) programming goals, (c) scheduling of events, (d) budget planning, fee structure, and allocation priorities, (e) employment policies, (f) space allocation priorities, and (g) hours of operation.

The CU must assure that outsourced programs and services comply with the goals, policies, and procedures of the CU and the institution.

The CU must have an emergency preparedness plan and a business continuity plan. The emergency preparedness plan must be compatible with the institution's emergency preparedness plan. The business continuity plan must be in place to respond after an emergency that compromises essential services and access to the facility.

Procedures must be in place to assess and manage events with large numbers of participants, potential volatile content, or dangerous materials and equipment.

Part 10. CAMPUS and EXTERNAL RELATIONS

The College Union (CU) must reach out to relevant individuals, campus offices, and external agencies to:
- establish, maintain, and promote effective relations
- disseminate information about their own and other related programs and services
- coordinate and collaborate, where appropriate, in offering programs and services to meet the needs of students and promote their achievement of student learning and development outcomes

Examples of relevant individuals, campus offices, and external agencies include students; student organizations, especially student government and program board(s); faculty members; administrative offices; alumni; local community members; contracted service providers, including lessees; and campus safety offices.

The CU should use relevant and appropriate student and campus marketing and outreach resources to inform the campus community about CU programs and services. Staff and volunteers throughout the CU should be considered for membership on various institutional committees and governing bodies.

The CU must have procedures and guidelines consistent with institutional policy for responding to threats, emergencies, and crisis situations. Systems and procedures must be in place to disseminate timely and accurate information to students and other members of the campus community during emergency situations.

The CU must have procedures and guidelines consistent with institutional policy for communicating with the media.

Part 11. FINANCIAL RESOURCES

The College Union (CU) must have adequate funding to accomplish their mission and goals. In establishing funding priorities and making significant changes, a comprehensive analysis, which includes relevant expenditures, external and internal resources, and impact on the campus community, must be conducted.

The CU must demonstrate fiscal responsibility and cost effectiveness consistent with institutional protocols.

The CU should have financial resources to ensure reasonable pricing of services and adequate programming, staffing, maintenance, and professional development.

When handling student fee funds, the CU must manage fees in accordance with approved accounting methods of the institution.

Student fee funds should be used to benefit students directly.

The institution should consider various methods and sources of financial support including, but not limited to: (a) direct institutional support (e.g., salaries, utilities, housekeeping, maintenance, and membership fees); (b) student fees; (c) income from sales, services, rentals, and leases; and (d) fundraising initiatives.

Part 12. TECHNOLOGY

The College Union (CU) must have adequate technology to support their mission. The technology and its use must comply with institutional policies and procedures and be evaluated for compliance with relevant federal, state/provincial, and local requirements.

The CU must maintain policies and procedures that address the security and back up of data.

When technology is used to facilitate student learning and development, the CU must select technology that reflects current best pedagogical practices.

Technology, as well as any workstations or computer labs maintained by the CU for student use, must be accessible and must meet established technology standards for delivery to persons with disabilities.

When the CU provide student access to technology, they must provide:
- access to policies that are clear, easy to understand, and available to all students
- access to instruction or training on how to use the technology
- access to information on the legal and ethical implications of misuse as it pertains to intellectual

property, harassment, privacy, and social networks.

Student violations of technology policies must follow established institutional student disciplinary procedures.

Students who experience negative emotional or psychological consequences from the use of technology must be referred to support services provided by the institution.

The CU should use current and appropriate technology to facilitate, improve, assess, and extend access to its programs, products, services, and facilities.

Part 13. FACILITIES and EQUIPMENT

The College Union (CU) must have adequate, accessible, suitably located facilities and equipment to support their mission and goals. If acquiring capital equipment as defined by the institution, the CU must take into account expenses related to regular maintenance and life cycle costs. Facilities and equipment must be evaluated regularly, including consideration of sustainability, and be in compliance with relevant federal, state/provincial, and local requirements to provide for access, health, safety, and security.

Recycling, energy conservation, and other sustainability efforts must be addressed throughout the CU.

The CU facility should be proportional in size to the needs of the campus community and be centrally located.

The CU should provide appropriate spaces that meet the unique needs of diverse groups, while simultaneously promoting interaction and community.

Facilities must be accessible, clean, reasonably priced, well maintained, and have adequate safety and security features.

New construction and renovation projects should be responsive to the current and future needs of the campus community. Decisions about new construction and renovation should be based upon clearly defined needs and consistent with the mission of the institution, which may include adherence to institutional standards for sustainability, accessibility, beautification, debt coverage, and historic preservation.

Members of the campus community and the CU staff should be involved in program development of new and renovated facilities. Such planning efforts should include representation by students, faculty, and staff.

Systematically planned replacement cycles should exist for furnishings, mechanical and electrical systems, maintenance equipment, floor/wall/window treatments, technology, and service equipment.

CU Staff members must have work space that is well-equipped, adequate in size, and designed to support their work and responsibilities. For conversations requiring privacy, staff members must have access to a private space.

CU Staff members who share work space must have the

ability to secure their work adequately.

The design of the facilities must guarantee the security of records and ensure the confidentiality of sensitive information.

The location and layout of the facilities must be sensitive to the special needs of persons with disabilities as well as the needs of constituencies served.

The CU must ensure that staff members are knowledgeable of and trained in safety and emergency procedures for securing and vacating the facilities.

Part 14. ASSESSMENT and EVALUATION

The College Union (CU) must establish systematic plans and processes to meet internal and external accountability expectations with regard to program as well as student learning and development outcomes. The CU must conduct regular assessment and evaluations. Assessments must include qualitative and quantitative methodologies as appropriate, to determine whether and to what degree the stated mission, goals, and student learning and development outcomes are being met. The process must employ sufficient and sound measures to ensure comprehensiveness. Data collected must include responses from students and other affected constituencies.

The CU must evaluate regularly how well they complement and enhance the institution's stated mission and educational effectiveness.

Results of these evaluations must be used in revising and improving programs and services, identifying needs and interests in shaping directions of program and service design, and recognizing staff performance.

Evaluation should include goal-related progress on such considerations as student satisfaction, attendance at programs, cash flow, appearance of facilities, and vitality of volunteer groups such as programming and governing boards.

Results and summary data from assessment and evaluation should be broadly shared with all appropriate constituencies including students, faculty and staff members, cabinet members, and board members.

General Standards revised in 2008;
CU content developed/revised in 1986, 1997, 1998, & 2009

The Role of Commuter and Off-Campus Living Programs
CAS Standards Contextual Statement

Commuter and off-campus students, defined as those who do not live in institution-owned housing on campus, account for over 80 percent of college students in the U.S. (Jacoby, 2000). Commuter and off-campus students attend virtually every institution of higher education. Their numbers include students who live at home with their parents, in rental housing, or with their own families. They may attend college full time, part time, or alternate between the two. They may live near the campus or far away; they may commute by car, public transportation, walking, or bicycle. They may represent a small minority of students at a private, residential liberal arts college or the entire population of the community college or urban institution. The majority of commuter and off-campus students work, mostly off-campus, and some are employed the equivalent of full-time and/or at more than one job.

Regardless of differences in backgrounds, living arrangements, and educational goals, commuter and off-campus students face common needs and concerns, such as finding safe and reliable transportation, managing multiple life roles, integrating their off-campus support systems into their higher education experience, and developing a sense of belonging in their campus community. Whether they attend a predominantly residential or commuter institution, the fact that they reside off-campus profoundly affects the nature of their educational experience.

Despite the overwhelming numbers of commuter and off-campus students, the long-standing residential tradition of American higher education has often impeded effective, comprehensive institutional responses to their wide range of lifestyles. Historically, the relationship of commuter and off-campus students to the institution has been neither well understood nor incorporated into the design of policies, programs, and practices. *The CAS Standards and Guidelines take the approach that all students must have equitable access to institutional services, engagement opportunities, and the total educational process regardless of place of residence.*

To begin correcting the inequities that have been built into policies and programs, institutions must critically and comprehensively examine their practices from the point of view of all types of commuter and off-campus students. In addition, because the commuter and off-campus student population is so diverse and because each institution's population is unique, it is important that each college and university regularly collect data about its commuter and off-campus students and the nature of their college experience. These standards and guidelines provide a basis for institutional self-assessment and program development.

References, Readings, and Resources

American College Personnel Association, Commission for Commuter Students and Adult Learners, One Dupont Circle NW, Suite 300, Washington DC 20036. (202) 835-2272. Http://www.acpa.nche.edu

Chickering, A.W. (1974). *Commuting versus resident students.* San Francisco: Jossey-Bass.

Jacoby, B. (Ed.). (2000). *Involving commuter students in learning.* New Directions for Higher Education #109.. San Francisco: Jossey-Bass.

Jacoby, B. (2004). Engaging first-year commuter students in learning. *Metropolitan Universities, 15*(2)..

Jacoby, B., & Garland, J. (2004). Strategies for enhancing commuter student success., *Journal of College Student Retention, 6*(1).

Jacoby, B. (1989). *The student as commuter: Developing a comprehensive institutional response.* ASHE-ERIC Higher Education Report No. 7. Washington, DC: School of Education and Human Development, The George Washington University.

Jacoby, B., & Girrell, K. (1981). A model for improving service and programs for commuter students (The SPAR Model). *NASPA Journal, 18*(3).

Schlossberg, N.K., Lynch, A.Q., & Chickering, A.W. (1989). *Improving higher education environments for adults.* San Francisco: Jossey-Bass.

Stewart, S.S. (Ed.). (1983). *Commuter students: Enhancing their educational experience.* New Directions for Student Services # 24.. San Francisco: Jossey-Bass.

National Clearinghouse for Commuter Programs, Stamp Student Union, University of Maryland, College Park, MD 20742, (301) 405-0986, www.umd.edu/nccp

Contributor:
Barbara Jacoby, University of Maryland, NCCP

Commuter and Off-Campus Living Programs
CAS Standards and Guidelines

Part 1. MISSION

The primary mission of Commuter and Off-Campus Living Programs (COCLP) is to ensure that all students have equitable access to programs, services, and engagement opportunities regardless of place of residence.

In addition, COCLP must:
- provide services and facilities to meet the basic needs of commuter and off-campus students as determined by institutional assessment
- ensure that all students benefit equitably from the institution's educational programs
- provide engagement opportunities to assist commuter and off-campus students and promote learning and development
- support the institution's vision for the student learning experience

COCLP must develop, disseminate, implement, and regularly review their mission. Mission statements must be consistent with the mission of the institution and with professional standards. COCLP in higher education must enhance overall educational experiences by incorporating student learning and development outcomes in their mission.

The COCLP mission should address not only programs and services but also education and advocacy on behalf of commuter and off-campus students.

Commuter and off-campus students may be defined differently at individual institutions; however, this document focuses on the equitable access of all students to institutional resources.

The number of commuter and off-campus students may range from a small minority to the entire student population. The commuter and off-campus students in any higher educational institution should have equitable benefits of the curricular and co-curricular programs and services offered, regardless of full-time or part-time credit load, family status, age, proximity to campus, day or evening enrollment, or dependent versus independent living status.

Part 2. PROGRAM

Commuter and Off-Campus Living Programs (COCLP) must provide direct delivery of essential programs and services meeting a wide variety of needs and interests, whether organized as a single office or distributed throughout the institution. In either case, these services and programs must be evaluated to ensure that all students have equitable access to programs, services, and engagement opportunities regardless of place of residence.

The formal education of students, consisting of the curriculum and the co-curriculum, must promote student learning and development outcomes that are purposeful and holistic and that prepare students for satisfying and productive lifestyles, work, and civic participation. The student learning and development outcome domains and their related dimensions are:

- knowledge acquisition, integration, construction, and application
    - Dimensions: understanding knowledge from a range of disciplines; connecting knowledge to other knowledge, ideas, and experiences; constructing knowledge; and relating knowledge to daily life

- cognitive complexity
    - Dimensions: critical thinking; reflective thinking; effective reasoning; and creativity

- intrapersonal development
    - Dimensions: realistic self-appraisal, self-understanding, and self-respect; identity development; commitment to ethics and integrity; and spiritual awareness

- interpersonal competence
    - Dimensions: meaningful relationships; interdependence; collaboration; and effective leadership

- humanitarianism and civic engagement
    - Dimensions: understanding and appreciation of cultural and human differences; social responsibility; global perspective; and sense of civic responsibility

- practical competence
    - Dimensions: pursuing goals; communicating effectively; technical competence; managing personal affairs; managing career development; demonstrating professionalism; maintaining health and wellness; and living a purposeful and satisfying life

[See The Council for the Advancement of Standards Learning and Developmental Outcomes statement for examples of outcomes related to these domains and dimensions.]

Consistent with the institutional mission, COCLP must identify relevant and desirable student learning and development outcomes from among the six domains and related dimensions. When creating opportunities for student learning and development, COCLP must explore possibilities for collaboration with faculty members and other colleagues.

COCLP must assess relevant and desirable student learning and development outcomes and provide evidence of their impact on student learning and development. COCLP must articulate how they contribute to or support students' learning and development in the domains not specifically assessed.

COCLP must be:

- integrated into the life of the institution
- intentional and coherent
- guided by theories and knowledge of learning and development
- reflective of developmental and demographic profiles of the student population
- responsive to needs of individuals, diverse and special populations, and relevant constituencies

COCLP must assist students with access to institutional resources and in meeting basic needs such as housing, transportation, parking, security, information and referral, facilities, food, computer and internet access, and childcare.

COCLP should assist students in making informed choices about housing and should provide information about available housing, tenants' rights and responsibilities, utilities, and legal advice and assistance.

Provisions should be made for parking; carpools; emergency vehicle assistance; and walkway, bike path, and parking lot security. Information about transportation alternatives to campus should be provided.

Information about campus services, programs, and current events should be disseminated in a variety of media and formats. Access to services such as course registration should be available via the internet and telephone as well as in traditional modes.

Students should have adequate study and lounge spaces in convenient locations around the campus. These should include access to computers, printers, copiers, and lockers.

Food service should be available in convenient locations at hours when students are on campus, including evenings and weekends.

Institutions should address commuter and off-campus students' need for high-speed internet access for accomplishing course work, and should ensure equitable access to informational resources.

Institutions should provide adequate childcare services, either through the institution or through referrals to community childcare providers. On-campus facilities for infant feeding and changing should be available.

COCLP should work to ensure that all institutional services are available equitably to commuter and off-campus students, including scheduling of classes, events, campus employment, and office hours to accommodate students' varied schedules.

COCLP must provide programs that meet the specific needs of commuter and off-campus students and ensure that all students have equitable access to all educational, recreational, and social programming.

COCLP should provide educational programs that inform students of tenancy ordinances, tenants and landlord rights and responsibilities, legal advice and assistance, personal financial management, roommate and neighbor relations, and conflict-resolution skills. Additional educational programs can include defensive driving, personal security, proper nutrition, and time management.

COCLP should offer programs, or encourage the institution to offer programs, that enable commuter and off-campus students to achieve learning and development outcomes. These include opportunities for interaction with faculty members and peers, activities scheduled at times convenient for commuter and off-campus students, peer mentoring, learning communities that do not require on-campus residence, experiential education, family-oriented activities, programs offered in off-campus locations with dense student populations, and programming using technology (e.g., virtual communities).

Institutions must include the commuter and off-campus student perspective at all appropriate levels of campus planning, policy making, budgeting, program delivery, and governance.

Commuter and off-campus student advocacy should focus on:
- access to comprehensive academic advising, student support services, and information
- recognition of the diverse subgroups of the commuter and off-campus student population, including students who are older, married, fully employed, part-time, evening, veterans, or who live at home with parents or guardian.
- equitable fee structure for campus services
- fair representation of all types of commuter and off-campus students in areas of campus employment, internships, and financial aid awards
- faculty and institutional research programs that enhance understanding of the demographic characteristics and unique needs of commuter and off-campus students
- inclusion of the commuter and off-campus student perspective in community decision-making (e.g., transportation route planning, police coverage, and local ordinances)
- minimum standards for use as criteria for listing off-campus housing options

COCLP must collect data and encourage institutional research to understand the characteristics, needs, and experiences of commuter and off-campus students.

Research efforts may include demographic studies, needs assessments, retention studies, environmental assessments, involvement and satisfaction measures, longitudinal studies, and commuter-resident comparisons.

Part 3. LEADERSHIP

Because effective and ethical leadership is essential to the success of all organizations, Commuter and Off-Campus Living Programs (COCLP) leaders with organizational authority for the programs and services must:
- **articulate a vision and mission for their programs and services**
- **set goals and objectives based on the needs of the population served and desired student learning and development outcomes**
- **advocate for their programs and services**
- **promote campus environments that provide meaningful opportunities for student learning, development, and**

integration
- identify and find means to address individual, organizational, or environmental conditions that foster or inhibit mission achievement
- advocate for representation in strategic planning initiatives at appropriate divisional and institutional levels
- initiate collaborative interactions with stakeholders who have legitimate concerns and interests in the functional area
- apply effective practices to educational and administrative processes
- prescribe and model ethical behavior
- communicate effectively
- manage financial resources, including planning, allocation, monitoring, and analysis
- incorporate sustainability practices in the management and design of programs, services, and facilities
- manage human resource processes including recruitment, selection, development, supervision, performance planning, and evaluation
- empower professional, support, and student staff to accept leadership opportunities
- encourage and support scholarly contribution to the profession
- be informed about and integrate appropriate technologies into programs and services
- be knowledgeable about federal, state/provincial, and local laws relevant to the programs and services and ensure that staff members understand their responsibilities by receiving appropriate training
- develop and continuously improve programs and services in response to the changing needs of students and other populations served and the evolving institutional priorities
- recognize environmental conditions that may negatively influence the safety of staff and students and propose interventions that mitigate such conditions

Part 4. HUMAN RESOURCES

Commuter and Off-Campus Living Programs (COCLP) must be staffed adequately by individuals qualified to accomplish the mission and goals. Within institutional guidelines, COCLP must establish procedures for staff selection, training, and evaluation; set expectations for supervision; and provide appropriate professional development opportunities to improve the leadership ability, competence, and skills of all employees.

COCLP professional staff members must hold an earned graduate or professional degree in a field relevant to the position they hold or must possess an appropriate combination of educational credentials and related work experience.

Degree- or credential-seeking interns must be qualified by enrollment in an appropriate field of study and by relevant

experience. These individuals must be trained and supervised adequately by professional staff members holding educational credentials and related work experience appropriate for supervision.

COCLP professional staff should possess the academic preparation, experience, abilities, professional interests, and competencies essential for the efficient operation of the office as charged, as well as the ability to identify and address needs of the commuter and off-campus student population. They should possess the following knowledge and skills:
- ability to work with diverse students
- knowledge of history and current trends in higher education
- knowledge of organizational development, group dynamics, strategies for changes and principles of community development
- ability to design and evaluate programs to meet desired outcomes
- effective written and oral communication skills
- knowledge of theories of college student learning and development
- knowledge of management and budgeting
- ability to work effectively with internal and external agencies
- ability to serve as an effective advocate

Student employees and volunteers must be carefully selected, trained, supervised, and evaluated. They must be educated on how and when to refer those in need of additional assistance to qualified staff members and must have access to a supervisor for assistance in making these judgments. Student employees and volunteers must be provided clear and precise job descriptions, pre-service training based on assessed needs, and continuing staff development.

Employees and volunteers must receive specific training on institutional policies and privacy laws regarding their access to student records and other sensitive institutional information (e.g., in the USA, Family Educational Rights and Privacy Act, FERPA, or equivalent privacy laws in other states/provinces or countries).

COCLP must have technical and support staff members adequate to accomplish their mission. All members of the staff must be technologically proficient and qualified to perform their job functions, be knowledgeable about ethical and legal uses of technology, and have access to training and resources to support the performance of their assigned responsibilities.

All members of the staff must receive training on policies and procedures related to the use of technology to store or access student records and institutional data.

COCLP must ensure that staff members are knowledgeable about and trained in emergency procedures, crisis response, and prevention efforts. Prevention efforts must address identification of threatening conduct or behavior of students, faculty members, staff, and others and must incorporate a system or procedures for responding, including but not limited to reporting them to the appropriate campus officials.

Salary levels and benefits for all staff members must be commensurate with those for comparable positions within the institution, in similar institutions, and in the relevant geographic area.

COCLP must maintain position descriptions for all staff members.

To create a diverse staff, COCLP must institute hiring and promotion practices that are fair, inclusive, proactive, and non-discriminatory.

COCLP must conduct regular performance planning and evaluation of staff members. COCLP must provide access to continuing and advanced education and professional development opportunities.

Part 5. ETHICS

Persons involved in the delivery of Commuter and Off-Campus Living Programs (COCLP) must adhere to the highest principles of ethical behavior. COCLP must review relevant professional ethical standards and develop or adopt and implement appropriate statements of ethical practice. COCLP must publish these statements and ensure their periodic review by relevant constituencies.

COCLP must orient new staff members to relevant ethical standards and statements of ethical practice.

COCLP staff members must ensure that privacy and confidentiality are maintained with respect to all communications and records to the extent that such records are protected under the law and appropriate statements of ethical practice. Information contained in students' education records must not be disclosed except as allowed by relevant laws and institutional policies. COCLP staff members must disclose to appropriate authorities information judged to be of an emergency nature, especially when the safety of the individual or others is involved, or when otherwise required by institutional policy or relevant law.

COCLP staff members must be aware of and comply with the provisions contained in the institution's policies pertaining to human subjects research and student rights and responsibilities, as well as those in other relevant institutional policies addressing ethical practices and confidentiality of research data concerning individuals.

COCLP staff members must recognize and avoid personal conflicts of interest or appearance thereof in the performance of their work.

COCLP staff members must strive to insure the fair, objective, and impartial treatment of all persons with whom they interact.

When handling institutional funds, COCLP staff members must ensure that such funds are managed in accordance with established and responsible accounting procedures and the fiscal policies or processes of the institution.

Promotional and descriptive information must be accurate and free of deception.

COCLP staff members must perform their duties within the limits of their training, expertise, and competence. When these limits are exceeded, individuals in need of further assistance must be referred to persons possessing appropriate qualifications.

COCLP staff members must use suitable means to confront and otherwise hold accountable other staff members who exhibit unethical behavior.

COCLP staff members must be knowledgeable about and practice ethical behavior in the use of technology.

Part 6. LEGAL RESPONSIBILITIES

Commuter and Off-Campus Living Programs (COCLP) staff members must be knowledgeable about and responsive to laws and regulations that relate to their respective responsibilities and that may pose legal obligations, limitations, or ramifications for the institution as a whole. As appropriate, staff members must inform users of programs and services, as well as officials, of legal obligations and limitations including constitutional, statutory, regulatory, and case law; mandatory laws and orders emanating from federal, state/provincial, and local governments; and the institution's policies.

COCLP must have written policies on all relevant operations, transactions, or tasks that may have legal implications.

COCLP staff members must neither participate in nor condone any form of harassment or activity that demeans persons or creates an intimidating, hostile, or offensive campus environment.

COCLP staff members must use reasonable and informed practices to limit the liability exposure of the institution and its officers, employees, and agents. COCLP staff members must be informed about institutional policies regarding risk management, personal liability, and related insurance coverage options and must be referred to external sources if coverage is not provided by the institution.

The institution must provide access to legal advice for COCLP staff members as needed to carry out assigned responsibilities.

The institution must inform COCLP staff and students in a timely and systematic fashion about extraordinary or changing legal obligations and potential liabilities.

Part 7. EQUITY and ACCESS

Commuter and Off-Campus Living Programs (COCLP) must be provided on a fair, equitable, and non-discriminatory basis in accordance with institutional policies and with all applicable state/provincial and federal statutes and regulations. COCLP must maintain an educational and work environment free from discrimination in accordance with law and institutional policy.

Discrimination must be avoided on the basis of age; cultural heritage; disability; ethnicity; gender identity and expression; nationality; political affiliation; race; religious affiliation; sex; sexual orientation; economic, marital, social, or veteran status; and any other bases included in local, state/provincial, or federal laws.

Consistent with the mission and goals, COCLP must take action to remedy significant imbalances in student participation and staffing patterns.

COCLP must ensure physical and program access for persons with disabilities. COCLP must be responsive to the needs of all students and other populations served when establishing hours of operation and developing methods of delivering programs and services.

COCLP must recognize the needs of distance learning students by providing appropriate and accessible services and assisting them in identifying and gaining access to other appropriate services in their geographic region.

Part 8. DIVERSITY

Within the context of each institution's unique mission, diversity enriches the community and enhances the collegiate experience for all; therefore, Commuter and Off-Campus Living Programs (COCLP) must create and nurture environments that are welcoming to and bring together persons of diverse backgrounds.

COCLP must promote environments that are characterized by open and continuous communication that deepens understanding of one's own identity, culture, and heritage, as well as that of others. COCLP must recognize, honor, educate, and promote respect about commonalties and differences among people within their historical and cultural contexts.

COCLP must address the characteristics and needs of a diverse population when establishing and implementing policies and procedures.

Part 9. ORGANIZATION and MANAGEMENT

To promote student learning and development outcomes, Commuter and Off-Campus Living Programs (COCLP) must be structured purposefully and managed effectively to achieve stated goals. Evidence of appropriate structure must include current and accessible policies and procedures, written performance expectations for all employees, functional workflow graphics or organizational charts, and clearly stated program and service delivery expectations.

COCLP must monitor websites used for distributing information to ensure that the sites are current, accurate,

appropriately referenced, and accessible.

Evidence of effective management must include use of comprehensive and accurate information for decisions, clear sources and channels of authority, effective communication practices, procedures for decision-making and conflict resolution, responses to changing conditions, systems of accountability and evaluation, and processes for recognition and reward. COCLP must align policies and procedures with those of the institution and provide channels within the organization for their regular review.

Part 10. CAMPUS and EXTERNAL RELATIONS

Commuter and Off-Campus Living Programs (COCLP) must reach out to relevant individuals, campus offices, and external agencies to:
- establish, maintain, and promote effective relations
- disseminate information about their own and other related programs and services
- coordinate and collaborate, where appropriate, in offering programs and services to meet the needs of students and promote their achievement of student learning and development outcomes

COCLP must have procedures and guidelines consistent with institutional policy for responding to threats, emergencies, and crisis situations. Systems and procedures must be in place to disseminate timely and accurate information to students and other members of the campus community during emergency situations.

COCLP must have procedures and guidelines consistent with institutional policy for communicating with the media.

COCLP must maintain a high degree of visibility within the campus community through direct promotion and delivery of services, involvement with campus programs, and educational efforts to increase all campus community members' understanding of the needs of commuter and off-campus students.

COCLP should coordinate their activities with all offices and agencies whose efforts directly affect commuter and off-campus students. These include such areas as campus safety and security, transportation and parking, campus information and referral services, and other relevant offices and campus committees.

COCLP should maintain active relationship with various community agencies to ensure the inclusion of the commuter and off-campus student perspective in community decision-making.

Part 11. FINANCIAL RESOURCES

Commuter and Off-Campus Living Programs (COCLP) must have adequate funding to accomplish their mission and goals. In establishing funding priorities and making significant changes, a comprehensive analysis, which includes relevant expenditures, external and internal resources, and impact on the campus community, must be conducted.

COCLP must demonstrate fiscal responsibility and cost effectiveness consistent with institutional protocols.

Fee-paying students should benefit equitably from fee-supported services. This is especially important regarding access to electronic services such as computer/internet and campus cable television systems.

Part 12. TECHNOLOGY

Commuter and Off-Campus Living Programs (COCLP) must have adequate technology to support their mission. The technology and its use must comply with institutional policies and procedures and be evaluated for compliance with relevant federal, state/provincial, and local requirements.

COCLP must maintain policies and procedures that address the security and back up of data.

When technology is used to facilitate student learning and development, COCLP must select technology that reflects current best pedagogical practices.

Technology, as well as any workstations or computer labs maintained by the COCLP for student use, must be accessible and must meet established technology standards for delivery to persons with disabilities.

Institutions that provide high speed internet access or campus based cable television programming to residential students should also consider options to increase accessibility to such services to commuter and off-campus students.

When COCLP provide student access to technology, they must provide:
- access to policies that are clear, easy to understand, and available to all students
- access to instruction or training on how to use the technology
- access to information on the legal and ethical implications of misuse as it pertains to intellectual property, harassment, privacy, and social networks

Student violations of technology policies must follow established institutional student disciplinary procedures.

Students who experience negative emotional or psychological consequences from the use of technology must be referred to support services provided by the institution.

Part 13. FACILITIES and EQUIPMENT

Commuter and Off-Campus Living Programs (COCLP) must have adequate, accessible, suitably located facilities and equipment to support their mission and goals. If acquiring capital equipment as defined by the institution, COCLP must take into account expenses related to regular maintenance and life cycle costs. Facilities and equipment must be evaluated regularly, including consideration of sustainability, and be in compliance with relevant federal, state/provincial, and local requirements to provide for access, health, safety, and security.

COCLP staff members must have work space that is well-equipped, adequate in size, and designed to support their work and responsibilities. For conversations requiring privacy, staff members must have access to a private space.

COCLP staff members who share work space must have the ability to secure their work adequately.

The design of the facilities must guarantee the security of records and ensure the confidentiality of sensitive information.

The location and layout of the facilities must be sensitive to the special needs of persons with disabilities as well as the needs of constituencies served.

COCLP must ensure that staff members are knowledgeable of and trained in safety and emergency procedures for securing and vacating the facilities.

The campus must provide adequate facilities for the use of commuter and off-campus students, including recreational, study, and lounge space; computer and internet access; and dining facilities.

Because commuter and off-campus students do not have a residence on campus in which to spend time before, between, and after classes, a variety of comfortable spaces should be provided for their use. These spaces should be in classroom buildings, as well as in college union and student center buildings, and should include individual lockers, computer and copier access, food preparation facilities, and family support services (e.g., infant feeding and changing areas).

Part 14. ASSESSMENT and EVALUATION

Commuter and Off-Campus Living Programs (COCLP) must establish systematic plans and processes to meet internal and external accountability expectations with regard to program as well as student learning and development outcomes. COCLP must conduct regular assessment and evaluations. Assessments must include qualitative and quantitative methodologies as appropriate, to determine whether and to what degree the stated mission, goals, and student learning and development outcomes are being met. The process must employ sufficient and sound measures to ensure comprehensiveness. Data collected must include responses from students and other affected constituencies.

COCLP must evaluate regularly how well they complement and enhance the institution's stated mission and educational effectiveness.

Results of these evaluations must be used in revising and improving programs and services, identifying needs and interests in shaping directions of program and service design, and recognizing staff performance.

General Standards revised 2008;
COCLP (formerly Commuter Student Programs) content developed/ revised 1986, 1997, & 2005

The Role of Conference and Event Programs
CAS Standards Contextual Statement

A higher education campus is a community where people gather to learn, share, and discuss issues of interest in an open, non-threatening, and enlightened atmosphere. It is a place where topics important to society are addressed freely in a number of formats and settings. Campuses are centers for symposia, lectures, public events, demonstrations, conferences, and other teaching and learning programs attended by people from all walks of life, generations, occupations, and education levels. These events help to identify the campus as a place where scholarly, cultural, social, artistic, athletic, and other activities can freely occur. As institutions become less constrained by physical borders, they have also become the source and home of conferences and events. A department responsible for developing, coordinating, and promoting on- and off-campus conferences and events is typically found at the core of this important educational responsibility.

Conference and event programs address a broad range of organizing, hosting, and logistical service needs. Services are provided to a variety of constituents and include program planning; managing conference centers; developing conferences in conjunction with faculty and staff members; providing services and support for summer youth camps; coordinating guest services and special celebrations; scheduling facilities; and organizing donor events, inaugurations, groundbreakings, commencements, homecomings, parents weekends, and other traditional gatherings.

Although the portfolios of program responsibilities will vary from campus to campus, one common element is that of helping institutions expand their activities, presence, and influence beyond the traditional roles of faculty, students, and staff. Conference and events programs make the campus a more effective and user-friendly place for all types of learners. They enhance diverse campus cultures; conference subject matter adds depth and variety to campus dialogue. They support institutional efforts to function as a center for celebrations and non-traditional educational activities. They provide a forum for free-speech, venues for cultural events, opportunities for students and scholars to be exposed to research findings, and a chance for more people to observe what higher education is all about.

Conference and event programs provide activities during periods when fewer students are present to optimize efficient use of campus resources. They provide institutions with additional sources of revenue and contribute to the availability and continuity of employment for faculty and staff.

In recent years, institutions have increased their number of short-term learning opportunities for pre-college and professional students, whose needs for support services vary greatly. Many of the roles associated with student affairs are now tailored to these students through a single conference and event programs office.

The Association of Collegiate Conference and Event Directors—International (ACCED-I) estimates that more than 1,500 U.S. institutions of higher learning have offices providing conference and event planning. Their operations may include overseeing the summer operation of residence halls and classrooms; year-round management of full-service conference centers; coordination of large public events held in campus arenas and stadiums; and procurement of services and facilities at off-campus locations. Today, conference and event staff members provide everything from multi-department coordination of services to year-round academic support services and professional event planning consultation.

In recent years, a global increase in complex campuses has resulted in a growing need to formalize and standardize conference and event services. Several associations for campus conference and event professionals have come into being and flourished. As these associations matured, the need for professional standards became abundantly clear in dialogue among members. In the mid-1990s, a study of service practices by the Canadian University and College Conference Officers Association (CUCCOA) culminated in a summary report that called for establishing international standards for practitioners. In 1997 ACCED-I, CUCCOA, the Association of College and University Housing Officers-International (ACUHO-I), and the British Universities Accommodation Consortium (BUAC), now named VENUEMASTERS, collectively agreed on the need for developing professional standards in collaboration with the CAS standards development initiative.

By establishing professional standards in conjunction with CAS, institutional conference and event programs can become increasingly interconnected, forming a basis on which industry-defined service standards may become a reality. The CAS standards and guidelines that follow provide a professional context for the campus conference and event industry and will serve as a useful tool for all who wish to provide conference and event programs in higher education settings.

References, Readings, and Resources

Association of College and University Housing Officers-International (ACUHO-I): http://www.acuho.ohio-state.edu/

Association of Collegiate Conference and Event Directors—International (ACCED-I): http://www.acced-i.com/

Canadian University and College Conference Officers Association (CUCCOA): http://www.cuccoa.org/

United Kingdom: VENUEMASTERS: http://www.venuemasters.co.uk/

Contributor:

Patrick Perfetto, University of Maryland, ACCED-I

Conference and Event Programs
CAS Standards and Guidelines

Part 1. MISSION

The primary mission of Conference and Event Programs (CEP) is to provide on and off campus constituents opportunity and access to educational conferences, workshops, events, and activities that are relevant and complementary to the mission of the institution.

CEP must develop, disseminate, implement, and regularly review their mission. Mission statements must be consistent with the mission of the institution and with professional standards. CEP in higher education must enhance overall educational experiences by incorporating student learning and development outcomes in their mission.

The program mission must recognize and accommodate, as appropriate, relevant goals of other campus agencies that are integral providers of important services, or are major users of conference and event services.

Part 2. PROGRAM

Conference and Event Programs (CEP) must provide leadership within and for the institution relative to conference and event planning and management.

To accomplish this, the CEP office may:
- serve as a point of contact for multiple campus services
- provide effective coordination of multiple services
- collaborate with clients and service providers to assure that programs have a positive and compatible presence in the campus community
- create opportunities for student affairs and other campus departments to fulfill their programmatic goals for students and other learners
- create opportunities for campus departments to extend employment for employees during periods outside of the regular academic calendar
- provide additional revenue derived from campus income-producing facilities and services
- provide employment and experiential opportunities for students
- ensure that scheduled and routine campus activities are free from undue interference or interruption by activities related to conferences, events, and similar programs
- ascertain the appropriateness and compatibility of conferences, events, and similar activities with the institution's mission
- know, articulate, and exercise state-of-the-art meeting/event planning concepts and procedures
- provide one-stop access to and coordination of services to planners of conferences, events, and similar gatherings
- be a knowledgeable source of information about student services, campus facilities, and support services
- exercise appropriate authority with regard to campus resources

necessary to support conferences and events in collaboration with campus service providers, through agreements and memoranda of understanding
- communicate effectively among campus agencies as to specially scheduled or on-going campus activities that might influence or conflict with planned or potential conferences/events
- provide clear description of activities on campus events and calendars

The formal education of students, consisting of the curriculum and the co-curriculum, must promote student learning and development outcomes that are purposeful and holistic and that prepare students for satisfying and productive lifestyles, work, and civic participation. The student learning and development outcome domains and their related dimensions are:

- **knowledge acquisition, integration, construction, and application**
  - o **Dimensions: understanding knowledge from a range of disciplines; connecting knowledge to other knowledge, ideas, and experiences; constructing knowledge; and relating knowledge to daily life**

- **cognitive complexity**
  - o **Dimensions: critical thinking; reflective thinking; effective reasoning; and creativity**

- **intrapersonal development**
  - o **Dimensions: realistic self-appraisal, self-understanding, and self-respect; identity development; commitment to ethics and integrity; and spiritual awareness**

- **interpersonal competence**
  - o **Dimensions: meaningful relationships; interdependence; collaboration; and effective leadership**

- **humanitarianism and civic engagement**
  - o **Dimensions: understanding and appreciation of cultural and human differences; social responsibility; global perspective; and sense of civic responsibility**

- **practical competence**
  - o **Dimensions: pursuing goals; communicating effectively; technical competence; managing personal affairs; managing career development; demonstrating professionalism; maintaining health and wellness; and living a purposeful and satisfying life**

[See *The Council for the Advancement of Standards Learning and Developmental Outcomes* statement for examples of outcomes related to these domains and dimensions.]

Consistent with the institutional mission, CEP must identify relevant and desirable student learning and

development outcomes from among the six domains and related dimensions. When creating opportunities for student learning and development, CEP must explore possibilities for collaboration with faculty members and other colleagues.

CEP must assess relevant and desirable student learning and development outcomes and provide evidence of their impact on student learning and development. CEP must articulate how they contribute to or support students' learning and development in the domains not specifically assessed.

CEP must promote student learning and development through the creation, marketing, and staffing of conferences, events, and similar educational activities.

CEP must be:
- integrated into the life of the institution
- intentional and coherent
- guided by theories and knowledge of learning and development
- reflective of developmental and demographic profiles of the student population
- responsive to needs of individuals, diverse and special populations, and relevant constituencies

Part 3. LEADERSHIP

Because effective and ethical leadership is essential to the success of all organizations, Conference and Event Programs (CEP) leaders with organizational authority for the programs and services must:
- articulate a vision and mission for their programs and services
- set goals and objectives based on the needs of the population served and desired student learning and development outcomes
- advocate for their programs and services
- promote campus environments that provide meaningful opportunities for student learning, development, and integration
- identify and find means to address individual, organizational, or environmental conditions that foster or inhibit mission achievement
- advocate for representation in strategic planning initiatives at appropriate divisional and institutional levels
- initiate collaborative interactions with stakeholders who have legitimate concerns and interests in the functional area
- apply effective practices to educational and administrative processes
- prescribe and model ethical behavior
- communicate effectively
- manage financial resources, including planning, allocation, monitoring, and analysis
- incorporate sustainability practices in the management and design of programs, services, and facilities
- manage human resource processes including recruitment,

selection, development, supervision, performance planning, and evaluation
- empower professional, support, and student staff to accept leadership opportunities
- encourage and support scholarly contribution to the profession
- be informed about and integrate appropriate technologies into programs and services
- be knowledgeable about federal, state/provincial, and local laws relevant to the programs and services and ensure that staff members understand their responsibilities by receiving appropriate training
- develop and continuously improve programs and services in response to the changing needs of students and other populations served and the evolving institutional priorities
- recognize environmental conditions that may negatively influence the safety of staff and students and propose interventions that mitigate such conditions

Because of the likely involvement of multiple campus units in the delivery of conference and event services, special attention may be required to properly empower the program leaders to exercise necessary authority over resources.

Special attention should be given to the changing needs of conference and event client and service providers.

CEP leaders should provide guidance on:
- effective and appropriate strategies for communicating with prospective program participants
- student needs, issues, and perspectives
- cultivating relations with academic departments
- working with student, campus, and academic leaders and organizations
- efficient and appropriate use of campus resources
- promoting equal access for all students and program participants

Part 4. HUMAN RESOURCES

Conference and Event Programs (CEP) must be staffed adequately by individuals qualified to accomplish the mission and goals. Within institutional guidelines, CEP must establish procedures for staff selection, training, and evaluation; set expectations for supervision; and provide appropriate professional development opportunities to improve the leadership ability, competence, and skills of all employees.

CEP staff members must be proficient in effective customer service techniques.

CEP staff members should be knowledgeable about services offered directly and by relevant campus agencies and facilities such as housing, dining, recreation, parking, and technology services.

CEP professional staff members must hold an earned graduate or professional degree in a field relevant to the position they hold or must possess an appropriate combination of educational credentials and related work experience.

Degree- or credential-seeking interns must be qualified by enrollment in an appropriate field of study and by relevant experience. These individuals must be trained and supervised adequately by professional staff members holding educational credentials and related work experience appropriate for supervision.

Student employees and volunteers must be carefully selected, trained, supervised, and evaluated. They must be educated on how and when to refer those in need of additional assistance to qualified staff members and must have access to a supervisor for assistance in making these judgments. Student employees and volunteers must be provided clear and precise job descriptions, pre-service training based on assessed needs, and continuing staff development.

Employees and volunteers must receive specific training on institutional policies and privacy laws regarding their access to student records and other sensitive institutional information (e.g., in the USA, Family Educational Rights and Privacy Act, FERPA, or equivalent privacy laws in other states/provinces or countries).

CEP must have technical and support staff members adequate to accomplish their mission. All members of the staff must be technologically proficient and qualified to perform their job functions, be knowledgeable about ethical and legal uses of technology, and have access to training and resources to support the performance of their assigned responsibilities.

All members of the staff must receive training on policies and procedures related to the use of technology to store or access student records and institutional data.

CEP must ensure that staff members are knowledgeable about and trained in emergency procedures, crisis response, and prevention efforts. Prevention efforts must address identification of threatening conduct or behavior of students, faculty members, staff, and others and must incorporate a system or procedures for responding, including but not limited to reporting them to the appropriate campus officials.

Salary levels and benefits for all staff members must be commensurate with those for comparable positions within the institution, in similar institutions, and in the relevant geographic area.

CEP must maintain position descriptions for all staff members.

To create a diverse staff, CEP must institute hiring and promotion practices that are fair, inclusive, proactive, and non-discriminatory.

CEP must conduct regular performance planning and evaluation of staff members. CEP must provide access to continuing and advanced education and professional development opportunities.

Part 5. ETHICS

Persons involved in the delivery of Conference and Event Programs (CEP) must adhere to the highest principles of ethical behavior. CEP must review relevant professional ethical standards and develop or adopt and implement appropriate statements of ethical practice. CEP must publish these statements and ensure their periodic review by relevant constituencies.

CEP should consider the ethical standards of constituents to whom it provides services and with whom it partners.

CEP must orient new staff members to relevant ethical standards and statements of ethical practice.

CEP staff members must ensure that privacy and confidentiality are maintained with respect to all communications and records to the extent that such records are protected under the law and appropriate statements of ethical practice. Information contained in students' education records must not be disclosed except as allowed by relevant laws and institutional policies. CEP staff members must disclose to appropriate authorities information judged to be of an emergency nature, especially when the safety of the individual or others is involved, or when otherwise required by institutional policy or relevant law.

Advice and information disclosed by clients, students, faculty members, and staff in the course of conducting business should be considered confidential.

CEP staff members must be aware of and comply with the provisions contained in the institution's policies pertaining to human subjects research and student rights and responsibilities, as well as those in other relevant institutional policies addressing ethical practices and confidentiality of research data concerning individuals.

CEP staff members must recognize and avoid personal conflicts of interest or appearance thereof in the performance of their work.

CEP staff members must strive to insure the fair, objective, and impartial treatment of all persons with whom they interact.

When handling institutional funds, CEP staff members must ensure that such funds are managed in accordance with established and responsible accounting procedures and the fiscal policies or processes of the institution.

Promotional and descriptive information must be accurate and free of deception.

CEP staff members must perform their duties within the limits of their training, expertise, and competence. When these limits are exceeded, individuals in need of further assistance must be referred to persons possessing appropriate qualifications.

CEP staff members must use suitable means to confront and otherwise hold accountable other staff members who exhibit unethical behavior.

CEP staff members must be knowledgeable about and practice ethical behavior in the use of technology.

Part 6. LEGAL RESPONSIBILITIES

Conference and Event Programs (CEP) staff members must be knowledgeable about and responsive to laws and regulations that relate to their respective responsibilities and that may pose legal obligations, limitations, or ramifications for the institution as a whole. As appropriate, staff members must inform users of programs and services, as well as officials, of legal obligations and limitations including constitutional, statutory, regulatory, and case law; mandatory laws and orders emanating from federal, state/provincial, and local governments; and the institution's policies.

CEP staff members should inform conference/event planners, participants, institutional staff and students in a timely, systematic, and forthright fashion, about extraordinary or changing conditions, legal obligations, potential liabilities, risks, and security.

CEP must have written policies on all relevant operations, transactions, or tasks that may have legal implications.

CEP staff members must neither participate in nor condone any form of harassment or activity that demeans persons or creates an intimidating, hostile, or offensive campus environment.

CEP staff members must use reasonable and informed practices to limit the liability exposure of the institution and its officers, employees, and agents. CEP staff members must be informed about institutional policies regarding risk management, personal liability, and related insurance coverage options and must be referred to external sources if coverage is not provided by the institution.

Although participation in conferences, events, and similar activities is a voluntary action, program leaders should monitor liability for wrongful or negligent acts.

The institution must provide access to legal advice for CEP staff members as needed to carry out assigned responsibilities.

The institution must inform CEP staff and students in a timely and systematic fashion about extraordinary or changing legal obligations and potential liabilities.

Part 7. EQUITY and ACCESS

Conference and Event Programs (CEP) must be provided on a fair, equitable, and non-discriminatory basis in accordance with institutional policies and with all applicable state/provincial and federal statutes and regulations. CEP must maintain an educational and work environment free from discrimination in accordance with law and institutional policy.

Discrimination must be avoided on the basis of age; cultural heritage; disability; ethnicity; gender identity and expression; nationality; political affiliation; race; religious affiliation; sex; sexual orientation; economic, marital, social, or veteran status; and any other bases included in local, state/provincial, or federal laws.

CEP should provide services and information through a variety of appropriate formats including web site, e-mail, in person through office hours, telephone, and individual appointments, and customer service systems with a goal of maximizing one-stop shopping.

Consistent with the mission and goals, CEP must take action to remedy significant imbalances in student participation and staffing patterns.

Staff members should ensure that program services provided through third parties are offered on a fair and equitable basis.

CEP must ensure physical and program access for persons with disabilities. CEP must be responsive to the needs of all students and other populations served when establishing hours of operation and developing methods of delivering programs and services.

CEP must recognize the needs of distance learning students by providing appropriate and accessible services and assisting them in identifying and gaining access to other appropriate services in their geographic region.

Part 8. DIVERSITY

Within the context of each institution's unique mission, diversity enriches the community and enhances the collegiate experience for all; therefore, Conference and Event Programs (CEP) must create and nurture environments that are welcoming to and bring together persons of diverse backgrounds.

CEP must promote environments that are characterized by open and continuous communication that deepens understanding of one's own identity, culture, and heritage, as well as that of others. CEP must recognize, honor, educate, and promote respect about commonalties and differences among people within their historical and cultural contexts.

CEP must address the characteristics and needs of a diverse population when establishing and implementing policies and procedures.

CEP should make reasonable effort to educate the campus community concerning cultural aspects that are unique to individual conferences and events.

Part 9. ORGANIZATION and MANAGEMENT

To promote student learning and development outcomes, Conference and Event Programs (CEP) must be structured purposefully and managed effectively to achieve stated goals. Evidence of appropriate structure must include current and accessible policies and procedures, written performance expectations for all employees, functional workflow graphics or organizational charts, and clearly stated program and service delivery expectations.

CEP must monitor websites used for distributing information to ensure that the sites are current, accurate, appropriately referenced, and accessible.

Evidence of effective management must include use of comprehensive and accurate information for decisions, clear sources and channels of authority, effective communication practices, procedures for decision-making and conflict resolution, responses to changing conditions, systems of accountability and evaluation, and processes for recognition and reward. CEP must align policies and procedures with those of the institution and provide channels within the organization for their regular review.

CEP must maintain accurate and current documentation on operational policies and procedures, agreements and memoranda of understanding with service providers, standards of performance and other expectations of service providers, and access provisions for clients with disabilities.

Other areas for consideration in determining structure and management of conference and event offices may include:
- availability and characteristics of facilities
- size, nature, and mission of the institution
- scope of related academic services
- philosophy and delivery system for services
- variety of delivery methods being employed or available to the institution
- degree of integration with academic disciplines and academic service units

Part 10. CAMPUS and EXTERNAL RELATIONS

Conference and Event Programs (CEP) must reach out to relevant individuals, campus offices, and external agencies to:
- **establish, maintain, and promote effective relations**
- **disseminate information about their own and other related programs and services**
- **coordinate and collaborate, where appropriate, in offering programs and services to meet the needs of students and promote their achievement of student learning and development outcomes**

CEP must have procedures and guidelines consistent with institutional policy for responding to threats, emergencies, and crisis situations. Systems and procedures must be in place to disseminate timely and accurate information to students and other members of the campus community during emergency situations.

CEP must have procedures and guidelines consistent with institutional policy for communicating with the media.

The program should develop institutional support by:
- establishing cooperative relationships with other offices

(in addition to direct service providers) such as alumni, enrollment management, athletics, institutional advancement, communications, public relations, campus information visitor services, to share information, to stimulate program opportunities, and to enhance institutional visibility
- encouraging staff participation in civic and community organizations such as a Chamber of Commerce or Rotary International as well as involvement in professional associations

CEP should adhere to institution-wide processes that systematically involve academic affairs, student affairs, and administrative units such as police, physical plant and business offices.

CEP should collaborate with campus agencies, as appropriate, and meet regularly with service providers to coordinate schedules and facility use, and to review conferences and events under development.

CEP should serve as a resource providing professional advice on conference/event-related issues and activities.

Part 11. FINANCIAL RESOURCES

Conference and Event Programs (CEP) must have adequate funding to accomplish their mission and goals. In establishing funding priorities and making significant changes, a comprehensive analysis, which includes relevant expenditures, external and internal resources, and impact on the campus community, must be conducted.

CEP must demonstrate fiscal responsibility and cost effectiveness consistent with institutional protocols.

Funds to support the CEP, insofar as possible and desirable, should be self-generated from fees set at fair market rates.

For self-support programs, when higher than expected revenue in any one year results in a surplus, CEP should be authorized to establish reserve funds as a buffer against future shortfalls.

Part 12. TECHNOLOGY

Conference and Event Programs (CEP) must have adequate technology to support their mission. The technology and its use must comply with institutional policies and procedures and be evaluated for compliance with relevant federal, state/ provincial, and local requirements.

CEP must maintain policies and procedures that address the security and back up of data.

When technology is used to facilitate student learning and development, CEP must select technology that reflects current best pedagogical practices.

Technology, as well as any workstations or computer labs maintained by the CEP for student use, must be accessible and must meet established technology standards for delivery to persons with disabilities.

When CEP provide student access to technology, they must

provide:

- access to policies that are clear, easy to understand, and available to all students
- access to instruction or training on how to use the technology
- access to information on the legal and ethical implications of misuse as it pertains to intellectual property, harassment, privacy, and social networks.

Student violations of technology policies must follow established institutional student disciplinary procedures.

Students who experience negative emotional or psychological consequences from the use of technology must be referred to support services provided by the institution.

Part 13. FACILITIES and EQUIPMENT

Conference and Event Programs (CEP) must have adequate, accessible, suitably located facilities and equipment to support their mission and goals. If acquiring capital equipment as defined by the institution, CEP must take into account expenses related to regular maintenance and life cycle costs. Facilities and equipment must be evaluated regularly, including consideration of sustainability, and be in compliance with relevant federal, state/provincial, and local requirements to provide for access, health, safety, and security.

CEP staff members must have work space that is well-equipped, adequate in size, and designed to support their work and responsibilities. For conversations requiring privacy, staff members must have access to a private space.

CEP staff members who share work space must have the ability to secure their work adequately.

The design of the facilities must guarantee the security of records and ensure the confidentiality of sensitive information.

The location and layout of the facilities must be sensitive to the special needs of persons with disabilities as well as the needs of constituencies served.

CEP must ensure that staff members are knowledgeable of and trained in safety and emergency procedures for securing and vacating the facilities.

Housing, dining, meeting space, athletic, parking, and recreation facilities sufficient to meet the needs of conference programs should be available consistent with agreements among and between the institutional collaboratives.

Part 14. ASSESSMENT and EVALUATION

Conference and Event Programs (CEP) must establish systematic plans and processes to meet internal and external accountability expectations with regard to program as well as student learning and development outcomes. CEP must conduct regular assessment and evaluations. Assessments must include qualitative and quantitative methodologies as appropriate, to determine whether and to what degree the stated mission, goals, and student learning and development outcomes are being met. The process must employ sufficient and sound measures to ensure comprehensiveness. Data collected must include responses from students and other affected constituencies.

CEP must evaluate regularly how well they complement and enhance the institution's stated mission and educational effectiveness.

CEP should collaborate with institutional research units to generate data that could project contributions to the local economy, increase student enrollment, or stimulate additional research or related programs, given conference and event activities.

A representative cross-section of appropriate people from campus communities should be involved in reviewing the conference and event program.

CEP should generate and disseminate an annual report identifying overall goals, activities and programs served, financial contributions, regular feedback from participants, and opportunities that contribute to the overall visibility and promotion of the institution.

CEP must assess and evaluate regularly its effectiveness in providing students with quality learning and development opportunities.

Results of these evaluations must be used in revising and improving programs and services, identifying needs and interests in shaping directions of program and service design, and recognizing staff performance.

General Standards revised in 2008;
CEP content developed/revised in 2002

The Role of Counseling Services
CAS Standards Contextual Statement

The face of college counseling is changing to meet the needs of today's students. It continues to represent the integration of a helping profession activity with an educational environment (Dean & Meadows, 1995). The arrival of the current high-achieving generation of traditional college students, along with the influx of nontraditional, under-represented, and first generation students, enhances the campus environment but also brings greater levels of anxiety, depression, and even suicidal ideation (Howard, Schiraldi, Pineda, & Campanella, 2006; Twenge, 2006).

The nature and type of the higher educational environment and its effects on students are important tools for college counselors. Steenbarger (1990) noted that college counseling exemplifies the developmental framework that has produced a history of creative outreach and support work on campuses. The delivery of counseling services to students in higher education has and is evolving to respond effectively to clientele in an ever-changing environment.

Historically, the role and function of college counseling has changed in response to both external and internal factors. Social needs, political environment, national economy, and changing demographics all exert shifting influences to which counseling services must respond. Change also occurs in response to internal factors unique to each campus environment (e.g., location of the counseling center within health services versus an office that combines the counseling center with career services or academic advising). As a result, the breadth and depth of counseling services reflect the intersection of these influences. Davis and Humphrey's (2000) comprehensive work provided a thorough review of the history of college counseling roles and service delivery models, the changing demographics of higher education, and implications for the future. With the rapid technological and cultural changes in our society, the counseling profession among other helping professions has put forth standards of practice to meet the ever-changing needs of higher education clientele. College counselors have a responsibility to stay informed with a strong knowledge of current student needs (Upcraft, Gardner, Barefoot, 2005).

The current challenges are created by external forces including changing ethnic, racial, national, and experiential backgrounds of students; increasing psychological, health, safety, and financial needs of students; increasing competition for resources in higher education; increased emphasis on accountability; new and changing regulations regarding client privacy; and the implications of health and mental health care reform (American College Health Association, 2007; Gallagher, 2007; Kadison & DiGeronimo, 2004; Magoon, 2002). Moreover, the aftermath of 9/11, Virginia Tech and other global traumatic events highlight the necessity for college counseling programs to be responsive to unanticipated factors. The level of severity of college students' presenting concerns is much greater than the traditional presenting problems of adjustment issues and individuation that were typically identified in counseling center research from the 1950s through the early 1980s (Pledge, et al., 1998). Recent research indicates that the level of severity of presenting problems and the complexity of problems continue to increase (ACHA, 2007; Benton et al., 2003; Kadison, 2006). As the severity and complexity of clients' problems expand, it is increasingly important for college counseling professionals to be prepared to work with physicians, community mental health workers, other campus departments, and other health care professionals. An increased focus on retention and outcomes assessment, generated in part by accreditation agencies, has challenged college counseling programs to be more intentional about demonstrating efficacy (Boyer, 2005; Dean & Meadows, 1995; Lifton, Seay, Bushko, 2004; Tinto, 2006-07).

Based on these challenges, Stone and Archer (1990) stressed a need for counseling centers to (a) clearly define boundaries on the types of problems and degree of severity of those clients for whom the counseling center will provide services and (b) develop and identify extensive referral and outreach services to transition effectively more severe clients to appropriate community resources. At the same time, college counselors strive to maintain the developmental, preventive, and consultative services that are integral to their work. As Stone and Archer (1990) noted, the concepts of working within limits and achieving balance between demands and resources are significant for college counseling services. Archer and Cooper (1998) further recognized the importance of demonstrating to institutions the positive outcomes of helping students maintain psychological health and develop personally in ways that support retention.

College counseling services work with other student support services to promote students' personal and educational success through activities that complement formal academic programs. College counselors offer remedial, preventive, crisis, outreach, and consultative services, depending on the nature of the campus and students served. A strong commitment to professional development, whether through conducting research, providing training and supervision, maintaining professional credentials, upholding ethical standards of practice, or actively participating in professional organizations or other scholarly activities, is the catalyst for competent responses to the changing social issues and complex developmental, psychosocial, and mental health concerns of students (Boyd, et al., 2003).

College attendance creates a unique set of circumstances and stresses that can stimulate significant student growth and development, especially when the many student support functions are well coordinated and working together. As students experience change, they often need to address personal issues, work through challenges, and deal with the implications of growth and change. The rapid changes that characterize today's society, compounded by the impact of global crisis, catastrophic natural events, and economic decline can exacerbate students' personal and psychological problems (Davis & Humphrey, 2000; Kadison & DiGeronimo, 2004). However, students' access to and success in higher education are maximized as counseling services embrace and utilize medical, technological, and psychological advances. Humphrey, Kitchens, and Patrick (2000) encouraged counseling services to expand and embrace the use of interactional and Internet-based technologies for additional service delivery options; this is particularly important as more students enroll through distance education options. Counseling centers must offer services and resources to students through innovative means in order to serve the needs of all students.

The CAS Counseling Services Standards and Guidelines that follow provide college counselors with criteria to develop, enhance, evaluate, and judge the quality of campus counseling services offered.

References, Readings, and Resources

American College Health Association. (2007). American College Health Association — National College Health Assessment: Reference Group Executive Summary Fall 2007. Baltimore, MD: American College Health Association.

Archer, J., Jr., & Cooper, S. (1998). *Counseling and mental health services on campus: A handbook of contemporary practices and challenges*. San Francisco: Jossey-Bass.

Benton, S., Robertson, J., Tseng, W., Newton, F., & Benton, S. (2003). Changes in counseling center client problems across 13 years, *Professional Psychology: Research and Practice, 34*, 66-72.

Boyd, V., Hattauer, E., Brandel, I. W., Buckles, N., Davidshofer, C., Deakin, S., et al. (2003).Accreditation standards for university and college counseling centers. *Journal of Counseling and Development, 81*, 168-177.

Boyer, P. G. (2005). College student persistence of first-time freshmen at a midwest university: A longitudinal study. *Research for Educational Reform, 10 (1)*, 16-27.

Dean, L. A., & Meadows, M. E. (1995). College counseling: Union and intersection. *Journal of Counseling and Development, 74*, 139-142.

Davis, D., & Humphrey, K. (2000). *College counseling: Issues and strategies for a new millennium*. Alexandria, VA: American Counseling Association.

Gallagher, R. P. (2006). *National survey of counseling center directors*. Alexandria, VA: International Association of Counseling Services.

Humphrey, K., Kitchens, H., & Patrick, J. (2000). Trends in college counseling in the 21st century. In D. Davis & K. Humphrey, (Eds.) *College counseling: Issues and strategies for a new millennium* (pp.289-305). Alexandria, VA: American Counseling Association.

Kadison, R. D. (2006). College psychiatry 2006: Challenges and opportunities. *Journal of American College Health, 54*(6), 338-340.

Kadison, R. D., & DiGeronimo, T. F. (2004). *College of the overwhelmed: The campus mental health crisis and what to do about it*. San Francisco: Jossey-Bass.

Lifton, D. E., Seay, S. & Bushko, A. (2004). Measuring undergraduate hardiness as an indicator of persistence to graduation within four years. In I. M. Duranczyk, J. L. Higbee, & D. B. Lundell (Eds.). *Best Practices for Access and Retention in Higher Education*. Minneapolis, MN: Center for Research on Developmental Education and Urban Literacy, General College, University of Minnesota.

Magoon, T. (2002). *College and university counseling center directors' 2001-2002 data bank*. College Park, MD: University of Maryland.

Pledge, D., Lapan, R., Heppner, P., Kivlighan, D., and Roehlke, H. (1998). Stability and severity of presenting problems at a university counseling center: A six year analysis. *Professional Psychology: Research and Practice, 29*, 386-389.

Upcraft, M.L., Gardner, J.N., & Barefood, B.O. (2005). *Challenging and supporting the first-year student: A handbook for improving the first-year of college*. San Francisco: Jossey-Bass.

Steenbarger, B. N. (1990). Toward a developmental understanding of the counseling specialty. *Journal of Counseling and Development, 68*, 435-437.

Stone, G. L., & Archer, J., Jr. (1990). College and university counseling centers in the 1990s: Challenges and limits. *The Counseling Psychologist, 18*, 539-607.

Tinto, V. (2006-2007). Research and practice of retention: What next? *Journal of College Student Retention, 8 (1)*, 1-19.

Twenge, J. M. (2004). *Generation me: Why today's young American's are more confident, assertive, entitled — and more miserable than ever before*. New York: Free Press.

Additional Resources:

American College Counseling Association (ACCA): http://www.collegecounseling.org.

American College Health Association (ACHA): http://www.acha.org

American College Personnel Association (ACPA): http://myacpa.org;

Commission VII: Counseling & Psychological Services: http://myacpa.org

American Counseling Association (ACA) http://www.counseling.org.

American Psychological Association (APA): http://www.apa.org/ and Division 17, Counseling Psychology http://www.apa.org/about/division/div17.html

Association for the Coordination of Counseling Center Clinical Services:
http://accccs.appstate.edu/

Association of Counseling Center Training Agents (ACCTA).

Association of Counselor Education and Supervision (ACES): http://www.acesonline.net/.

Association of Psychology Postdoctoral and Internship Centers (APPIC): http://www.appic.org/index.html

Association for University and College Counseling Center Directors (AUCCCD):
http://www.aucccd.org.

Clearinghouse for Structured/Thematic Groups & Innovative Programs, University of Texas at Austin: http://www.utexas.edu/student/cmhc/clearinghouse/index.html

Counseling Center Village: http://ub-counseling.buffalo.edu/ccv.html.

International Association of Counseling Services (IACS): An Accreditation Association: http://www.iacsinc.org/.

Contributors:

Current Edition:
Carolyn W. Kern, University of North Texas
Angela Shores, Meredith College

Previous editions:
Laura A. Dean, University of Georgia, ACCA
Michelle (Stefanisko) Cooper, Western Carolina University

Counseling Services
CAS Standards and Guidelines

Part 1. MISSION

Counseling Services (CS) must develop, disseminate, implement, and regularly review their mission. Mission statements must be consistent with the mission of the institution and with professional standards. CS in higher education must enhance overall educational experiences by incorporating student learning and development outcomes in their mission.

The mission of CS is to assist students to define and accomplish personal, academic, and career goals.   To accomplish the mission, the scope of CS must include:

- **high quality individual and group counseling services to students who may be experiencing psychological, behavioral, or learning difficulties**
- **programming focused on the developmental needs of college students to maximize the potential of students to benefit from the academic environment and experience**
- **consultative services to the institution to help foster an environment supportive of the intellectual, emotional, spiritual and physical development of students**
- **assessment services to identify student needs and appropriate services and referrals**

A wide variety of counseling, consultative, evaluative, and training functions may be performed by CS as an expression of its institutional mission.

To effectively respond to the educational needs of the institution and of students, CS should have the following complementary functions:

Developmental. The developmental function is to help students enhance their growth. Developmental interventions help students benefit from the academic environment. To do so, the counseling services promote student growth by encouraging positive and realistic self-appraisal, intellectual development, appropriate personal and occupational choices, the ability to relate meaningfully and mutually with others, and the capacity to engage in a personally satisfying and effective style of living.

Remedial. The remedial function recognizes that some students experience significant problems, ranging from serious adjustment issues to more severe psychological disorders that require immediate professional attention. This function includes assisting students in overcoming current specific personal and educational problems and, in some cases, remedying current academic skill deficiencies.

Preventive. The preventive function is to anticipate environmental conditions and developmental processes that may negatively influence students' well being and initiate interventions that will promote personal adjustment and growth.

While there are basic similarities in the overall goals of various types of institutions, differences in student populations and institutional priorities may affect emphases of functions within individual counseling services. For these reasons, counseling services at two given institutions may emphasize different combinations of personal counseling, academic counseling, career counseling, or student development services.

CS should be organized based on institutional characteristics, priorities, and organizational structures.   Accordingly, not all functions may exist within the same administrative unit. In such cases, coordination among the units is essential to insure a cohesive system of services for students.

Part 2. PROGRAM

The formal education of students, consisting of the curriculum and the co-curriculum, must promote student learning and development outcomes that are purposeful and holistic and that prepare students for satisfying and productive lifestyles, work, and civic participation. The student learning and development outcome domains and their related dimensions are:

- **knowledge acquisition, integration, construction, and application**
  - o **Dimensions: understanding knowledge from a range of disciplines; connecting knowledge to other knowledge, ideas, and experiences; constructing knowledge; and relating knowledge to daily life**

- **cognitive complexity**
  - o **Dimensions: critical thinking; reflective thinking; effective reasoning; and creativity**

- **intrapersonal development**
  - o **Dimensions: realistic self-appraisal, self-understanding, and self-respect; identity development; commitment to ethics and integrity; and spiritual awareness**

- **interpersonal competence**
  - o **Dimensions: meaningful   relationships; interdependence; collaboration; and effective leadership**

- **humanitarianism and civic engagement**
  - o **Dimensions: understanding and appreciation of cultural and human differences; social responsibility; global perspective; and sense of civic responsibility**

- **practical competence**
  - o **Dimensions: pursuing goals; communicating effectively; technical competence; managing personal affairs; managing career development; demonstrating professionalism; maintaining health and wellness; and living a purposeful and satisfying life**

[See *The Council for the Advancement of Standards Learning and Developmental Outcomes* statement for examples of outcomes related to these domains and dimensions.]

Consistent with the institutional mission, Counseling Services (CS) must identify relevant and desirable student learning and development outcomes from among the six domains and related dimensions. When creating opportunities for student learning and development, CS must explore possibilities for collaboration with faculty members and other colleagues.

CS must assess relevant and desirable student learning and development outcomes and provide evidence of their impact on student learning and development. CS must articulate how they contribute to or support students' learning and development in the domains not specifically assessed.

CS must be:
- integrated into the life of the institution
- intentional and coherent
- guided by theories and knowledge of learning and development
- reflective of developmental and demographic profiles of the student population
- responsive to needs of individuals, diverse and special populations, and relevant constituencies

To effectively fulfill its mission, CS must provide directly, through referral, or in collaboration:
- individual counseling and/or psychotherapy in areas of personal, educational, career development/vocational choice, interpersonal relationships, family, social, and psychological issues
- group interventions (e.g., counseling, psychotherapy, support) to help students establish satisfying personal relationships and to become more effective in areas such as interpersonal processes, communication skills, decision-making concerning personal relationships and educational or career matters, and the establishment of personal values
- psychological testing and other assessment techniques to foster client self-understanding and decision-making
- outreach efforts to address developmental needs and concerns of students
- counseling support to help students assess and overcome specific deficiencies in educational preparation or skills
- psychiatric consultation, evaluation, and support services for students needing maintenance or monitoring of psychotropic medications
- crisis intervention and emergency coverage
- staff and faculty professional development programs

In those cases where other campus agencies address similar issues, such as career counseling and educational counseling, CS should establish cooperative relationships and maintain appropriate mutual referrals. In those cases where specialized and needed expertise is not available within counseling services, staff members should make full and active use of referral resources within the institution and the local community.

CS should play an active role in interpreting and, when appropriate, advocating for addressing the needs of students to administration, faculty, and staff of the institution. CS can provide a needed perspective for campus administrative leaders, reflecting an appropriate balance between administrative requirements and the special needs and interests of students. CS should interpret the institutional environment to students and intervene to either improve the quality of the environment or facilitate the development of better interactions between the student and environment. CS should be sensitive to the needs of traditionally under-served and special populations.

CS may engage in research that contributes to knowledge of student characteristics and needs and evaluation of student outcomes in its programs. CS may assist students, faculty and staff members who conduct individual research on student characteristics or on the influence of specific student development activities.

CS should provide consultation, supervision, and in-service professional development for faculty members, administrators, staff and student staff members, and paraprofessionals.

Training and supervision of paraprofessionals, practicum students, and interns is an appropriate and desirable responsibility of CS.

Part 3. LEADERSHIP

Because effective and ethical leadership is essential to the success of all organizations, Counseling Services (CS) leaders with organizational authority for the programs and services must:
- articulate a vision and mission for their programs and services
- set goals and objectives based on the needs of the population served and desired student learning and development outcomes
- advocate for their programs and services
- promote campus environments that provide meaningful opportunities for student learning, development, and integration
- identify and find means to address individual, organizational, or environmental conditions that foster or inhibit mission achievement
- advocate for representation in strategic planning initiatives at appropriate divisional and institutional levels
- initiate collaborative interactions with stakeholders who have legitimate concerns and interests in the functional area
- apply effective practices to educational and administrative processes
- prescribe and model ethical behavior
- communicate effectively
- manage financial resources, including planning, allocation, monitoring, and analysis
- incorporate sustainability practices in the management and design of programs, services, and facilities
- manage human resource processes including recruitment, selection, development, supervision, performance

planning, and evaluation

- empower professional, support, and student staff to accept leadership opportunities
- encourage and support scholarly contribution to the profession
- be informed about and integrate appropriate technologies into programs and services
- be knowledgeable about federal, state/provincial, and local laws relevant to the programs and services and ensure that staff members understand their responsibilities by receiving appropriate training
- develop and continuously improve programs and services in response to the changing needs of students and other populations served and the evolving institutional priorities
- recognize environmental conditions that may negatively influence the safety of staff and students and propose interventions that mitigate such conditions

Part 4. HUMAN RESOURCES

Counseling Services (CS) must be staffed adequately by individuals qualified to accomplish the mission and goals. Within institutional guidelines, CS must establish procedures for staff selection, training, and evaluation; set expectations for supervision; and provide appropriate professional development opportunities to improve the leadership ability, competence, and skills of all employees.

Counseling functions must be performed by professionals from disciplines such as counseling and clinical psychology, counselor education, psychiatry, and clinical social work, and by others with appropriate training, credentials, and supervised experience.

CS professional staff members must hold an earned graduate or professional degree in a field relevant to the position they hold or must possess an appropriate combination of educational credentials and related work experience.

Degree- or credential-seeking interns must be qualified by enrollment in an appropriate field of study and by relevant experience. These individuals must be trained and supervised adequately by professional staff members holding educational credentials and related work experience appropriate for supervision.

Student employees and volunteers must be carefully selected, trained, supervised, and evaluated. They must be educated on how and when to refer those in need of additional assistance to qualified staff members and must have access to a supervisor for assistance in making these judgments. Student employees and volunteers must be provided clear and precise job descriptions, pre-service training based on assessed needs, and continuing staff development.

Employees and volunteers must receive specific training on institutional policies and privacy laws regarding their access to student records and other sensitive institutional information (e.g., in the USA, Family Educational Rights and Privacy Act, FERPA, or equivalent privacy laws in other states/provinces or countries).

CS must have technical and support staff members adequate to accomplish their mission. All members of the staff must be technologically proficient and qualified to perform their job functions, be knowledgeable about ethical and legal uses of technology, and have access to training and resources to support the performance of their assigned responsibilities.

All members of the staff must receive training on policies and procedures related to the use of technology to store or access student records and institutional data.

CS must ensure that staff members are knowledgeable about and trained in emergency procedures, crisis response, and prevention efforts. Prevention efforts must address identification of threatening conduct or behavior of students, faculty members, staff, and others and must incorporate a system or procedures for responding, including but not limited to reporting them to the appropriate campus officials.

Salary levels and benefits for all staff members must be commensurate with those for comparable positions within the institution, in similar institutions, and in the relevant geographic area.

CS must maintain position descriptions for all staff members.

To create a diverse staff, CS must institute hiring and promotion practices that are fair, inclusive, proactive, and non-discriminatory.

CS must conduct regular performance planning and evaluation of staff members. CS must provide access to continuing and advanced education and professional development opportunities.

CS should maintain an in-service and staff development program which includes supervision, case presentations, research reports, and discussion of relevant professional issues. Institutional budgetary support should be available to provide for in-service and professional development activities.

The director of counseling services must have an appropriate combination of graduate course work, formal training, and supervised experience.

The director of CS should have a doctoral degree in counseling psychology, clinical psychology, counselor education, or other related discipline from an accredited institution, with a minimum of a master's degree in such areas. The director should hold or be eligible for state licensure or certification where such exists or should pursue such credentials. It is highly desirable that the director has a minimum of three years experience as a staff member or administrator in counseling services within higher education. The director should have received supervision (either pre- or post-doctoral) in counseling within higher education.

The director should have the ability to interact effectively with administrators, faculty and staff members, students, colleagues, and community members and should possess all the general qualifications of a counseling staff member.

The responsibilities of the director should include:
- overall administration and coordination of counseling activities
- coordination, recruitment, training, supervision, development, and evaluation of counseling and support staff personnel
- preparation and administration of budget
- preparation of annual reports
- provision of counseling information and services to students, faculty members, and staff in accordance with the mission of CS and the institution, to the community
- evaluation of services
- provision of consultation/leadership in policy formation and program development
- education of staff members regarding legal issues in mental health, medicine, and higher education, as well as legal issues governing the delivery of counseling services

Counseling staff members must have an appropriate combination of graduate course work, formal training, and supervised experience.

The minimum qualification for counseling staff members should be a master's degree from a regionally accredited institution in a relevant discipline such as counseling psychology, clinical psychology, counseling and personnel services, mental health counseling, and clinical social work, with a supervised practicum/internship at the graduate level, preferably in the counseling of students within a higher education setting, or should be appropriately supervised until they can transfer their skills to this setting. Counseling staff members should hold, or be eligible for, state/provincial licensure or certification in their chosen discipline (e.g., counseling, psychology, social work), where such exists.

Counseling staff members should have appropriate course work and training in psychological assessment, theories of personality, abnormal psychology or psychopathology, career development, multicultural counseling, legal and ethical issues in counseling, and learning theory. Counseling staff members should keep abreast of current research, including outcome research. Counseling staff members should also demonstrate knowledge of technology, leadership, organization development, consultation, and relevant federal, regional, and state/provincial statutes.

In cases where counseling staff members are responsible for the supervision of colleagues or graduate interns, the counseling staff members should have doctoral degrees or hold degrees commensurate with those being supervised.

Counseling staff members should participate in appropriate professional organizations and should have the budgetary support to do so. Counseling staff members should be encouraged to participate in community activities related to their profession.

Practicum students and interns, as well as paraprofessional assistants, may perform, under supervision, such counseling functions as are appropriate to their preparation and experience.

The level of CS staffing must be established and reviewed regularly with regard to service demands, enrollment, user surveys, diversity of services offered, institutional resources, and other mental health and student services that may be available on the campus and in the local community.

In addition to providing direct services, it is important that staff time be allowed for preparation of interviews and reports, updating institutional information, research, faculty and staff contacts, staff meetings, training and supervision, personal and professional development, consultation, and walk-in and emergency counseling interventions, in accordance with individual staff members' qualifications and task assignments. Similarly, teaching, administration, research, and other such responsibilities should be identified as relevant staff functions.

CS must have technical and support staff members adequate to accomplish its mission. CS staff members must be technologically proficient and qualified to perform their job functions, be knowledgeable of ethical and legal uses of technology, and have access to training. The level of staffing and workloads must be adequate and appropriate for program and service demands.

Clerical employees who deal directly with students should be carefully selected, since they play an important role in the students' impressions of the counseling services and often must make some preliminary client-related decisions.

Part 5. ETHICS

Persons involved in the delivery of Counseling Services (CS) must adhere to the highest principles of ethical behavior. CS must review relevant professional ethical standards and develop or adopt and implement appropriate statements of ethical practice. CS must publish these statements and ensure their periodic review by relevant constituencies.

CS must orient new staff members to relevant ethical standards and statements of ethical practice.

CS staff members must ensure that privacy and confidentiality are maintained with respect to all communications and records to the extent that such records are protected under the law and appropriate statements of ethical practice. Information contained in students' education records must not be disclosed except as allowed by relevant laws and institutional policies. CS staff members must disclose to appropriate authorities information judged to be of an emergency nature, especially when the safety of the individual or others is involved, or when otherwise required by institutional policy or relevant law.

CS staff members must be aware of and comply with the provisions contained in the institution's policies pertaining to human subjects research and student rights and responsibilities, as well as those in other relevant institutional policies addressing ethical practices and confidentiality of

research data concerning individuals.

CS staff members must recognize and avoid personal conflicts of interest or appearance thereof in the performance of their work.

CS staff members must strive to insure the fair, objective, and impartial treatment of all persons with whom they interact.

When handling institutional funds, CS staff members must ensure that such funds are managed in accordance with established and responsible accounting procedures and the fiscal policies or processes of the institution.

Promotional and descriptive information must be accurate and free of deception.

CS staff members must perform their duties within the limits of their training, expertise, and competence. When these limits are exceeded, individuals in need of further assistance must be referred to persons possessing appropriate qualifications.

CS staff members must use suitable means to confront and otherwise hold accountable other staff members who exhibit unethical behavior.

CS staff members must be knowledgeable about and practice ethical behavior in the use of technology.

CS staff members must conform to relevant federal, state/provincial, and local statutes which govern the delivery of counseling and psychological services.

CS staff members must be familiar with and adhere to relevant ethical standards in the field, including those professional procedures for intake, assessment, case notes, termination summaries and the preparation, use, and distribution of psychological tests.

Client status and information disclosed in individual counseling sessions must remain confidential, unless written permission to divulge the information is given by the student.

Clients must be made aware of issues such as the limits to confidentiality during intake or early in the counseling process so they can participate from a position of informed consent.

Consultation regarding individual students, as requested or needed with faculty and other campus personnel, is offered in the context of preserving the student's confidential relationship with the counseling services. Consultation with parents, spouses, and public and private agencies that bear some responsibility for particular students may occur within the bounds of a confidential counseling relationship.

When the condition of a client is indicative of clear and imminent danger to the client or to others, counseling staff members must take reasonable personal action that may involve informing responsible authorities, and when possible, consulting with other professionals. In such cases, counseling staff members must be cognizant of pertinent ethical principles, state/provincial or federal statutes, and local mental health guidelines that stipulate the limits of confidentiality.

Information should be released only at the written request or concurrence of a client who has full knowledge of the nature of the information that is being released and of the parties to whom it is released. Instances of limited confidentiality should be clearly articulated. The decision to release information without consent should occur only after careful consideration and under the conditions described above.

CS must maintain records in a confidential and secure manner while specifying procedures to monitor access, use, and maintenance of the records.

Part 6. LEGAL RESPONSIBILITIES

Counseling Services (CS) staff members must be knowledgeable about and responsive to laws and regulations that relate to their respective responsibilities and that may pose legal obligations, limitations, or ramifications for the institution as a whole. As appropriate, staff members must inform users of programs and services, as well as officials, of legal obligations and limitations including constitutional, statutory, regulatory, and case law; mandatory laws and orders emanating from federal, state/provincial, and local governments; and the institution's policies.

CS must have written policies on all relevant operations, transactions, or tasks that may have legal implications.

CS staff members must neither participate in nor condone any form of harassment or activity that demeans persons or creates an intimidating, hostile, or offensive campus environment.

CS staff members must use reasonable and informed practices to limit the liability exposure of the institution and its officers, employees, and agents. CS staff members must be informed about institutional policies regarding risk management, personal liability, and related insurance coverage options and must be referred to external sources if coverage is not provided by the institution.

The institution must provide access to legal advice for CS staff members as needed to carry out assigned responsibilities.

The institution must inform CS staff and students in a timely and systematic fashion about extraordinary or changing legal obligations and potential liabilities.

Part 7. EQUITY and ACCESS

Counseling Services (CS) must be provided on a fair, equitable, and non-discriminatory basis in accordance with institutional policies and with all applicable state/provincial and federal statutes and regulations. CS must maintain an educational and work environment free from discrimination in accordance with law and institutional policy.

Discrimination must be avoided on the basis of age; cultural heritage; disability; ethnicity; gender identity and expression; nationality; political affiliation; race; religious affiliation; sex; sexual orientation; economic, marital, social, or veteran status; and any other bases included in local, state/provincial, or federal laws.

Consistent with the mission and goals, CS must take action to remedy significant imbalances in student participation and staffing patterns.

CS must ensure physical and program access for persons with disabilities. CS must be responsive to the needs of all students and other populations served when establishing hours of operation and developing methods of delivering programs and services.

CS must recognize the needs of distance learning students by providing appropriate and accessible services and assisting them in identifying and gaining access to other appropriate services in their geographic region.

Part 8. DIVERSITY

Within the context of each institution's unique mission, diversity enriches the community and enhances the collegiate experience for all; therefore, Counseling Services (CS) must create and nurture environments that are welcoming to and bring together persons of diverse backgrounds.

CS must promote environments that are characterized by open and continuous communication that deepens understanding of one's own identity, culture, and heritage, as well as that of others. CS must recognize, honor, educate, and promote respect about commonalties and differences among people within their historical and cultural contexts.

CS must address the characteristics and needs of a diverse population when establishing and implementing policies and procedures.

Part 9. ORGANIZATION and MANAGEMENT

To promote student learning and development outcomes, Counseling Services (CS) must be structured purposefully and managed effectively to achieve stated goals. Evidence of appropriate structure must include current and accessible policies and procedures, written performance expectations for all employees, functional workflow graphics or organizational charts, and clearly stated program and service delivery expectations.

CS must monitor websites used for distributing information to ensure that the sites are current, accurate, appropriately referenced, and accessible.

Evidence of effective management must include use of

comprehensive and accurate information for decisions, clear sources and channels of authority, effective communication practices, procedures for decision-making and conflict resolution, responses to changing conditions, systems of accountability and evaluation, and processes for recognition and reward. CS must align policies and procedures with those of the institution and provide channels within the organization for their regular review.

Because the functions of CS are essential to the overall mission of an institution, their value and impact should be clearly articulated to the campus and their placement within the organizational structure should be such that it facilitates significant interaction with unit heads in academic and student affairs.

CS should function independently of units directly responsible for making decisions concerning students' official matriculation status, such as judicial actions, academic probation, and admissions or re-admissions actions.

Part 10. CAMPUS and EXTERNAL RELATIONS

Counseling Services (CS) must reach out to relevant individuals, campus offices, and external agencies to:
- establish, maintain, and promote effective relations
- disseminate information about their own and other related programs and services
- coordinate and collaborate, where appropriate, in offering programs and services to meet the needs of students and promote their achievement of student learning and development outcomes

CS must have procedures and guidelines consistent with institutional policy for responding to threats, emergencies, and crisis situations. Systems and procedures must be in place to disseminate timely and accurate information to students and other members of the campus community during emergency situations.

CS must have procedures and guidelines consistent with institutional policy for communicating with the media.

It is desirable that CS develop close cooperation with campus referral sources and with potential consumers of counseling services consultations. CS should also work closely with all other segments of the institution whose goal is the promotion of psychological, emotional, and career development.

CS should work closely with the chief student affairs and chief academic affairs administrators to insure the meeting of institutional goals and objectives.

Within the campus community, CS should establish close cooperation with career services, academic advising, special academic support units (e.g., reading and study skills programs, learning assistance programs) and specialized student services (e.g., services for students with disabilities, international and minority students, TRIO programs, women, veterans, returning adult students).

CS should establish relationships with a wide range of student groups (e.g., student government; gay, lesbian, bisexual, transgender groups; fraternities and sororities) to promote visibility and serve as a resource to them.

CS should establish and maintain a close working relationship with student health services as counseling staff members are often called upon to refer clients for medical concerns or hospitalization, or to serve as consultants to, or to seek consultation from, health services professionals.

CS should foster relationships with academic units and with campus professionals in admissions, registrar's office, student activities, athletics, and residence halls, where appropriate.

CS should establish effective relationships with the institutional legal counsel and the legal staff of relevant professional organizations in order to effectively respond to pertinent legal issues and precedents which underlie the delivery components of CS.

Where adequate mental health resources are not available on campus, CS must establish and maintain close working relationships with off-campus community mental health resources.

CS should have procedures for the referral of students who require counseling beyond the scope of institutional CS.

Part 11. FINANCIAL RESOURCES

Counseling Services (CS) must have adequate funding to accomplish their mission and goals. In establishing funding priorities and making significant changes, a comprehensive analysis, which includes relevant expenditures, external and internal resources, and impact on the campus community, must be conducted.

CS must demonstrate fiscal responsibility and cost effectiveness consistent with institutional protocols.

Part 12. TECHNOLOGY

Counseling Services (CS) must have adequate technology to support their mission. The technology and its use must comply with institutional policies and procedures and be evaluated for compliance with relevant federal, state/provincial, and local requirements.

CS must maintain policies and procedures that address the security and back up of data.

When technology is used to facilitate student learning and development, CS must select technology that reflects current best pedagogical practices.

Technology, as well as any workstations or computer labs maintained by the CS for student use, must be accessible and must meet established technology standards for delivery to persons with disabilities.

When CS provide student access to technology, they must provide:
- **access to policies that are clear, easy to understand, and available to all students**
- **access to instruction or training on how to use the technology**
- **access to information on the legal and ethical implications of misuse as it pertains to intellectual property, harassment, privacy, and social networks.**

Student violations of technology policies must follow established institutional student disciplinary procedures.

Students who experience negative emotional or psychological consequences from the use of technology must be referred to support services provided by the institution.

Part 13. FACILITIES and EQUIPMENT

Counseling Services (CS) must have adequate, accessible, suitably located facilities and equipment to support their mission and goals. If acquiring capital equipment as defined by the institution, CS must take into account expenses related to regular maintenance and life cycle costs. Facilities and equipment must be evaluated regularly, including consideration of sustainability, and be in compliance with relevant federal, state/provincial, and local requirements to provide for access, health, safety, and security.

CS staff members must have work space that is well-equipped, adequate in size, and designed to support their work and responsibilities. For conversations requiring privacy, staff members must have access to a private space.

CS staff members who share work space must have the ability to secure their work adequately.

The design of the facilities must guarantee the security of records and ensure the confidentiality of sensitive information.

The location and layout of the facilities must be sensitive to the special needs of persons with disabilities as well as the needs of constituencies served.

CS must ensure that staff members are knowledgeable of and trained in safety and emergency procedures for securing and vacating the facilities.

CS must maintain a physical and social environment that facilitates optimal functioning and insures appropriate confidentiality.

CS, when feasible, should be physically separate from administrative offices, campus police, and judicial units.

Individual offices for counseling staff members should be provided and appropriately equipped and soundproof. The offices should be designed to accommodate the functions performed by counseling staff members.

There should be a reception area that provides a comfortable and private waiting area for clients.

CS should maintain or have ready access to professional resource materials.

In those instances where counseling services include a career development unit, there should be a resource center that holds institutional catalogs and occupation and career information.

An area suitable for individual and group testing procedures should be available.

CS should maintain, or have ready access to, group meeting space.

CS should maintain equipment that is capable of providing modern technical approaches to treatment and record keeping and have access to equipment for research and media presentations.

CS with training components should have adequate facilities for recording, and, where possible, for direct observations.

Part 14. ASSESSMENT and EVALUATION

Counseling Services (CS) must establish systematic plans and processes to meet internal and external accountability expectations with regard to program as well as student learning and development outcomes. CS must conduct regular assessment and evaluations. Assessments must include qualitative and quantitative methodologies as appropriate, to determine whether and to what degree the stated mission, goals, and student learning and development outcomes are being met. The process must employ sufficient and sound measures to ensure comprehensiveness. Data collected must include responses from students and other affected constituencies.

CS must evaluate regularly how well they complement and enhance the institution's stated mission and educational effectiveness.

Results of these evaluations must be used in revising and improving programs and services, identifying needs and interests in shaping directions of program and service design, and recognizing staff performance.

General Standards revised in 2008;
CS content developed/revised in 1986, 1997, & 1999

The Role of Dining Services Programs
CAS Standards Contextual Statement

Institutions of higher education have provided a dining services program, initially as a component of student housing, since the first residential colleges were founded. Over the years the quality and variety of services provided varied greatly depending upon the specific institution. In 1958, with the creation of the National Association of College and University Food Services (NACUFS), the professionalism of those employed in dining services was enhanced, and the potential for the overall improvement of dining services was increased.

The basic principles that underlie any dining services program are to provide students, faculty, staff, and guests with high quality food service and products in a pleasant environment at a reasonable cost. Those principles are shared by professionals throughout the college and university arena, although the specific focus may vary from campus to campus. While the original scope of the dining services program encompassed simply the providing of nourishment, currently that is only one of the basic elements of a quality program. Meals are important times and places for students, faculty, and staff to exchange ideas, discuss current issues, and share experiences, and the design of facilities and menus needs to accommodate these functions. While reasonable cost to the consumer is an expectation, providing a source of revenue to the institution is also usually a desired outcome. Balancing those two imperatives is critical to the success of any program.

Additionally, modern dining services programs must address the dietary needs and wants of an increasingly diverse population. It is no longer sufficient to provide only good nutrition. Programs must address the rising sophistication of students in higher education and the dining experiences they bring with them to campus. Life-style choices must also be addressed in addition to dietary needs. Vegetarian/vegan and/or religious-based diets are but two of an ever-growing list of eating choices made by today's student that must be accommodated successfully.

As dining services programs have dealt positively with the transition from supplying basic needs to providing for expanded expectations, they are now addressing an increasing list of current issues. Among these is the practice of outsourcing of the dining services program. It is incumbent upon the administration of each institution to make the decision to self-operate or privatize based on what is in the best interest of that particular institution and its students, faculty, and staff. Sustainability is an issue that has recently emerged on many campuses. These institutions are trying to provide products and services that support local businesses and industries in a manner that encourages the continued existence of those resources while balancing the budget. Increasingly, students with food allergies are being served by dining services programs. One of the challenges in this area is to provide a specialized diet without students feeling as if they are being singled out as different. Finally, as mentioned above, students bring an increasingly sophisticated and diverse set of dining experiences to campus. Developing a "retail orientation" to better address these expectations is one of the more prevalent changes being implemented across campuses. There is a continuing need to provide a wide variety of services. At times, students may benefit from all-you-care-to-eat service; at other times, they prefer take-out services. Often, late-night service is a need. In other words, today's students want what they want, where they want it, and when they want it. It is the role of dining services to maintain high quality programs while seeking ways to meet these changing needs and expectations. The standards and guidelines that follow offer guidance for the development and assessment of such high quality dining services programs.

References, Readings, and Resources

Administering Food Service Contracts: A Handbook for Contract Administrators in College and University Food Services. (n.d.). Okemos, MI: National Association of College and University Food Services (NACUFS).

American Dietetic Association. http://www.eatright.org

Educational Foundation of the National Restaurant Association http://www.nraef.org

Foodservice Systems Management Education Council. http://www.fsmec.org

Journal of The National Association of College & University Food Services. (n.d.). Okemos, MI: National Association of College and University Food Services (NACUFS).

Professional Practices in College and University Food Services (5th ed.). Okemos, MI: National Association of College and University Food Services (NACUFS).

The National Association of College and University Food Services. http://www.nacufs.org

Contributors:
Russ Myer, University of Nevada, Reno; NACUFS
Joe Spina, NACUFS

Dining Services Programs
CAS Standards and Guidelines

Part 1. MISSION

The mission of Dining Services Programs (DSP) must address:

- a dining environment that encourages both individual and community development
- engagement of students in learning about sound nutrition practices
- safe and secure facilities that are clean, attractive, well-maintained, and comfortable
- management services that ensure the orderly and effective administration and operation of all aspects of the program
- reasonably priced, quality, safe, diverse, and nutritious food offerings

DSP must develop, disseminate, implement, and regularly review their mission. Mission statements must be consistent with the mission of the institution and with professional standards. DSP in higher education must enhance overall educational experiences by incorporating student learning and development outcomes in their mission.

DSP should clearly define and communicate its vision and mission to staff members and students, to provide the focus for departmental practices.

The institution, when outsourcing, should clearly define what role the contractor has in developing a mission statement or supporting the institution's mission statement.

In addition to dining services, the DSP mission must include, either directly or through collaboration, a provision for educational programs and services and management services.

Part 2. PROGRAM

The formal education of students, consisting of the curriculum and the co-curriculum, must promote student learning and development outcomes that are purposeful and holistic and that prepare students for satisfying and productive lifestyles, work, and civic participation. The student learning and development outcome domains and their related dimensions are:

- knowledge acquisition, integration, construction, and application
  - Dimensions: understanding knowledge from a range of disciplines; connecting knowledge to other knowledge, ideas, and experiences; constructing knowledge; and relating knowledge to daily life

- cognitive complexity
  - Dimensions: critical thinking; reflective thinking; effective reasoning; and creativity

- intrapersonal development
  - Dimensions: realistic self-appraisal, self-understanding, and self-respect; identity development; commitment to ethics and integrity; and spiritual awareness

- interpersonal competence
  - Dimensions: meaningful relationships; interdependence; collaboration; and effective leadership

- humanitarianism and civic engagement
  - Dimensions: understanding and appreciation of cultural and human differences; social responsibility; global perspective; and sense of civic responsibility

- practical competence
  - Dimensions: pursuing goals; communicating effectively; technical competence; managing personal affairs; managing career development; demonstrating professionalism; maintaining health and wellness; and living a purposeful and satisfying life

[See *The Council for the Advancement of Standards Learning and Developmental Outcomes* statement for examples of outcomes related to these domains and dimensions.]

Consistent with the institutional mission, Dining Services Programs (DSP) must identify relevant and desirable student learning and development outcomes from among the six domains and related dimensions. When creating opportunities for student learning and development, DSP must explore possibilities for collaboration with faculty members and other colleagues.

DSP must assess relevant and desirable student learning and development outcomes and provide evidence of their impact on student learning and development. DSP must articulate how they contribute to or support students' learning and development in the domains not specifically assessed.

DSP must be:
- integrated into the life of the institution
- intentional and coherent
- guided by theories and knowledge of learning and development
- reflective of developmental and demographic profiles of the student population
- responsive to needs of individuals, diverse and special populations, and relevant constituencies

To fulfill its mission and goals effectively, DSP must provide students with access to experiences, services, and programs that facilitate:
- interaction with faculty and staff members
- respect for self, others, and property
- appreciation of new ideas
- appreciation of cultural differences and other forms of

diversity
- **development of a balanced lifestyle embracing wellness**
- **orientation to community expectations, facilities, services, and staff**
- **understanding of institutional and dining policies, procedures, and expectations, including the potential consequences for violation**
- **involvement in programming and policy development**
- **responsibility for their community through confrontation of inappropriate or disruptive behavior**

DSP should support and respond to student dietary and medical requirements, such as vegan diets and food allergies.

DSP should provide access to a registered dietician to assist students in meeting their dietary and medical needs.

DSP must establish appropriate policies and procedures for responding to emergency situations, especially where DSP facilities, personnel, and resources could assist the institution.

Dining Services should be involved in institution emergency planning.

DSP should provide an organizational avenue such as a food advisory board and should have a relationship with appropriate student governance organizations.

Part 3. LEADERSHIP

Because effective and ethical leadership is essential to the success of all organizations, leaders with organizational authority for the programs and services must:
- **articulate a vision and mission for their programs and services**
- **set goals and objectives based on the needs of the population served and desired student learning and development outcomes**
- **advocate for their programs and services**
- **promote campus environments that provide meaningful opportunities for student learning, development, and integration**
- **identify and find means to address individual, organizational, or environmental conditions that foster or inhibit mission achievement**
- **advocate for representation in strategic planning initiatives at appropriate divisional and institutional levels**
- **initiate collaborative interactions with stakeholders who have legitimate concerns and interests in the functional area**
- **apply effective practices to educational and administrative processes**
- **prescribe and model ethical behavior**
- **communicate effectively**
- **manage financial resources, including planning, allocation, monitoring, and analysis**
- **incorporate sustainability practices in the management**

and design of programs, services, and facilities
- **manage human resource processes including recruitment, selection, development, supervision, performance planning, and evaluation**
- **empower professional, support, and student staff to accept leadership opportunities**
- **encourage and support scholarly contribution to the profession**
- **be informed about and integrate appropriate technologies into programs and services**
- **be knowledgeable about federal, state/provincial, and local laws relevant to the programs and services and ensure that staff members understand their responsibilities by receiving appropriate training**
- **develop and continuously improve programs and services in response to the changing needs of students and other populations served and the evolving institutional priorities**
- **recognize environmental conditions that may negatively influence the safety of staff and students and propose interventions that mitigate such conditions.**

DSP must promote professionalism, integrity, and ethical behavior in dealing with colleagues, students, administration, faculty, vendors, and the public.

The institution must clearly articulate whether DSP is to be subsidized, self-sustaining, or revenue generating.

Institutions with significant commuter-based populations or other unique circumstances should recognize that subsidizing the operation may be required, depending upon the level of service desired.

The institution, when outsourcing, must clearly state that the relationship is to be mutually beneficial.

It should recognize that when outsourced, the food service provider has a reasonable expectation of profit and should work with the institution to achieve mutual benefit.

DSP must comply with laws, regulations, and policies, with particular attention to health and safety requirements.

DSP should promote a positive relationship with all internal and external customers, especially students, and openly solicit comments from all customers.

DSP must have internal service control systems in place throughout the department to protect the customer and the department without sacrificing the underlying commitment to customer service.

Part 4. HUMAN RESOURCES

Dining Services Programs (DSP) must be staffed adequately by individuals qualified to accomplish the mission and goals. Within institutional guidelines, DSP must establish procedures for staff selection, training, and evaluation; set expectations for supervision; and provide appropriate professional

development opportunities to improve the leadership ability, competence, and skills of all employees.

DSP professional staff members must hold an earned graduate or professional degree in a field relevant to the position they hold or must possess an appropriate combination of educational credentials and related work experience.

Degree- or credential-seeking interns must be qualified by enrollment in an appropriate field of study and by relevant experience. These individuals must be trained and supervised adequately by professional staff members holding educational credentials and related work experience appropriate for supervision.

Student employees and volunteers must be carefully selected, trained, supervised, and evaluated. They must be educated on how and when to refer those in need of additional assistance to qualified staff members and must have access to a supervisor for assistance in making these judgments. Student employees and volunteers must be provided clear and precise job descriptions, pre-service training based on assessed needs, and continuing staff development.

Employees and volunteers must receive specific training on institutional policies and privacy laws regarding their access to student records and other sensitive institutional information (e.g., in the USA, Family Educational Rights and Privacy Act, FERPA, or equivalent privacy laws in other states/provinces or countries).

DSP must have technical and support staff members adequate to accomplish their mission. All members of the staff must be technologically proficient and qualified to perform their job functions, be knowledgeable about ethical and legal uses of technology, and have access to training and resources to support the performance of their assigned responsibilities.

All members of the staff must receive training on policies and procedures related to the use of technology to store or access student records and institutional data.

DSP must ensure that staff members are knowledgeable about and trained in emergency procedures, crisis response, and prevention efforts. Prevention efforts must address identification of threatening conduct or behavior of students, faculty members, staff, and others and must incorporate a system or procedures for responding, including but not limited to reporting them to the appropriate campus officials.

Salary levels and benefits for all staff members must be commensurate with those for comparable positions within the institution, in similar institutions, and in the relevant geographic area.

DPS must maintain position descriptions for all staff members.

To create a diverse staff, DSP must institute hiring and promotion practices that are fair, inclusive, proactive, and non-discriminatory.

Student employees should be considered as a part of the DSP staff.

Because student employment is an important component of student development, DSP should have an effective program for the recruitment, training, education, development, evaluation, and promotion of student employees.

DSP must maintain up-to-date, accurate, and complete personnel, payroll, and certification records for each staff member of the department.

DSP must provide emergency response training opportunities for staff to learn to respond to emergencies.

These opportunities could include CPR training, Heimlich maneuver, and basic first aid.

DSP should provide all new staff members, including students, a formal orientation, including policies, procedures, rules, and benefits that apply to them.

DSP should use a formal system for providing standardized and consistent job-specific training for staff members, including students.

Staff members include student staff where applicable.

DSP must follow an orderly system for salary and wage administration that complies with federal and state/provincial laws and institutional policies and procedures.

DSP should provide personnel benefits beyond wage and salary that provide for the basic needs of all eligible staff members.

DSP should promote long-term career opportunities for all staff members.

DSP management should practice positive approaches to staff management designed to increase productivity, minimize turnover, and contribute to a high level of morale.

DSP should use a system for reviewing the job performance of all staff members, including student employees, on a scheduled basis as an integral part of a proactive human resource development process.

DSP should provide special recognition for staff members, including student employees, whose performance is superior as an incentive to all staff members to maximize their potential.

DSP must have a system for administering discipline on an objective and fair basis with a clear focus on human resource development.

DSP must provide procedures for filing, processing, and hearing employee grievances. All staff members, including students, must be aware of and support the goals, objectives, and philosophy of DSP.

Where collective bargaining agreements exist, DSP management must administer them in good faith and strive to maintain a positive working relationship between management and union staff members.

DSP must comply with federal, state/provincial, and local laws and regulations and institutional and department policies regarding posting of information for staff members, including students, about their rights and responsibilities.

DSP should have orderly separation procedures that follow institutional policies for processing resignations and involuntary termination of employment.

DSP must conduct regular performance planning and evaluation of staff members. DSP must provide access to continuing and advanced education and professional development opportunities.

Part 5. ETHICS

Persons involved in the delivery of Dining Services Programs (DSP) must adhere to the highest principles of ethical behavior. DSP must review relevant professional ethical standards and develop or adopt and implement appropriate statements of ethical practice. DSP must publish these statements and ensure their periodic review by relevant constituencies.

DSP must orient new staff members to relevant ethical standards and statements of ethical practice.

DSP staff members must ensure that privacy and confidentiality are maintained with respect to all communications and records to the extent that such records are protected under the law and appropriate statements of ethical practice. Information contained in students' education records must not be disclosed except as allowed by relevant laws and institutional policies. DSP staff members must disclose to appropriate authorities information judged to be of an emergency nature, especially when the safety of the individual or others is involved, or when otherwise required by institutional policy or relevant law.

DSP staff members must be aware of and comply with the provisions contained in the institution's policies pertaining to human subjects research and student rights and responsibilities, as well as those in other relevant institutional policies addressing ethical practices and confidentiality of research data concerning individuals.

DSP staff members must recognize and avoid personal conflicts of interest or appearance thereof in the performance of their work.

DSP staff members must strive to insure the fair, objective, and impartial treatment of all persons with whom they interact.

When handling institutional funds, DSP staff members must ensure that such funds are managed in accordance with established and responsible accounting procedures and the fiscal policies or processes of the institution.

Promotional and descriptive information must be accurate

and free of deception.

DSP staff members must perform their duties within the limits of their training, expertise, and competence. When these limits are exceeded, individuals in need of further assistance must be referred to persons possessing appropriate qualifications.

DSP staff members must use suitable means to confront and otherwise hold accountable other staff members who exhibit unethical behavior.

DSP staff members must be knowledgeable about and practice ethical behavior in the use of technology.

Part 6. LEGAL RESPONSIBILITIES

Dining Services Programs (DSP) staff members must be knowledgeable about and responsive to laws and regulations that relate to their respective responsibilities and that may pose legal obligations, limitations, or ramifications for the institution as a whole. As appropriate, staff members must inform users of programs and services, as well as officials, of legal obligations and limitations including constitutional, statutory, regulatory, and case law; mandatory laws and orders emanating from federal, state/provincial, and local governments; and the institution's policies.

DSP must have written policies on all relevant operations, transactions, or tasks that may have legal implications.

DSP staff members must neither participate in nor condone any form of harassment or activity that demeans persons or creates an intimidating, hostile, or offensive campus environment.

DSP staff members must use reasonable and informed practices to limit the liability exposure of the institution and its officers, employees, and agents. DSP staff members must be informed about institutional policies regarding risk management, personal liability, and related insurance coverage options and must be referred to external sources if coverage is not provided by the institution.

The institution must provide access to legal advice for DSP staff members as needed to carry out assigned responsibilities.

The institution must inform DSP staff and students in a timely and systematic fashion about extraordinary or changing legal obligations and potential liabilities.

Part 7. EQUITY and ACCESS

Dining Services Programs (DSP) must be provided on a fair, equitable, and non-discriminatory basis in accordance with institutional policies and with all applicable state/provincial and federal statutes and regulations. DSP must maintain an educational and work environment free from discrimination in accordance with law and institutional policy.

Discrimination must be avoided on the basis of age; cultural heritage; disability; ethnicity; gender identity and expression; nationality; political affiliation; race; religious affiliation; sex; sexual orientation; economic, marital, social, or veteran status; and any other bases included in local, state/provincial, or federal laws.

Consistent with the mission and goals, DSP must take action to remedy significant imbalances in student participation and staffing patterns.

DSP must ensure physical and program access for persons with disabilities. DSP must be responsive to the needs of all students and other populations served when establishing hours of operation and developing methods of delivering programs and services.

DSP must recognize the needs of distance learning students by providing appropriate and accessible services and assisting them in identifying and gaining access to other appropriate services in their geographic region.

Part 8. DIVERSITY

Within the context of each institution's unique mission, diversity enriches the community and enhances the collegiate experience for all; therefore, Dining Services Programs (DSP) must create and nurture environments that are welcoming to and bring together persons of diverse backgrounds.

DSP structure should reflect an unbiased commitment to diversity and maximize the potential of all staff members, including students.

DSP should acknowledge that it serves a multicultural community and provide products and services that recognize this ethnic and cultural diversity.

DSP must promote environments that are characterized by open and continuous communication that deepens understanding of one's own identity, culture, and heritage, as well as that of others. DSP must recognize, honor, educate, and promote respect about commonalties and differences among people within their historical and cultural contexts.

DSP must address the characteristics and needs of a diverse population when establishing and implementing policies and procedures.

DSP should plan promotions that recognize religious or ethnic events, considering student body diversity, institutional support, and community diversity.

Part 9. ORGANIZATION and MANAGEMENT

To promote student learning and development outcomes, Dining Services Programs (DSP) must be structured purposefully and managed effectively to achieve stated goals. Evidence of appropriate structure must include current and accessible policies and procedures, written performance expectations for all employees, functional workflow graphics or organizational charts, and clearly stated program and service delivery expectations.

DSP must monitor websites used for distributing information to ensure that the sites are current, accurate, appropriately referenced, and accessible.

Evidence of effective management must include use of comprehensive and accurate information for decisions, clear sources and channels of authority, effective communication practices, procedures for decision-making and conflict resolution, responses to changing conditions, systems of accountability and evaluation, and processes for recognition and reward. DSP must align policies and procedures with those of the institution and provide channels within the organization for their regular review.

DSP should have clear lines of authority and responsibility, assignment of span of control, and delineation of individual job responsibilities to achieve the mission of the department while maximizing efficient and effective use of human resources.

DSP must plan and conduct all activities around a fundamental commitment to providing quality service.

Resident dining and retail operations should provide a variety of features, offerings, and themes that deliver a quality food service experience, meet the expectations of customers, and contribute positively to the department and institution.

Nutrition education provided by the department should address the assessed needs of customers and staff and contribute to the overall health of the campus community.

Catering services should provide quality products and customer-centered services.

DSP must have written up-to-date internal policies and procedures covering each aspect of the operation.

Where the management of DSP is divided among different offices within the institution and/or contracted to an outside vendor, institutional leaders, stakeholders, and contractors must establish and maintain productive working relationships.

When DSP is contracted for or outsourced, the institution must identify the individual(s) responsible for administering the contract, supervising the service, and the conditions for the contract's continuance or renewal.

The institution and DSP, whether self-operated, contracted, or a combination of self-operated and contracted, must collaborate in providing a balanced dining services program that meets the nutritional, educational, and social needs of students and the college or university community.

DSP should participate in campus emergency planning efforts to ensure that appropriate contingency plans are in place to feed students.

To fulfill its mission and goals effectively, DSP must maintain well-structured management functions, including planning, personnel, property management, purchasing, contract administration, financial control, and information systems.

DSP should use a planning process that increases the probability that the department will successfully accomplish its mission.

DSP should have a formal, written long-range strategic planning document that provides a vision of the future, reflects the department's long-range decision-making process, and supports its short-term operational planning.

DSP and each of its units should prepare operating or action plans for short-term periods that are consistent with the approved long-term plans.

DSP should develop capital improvement plans, guided by the department's long-term strategic plan, by working in cooperation with the institution to meet the projected needs for dining service facilities and programs that will support the future student enrollment of the institution.

DSP should conduct market research to provide an objective basis for planning how to market and manage the department to maximize customer satisfaction and achieve fiscal goals.

DSP should use a menu-planning process that results in a variety of appealing and wholesome food and beverage choices to meet the dining and nutritional needs of customers within the food cost budget goals.

DSP must use safe and effective procedures for preparing, presenting, and holding foods and maintaining the safety, appearance, and nutritional quality of the products.

DSP should have well-organized food production systems in place.

The organization of work flow within dining services should permit the efficient and safe movement of food and beverage products from receiving through storage, issue, preparation, production, holding, distribution, service, and storage of leftovers.

DSP should organize the purchasing functions to ensure the orderly and timely procurement of food products, supplies, services, and equipment at the defined quantity, cost, and quality levels to support the mission of the department.

DSP must fully comply with all applicable federal, state/ provincial, and local food safety codes; compliance focuses on managing the food safety risk at critical control points in a manner consistent with a Hazard Analysis Critical Control Point (HACCP) or similar food safety system.

Part 10. CAMPUS and EXTERNAL RELATIONS

Dining Services Programs (DSP) must reach out to relevant individuals, campus offices, and external agencies to:
- **establish, maintain, and promote effective relations**
- **disseminate information about their own and other related programs and services**
- **coordinate and collaborate, where appropriate, in offering programs and services to meet the needs of students and promote their achievement of student learning and development outcomes**

DSP must have procedures and guidelines consistent with institutional policy for responding to threats, emergencies, and crisis situations. Systems and procedures must be in place to disseminate timely and accurate information to students and other members of the campus community during emergency situations.

DSP must have procedures and guidelines consistent with institutional policy for communicating with the media.

DSP must comply with these standards even when contracted for or outsourced by the institution.

DSP should make a positive contribution to the educational, social, and economic development of the campus and local community.

The success of DSP is dependent on the maintenance of good relationships with students, faculty, administrators, alumni, the community at large, contractors, and support agencies. Staff members should encourage participation in campus programs by relevant groups.

When appropriate within the policies and procedures of the institution and department, DSP should sponsor campus and community nonprofit activities to promote goodwill and enhance the nonprofit mission of the community organization.

DSP departmental managers should encourage staff members, including students, to volunteer for community nonprofit and campus causes and activities in the name of the department to promote the community image of the department and enhance the quality of life of the volunteers.

Part 11. FINANCIAL RESOURCES

Dining Services Programs (DSP) must have adequate funding to accomplish their mission and goals. In establishing funding priorities and making significant changes, a comprehensive analysis, which includes relevant expenditures, external and internal resources, and impact on the campus community, must be conducted.

DSP must demonstrate fiscal responsibility and cost effectiveness consistent with institutional protocols.

DSP must have in place an effective system of financial accountability controls to ensure responsible fiscal management.

The institution should recognize that when outsourced, the food service provider has a reasonable expectation of making profit.

DSP should prepare annual operating budgets to project income and expenses for the year for each component of the operation and break down the budget to accurately forecast financial performance by accounting periods. DSP should strive to balance revenue and institutional expectations to provide necessary and desirable services.

DSP must use an accounting system that accurately accounts

for all income and expenses, as approved by the institution, the department's controller, and auditors, as applicable.

Part 12. TECHNOLOGY

Dining Services Programs (DSP) must have adequate technology to support their mission. The technology and its use must comply with institutional policies and procedures and be evaluated for compliance with relevant federal, state/provincial, and local requirements.

DSP must maintain policies and procedures that address the security and back up of data.

When technology is used to facilitate student learning and development, DSP must select technology that reflects current best pedagogical practices.

Technology, as well as any workstations or computer labs maintained by the DSP for student use, must be accessible and must meet established technology standards for delivery to persons with disabilities.

When DSP provide student access to technology, they must provide:
- access to policies that are clear, easy to understand, and available to all students
- access to instruction or training on how to use the technology
- access to information on the legal and ethical implications of misuse as it pertains to intellectual property, harassment, privacy, and social networks.

Student violations of technology policies must follow established institutional student disciplinary procedures.

Students who experience negative emotional or psychological consequences from the use of technology must be referred to support services provided by the institution.

DSP should use an objective process for evaluating technology needs and staying current with appropriate new information technologies. Areas for consideration include menu and inventory management, nutritional analysis, catering, event management, point-of-sale systems, concessions management, accounting systems, email, office production systems and services, and other specialty software such as that used for time and attendance.

DSP should make appropriate selections of technology systems, including hardware and software, to meet clearly-defined needs within budgetary limitations.

DSP should use a system for maintaining electronic and other computerized equipment and software.

Part 13. FACILITIES and EQUIPMENT

Dining Services Programs (DSP) must have adequate, accessible, suitably located facilities and equipment to support their mission and goals. If acquiring capital equipment as defined by the institution, DSP must take into account expenses related to regular maintenance and life cycle costs. Facilities and equipment must be evaluated regularly, including consideration of sustainability, and be in compliance with relevant federal, state/provincial, and local requirements to provide for access, health, safety, and security.

DSP staff members must have work space that is well-equipped, adequate in size, and designed to support their work and responsibilities. For conversations requiring privacy, staff members must have access to a private space.

DSP staff members who share work space must have the ability to secure their work adequately.

The design of the facilities must guarantee the security of records and ensure the confidentiality of sensitive information.

The location and layout of the facilities must be sensitive to the special needs of persons with disabilities as well as the needs of constituencies served.

DSP must ensure that staff members are knowledgeable of and trained in safety and emergency procedures for securing and vacating the facilities.

The facilities managed by DSP must be in full compliance with applicable federal, state/provincial, and local building codes, as well as institutional policies.

DSP should share dining facility spaces for campus programs and events, such as study halls and social events.

DSP should take extra precautions to provide a secure environment for customers and staff members.

DSP should have a capital improvement budget that supports the long-term strategic plan.

DSP must comply with all applicable federal, state/provincial, and local statutes, regulations, and codes when undertaking capital improvements, including new construction, renovations, and equipment installation.

DSP should use current sources of information in planning for capital equipment purchases, installation, and implementation to support the mission of the department within applicable federal, state/provincial, and local codes and regulations.

DSP facilities must be accessible, clean, attractive, properly designed, well-maintained, comfortable, conducive to a positive dining experience, and must have appropriate safety and security features.

DSP must maintain a high level of facilities sanitation through effective housekeeping.

DSP should have on-going programs of planned and preventive maintenance to extend the life of facilities and equipment, ensure optimum working condition, and enhance safety and appearance.

Spaces must include adequate areas for seating as well as for service, preparation, storage, and receiving of food, and for disposal of waste.

DSP should design its facilities to support the mission of the department with optimum efficiency, while enhancing customer and staff satisfaction.

DSP must have a program for managing solid and liquid waste that complies with federal, state/provincial, and local regulations and coordinates the program with other solid and liquid waste efforts of the institution or community.

The focus of all capital improvement projects should be on designing for the future, based on the best available information and projections concerning future enrollment, shifts in student housing patterns, changes in the diversity of the student body, trends in college and university dining services, and market research of the off-campus dining service trends in the surrounding community.

Part 14. ASSESSMENT and EVALUATION

Dining Services Programs (DSP) must establish systematic plans and processes to meet internal and external accountability expectations with regard to program as well as student learning and development outcomes. DSP must conduct regular assessment and evaluations. Assessments must include qualitative and quantitative methodologies as appropriate, to determine whether and to what degree the stated mission, goals, and student learning and development outcomes are being met. The process must employ sufficient and sound measures to ensure comprehensiveness. Data collected must include responses from students and other affected constituencies.

DSP should conduct market research such as comparing prices, offerings, menu, hours, and service levels.

DSP should promote a positive relationship with all internal and external customers, especially students, and openly solicit comments from all customers about how to improve the dining services program.

DSP must evaluate regularly how well they complement and enhance the institution's stated mission and educational effectiveness.

DSP must also evaluate customer satisfaction.

Results of these evaluations must be used in revising and improving programs and services, identifying needs and interests in shaping directions of program and service design, and recognizing staff performance.

General Standards revised in 2008;
DSP content developed in 2006

The Role of Disability Support Services
CAS Standards Contextual Statement

Students with disabilities have always been present in the college/university environment. Examples range from students with notoriety (Helen Keller entered Radcliffe College in 1900) to the early support programs at the University of Illinois which began with World War II veterans studying through the GI Bill.

Beginning in 1973 with the passage of Section 504 of the Rehabilitation Act, "no otherwise qualified individual with a disability shall, solely by reason of his/her disability, be excluded from the participation in, be denied the benefits of, or be subjected to discrimination under any program or activity of a public entity." As the result of this legislation, U.S. colleges and universities receiving federal funds were required to provide nondiscriminatory, equal access to programs and facilities for individuals with disabilities. The Americans with Disabilities Act of 1990 (ADA) broadened this legislation to include public entities such as restaurants, hotels, stores, transportation, and communication systems. In these areas, oversight of the ADA is not dependent on the receipt of federal funds as it is with institutions of higher education.

Universities and colleges looked to each other to help define the growing need for services. Thus the field of "Disability Services" evolved and in response to that need, a uniquely challenged and experienced cadre of professional disability service providers created what is today, the Association on Higher Education and Disability (AHEAD) in 1977.

Colleges and universities worked to design services appropriate to the mission of individual campuses. Disability Services were often housed in student affairs. As a result, many of the earliest service providers were re-assigned from student life, counseling, academic advising, or the Dean of Students' office. Other campuses chose to house the office in affirmative action or in an academic department such as psychology, counseling, special education or education; however, administrative location is immaterial and remains an institution's prerogative. What is important is that Disability Services offices should have their own financial resources and staff in order to meet the institutional commitment to access and compliance with federal laws.

The difference in legislative focus between K-12 (in the U.S., IDEA, which is success-oriented) and higher education (Section 504 — Rehabilitation Act and ADA, which are access-oriented) often results in students with disabilities who are not prepared to enter higher education as strong advocates for themselves. From the mid-1980s through 2000 most campuses experienced a significant growth in the number of students who self-identified as having a learning disability (LD) and Attention Deficit (Hyperactivity) Disorder (ADD/ADHD) and requested reasonable accommodations. Additionally, current issues facing those who work in disability support services include: advanced assistive technology (e.g., screen readers, speech output), study abroad, online/distance education, increasing numbers of students with psychological/psychiatric conditions and autism spectrum disorders, campus safety, technical standards, performance demands of graduate and professional schools, returning injured veterans, and transition to work. These issues are examples of the ever-changing demands of a field that requires greater comprehension of the impact of medical conditions, assessment of abilities, and programmatic standards/requirements on the part of the disability service provider to ensure the institution is able to realistically and reasonably provide access to students with disabilities. The standards and guidelines that follow are designed to assist in the development and assessment of disability services that are equipped to meet these challenges.

References, Readings and Resources

American Council on Education (1994).*Educating students with disabilities on campus: Strategies of successful projects.* Washington, DC: Author.

American Council on Education. (1995). *College freshmen with disabilities: A triennial statistical profile.* Washington, DC: Author.

Association on Higher Education and Disability (AHEAD *P.O. Box 540666, Waltham, MA 02454 USA, tel/tty: 781-788-0003 fax: 781-788-0033,* www.ahead.org

Disability Compliance for Higher Education Newsletter. Dan Gephart, Managing Editor, LRP Publications, Horsheim, PA.

Disability Compliance for Higher Education: Newsletter published monthly by LRP Publishers, http://www.lrp.com/

HEATH Resource Center, National Clearinghouse on Postsecondary Education housed at the George Washington University, http://www.heath.gwu.edu

Helen Keller: Biographical notes: /http://www.rnib.org.uk/xpedio/groups/public/documents/publicwebsite/public_keller.hcsp#P69_9224

Heyward, S. M. (1996). *Frequently asked questions: Postsecondary education and disability.* Cambridge, MA: Heyward, Lawton and Associates.

Journal of Postsecondary Education and Disability. Association on Higher Education and Disability, Boston, Mass. www.ahead.org

Kroeger, S., & Schuck, J. (Eds.) (1993). *Responding to disability issues in student affairs,* no. 64. New Directions For Student Services. San Francisco: Jossey-Bass.

Latham, J. D., & Latham, P. H. (1996). *Documentation and the law for professionals concerned with ADD/LD and those they serve.* Washington, DC: JKL Communications.

Ryan, D, & McCarthy, M. (Eds.) (1994). *A student affairs guide to the ADA and disability issues,* Monograph 17. Washington, DC: National Association of Student Personnel Administrators.

U.S. Department of Education - Office for Civil Rights (OCR): www.ed.gov/offices/OCR

U.S. Department of Education: www.ed.gov/policy/speced/guid/idea/idea2004.html

U.S. Department of Justice — ADA Home Page: www.usdoj.gov/crt/ada/adahom1.htm

Walling, L. L. (Ed.) (1996). *Hidden abilities in higher education: New college students with disabilities.* Monograph series no. 21, National Resource Center for the Freshman Year Experience and Students in Transition. Columbia, SC: University of South Carolina.

Contributor:

Beth Hunsinger, The Community College of Baltimore Maryland, AHEAD

Disability Support Services
CAS Standards and Guidelines

Part 1. MISSION

The primary mission of Disability Support Services (DSS) is to ensure equal access for students with disabilities to all curricular and co-curricular opportunities offered by the institution.

In addition, the mission of DSS must:
- Provide leadership to the campus community to enhance understanding and support of DSS
- Provide guidance to the campus community to ensure compliance with legal requirements for access
  Relevant legal requirements may vary among governmental jurisdictions but would include minimally for U.S. institutions the requirements defined under Section 504 of the Rehabilitation Act of 1973, and the Americans with Disabilities Act of 1990.
- Establish a clear set of policies and procedures that define the responsibilities of both the institution and the person eligible for accommodations

DSS must develop, disseminate, implement, and regularly review their mission. Mission statements must be consistent with the mission of the institution and with professional standards. DSS in higher education must enhance overall educational experiences by incorporating student learning and development outcomes in their mission.

To accomplish its mission, DSS must:
- ensure that qualified individuals with disabilities receive reasonable and appropriate accommodations so as to have equal access to all institutional programs and services regardless of the type and extent of the disability
- possess a clear set of policies and procedures
- inform the campus community about the location of disability services, the availability of equipment and technology helpful to those with disabilities, and identification of key individuals within the institution who can provide services to students with disabilities
- define and describe the procedures for obtaining services and accommodations
- provide guidance and training for institutional staff and faculty members in the understanding of disability issues
- Institutional staff and faculty members should be educated about the stereotypes surrounding people with disabilities as well as appropriate protocols and language.
- advocate for equal access, accommodations, and respect for students with disabilities within the campus community

Part 2. PROGRAM

The formal education of students, consisting of the curriculum and the co-curriculum, must promote student learning and development outcomes that are purposeful and holistic and that prepare students for satisfying and productive lifestyles, work, and civic participation. The student learning and development outcome domains and their related dimensions are:

- knowledge acquisition, integration, construction, and application
  o Dimensions: understanding knowledge from a range of disciplines; connecting knowledge to other knowledge, ideas, and experiences; constructing knowledge; and relating knowledge to daily life

- cognitive complexity
  o Dimensions: critical thinking; reflective thinking; effective reasoning; and creativity

- intrapersonal development
  o Dimensions: realistic self-appraisal, self-understanding, and self-respect; identity development; commitment to ethics and integrity; and spiritual awareness

- interpersonal competence
  o Dimensions: meaningful relationships; interdependence; collaboration; and effective leadership

- humanitarianism and civic engagement
  o Dimensions: understanding and appreciation of cultural and human differences; social responsibility; global perspective; and sense of civic responsibility

- practical competence
  o Dimensions: pursuing goals; communicating effectively; technical competence; managing personal affairs; managing career development; demonstrating professionalism; maintaining health and wellness; and living a purposeful and satisfying life

[See *The Council for the Advancement of Standards Learning and Developmental Outcomes* statement for examples of outcomes related to these domains and dimensions.]

Consistent with the institutional mission, Disability Support Services (DSS) must identify relevant and desirable student learning and development outcomes from among the six domains and related dimensions. When creating opportunities for student learning and development, DSS must explore possibilities for collaboration with faculty members and other colleagues.

DSS must assess relevant and desirable student learning and development outcomes and provide evidence of their impact on student learning and development. DSS must articulate how they contribute to or support students' learning and development in the domains not specifically assessed.

DSS must be:

- integrated into the life of the institution
- intentional and coherent
- guided by theories and knowledge of learning and development
- reflective of developmental and demographic profiles of the student population
- responsive to needs of individuals, diverse and special populations, and relevant constituencies

If a formal DSS program does not exist, it must be the responsibility of the institution to ensure that the primary mission is accomplished, either through the direct delivery of essential programs and services by the person(s) designated by the institution as the point of contact for students or by assisting other offices in meeting those needs.

Institutions must make effective use of existing administrative structures and resources to avoid unnecessary duplication of services and to ensure that all campus offices and services have as a part of their mission the responsibility to meet the needs of persons with disabilities.

Depending on the institution, students with disabilities should be served within a decentralized system, with a central office providing those services not provided elsewhere on campus.

DSS must identify environmental conditions that negatively influence persons with disabilities and propose interventions that are designed to ameliorate such conditions.

The institution must regularly evaluate the campus for physical access. Maps and signage must reflect accessible routes, handicapped parking, building accessibility, entrances, and restroom facilities. Parking and transportation must comply with applicable accessibility regulations and laws.

The major components of DSS, each of which must be clearly identified to the campus and to the potential and current users of the services, include:

- a procedure for disclosure

  Persons with disabilities should be given the opportunity to self-disclose to a disability services provider who is trained to evaluate the information and who understands and respects the confidentiality of the individual.

  Each person requesting services should be screened during an intake interview, should have documentation from a qualified professional, and should ensure that the service provider receives the documentation. The documentation should be current, state a diagnosis, and give evidence to support the impact of the disability and its effect on the academic or work environment. A referral list of qualified and competent professionals should be maintained for students who need more current or new documentation.

- direct assistance to persons with disabilities.

Services to qualified individuals should ensure equal access and also meet the requirements as required by current law and institutional policy. The actual services provided will vary among institutions based on the specific disability and on the location of services provided by other campus offices or the community. Staff members provide for accommodations that assist persons with disabilities in the accomplishment of educational, personal, social, and work goals.

Examples of accommodation can include testing accommodations, readers, scribes, interpreters, note takers, brailed materials, screen magnification systems, text-to-speech, screen reading, voice dictation, and /or optical character recognition systems.

- consultation to the campus community

  DSS should act as a consultant and advocate to the campus community in ensuring physical and programmatic access to all institutional resources. This would include collaboration with faculty members about teaching and testing techniques for academic departments. DSS should work to ensure equal access to electronic communication and distance learning materials as well as access to print.

- advising, counseling, and support for persons with disabilities

  DSS should assist individuals in devising strategies to adjust to and succeed in higher education. When strategies include reasonable accommodations, the program should provide information about how to acquire them.

- professional and community education

  DSS should offer training and educational activities to faculty members, staff, and students and other community members that promotes understanding, awareness, and advocacy.

- dissemination of Information

  Information should include access issues, accommodations, and legal rights of persons with disabilities to the campus community. Information regarding the laws, the procedures for receiving services, documentation guidelines, and other related policies should be made readily available in both print and electronic formats. Additionally, general information about location, available hours, contact information, and procedures should be made widely available especially in institutional print and electronic publications including, but not limited to, course schedules, catalogs, bulletins, recruitment materials, student and faculty handbooks, and residence life publications. On-line information about DSS should be accessible with the use of assistive technology and must provide appropriate links to other useful services such as financial aid, admissions, residence life, security, parking, and campus information.

- collaboration on institutional safety policies and procedures

  The program should collaborate with appropriate campus offices and community agencies on the development and dissemination of safety, evacuation, and other emergency response plans.

Part 3. LEADERSHIP

Because effective and ethical leadership is essential to the success of all organizations, Disability Support Services (DSS) leaders with organizational authority for the programs and services must:

- articulate a vision and mission for their programs and services
- set goals and objectives based on the needs of the population served and desired student learning and development outcomes
- advocate for their programs and services
- promote campus environments that provide meaningful opportunities for student learning, development, and integration
- identify and find means to address individual, organizational, or environmental conditions that foster or inhibit mission achievement
- advocate for representation in strategic planning initiatives at appropriate divisional and institutional levels
- initiate collaborative interactions with stakeholders who have legitimate concerns and interests in the functional area
- apply effective practices to educational and administrative processes
- prescribe and model ethical behavior
- communicate effectively
- manage financial resources, including planning, allocation, monitoring, and analysis
- incorporate sustainability practices in the management and design of programs, services, and facilities
- manage human resource processes including recruitment, selection, development, supervision, performance planning, and evaluation
- empower professional, support, and student staff to accept leadership opportunities
- encourage and support scholarly contribution to the profession
- be informed about and integrate appropriate technologies into programs and services
- be knowledgeable about federal, state/provincial, and local laws relevant to the programs and services and ensure that staff members understand their responsibilities by receiving appropriate training
- develop and continuously improve programs and services in response to the changing needs of students and other populations served and the evolving institutional priorities
- recognize environmental conditions that may negatively influence the safety of staff and students and propose interventions that mitigate such conditions

The leaders of a DSS must keep abreast of current litigation, interpretation of case law, changes in the field of medicine and diseases, changes in documenting disabilities, and trends in the field of secondary special education, and must use this information to advise their institutions and community how to best respond and react to these changes. Also, leaders must be informed of best practices within the field of disability services.

Part 4. HUMAN RESOURCES

Disability Support Services (DSS) must be staffed adequately by individuals qualified to accomplish the mission and goals. Within institutional guidelines, DSS must establish procedures for staff selection, training, and evaluation; set expectations for supervision; and provide appropriate professional development opportunities to improve the leadership ability, competence, and skills of all employees.

DSS professional staff members must hold an earned graduate or professional degree in a field relevant to the position they hold or must possess an appropriate combination of educational credentials and related work experience.

Designated staff members may serve as practicum instructors or intern supervisors.

Degree- or credential-seeking interns must be qualified by enrollment in an appropriate field of study and by relevant experience. These individuals must be trained and supervised adequately by professional staff members holding educational credentials and related work experience appropriate for supervision.

Student employees and volunteers must be carefully selected, trained, supervised, and evaluated. They must be educated on how and when to refer those in need of additional assistance to qualified staff members and must have access to a supervisor for assistance in making these judgments. Student employees and volunteers must be provided clear and precise job descriptions, pre-service training based on assessed needs, and continuing staff development.

Employees and volunteers must receive specific training on institutional policies and privacy laws regarding their access to student records and other sensitive institutional information (e.g., in the USA, Family Educational Rights and Privacy Act, FERPA, or equivalent privacy laws in other states/provinces or countries).

DSS must have technical and support staff members adequate to accomplish their mission. All members of the staff must be technologically proficient and qualified to perform their job functions, be knowledgeable about ethical and legal uses of technology, and have access to training and resources to support the performance of their assigned responsibilities.

Administrative and support staff must be provided with disability awareness training and possess knowledge and understanding of the needs of persons with disabilities.

All members of the staff must receive training on policies and procedures related to the use of technology to store or access student records and institutional data.

DSS must ensure that staff members are knowledgeable about and trained in emergency procedures, crisis response, and prevention efforts. Prevention efforts must address identification of threatening conduct or behavior of students, faculty members, staff, and others and must incorporate a system or procedures for responding, including but not limited to reporting them to the appropriate campus officials.

Salary levels and benefits for all staff members must be commensurate with those for comparable positions within the institution, in similar institutions, and in the relevant geographic area.

DSS must maintain position descriptions for all staff members.

To create a diverse staff, DSS must institute hiring and promotion practices that are fair, inclusive, proactive, and non-discriminatory.

Staff assignments should take into account the benefits of employing persons with disabilities.

Sign language and oral interpreters must have appropriate qualifications, including appropriate coursework and certification.

DSS must conduct regular performance planning and evaluation of staff members. DSS must provide access to continuing and advanced education and professional development opportunities.

Part 5. ETHICS

Persons involved in the delivery of Disability Support Services (DSS) must adhere to the highest principles of ethical behavior. DSS must review relevant professional ethical standards and develop or adopt and implement appropriate statements of ethical practice. DSS must publish these statements and ensure their periodic review by relevant constituencies.

Ethical standards or other statements from relevant professional associations should also be considered.

DSS must orient new staff members to relevant ethical standards and statements of ethical practice.

DSS staff members must ensure that privacy and confidentiality are maintained with respect to all communications and records to the extent that such records are protected under the law and appropriate statements of ethical practice. Information contained in students' education records must not be disclosed except as allowed by relevant laws and institutional policies. DSS staff members must disclose to appropriate authorities information judged to be of an emergency nature, especially when the safety of the individual or others is involved, or when otherwise required by institutional policy or relevant law.

Staff members must be aware of and comply with the provisions contained in the institution's policies pertaining

to human subjects research and student rights and responsibilities, as well as those in other relevant institutional policies addressing ethical practices and confidentiality of research data concerning individuals.

DSS staff members must recognize and avoid personal conflicts of interest or appearance thereof in the performance of their work.

DSS staff members must strive to insure the fair, objective, and impartial treatment of all persons with whom they interact.

When handling institutional funds, DSS staff members must ensure that such funds are managed in accordance with established and responsible accounting procedures and the fiscal policies or processes of the institution.

Promotional and descriptive information must be accurate and free of deception.

DSS staff members must perform their duties within the limits of their training, expertise, and competence. When these limits are exceeded, individuals in need of further assistance must be referred to persons possessing appropriate qualifications.

DSS staff members must use suitable means to confront and otherwise hold accountable other staff members who exhibit unethical behavior.

DSS staff members must be knowledgeable about and practice ethical behavior in the use of technology.

Part 6. LEGAL RESPONSIBILITIES

Disability Support Services (DSS) staff members must be knowledgeable about and responsive to laws and regulations that relate to their respective responsibilities and that may pose legal obligations, limitations, or ramifications for the institution as a whole. As appropriate, staff members must inform users of programs and services, as well as officials, of legal obligations and limitations including constitutional, statutory, regulatory, and case law; mandatory laws and orders emanating from federal, state/provincial, and local governments; and the institution's policies.

DSS must have written policies on all relevant operations, transactions, or tasks that may have legal implications.

DSS staff members must neither participate in nor condone any form of harassment or activity that demeans persons or creates an intimidating, hostile, or offensive campus environment.

DSS staff members must use reasonable and informed practices to limit the liability exposure of the institution and its officers, employees, and agents. DSS staff members must be informed about institutional policies regarding risk management, personal liability, and related insurance coverage options and must be referred to external sources if coverage is not provided by the institution.

The institution must provide access to legal advice for DSS staff members as needed to carry out assigned responsibilities.

Staff members must be aware of and seek advice from the institution's legal counsel on privacy and disclosure of student information contained in educational records, defamation law regarding references and recommendations on behalf of students, affirmative action laws, protective health information laws, and regulations regarding programs and liability issues pertaining to sponsored programs.

The institution must inform DSS staff and students in a timely and systematic fashion about extraordinary or changing legal obligations and potential liabilities.

Higher education institutions must adhere to the law in appointing a disability compliance officer.

The DSS staff must, in conjunction with legal counsel, work to develop policies, procedures, and guidelines as required under relevant disability laws.

Interpretation of the laws and their application to the campus should be a coordinated effort with institutional legal counsel.

Part 7. EQUITY and ACCESS

Disability Support Services (DSS) must be provided on a fair, equitable, and non-discriminatory basis in accordance with institutional policies and with all applicable state/provincial and federal statutes and regulations. Programs and services must maintain an educational and work environment free from discrimination in accordance with law and institutional policy.

Discrimination must be avoided on the basis of age; cultural heritage; disability; ethnicity; gender identity and expression; nationality; political affiliation; race; religious affiliation; sex; sexual orientation; economic, marital, social, or veteran status; and any other bases included in local, state/provincial, or federal laws.

Consistent with the mission and goals, DSS must take action to remedy significant imbalances in student participation and staffing patterns.

DSS must ensure physical and program access for persons with disabilities. DSS must be responsive to the needs of all students and other populations served when establishing hours of operation and developing methods of delivering programs and services.

DSS must educate the campus community about ensuring opportunities for individuals with disabilities in all facets of the institution.

DSS must recognize the needs of distance learning students by providing appropriate and accessible services and assisting them in identifying and gaining access to other appropriate services in their geographic region.

Part 8. DIVERSITY

Within the context of each institution's unique mission, diversity enriches the community and enhances the collegiate experience for all; therefore, Disability Support Services (DSS) must create and nurture environments that are welcoming to and bring together persons of diverse backgrounds.

DSS must promote environments that are characterized by open and continuous communication that deepens understanding of one's own identity, culture, and heritage, as well as that of others. DSS must recognize, honor, educate, and promote respect about commonalties and differences among people within their historical and cultural contexts.

DSS must address the characteristics and needs of a diverse population when establishing and implementing policies and procedures.

Part 9. ORGANIZATION and MANAGEMENT

To promote student learning and development outcomes, Disability Support Services (DSS) must be structured purposefully and managed effectively to achieve stated goals. Evidence of appropriate structure must include current and accessible policies and procedures, written performance expectations for all employees, functional workflow graphics or organizational charts, and clearly stated program and service delivery expectations.

DSS must monitor websites used for distributing information to ensure that the sites are current, accurate, appropriately referenced, and accessible.

Evidence of effective management must include use of comprehensive and accurate information for decisions, clear sources and channels of authority, effective communication practices, procedures for decision-making and conflict resolution, responses to changing conditions, systems of accountability and evaluation, and processes for recognition and reward. DSS must align policies and procedures with those of the institution and provide channels within the organization for their regular review.

DSS must be situated within the administrative structure to develop and direct program activities effectively. Adequate staff, funding, and resources must be provided.

Such services normally function within divisions of student affairs or academic affairs. The services should involve advisory bodies which include students, faculty and staff members with disabilities.

Part 10. CAMPUS and EXTERNAL RELATIONS

Disability Support Services (DSS) must reach out to relevant individuals, campus offices, and external agencies to:
- establish, maintain, and promote effective relations
- disseminate information about their own and other related programs and services
- coordinate and collaborate, where appropriate, in

offering programs and services to meet the needs of students and promote their achievement of student learning and development outcomes

Such agencies would include vocational rehabilitation, the medical community, veterans administration, school districts, and social services agencies.

DSS must also work to maintain positive relations with students, faculty members, staff, the institutional legal counsel, the administration, all support offices, community agencies, the medical community, diagnosticians, and equal opportunity compliance officers.

DSS should take an active role in the coordination of the institution's response to the needs of persons with disabilities. This is essential to ensure the continuity of services, resource management, consistent institutional policies, and the integration of persons with disabilities into the total campus experience.

DSS should maintain a high degree of visibility with the academic units through the promotion and delivery of services, through involvement in determining what constitutes reasonable accommodations, and through promoting increased understanding of, and responsiveness to, the needs of persons with disabilities.

DSS should be informed about, and actively involved in, influencing and affecting the policies, practices, and planning of other units, which directly affect persons with disabilities.

DSS staff members must be available to participate in appropriate campus-wide committees.

Disability support service staff members may act as liaisons between student services, academic services, and community services on the behalf of persons with disabilities.

DSS must have procedures and guidelines consistent with institutional policy for responding to threats, emergencies, and crisis situations. Systems and procedures must be in place to disseminate timely and accurate information to students and other members of the campus community during emergency situations.

DSS must have procedures and guidelines consistent with institutional policy for communicating with the media.

Part 11. FINANCIAL RESOURCES

Disability Support Services (DSS) must have adequate funding to accomplish their mission and goals. In establishing funding priorities and making significant changes, a comprehensive analysis, which includes relevant expenditures, external and internal resources, and impact on the campus community, must be conducted.

DSS must demonstrate fiscal responsibility and cost effectiveness consistent with institutional protocols.

DSS should be funded as a separate institutional budget item. The institution must provide appropriate funding to carry out its stated mission and goals.

The allocation of financial resources must be adequate to meet the obligations of the institution under relevant national, state/provincial, and local laws.

In addition to normal budget categories, the DSS program may have unusual budgetary requirements that can vary from term to term. These may include readers, interpreters, and special equipment such as a TTY/TDD (telephone communication devices for the deaf), screen readers, voice synthesizers, reading machines, device for enlarging print, Braille capabilities, additional technology to provide accommodated exams, and variable speed tape recorders. The institution is not obligated to provide personal equipment such as wheelchairs, hearing aids, or prosthetics. The number and nature of the devices can be determined based on the population of persons with disabilities requesting services.

The decision of whether to purchase mandated devices should not be weighed against competing departmental needs, such as additional computers or staff. Funding for disability accommodations should come from a centralized institutional source rather than from any one individual department.

Part 12. TECHNOLOGY

Disability Support Services (DSS) must have adequate technology to support their mission. The technology and its use must comply with institutional policies and procedures and be evaluated for compliance with relevant federal, state/provincial, and local requirements.

DSS must maintain policies and procedures that address the security and back up of data.

When technology is used to facilitate student learning and development, DSS must select technology that reflects current best pedagogical practices.

Technology, as well as any workstations or computer labs maintained by the DSS for student use, must be accessible and must meet established technology standards for delivery to persons with disabilities.

When DSS provide student access to technology, they must provide:
- access to policies that are clear, easy to understand, and available to all students
- access to instruction or training on how to use the technology
- access to information on the legal and ethical implications of misuse as it pertains to intellectual property, harassment, privacy, and social networks

Student violations of technology policies must follow established institutional student disciplinary procedures.

Students who experience negative emotional or psychological consequences from the use of technology must be referred to support services provided by the institution.

Part 13. FACILITIES and EQUIPMENT

Disability Support Services (DSS) must have adequate, accessible, suitably located facilities and equipment to support their mission and goals. If acquiring capital equipment as defined by the institution, DSS must take into account expenses related to regular maintenance and life cycle costs. Facilities and equipment must be evaluated regularly, including consideration of sustainability, and be in compliance with relevant federal, state/provincial, and local requirements to provide for access, health, safety, and security.

DSS staff members must have work space that is well-equipped, adequate in size, and designed to support their work and responsibilities. For conversations requiring privacy, staff members must have access to a private space.

DSS staff members who share work space must have the ability to secure their work adequately.

The design of the facilities must guarantee the security of records and ensure the confidentiality of sensitive information.

The location and layout of the facilities must be sensitive to the special needs of persons with disabilities as well as the needs of constituencies served.

Facilities available to DSS units should include:

- offices and programmatic spaces within an accessible facility
- private offices for conducting intake interviews, counseling, or other meetings of a confidential nature
- private and quiet space for tape recording materials, and scribing or taking exams
- a receptionist area with accessible counter heights and TTY/TDD
- storage area to ensure the confidentiality of records
- conference room and training space adequate to accommodate persons in wheelchairs
- nearby availability of accessible rest rooms, water fountains, elevators, and corridors
- adequate handicapped parking convenient to the facility
- coat racks and bulletin boards
- warning devices such as strobe/buzzer fire alarms for emergencies.

DSS must ensure that staff members are knowledgeable of and trained in safety and emergency procedures for securing and vacating the facilities.

Part 14. ASSESSMENT and EVALUATION

Disability Support Services (DSS) must establish systematic plans and processes to meet internal and external accountability expectations with regard to program as well as student learning and development outcomes. DSS must conduct regular assessment and evaluations. Assessments must include qualitative and quantitative methodologies as appropriate, to determine whether and to what degree the stated mission, goals, and student learning and development outcomes are being met. The process must employ sufficient and sound measures to ensure comprehensiveness. Data collected must include responses from students and other affected constituencies.

DSS must evaluate regularly how well they complement and enhance the institution's stated mission and educational effectiveness.

Results of these evaluations must be used in revising and improving programs and services, identifying needs and interests in shaping directions of program and service design, and recognizing staff performance.

Comprehensive, systematic, and periodic assessments should be conducted to address the academic, social, and physical needs of students as well as the psychological and physical environments of the campus. In turn, findings should be used to influence how present services should change for future development.

To determine the effectiveness of the organization and administration of the services, a data collection system should be developed and implemented. Program evaluations should be obtained from designated staff members, students, faculty members, and community.

Analyses of population characteristics and trends in the use of services should be performed regularly. Although not the sole measure of program's success, data may be compiled annually on attrition and graduation rates of students using the services.

General Standards revised in 2008;
DSS content developed/revised in 1986, 1997, & 2003

The Role of Distance Education Programs
CAS Standards Contextual Statement

Distance learning has increasingly become a major educational issue in recent years. Although it has been defined in various ways by a number of educational authorities, the simplest definition is that "distance learning takes place when the instructor and student are not in the same room but instead are separated by physical distance" (Connick, 1999, p. 3). Distance learning often occurs when the student and instructor are separated by time as well.

Distance education refers to the various methods of instruction that have been intentionally designed to be applied in distance learning settings. Interestingly, distance education has its roots in the correspondence study movement, which began in Europe during the mid-1880s. By 1873, correspondence courses were being offered in the United States, and the University of Chicago had established a strong academic credit correspondence division by 1892 (Watkins, 1991).

Although higher education correspondence courses, sometimes referred to as "independent study programs," remain a viable alternative for many students today, developments in electronic communications have provided new technology-supported options for distance learners. In addition to correspondence study, the most common distance learning technologies include:

- Computer or on-line courses taught via the Internet or CD-ROM
- Interactive video systems in which two or more locations are connected, allowing student and instructor to see and hear one another from a distance
- Tele-courses wherein instructional television courses are videotaped and broadcast over public or cable television stations

Many of these new teaching methods have gained recognition and acceptance throughout higher education, including at some of the most traditional academic institutions. Concurrently, regional accrediting bodies are awarding accreditation to both degree programs and institutions that offer instruction completely on-line. In the "Statement of Commitment by the Regional Accrediting Commissions for the Evaluation of Electronically Offered Degree and Certificate Programs" (Regional Accrediting, 2001b), the accrediting commissions collectively affirmed that although a growing number of colleges and universities are going on-line with academic programs, the "new delivery systems test conventional assumptions, raising fresh questions as to the essential nature and content of an educational experience and the resources required to support it" (p. 1). Not only are there questions about teaching and learning, but distance education also poses challenges to student affairs programs and related student support services to meet the needs of distance learners even though these students may never set foot on campus.

During the past century, student affairs practitioners have sought to learn how best to provide both resident and commuter students with effective programs and services designed to enhance student learning and personal development. As colleges and universities develop programs that implement distance education technologies, the entire campus community must find ways to serve the special needs of distance learners. In response to the growth of technologically mediated instruction, the Student Support section of the regional accrediting commission's *Best Practices* (2001a) asserts that "the institution recognizes that appropriate services must be available for students of electronically offered programs, using the working assumption that these students will not be physically present on campus" (p 12).

The *Best Practices* were initially developed by the Western Cooperative for Educational Telecommunications www.wiche.edu/telecom/ , an organization widely recognized for its expertise in the field of distance learning. Staff members of this cooperative were consulted in the development of the CAS Standards for Educational Services for Distance Learners that follow.

References, Readings, and Resources

Connick, G. P. (Ed.) (1999). *The distance learner's guide.* Upper Saddle River, NJ.: Prentice Hall.

Regional Accrediting Commissions (2001a). *Best Practices for electronically offered degree and certificate programs.* http://www.wiche.edu/telecom/Article1.htm

Regional Accrediting Commissions (2001b). *Statement of commitment by the regional accrediting commissions for the evaluation of electronically offered degree and certificate programs* http://www.wiche.edu/telecom/Article1.htm

Schwitzer, A.M., Ancis, J.R., & Brown, N. (2001). *Promoting student learning and student development at a distance.* lanham, MD: American College Personnel Association.

Watkins, B.L, & Wright, S.J. (eds.) (1991). *The Foundations of American Distance Education.* Dubuque, Iowa: Kendall/Hunt.

Western Cooperative for Educational Telecommunications (1999). *Guide to developing online student services.* http://www.wcet.info/resources/publications/guide/guide.htm

American Association for Collegiate Independent Study, http://www.aacis.org/

Western Cooperative for Educational Telecommunications, P.O. Box 9752, Boulder, CO 80301; 1540 30th Street, Boulder, CO 80303; (303)541-0231; (303)541-0291 (fax) http://www.wiche.edu/telecom/

Contributor:

Nancy Thompson, University of Georgia

Distance Education Programs
CAS Standards and Guidelines

Part 1. MISSION and PROGRAM

Distance education, for purposes of these standards, refers to any formal educational process provided by or contracted for an institution of higher education in which the student and faculty member are separated by time and/or space.

Distance education may be delivered by a variety of methods including the Internet, radio and telecommunication, CD-ROM, television, video, and/or print. An institution may be a traditional higher education institution, a consortium of such institutions, or other education entity.

Distance Education Programs (DEP) must develop, disseminate, implement, and regularly review their mission. Mission statements must be consistent with the mission of the institution and with professional standards. DEP in higher education must enhance overall educational experiences by incorporating student learning and development outcomes in their mission.

Institutions providing DEP must offer commensurate educational services as outlined throughout this document to assist distance learners to achieve their goals. Such services must be comparable to educational services provided to conventional learners and they must meet standards comparable to those of other institutional offerings. Institutions must recognize, however, that the students who select distance education might have different needs than those enrolled in campus-based instruction.

Institutions must identify the characteristics of their distance students and adapt services to meet the needs of the particular populations they serve.

Part 2. CONGRUENCY of MISSION and PROGRAMS

The mission of Distance Education Programs (DEP) must be clearly and explicitly stated. Institutional missions must be approved by appropriate governing bodies such as boards of trustees and state/provincial coordinating or governing agencies, and regularly reviewed by the institution and its regional and specialized accrediting agencies. The purposes or mission of distance education must be congruent with its host institution's purposes and must gain explicit approval of the relevant governance bodies of the institution. Primary oversight of the compatibility of distance education purposes and those of the institution rests with the institution and its governance system.

Evidence of effective management must include use of comprehensive and accurate information for decisions, clear sources and channels of authority, effective communication practices, procedures for decision-making and conflict resolution, responses to changing conditions, systems of accountability and evaluation, and processes for recognition and reward. DEP must align policies and procedures with those of the institution and provide channels within the organization for their regular review.

To promote student learning and development outcomes, DEP must be structured purposefully and managed effectively to achieve stated goals. Evidence of appropriate structure must include current and accessible policies and procedures, written performance expectations for all employees, functional workflow graphics or organizational charts, and clearly stated program and service delivery expectations.

DEP must monitor websites used for distributing information to ensure that the sites are current, accurate, appropriately referenced, and accessible.

Authority over the distance education curriculum must be clearly articulated. Goals of DEP must be stated in terms of outcomes to be achieved by students in the program.

The formal education of students, consisting of the curriculum and the co-curriculum, must promote student learning and development outcomes that are purposeful and holistic and that prepare students for satisfying and productive lifestyles, work, and civic participation. The student learning and development outcome domains and their related dimensions are:

- knowledge acquisition, integration, construction, and application
  o Dimensions: understanding knowledge from a range of disciplines; connecting knowledge to other knowledge, ideas, and experiences; constructing knowledge; and relating knowledge to daily life

- cognitive complexity
  o Dimensions: critical thinking; reflective thinking; effective reasoning; and creativity

- intrapersonal development
  o Dimensions: realistic self-appraisal, self-understanding, and self-respect; identity development; commitment to ethics and integrity; and spiritual awareness

- interpersonal competence
  o Dimensions: meaningful relationships; interdependence; collaboration; and effective leadership

- humanitarianism and civic engagement
  o Dimensions: understanding and appreciation of cultural and human differences; social responsibility; global perspective; and sense of civic responsibility

- practical competence
  o Dimensions: pursuing goals; communicating effectively; technical competence; managing personal

affairs; managing career development; demonstrating professionalism; maintaining health and wellness; and living a purposeful and satisfying life

[See *The Council for the Advancement of Standards Learning and Developmental Outcomes* statement for examples of outcomes related to these domains and dimensions.]

Consistent with the institutional mission, DEP must identify relevant and desirable student learning and development outcomes from among the six domains and related dimensions. When creating opportunities for student learning and development, DEP must explore possibilities for collaboration with faculty members and other colleagues.

DEP must assess relevant and desirable student learning and development outcomes and provide evidence of their impact on student learning and development. DEP must articulate how they contribute to or support students' learning and development in the domains not specifically assessed.

DEP must be:
- integrated into the life of the institution
- intentional and coherent
- guided by theories and knowledge of learning and development
- reflective of developmental and demographic profiles of the student population
- responsive to needs of individuals, diverse and special populations, and relevant constituencies

Part 3. LEADERSHIP

Because effective and ethical leadership is essential to the success of all organizations, Distance Education Programs (DEP) leaders with organizational authority for the programs and services must:
- articulate a vision and mission for their programs and services
- set goals and objectives based on the needs of the population served and desired student learning and development outcomes
- advocate for their programs and services
- promote campus environments that provide meaningful opportunities for student learning, development, and integration
- identify and find means to address individual, organizational, or environmental conditions that foster or inhibit mission achievement
- advocate for representation in strategic planning initiatives at appropriate divisional and institutional levels
- initiate collaborative interactions with stakeholders who have legitimate concerns and interests in the functional area
- apply effective practices to educational and administrative processes
- prescribe and model ethical behavior
- communicate effectively

- manage financial resources, including planning, allocation, monitoring, and analysis
- incorporate sustainability practices in the management and design of programs, services, and facilities
- manage human resource processes including recruitment, selection, development, supervision, performance planning, and evaluation
- empower professional, support, and student staff to accept leadership opportunities
- encourage and support scholarly contribution to the profession
- be informed about and integrate appropriate technologies into programs and services
- be knowledgeable about federal, state/provincial, and local laws relevant to the programs and services and ensure that staff members understand their responsibilities by receiving appropriate training
- develop and continuously improve programs and services in response to the changing needs of students and other populations served and the evolving institutional priorities
- recognize environmental conditions that may negatively influence the safety of staff and students and propose interventions that mitigate such conditions

Part 4. FACULTY QUALITY and SUPPORT

The key ingredient of the quality of academic programs is the caliber of faculty members. The institution must provide adequate faculty support for distance education courses and programs.

Leaders must ensure that faculty members are competent in their disciplines and/or fields of study and capable of teaching students in using a variety of pedagogical methods consistent with qualifications required of non-distance education faculty.

Faculty members must possess demonstrable skill in the appropriate uses of the methods used to deliver instruction.

These methods may include the Internet, CD-ROM, television, video, and/or print.

To ensure the quality of instruction, the institution must provide adequate support to faculty in the design and teaching of distance education courses and programs including training in the effective uses of the delivery methods to be used in providing instruction. This support must include access to individuals with special knowledge of the pedagogy of various forms of distance education and to technical personnel.

Faculty members must be educated about the special issues associated with teaching at a distance, including physical, emotional, social, and psychological issues.

In electronically delivered teaching, for example, teachers may need training in how to identify problems of distance students that interfere with learning and how to help students when there is little or no opportunity for face-to-face interaction. The distance education environment poses special challenges with respect to the manner in which educational materials are distributed and shared. Distance education faculty members should receive special training on copyright laws and the use of copyrighted materials. Devising ways to ensure academic integrity is another area of difficulty in the distance education environment. Institutions should regularly share best practices in this area with all faculty members teaching distance education courses.

Institutional policies concerning teaching load, class size, time needed for course preparation, and sharing of instructional responsibilities must be adapted to appropriately support distributed education models. Because the number of hours required for the preparation and delivery of electronic courses may exceed similar requirements for face-to-face delivery, institutional policies must accommodate these requirements.

Faculty members are the primary contact between the institution and the distance student; therefore, they must be able to provide appropriate support and guidance. To accomplish this, the institution must provide faculty access to computer service technicians, advisors, counselors, disability services, student affairs professionals, site administrators, distribution clerks, and library resource personnel.

Part 5. RESOURCES FOR LEARNING

Distance Education Programs (DEP) must have adequate funding to accomplish their mission and goals. In establishing funding priorities and making significant changes, a comprehensive analysis, which includes relevant expenditures, external and internal resources, and impact on the campus community, must be conducted.

DEP must demonstrate fiscal responsibility and cost effectiveness consistent with institutional protocols.

DEP must have adequate technology to support their mission. The technology and its use must comply with institutional policies and procedures and be evaluated for compliance with relevant federal, state/provincial, and local requirements.

DEP must maintain policies and procedures that address the security and back up of data.

When technology is used to facilitate student learning and development, DEP must select technology that reflects current best pedagogical practices.

Technology, as well as any workstations or computer labs maintained by the DEP for student use, must be accessible and must meet established technology standards for delivery to persons with disabilities.

When DEP provide student access to technology, they must provide:

- access to policies that are clear, easy to understand, and available to all students
- access to instruction or training on how to use the technology
- access to information on the legal and ethical implications of misuse as it pertains to intellectual property, harassment, privacy, and social networks.

Student violations of technology policies must follow established institutional student disciplinary procedures.

Students who experience negative emotional or psychological consequences from the use of technology must be referred to support services provided by the institution.

DEP must have adequate, accessible, suitably located facilities and equipment to support their mission and goals. If acquiring capital equipment as defined by the institution, DEP must take into account expenses related to regular maintenance and life cycle costs. Facilities and equipment must be evaluated regularly, including consideration of sustainability, and be in compliance with relevant federal, state/provincial, and local requirements to provide for access, health, safety, and security.

DEP staff members must have work space that is well-equipped, adequate in size, and designed to support their work and responsibilities. For conversations requiring privacy, staff members must have access to a private space.

DEP staff members who share work space must have the ability to secure their work adequately.

The design of the facilities must guarantee the security of records and ensure the confidentiality of sensitive information.

The location and layout of the facilities must be sensitive to the special needs of persons with disabilities as well as the needs of constituencies served.

DEP must ensure that staff members are knowledgeable of and trained in safety and emergency procedures for securing and vacating the facilities.

Facilities, equipment, and other resources associated with the viability and effectiveness of distance education programs should be reflected in the institution's long range planning, budgeting, and policy development processes.

DEP must have technical and support staff members adequate to accomplish their mission. All members of the staff must be technologically proficient and qualified to perform their job functions, be knowledgeable about ethical and legal uses of technology, and have access to training and resources to support the performance of their assigned responsibilities.

All members of the staff must receive training on policies and procedures related to the use of technology to store or access student records and institutional data.

DEP must be staffed adequately by individuals qualified to accomplish the mission and goals. Within institutional guidelines, DEP must establish procedures for staff selection, training, and evaluation; set expectations for supervision; and provide appropriate professional development opportunities to improve the leadership ability, competence, and skills of all employees.

DEP staff positions must be filled based on a defined set of qualifications such as level of education, work experience, and personal characteristics (for example, integrity, communication skills, and leadership ability).

DEP professional staff members must hold an earned graduate or professional degree in a field relevant to the position they hold or must possess an appropriate combination of educational credentials and related work experience.

Degree- or credential-seeking interns must be qualified by enrollment in an appropriate field of study and by relevant experience. These individuals must be trained and supervised adequately by professional staff members holding educational credentials and related work experience appropriate for supervision.

Student employees and volunteers must be carefully selected, trained, supervised, and evaluated. They must be educated on how and when to refer those in need of additional assistance to qualified staff members and must have access to a supervisor for assistance in making these judgments. Student employees and volunteers must be provided clear and precise job descriptions, pre-service training based on assessed needs, and continuing staff development.

Employees and volunteers must receive specific training on institutional policies and privacy laws regarding their access to student records and other sensitive institutional information (e.g., in the USA, Family Educational Rights and Privacy Act, FERPA, or equivalent privacy laws in other states/provinces or countries).

DEP must ensure that staff members are knowledgeable about and trained in emergency procedures, crisis response, and prevention efforts. Prevention efforts must address identification of threatening conduct or behavior of students, faculty members, staff, and others and must incorporate a system or procedures for responding, including but not limited to reporting them to the appropriate campus officials.

Salary levels and benefits for all staff members must be commensurate with those for comparable positions within the institution, in similar institutions, and in the relevant geographic area.

DEP must maintain position descriptions for all staff members.

To create a diverse staff, DEP must institute hiring and promotion practices that are fair, inclusive, proactive, and non-discriminatory.

DEP must conduct regular performance planning and evaluation of staff members. DEP must provide access to continuing and advanced education and professional development opportunities.

It is especially crucial that administrators, managers, and coordinators possess technical proficiency and a thorough understanding of how distance education programs are linked to institutional mission. These personnel also should be talented in communication skills to prepare them for effective involvement with other administrators, faculty members, students, and staff of distance education programs. They also should be able to facilitate collaborative relationships among faculty and staff to achieve program goals and to enable program evaluation.

Adequate library resources must be available and accessible to distance students. Institutions must own the library/learning resources or have formal agreements with other institutions' library/learning resources to ensure adequate access to all distance education students.

Part 6. ETHICAL TEACHING and LEARNING

Persons involved in the delivery of Distance Education Programs (DEP) must adhere to the highest principles of ethical behavior. DEP must review relevant professional ethical standards and develop or adopt and implement appropriate statements of ethical practice. DEP must publish these statements and ensure their periodic review by relevant constituencies.

DEP must orient new staff members to relevant ethical standards and statements of ethical practice.

Students must be informed of the applicable ethical standards at the time of their initial enrollment.

Training on ethical principles and guidelines for professionals who deliver the instructional services must be provided. Training on principles and guidelines must be promulgated and enforced by the institution.

Professional association statements of ethical principles and guidelines also are suitable.

DEP staff members must ensure that privacy and confidentiality are maintained with respect to all communications and records to the extent that such records are protected under the law and appropriate statements of ethical practice. Information contained in students' education records must not be disclosed except as allowed by relevant laws and institutional policies. DEP staff members must disclose to appropriate authorities information judged to be of an emergency nature, especially when the safety of the individual or others is involved, or when otherwise required by institutional policy or relevant law.

DEP staff members must be aware of and comply with the provisions contained in the institution's policies pertaining to human subjects research and student rights and responsibilities, as well as those in other relevant institutional policies addressing ethical practices and confidentiality of research data concerning individuals.

DEP staff members must recognize and avoid personal conflicts of interest or appearance thereof in the performance of their work.

DEP staff members must strive to ensure the fair, objective, and impartial treatment of all persons with whom they interact.

When handling institutional funds, DEP staff members must ensure that such funds are managed in accordance with established and responsible accounting procedures and the fiscal policies or processes of the institution.

Promotional and descriptive information must be accurate and free of deception.

DEP staff members must perform their duties within the limits of their training, expertise, and competence. When these limits are exceeded, individuals in need of further assistance must be referred to persons possessing appropriate qualifications.

DEP staff members must use suitable means to confront and otherwise hold accountable other staff members who exhibit unethical behavior.

DEP staff members must be knowledgeable about and practice ethical behavior in the use of technology.

Part 7. LEGAL RESPONSIBILITIES

Distance Education Programs (DEP) staff members must be knowledgeable about and responsive to laws and regulations that relate to their respective responsibilities and that may pose legal obligations, limitations, or ramifications for the institution as a whole. As appropriate, staff members must inform users of programs and services, as well as officials, of legal obligations and limitations including constitutional, statutory, regulatory, and case law; mandatory laws and orders emanating from federal, state/provincial, and local governments; and the institution's policies.

DEP must have written policies on all relevant operations, transactions, or tasks that may have legal implications.

DEP staff members must neither participate in nor condone any form of harassment or activity that demeans persons or creates an intimidating, hostile, or offensive campus environment.

DEP staff members must use reasonable and informed practices to limit the liability exposure of the institution and its officers, employees, and agents. DEP staff members must be informed about institutional policies regarding risk management, personal liability, and related insurance coverage options and must be referred to external sources if coverage is not provided by the institution.

The institution must provide access to legal advice for DEP staff members as needed to carry out assigned responsibilities.

The institution must inform DEP staff and students in a timely and systematic fashion about extraordinary or changing legal obligations and potential liabilities.

Part 8. EQUITY and ACCESS

Distance Education Programs (DEP) must be provided on a fair, equitable, and non-discriminatory basis in accordance with institutional policies and with all applicable state/provincial and federal statutes and regulations. DEP must maintain an educational and work environment free from discrimination in accordance with law and institutional policy.

Discrimination must be avoided on the basis of age; cultural heritage; disability; ethnicity; gender identity and expression; nationality; political affiliation; race; religious affiliation; sex; sexual orientation; economic, marital, social, or veteran status; and any other bases included in local, state/provincial, or federal laws.

Consistent with the mission and goals, DEP must take action to remedy significant imbalances in student participation and staffing patterns.

DEP must ensure physical and program access for persons with disabilities. DEP must be responsive to the needs of all students and other populations served when establishing hours of operation and developing methods of delivering programs and services.

DEP must recognize the needs of distance learning students by providing appropriate and accessible services and assisting them in identifying and gaining access to other appropriate services in their geographic region.

Part 9. DIVERSITY

Within the context of each institution's unique mission, diversity enriches the community and enhances the collegiate experience for all; therefore, Distance Education Programs (DEP) must create and nurture environments that are welcoming to and bring together persons of diverse backgrounds.

DEP must promote environments that are characterized by open and continuous communication that deepens understanding of one's own identity, culture, and heritage, as well as that of others. DEP must recognize, honor, educate, and promote respect about commonalties and differences among people within their historical and cultural contexts.

DEP must address the characteristics and needs of a diverse population when establishing and implementing policies and procedures.

Part 10. CAMPUS and EXTERNAL RELATIONS

Distance Education Programs (DEP) must reach out to relevant individuals, campus offices, and external agencies

to:
- establish, maintain, and promote effective relations
- disseminate information about their own and other related programs and services
- coordinate and collaborate, where appropriate, in offering programs and services to meet the needs of students and promote their achievement of student learning and development outcomes

Leaders should pursue partnering opportunities with agencies, remote facility managers, and campus stakeholders to offer and improve distance education services.

DEP must have procedures and guidelines consistent with institutional policy for responding to threats, emergencies, and crisis situations. Systems and procedures must be in place to disseminate timely and accurate information to students and other members of the campus community during emergency situations.

DEP must have procedures and guidelines consistent with institutional policy for communicating with the media.

Part 11.
CURRICULUM, COURSE, and DEGREE REQUIREMENTS

Information about courses, programs, and degree requirements must be clear and understandable and accessible to all participants.

Preferably, this information should be published in written form and distributed widely, using a variety of media.

The institutional catalog must clearly state the distance education opportunities available to students. It must present a clear and accurate statement of the instructional delivery systems, learning formats, prerequisites, expected learning outcomes, completion requirements, and other relevant requirements.

Effective distance education programs should employ faculty teamwork, collaborative learning, focused outcomes and shared goals, active creation of knowledge and meaning, and meaningful interaction and feedback. Curriculum design should recognize these components of quality distance education experiences and provide for them intentionally and systematically.

Part 12. FACULTY/STUDENT INTERACTIONS

Distance education programs must provide for appropriate and effective faculty and student interactions.

These interactions may use one or more media, but should be relevant to the course activities and accessible to all students.

Faculty members must provide for interchange among students, when possible, and with students in all cases.

These interactions must be learning-oriented and ideally should lead to a sense of community among learners and faculty members.

Part 13. TECHNOLOGICAL COMPETENCE of STUDENTS

Distance students must be competent in appropriate technologies or instructional delivery approaches used in the distance education programs of the institution.

Students in distance education programs should possess attributes associated with their ability to succeed in educational programs equal to that of other students admitted elsewhere to the institution.

Part 14.
ACCESS TO STUDENT and ACADEMIC SERVICES

Institutions must provide appropriate student services for all students enrolled in distance education programs. These services must be sufficiently comprehensive to be responsive to the special needs of all distance students.

The needs of distance students should be carefully analyzed. Programs and services to aid these students should be carefully designed to meet their particular needs.

Institutions offering distance education programs must provide a fully functioning program of distributed education services.

Distributed educational services are those designed to be delivered in learning environments where student and teacher are separated by time and/or space. These services may be divided into three levels of service. The first level provides comprehensive and thorough information about the institution, programs, and services. The second level includes links to other relevant information sources, frequently asked questions about programs of study, and direct access to human resources including phone numbers and e-mail addresses. The third level should provide access to mechanisms to permit the formation of virtual communities of learners.

Services to students must be of comparable quality to services provided to on-campus students.

In many areas, the services to distance students are nearly identical to those provided to on-campus students. Services in admission, financial aid, and registration, for example, might be indistinguishable from those provided to on-campus students. Other services, however, such as advising, counseling, tutoring, career services, wellness programs, and opportunities to engage in aesthetic and culturally enriching activities, may require significant modification to services provided to on-campus students.

Part 15. EDUCATIONAL SUPPORT SERVICES

The required program of distributed educational services must include at least the following:

15.A. Information for Prospective Students

Information must be provided in anticipation that the prospective distance student will need to make decisions about whether to undertake study in this form. This information must include the following:

Subpart 15.AA

Pre-admission. **Information must be no less comprehensive than that available to students during campus visits prior to admission. Information about what it is like to be a distance learner in general, and what it is like to be a distance learner specifically at the institution offering the services, must be accessible and effectively communicated.**

Web pages may be a good vehicle for making information available to distance learners.

Subpart 15.AB

Enrollment. **Certain materials and processes must be described and provided through other suitable and readily accessible formats.**

Among these may be the catalog, academic advising, registration, the student handbook, and information related to services provided specifically for, and expectations of, distance learners.

Policies applicable to all students, such as the academic dishonesty policy and other information mandated by law, must be distributed and include information concerning how the institution manages such issues for students studying via distance education.

Subpart 15.AC

Academic Program Information. **Prospective students must have access to full descriptive materials about all courses and programs. Requirements of students, including all course prerequisites and technical competence and equipment, must be stated clearly.**

Information should:
- be easily identified and highly visible and clearly organized on web pages
- provide a credible presentation of the institution and its distance learning programs
- provide prospective students with an opportunity to assess their personal readiness for distance learning
- provide students the tools to assess their hardware and software requirements and capabilities
- include costs, transferability, course sequencing, and equipment requirements
- contact sources

15.B. Admission

Applications for admission must be provided in a manner that is practical and that can be completed without undue assistance. These applications must be processed in a manner equitable with that of resident students. Application and admission counseling must be made available to distance learners.

The admission process should be described in a detailed, step-by-step fashion. Admission requirements should be specified clearly. Criteria used in admission decisions should be specified clearly. Applications should be provided in several forms (e.g., printed, online), along with clear instructions. Deadlines should be specific and explicit.

15.C. Financial Aid

Information about financial aid must be provided to distance students and the application process must be described clearly. Eligibility requirements must be specifically outlined including all institutional financial aid policies. Deadlines for application for financial aid must be clearly stated. Student enrollment in multiple institutions must be recognized and applications for financial aid properly administered.

Distance students applying for financial aid should be provided with the following:
- general information about financial aid
- clearly described types of financial aid available
- specified costs of attendance
- information about average percent of financial need met
- other relevant forms
- online information when appropriate, but also available in print form

15.D. Registration

Distance students must be provided registration services for each new term or course in a clear, timely, and user-friendly manner. Registration services must accommodate students enrolled in courses and programs taught asynchronously.

Registration policies and processes should be clearly described. Alternative registration methods (e.g., online, print, fax, walk-in) should be identified and provided.

15.E. Orientation Services

Orientation to the institution and to the processes of learning required of new distance students must be offered.

The orientation program should be interactive. As with the delivery of instructional services, orientation may employ a variety of methods of communication and should be accessible.

The orientation process should be interactive and must provide opportunities for student-to-student where possible and faculty (or other staff) member-to-student exchanges.
Any qualified member of the faculty or staff may deliver this interactive orientation.

All requirements for new distance students must be specified in the orientation program. All services available to new students must be specified.

Prospective learners should be provided a sense of the nature of distance learning along with tips for success.

Academic integrity and related policy issues must be covered in orientation. All applicable student codes must be communicated.

15.F. Academic Advising

Academic advising must be readily available throughout the academic year and convenient to both students and advisors.

The academic advising program developed for distance students should be designed around their particular needs.

Advising services must be commensurate with services provided to on-campus students in course selection and registration. Additional services to assist students in goal setting and educational and life planning must be provided as needed.

The academic advising services should include:
- one-on-one access to advisors by phone, internet, or other communication tools
- all general education and major requirements
- self-help pointers to educational planning and course selection
- articulation information between programs and institutions
- advising guidelines, such as curriculum guides
- access to personal academic records (e.g., courses taken and completed, grades, GPA)

15.G. Technical Support

The institution must provide information concerning the equipment, software, and type of Internet service provider students will need to participate fully in their courses and programs.

The institution must take steps to ensure that students have the technical skills necessary to participate fully in the academic program and must provide an introduction to the specific applications students will need.

Technical support must be available at times convenient to the students enrolled in distance education courses and programs.

Technical support should include:
- eligibility for technical support
- tutorials for dealing with common technical difficulties
- self-help tools
- a help line/help service

15.H. Career Services

Career services must be provided for distance students appropriate to their needs. Their eligibility to receive them must be made clear.

Information about career service processes should be accessible to all students in a form consistent with the format of interaction.

These services may include, but are not limited to, self-exploration, self-assessment, goal setting, decision-making, educational planning, career planning, career information, co-op education, and job search services. Self-help tools for career decision-making and on-line searches for positions should be provided.

Opportunities for experiential learning, such as internships, service learning, cooperative education, and part-time jobs, should be effectively marketed and accessible for distance learners.

15.I. Library Services

The institution must provide an orientation to library services, which includes effective on-line search strategies geared to the programs of study offered at a distance. Service expectations must be defined.

Access to reference materials, periodicals, and books needed to fulfill course requirements must be readily available. Courses with unique or significant needs for library access must provide this information as part of the introduction to the course. Reference services must be available to individual students.

Library services should include:
- reference support
- convenient access to document delivery services
- online tutorials on conducting library research
- procedures that allow students to obtain necessary books and materials within a reasonable time period should be operable

15.J. Services for Students with Disabilities

Accessible services to distance students with disabilities must be provided. The institution's policies concerning reasonable and appropriate accommodations must be provided to the student.

Web pages should conform to World Wide Web (W3C) Content Accessibility Guidelines that explain how to make web pages content accessible to people with disabilities. These guidelines emphasize the importance of providing text equivalents of non-text content such as images, pre-recorded audio, and video.

Assistance in the availability and use of assistive technology must be provided.

15.K. Personal Counseling

Counseling services essential to assist distance students to achieve their goals must be provided.

Reasonable efforts should be made to extend comparable counseling services to distance education students. Counseling services, especially in their traditional forms that require face-to-face interaction, cannot be delivered in most distance education formats; however, services that effectively use electronic technologies should be offered when appropriate.

Counseling services for distance education students must be offered in accordance with applicable ethical standards, including ethical guidelines and standards for practice for counseling online. Counselors must develop or adopt ethical standards for their services.

These counseling services should include:
- descriptions of available counseling services
- for those experiencing a mental health crisis, contact with a personal counselor on campus, referrals to local
- emergency care resources, and phone numbers for crisis

hotlines
- self-help tools, including on-line links to appropriate Internet sites and information about finding local referral assistance

15.L. Academic Support Services

Information concerning academic support services must be made available.

Distance learning students should have opportunities for developing learning strategies and getting assistance with content comprehension. Tutoring services, supplemental instruction, and other academic support services should be available to all distance education students. These services should conform to the CAS Standards for Learning Assistance Programs in terms of their quality.

15.M. Instructional Materials

Convenient delivery of instructional materials must be provided to all distance students.

Where campus bookstores are available, their services should include:
- merchandise displayed visually
- relevant policies about bookstore operations
- on-line methods for locating course textbooks and materials
- alternative methods for ordering books and supplies

15.N. Promoting Identity with the Institution

Distance learners must be provided a reasonable opportunity to connect with other students and their instructors. Means of regular communication among students and their instructors must be provided.

Regular communication with distance learners, such as in newsletters, should be offered. Frequent announcements to distance learners though such means as web pages should be provided. Efforts to create virtual communities among distance learners should be made, when appropriate.

Creative use of electronic or other messages that would likely promote an enhanced sense of community such as bulletin boards, special events, institutional news briefs, and opportunities in special interest groups or projects may be provided.

15.O. Other Student Services

Additional student services deemed to be necessary or appropriate to the circumstances of each institution's distance education programs must be provided.

Traditional campus services such as leadership development programs and housing services may not be necessarily appropriate or necessary to distance students. Where indicated, however, they should be provided in forms equivalent to those on campus.

Information about health and wellness programs should be made available to distance education students. Referrals to local health-care providers and prescriptions by mail may be examples of services to be provided.

Information about student activities, including organizations, leisure and recreational activities, and cultural and entertainment events may be provided to distance education students when possible.

Part 16. ASSESSMENT and EVALUATION

Distance Education Programs (DEP) must establish systematic plans and processes to meet internal and external accountability expectations with regard to program as well as student learning and development outcomes. DEP must conduct regular assessment and evaluations. Assessments must include qualitative and quantitative methodologies as appropriate, to determine whether and to what degree the stated mission, goals, and student learning and development outcomes are being met. The process must employ sufficient and sound measures to ensure comprehensiveness. Data collected must include responses from students and other affected constituencies.

DEP must evaluate regularly how well they complement and enhance the institution's stated mission and educational effectiveness.

Results of these evaluations must be used in revising and improving programs and services, identifying needs and interests in shaping directions of program and service design, and recognizing staff performance.

Program evaluation must address student retention and attrition of distance learners.

Evaluations should be clearly focused. Evaluations should include course content and quality of instruction apart from mode of delivery and use of technologies.

General Standards revised in 2008;
DEP content developed in 2000

The Role of Education Abroad Programs and Services
CAS Standards Contextual Statement

According to the Institute of International Education's *Open Doors* publication, during the 2006-2007 academic year a record 241,791 college students from colleges and universities in the United States participated in an education abroad program for academic credit. This figure marks an 8% rise from the preceding year and a nearly 150% increase from 1996-1997 totals. In addition to the student numbers listed in *Open Doors*, U.S. students participated in experiential, volunteer, service-learning, and internship programs abroad. This visible trend toward greater interest and participation in education abroad among college students, both in the U.S. and in other countries, has happened concurrent to the proliferation of education abroad opportunities. Education abroad participants may now choose from a variety of programs that differ according to program location, type, duration, academic focus, method of instruction, and coordinating entity.

Given the array of programs and the increasing interest in global education among students, their parents, educational institutions, state/provincial governments, and federal governments, as well as in other countries throughout the world, the need for Education Abroad Programs and Services (EAPS) offices to have and meet standards cannot be overstated.

For more than 40 years, guidelines and standards for providing EAPS have been developed by various groups, such as NAFSA: Association of International Educators, the Council on International Educational Exchange, the Institute for International Education, accreditation associations such as the Middle States Association, the Institute for the International Education of Students, and The Forum on Education Abroad. NAFSA and The Forum include developing and disseminating professional standards as part of their mission, and The Forum is registered as the Standards Development Organization for education abroad with the Department of Justice and the Federal Trade Commission. CAS drew heavily on the publications of these groups in developing the CAS standards for EAPS. See the Resources section below for access to these organizations and some of their standards materials. They provide essential additional perspectives to any standards assessment of an education abroad office or organization.

On college and university campuses, EAPS responsibilities may be centralized in one office on campus or dispersed in multiple schools and departments across the institution.

Education abroad directors and advisers must be familiar with a broad spectrum of campus services, processes and systems, including but not limited to academic advising services, financial aid, registration, residence life, health services, counseling services, off-campus regulations and guidelines, disability services, risk management, judicial affairs, career services, alumni services, and development.

In times of global and economic uncertainty, education abroad directors and advisers must pay special attention to matters of safety, security, currency and market fluctuations, and access to financial assistance. These matters are of concern both to students and their families as well as program development and management.

Assessment is a critical aspect of ensuring the integrity of EAPS. Among other areas, EAPS should systematically assess student learning outcomes. An example of one such assessment model is the *IES MAP (Model Assessment Project) for Study Abroad* (see resources). CAS users are encouraged to review the IES assessment definitions.

Some education abroad opportunities are administered by the student's home campus, some by other institutions, and some by organizations. Whenever the programs are not administered by the home campus, the EAPS is responsible for investigating and approving the programs before allowing students to participate in and receive credit through them.

The following standards and guidelines are aimed at home-country campus-based offices, although non-campus based EAPS organizations and overseas institutions will find many of the sections helpful. The provision of Education Abroad Programs and Services has become a global enterprise.

References, Readings, and Resources

Forum on education abroad: Standards of good practice for education abroad, 2008. Available at http://www.forumea.org/standards-standards.cfm

IES MAP for study abroad: Charting a course for quality (4th ed.). (2008). Chicago: Institute for the International Education of Students. Available at https://www.iesabroad.org/IES/Advisors_and_Faculty/iesMap.html

Institute of International Education. (published annually). *Open doors report 2008: Report on international educational exchange*. See http://opendoors.iienetwork.org/

Martin, P.C., Brockington, J. L., & Hoffa W. W. (2005). *NAFSA's guide to education abroad for advisers and administrators*

(3rd ed.).. Washington, D.C.: NAFSA: Association of International Educators.

NAFSA's Statement of Ethics: http://www.nafsa.org/about.sec/ governance_leadership/ethics_standards/nafsa_s_ code_of_ethics

Spencer, S. E., & Tuma, K. (Eds.). (2007). *The guide to successful short-term programs abroad (2nd ed.)*. Washington, D.C.: NAFSA: Association of International Educators.

Strengthening study abroad: Recommendations for effective institutional management. (2008). Washington, D.C.: NAFSA: Association of International Educators. Available at http://www.nafsa.org/imsa

Alliance for International Educational and Cultural Exchange: http:// www.alliance-exchange.org/

American International Education Foundation: http://www.ief-usa. org/

Association for Studies in International Education: http://www.asie. org/index.htm

Frontiers, The Interdisciplinary Journal of Study Abroad: http:// www.frontiersjournal.com/

IES MAP (Model Assessment Program): https://www.iesabroad. org/IES/Advisors_and_Faculty/iesMap.html

Institute of International Education Annual Report *Open Doors*: http://opendoors.iienetwork.org/

Institute of International Education: http://www.iienetwork.org/

NAFSA: Association of International Educators: http://www.nafsa. org/

The Center for Global Education: http://www.lmu.edu/globaled/ index.html

The Forum on Education Abroad: http://www.forumea.org/

Contributor:
Current Edition: Sandy Tennies, NAFSA
Previous Editions: Susan Komives, University of Maryland, ACPA

Education Abroad Programs and Services
CAS Standards and Guidelines

Part 1. MISSION

Education Abroad Programs and Services (EAPS) facilitate and oversee student participation in educational experiences that occur in countries outside the institution's home country.

EAPS must develop, disseminate, implement, and regularly review their mission. Mission statements must be consistent with the mission of the institution and with professional standards. EAPS in higher education must enhance overall educational experiences by incorporating student learning and development outcomes in their mission.

EAPS overall mission should address the following:
- whom the program serves
- what the program values
- what the program seeks to accomplish (goals and objectives)
- a commitment to providing an appropriate variety of types of education abroad programs, in a variety of locations for academic credit
- a commitment to supporting students prior to, during, and after their education abroad experience
- a commitment to collaborating with internal and external stakeholders

Part 2. PROGRAM

The formal education of students, consisting of the curriculum and the co-curriculum, must promote student learning and development outcomes that are purposeful and holistic and that prepare students for satisfying and productive lifestyles, work, and civic participation. The student learning and development outcome domains and their related dimensions are:

- **knowledge acquisition, integration, construction, and application**
  - o Dimensions: understanding knowledge from a range of disciplines; connecting knowledge to other knowledge, ideas, and experiences; constructing knowledge; and relating knowledge to daily life

- **cognitive complexity**
  - o Dimensions: critical thinking; reflective thinking; effective reasoning; and creativity

- **intrapersonal development**
  - o Dimensions: realistic self-appraisal, self-understanding, and self-respect; identity development; commitment to ethics and integrity; and spiritual awareness

- **interpersonal competence**
  - o Dimensions: meaningful relationships; interdependence; collaboration; and effective leadership

- **humanitarianism and civic engagement**
  - o Dimensions: understanding and appreciation of cultural and human differences; social responsibility; global perspective; and sense of civic responsibility

- **practical competence**
  - o Dimensions: pursuing goals; communicating effectively; technical competence; managing personal affairs; managing career development; demonstrating professionalism; maintaining health and wellness; and living a purposeful and satisfying life

[See *The Council for the Advancement of Standards Learning and Developmental Outcomes* statement for examples of outcomes related to these domains and dimensions.]

Consistent with the institutional mission, Education Abroad Programs and Services (EAPS) must identify relevant and desirable student learning and development outcomes from among the six domains and related dimensions. When creating opportunities for student learning and development, EAPS must explore possibilities for collaboration with faculty members and other colleagues.

EAPS must assess relevant and desirable student learning and development outcomes and provide evidence of their impact on student learning and development. EAPS must articulate how they contribute to or support students' learning and development in the domains not specifically assessed.

EAPS must be:
- integrated into the life of the institution
- intentional and coherent
- guided by theories and knowledge of learning and development
- reflective of developmental and demographic profiles of the student population
- responsive to needs of individuals, diverse and special populations, and relevant constituencies

The EAPS should facilitate student participation in a variety of types of education abroad programs such as:
- programs where the student mobility is from the home institution (the school at which the student is seeking the degree) to a host institution (the school outside the institution's home country at which the student receives instruction and services while abroad)
- institutional exchanges where students from the home institution trade places with students from the host institution
- consortia programs that involve two or more institutions
- third-party programs where the program is administered outside the institution

To fulfill its mission and goals effectively, EAPS must include the following elements:

- **Clear and consistent academic policies and guidelines for home and host institutions**

  Admissions policies and procedures should be clearly articulated to students. Academic policies and procedures for awarding credit and understanding course grade equivalencies should also be clearly articulated to students before they depart for an education abroad program. Guidance with course selection should be offered regarding course transferability and equivalency. Coursework should be appropriately challenging; course requirements and methods of evaluating performance should be clearly stated; feedback should be provided to students periodically, in keeping with host country norms. Opportunities should be provided that allow the learning that occurs as a result of the EAPS experience to be integrated into subsequent educational experiences.

- **Curricular and co-curricular opportunities that are related to the mission and purpose of the specific education abroad program**

  The curricular and co-curricular components of each education abroad opportunity should make effective use of the location and resources of the host country; students should be encouraged to engage with the host culture and to reflect on the differences and similarities between the intellectual, political, cultural, spiritual, and social institutions of the home and host countries. Students' curricular and co-curricular experiences should contribute to their appreciation and respect for cultural differences in general. Students should be encouraged to immerse themselves in the host culture, interact with host nationals, practice and improve their language and intercultural communication abilities, and reflect on their value systems in the context of living in another culture.

  EAPS should provide opportunities for internships, service-learning, and other field study experiences that are related to the mission and purpose of the specific education abroad program. EAPS should incorporate opportunities to synthesize the learning that occurs as a result of these out-of-classroom experiences into future educational and life experiences. **Where field opportunities exist, they must be appropriately supervised and evaluated and must relate to the mission of the EAPS and institution. Awarding of credit for internships or field studies must be consistent with the policies of the home institution.**

- **Pre-departure advising and orientation programs**

  Pre-departure advising and orientation sessions must inform students about program requirements, academic credit and transfer policies, visa and passport requirements, and housing and travel arrangements, as well as financial, health, liability, insurance, safety, and security information. International students at the home institution must be advised to determine their re-entry status. Students must be asked directly and encouraged strongly to share information about any on-going health concerns before departing for their program locations. Home and host institution codes of conduct that apply to students while abroad must be clearly articulated; consequences of not following these codes of conduct must be clearly defined and communicated. Students must be provided with an introduction to intercultural communication and preparation for the cultural transition, including resources on culture shock and cultural adjustment. Orientation programs must identify resources for students so that they may educate themselves about the culture, customs, and laws of the host countries. EAPS must provide students with the contact the information of their home country's embassy or consulate at their host site.

  Students should be advised to utilize the appropriate campus or community resources (e.g., travel medicine, financial aid, immigration status) before departure.

- **Information about student financial assistance**

- **On-going advising and support services for students while they are abroad**

  On-going advising and support services throughout the duration of the education abroad program should be provided either through the home or host institution.

- **Re-entry support and orientation programs for returning students**

  Upon return, re-entry programs and services must support re-acculturation to the home country, relationships, and the institution.

  Returning students should be encouraged to integrate their experience abroad into their continued learning, including sharing their stories and experiences with other students, faculty members, and staff members.

Part 3. LEADERSHIP

Because effective and ethical leadership is essential to the success of all organizations, Education Abroad Programs and Services (EAPS) leaders with organizational authority for the programs and services must:

- articulate a vision and mission for their programs and services
- set goals and objectives based on the needs of the population served and desired student learning and development outcomes
- advocate for their programs and services
- promote home and host campus environments that provide meaningful opportunities for student learning, development, and integration
- identify and find means to address individual, organizational, or environmental conditions that foster or inhibit mission achievement
- advocate for representation in strategic planning initiatives at appropriate divisional and institutional levels
- initiate collaborative interactions with stakeholders who have legitimate concerns and interests in the functional

area
- apply effective practices to educational and administrative processes
- prescribe and model ethical behavior
- communicate effectively
- manage financial resources, including planning, allocation, monitoring, and analysis
- incorporate sustainability practices in the management and design of programs, services, and facilities
- manage human resource processes including recruitment, selection, development, supervision, performance planning, and evaluation
- empower professional, support, and student staff to accept leadership opportunities
- encourage and support scholarly contribution to the profession
- be informed about and integrate appropriate technologies into programs and services
- be knowledgeable about federal, state/provincial, and local laws relevant to the programs and services and ensure that staff members understand their responsibilities by receiving appropriate training
- develop and continuously improve programs and services in response to the changing needs of students and other populations served and the evolving institutional priorities
- recognize environmental conditions that may negatively influence the safety of staff and students and propose interventions that mitigate such conditions

EAPS leaders should establish working relationships with institutional agents, including provosts, academic deans, department chairs, risk managers, academic advisors, and student affairs professionals on the home campus to promote programs and engender support.

Part 4. HUMAN RESOURCES

Education Abroad Programs and Services (EAPS) must be staffed adequately by individuals qualified to accomplish the mission and goals. Within institutional guidelines, EAPS must establish procedures for staff selection, training, and evaluation; set expectations for supervision; and provide appropriate professional development opportunities to improve the leadership ability, competence, and skills of all employees.

EAPS professional staff members must hold an earned graduate or professional degree in a field relevant to the position they hold or must possess an appropriate combination of educational credentials and related work experience.

EAPS staff should have experience living or studying abroad. Entry into the profession by educators from a variety of academic backgrounds is encouraged.

EAPS professional staff members must be knowledgeable and competent in the following areas:
- cultural sensitivity

- intercultural communication
- culture shock, reverse culture shock, and cultural adjustment
- student advising and counseling
- crisis management
- budgetary and financial management
- collaboration with faculty members and academic departments at home and host institutions
- organizational policies (e.g., admissions, credit transfer, financial aid, travel regulations, immigration policies, insurance)
- pre-departure and re-entry issues
- travel and living abroad
- technology
- country specific health, safety, and security concerns

EAPS professional staff members should be knowledgeable and competent in such areas as:
- foreign language(s)
- countries, cultures, and regions where their students most frequently study (e.g. culture, customs, language, art, geography, political system, economic system, history, traditions, values, laws)
- other countries' educational systems
- human development
- marketing and promoting education abroad programs
- experiential education

Degree- or credential-seeking interns must be qualified by enrollment in an appropriate field of study and by relevant experience. These individuals must be trained and supervised adequately by professional staff members holding educational credentials and related work experience appropriate for supervision.

Student employees and volunteers must be carefully selected, trained, supervised, and evaluated. They must be educated on how and when to refer those in need of additional assistance to qualified staff members and must have access to a supervisor for assistance in making these judgments. Student employees and volunteers must be provided clear and precise job descriptions, pre-service training based on assessed needs, and continuing staff development.

Employees and volunteers must receive specific training on institutional policies and privacy laws regarding their access to student records and other sensitive institutional information (e.g., in the USA, Family Educational Rights and Privacy Act, FERPA, or equivalent privacy laws in other states/provinces or countries).

EAPS must have technical and support staff members adequate to accomplish their mission. All members of the staff must be technologically proficient and qualified to perform their job functions, be knowledgeable about ethical and legal uses of technology, and have access to training and resources to support the performance of their assigned responsibilities.

All members of the staff must receive training on policies and procedures related to the use of technology to store or access student records and institutional data.

EAPS must ensure that staff members are knowledgeable about and trained in emergency procedures, crisis response, and prevention efforts. Prevention efforts must address identification of threatening conduct or behavior of students, faculty members, staff, and others and must incorporate a system or procedures for responding, including but not limited to reporting them to the appropriate campus officials.

Salary levels and benefits for all staff members must be commensurate with those for comparable positions within the institution, in similar institutions, and in the relevant geographic area.

EAPS must maintain position descriptions for all staff members.

To create a diverse staff, EAPS must institute hiring and promotion practices that are fair, inclusive, proactive, and non-discriminatory.

EAPS must conduct regular performance planning and evaluation of staff members. EAPS must provide access to continuing and advanced education and professional development opportunities.

Part 5. ETHICS

Persons involved in the delivery of Education Abroad Programs and Services (EAPS) must adhere to the highest principles of ethical behavior. EAPS must review relevant professional ethical standards and develop or adopt and implement appropriate statements of ethical practice. EAPS must publish these statements and ensure their periodic review by relevant constituencies.

EAPS must orient new staff members to relevant ethical standards and statements of ethical practice.

EAPS staff members must ensure that privacy and confidentiality are maintained with respect to all communications and records to the extent that such records are protected under the law and appropriate statements of ethical practice. Information contained in students' education records must not be disclosed except as allowed by relevant laws and institutional policies. EAPS staff members must disclose to appropriate authorities information judged to be of an emergency nature, especially when the safety of the individual or others is involved, or when otherwise required by institutional policy or relevant law.

EAPS staff members must be aware of and comply with the provisions contained in the institution's policies pertaining to human subjects research and student rights and responsibilities, as well as those in other relevant institutional policies addressing ethical practices and confidentiality of research data concerning individuals.

EAPS staff members must recognize and avoid personal conflicts of interest or appearance thereof in the performance of their work.

EAPS staff members must strive to insure the fair, objective, and impartial treatment of all persons with whom they interact.

When handling institutional funds, EAPS staff members must ensure that such funds are managed in accordance with established and responsible accounting procedures and the fiscal policies or processes of the institution.

Promotional and descriptive information must be accurate and free of deception.

EAPS staff members must perform their duties within the limits of their training, expertise, and competence. When these limits are exceeded, individuals in need of further assistance must be referred to persons possessing appropriate qualifications.

EAPS staff members must use suitable means to confront and otherwise hold accountable other staff members who exhibit unethical behavior.

EAPS staff members must be knowledgeable about and practice ethical behavior in the use of technology.

EAPS home and host staff members must have ethical and unbiased procedures in place for terminating participants.

Termination procedures should be made public and provided to participants prior to their participation in an education abroad program.

EAPS home and host staff members must have ethical guidelines in place for advising and interacting with students and their families.

In addition to standard records privacy and confidentiality policies, EAPS should develop procedures to assure the long-term protection of students' records.

Part 6. LEGAL RESPONSIBILITIES

Education Abroad Programs and Services (EAPS) staff members must be knowledgeable about and responsive to laws and regulations that relate to their respective responsibilities and that may pose legal obligations, limitations, or ramifications for the institution as a whole. As appropriate, staff members must inform users of programs and services, as well as officials, of legal obligations and limitations including constitutional, statutory, regulatory, and case law; mandatory laws and orders emanating from federal, state/provincial, and local governments; and the institution's policies.

EAPS staff members must know where to refer program participants for information on host country laws and host institution policies and procedures. EAPS staff members must make participants aware of home institution consequences of breaking these laws, policies, and procedures.

EAPS must have written policies on all relevant operations, transactions, or tasks that may have legal implications.

EAPS staff members must neither participate in nor condone any form of harassment or activity that demeans persons or creates an intimidating, hostile, or offensive campus environment.

EAPS staff members must use reasonable and informed practices to limit the liability exposure of the institution and its officers, employees, and agents. EAPS staff members must be informed about institutional policies regarding risk management, personal liability, and related insurance coverage options and must be referred to external sources if coverage is not provided by the institution.

The institution must provide access to legal advice for EAPS staff members as needed to carry out assigned responsibilities.

The institution must inform EAPS staff and students in a timely and systematic fashion about extraordinary or changing legal obligations and potential liabilities.

EAPS staff members must ensure that expectations for participant conduct - including but not limited to drug and alcohol abuse, sexual assault and harassment, academic integrity, and social conduct - are clearly articulated in program materials and in pre-departure and on-site orientations.

EAPS must have a clearly defined crisis management program.

The home institution should have a clearly defined crisis management program that integrates and supports the EAPS plan. The home institution should obtain the host institution crisis management plan.

EAPS staff members should develop collaborative relationships with relevant home and host institutional departments (e.g., general counsel, student conduct programs) in order to assess and minimize risk and develop appropriate resources for students.

Part 7. EQUITY and ACCESS

Education Abroad Programs and Services (EAPS) must be provided on a fair, equitable, and non-discriminatory basis in accordance with institutional policies and with all applicable state/provincial and federal statutes and regulations. EAPS must maintain an educational and work environment free from discrimination in accordance with law and institutional policy.

Discrimination must be avoided on the basis of age; cultural heritage; disability; ethnicity; gender identity and expression; nationality; political affiliation; race; religious affiliation; sex; sexual orientation; economic, marital, social, or veteran status; and any other bases included in local, state/provincial,

or federal laws.

Consistent with the mission and goals, EAPS must take action to remedy significant imbalances in student participation and staffing patterns.

EAPS must ensure physical and program access for persons with disabilities. EAPS must be responsive to the needs of all students and other populations served when establishing hours of operation and developing methods of delivering programs and services.

EAPS must recognize the needs of distance learning students by providing appropriate and accessible services and assisting them in identifying and gaining access to other appropriate services in their geographic region.

EAPS should encourage students from under-represented groups (e.g., gender, ethnicity, age, disability, marital status, socioeconomic status, academic major, religious affiliation, sexual orientation) to apply and participate in education abroad programs.

Part 8. DIVERSITY

Within the context of each institution's unique mission, diversity enriches the community and enhances the collegiate experience for all; therefore, Education Abroad Programs and Services (EAPS) must create and nurture environments that are welcoming to and bring together persons of diverse backgrounds.

EAPS must promote environments that are characterized by open and continuous communication that deepens understanding of one's own identity, culture, and heritage, as well as that of others. EAPS must recognize, honor, educate, and promote respect about commonalties and differences among people within their historical and cultural contexts.

EAPS must address the characteristics and needs of a diverse population when establishing and implementing policies and procedures.

EAPS must intentionally foster students' understanding of cross-cultural differences and encourage participants to reflect on these differences at home and abroad.

EAPS must intentionally prepare participants for living and studying in the intended host country.

EAPS staff members must actively work with all interested participants to select an education abroad program suitable to their needs, skills, and eligibility.

EAPS should intentionally seek and promote diversity within education abroad program participants (including under-represented groups), faculty program leaders, and staff members.

Part 9. ORGANIZATION and MANAGEMENT

To promote student learning and development outcomes, Education Abroad Programs and Services (EAPS) must be structured purposefully and managed effectively to achieve stated goals. Evidence of appropriate structure must include current and accessible policies and procedures, written performance expectations for all employees, functional workflow graphics or organizational charts, and clearly stated program and service delivery expectations.

EAPS must monitor websites used for distributing information to ensure that the sites are current, accurate, appropriately referenced, and accessible.

Evidence of effective management must include use of comprehensive and accurate information for decisions, clear sources and channels of authority, effective communication practices, procedures for decision-making and conflict resolution, responses to changing conditions, systems of accountability and evaluation, and processes for recognition and reward. EAPS must align policies and procedures with those of the institution and provide channels within the organization for their regular review.

To fulfill its mission and goals effectively, EAPS must:
- provide leadership for integrating education abroad into the wider administrative and academic structure of the institution
- efficiently and effectively administer the programs they coordinate
- advise students appropriately, based on their interests, needs, financial ability, language proficiency, and academic background, as they choose an education abroad program

EAPS should be housed within a centralized unit.

Information about education abroad opportunities and related institutional policies must be easily accessible.

Part 10. CAMPUS and EXTERNAL RELATIONS

Education Abroad Programs and Services (EAPS) must reach out to relevant individuals, campus offices, and external agencies to:
- establish, maintain, and promote effective relations
- disseminate information about their own and other related programs and services
- coordinate and collaborate, where appropriate, in offering programs and services to meet the needs of students and promote their achievement of student learning and development outcomes

EAPS must have procedures and guidelines consistent with institutional policy for responding to threats, emergencies, and crisis situations. Systems and procedures must be in place to disseminate timely and accurate information to students and other members of the campus community during emergency situations.

EAPS must have procedures and guidelines consistent with institutional policy for communicating with the media.

EAPS staff members should collaborate with:

- departments on the home campus (i.e., academic departments and programs, registrar, academic affairs, financial aid, financial services, student affairs, international student and scholar services, admissions, career advising, clinical health services, counseling services, institutional advancement, disability support services, multicultural centers, residential life)
- consulates of host countries
- home country embassies and consulates abroad
- faculty members at home and abroad who teach or do research in fields related to home institution education abroad opportunities
- administrative staff at the host institution responsible for students from abroad
- external program providers

EAPS staff members should collaborate with third-party program providers as appropriate to sustain existing programs and establish new opportunities to increase the diversity of options for students. Interested individuals (faculty members or other campus personnel) should be encouraged to become involved in education abroad by suggesting possible opportunities, proposing specific programs, or presenting and encouraging discussions about education abroad.

Agreements between EAPS and other institutions to promote education abroad, whether exchange agreements or co-sponsorship of programs, should be supportive of the institution's overall mission and collaborative with regard to academic objectives and standards.

EAPS should ensure that faculty members, administrators, staff members, and students are aware of education abroad opportunities. EAPS should work to ensure that programs are accurately described in advisory and promotional materials and that their purposes, financial implications, and educational objectives are clearly stated.

Part 11. FINANCIAL RESOURCES

Education Abroad Programs and Services (EAPS) must have adequate funding to accomplish their mission and goals. In establishing funding priorities and making significant changes, a comprehensive analysis, which includes relevant expenditures, external and internal resources, and impact on the campus community, must be conducted.

EAPS must demonstrate fiscal responsibility and cost effectiveness consistent with institutional protocols.

EAPS should offer education abroad programs to students at affordable costs.

EAPS should consider grant writing and fundraising efforts to increase their financial resources, including funding for need-based student scholarships.

EAPS should encourage their institution to create institutional education abroad scholarships and grants, both need and merit-based.

Part 12. TECHNOLOGY

Education Abroad Programs and Services (EAPS) must have adequate technology to support their mission. The technology and its use must comply with institutional policies and procedures and be evaluated for compliance with relevant federal, state/provincial, and local requirements.

EAPS must maintain policies and procedures that address the security and back up of data.

When technology is used to facilitate student learning and development, EAPS must select technology that reflects current best pedagogical practices.

Technology, as well as any workstations or computer labs maintained by the EAPS for student use, must be accessible and must meet established technology standards for delivery to persons with disabilities.

When EAPS provide student access to technology, they must provide:
- access to policies that are clear, easy to understand, and available to all students
- access to instruction or training on how to use the technology
- access to information on the legal and ethical implications of misuse as it pertains to intellectual property, harassment, privacy, and social networks

Student violations of technology policies must follow established institutional student disciplinary procedures.

Students who experience negative emotional or psychological consequences from the use of technology must be referred to support services provided by the institution.

Part 13. FACILITIES and EQUIPMENT

Education Abroad Programs and Services (EAPS) must have adequate, accessible, suitably located facilities and equipment to support their mission and goals. If acquiring capital equipment as defined by the institution, EAPS must take into account expenses related to regular maintenance and life cycle costs. Facilities and equipment must be evaluated regularly, including consideration of sustainability, and be in compliance with relevant federal, state/provincial, and local requirements to provide for access, health, safety, and security.

EAPS staff members must have work space that is well-equipped, adequate in size, and designed to support their work and responsibilities. For conversations requiring privacy, staff members must have access to a private space.

EAPS staff members who share work space must have the ability to secure their work adequately.

The design of the facilities must guarantee the security of records and ensure the confidentiality of sensitive information.

The location and layout of the facilities must be sensitive to the special needs of persons with disabilities as well as the needs of constituencies served.

EAPS must ensure that staff members are knowledgeable of and trained in safety and emergency procedures for securing and vacating the facilities.

Office facilities at home and host institutions must be provided to accommodate EAPS goals. Home and host campus facilities must allow for privacy during student advising.

Residential and non-residential student facilities at host institutions must be provided to accommodate program goals, be safe and secure, and be maintained to meet student needs.

Residential and non-residential student facilities should be located conveniently at host institutions.

Host institutions should provide students with services equivalent to the services provided to host institution students (e.g., telephone, computer, Internet) at similar costs.

Part 14. ASSESSMENT and EVALUATION

Education Abroad Programs and Services (EAPS) must establish systematic plans and processes to meet internal and external accountability expectations with regard to program as well as student learning and development outcomes. EAPS must conduct regular assessment and evaluations. Assessments must include qualitative and quantitative methodologies as appropriate, to determine whether and to what degree the stated mission, goals, and student learning and development outcomes are being met. The process must employ sufficient and sound measures to ensure comprehensiveness. Data collected must include responses from students and other affected constituencies.

EAPS must evaluate regularly how well they complement and enhance the institution's stated mission and educational effectiveness.

Results of these evaluations must be used in revising and improving programs and services, identifying needs and interests in shaping directions of program and service design, and recognizing staff performance.

General Standards revised in 2008;
EAPS content developed in 2005

Financial Aid Programs

The CAS Financial Aid Standards and Guidelines, as well as the accompanying contextual statement and self-assessment guide, are undergoing revision at the time of publication. Because of the significant amount of change related to the financial aid field since the previous edition of the standards, and the desire to reflect current issues, trends, and practices accurately, the Financial Aid materials are not being published at this time. They will be made available through the CAS website when they are complete. Anyone needing copies for historical or research purposes should contact the CAS office or refer to the 2006 CAS publications.

The Role of Fraternity and Sorority Advising Programs
CAS Standards Contextual Statement

Advising undergraduate fraternal organizations is a multifaceted function within student life. Professionals not only support individual student development but also work to advance organizational and community goals. Persons working with fraternity and sorority life (FSL) also work with a range of stakeholders outside of the college or university. Stakeholders include students, alumni, inter/national fraternity/sorority staff and volunteers, parents, police and fire officials, and community members, among others (Mamarchev, Sina, & Heida, 2003). A question to be answered by fraternity/sorority professionals is to what extent these organizations augment the institution's educational mission.

Fraternities and sororities have been a part of the fabric of student life on some campuses for more than two centuries, but the nature of this relationship is debated (Gregory, 2003; Rudolph, 1962; Whipple & Sullivan, 1998). The primary role for fraternity/sorority professionals is aiding stakeholders in positioning these organizations as a valued and relevant part of campus life (Bureau, 2007). With this charge in mind, we present the following model: identify the issues, generate ideas, and act with intention. This model can provide a basis for enacting the CAS Standards for Fraternity and Sorority Advising - supporting the holistic development of students and helping FSL ensure its future on college/university campuses.

Issues
Organizational culture is certainly complex (Kuh & Whitt, 1988). Any collection of organized individuals can provide challenges for student life professionals; however, some argue the long standing traditions in FSL can make this culture particularly difficult to manage (Jelke & Kuh, 2003; Whipple & Sullivan, 1998). FSL culture is shaped in part by students but is also molded by stakeholders' influence. Therefore, the issues are confounded by multiple agents, all of whom can make cultural change difficult. It may be too simplistic to divide the challenges and opportunities affecting the undergraduate fraternal movement into internal and external and furthermore into three different levels of individual, organization, and community, but this delineation may be the most effective way to understand the issues facing FSL.

Internal issues are those that immediate stakeholders must address to support student needs, organizational functions, and community-wide advancement. These include the challenges associated with alcohol misuse and abuse, hazing, recruitment and intake activities, and new member education practices. This is made more complex when there is a lack of collaboration amongst diverse fraternal organizations in the enactment of community policies and procedures. It can sometimes feel impossible to manage the different responsibilities that come with such dynamic organizations.

There are also opportunities to take an ordinary college experience and transform it into a powerful learning experience. Students learn through involvement in civic engagement and philanthropic activities, leadership development, academic support, and friendships built on common values. Ultimately these experiences offer students a unique challenge of managing individual and organizational expectations.

There are also issues within the international fraternal movement that impact FSL on campuses: the management role of umbrella groups, ensuring that professionals have the skills necessary to support fraternities and sororities (such as those outlined in the *CAS Standards for Fraternity and Sorority Advising* and the *AFA Core Competencies for Excellence in the Profession*) and a sometimes politically charged and potentially disjointed effort to assess the quality of the undergraduate fraternal experience.

External issues are those that influence FSL in the larger scope of student affairs, higher education, and society. Challenges include institutional funding and staffing of student life, accountability and assessment in higher education, assessment of student learning outcomes, and the role of student affairs in supporting the mission of higher education (Sandeen & Barr, 2006). Student Affairs must align its activities with the mission of student learning (Schuh & Upcraft, 2001); therefore, as a part of a larger student affairs division, FSL must demonstrate the degree to which it accomplishes this important task.

Within society, the perceptions of fraternities/sororities vary. Ardent supporters value the role these organizations can play in the development of students. The loudest critics question how FSL adds value to the student experience (Gregory, 2003).

Ultimately, fraternities and sororities influence and are influenced by the aforementioned issues. With the many challenges in mind, efforts to solve the problems and accentuate the contributions of FSL require new and innovative ideas.

Ideas

If the consistently problematic issues could be easily solved, then the ills of FSL would have been cured years ago. There is certainly a population of people who are committed to improving these organizations and aligning them with the mission of higher education. However, students bring with them a world of ideas and expectations about fraternities and sororities. These perceptions and expectations will be difficult to alter. With this challenge in mind, new ideas are needed. A list of actions is beyond the scope of this statement; however the accomplishment of any idea must involve collaboration, embrace the never-ending process of change, and apply creativity and innovation.

As professionals support the advancement of their respective fraternity and sorority community, some comfort may be found in the idea that many are invested in the future of fraternities and sororities. Partnerships with fellow staff, faculty, alumni volunteers, (inter)national fraternity/sorority professionals and volunteers, parents, and local service agencies and businesses can be forged to support the development of the students and the organizations.

Applying new ideas can be tricky. However, innovation is required to make change stick (Koepsell, 2008). Tactics such as grounding policy discussions from a values-perspective, implementing activities that allow for students and stakeholders to imagine reinventing the fraternity and sorority community, and transforming educational efforts to move from a *symptom approach* (for example, alcohol misuse and abuse) to a broader *disease approach* (people drink too much because they have low self-esteem) could be viewed as innovative. Even small tactics of innovation can make a difference in how fraternities and sororities contribute to the campus environment (Bureau, 2007).

Intentionality

With the issues and ideas in mind, we must be purposeful in our support of the positive development of students in fraternities and sororities. Student development theory is widely applied in student affairs to aid in the explanation of how students function (Hamrick, Evans & Schuh, 2002). Additionally, organizational theory can guide practice (Jelke & Kuh, 2003). When practitioners intentionally apply the theoretical foundations of student affairs they can be most focused on student development.

In addition to theories, FSL professionals can be effective in their roles if they understand the models and frameworks that guide good practice. There are many to consider (Gregory, 2003; Marmarchev, Sina & Heida, 2003). One effective framework is that of assessment. Assessment is one way to be most intentional in how student affairs professionals conduct their

work (Sandeen & Barr, 2006). Schuh and Upcraft (2001) provide guidance on how to support assessment in fraternity and sorority communities.

Conclusion

The *CAS Standards for Fraternity and Sorority Advising* can be a powerful tool to enhance the fraternal experience. It addresses the issues challenging the movement, brings forth a framework to apply new ideas, and is an intentional approach to managing these complex organizations. Challenges exist but the application of the *CAS Standards for Fraternity and Sorority Advising* can support efforts for student development in the context of fraternities and sororities and increase their relevance on college and university campuses.

References, Readings, and Resources

Association of Fraternity Advisors (2007). Core competencies for excellence in the profession. Retrieved September 9, 2008 from http://www.fraternityadvisors.org/Business/CoreCompetencies.aspx

Bureau, D. (2007, Summer). Beyond the rhetoric and into the action of the values movement. Perspectives, 20-22

Bureau, D. (2007, Winter). Barriers to greatness: Using the concept of relevancy to create urgency for change. Perspectives, 8-11.

Gregory, D. E. (2003). The dilemma facing fraternal organizations at the Millennium. In D. E. Gregory & Associates, The administration of fraternal organizations on North American campuses, 1-21. Asheville, N.C.: College Administration Publications.

Hamrick, F. A., Evans, N. J., & Schuh, J. H. (2002). Foundations of student affairs practice. San Francisco: John Wiley & Sons.

Jelke, T. & Kuh, G. (2003). High performing fraternities and sororities. In D. E. Gregory & Associates, The administration of fraternal organizations on North American campuses, 1-21. Asheville, N.C.: College Administration Publications.

Koepsell, M. (2008, May). Utilizing community standards to align accountability, assessment and performance. Essentials. Retrieved September 9, 2008 from http://www.fraternityadvisors.org/Essentials/200805_Community_Standards.aspx (members only)

Kuh, G. D., & Whitt, E. J. (1988). The invisible tapestry: Culture in American colleges and universities. ASHE-ERIC Higher Education Report Series, No. 1. Washington, DC: Association for the Study of Higher Education.

Mamarchev, H.L., Sina, J.A., & Heida, D.E. (2003). Creating and managing a campus oversight plan: Do they work? What are the alternatives? In Gregory & Associates, The administration of fraternal organizations on North American campuses, 1-21. Asheville, N.C.: College Administration Publications.

Rudolph, F. (1990). The American college and university (2nd ed.). Athens, GA. The University of Georgia Press.

Sandeen, A., & Barr, M. J. (2006). Critical issues for student affairs: Challenges and opportunities. San Francisco: Jossey-Bass.

Schuh, J. H., & Upcraft, M. L. (2001). Assessment practice in student affairs: An applications manual. San Francisco: Jossey-Bass.

Whipple, E.G., & Sullivan, E.G. (1998). Greek-letter organizations: A community of learners? In E. G. Whipple (Ed.). New challenges for Greek-letter organizations: Transforming fraternities and sororities into learning communities. San Francisco, CA: Jossey-Bass.

Main Contributor:

Dan Bureau, Indiana University, AFA

Contributors:
Tanner Marcantel, Vanderbilt University
Monica Miranda Smalls, University of Rochester
Emily Perlow, Worcester Polytechnic Institute
Jeremiah Shinn, Indiana University

Reviewed by:
AFA Executive Board and Staff

Fraternity and Sorority Advising Programs
CAS Standards and Guidelines

Part 1. MISSION

Fraternity and Sorority Advising Programs (FSAP) must develop, disseminate, implement, and regularly review their mission. Mission statements must be consistent with the mission of the institution and with professional standards. FSAP in higher education must enhance overall educational experiences by incorporating student learning and development outcomes in their mission.

FSAP must promote academic and personal growth and development of students who affiliate with fraternities and sororities and promote the fraternity and sorority community as an integral and productive part of the institution.

To accomplish its mission, FSAP must:
- promote the intellectual, social, spiritual, moral, civic, and career development, and wellness of students
- provide education and experience in leadership, group dynamics, and organization development
- promote student involvement in co-curricular activities
- promote sponsorship of and participation in community service and philanthropic projects
- promote an appreciation for different lifestyles including cultural and religious heritages
- recognize and encourage the positive learning experiences that are possible in a fraternity and sorority community that has a diversified membership

Participation in a campus chapter represents one of several group affiliation options for college students. Fraternity and sorority affiliation may include: a recruitment process, new/associate member education, initiation (formal induction into the organization), on-going membership development programming, and lifelong affiliation. Professional staff members should promote student development in all affiliation processes.

Staff members should develop a comprehensive program to promote the education and welfare of participating students and coordinate resources and activities with others in the campus community.

Participation in a fraternity or sorority must promote responsible membership in both the organization and the institution.

Part 2. PROGRAM

The formal education of students, consisting of the curriculum and the co-curriculum, must promote student learning and development outcomes that are purposeful and holistic and that prepare students for satisfying and productive lifestyles, work, and civic participation. The student learning and development outcome domains and their related dimensions are:

- knowledge acquisition, integration, construction, and application
  - o Dimensions: understanding knowledge from a range of disciplines; connecting knowledge to other knowledge, ideas, and experiences; constructing knowledge; and relating knowledge to daily life

- cognitive complexity
  - o Dimensions: critical thinking; reflective thinking; effective reasoning; and creativity

- intrapersonal development
  - o Dimensions: realistic self-appraisal, self-understanding, and self-respect; identity development; commitment to ethics and integrity; and spiritual awareness

- interpersonal competence
  - o Dimensions: meaningful relationships; interdependence; collaboration; and effective leadership

- humanitarianism and civic engagement
  - o Dimensions: understanding and appreciation of cultural and human differences; social responsibility; global perspective; and sense of civic responsibility

- practical competence
  - o Dimensions: pursuing goals; communicating effectively; technical competence; managing personal affairs; managing career development; demonstrating professionalism; maintaining health and wellness; and living a purposeful and satisfying life

[See *The Council for the Advancement of Standards Learning and Developmental Outcomes* statement for examples of outcomes related to these domains and dimensions.]

Consistent with the institutional mission, Fraternity and Sorority Advising Programs (FSAP) must identify relevant and desirable student learning and development outcomes from among the six domains and related dimensions. When creating opportunities for student learning and development, FSAP must explore possibilities for collaboration with faculty members and other colleagues.

FSAP must assess relevant and desirable student learning and development outcomes and provide evidence of their impact on student learning and development. FSAP must articulate how they contribute to or support students' learning and development in the domains not specifically assessed.

FSAP must be:
- integrated into the life of the institution
- intentional and coherent
- guided by theories and knowledge of learning and development
- reflective of developmental and demographic profiles of the student population

- **responsive to needs of individuals, diverse and special populations, and relevant constituencies**

The FSAP must include the following elements:

- **Educational programming that enhances member knowledge, understanding, and competencies essential for academic success, personal development, and the exercise of leadership. Educational programming must complement the academic curriculum.**

  Activities that improve the student's chances of academic success are particularly important. Programs should address the maturation and development of students and facilitate the application of knowledge and skills through experiential opportunities.

- **Staff members who provide programs that encourage faculty, staff, and administrator involvement and interaction with students**

  Leadership programs should help the individual effectively understand and manage group processes, particularly the relevant aspects of self-governance and accountability. Leadership programs also should enable students to gain knowledge about assessing leadership and management skills.

  Good citizenship development programs, including opportunities for self-learning, should assist students in becoming responsible and involved community members.

- **Social and recreational programming that enhances the members' knowledge, understanding, and skills necessary for success and the productive use of leisure time**

  Social skills programs should assist individuals in developing more mature and satisfying interpersonal relationships.

  Educational programs should promote wellness, teamwork, sportsmanship, and healthy competition.

- **Opportunities for recognition by the institution as appropriate**

- **The institution and the fraternities and sororities must jointly define their relationship. The relationship statement must be formalized, documented, and disseminated.**

  Campus chapters should participate in the same student organization registration and recognition process as other campus student groups. Additional statements regarding relationships between the institution and its chapters may be defined as appropriate for the campus. Areas of consideration may include:
  - a description of the community
  - historical relationships
  - educational role of fraternities and sororities
  - conditions and responsibilities of affiliation
  - housing and other facilities
  - support and program orientation
  - governance and authority (e.g., national and international organization affiliation and expansion)
  - reference to comprehensive policy documents

  - expectations of the institution and the fraternity and sorority community
  - accountability to other student governing bodies

- **Educational programming that addresses aspects of the fraternity and sorority community that are currently or historically problematic to the institution, including housing safety, hazing, alcohol and other drug abuse, sexual harassment, racism, intolerance based on religion or sexual orientation, and other practices and attitudes that diminish human dignity or the physical and social security of the host institution or host community.**

- **Professional staff members who assist students to function productively within the institution and to understand fully the rights and responsibilities of individuals and groups.**

  This may include such activities as interpreting institutional policies, administering a disciplinary system that safeguards due process, conducting performance evaluations, and providing outreach programming to familiarize other departments and community agencies with fraternity and sorority life. Staff members should avoid social situations or appearance of preferential treatment that may pose conflicts of interest.

  The program may include awards for academic and service achievement as well as chapter/community monitoring.

- **Enforcement of applicable laws as well as institutional policies with particular attention paid to housing safety, hazing, the use and possession of alcohol and other drugs, sexual harassment, racism, intolerance based on religion or sexual orientation, and other practices and attitudes that diminish human dignity.**

- **Advising chapters, their individual members, their officers, and their alumni regarding leadership roles and responsibilities.**

  Advising services to chapters may include:
  - monitoring scholastic standing of chapter members individually and collectively and recommending programs for scholastic improvement
  - meeting with chapter leaders to discuss individual and chapter goals and developmental needs
  - assisting student members to understand their responsibilities to the group and to the future of the organization
  - attending chapter meetings on a periodic basis
  - encouraging chapter members' attendance at regional and national or international conferences
  - evaluating chapter development and recommending programs for improvement
  - providing assistance and advice in planning chapter programs (e.g., fund raising, fiscal management)

  Advising services for the fraternity and sorority system (e.g., chapter advisors, house corporation members, chapter presidents, institutional administrators) may include:
  - providing workshops, programs, retreats, and seminars on relevant topics (e.g., human relations, sexual responsibility, eating disorders/body image)
  - coordinating information gathering and dissemination

regarding fraternity and sorority life via monthly meetings, newsletters, and/or information bulletins to the various entities involved in fraternity and sorority life
- acquiring resources for and promoting service projects
- advising governing bodies
- providing assistance and advice in the planning of fraternity and sorority community programs (e.g., Fraternity and Sorority Week)
- publishing documents that focus on current events, leadership opportunities, and other information regarding fraternity and sorority life
- developing and distributing a speakers' directory for distribution that focuses on educational programs
- coordinating annual fire prevention and energy conservation programs in conjunction with local agencies for housed organizations
- coordinating cooperative buying efforts in conjunction with local chapters and/or councils
- monitoring of membership statistics and academic retention by chapter and community

Advising services with other agencies may include:
- collaborating with national or international organizations when applicable/appropriate
- establishing and coordinating communication with local alumni volunteers
- serving as an immediate information resource for students, alumni, and administrators

Part 3. LEADERSHIP

Because effective and ethical leadership is essential to the success of all organizations, Fraternity and Sorority Advising Programs (FSAP) leaders with organizational authority for the programs and services must:
- **articulate a vision and mission for their programs and services**
- **set goals and objectives based on the needs of the population served and desired student learning and development outcomes**
- **advocate for their programs and services**
- **promote campus environments that provide meaningful opportunities for student learning, development, and integration**
- **identify and find means to address individual, organizational, or environmental conditions that foster or inhibit mission achievement**
- **advocate for representation in strategic planning initiatives at appropriate divisional and institutional levels**
- **initiate collaborative interactions with stakeholders who have legitimate concerns and interests in the functional area**
- **apply effective practices to educational and administrative processes**
- **prescribe and model ethical behavior**
- **communicate effectively**

- **manage financial resources, including planning, allocation, monitoring, and analysis**
- **incorporate sustainability practices in the management and design of programs, services, and facilities**
- **manage human resource processes including recruitment, selection, development, supervision, performance planning, and evaluation**
- **empower professional, support, and student staff to accept leadership opportunities**
- **encourage and support scholarly contribution to the profession**
- **be informed about and integrate appropriate technologies into programs and services**
- **be knowledgeable about federal, state/provincial, and local laws relevant to the programs and services and ensure that staff members understand their responsibilities by receiving appropriate training**
- **develop and continuously improve programs and services in response to the changing needs of students and other populations served and the evolving institutional priorities**
- **recognize environmental conditions that may negatively influence the safety of staff and students and propose interventions that mitigate such conditions**

Part 4. HUMAN RESOURCES

Fraternity and Sorority Advising Programs (FSAP) must be staffed adequately by individuals qualified to accomplish the mission and goals. Within institutional guidelines, FSAP must establish procedures for staff selection, training, and evaluation; set expectations for supervision; and provide appropriate professional development opportunities to improve the leadership ability, competence, and skills of all employees.

FSAP professional staff members must hold an earned graduate or professional degree in a field relevant to the position they hold or must possess an appropriate combination of educational credentials and related work experience.

Appropriate preparatory graduate level coursework may include organizational behavior and development, oral and written communication, research and evaluation, ethics, appraisal of educational practices, group dynamics, budgeting, counseling techniques, leadership development, learning and human development theories, higher education administration, performance appraisal and supervision, administrative uses of computers, legal issues in higher education, and student affairs functions.

Effective management is critical to the success of the program, with expertise often required in the areas of housing, dining, accounting, safety and risk management, alumni relations, and programming. In addition, professional staff members should have experience in the development and implementation of educational programs for students. Staff members should be qualified to work with various internal and external agencies in formulating goals and directions for the chapters and community that are consistent with institutional policies.

Degree- or credential-seeking interns must be qualified by enrollment in an appropriate field of study and by relevant experience. These individuals must be trained and supervised adequately by professional staff members holding educational credentials and related work experience appropriate for supervision.

Student employees and volunteers must be carefully selected, trained, supervised, and evaluated. They must be educated on how and when to refer those in need of additional assistance to qualified staff members and must have access to a supervisor for assistance in making these judgments. Student employees and volunteers must be provided clear and precise job descriptions, pre-service training based on assessed needs, and continuing staff development.

The use of graduate assistants and interns may be a way to expand staff capabilities and to provide valuable experience for professionals who have an interest in the field of fraternity and sorority advising.

When appropriate, student employees or volunteers may be utilized and assigned responsibilities for specific projects that are administered or coordinated within the program. Students can lend a valuable perspective to educational programming efforts.

Employees and volunteers must receive specific training on institutional policies and privacy laws regarding their access to student records and other sensitive institutional information (e.g., in the USA, Family Educational Rights and Privacy Act, FERPA, or equivalent privacy laws in other states/provinces or countries).

FSAP must have technical and support staff members adequate to accomplish their mission. All members of the staff must be technologically proficient and qualified to perform their job functions, be knowledgeable about ethical and legal uses of technology, and have access to training and resources to support the performance of their assigned responsibilities.

All members of the staff must receive training on policies and procedures related to the use of technology to store or access student records and institutional data.

FSAP must ensure that staff members are knowledgeable about and trained in emergency procedures, crisis response, and prevention efforts. Prevention efforts must address identification of threatening conduct or behavior of students, faculty members, staff, and others and must incorporate a system or procedures for responding, including but not limited to reporting them to the appropriate campus officials.

Salary levels and benefits for all staff members must be commensurate with those for comparable positions within the institution, in similar institutions, and in the relevant geographic area.

FSAP must maintain position descriptions for all staff members.

To create a diverse staff, FSAP must institute hiring and promotion practices that are fair, inclusive, proactive, and non-discriminatory.

FSAP must conduct regular performance planning and evaluation of staff members. FSAP must provide access to continuing and advanced education and professional development opportunities.

FSAP professional staff members must engage in professional development opportunities to keep abreast of research, theories, legislation, policies, and developments that affect fraternity and sorority advising.

These activities may include participation in in-service training programs, professional conferences, workshops, and other continuing education activities.

The level of FSAP services must be established and reviewed regularly with regard to demands, enrollment, user surveys, diversity of services offered, institutional resources, and other services available on the campus and in the local community.

Part 5. ETHICS

Persons involved in the delivery of Fraternity and Sorority Advising Programs (FSAP) must adhere to the highest principles of ethical behavior. FSAP must review relevant professional ethical standards and develop or adopt and implement appropriate statements of ethical practice. FSAP must publish these statements and ensure their periodic review by relevant constituencies.

FSAP must orient new staff members to relevant ethical standards and statements of ethical practice.

FSAP staff members must ensure that privacy and confidentiality are maintained with respect to all communications and records to the extent that such records are protected under the law and appropriate statements of ethical practice. Information contained in students' education records must not be disclosed except as allowed by relevant laws and institutional policies. FSAP staff members must disclose to appropriate authorities information judged to be of an emergency nature, especially when the safety of the individual or others is involved, or when otherwise required by institutional policy or relevant law.

FSAP staff members must be aware of and comply with the provisions contained in the institution's policies pertaining to human subjects research and student rights and responsibilities, as well as those in other relevant institutional policies addressing ethical practices and confidentiality of research data concerning individuals.

FSAP staff members must recognize and avoid personal conflicts of interest or appearance thereof in the performance of their work.

FSAP staff members must strive to insure the fair, objective, and impartial treatment of all persons with whom they interact.

When handling institutional funds, FSAP staff members must ensure that such funds are managed in accordance with established and responsible accounting procedures and the fiscal policies or processes of the institution.

Promotional and descriptive information must be accurate and free of deception.

FSAP staff members must perform their duties within the limits of their training, expertise, and competence. When these limits are exceeded, individuals in need of further assistance must be referred to persons possessing appropriate qualifications.

FSAP staff members must use suitable means to confront and otherwise hold accountable other staff members who exhibit unethical behavior.

FSAP staff members must be knowledgeable about and practice ethical behavior in the use of technology.

FSAP staff members must be familiar with, adhere to, advocate for, and model relevant ethical standards in the field.

FSAP staff members must demonstrate a high level of ethical conduct. The program must adopt a statement of ethics that strives to:
- treat fairly all students who wish to affiliate
- eliminate illegal discrimination associated with the selection of members
- uphold applicable standards of conduct expressed by the institution and by the respective national or international organizations

Part 6. LEGAL RESPONSIBILITIES

Fraternity and Sorority Advising Programs (FSAP) staff members must be knowledgeable about and responsive to laws and regulations that relate to their respective responsibilities and that may pose legal obligations, limitations, or ramifications for the institution as a whole. As appropriate, staff members must inform users of programs and services, as well as officials, of legal obligations and limitations including constitutional, statutory, regulatory, and case law; mandatory laws and orders emanating from federal, state/provincial, and local governments; and the institution's policies.

FSAP must have written policies on all relevant operations, transactions, or tasks that may have legal implications.

FSAP staff members must neither participate in nor condone any form of harassment or activity that demeans persons or creates an intimidating, hostile, or offensive campus environment.

FSAP staff members must use reasonable and informed practices to limit the liability exposure of the institution and its officers, employees, and agents. FSAP staff members must be informed about institutional policies regarding risk management, personal liability, and related insurance coverage options and must be referred to external sources if coverage is not provided by the institution.

The institution must provide access to legal advice for FSAP staff members as needed to carry out assigned responsibilities.

The institution must inform FSAP staff and students in a timely and systematic fashion about extraordinary or changing legal obligations and potential liabilities.

Part 7. EQUITY and ACCESS

Fraternity and Sorority Advising Programs (FSAP) must be provided on a fair, equitable, and non-discriminatory basis in accordance with institutional policies and with all applicable state/provincial and federal statutes and regulations. FSAP must maintain an educational and work environment free from discrimination in accordance with law and institutional policy.

Discrimination must be avoided on the basis of age; cultural heritage; disability; ethnicity; gender identity and expression; nationality; political affiliation; race; religious affiliation; sex; sexual orientation; economic, marital, social, or veteran status; and any other bases included in local, state/provincial, or federal laws.

Consistent with the mission and goals, FSAP must take action to remedy significant imbalances in student participation and staffing patterns.

FSAP must ensure physical and program access for persons with disabilities. FSAP must be responsive to the needs of all students and other populations served when establishing hours of operation and developing methods of delivering programs and services.

FSAP must recognize the needs of distance learning students by providing appropriate and accessible services and assisting them in identifying and gaining access to other appropriate services in their geographic region.

FSAP must advocate for the needs of specific under-represented populations.

Part 8. DIVERSITY

Within the context of each institution's unique mission, diversity enriches the community and enhances the collegiate experience for all; therefore, Fraternity and Sorority Advising Programs (FSAP) must create and nurture environments that are welcoming to and bring together persons of diverse backgrounds.

FSAP must promote environments that are characterized

by open and continuous communication that deepens understanding of one's own identity, culture, and heritage, as well as that of others. FSAP must recognize, honor, educate, and promote respect about commonalties and differences among people within their historical and cultural contexts.

FSAP must address the characteristics and needs of a diverse population when establishing and implementing policies and procedures.

FSAP must enhance students' knowledge, understanding, skills, and responsibilities associated with being a member of a pluralistic society. The program must provide educational efforts that focus on awareness of cultural, religious, sexual orientation, and gender identity differences.

These efforts should also include assessment of possible prejudices and desirable behavioral changes.

FSAP must include outreach to under-represented populations in membership recruitment activities.

Part 9. ORGANIZATION and MANAGEMENT

To promote student learning and development outcomes, Fraternity and Sorority Advising Programs (FSAP) must be structured purposefully and managed effectively to achieve stated goals. Evidence of appropriate structure must include current and accessible policies and procedures, written performance expectations for all employees, functional workflow graphics or organizational charts, and clearly stated program and service delivery expectations.

FSAP must monitor websites used for distributing information to ensure that the sites are current, accurate, appropriately referenced, and accessible.

Evidence of effective management must include use of comprehensive and accurate information for decisions, clear sources and channels of authority, effective communication practices, procedures for decision-making and conflict resolution, responses to changing conditions, systems of accountability and evaluation, and processes for recognition and reward. FSAP must align policies and procedures with those of the institution and provide channels within the organization for their regular review.

FSAP must be organized to encourage positive relationships with students.

The administrative organization of the fraternity and sorority advising program should organized by the size, nature, and mission of the institution. This may include special living arrangements for various levels of affiliation. Fraternities and sororities should be a fully integrated institutional component provided with the necessary resources and support to effect the desired student outcomes. The program should be organized and administered in a manner that permits its stated mission to be fulfilled. The administrative leader of the program should be responsible to the chief student affairs officer or designee.

Part 10. CAMPUS and EXTERNAL RELATIONS

Fraternity and Sorority Advising Programs (FSAP) must reach out to relevant individuals, campus offices, and external agencies to:
- establish, maintain, and promote effective relations
- disseminate information about their own and other related programs and services
- coordinate and collaborate, where appropriate, in offering programs and services to meet the needs of students and promote their achievement of student learning and development outcomes

FSAP must have procedures and guidelines consistent with institutional policy for responding to threats, emergencies, and crisis situations. Systems and procedures must be in place to disseminate timely and accurate information to students and other members of the campus community during emergency situations.

FSAP must have procedures and guidelines consistent with institutional policy for communicating with the media.

FSAP staff members must seek out and utilize multiple learning resource opportunities in the delivery of services and programs. These include the national or international headquarters staff, alumni, chapter officers and members, faculty members, institutional administrators, and community resources.

FSAP must maintain effective contact with its local chapters' national and international representatives.

A team approach in working with students in the local chapters should be a common goal of advisors, alumni, and national or international representatives.

Faculty and staff members are valuable as chapter advisors and role models for students. They may serve on committees that focus on institutional issues affecting the fraternity and sorority community. Further, faculty members can help shape the institutional policy with regard to the fraternity and sorority community. Effective and consistent communications among faculty and staff members, fraternity and sorority chapter members, and chapter advisors can enhance the creation of meaningful learning experiences to improve academic success   and increase understanding of educational goals.

Because alumni can serve as valuable resources, program staff members should encourage and enlist a productive level of alumni involvement and assist with information exchange and collaborative programming efforts.

The staff member is typically the principal representative of the administration to the fraternity and sorority community as well as the principal advocate for the fraternity and sorority community within the administration.

Particularly when houses are located in community neighborhoods, good working relationships with neighbors, merchants, and community leaders must be maintained to promote cooperative solutions to problems that may arise.

Chapter houses may be governed by the local community and have access to its services and agencies.

FSAP must assist students in maintaining responsible community living.

Attention should be paid to issues such as fire safety, noise control, parking, trash removal, security, facility and property maintenance, and life safety and health code compliance.

Philanthropic activities and community volunteer involvement, which have been traditional components of fraternity and sorority programs, should be developed, maintained, and encouraged.

Part 11. FINANCIAL RESOURCES

Fraternity and Sorority Advising Programs (FSAP) must have adequate funding to accomplish their mission and goals. In establishing funding priorities and making significant changes, a comprehensive analysis, which includes relevant expenditures, external and internal resources, and impact on the campus community, must be conducted.

FSAP must demonstrate fiscal responsibility and cost effectiveness consistent with institutional protocols.

When any special institutional or fraternity and sorority funding or expenditure accounts are used, professional staff members should provide for the collection and disbursement of funds and follow the institution's accounting procedures.

Part 12. TECHNOLOGY

Fraternity and Sorority Advising Programs (FSAP) must have adequate technology to support their mission. The technology and its use must comply with institutional policies and procedures and be evaluated for compliance with relevant federal, state/provincial, and local requirements.

FSAP must maintain policies and procedures that address the security and back up of data.

When technology is used to facilitate student learning and development, FSAP must select technology that reflects current best pedagogical practices.

Technology, as well as any workstations or computer labs maintained by the FSAP for student use, must be accessible and must meet established technology standards for delivery to persons with disabilities.

When FSAP provide student access to technology, they must provide:

- **access to policies that are clear, easy to understand, and available to all students**
- **access to instruction or training on how to use the technology**
- **access to information on the legal and ethical implications of misuse as it pertains to intellectual property, harassment, privacy, and social networks.**

Student violations of technology policies must follow established institutional student disciplinary procedures.

Students who experience negative emotional or psychological consequences from the use of technology must be referred to support services provided by the institution.

Part 13. FACILITIES and EQUIPMENT

Fraternity and Sorority Advising Programs (FSAP) must have adequate, accessible, suitably located facilities and equipment to support their mission and goals. If acquiring capital equipment as defined by the institution, FSAP must take into account expenses related to regular maintenance and life cycle costs. Facilities and equipment must be evaluated regularly, including consideration of sustainability, and be in compliance with relevant federal, state/provincial, and local requirements to provide for access, health, safety, and security.

FSAP staff members must have work space that is well-equipped, adequate in size, and designed to support their work and responsibilities. For conversations requiring privacy, staff members must have access to a private space.

FSAP staff members who share work space must have the ability to secure their work adequately.

The design of the facilities must guarantee the security of records and ensure the confidentiality of sensitive information.

The location and layout of the facilities must be sensitive to the special needs of persons with disabilities as well as the needs of constituencies served.

FSAP must ensure that staff members are knowledgeable of and trained in safety and emergency procedures for securing and vacating the facilities.

Contracts with outside vendors must include adherence to ethical and institutional policies.

Houses or common rooms that are owned, rented, or otherwise assigned to fraternities and sororities for their use must be managed in accordance with all applicable regulatory and statutory requirements of the host institution and relevant government authorities.

To effectively carry out essential activities, services, and programs, adequate space should be provided for private consultation, work areas, equipment storage, and resource library. Any space should be accessible and integrated with other institutional student support services.

Part 14. ASSESSMENT and EVALUATION

Fraternity and Sorority Advising Programs (FSAP) must establish systematic plans and processes to meet internal and external accountability expectations with regard to program as well as student learning and development outcomes. FSAP must conduct regular assessment and evaluations. Assessments must include qualitative and

quantitative methodologies as appropriate, to determine whether and to what degree the stated mission, goals, and student learning and development outcomes are being met. The process must employ sufficient and sound measures to ensure comprehensiveness. Data collected must include responses from students and other affected constituencies.

FSAP must evaluate regularly how well they complement and enhance the institution's stated mission and educational effectiveness.

Results of these evaluations must be used in revising and improving programs and services, identifying needs and interests in shaping directions of program and service design, and recognizing staff performance.

FSAP must seek evaluative feedback from relevant administrative units, community agencies, alumni, students, faculty, and national or international headquarters staff. Selected critical aspects of evaluations should be recorded and maintained by the institution.

Evaluations should address the fraternity and sorority community, programs, services, and activities.

Evaluations should be conducted to determine the strength of leadership, the fulfillment of the community's purposes and priorities, the effectiveness of self-governance procedures, individual chapter congruence with institutional and system purposes, the effectiveness of programs, and the availability and stability of resources.

Periodic assessment and evaluation of chapter needs, goals, and objectives should include chapter vitality and evaluation of each chapter's leadership, self-sufficiency, accountability to purpose, and productive activities.

The living environment of each chapter should be assessed including annual or as-needed safety, sanitation, and quality of life inspections of all housing facilities, kitchens, building electrical systems, heating systems, and fire control equipment.

Research also should be a part of the program. Research topics should include:
- how student development is influenced by fraternity or sorority membership
- influence of participation in members' values
- skill development among members at various stages of membership
- the effect of participation in fraternities and sororities on members' academic performance, retention, and matriculation

General Standards revised in 2008;
FSAP content developed/revised in 1986 &1996

The Role of Graduate and Professional Student Programs
CAS Standards Contextual Statement

Historically, research on students and the programs and services designed to support them has focused on the undergraduate experience. In the mid-1990s the higher education community began to recognize the unique needs, challenges and experiences of graduate and professional students — a growing and often underserved population at many colleges and universities. Today, institutions are addressing the academic, personal and professional needs and interests of graduate and professional students in a variety of ways: through a centralized graduate office; through offices reporting to academic departments, schools or colleges; or in collaboration with student other institutional units. The variations in programs and services, organizational structures, and backgrounds of the professional administrators, coupled with the differences in the student populations served (e.g., degrees pursued, academic disciplines), present unique challenges in development of standards and guidelines for graduate and professional student programs and services and underscores the need for these standards.

Since the 1990s, several notable initiatives occurred to address the challenges of graduate and professional students (Brandes, 2007). They include publications such as: the report, "Reshaping the Education of Scientists and Engineers" (Committee on Science, Engineering, and Public Policy, 1995), recommending a more student-centered model of education with attention on diversity and student professional development; and the first major monograph to address services for graduate and professional students, *Student Services for the Changing Graduate Student Population* (Logan and Isaac, 1995). A second monograph, *Supporting Graduate and Professional Students: The Role of Student Affairs* (Guentzel and Nesheim) was published in 2006. Universities such as Harvard, Cornell and Yale, took the lead in the latter half of the 1990s by establishing graduate student centers and appointing student affairs professionals (Brandes, 2007). These new professionals in graduate student affairs provided the vision and impetus for the formation in 1999 of a professional network within the National Association of Student Personnel Administrators (NASPA), which continues today as the Administrators in Graduate and Professional Student Services (AGAPSS). Several years later, the American College Personnel Association (ACPA) established its Commission for Graduate and Professional School Educators (Brandes, 2007).

Among the emerging topics appearing in research studies and publications and at conferences and other gatherings of faculty and higher education administrators are the following:

- recruitment and retention of graduate and professional students, e.g., persistence to degree completion, especially among doctoral students; attrition rates; academic job shortages and decline in students pursuing academic careers,

- students' socialization to a profession and how to best structure and deliver programs, services and experience that involve and engage students and lead to their professional development,

- attitudes that institutions only need to attend to the basic academic experience of graduate and professional students; that graduate students do not require the student services provided to undergraduates or places and opportunities for community building, involvement and social integration,

- the increasingly heterogeneous graduate and professional student population, e.g., more diverse, nontraditional, commuting, part-time, full-time employed students; students with distinct needs pursuing different degrees, i.e., masters, doctoral, professional degrees; groups of students feeling marginalized, e.g., international students,

- how to address the distinct needs of an increasingly heterogeneous graduate and professional student population enrolled in a growing number of masters, doctoral, professional and certificate programs. Today's students are more diverse, multicultural, and nontraditional. Many pursue their degree on a part-time basis while working full-time. And a growing number of students, e.g. international, feel marginalized or minimally engaged with fellow students and faculty,

- lack of research on developmental needs of graduate students and application of developmental theories and recommended practices to this population,

- failure to address mental health, emotional or stress-related problems that are common among graduate and professional students,

- the focus of many divisions of student affairs on the undergraduate experience, resulting in lack of resources to address needs of graduate students,

- the differences and variety of organizational and reporting structures, services offered and locations of offices responsible for provision of services to graduate and professional students,

- the varied knowledge, backgrounds and experiences of professionals responsible for providing services and support to graduate and professional students,

- how to build the professional communities and standards of practice for individuals with primary responsibility for student support services for graduate and professional students.

The growing awareness of the unique needs of graduate and professional students led the authors of ACPA's and NASPA's seminal publication, *Learning Reconsidered: A Campus-Wide Focus on the Student Experience* (2004) to recommend that "Faculty members, student affairs professionals, academic administrators, and representative graduate students should work together to define strategies and resources that will support the comprehensive, holistic learning of graduate students" (p. 29). Other studies and findings, most notably Elkins Nesheim et al., 2007) also suggest that programs for graduate students are often most successful when delivered through partnerships between student affairs and academic affairs professionals.

In order to develop support at their institutions for a comprehensive and holistic approach to graduate student learning and development, members of NASPA's and ACPA's graduate and professional student services communities began discussions about the need for standards and practices to guide and support the development, assessment, and improvement of programs and services. Although CAS had developed separate standards for many of the programs and services that graduate and professional student services administer, e.g., admissions, advising, career services, orientation, etc., trying to apply these multiple standards to graduate and professional student services seemed daunting and difficult. The existing standards tended toward the undergraduate student services; did not take into account the wide-ranging roles and organizational structures of graduate and professional student services or the relationship to academic disciplines; and did not address the varied and specialized needs of graduate and professional students and their experiences.

In April 2007 CAS approved formation of a committee to develop standards for graduate and professional student programs and services. Members of NASPA's AGAPSS and ACPA's Commission for Graduate and Professional School Educators actively participated in the development of these standards and guidelines.

References, Readings, and Resources

American College Personnel Association & National Association of Student Personnel Administrators. (2004). *Learning reconsidered: A campus-wide focus on the student experience*. Washington, D.C.: American College Personnel Association and National Association of Student Personnel Administrators.

American College Student Personnel Association (ACPA) — Commission for Graduate and Professional School Educators, www.myacpa.org/comm/graduate

Brandes, L. C. O. (2007). Recent graduate and professional education issues: A timeline. Prepared for NASPA AGAPSS Preconference workshop at Harvard University, March 2007

Committee on Science, Engineering and Public Policy. (1995). *Reshaping the education of scientists and engineers.* Washington, D.C.: National Academy of Sciences.

Elkins Nesheim, B., Guentzel, M.J., Kellogg. A.H., McDonald, W.M., Wells, C.A., & Whitt, E.J. (2007). Outcomes for student affairs-academic affairs partnership programs. *Journal of College Student Development, 48*(4), 435-454.

Gardner S.K & Barnes, B.J. (2007). Graduate student involvement: Socialization for the professional role. *Journal of College Student Development, 48*(4), 369-387.

Guentzel, M.J. & Nesheim, B.E. (2006). *Supporting graduate and professional students: The role of student affairs: New Directions in Student Services (No.115).* San Francisco: Jossey Bass.

Hesli, V.L., Fink, E.C., & Duffy, D.M. (2003). The role of faculty in creating a positive graduate experience: survey results from the Midwest region, part II. *Political Science and Politics,* 3694), 801-804.

Hyun, J.K., Quinn, B.C., Madon, T., & Lustig, S. (2006). Graduate student mental health: Needs assessment and utilization of counseling services. *Journal of College Student Development,* 47(3), 247-266.

Logan, A.P. & Isaac, P.D. (1995). *Student services for the changing graduate student population: New Directions in Student Services (No.42).* San Francisco: Jossey Bass.

National Association of Student Personnel Administrators (NASPA) — Administrators in Graduate and Professional Student Services (AGAPSS), www.naspa.org/kc/agapss/default.cfm

Polson, C.J. (2003, Summer). Adult graduate student challenge institutions to change. *New Directions for Student Services,* 102, 59-68.

Poock, M.C. (2004, Spring). Graduate student orientation practices: Results from a national survey. *NASPA Journal 41*(3), 470-486

Contributors:

Lisa Brandes, Yale University, NASPA-AGAPSS
Pat Carretta, George Mason University, NACE
Lori Cohen, George Mason University
Eva DeCourcey, George Mason University

Graduate and Professional Student Programs and Services
CAS Standards and Guidelines

Part 1. MISSION

The mission of Graduate and Professional Student Programs and Services (GPSPS) is to promote academic, personal, and professional growth and development of students enrolled in graduate and professional schools. In support of successful degree completion and achievement of other academic goals, GPSPS must ensure student access to programs and services that address students' needs, provide opportunities for involvement and engagement with students, staff, and faculty members, and facilitate community building and social integration across disciplines. Central to this mission is the necessity to connect students with appropriate resources through collaboration with campus partners and experts when services are not centrally provided by a GPSPS office.

GPSPS must develop, disseminate, implement, and regularly review their mission. Mission statements must be consistent with the mission of the institution and with professional standards. GPSPS in higher education must enhance overall educational experiences by incorporating student learning and development outcomes in their mission.

Part 2. PROGRAM

Graduate and Professional Student Programs and Services (GPSPS) must provide programs and services to meet the academic, personal, and professional needs and interests of graduate and professional students, whether organized as a central office; located within an academic department, school, or college; or offered in collaboration with other student and academic affairs offices. GPSPS must use data about their graduate and professional students and their experiences to tailor programs and services for those students.

GPSPS should offer programs that reflect the diversity of their students. Demographics to consider include heterogeneity of students who are seeking degrees, disciplines studied, and the different types of institutions they have previously attended.

The formal education of students, consisting of the curriculum and the co-curriculum, must promote student learning and development outcomes that are purposeful and holistic and that prepare students for satisfying and productive lifestyles, work, and civic participation. The student learning and development outcome domains and their related dimensions are:

- knowledge acquisition, integration, construction, and application
  - Dimensions: understanding knowledge from a range of disciplines; connecting knowledge to other knowledge, ideas, and experiences; constructing knowledge; and relating knowledge to daily life

- cognitive complexity
  - Dimensions: critical thinking; reflective thinking; effective reasoning; and creativity

- intrapersonal development
  - Dimensions: realistic self-appraisal, self-understanding, and self-respect; identity development; commitment to ethics and integrity; and spiritual awareness

- interpersonal competence
  - Dimensions: meaningful relationships; interdependence; collaboration; and effective leadership

- humanitarianism and civic engagement
  - Dimensions: understanding and appreciation of cultural and human differences; social responsibility; global perspective; and sense of civic responsibility

- practical competence
  - Dimensions: pursuing goals; communicating effectively; technical competence; managing personal affairs; managing career development; demonstrating professionalism; maintaining health and wellness; and living a purposeful and satisfying life

[See *The Council for the Advancement of Standards Learning and Developmental Outcomes* statement for examples of outcomes related to these domains and dimensions.]

Consistent with the institutional mission, GPSPS must identify relevant and desirable student learning and development outcomes from among the six domains and related dimensions. When creating opportunities for student learning and development, GPSPS must explore possibilities for collaboration with faculty members and other colleagues.

GPSPS must assess relevant and desirable student learning and development outcomes and provide evidence of their impact on student learning and development. Programs and services must articulate how they contribute to or support students' learning and development in the domains not specifically assessed.

Because of the potential impact on graduate student success, GPSPS must offer programs and services that promote students' continued cognitive, emotional, ethical, and social development.

GPSPS must provide opportunities for students to develop knowledge, skills, professional ethics, and values necessary for entry into and progress through the profession or career for which the graduate or professional degree programs offer preparation.

GPSPS must ensure that students have access to programs and services to assist in navigating the issues and coping with stress often associated with the transition into and progress through graduate or professional education. GPSPS must develop support systems for fostering retention and persistence.

Programs should address changes in lifestyle, relationships, work, and finances, as well as isolation and lack of support networks.

GPSPS should provide resources, services, and support to students who are or who become parents during their graduate program and should ensure that policies do not place an unfair burden on students who are parents.

GPSPS must offer programs and services that promote individual and community responsibility, academic integrity, and ethical practices.

GPSPS must advocate that students involved in research, teaching, or clinical work receive supervision and information, guidelines, and training on appropriate practices and policies.

GPSPS must be:
- integrated into the life of the institution
- intentional and coherent
- guided by theories and knowledge of learning and development
- reflective of developmental and demographic profiles of the student population
- responsive to needs of individuals, diverse and special populations, and relevant constituencies

GPSPS should be especially responsive to the needs of international, multicultural, women, and LGBT students and students with disabilities.

GPSPS must include an admissions function or work closely with admissions staff to:
- ensure timely dissemination of information and materials
- provide equal access for all prospective students interested in and capable of pursuing graduate or professional education at the institution
- work with stakeholders to develop enrollment goals, related strategies, and resources that are needed to reach those goals
- coordinate programs for prospective students that present the realities of graduate education and promote deliberate educational planning

GPSPS must orient students to the academic unit, school/college, institution, and community or work closely with appropriate staff and resources to offer information in formats compatible with multiple constituencies, including residential, commuter, and distance learning students.

GPSPS should coordinate a series of orientation activities and transition services for new students that address the realities, norms, and expectations of graduate education; policies and regulations; resources within the academic department or school/college; and

other campus and community resources beyond the department or school/college that offer programs and services essential or of interest to their students. GPSPS should provide information about student organizations and other formal or informal support groups and opportunities for involvement for all graduate students and especially for underrepresented students. GPSPS should employ the assistance of advanced graduate and professional students in planning and implementing the orientation program.

GPSPS must offer financial aid services or provide access to appropriate staff and resources to:
- provide comprehensive and accurate information for students to make informed decisions on financing their education, managing loans and debt, research and training grants, and other financial matters while in graduate or professional school
- ensure clear and transparent procedures and policies for awarding financial aid
- ensure timeliness of delivery of financial aid offered by the academic department, school/college, or institution

GPSPS must assist students in adjusting to the academic demands of graduate or professional education or provide access to appropriate staff and resources.

GPSPS may:
- provide information about grading and other policies; academic writing and citation style; the pace for learning; and other realities about academic demands and performance in their program of study
- provide professional development programs, resources, or referral to services on studying, test-taking, intellectual property, research methodologies, and research protocol
- arrange or facilitate study or tutor groups
- refer students with disabilities to staff or others who can conduct assessments and arrange accommodations
- discuss and clarify educational, career, and life goals and advise on the selection of appropriate courses and other educational experiences
- provide opportunities to assess appropriateness of academic program choice
- evaluate and monitor student academic progress and the impact on achievement of goals and degree completion
- support or refer students with supervisory, assistantship, or advising issues
- direct students with personal concerns to resources and programs on the campus or in the community
- provide information and referral to programs to improve oral communication and conversation skills
- encourage departments and students to develop strong mentorship programs

GPSPS must offer or provide access to resources that enhance the career and professional development of its students. Program components must be designed for and be reflective of the needs and interests of students.

GPSPS program components should include:
- career counseling or coaching

- information and resources on careers, specializations within fields and professions, further education and training opportunities, and fellowships
- opportunities to explore career options available to those with graduate or professional degrees
- opportunities to gain experience related to the field or profession through internships, practica, summer or part-time jobs, job shadowing, or volunteer work
- job search services
- access to advice and guidance from faculty, peer mentors, alumni, and other professionals
- information and support for travel grants and professional presentations

GPSPS may also encompass:
- academic advising
- academic integrity and student conduct
- counseling and psychological services
- assistance with housing on and off campus
- disability services
- professional development programs in teaching, presentation of research, academic and research integrity, thesis and dissertation preparation, grant writing, ethical conduct, preparing future faculty, diversity training, and related topics
- information and advice on applying for scholarships and fellowships
- disciplinary or interdisciplinary scholarly events
- student organizations, governance support, and leadership development
- social and networking activities and programs
- international student programs and services
- multicultural activities and events
- access to sports events, recreation, and fitness and wellness activities
- community service opportunities
- services and accommodations for students with families including children
- graduation activities
- graduate alumni activities
- post-doctoral training and support services

GPSPS must disseminate relevant information about campus services, programs, and current events in a variety of media and formats.

Access to GPSPS services should be available via the Internet and telephone as well as through other channels of communication appropriate to the institution and community.

GPSPS must facilitate opportunities for community building and multicultural interaction within and across academic units.

GPSPS should offer students opportunities for interaction with faculty and staff members and peers within and outside their fields of study. GPSPS should encourage and support formation of student organizations and activities, multicultural communities, special-interest student organizations, honoraries, mentoring, and leadership programs.

Graduate and professional students should have adequate study, meeting, and lounge spaces that serve as gathering and community building spaces for students from different departments and academic programs. These spaces should encourage and support informal meetings, study groups, quiet study space, student organization activities, and co-curricular programs.

GPSPS should partner with graduate faculty members to offer discipline specific co-curricular programs or collaborate with other departments, faculty members, and staff from related disciplines to offer such programs to a larger population of graduate students.

GPSPS must promote representation of graduate and professional students on all appropriate levels of campus planning, policy-making, budgeting, program delivery, and governance.

GPSPS must advocate for students and empower students to advocate for themselves.

Graduate and professional student advocacy should focus on:
- access to comprehensive academic and student support services and information
- recognition of diverse subgroups within the graduate student population
- availability and equitable distribution of funds in support of student organizations, governance, conference travel, and research
- institutional research and assessment that enhance understanding of the demographic characteristics and special needs of graduate and professional students
- provision of on-campus housing designed for graduate and professional students, including housing for married students, students with domestic partners, older single students, and students with children
- assistance in locating accessible, affordable, and safe off-campus housing
- provision of child care services
- expanded access to libraries, laboratories, and studios as needed days, nights, and weekends throughout the year
- coordination of campus and community transit, parking, and security to access classes, libraries, laboratories, and studios

Part 3. LEADERSHIP

Because effective and ethical leadership is essential to the success of all organizations, leaders with organizational authority for Graduate and Professional Student Programs and Services (GPSPS) must:
- **articulate a vision and mission for their programs and services**
- **set goals and objectives based on the needs of the population served and desired student learning and development outcomes**
- **advocate for their programs and services**
- **promote campus environments that provide meaningful opportunities for student learning, development, and integration**
- **identify and find means to address individual,**

organizational, or environmental conditions that foster or inhibit mission achievement

- advocate for representation in strategic planning initiatives at appropriate divisional and institutional levels
- initiate collaborative interactions with stakeholders who have legitimate concerns and interests in the functional area
- apply effective practices to educational and administrative processes
- prescribe and model ethical behavior
- communicate effectively
- manage financial resources, including planning, allocation, monitoring, and analysis
- incorporate sustainability practices in the management and design of programs, services, and facilities
- manage human resource processes including recruitment, selection, development, supervision, performance planning, and evaluation
- empower professional, support, and student staff to accept leadership opportunities
- encourage and support scholarly contribution to the profession
- be informed about and integrate appropriate technologies into programs and services
- be knowledgeable about federal, state/provincial, and local laws relevant to the programs and services and ensure that staff members understand their responsibilities by receiving appropriate training
- develop and continuously improve programs and services in response to the changing needs of students and other populations served and the evolving institutional priorities
- recognize environmental conditions that may negatively influence the safety of staff and students and propose interventions that mitigate such conditions

GPSPS leaders must collaborate with institutional leaders; academic departments within their college, school, or division; colleagues in other graduate programs at their institution; and with graduate offices, enrollment services, student affairs, academic support services, and alumni affairs for the purpose of developing strategies for connecting students to the larger community and positively affecting graduate student learning and development in and outside the classroom.

Part 4. HUMAN RESOURCES

Graduate and Professional Student Programs and Services (GPSPS) must be staffed adequately by individuals qualified to accomplish the mission and goals. Within institutional guidelines, GPSPS must establish procedures for staff selection, training, and evaluation; set expectations for supervision; and provide appropriate professional development opportunities to improve the leadership ability, competence, and skills of all employees.

GPSPS professional staff members must hold an earned graduate or professional degree in a field relevant to the position they hold or must possess an appropriate combination of educational credentials and related work experience.

GPSPS professional staff should be educated in student/academic services in order to design and implement intentional support and services for graduate and professional students.

Degree- or credential-seeking interns must be qualified by enrollment in an appropriate field of study and by relevant experience. These individuals must be trained and supervised adequately by professional staff members holding educational credentials and related work experience appropriate for supervision.

Student employees and volunteers must be carefully selected, trained, supervised, and evaluated. They must be educated on how and when to refer those in need of additional assistance to qualified staff members and must have access to a supervisor for assistance in making these judgments. Student employees and volunteers must be provided clear and precise job descriptions, pre-service training based on assessed needs, and continuing staff development.

Employees and volunteers must receive specific training on institutional policies and privacy laws regarding their access to student records and other sensitive institutional information (e.g., in the USA, Family Educational Rights and Privacy Act, FERPA, or equivalent privacy laws in other states/provinces or countries).

GPSPS must have technical and support staff members adequate to accomplish their mission. All members of the staff must be technologically proficient and qualified to perform their job functions, be knowledgeable about ethical and legal uses of technology, and have access to training and resources to support the performance of their assigned responsibilities.

All members of the staff must receive training on policies and procedures related to the use of technology to store or access student records and institutional data.

GPSPS must ensure that staff members are knowledgeable about and trained in emergency procedures, crisis response, and prevention efforts. Prevention efforts must address identification of threatening conduct or behavior of students, faculty members, staff, and others and must incorporate a system or procedures for responding, including but not limited to reporting them to the appropriate campus officials.

Salary levels and benefits for all staff members must be commensurate with those for comparable positions within the institution, in similar institutions, and in the relevant geographic area.

GPSPS must maintain position descriptions for all staff members.

To create a diverse staff, GPSPS must institute hiring and promotion practices that are fair, inclusive, proactive, and non-discriminatory.

GPSPS must conduct regular performance planning and evaluation of staff members. GPSPS must provide access to continuing and advanced education and professional development opportunities.

Part 5. ETHICS

Persons involved in the delivery of Graduate and Professional Student Programs and Services (GPSPS) must adhere to the highest principles of ethical behavior. GPSPS must review relevant professional ethical standards and develop or adopt and implement appropriate statements of ethical practice. GPSPS must publish these statements and ensure their periodic review by relevant constituencies.

GPSPS must orient new staff members to relevant ethical standards and statements of ethical practice.

GPSPS staff members must ensure that privacy and confidentiality are maintained with respect to all communications and records to the extent that such records are protected under the law and appropriate statements of ethical practice. Information contained in students' education records must not be disclosed except as allowed by relevant laws and institutional policies. GPSPS staff members must disclose to appropriate authorities information judged to be of an emergency nature, especially when the safety of the individual or others is involved, or when otherwise required by institutional policy or relevant law.

GPSPS staff members must be aware of and comply with the provisions contained in the institution's policies pertaining to human subjects research and student rights and responsibilities, as well as those in other relevant institutional policies addressing ethical practices and confidentiality of research data concerning individuals.

GPSPS staff members must recognize and avoid personal conflicts of interest or appearance thereof in the performance of their work.

GPSPS staff members must strive to insure the fair, objective, and impartial treatment of all persons with whom they interact.

When handling institutional funds, GPSPS staff members must ensure that such funds are managed in accordance with established and responsible accounting procedures and the fiscal policies or processes of the institution.

Promotional and descriptive information must be accurate and free of deception.

GPSPS staff members must perform their duties within the limits of their training, expertise, and competence. When these limits are exceeded, individuals in need of further assistance must be referred to persons possessing appropriate qualifications.

GPSPS staff members must use suitable means to confront and otherwise hold accountable other staff members who exhibit unethical behavior.

GPSPS staff members must be knowledgeable about and practice ethical behavior in the use of technology.

Part 6. LEGAL RESPONSIBILITIES

Graduate and Professional Student Programs and Services (GPSPS) staff members must be knowledgeable about and responsive to laws and regulations that relate to their respective responsibilities and that may pose legal obligations, limitations, or ramifications for the institution as a whole. As appropriate, staff members must inform users of programs and services, as well as officials, of legal obligations and limitations including constitutional, statutory, regulatory, and case law; mandatory laws and orders emanating from federal, state/provincial, and local governments; and the institution's policies.

GPSPS must have written policies on all relevant operations, transactions, or tasks that may have legal implications.

GPSPS staff members must neither participate in nor condone any form of harassment or activity that demeans persons or creates an intimidating, hostile, or offensive campus environment.

GPSPS staff members must use reasonable and informed practices to limit the liability exposure of the institution and its officers, employees, and agents. GPSPS staff members must be informed about institutional policies regarding risk management, personal liability, and related insurance coverage options and must be referred to external sources if coverage is not provided by the institution.

The institution must provide access to legal advice for GPSPS staff members as needed to carry out assigned responsibilities.

The institution must inform GPSPS staff and students in a timely and systematic fashion about extraordinary or changing legal obligations and potential liabilities.

Part 7. EQUITY and ACCESS

Graduate and Professional Student Programs and Services (GPSPS) must be provided on a fair, equitable, and non-discriminatory basis in accordance with institutional policies and with all applicable state/provincial and federal statutes and regulations. GPSPS must maintain an educational and work environment free from discrimination in accordance with law and institutional policy.

Discrimination must be avoided on the basis of age; cultural heritage; disability; ethnicity; gender identity and expression; nationality; political affiliation; race; religious affiliation; sex; sexual orientation; economic, marital, social, or veteran status; and any other bases included in local, state/provincial, or federal laws.

Consistent with the mission and goals, GPSPS must take action to remedy significant imbalances in student participation and staffing patterns.

GPSPS must ensure physical and program access for persons with disabilities. GPSPS must be responsive to the needs of all students and other populations served when establishing hours of operation and developing methods of delivering programs and services.

GPSPS must recognize the needs of distance learning students by providing appropriate and accessible services and assisting them in identifying and gaining access to other appropriate services in their geographic region.

Part 8. DIVERSITY

Within the context of each institution's unique mission, diversity enriches the community and enhances the collegiate experience for all; therefore, Graduate and Professional Student Programs and Services (GPSPS) must create and nurture environments that are welcoming to and bring together persons of diverse backgrounds.

GPSPS must promote environments that are characterized by open and continuous communication that deepens understanding of one's own identity, culture, and heritage, as well as that of others. GPSPS must recognize, honor, educate, and promote respect about commonalties and differences among people within their historical and cultural contexts.

GPSPS must address the characteristics and needs of a diverse population when establishing and implementing policies and procedures.

Part 9. ORGANIZATION and MANAGEMENT

To promote student learning and development outcomes, Graduate and Professional Student Programs and Services (GPSPS) must be structured purposefully and managed effectively to achieve stated goals. Evidence of appropriate structure must include current and accessible policies and procedures, written performance expectations for all employees, functional workflow graphics or organizational charts, and clearly stated program and service delivery expectations.

Staffing and reporting structures of GPSPS may vary. Whatever the structure, GPSPS should develop collaborative mechanisms, working groups, or relationships to coordinate their work to benefit all graduate and professional students.

GPSPS must monitor websites used for distributing information to ensure that the sites are current, accurate, appropriately referenced, and accessible.

Evidence of effective management must include use of comprehensive and accurate information for decisions, clear sources and channels of authority, effective communication practices, procedures for decision-making and conflict resolution, responses to changing conditions, systems of accountability and evaluation, and processes for recognition and reward. GPSPS must align policies and procedures with those of the institution and provide channels within the organization for their regular review.

Part 10. CAMPUS and EXTERNAL RELATIONS

Graduate and Professional Student Programs and Services (GPSPS) must reach out to relevant individuals, campus offices, and external agencies to:
- establish, maintain, and promote effective relations
- disseminate information about their own and other related programs and services
- coordinate and collaborate, where appropriate, in offering programs and services to meet the needs of students and promote their achievement of student learning and development outcomes

The staff of GPSPS must work collaboratively with colleagues in other graduate programs at their institution and with departments including but not limited to graduate offices, enrollment services, international student services, student affairs, academic support services, research and grants offices, development, and alumni affairs.

GPSPS must have procedures and guidelines consistent with institutional policy for responding to threats, emergencies, and crisis situations. Systems and procedures must be in place to disseminate timely and accurate information to students and other members of the campus community during emergency situations.

GPSPS must have procedures and guidelines consistent with institutional policy for communicating with the media.

Part 11. FINANCIAL RESOURCES

Graduate and Professional Student Programs and Services (GPSPS) must have adequate funding to accomplish their mission and goals. In establishing funding priorities and making significant changes, a comprehensive analysis, which includes relevant expenditures, external and internal resources, and impact on the campus community, must be conducted.

GPSPS must demonstrate fiscal responsibility and cost effectiveness consistent with institutional protocols.

Part 12. TECHNOLOGY

Graduate and Professional Student Programs and Services (GPSPS) must have adequate technology to support their mission. The technology and its use must comply with institutional policies and procedures and be evaluated for compliance with relevant federal, state/provincial, and local requirements.

GPSPS must maintain policies and procedures that address the security and back up of data.

When technology is used to facilitate student learning and development, GPSPS must select technology that reflects current best pedagogical practices.

Technology, as well as any workstations or computer labs maintained by the GPSPS for student use, must be accessible and must meet established technology standards for delivery to persons with disabilities.

When GPSPS provide student access to technology, they must provide:

- access to policies that are clear, easy to understand, and available to all students
- access to instruction or training on how to use the technology
- access to information on the legal and ethical implications of misuse as it pertains to intellectual property, harassment, privacy, and social networks

Student violations of technology policies must follow established institutional student disciplinary procedures.

Students who experience negative emotional or psychological consequences from the use of technology must be referred to support services provided by the institution.

Part 13. FACILITIES and EQUIPMENT

Graduate and Professional Student Programs and Services (GPSPS) must have adequate, accessible, suitably located facilities and equipment to support their mission and goals. If acquiring capital equipment as defined by the institution, GPSPS must take into account expenses related to regular maintenance and life cycle costs. Facilities and equipment must be evaluated regularly, including consideration of sustainability, and be in compliance with relevant federal, state/provincial, and local requirements to provide for access, health, safety, and security.

GPSPS staff members must have work space that is well-equipped, adequate in size, and designed to support their work and responsibilities. For conversations requiring privacy, staff members must have access to a private space.

GPSPS staff members who share work space must have the ability to secure their work adequately.

GPSPS should advocate for adequate office and work space for research and teaching assistants located where meaningful interactions with students, faculty members, and staff members may take place.

GPSPS should ensure that graduate and professional students have adequate spaces for study groups; for socializing and networking with peers, faculty and staff members; and for holding co-curricular programs and events. These spaces should be for the specific use by graduate and professional students.

GPSPS should provide space for graduate student organizations and governance councils.

The design of the facilities must guarantee the security of records and ensure the confidentiality of sensitive information.

The location and layout of the facilities must be sensitive to the special needs of persons with disabilities as well as the needs of constituencies served.

GPSPS must ensure that staff members are knowledgeable of and trained in safety and emergency procedures for securing and vacating the facilities.

Part 14. ASSESSMENT and EVALUATION

Graduate and Professional Student Programs and Services (GPSPS) must establish systematic plans and processes to meet internal and external accountability expectations with regard to program as well as student learning and development outcomes. GPSPS must conduct regular assessment and evaluations.

These should include assessment of:

- demographics and characteristics of the students
- student needs, experiences, and learning outcomes
- overall use of and satisfaction with programs and services
- attrition and persistence rates, such as time to degree completion and reasons for leaving prior to completion
- post-graduation career plans and outcomes
- adherence to national standards
- certification and licensing examination passing rates
- overall satisfaction with services and environment

Assessments must include qualitative and quantitative methodologies as appropriate, to determine whether and to what degree the stated mission, goals, and student learning and development outcomes are being met. The process must employ sufficient and sound measures to ensure comprehensiveness. Data collected must include responses from students and other affected constituencies.

GPSPS must evaluate regularly how well they complement and enhance the institution's stated mission and educational effectiveness.

Results of these evaluations must be used in revising and improving programs and services, identifying needs and interests in shaping directions of program and service design, and recognizing staff performance.

General Standards revised in 2008;
GPSPS content developed in 2008

The Role of Health Promotion Services
CAS Standards Contextual Statement

Student learning is both the core goal and the primary outcome of the work of higher education. Health promotion services, sometimes called wellness services, are directed towards the student population and serves the learning mission of the institution by enhancing students' capability to be effective, engaged learners; by creating supportive living-learning environments; and by advocating for more socially just campus communities in which students, faculty, and staff, regardless of identity or background, are given equitable access to available opportunities. Professionals from many different disciplines and departments work to enhance health and reduce risk at the community, campus, and individual levels. Professional health educators; staff from residence life, student activities, campus recreation, orientation and other student affairs departments; nurses, physicians, and counselors; as well as other interested students, faculty, and staff, often lead or collaborate on health promotion and wellness initiatives. Together, they build environments and establish policies that promote normal sleep hygiene, reduce alcohol misuse and abuse, enhance safety and community, support regular exercise, and reduce unnecessary stressors, which are increasingly viewed as campus-wide concerns that affect the productivity of faculty and staff, as well as student success, retention, and academic progress

To better understand the functional area of health promotion services on a higher education campus, three definitions are essential: learning, health, and wellness.

1. LEARNING. Learning is defined in the document *Learning Reconsidered* as a comprehensive, holistic, transformative activity that integrates academic learning and student development, processes that have often been considered separate and even independent of each other (ACPA/NASPA, 2006).). The correlation between learning and health has been documented. Graduation from high school is associated with an increase in average lifespan of six to nine years (Wong, et al., 2002). Less is understood about the effects of health on learning.
2. HEALTH. In 1948, in its constitution, the World Health Organization (WHO) defined health as "a state of complete physical, mental and social well-being and not merely the absence of disease or infirmity." In more recent years, this statement has been modified to include the ability to lead a "socially and economically productive life." From a population health perspective, health has been defined not simply as a state free from disease but as "the capacity of people to adapt to,

respond to, or control life's challenges and changes." (Frankish, et al., 1996). Health may be found in capacity -- the ability to love, to work, to know yourself, and to be, in some way, centered - whether or not you have a chronic illness (Keeling, 1995).

3. WELLNESS. Wellness is defined as a multi-dimensional model for the understanding of and approach to health that goes beyond the absence of disease or infirmity and includes the integration of social, mental, emotional, spiritual, and physical aspects of health. The concept of wellness was first introduced in the United States in the 1970s as an expanding experience of purposeful and enjoyable living. Wellness refers to a positive state, illness to a negative state (Modeste, 1996). In some circles, wellness is used as a synonym for health.

Each of these concepts -- learning, health, and wellness -- are critical to the work of health promotion. In addition to definitions, it is critical to understand the diverse models and theoretical structures that drive health promotion and wellness services. The socio-ecological, public health, and community development models are all important to this functional area.

In 1996, the American College Health Association (ACHA) appointed the Task Force on Health Promotion in Higher Education to study the scope and practice of health promotion for students in colleges and universities (Zimmer, Hill, & Sonnad, 2003). In 2006, the *Journal of American College Health* published *Standards of Practice for Health Promotion in Higher Education* to guide daily efforts, facilitate the assessment of individual skills and capacities, and assist in decisions to improve practice through professional development, and also to delineate a set of indicators to evaluate comprehensive health promotion programs and guide accreditation of those programs (Allen, et al., 2006). The standards are guided by several premises about the mission and scope of practice of health promotion or wellness services in higher education as well as about health itself.

These premises include the following:

1. Health, in the broadest sense, encompasses the capacity of individuals and communities to reach their full potential; transcends individual factors; and includes cultural, institutional, socioeconomic, environmental and political influences. This definition challenges the prevailing societal view that health is solely a biomedical quality measured through clinical

indicators which are divorced from context and the built environment.

2. The mission of health promotion services in higher education is not only to foster wellness focused campus communities by empowering individuals to reach their full potential and taking responsibility for themselves and others, but also to advance the health of students and to contribute to the creation of healthy and socially just learning environment . Thus, the professionals working in these services create opportunities, programs, and policies to help students and communities reduce risk for illness and injury, enhance health as a strategy to support student learning, and advocate for safety, social justice, economic opportunity, and human dignity.

3. Health and social justice are inextricably connected; therefore, these services strive to identify and address the complex social, cultural, economic, and political factors that may contribute to or compromise the health of individuals or communities; advocate for inclusive and equitable access to resources and services; and eliminate health disparities and increase the quality and years of healthy life for all.

4. The scope of practice of health promotion on college campuses includes both individual and environmental approaches. Thus, professionals develop and implement initiatives, services, programs and policies to reduce the risk of individual illness and injury, as well as build individual capacity, and address larger institutional issues, community factors, and public policies that shape health-related decisions.

Health promotion as wellness, health enhancement, risk reduction, employee productivity, and prevention of illness and injury serves as a natural ally to the achievement of the academic mission of higher education. Physical facility, policy, tradition, the demographics of the student body, the geography of the surrounding community, and the employees as faculty or staff are some of the variables that contribute to environment of an institution of higher education. Environmental factors are ascending as a focus of effective intervention. Many institutions use a purposeful employee wellness program as the environmental foundation for establishing an environment that values both productivity and the health of the individuals as well as the institution. Health promotion services in colleges and universities support the academic mission by engaging students, faculty, and staff in leading healthier lives and building supportive and sustainable environments, so that health can advance the capacity to learn and work.

Health promotion services are defined as primary or universal prevention and wellness policies or initiatives designed to enhance student learning, employee productivity, and the overall learning environment.

References, Readings, and Resources

Allen, N., Fabiano, P., Hong, L., Kennedy, S., Kenzig, M., Kodama, C., Swinford, P. L., & Zimmer, C. (2007). Introduction to the American College Health Association's "Standards of practice for health promotion in higher education." *Journal of American College Health, 55*(6), 374-379.

American College Health Association. (2005). *Vision into action: tools for professional and program development.* Based on the Standards of Practice for Health Promotion in Higher Education. Baltimore: Author.

American College Health Association-National College Health Assessment (ACHA-NCHA) Spring 2007 Reference Group Data Report (Abridged). *Journal of American College Health, 56*(5), 469-480.

American College Health Association [ACHA]. ACHA National Office, P.O. Box 28937. Baltimore, MD 21240-8937. (410) 859-1500; Fax (410) 859-1510. www.acha.org

American College Personnel Association and National Association of Student Personnel Administrators. (2006). *Learning reconsidered 2: A practical guide to implementing a campus-wide focus on the student experience.* Washington, DC: ACPA and NASPA.

Frankish, C. J., Green, L. W., Ratner, P. A., Chomik, T., & Larsen, C.. (1996). *Health impact assessment as a tool for population health promotion and public policy.* Vancouver: Institute of Health Promotion Research, University of British Columbia.

Glantz, K., Lewis, F. M., & Rimer, B. K. (Eds.). (1997). *Health behavior and health education: Theory, research, and practice* (2nd ed.). San Francisco: Jossey-Bass.

Green L. W., & Kreuter, M. W. (1999). *Health promotion planning: An educational and ecological approach* (3rd ed). Boston: Mayfield Publishing Company.

Keeling, R. P. (1995). *The search for sexual health.* Article based on his keynote address at American Social Health Association, Canadian HELP Group Conference in June 1995. Available online at http://www.herpes.com/sexualHealth.html

Miller, W. R., & Rollnick, S. (2002). *Motivational interviewing: Preparing people for change.* New York: The Guilford Press.

Modeste, N. (1996). *Dictionary of public health promotion and education: Terms and concepts.* Thousand Oaks, CA: Sage Publications.

National Association of Student Personnel Administrators and American College Health Association. (2004). *Leadership for a healthy campus: An ecological approach to student success.* Washington, DC: Author.

National Association of Student Personnel Administrators [NASPA]. NASPA National Office, 1875 Connecticut Ave., N.W., Suite 418. Washington, DC 20009. (202) 265-7500. www.naspa. org

National Commission for Health Education Credentialing, 1541 Alta Drive, Suite 303, Whitehall, PA 18052-5642. (888) 624-3248. www.nchec.org

National Research Council. (Bransford, J., Brown, A., & Cocking, R., Eds.) (2000). *How people learn: Brain, mind experience and school: Expanded edition.* Washington, DC: National Academy Press.

Prochaska, J., Norcross, J., & DiClemente, C. (1994). *Changing for good: The revolutionary program that explains the six stages of change and teaches you how to free yourself from bad habits.* New York: Avon Books.

Silverman, D., Underhile, R., & Keeling, R. (2008). Student health reconsidered: A radical proposal for thinking differently about health-related programs and services for students. *Student Health Spectrum,* June 2008, 4-11.

Student Health Spectrum. (November 2005). *Health education and health promotion: Primary prevention and student health,* S. C. Caulfield (Ed.). Cambridge, MA: The Chickering Group.

Swinford, P. (2002). Advancing the health of students: A rationale for college health programs, *Journal of American College Health, 50*(6), 309-312.

Task Force of the National Advisory Council on Alcohol Abuse and Alcoholism. (2002). *A call to action: Changing the culture of drinking at US colleges.* Washington, DC: National Institutes of Health, US Department of Health and Human Services. Available at www.collegedrinkingprevention.gov.

U.S. Department of Human Services. (2000). *Healthy People 2010, 2nd ed.: Understanding and improving health & objectives for improving health* (Vols. 1-2). Washington, DC: U.S. Government Printing Office.

Wong, M., Shapiro, M., Boscardin, W., & Ettner, S. (2002). Contribution of major disease to disparities in mortality. *New England Journal of Medicine* (347), 1585-1592.

WHO. Constitution of the World Health Organization, Geneva, 1946. Retrieved May 20, 2009, from http://www.who.int/governance/eb/who_constitution_en.pdf

Zimmer, C. G., Hill, M. H., & Sonnad, S. R. (2003). A scope-of-practice survey leading to the development of standards of practice for health promotion in higher education. *Journal of American College Health, 51(6),* 247-54.

Zimmer, C. G. (2002). Health promotion in higher education. In S. Turner & J. Hurley (Eds.), *The history and practice of college health.* Lexington, KY: The University Press of Kentucky, 311-327.

Contributors:

Patricia Fabiano, Western Washington University
Susan Kennedy, Pennsylvania State University
Nancy Allen, Michigan State University
Daisye Orr, Washington State Public Health Department
Paula Swinford, University of Southern California, ACHA
Dixie Bennett, Loyola University Chicago, NIRSA
Cathy Kodoma, University of California at Berkeley
Luoluo Hong, Arizona State University
Gina Baral Abrams, Princeton University

Health Promotion Services
CAS Standards and Guidelines

Part 1. MISSION

The mission and scope of practice of health promotion, sometimes referred to as wellness, must be reflective of the following fundamental assumptions about the role of health in higher education:

- there is a reciprocal relationship between learning and health, as well as a direct connection between the academic mission of higher education and the well-being of students
- in the broadest sense, health encompasses the capacity of individuals and communities to reach their potential
- health transcends individual factors and includes cultural, institutional, socioeconomic, and political influences
- health is not solely a biomedical quality measured through clinical indicators
- health and social justice are inextricably connected
- both individual and environmental approaches to health are critical

Health Promotion Services (HPS) must develop, disseminate, implement, and regularly review their mission. Mission statements must be consistent with the mission of the institution and with professional standards. HPS in higher education must enhance overall educational experiences by incorporating student learning and development outcomes in their mission.

Part 2. PROGRAM

The formal education of students, consisting of the curriculum and the co-curriculum, must promote student learning and development outcomes that are purposeful and holistic and that prepare students for satisfying and productive lifestyles, work, and civic participation. The student learning and development outcome domains and their related dimensions are:

- knowledge acquisition, integration, construction, and application
    o Dimensions: understanding knowledge from a range of disciplines; connecting knowledge to other knowledge, ideas, and experiences; constructing knowledge; and relating knowledge to daily life

- cognitive complexity
    o Dimensions: critical thinking; reflective thinking; effective reasoning; and creativity

- intrapersonal development
    o Dimensions: realistic self-appraisal, self-understanding, and self-respect; identity development; commitment to ethics and integrity; and spiritual awareness

- interpersonal competence
    o Dimensions: meaningful relationships; interdependence; collaboration; and effective leadership

- humanitarianism and civic engagement
    o Dimensions: understanding and appreciation of cultural and human differences; social responsibility; global perspective; and sense of civic responsibility

- practical competence
    o Dimensions: pursuing goals; communicating effectively; technical competence; managing personal affairs; managing career development; demonstrating professionalism; maintaining health and wellness; and living a purposeful and satisfying life

[See *The Council for the Advancement of Standards Learning and Developmental Outcomes* statement for examples of outcomes related to these domains and dimensions.]

Consistent with the institutional mission, Health Promotion Services (HPS) must identify relevant and desirable student learning and development outcomes from among the six domains and related dimensions. When creating opportunities for student learning and development, HPS must explore possibilities for collaboration with faculty members and other colleagues.

HPS must assess relevant and desirable student learning and development outcomes and provide evidence of their impact on student learning and development. HPS must articulate how they contribute to or support students' learning and development in the domains not specifically assessed.

HPS must be:
- integrated into the life of the institution
- intentional and coherent
- guided by theories and knowledge of learning and development
- reflective of developmental and demographic profiles of the student population
- responsive to needs of individuals, diverse and special populations, and relevant constituencies

HPS must advance the health of students and contribute to the creation an institutional and community climate of health and social justice.

HPS must review health promotion research and theories from interdisciplinary sources as a guide for the development of initiatives.

HPS must articulate the theoretical frameworks used in setting priorities and decision-making to the campus community.

HPS must apply professionally recognized constructs, tested

theories, and evidence based strategies to the development of initiatives designed to improve the health of individuals and the campus environment.

HPS must involve students, faculty members, staff members, and community constituents to advance the health of students and to create campus and community environments that support students' health.

HPS professionals should strive to reduce risk, incidence, and severity for individual mental and physical distress, illness and injury; enhance health as a strategy to support student learning; and advocate for safety, social justice, economic opportunity, and human dignity.

HPS must acknowledge that health and social justice are inextricably connected.

HPS professionals should strive to identify and address the complex social, cultural, economic, and political factors that may contribute to or compromise the health of individuals or communities; advocate for inclusive and equal access to resources and services; and eliminate health disparities and increase the quality and years of healthy life for all.

HPS must include both individual and environmental prevention strategies.

HPS professionals should strive to reduce the risk of individual illness and injury, as well as build individual capacity and address larger institutional issues, priority health issues, community factors, and public policies that affect the health of students.

HPS professionals must advance the connection between the academic mission of higher education and the well-being of students.

HPS professionals should support the academic mission of student learning by assisting students in leading healthier lives and engaging individuals who will become political, social, and economic decision makers, thereby advancing the collective health of the community.

Part 3. LEADERSHIP

Because effective and ethical leadership is essential to the success of all organizations, Health Promotion Services (HPS) leaders with organizational authority for the programs and services must:

- **articulate a vision and mission for their programs and services**
- **set goals and objectives based on the needs of the population served and desired student learning and development outcomes**
- **advocate for their programs and services**
- **promote campus environments that provide meaningful opportunities for student learning, development, and integration**
- **identify and find means to address individual, organizational, or environmental conditions that foster or inhibit mission achievement**
- **advocate for representation in strategic planning**

initiatives at appropriate divisional and institutional levels
- **initiate collaborative interactions with stakeholders who have legitimate concerns and interests in the functional area**
- **apply effective practices to educational and administrative processes**
- **prescribe and model ethical behavior**
- **communicate effectively**
- **manage financial resources, including planning, allocation, monitoring, and analysis**
- **incorporate sustainability practices in the management and design of programs, services, and facilities**
- **manage human resource processes including recruitment, selection, development, supervision, performance planning, and evaluation**
- **empower professional, support, and student staff to accept leadership opportunities**
- **encourage and support scholarly contribution to the profession**
- **be informed about and integrate appropriate technologies into programs and services**
- **be knowledgeable about federal, state/provincial, and local laws relevant to the programs and services and ensure that staff members understand their responsibilities by receiving appropriate training**
- **develop and continuously improve programs and services in response to the changing needs of students and other populations served and the evolving institutional priorities**
- **recognize environmental conditions that may negatively influence the safety of staff and students and propose interventions that mitigate such conditions**

Leaders of HPS must also:
- **develop health-related programs and policies that support student learning**
- **gather relevant data and review current literature**
- **develop strategic, operational, and resource utilization plans and policies**

Leaders of HPS should advocate for campus-wide understanding of the connections between learning, culture, identity, social justice, and health.

Leaders of HPS should support others in strengthening their health promotion skills.

Part 4. HUMAN RESOURCES

Health Promotion Services (HPS) must be staffed adequately by individuals qualified to accomplish the mission and goals. Within institutional guidelines, HPS must establish procedures for staff selection, training, and evaluation; set expectations for supervision; and provide appropriate professional development opportunities to improve the leadership ability, competence, and skills of all employees.

HPS should encourage professional staff members to participate in regular self-reflection, assessment, and professional development planning to improve health promotion practice.

HPS should provide personnel with convenient access to on-line and other reference services that include materials pertinent to the operational, administrative, institutional, and research services offered by the institution.

HPS professional staff members must hold an earned graduate or professional degree in a field relevant to the position they hold or must possess an appropriate combination of educational credentials and related work experience.

Professional staff members should have appropriate professional preparation and competencies in both theory and evidence-based practice for promoting health, advancing student learning, and contributing to student development.

The director of HPS should have an advanced degree in health education, public health, higher education administration, or other related discipline from an accredited institution.

The preferred qualification for HPS staff members should be an advanced degree from an accredited institution in a relevant discipline such as health education, public health, higher education administration, counseling, or community development with experience in higher education.

HPS staffing requirements must be established and reviewed regularly with regard to size of campus, institutional resources, student needs, and interdisciplinary health promotion collaborations on campus.

Degree- or credential-seeking interns must be qualified by enrollment in an appropriate field of study and by relevant experience. These individuals must be trained and supervised adequately by professional staff members holding educational credentials and related work experience appropriate for supervision.

Student employees and volunteers must be carefully selected, trained, supervised, and evaluated. They must be educated on how and when to refer those in need of additional assistance to qualified staff members and must have access to a supervisor for assistance in making these judgments. Student employees and volunteers must be provided clear and precise job descriptions, pre-service training based on assessed needs, and continuing staff development.

Employees and volunteers must receive specific training on institutional policies and privacy laws regarding their access to student records and other sensitive institutional information (e.g., in the USA, Family Educational Rights and Privacy Act, FERPA, or equivalent privacy laws in other states/provinces or countries).

HPS staff members must participate in training sessions and professional development that address gender, sexual orientation, racial, cultural, religious and/or spiritual, and ethnic sensitivity.

HPS staff members should be encouraged to demonstrate their commitment to these issues that affect individuals, the campus, and the community by participating in relevant events.

HPS staff members must demonstrate trust when dealing sensitive information and a strict regard for confidentiality.

HPS must have technical and support staff members adequate to accomplish their mission. All members of the staff must be technologically proficient and qualified to perform their job functions, be knowledgeable about ethical and legal uses of technology, and have access to training and resources to support the performance of their assigned responsibilities.

All members of the staff must receive training on policies and procedures related to the use of technology to store or access student records and institutional data.

HPS must ensure that staff members are knowledgeable about and trained in emergency procedures, crisis response, and prevention efforts. Prevention efforts must address identification of threatening conduct or behavior of students, faculty members, staff, and others and must incorporate a system or procedures for responding, including but not limited to reporting them to the appropriate campus officials.

Salary levels and benefits for all staff members must be commensurate with those for comparable positions within the institution, in similar institutions, and in the relevant geographic area.

HPS must maintain position descriptions for all staff members.

To create a diverse staff, HPS must institute hiring and promotion practices that are fair, inclusive, proactive, and non-discriminatory.

HPS must conduct regular performance planning and evaluation of staff members. HPS must provide access to continuing and advanced education and professional development opportunities.

Specific aspects of professional development should include theories of health promotion, student learning, and student development; assessment and evaluation; service delivery; coalition building; collaboration; and business and financial management.

HPS should maintain and financially support an in-service and staff development program, and budgetary support should be available to provide for in-service and professional development activities.

Part 5. ETHICS

Persons involved in the delivery of Health Promotion Services (HPS) must adhere to the highest principles of ethical behavior. HPS must review relevant professional ethical standards and develop or adopt and implement appropriate statements of ethical practice. HPS must publish these statements and ensure their periodic review by relevant constituencies.

HPS must orient new staff members to relevant ethical standards and statements of ethical practice.

HPS staff members must ensure that privacy and confidentiality are maintained with respect to all communications and records to the extent that such records are protected under the law and appropriate statements of ethical practice. Information contained in students' education records must not be disclosed except as allowed by relevant laws and institutional policies. HPS staff members must disclose to appropriate authorities information judged to be of an emergency nature, especially when the safety of the individual or others is involved, or when otherwise required by institutional policy or relevant law.

HPS staff members must be aware of and comply with the provisions contained in the institution's policies pertaining to human subjects research and student rights and responsibilities, as well as those in other relevant institutional policies addressing ethical practices and confidentiality of research data concerning individuals.

HPS staff members must recognize and avoid personal conflicts of interest or appearance thereof in the performance of their work.

HPS staff members must strive to insure the fair, objective, and impartial treatment of all persons with whom they interact.

When handling institutional funds, HPS staff members must ensure that such funds are managed in accordance with established and responsible accounting procedures and the fiscal policies or processes of the institution.

Promotional and descriptive information must be accurate and free of deception.

HPS staff members must perform their duties within the limits of their training, expertise, and competence. When these limits are exceeded, individuals in need of further assistance must be referred to persons possessing appropriate qualifications.

HPS staff members must use suitable means to confront and otherwise hold accountable other staff members who exhibit unethical behavior.

HPS staff members must be knowledgeable about and practice ethical behavior in the use of technology.

Part 6. LEGAL RESPONSIBILITIES

Health Promotion Services (HPS) staff members must be knowledgeable about and responsive to laws and regulations that relate to their respective responsibilities and that may pose legal obligations, limitations, or ramifications for the institution as a whole. As appropriate, staff members must inform users of programs and services, as well as officials, of legal obligations and limitations including constitutional, statutory, regulatory, and case law; mandatory laws and orders emanating from federal, state/provincial, and local governments; and the institution's policies.

HPS must have written policies on all relevant operations, transactions, or tasks that may have legal implications.

HPS staff members must neither participate in nor condone any form of harassment or activity that demeans persons or creates an intimidating, hostile, or offensive campus environment.

HPS staff members must use reasonable and informed practices to limit the liability exposure of the institution and its officers, employees, and agents. HPS staff members must be informed about institutional policies regarding risk management, personal liability, and related insurance coverage options and must be referred to external sources if coverage is not provided by the institution.

The institution must provide access to legal advice for HPS staff members as needed to carry out assigned responsibilities.

The institution must inform HPS staff and students in a timely and systematic fashion about extraordinary or changing legal obligations and potential liabilities.

Part 7. EQUITY and ACCESS

Health Promotion Services (HPS) must be provided on a fair, equitable, and non-discriminatory basis in accordance with institutional policies and with all applicable state/provincial and federal statutes and regulations. HPS must maintain an educational and work environment free from discrimination in accordance with law and institutional policy.

Discrimination must be avoided on the basis of age; cultural heritage; disability; ethnicity; gender identity and expression; nationality; political affiliation; race; religious affiliation; sex; sexual orientation; economic, marital, social, or veteran status; and any other bases included in local, state/provincial, or federal laws.

Consistent with the mission and goals, HPS must take action to remedy significant imbalances in student participation and staffing patterns.

HPS must ensure physical and program access for persons with disabilities. HSP must be responsive to the needs of all students and other populations served when establishing hours of operation and developing methods of delivering programs and services.

HSP must recognize the needs of distance learning students by providing appropriate and accessible services and assisting them in identifying and gaining access to other appropriate services in their geographic region.

HPS should help identify any social, cultural, political, and economic disparities that influence the health of students so that any disparities may be adequately addressed to improve equity and access to health-related services.

Part 8. DIVERSITY

Within the context of each institution's unique mission, diversity enriches the community and enhances the collegiate experience for all; therefore, Health Promotion Services (HPS) must create and nurture environments that are welcoming to and bring together persons of diverse backgrounds.

HPS must promote environments that are characterized by open and continuous communication that deepens understanding of one's own identity, culture, and heritage, as well as that of others. HPS must recognize, honor, educate, and promote respect about commonalties and differences among people within their historical and cultural contexts.

HPS must address the characteristics and needs of a diverse population when establishing and implementing policies and procedures.

HPS staff members must demonstrate cultural competency and inclusiveness in advancing the health of individuals and communities.

HPS should identify the social, cultural, and economic disparities that influence the health of students.

HPS should design health promotion initiatives that reflect the social, cultural, and economic diversity of students.

HPS should create health promotion mission statements, program policies, staff member recruitment and retention practices, and professional development goals that reflect the social, cultural, and economic diversity of the campus.

HPS should provide leadership for campus-wide understanding of the connection between culture, identity, social justice, and health status.

Part 9. ORGANIZATION and MANAGEMENT

To promote student learning and development outcomes, Health Promotion Services (HPS) must be structured purposefully and managed effectively to achieve stated goals. Evidence of appropriate structure must include current and accessible policies and procedures, written performance expectations for all employees, functional workflow graphics or organizational charts, and clearly stated program and service delivery expectations.

HPS must monitor websites used for distributing information to ensure that the sites are current, accurate, appropriately referenced, and accessible.

Evidence of effective management must include use of comprehensive and accurate information for decisions, clear sources and channels of authority, effective communication practices, procedures for decision-making and conflict resolution, responses to changing conditions, systems of accountability and evaluation, and processes for recognition and reward. HPS must align policies and procedures with those of the institution and provide channels within the organization for their regular review.

The HPS director must be placed within the institution's organizational structures so as to be able to promote cooperative interaction with appropriate campus and community entities and to develop the support of high-level administrators for the creation of safe and healthy campus environments. The placement of HPS within the organizational structure must clearly articulate the value of enhancing well-being and health promotion as essential to the overall mission of an institution.

HPS organizational placement should facilitate significant interaction with unit heads in academic and student affairs.

HPS must be located in an organizational structure to best provide for effective programs and services to achieve its mission.

HPS must play a principal role in creating and implementing institutional policies and programs in response to assessed student needs and capabilities.

HPS should function independent of clinical health services to ensure adequate attention is paid to prevention.

Part 10. CAMPUS and EXTERNAL RELATIONS

Health Promotion Services (HPS) must reach out to relevant individuals, campus offices, and external agencies to:
- establish, maintain, and promote effective relations
- disseminate information about their own and other related programs and services
- coordinate and collaborate, where appropriate, in offering programs and services to meet the needs of students and promote their achievement of student learning and development outcomes

Sustaining partnerships should include:
- advocating for a shared vision that health promotion is the responsibility of all campus and community members
- developing and participating in campus and community partnerships that advance health promotion initiatives
- utilizing campus and community resources to maximize the effectiveness of health promotion initiatives
- advocating for campus, local, state/provincial, national, and international policies that address campus and community health issues
- institutionalizing health promotion initiatives through inclusion in campus strategic planning and resource allocation processes

To ensure success, HPS must maintain productive relations with students, faculty members, staff members, alumni, the community at large, contractors, and support agencies.

HPS staff members should participate actively with their institutions in designing policies and practices and developing further resources and services that have direct effects on the health of the campus population.

HPS should work closely with the senior administrators to ensure the meeting of institutional goals and objectives.

HPS should establish relationships with a wide range of constituencies, such as student affairs professionals, faculty members, and student groups, to promote collaboration and serve as a resource.

HPS should foster relationships with academic units and campus professionals in residence halls, recreational facilities, student activities, and athletics, where appropriate.

HPS should foster reciprocal relationships with clinical health services and counseling services to refer students for medical concerns and to serve as colleagues and consultants.

HPS must have procedures and guidelines consistent with institutional policy for responding to threats, emergencies, and crisis situations. Systems and procedures must be in place to disseminate timely and accurate information to students and other members of the campus community during emergency situations.

HPS must have procedures and guidelines consistent with institutional policy for communicating with the media.

Part 11. FINANCIAL RESOURCES

Health Promotion Services (HPS) must have adequate funding to accomplish their mission and goals. In establishing funding priorities and making significant changes, a comprehensive analysis, which includes relevant expenditures, external and internal resources, and impact on the campus community, must be conducted.

HPS must demonstrate fiscal responsibility and cost effectiveness consistent with institutional protocols.

Funding for HPS should be provided and sustained by the institution's budget or through a designated health fee applied to all enrolled students.

Part 12. TECHNOLOGY

Health Promotion Services (HPS) must have adequate technology to support their mission. The technology and its use must comply with institutional policies and procedures and be evaluated for compliance with relevant federal, state/provincial, and local requirements.

HPS must maintain policies and procedures that address the security and back up of data.

When technology is used to facilitate student learning and development, HPS must select technology that reflects current best pedagogical practices.

Technology, as well as any workstations or computer labs maintained by the HPS for student use, must be accessible and must meet established technology standards for delivery to persons with disabilities.

When HPS provide student access to technology, they must provide:

- **access to policies that are clear, easy to understand, and available to all students**
- **access to instruction or training on how to use the technology**
- **access to information on the legal and ethical implications of misuse as it pertains to intellectual property, harassment, privacy, and social networks**

Student violations of technology policies must follow established institutional student disciplinary procedures.

Students who experience negative emotional or psychological consequences from the use of technology must be referred to support services provided by the institution.

Part 13. FACILITIES and EQUIPMENT

Health Promotion Services (HPS) must have adequate, accessible, suitably located facilities and equipment to support their mission and goals. If acquiring capital equipment as defined by the institution, HPS must take into account expenses related to regular maintenance and life cycle costs. Facilities and equipment must be evaluated regularly, including consideration of sustainability, and be in compliance with relevant federal, state/provincial, and local requirements to provide for access, health, safety, and security.

To promote holistic health, the facilities of HPS should include:
- a safe, functional, effective, and conveniently located positive environment for students, faculty and staff members, and community partners
- office space that is functionally autonomous rather than housed as a component of other units on campus
- office space that is physically separate from clinical health services
- quality space to ensure maximum effectiveness in providing health promotion resources for the campus community
- adequate meeting space for training student volunteers and supporting their work
- adequate physical facilities, equipment, and technology to monitor and report population health status data

HPS staff members must have work space that is well-equipped, adequate in size, and designed to support their work and responsibilities. For conversations requiring privacy, staff members must have access to a private space.

HPS staff members who share work space must have the ability to secure their work adequately.

The design of the facilities must guarantee the security of records and ensure the confidentiality of sensitive information.

The location and layout of the facilities must be sensitive to the special needs of persons with disabilities as well as the needs of constituencies served.

HPS must ensure that staff members are knowledgeable of

and trained in safety and emergency procedures for securing and vacating the facilities.

Part 14. ASSESSMENT and EVALUATION

Health Promotion Services (HPS) must establish systematic plans and processes to meet internal and external accountability expectations with regard to program as well as student learning and development outcomes. HSP must conduct regular assessment and evaluations. Assessments must include qualitative and quantitative methodologies as appropriate, to determine whether and to what degree the stated mission, goals, and student learning and development outcomes are being met. The process must employ sufficient and sound measures to ensure comprehensiveness. Data collected must include responses from students and other affected constituencies.

Assessment and evaluation should include:
- data gathered from published research on international, national, state/provincial, local, and campus health priorities
- population-based assessment of health status, needs, and assets of students
- environmental assessment of campus-community health needs and resources
- measurable goals and objectives for health promotion initiatives

HPS must evaluate regularly how well they complement and enhance the institution's stated mission and educational effectiveness.

Results of these evaluations must be used in revising and improving programs and services, identifying needs and interests in shaping directions of program and service design, and recognizing staff performance.

HPS should report evaluation data and research results to students, faculty members, staff members, and the campus community.

General Standards revised in 2008;
HPS content developed/revised in 2006

The Role of Housing and Residential Life Programs
CAS Standards Contextual Statement

Although U.S. institutions of higher learning have provided student housing in one form or another since the first colleges were founded (Frederiksen,1993), the professionalization of those employed in housing was greatly enhanced when the Association of College and University Housing Officers-International (ACUHO-I) held its first annual conference in 1949. This meeting marked a significant step forward in the development of college and university student housing programs as a profession.

Until the middle of the twentieth century, college and university "dormitories" were administered by "housemothers," often under the supervision of deans of men or women. These staff members assumed parental responsibility (*in loco parentis*) for the students housed in the residence halls. During the 1960s, dramatic changes in laws and education produced changes in the operation of residence halls. Housemothers were replaced by full-time staff with professional training in counseling and administration. These student affairs professionals focused on using the residence hall environment as a tool to complement formal classroom education. Since the 1960s, student housing has become increasingly more specialized and complex. However, the influence of the residential experience on the lives of students has been widely researched over the years.

> Group living influences maturation by exposing students to a variety of experiences and community-building activities. What distinguishes group living in campus residence from most other forms of housing is the involvement of both professional and paraprofessional staff members in providing intentional, as opposed to random, educational experiences for students. Students living in residence halls participate in more extracurricular, social, and cultural events; are more likely to graduate; and exhibit greater positive gains in psychosocial development, intellectual orientation, and self concept than students living at home or commuting. In addition, they demonstrate significantly greater increases in aesthetic, cultural, and intellectual values; social and political liberalism; and secularism. (Schroeder & Mable, 1993)

More recently, the quality of residence halls has been acknowledged as not only essential to the quality of campus life but as an increasingly important factor in attracting students to a given institution.   There has been a renaissance in college and university housing with many campuses significantly renovating halls and constructing new facilities to respond to today's students and to better meet expectations. Residence halls provide valuable opportunities for the development of learning communities which serve to integrate the more formal academic and student life experience, provide increased interaction between students and faculty, and provide critical avenues to enhance campus community building activities and traditions.

College and university student housing operations employ staff members with wide varieties of skills and functions. Areas administered by institutional housing and residence life programs include such functions as:

- Administration of various electronic media (residential cable TV channels, network access, internal movie and information channels, electronic access systems) and information technology resources (in-room connections, computer labs, learning resources centers, wireless capabilities)
- Apartment housing
- Conference and guest housing
- Education (e.g., leadership development, student government advising, student conduct, residential learning communities, joint programs with faculty and academic departments, community and individual development)
- Facilities management and maintenance
- Financial planning and administration
- Dining services (including catering and cash food operations)
- Marketing
- Off-campus rental referral and related educational services
- Planning and administration of the construction of new facilities
- Research, evaluation, and assessment
- Safety and security
- Identification and "one card" programs

Many institutional student housing operations are self-supported auxiliaries that do not receive financial support from the institution or other public sources; in effect, student housing in that context is an education "business." Regardless of the status of the operation, however, because of the wide scope and function of student housing, planning is usually initiated institution-wide. Likewise, although housing encompasses many functions, most administrations agree that students are best served when all housing and residence life functions fall under the responsibility of a single administrator, usually the director of housing and/or residential life.

As higher education prepares students with the knowledge and skills required for the challenges of the 21st century and as learning becomes more a lifetime responsibility, residence halls will continue to be a critical component of the undergraduate experience. The standards and guidelines that follow provide guidance to those who work in this field and accountability to the public they serve.

References, Readings, and Resources

American Association of Higher Education, American College Personnel Association, National Association of Student Personnel Administrators. (1998). *Powerful partnerships: A shared responsibility for learning.* Washington, DC: Authors.

American College Personnel Association. Commission on Housing and Residence Life. http://www.acpa.nche.edu/comms/comm03/index.html

American College Personnel Association and National Association of Student Personnel Administrators. (2004). *Learning reconsidered: A campus-wide focus on the student experience.* Washington DC: Authors.

Association of College and University Housing Officers-International (ACUHO-I). (1999). *Educational programming and student learning in college and university residence halls.* Columbus, OH: Author.

Association of College and University Housing Officers-International (ACUHO-I). (1992). *Ethical principles and standards for college and university housing professionals.* Columbus, OH: Author.

Frederiksen, C. F. (1993). A brief history of collegiate housing. In R. B. Winston, Jr., & S. Anchors (Eds.), *Student housing and residential life: A handbook for student affairs professionals committed to student development goals* (pp. 167-183). San Francisco: Jossey-Bass.

Keeling, R. P. (Ed.). (2006). *Learning reconsidered 2: A practical guide to implementing a campus-wide focus on the student experience.* Washington, D.C.: American College Personnel Association, Association of College and University Housing Officers International, Association of College Unions International, National Academic Advising Association, National Association of Campus Activities, National Association of Student Personnel Administrators, & National Intramural-Recreational Sports Association.

Kuh, G.D., Sheed, J.D., Whitt, E.J., & Associates. (1991). *Involving colleges: Successful approaches to fostering student learning and development outside the classroom.* San Francisco: Jossey-Bass.

Laufgraben, J. L., Shipiro, N. S., & Associates. (2004). *Sustaining and improving learning communities.* San Francisco: Jossey-Bass.

National Leadership Council for Liberal Education and America's Promise. (2007). *College learning for the new global century.* Washington, DC: Author.

Schroeder, C. C., Mable, P., & Associates. (1993). *Realizing the educational potential of residence halls.* San Francisco: Jossey-Bass.

Shuh, J. (Ed.). (1999). *Educational programming and student learning in college and university residence halls.* Columbus, OH: Association of College and University Housing Officers-International..

The Journal of College and University Student Housing. Published by the Association of College and University Housing Officers-International (ACUHO-I), 941 Chatham Lane, Suite 318 Columbus, OH 43221-2416 Phone: 614.292.0099 Fax: 614.292.3205

Winston, R. B, Jr., Anchors, S., & Associates. (1993). *Student housing and residential life: A handbook for student affairs professionals committed to student development goals.* San Francisco: Jossey-Bass.

Contributors:

Current edition:
Carole Henry, Old Dominion University, ACUHO-I

Previous editions:
Mike Eyster, University of Oregon

Housing and Residential Life Programs
CAS Standards and Guidelines

Part 1. MISSION

Housing and Residential Life Programs (HRLP) must develop, disseminate, implement, and regularly review their mission. Mission statements must be consistent with the mission of the institution and with professional standards. HRLP in higher education must enhance overall educational experiences by incorporating student learning and development outcomes in their mission.

The mission of HRLP is accomplished through the coordination of several interdependent specialized areas: residence education/programming, business operations, and housing/facilities management.

The standards in this document also apply to additional specialized areas that may include food services, apartment/family housing, special interest housing, conference housing, faculty/staff housing, and off-campus housing services.

The mission of HRLP must address:
- the living environment, including programs and services, that promotes learning and development in the broadest sense, with an emphasis on academic success
- reasonably priced living facilities that are clean, attractive, well-maintained, comfortable, and which include contemporary safety features maintained by systematic operations
- orderly and effective management of HRLP that consists of meeting the needs of students and other constituents in a courteous, efficient, and effective manner
- the provision of a variety of nutritious and pleasing meals, in pleasant surroundings, at a reasonable cost, and related services that effectively meet institutional goals (catering, retail/cash operations, convenience stores), in programs that include food services

Part 2. PROGRAM

The formal education of students, consisting of the curriculum and the co-curriculum, must promote student learning and development outcomes that are purposeful and holistic and that prepare students for satisfying and productive lifestyles, work, and civic participation. The student learning and development outcome domains and their related dimensions are:

- knowledge acquisition, integration, construction, and application
    - Dimensions: understanding knowledge from a range of disciplines; connecting knowledge to other knowledge, ideas, and experiences; constructing knowledge; and relating knowledge to daily life

- cognitive complexity
    - Dimensions: critical thinking; reflective thinking; effective reasoning; and creativity

- intrapersonal development
    - Dimensions: realistic self-appraisal, self-understanding, and self-respect; identity development; commitment to ethics and integrity; and spiritual awareness

- interpersonal competence
    - Dimensions: meaningful relationships; interdependence; collaboration; and effective leadership

- humanitarianism and civic engagement
    - Dimensions: understanding and appreciation of cultural and human differences; social responsibility; global perspective; and sense of civic responsibility

- practical competence
    - Dimensions: pursuing goals; communicating effectively; technical competence; managing personal affairs; managing career development; demonstrating professionalism; maintaining health and wellness; and living a purposeful and satisfying life

[See *The Council for the Advancement of Standards Learning and Developmental Outcomes* statement for examples of outcomes related to these domains and dimensions.]

Consistent with the institutional mission, Housing and Residential Life Programs (HRLP) must identify relevant and desirable student learning and development outcomes from among the six domains and related dimensions. When creating opportunities for student learning and development, HRLP must explore possibilities for collaboration with faculty members and other colleagues.

HRLP must assess relevant and desirable student learning and development outcomes and provide evidence of their impact on student learning and development. HRLP must articulate how they contribute to or support students' learning and development in the domains not specifically assessed.

HRLP must be:
- integrated into the life of the institution
- intentional and coherent
- guided by theories and knowledge of learning and development
- reflective of developmental and demographic profiles of the student population
- responsive to needs of individuals, diverse and special populations, and relevant constituencies

HRLP must provide educational opportunities for students and other members of the campus community that support the strategic initiatives of the institution.

Partnerships with faculty members, academic administrators, and other campus constituents should be developed to utilize student residences as an integral part of the educational experience. These activities may include offering any of the following: partnerships with enrollment management to attract and retain students; faculty-staff interaction with students through workshop and lecture presentations; scholars in residence programs, residential colleges, classrooms (traditional and electronic) and computer labs in the residence halls; opportunities for faculty to hold office hours and meet with students; partnerships with departments and colleges to offer living-learning communities by academic program, theme, or special interest; residentially-based tutoring programs, study skills, and related workshops; and activities that contribute to achieving the academic mission.

Staff members must provide a variety of educational opportunities that promote academic success and the achievement of learning and student development outcomes.

HRLP should provide an environment that assists residents to remain in good academic standing, earn higher GPAs, and be retained. This may occur through early alert intervention programs; educating staff and students about available campus academic resources; offering living-learning communities which can be linked with course blocking; transition or bridging programs; partnerships with first-year experience programs; or establishment of first-year interest groups, year-two programs, informal study groups, senior year experience programs, or other academic initiatives.

HRLP must provide access to experiences and services that facilitate:
- **a seamless learning environment**
- **opportunities to interact with faculty and staff members**
- **encouragement and assistance in forming study groups**
- **access to academic resources through technology**
- **opportunities to develop a mature style of relating to others and living cooperatively with others**
- **opportunities for analyzing, forming, and confirming values**
- **activities and educational opportunities that promote independence and self-sufficiency**
- **educational opportunities that assist residents in developing and confirming a sense of identity**
- **experiences that lead to the respect for self, others, and property**
- **experiences that promote a sense of justice and fair play**
- **opportunities to appreciate new ideas**
- **opportunities to appreciate cultural differences and other forms of diversity**
- **opportunities to apply knowledge, skills, and values**
- **opportunities for leadership development and decision-making**
- **opportunities to make career choices through planned activities**
- **opportunities to develop a balanced life style embracing wellness**
- **opportunities to learn life skills, e.g., personal finance and time management**

Educational and community development programming, advising and counseling, and administrative activities of the HRLP staff will vary according to assessed student needs and institutional priorities.

In education and community development programs, staff members must:
- **introduce and orient residents to community expectations, facilities, services, and staff**
- **document institutional and residential living policies, procedures, and expectations including the potential consequences for violation**
- **involve students in programming, policy development, and self-governance**
- **provide educational programs that focus on awareness of cultural differences and self-assessment of possible prejudices**
- **offer social, recreational, educational, cultural, and community service programs**
- **promote and provide education about the effects and risks of drug and alcohol use**
- **encourage residents to exercise responsibility for their community through confrontation of inappropriate or disruptive behavior**
- **encourage residents to participate in mediating conflict within the community**
- **encourage residents to learn about their rights as students, tenants, residents, and consumers**
  Off-campus housing services should include referrals to available housing opportunities, listings, information about leases, landlord/tenant law, information about local ordinances, community resources, and other related information.
- **promote appropriate student use of technological resources**

In advising, counseling, and crises intervention, staff members must:
- **provide individual advising or counseling support within the scope of their training and expertise, and make appropriate referrals**
- **create relationships with students that demonstrate genuine interest in students' educational and personal development**

In administrative activities, staff members must:
- **provide a clear and complete written agreement between the resident and the institution that conveys mutual commitments and responsibilities**
  The agreement should include contract eligibility and duration; room assignments and changes; rates and payment policies; dining options; procedures for canceling, subleasing, or being released from the housing and/or dining agreement; room entry and inspection procedures; and pertinent rules and regulations.

- encourage residents to participate in evaluating HRLP
- provide information on safety, security, and emergency procedures
- create and maintain an environment and atmosphere which is conducive to educational pursuits
- provide emergency response and crisis intervention management in coordination with relevant campus and community resources
- ensure that the safety and security of the residents and their property are taken into consideration as policies are developed
- assess needs of the housing population annually, specifically addressing the needs for special interest programming and for upgrading or modifying facilities

When food services is included within HRLP, it must include:
- high quality food products
- orderly, secure, and sanitary food storage
- compliance with all pertinent environmental, health, and safety codes as well as sanitation procedures
- timely delivery of services
- high quality customer services
- pleasant environment in dining areas
- materials that educate students about nutrition and its relationship to good health
- suggestions and input from users regarding menu selection, satisfaction, and
- on-going evaluation

When a residential dining program is included within HRLP, it must include the above standards and:
- menu planning to provide optimum nutrition and variety
- recipes and preparation processes that ensure appetizing food
- attention to students' cultural differences and special dietary needs
- hours of dining service operations sufficient to reasonably accommodate student needs
- dining meal plan options that are clear, affordable, and responsive to student needs
- involvement in educational programming that contributes to student learning and resident satisfaction

The standards and procedures developed and published by professional associations should be used for operating institutional food service operations.

Part 3. LEADERSHIP

Because effective and ethical leadership is essential to the success of all organizations, Housing and Residential Life Programs (HRLP) leaders with organizational authority for the programs and services must:
- articulate a vision and mission for their programs and services
- set goals and objectives based on the needs of the population served and desired student learning and development outcomes

- advocate for their programs and services
- promote campus environments that provide meaningful opportunities for student learning, development, and integration
- identify and find means to address individual, organizational, or environmental conditions that foster or inhibit mission achievement
- advocate for representation in strategic planning initiatives at appropriate divisional and institutional levels
- initiate collaborative interactions with stakeholders who have legitimate concerns and interests in the functional area
- apply effective practices to educational and administrative processes
- prescribe and model ethical behavior
- communicate effectively
- manage financial resources, including planning, allocation, monitoring, and analysis
- incorporate sustainability practices in the management and design of programs, services, and facilities
- manage human resource processes including recruitment, selection, development, supervision, performance planning, and evaluation
- empower professional, support, and student staff to accept leadership opportunities
- encourage and support scholarly contribution to the profession
- be informed about and integrate appropriate technologies into programs and services
- be knowledgeable about federal, state/provincial, and local laws relevant to the programs and services and ensure that staff members understand their responsibilities by receiving appropriate training
- develop and continuously improve programs and services in response to the changing needs of students and other populations served and the evolving institutional priorities
- recognize environmental conditions that may negatively influence the safety of staff and students and propose interventions that mitigate such conditions

Part 4. HUMAN RESOURCES

Housing and Residential Life Programs (HRLP) must be staffed adequately by individuals qualified to accomplish the mission and goals. Within institutional guidelines, HRLP must establish procedures for staff selection, training, and evaluation; set expectations for supervision; and provide appropriate professional development opportunities to improve the leadership ability, competence, and skills of all employees.

HRLP professional staff members must hold an earned graduate or professional degree in a field relevant to the position they hold or must possess an appropriate combination of educational credentials and related work experience.

There must be at least one professional staff member responsible for the administration and coordination of the department. This individual must be knowledgeable about the goals and mission of the program.

Individual residence halls and apartment areas should be supervised by professional staff that have earned a master's degree from accredited institutions in a field of study such as college student personnel, college counseling, or higher education administration, or other fields as appropriate.

Degree- or credential-seeking interns must be qualified by enrollment in an appropriate field of study and by relevant experience. These individuals must be trained and supervised adequately by professional staff members holding educational credentials and related work experience appropriate for supervision.

Demonstrated skills of leadership and communication, maturity, a well-developed sense of responsibility, sensitivity to individual differences, a positive self-concept, an understanding of how to promote student learning and academic success, and an obvious interest and enthusiasm for working with students are desirable characteristics for professional, pre-professional, and paraprofessional staff members.

Student employees and volunteers must be carefully selected, trained, supervised, and evaluated. They must be educated on how and when to refer those in need of additional assistance to qualified staff members and must have access to a supervisor for assistance in making these judgments. Student employees and volunteers must be provided clear and precise job descriptions, pre-service training based on assessed needs, and continuing staff development.

Employees and volunteers must receive specific training on institutional policies and privacy laws regarding their access to student records and other sensitive institutional information (e.g., in the USA, Family Educational Rights and Privacy Act, FERPA, or equivalent privacy laws in other states/provinces or countries).

Resident/community assistants and other paraprofessionals are expected to contribute to the accomplishment of the following functions: (a) educational programming, (b) administration, (c) group and activity advising, (d) leadership development, (e) discipline, (f) role modeling, (g) individual assistance and referral, and (h) providing information.

HRLP must have technical and support staff members adequate to accomplish their mission. All members of the staff must be technologically proficient and qualified to perform their job functions, be knowledgeable about ethical and legal uses of technology, and have access to training and resources to support the performance of their assigned responsibilities.

All members of the staff must receive training on policies and procedures related to the use of technology to store or access student records and institutional data.

HRLP must ensure that staff members are knowledgeable about and trained in emergency procedures, crisis response, and prevention efforts. Prevention efforts must address identification of threatening conduct or behavior of students, faculty members, staff, and others and must incorporate a system or procedures for responding, including but not limited to reporting them to the appropriate campus officials.

Salary levels and benefits for all staff members must be commensurate with those for comparable positions within the institution, in similar institutions, and in the relevant geographic area.

HRLP must provide procedures for filing, processing, and hearing employee grievances.

HRLP must maintain position descriptions for all staff members.

HRLP position descriptions should include adequate time for planning as well as for program implementation.

To create a diverse staff, HRLP must institute hiring and promotion practices that are fair, inclusive, proactive, and non-discriminatory.

HRLP must conduct regular performance planning and evaluation of staff members. HRLP must provide access to continuing and advanced education and professional development opportunities.

HRLP staff members should have a written personal development plan that reflects the goals and objectives of the organization and areas for professional growth.

HRLP staff members must have a working knowledge of all relevant policies and procedures, the rationale for policies and procedures, and the relationship of policies and procedures to the organization's mission statement, goals, and objectives.

HRLP policies and procedures are reviewed annually and updated as appropriate.

HRLP staff members must be knowledgeable about and remain current with respect to the obligations and limitations placed upon the institution by constitutional, statutory, and common law, by external governmental agencies, and by institutional policies.

Part 5. ETHICS

Persons involved in the delivery of Housing and Residential Life Programs (HRLP) must adhere to the highest principles of ethical behavior. HRLP must review relevant professional ethical standards and develop or adopt and implement appropriate statements of ethical practice. HRLP must publish these statements and ensure their periodic review by relevant constituencies.

HRLP must orient new staff members to relevant ethical standards and statements of ethical practice.

HRLP staff members must ensure that privacy and confidentiality are maintained with respect to all communications and records to the extent that such records are protected under the law and appropriate statements of ethical practice. Information contained in students' education records must not be disclosed except as allowed by relevant laws and institutional policies. HRLP staff members must disclose to appropriate authorities information judged to be of an emergency nature, especially when the safety of the individual or others is involved, or when otherwise required by institutional policy or relevant law.

HRLP staff members must be aware of and comply with the provisions contained in the institution's policies pertaining to human subjects research and student rights and responsibilities, as well as those in other relevant institutional policies addressing ethical practices and confidentiality of research data concerning individuals.

HRLP staff members must recognize and avoid personal conflicts of interest or appearance thereof in the performance of their work.

HRLP staff members must strive to insure the fair, objective, and impartial treatment of all persons with whom they interact.

When handling institutional funds, HRLP staff members must ensure that such funds are managed in accordance with established and responsible accounting procedures and the fiscal policies or processes of the institution.

Promotional and descriptive information must be accurate and free of deception.

HRLP staff members must perform their duties within the limits of their training, expertise, and competence. When these limits are exceeded, individuals in need of further assistance must be referred to persons possessing appropriate qualifications.

HRLP staff members must use suitable means to confront and otherwise hold accountable other staff members who exhibit unethical behavior.

HRLP staff members must be knowledgeable about and practice ethical behavior in the use of technology.

HRLP staff members should remain abreast of ethical codes and practices through involvement in professional associations.

Part 6. LEGAL RESPONSIBILITIES

Housing and Residential Life Program (HRLP) staff members must be knowledgeable about and responsive to laws and regulations that relate to their respective responsibilities and that may pose legal obligations, limitations, or ramifications for the institution as a whole. As appropriate, staff members must inform users of programs and services, as well as officials, of legal obligations and limitations including constitutional, statutory, regulatory, and case law; mandatory laws and orders emanating from federal, state/provincial, and local governments; and the institution's policies.

HRLP must have written policies on all relevant operations, transactions, or tasks that may have legal implications.

HRLP staff members must neither participate in nor condone any form of harassment or activity that demeans persons or creates an intimidating, hostile, or offensive campus environment.

HRLP staff members must use reasonable and informed practices to limit the liability exposure of the institution and its officers, employees, and agents. Staff members must be informed about institutional policies regarding risk management, personal liability, and related insurance coverage options and must be referred to external sources if coverage is not provided by the institution.

The institution must provide access to legal advice for HRLP staff members as needed to carry out assigned responsibilities.

The institution must inform HRLP staff and students in a timely and systematic fashion about extraordinary or changing legal obligations and potential liabilities.

Part 7. EQUITY and ACCESS

Housing and Residential Life Programs (HRLP) must be provided on a fair, equitable, and non-discriminatory basis in accordance with institutional policies and with all applicable state/provincial and federal statutes and regulations. HRLP must maintain an educational and work environment free from discrimination in accordance with law and institutional policy.

Discrimination must be avoided on the basis of age; cultural heritage; disability; ethnicity; gender identity and expression; nationality; political affiliation; race; religious affiliation; sex; sexual orientation; economic, marital, social, or veteran status; and any other bases included in local, state/provincial, or federal laws.

Consistent with the mission and goals, HRLP must take action to remedy significant imbalances in student participation and staffing patterns.

Policies must be in place to encourage the hiring and promotion of a diverse and multicultural staff.

HRLP must ensure physical and program access for persons with disabilities. HRLP must be responsive to the needs of all students and other populations served when establishing hours of operation and developing methods of delivering programs and services.

HRLP must recognize the needs of distance learning students

by providing appropriate and accessible services and assisting them in identifying and gaining access to other appropriate services in their geographic region.

Part 8. DIVERSITY

Within the context of each institution's unique mission, diversity enriches the community and enhances the collegiate experience for all; therefore, Housing and Residential Life Programs (HRLP) must create and nurture environments that are welcoming to and bring together persons of diverse backgrounds.

HRLP must promote environments that are characterized by open and continuous communication that deepens understanding of one's own identity, culture, and heritage, as well as that of others. HRLP must recognize, honor, educate, and promote respect about commonalties and differences among people within their historical and cultural contexts.

HRLP must address the characteristics and needs of a diverse population when establishing and implementing policies and procedures.

Part 9. ORGANIZATION and MANAGEMENT

To promote student learning and development outcomes, Housing and Residential Life Programs (HRLP) must be structured purposefully and managed effectively to achieve stated goals. Evidence of appropriate structure must include current and accessible policies and procedures, written performance expectations for all employees, functional workflow graphics or organizational charts, and clearly stated program and service delivery expectations.

An organizational chart should define both the responsibilities and relationships of staff members with the understanding that HRLP leadership should emphasize fluidity, adaptability, and cross-functional collaboration.

HRLP must monitor websites used for distributing information to ensure that the sites are current, accurate, appropriately referenced, and accessible.

Evidence of effective management must include use of comprehensive and accurate information for decisions, clear sources and channels of authority, effective communication practices, procedures for decision-making and conflict resolution, responses to changing conditions, systems of accountability and evaluation, and processes for recognition and reward. HRLP must align policies and procedures with those of the institution and provide channels within the organization for their regular review.

Where the management of the HRLP is divided among different agencies within the institution, it is the responsibility of institutional leaders to establish and maintain productive working relationships.

A unified organizational structure, including all housing and residential life functions, should be used so as to effectively deliver the services to users and to avoid multiple hierarchical lines of communication and authority.

HRLP must maintain well-structured management functions, including planning, personnel, property management, purchasing, contract administration, financial control, and information systems.

Evaluation of the organization is based on progress toward the achievement of short-range and long-range organizational goals. Planning must be adequate to project and accommodate both immediate and future needs.

Part 10. CAMPUS and EXTERNAL RELATIONS

Housing and Residential Life Programs (HRLP) must reach out to relevant individuals, campus offices, and external agencies to:
- establish, maintain, and promote effective relations
- disseminate information about their own and other related programs and services
- coordinate and collaborate, where appropriate, in offering programs and services to meet the needs of students and promote their achievement of student learning and development outcomes

Particular efforts should be made by the staff to develop positive relationships with campus and off-campus agencies responsible for judicial affairs, counseling services, learning assistance, disability services, student health services, student activities, security and safety, academic advising, admissions, campus mail and telephone services, physical plant services, institutional budgeting and planning, computer centers, vendors and suppliers of products used in residence and dining halls, and private housing operators.

Special attention must be paid to the relationships with those units who use housing facilities to carry out their programs, such as conference services.

HRLP staff should be aware of the importance of housing and residential life as a critical institutional asset, its opportunity to contribute to academic programs and the delivery of services, and its effect on attracting and retaining students.

HRLP staff must develop and maintain staff relationships in a climate of mutual respect, support, trust, and interdependence, recognizing the strengths and limitations of each colleague.

HRLP must have procedures and guidelines consistent with institutional policy for responding to threats, emergencies, and crisis situations. Systems and procedures must be in place to disseminate timely and accurate information to students and other members of the campus community during emergency situations.

HRLP must have procedures and guidelines consistent with institutional policy for communicating with the media.

Part 11. FINANCIAL RESOURCES

Housing and Residential Life Programs (HRLP) must have adequate funding to accomplish their mission and goals. In establishing funding priorities and making significant changes, a comprehensive analysis, which includes relevant expenditures, external and internal resources, and impact on the campus community, must be conducted.

HRLP must demonstrate fiscal responsibility and cost effectiveness consistent with institutional protocols.

Administration of funds must be handled in accordance with established, responsible accounting procedures.

Procedures should be present to ensure reconciliation between goods paid for and goods ordered and received.

Adequate and appropriate internal controls must exist to ensure full accountability of financial processes.

Financial reports must provide and reflect an accurate financial overview of the organization.

Financial reports should provide clear, understandable, timely data on which staff can plan and make informed decisions.

Purchasing procedures must be consistent with institutional policies and be cost effective.

The budget must be used as a planning and goal-setting document that reflects commitment to the mission and goals of the HRLP and of the institution.

Budgets should be flexible and capable of being adjusted during the year.

A portion of fees collected must be dedicated to the immediate support and long-term improvement of housing and residential life programs and facilities. Funding must be available to provide for the continuous upkeep of facilities, equipment and furnishings, on-going repairs, educational programming, and services to residents. Reserves must be available for major maintenance and renovation of facilities, replacement of equipment, and other capital improvements.

Student governance units (e.g., hall or campus-wide residential councils) should have access to accounting offices and services to carry out their functions effectively. Dues collected from students for programs and services should be managed within the institution.

Representatives of residence hall and apartment housing communities should be given opportunity to comment on proposed rate increases and the operating budget. Rate increases should be announced at least 90 days in advance of their implementation and discussed well in advance of their effective date.

Part 12. TECHNOLOGY

Housing and Residential Life Programs (HRLP) must have adequate technology to support their mission. The technology and its use must comply with institutional policies and

procedures and be evaluated for compliance with relevant federal, state/provincial, and local requirements.

HRLP must maintain policies and procedures that address the security and back up of data.

When technology is used to facilitate student learning and development, HRLP must select technology that reflects current best pedagogical practices.

Technology, as well as any workstations or computer labs maintained by the HRLP for student use, must be accessible and must meet established technology standards for delivery to persons with disabilities.

When HRLP provide student access to technology, they must provide:
- access to policies that are clear, easy to understand, and available to all students
- access to instruction or training on how to use the technology
- access to information on the legal and ethical implications of misuse as it pertains to intellectual property, harassment, privacy, and social networks

Student violations of technology policies must follow established institutional student disciplinary procedures.

Students who experience negative emotional or psychological consequences from the use of technology must be referred to support services provided by the institution.

Part 13. FACILITIES and EQUIPMENT

Housing and Residential Life Programs (HRLP) must have adequate, accessible, suitably located facilities and equipment to support their mission and goals. If acquiring capital equipment as defined by the institution, HRLP must take into account expenses related to regular maintenance and life cycle costs. Facilities and equipment must be evaluated regularly, including consideration of sustainability, and be in compliance with relevant federal, state/provincial, and local requirements to provide for access, health, safety, and security.

HRLP staff members must have work space that is well-equipped, adequate in size, and designed to support their work and responsibilities. For conversations requiring privacy, staff members must have access to a private space.

HRLP staff members who share work space must have the ability to secure their work adequately.

The design of the facilities must guarantee the security of records and ensure the confidentiality of sensitive information.

The location and layout of the facilities must be sensitive to the special needs of persons with disabilities as well as the needs of constituencies served.

HRLP must ensure that staff members are knowledgeable of

and trained in safety and emergency procedures for securing and vacating the facilities.

HRLP must ensure the physical environment is attractive, conducive to academic success and other learning opportunities, functional, in compliance with codes, and adequately provided with safety features.

Individual rooms and apartments must be furnished and equipped to accommodate the designated number of occupants.

Adequate space must be provided for student study, recreation, socializing, and group meetings.

Facilities should include private offices for counseling, advising, interviewing, or other meetings of a confidential nature, and office, reception, and storage space sufficient to accommodate assigned staff, supplies, equipment, library resources, conference rooms, classrooms, and meeting spaces.

Public, common, study, recreational areas and computer labs must be adequately furnished to accommodate the number of users.

Housekeeping programs must be required to provide a clean and orderly environment in all housing facilities. All community bathrooms, as well as public areas, must be cleaned and sanitized at least daily on weekdays.

A weekend housekeeping program should be in place.

Sufficient space for custodial work and storage must be available in close proximity to the assigned custodial area.

Maintenance and renovation programs must be implemented in all housing operations and include four major areas: (a) a preventive maintenance program designed to realize or exceed the projected life expectancy of the equipment and facilities, (b) a program designed to repair or upgrade equipment, facilities, and building systems as they become inoperable or obsolete, (c) a renovation program that modifies physical facilities and building systems to make them more accessible, effective, attractive, efficient, and safe, and (d) a program designed to provide emergency response 24 hours a day..

Periodic inspections must be made to: (a) ensure compliance with fire and safety codes; (b) identify and address potential safety and security hazards including fire extinguishers, exit doors, automatic door closers, outside building lighting; and (c) identify other potentially dangerous spaces. Data from inspections must be used for repair and replacement schedules.

A system of access control must be in place to provide for building security, monitoring of exterior doors, and stringent controls on the use of master keys/access cards.

Systematically planned equipment replacement programs must exist for furnishings; mechanical, fire safety, and electrical systems; maintenance equipment; carpeting; window coverings; and dining equipment where applicable.

Painting must be done on the basis of current need and a pre-planned cyclical schedule.

Waste disposal, recycling, and handling and storage of chemicals and hazardous materials must be in compliance with federal, state/provincial, and local health, safety, and environmental protection requirements. HRLP staff must identify work place hazards and strive to minimize the risk to employees through education, training, and provision of personal protective equipment.

Grounds, including streets, walks, recreational areas, and parking lots, must be attractively maintained, with attention given to safety features.

Appropriate parking policies should exist for resident students, be developed collaboratively, and define responsibility and options.

Student housing construction project planning must be responsive to the current and future needs of residents. HRLP staff must be involved in the design and development of new housing construction.

Students should be consulted on the design and development of new housing construction.

A master plan for maintaining and renovating all facilities must exist and include timelines for addressing specific needs.

Laundry facilities should be provided within or in close proximity to living areas, be well-maintained, and be reasonably priced.

Suggestions from residents should be regularly and consistently sought and considered regarding physical plant improvements and renovations to college/university housing and dining facilities.

A systematic energy conservation program should be implemented through assessment, programming, education, renovation, and replacement.

An up-to-date inventory of housing property and furnishings should be maintained.

Physical plant renovations should be scheduled to minimize disruption to residents and diners.

Acceptable accommodations and amenities should be provided for professional live-in staff members with appropriate consideration provided for the following needs: adequate living space for the staff member and any family, furnishings and equipment, telecommunications package, appropriate access, and parking.

Part 14. ASSESSMENT and EVALUATION

Housing and Residential Life Programs (HRLP) must establish systematic plans and processes to meet internal and external accountability expectations with regard to program as well as student learning and development outcomes. HRLP must conduct regular assessment and evaluations. Assessments must include qualitative and quantitative methodologies as appropriate, to determine whether and to what degree the stated mission, goals, and student learning and development outcomes are being met. The process must employ sufficient and sound measures to ensure comprehensiveness. Data collected must include responses from students and other affected constituencies.

HRLP must evaluate regularly how well they complement and enhance the institution's stated mission and educational effectiveness.

Results of these evaluations must be used in revising and improving programs and services, identifying needs and interests in shaping directions of program and service design, and recognizing staff performance.

General Standards revised in 2008;
HRLP content developed/revised in 1986, 1992, 1997, & 2004

The Role of International Student Programs and Services
CAS Standards Contextual Statement

During the 2007/08 academic year, more than 623,805 international students from over 200 countries studied at U.S. colleges and universities (IIE, 2008). International students studying in the United States pursue undergraduate and graduate degrees as well as English-language training, and are drawn to this country because of the high quality programs and the wide range of academic options offered in the United States. U.S. students study in other countries, as well, and as such are considered to be international students in their host countries. Regardless of their home countries, international students bring with them rich experiences and unique cross-cultural perspectives that help to internationalize the campus and give host country students first-hand opportunities to learn about the world. International students face unique challenges as they attempt to adjust to a different campus life and culture, master written and spoken languages, comply with immigration regulations, meet the requirements of their academic programs, and prepare to begin their careers.

The events of September 11, 2001, drew widespread attention and scrutiny of International Student Programs and Services (ISPS), resulting in dramatic changes to their roles and responsibilities, particularly in the U.S. A key change is the additional record-keeping and reporting that is necessary for an institution to remain in compliance with immigration regulations.

The functions and roles that ISPS play on campuses vary greatly. Some ISPS offices may serve only a handful of students, while others serve thousands, as well as the academic departments that enroll and depend on these students. Some offices only serve international students, while other offices serve both international students and visiting scholars. As more institutions open campuses in other countries, ISPS may be responsible for helping prepare institutional officials from both countries for the cross-cultural, procedural, and governmental issues that may arise. International student and scholar advising has progressed over the years from being an "add-on" activity for a faculty member or administrator to being a robust profession with a body of knowledge and any number of necessary key skill sets, including those listed below.

International advisers must: be current on immigration regulations and policies and be able to effectively communicate these regulations to students, scholars, and key campus community members; establish and maintain working relationships with individuals on and off-campus to address and advocate for students' and scholars' needs; be competent in crisis intervention in case of illness or serious legal, financial, or personal problems; have strong cross-cultural competencies to allow them to interact effectively with students and scholars from diverse cultures; understand how to develop effective and creative social and cultural programming; and be good at setting priorities and managing time and resources.

Advisers frequently serve as the liaison between international students and scholars, and all those with whom these students and scholars come into contact, including faculty members, students, and staff; local citizens; officials of host country and foreign government agencies; and the student's sponsor or family at home, representing the students' best interests and advising them accordingly. They should be knowledgeable and articulate about host country culture and how it differs from the cultures of other countries and should understand the social and psychological processes of cross-cultural adjustment. They should be familiar with the educational systems and political, economic, historical, and social issues and trends framing the contexts of the countries from which their students come.

As more campuses continue to emphasize internationalization efforts, International Student Programs and Services should be prepared to step forward and initiate partnerships that will advance these goals. Collaboration with education abroad, international studies and international education, and student affairs organizations will sustain these efforts. While this statement and the accompanying standards and guidelines are mostly focused on international students studying in the U.S., many of the challenges and other aspects described may also applies to any students who are studying outside their home country.

References, Readings, and Resources

Institute of International Education. (published annually). *Open doors* report 2008: Report on international educational exchange. See **http://opendoors.iienetwork.org/**

Institute of International Education: 809 United Nations Plaza, New York, NY 10017-3580 (212)883-8200, http://www.iie.org

NAFSA: Association of International Educators: 1307 New York Avenue, NW, 8th Floor, Washington, DC 20005-4701; (202)737-3699, http://www.nafsa.org

NAFSA's Knowledge Community for International Student and
Scholar Services:
http://www.nafsa.org/istanetwork
http://www.nafsa.org/iscanetwork
http://www.nafsa.org/ccpnetwork

NAFSA Adviser's Manual On-line: http://www.nafsa.org/am

U. S. Citizenship and Immigration Services: http://www.uscis.gov

U.S. Immigration and Customs Enforcement: http://www.ice.gov

U.S. Department of Homeland Security: http://www.dhs.gov

U.S. Department of State: http://travel.state.gov

Additional Resources:

From Intercultural Press
(http://www.interculturalpress.com)

The Aliens: Being a Foreign Student. (2001). (video) In this video, six
international students are interviewed about their experiences
coming to the United States and attending a U.S. American
college.

Bennett, Milton (Ed.). (1998). *Basic Concepts of Intercultural
Communication: Selected Readings.*

Cold Water. (1987). (video) This video is about cross-cultural
adaptation and culture shock and includes a comprehensive
instructional guide. Twelve Boston University international
students (plus one U.S. American student and three cross-
cultural specialists) are interviewed about the experience of
living and studying in a new culture.

Storti, Craig. (1998). *Figuring Foreigners Out: A Practical Guide.*

Lanier, Alison. (2004). *Living in the U.S.A.* (6th ed.). Revised by Jef
C. Davis.

From NAFSA: Association of International Educators
(http://www.nafsa.org):

Assaf, Masume and Linda Gentile (Eds.). (2004). *Basic F-1
Procedures for Beginners*

Burak, Patricia A. & William W. Hoffa. (Eds.). (2001). *Crisis
Management in a Cross-Cultural Setting*

Gooding, Marjory and Melinda Wood (Eds.). (2006). *Finding Your
Way: Navigational Tools For International Student and Scholar
Advisers*

O'Connell, Bill (Ed.). (1994). *Foreign Student Education at Two-
Year Colleges*

Althen, Gary (Ed.). (1994). *Learning Across Cultures*

Contributor:
Sandy Tennies, NAFSA

International Student Programs and Services
CAS Standards and Guidelines

Part 1. MISSION

The mission of International Student Programs and Services (ISPS) is to provide support and assistance necessary for international students to achieve their educational goals and to ensure institutional compliance with governmental immigration regulations. The ISPS must provide the documents for students to enter the country and maintain their legal status.

ISPS must develop, disseminate, implement, and regularly review their mission. Mission statements must be consistent with the mission of the institution and with professional standards. ISPS in higher education must enhance overall educational experiences by incorporating student learning and development outcomes in their mission.

Part 2. PROGRAM

The formal education of students, consisting of the curriculum and the co-curriculum, must promote student learning and development outcomes that are purposeful and holistic and that prepare students for satisfying and productive lifestyles, work, and civic participation. The student learning and development outcome domains and their related dimensions are:

• knowledge acquisition, integration, construction, and application
   o Dimensions: understanding knowledge from a range of disciplines; connecting knowledge to other knowledge, ideas, and experiences; constructing knowledge; and relating knowledge to daily life

• cognitive complexity
   o Dimensions: critical thinking; reflective thinking; effective reasoning; and creativity

• intrapersonal development
   o Dimensions: realistic self-appraisal, self-understanding, and self-respect; identity development; commitment to ethics and integrity; and spiritual awareness

• interpersonal competence
   o Dimensions: meaningful relationships; interdependence; collaboration; and effective leadership

• humanitarianism and civic engagement
   o Dimensions: understanding and appreciation of cultural and human differences; social responsibility; global perspective; and sense of civic responsibility

• practical competence
   o Dimensions: pursuing goals; communicating effectively; technical competence; managing personal affairs; managing career development; demonstrating

professionalism; maintaining health and wellness; and living a purposeful and satisfying life

[See *The Council for the Advancement of Standards Learning and Developmental Outcomes* statement for examples of outcomes related to these domains and dimensions.]

Consistent with the institutional mission, International Student Programs and Services (ISPS) must identify relevant and desirable student learning and development outcomes from among the six domains and related dimensions. When creating opportunities for student learning and development, ISPS must explore possibilities for collaboration with faculty members and other colleagues.

ISPS must assess relevant and desirable student learning and development outcomes and provide evidence of their impact on student learning and development. ISPS must articulate how they contribute to or support students' learning and development in the domains not specifically assessed.

ISPS must be:
▪ integrated into the life of the institution
▪ intentional and coherent
▪ guided by theories and knowledge of learning and development
▪ reflective of developmental and demographic profiles of the student population
▪ responsive to needs of individuals, diverse and special populations, and relevant constituencies

ISPS should provide the campus and larger community with multiple and varied opportunities for discussion to maximize learning, to minimize cultural conflict, or to deal with conflict.

ISPS must:
▪ assess the needs of the international student population and set priorities among those needs
▪ offer or provide access to professional services for students in the areas of immigration and other government regulations, financial matters, employment, obtaining health care insurance, navigating the health care system, host-country language needs, and personal and cultural concerns
▪ assure institutional compliance with government regulations and procedures, including record-keeping and reporting responsibilities
▪ interpret immigration policies to the campus and local communities
▪ develop and offer educational programs to the campus community to enhance positive interaction between domestic and international students, to develop sensitivity regarding cultural differences and international student needs, and to assist in the understanding of adjustment to a host country's

educational system and culture
- orient international students to the expectations, policies, and culture of the institution and to the educational system and culture of the host country
- facilitate the enrollment and retention of international students
- prepare students for re-entry and cultural re-adjustment related to the students' return home
- provide appropriate referrals for students whose individual needs may be in conflict with the home culture
- provide appropriate and timely referral services to other relevant agencies
- determine the educational goals; developmental levels; and social, emotional, and cultural needs of individual international students and specific populations
- collaborate effectively with other services areas, student organizations, and academic departments to meet international students' needs
- facilitate international students' participation in campus life
- advocate to all areas of the institution for the needs of international students
- facilitate sensitivity within the institution and the community at large to the cultural needs of international students

Part 3. LEADERSHIP

Because effective and ethical leadership is essential to the success of all organizations, International Student Programs and Services (ISPS) leaders with organizational authority for the programs and services must:
- articulate a vision and mission for their programs and services
- set goals and objectives based on the needs of the population served and desired student learning and development outcomes
- advocate for their programs and services
- promote campus environments that provide meaningful opportunities for student learning, development, and integration
- identify and find means to address individual, organizational, or environmental conditions that foster or inhibit mission achievement
- advocate for representation in strategic planning initiatives at appropriate divisional and institutional levels
- initiate collaborative interactions with stakeholders who have legitimate concerns and interests in the functional area
- apply effective practices to educational and administrative processes
- prescribe and model ethical behavior
- communicate effectively
- manage financial resources, including planning, allocation, monitoring, and analysis

- incorporate sustainability practices in the management and design of programs, services, and facilities
- manage human resource processes including recruitment, selection, development, supervision, performance planning, and evaluation
- empower professional, support, and student staff to accept leadership opportunities
- encourage and support scholarly contribution to the profession
- be informed about and integrate appropriate technologies into programs and services
- be knowledgeable about federal, state/provincial, and local laws relevant to the programs and services and ensure that staff members understand their responsibilities by receiving appropriate training
- develop and continuously improve programs and services in response to the changing needs of students and other populations served and the evolving institutional priorities
- recognize environmental conditions that may negatively influence the safety of staff and students and propose interventions that mitigate such conditions

Part 4. HUMAN RESOURCES

International Student Programs and Services (ISPS) must be staffed adequately by individuals qualified to accomplish the mission and goals. Within institutional guidelines, ISPS must establish procedures for staff selection, training, and evaluation; set expectations for supervision; and provide appropriate professional development opportunities to improve the leadership ability, competence, and skills of all employees.

ISPS professional staff members must hold an earned graduate or professional degree in a field relevant to the position they hold or must possess an appropriate combination of educational credentials and related work experience.

ISPS professional staff members must be knowledgeable about research and practice in areas related to international student programs and services and stay abreast of developments in policies, laws, and regulations affecting international students.

ISPS professional staff members must have an understanding of and demonstrate appreciation for various cultures served in the student population.

ISPS professional staff members must possess the required interpersonal skills and be competent in the areas of effective communication, group facilitation, leadership training and development, and crisis intervention.

ISPS professional staff members should be familiar with multicultural theory, organizational development, counseling theory and practice, group dynamics, leadership development, human development, and research and evaluation. ISPS professional staff members should have proficiency in a second language and extended travel and/or living experiences abroad.

Degree- or credential-seeking interns must be qualified by enrollment in an appropriate field of study and by relevant experience. These individuals must be trained and supervised adequately by professional staff members holding educational credentials and related work experience appropriate for supervision.

Student employees and volunteers must be carefully selected, trained, supervised, and evaluated. They must be educated on how and when to refer those in need of additional assistance to qualified staff members and have access to a supervisor for assistance in making these judgments. Student employees and volunteers must be provided clear and precise job descriptions, pre-service training based on assessed needs, and continuing staff development.

ISPS should hire graduate assistants and interns with an interest in international student programs and services. These individuals expand staff abilities, provide peer role models, and gain valuable pre-professional experience. Particular attention should be given to preparing assistants and interns to be sensitive to cultural differences and the special needs of international students.

Employees and volunteers must receive specific training on institutional policies and privacy laws regarding their access to student records and other sensitive institutional information (e.g., in the United States, Family Educational Rights and Privacy Act, FERPA, or equivalent privacy laws in other states/provinces or countries).

ISPS must have technical and support staff members adequate to accomplish their mission. All members of the staff must be technologically proficient and qualified to perform their job functions, be knowledgeable about ethical and legal uses of technology, and have access to training and resources to support the performance of their assigned responsibilities.

All members of the staff must receive training on policies and procedures related to the use of technology to store or access student records and institutional data.

ISPS must ensure that staff members are knowledgeable about and trained in emergency procedures, crisis response, and prevention efforts. Prevention efforts must address identification of threatening conduct or behavior of students, faculty members, staff, and others and must incorporate a system or procedures for responding, including but not limited to reporting them to the appropriate campus officials.

Salary levels and benefits for all staff members must be commensurate with those for comparable positions within the institution, in similar institutions, and in the relevant geographic area.

ISPS must maintain position descriptions for all staff members.

To create a diverse staff, ISPS must institute hiring and promotion practices that are fair, inclusive, proactive, and non-discriminatory.

ISPS must conduct regular performance planning and evaluation of staff members. ISPS must provide access to continuing and advanced education and professional development opportunities.

Part 5. ETHICS

Persons involved in the delivery of International Student Programs and Services (ISPS) must adhere to the highest principles of ethical behavior. ISPS must review relevant professional ethical standards and develop or adopt and implement appropriate statements of ethical practice. ISPS must publish these statements and ensure their periodic review by relevant constituencies.

ISPS must orient new staff members to relevant ethical standards and statements of ethical practice.

ISPS staff members must ensure that privacy and confidentiality are maintained with respect to all communications and records to the extent that such records are protected under the law and appropriate statements of ethical practice. Information contained in students' education records must not be disclosed except as allowed by relevant laws and institutional policies. ISPS staff members must disclose to appropriate authorities information judged to be of an emergency nature, especially when the safety of the individual or others is involved, or when otherwise required by institutional policy or relevant law.

ISPS must also make exceptions to privacy and confidentiality of information contained in students' education records when mandated by governmental regulations and legislation.

In the United States, this includes the U.S. Department of Homeland Security or the U.S. Department of State.

ISPS staff members must be aware of and comply with the provisions contained in the institution's policies pertaining to human subjects research and student rights and responsibilities, as well as those in other relevant institutional policies addressing ethical practices and confidentiality of research data concerning individuals.

ISPS staff members must recognize and avoid personal conflicts of interest or appearance thereof in the performance of their work.

ISPS staff members must strive to insure the fair, objective, and impartial treatment of all persons with whom they interact.

When handling institutional funds, ISPS staff members must ensure that such funds are managed in accordance with established and responsible accounting procedures and the fiscal policies or processes of the institution.

Promotional and descriptive information must be accurate and free of deception.

ISPS staff members must perform their duties within the limits of their training, expertise, and competence. When these limits are exceeded, individuals in need of further assistance must be referred to persons possessing appropriate qualifications.

ISPS staff members must use suitable means to confront and otherwise hold accountable other staff members who exhibit unethical behavior.

ISPS staff members must be knowledgeable about and practice ethical behavior in the use of technology.

Part 6. LEGAL RESPONSIBILITIES

International Student Programs and Services (ISPS) staff members must be knowledgeable about and responsive to laws and regulations that relate to their respective responsibilities and that may pose legal obligations, limitations, or ramifications for the institution as a whole. As appropriate, staff members must inform users of programs and services, as well as officials, of legal obligations and limitations including constitutional, statutory, regulatory, and case law; mandatory laws and orders emanating from federal, state/provincial, and local governments; and the institution's policies.

ISPS staff must be well-versed in and remain current on immigration laws and regulations that impact students. ISPS staff must understand and be able to communicate short-term issues related to and long-term impacts of immigration tracking systems, such as SEVIS, the Student and Exchange Visitor Information System.

ISPS staff must also be familiar with constitutional issues of due process, with rights and responsibilities afforded international students, and with privacy laws, and staff must be able to communicate such to students.

ISPS must have written policies on all relevant operations, transactions, or tasks that may have legal implications.

ISPS staff members must neither participate in nor condone any form of harassment or activity that demeans persons or creates an intimidating, hostile, or offensive campus environment.

ISPS staff members must use reasonable and informed practices to limit the liability exposure of the institution and its officers, employees, and agents. Staff members must be informed about institutional policies regarding risk management, personal liability, and related insurance coverage options and must be referred to external sources if coverage is not provided by the institution.

The institution must provide access to legal advice for ISPS staff members as needed to carry out assigned responsibilities.

Staff members should establish and maintain positive working relationships with the institution's legal counsel.

The institution must inform ISPS staff and students in a timely and systematic fashion about extraordinary or changing legal obligations and potential liabilities.

Part 7. EQUITY and ACCESS

International Student Programs and Services (ISPS) must be provided on a fair, equitable, and non-discriminatory basis in accordance with institutional policies and with all applicable state/provincial and federal statutes and regulations. ISPS must maintain an educational and work environment free from discrimination in accordance with law and institutional policy.

Discrimination must be avoided on the basis of age; cultural heritage; disability; ethnicity; gender identity and expression; nationality; political affiliation; race; religious affiliation; sex; sexual orientation; economic, marital, social, or veteran status; and any other bases included in local, state/provincial, or federal laws.

Consistent with the mission and goals, ISPS must take action to remedy significant imbalances in student participation and staffing patterns.

ISPS must ensure physical and program access for persons with disabilities. ISPS must be responsive to the needs of all students and other populations served when establishing hours of operation and developing methods of delivering programs and services.

ISPS must recognize the needs of distance learning students by providing appropriate and accessible services and assisting them in identifying and gaining access to other appropriate services in their geographic region.

Part 8. DIVERSITY

Within the context of each institution's unique mission, diversity enriches the community and enhances the collegiate experience for all; therefore, International Student Programs and Services (ISPS) must create and nurture environments that are welcoming to and bring together persons of diverse backgrounds.

ISPS must promote environments that are characterized by open and continuous communication that deepens understanding of one's own identity, culture, and heritage, as well as that of others. ISPS must recognize, honor, educate, and promote respect about commonalties and differences among people within their historical and cultural contexts.

ISPS must address the characteristics and needs of a diverse population when establishing and implementing policies and procedures.

ISPS must orient international students to the culture of the host country and promote and deepen international students' understanding of cross-cultural differences while building cross-cultural competencies.

ISPS should encourage coordinated efforts to promote multicultural sensitivity and the elimination of prejudicial behaviors in all functional areas.

Considering the long-term well-being of both individual international students and the institution's international educational exchange programs, ISPS staff members must anticipate and balance the wants, needs, and requirements of students with institutional policies, laws, and sponsors.

ISPS staff members should develop procedures to respond to anticipated conflicts between the needs of individual international students and institutional policies, governmental laws and regulations, or sponsor policies.

ISPS staff members should develop systems to address unanticipated conflicts between the needs of individual international students and institutional policies, governmental laws and regulations, or sponsor policies.

ISPS staff members must demonstrate a high degree of cross-cultural competency and sensitivity, while treating differences between value systems and cultures non-judgmentally and avoiding use of pejorative stereotypical statements.

Part 9. ORGANIZATION and MANAGEMENT

To promote student learning and development outcomes, International Student Programs and Services (ISPS) must be structured purposefully and managed effectively to achieve stated goals. Evidence of appropriate structure must include current and accessible policies and procedures, written performance expectations for all employees, functional workflow graphics or organizational charts, and clearly stated program and service delivery expectations.

Institutional compliance issues must be considered in creating and maintaining effective office organization structure and management.

The institution should be aware of and ready to respond to government requirements for enrolling international students. For instance, the institution may be required to designate specific employees who will ensure institutional compliance with government immigration regulations.

ISPS must monitor websites used for distributing information to ensure that the sites are current, accurate, appropriately referenced, and accessible.

Evidence of effective management must include use of comprehensive and accurate information for decisions, clear sources and channels of authority, effective communication practices, procedures for decision-making and conflict resolution, responses to changing conditions, systems of accountability and evaluation, and processes for recognition and reward. ISPS must align policies and procedures with those of the institution and provide channels within the organization for their regular review.

Part 10. CAMPUS and EXTERNAL RELATIONS

International Student Programs and Services (ISPS) must reach out to relevant individuals, campus offices, and external agencies to:
- establish, maintain, and promote effective relations
- disseminate information about their own and other related programs and services
- coordinate and collaborate, where appropriate, in offering programs and services to meet the needs of students and promote their achievement of student learning and development outcomes

ISPS must have procedures and guidelines consistent with institutional policy for responding to threats, emergencies, and crisis situations. Systems and procedures must be in place to disseminate timely and accurate information to students and other members of the campus community during emergency situations.

ISPS must have procedures and guidelines consistent with institutional policy for communicating with the media.

ISPS professional staff must be aware of and respond to changes in government activity affecting international students.

ISPS professional staff members should establish and maintain a positive working relationship with the institutional government liaison. Staff members should participate in advocacy as appropriate and necessary.

Part 11. FINANCIAL RESOURCES

International Student Programs and Services (ISPS) must have adequate funding to accomplish their mission and goals. In establishing funding priorities and making significant changes, a comprehensive analysis, which includes relevant expenditures, external and internal resources, and impact on the campus community, must be conducted.

ISPS must demonstrate fiscal responsibility and cost effectiveness consistent with institutional protocols.

When considering a special student fee as a means of supporting international student programs and services, ISPS should carefully review the related ethical issues of such a fee and bring them to the attention of appropriate institutional leaders.

Part 12. TECHNOLOGY

International Student Programs and Services (ISPS) must have adequate technology to support their mission. The technology and its use must comply with institutional policies and procedures and be evaluated for compliance with relevant federal, state/provincial, and local requirements.

ISPS must maintain policies and procedures that address the security and back up of data.

When technology is used to facilitate student learning and development, ISPS must select technology that reflects current best pedagogical practices.

Technology, as well as any workstations or computer labs maintained by the ISPS for student use, must be accessible and must meet established technology standards for delivery to persons with disabilities.

When ISPS provide student access to technology, they must provide:
- access to policies that are clear, easy to understand, and available to all students
- access to instruction or training on how to use the technology
- access to information on the legal and ethical implications of misuse as it pertains to intellectual property, harassment, privacy, and social networks

Student violations of technology policies must follow established institutional student disciplinary procedures.

Students who experience negative emotional or psychological consequences from the use of technology must be referred to support services provided by the institution.

Part 13. FACILITIES and EQUIPMENT

International Student Programs and Services (ISPS) must have adequate, accessible, suitably located facilities and equipment to support their mission and goals. If acquiring capital equipment as defined by the institution, ISPS must take into account expenses related to regular maintenance and life cycle costs. Facilities and equipment must be evaluated regularly, including consideration of sustainability, and be in compliance with relevant federal, state/provincial, and local requirements to provide for access, health, safety, and security.

ISPS staff members must have work space that is well-equipped, adequate in size, and designed to support their work and responsibilities. For conversations requiring privacy, staff members must have access to a private space.

ISPS staff members who share work space must have the ability to secure their work adequately.

The design of the facilities must guarantee the security of records and ensure the confidentiality of sensitive information.

The location and layout of the facilities must be sensitive to the special needs of persons with disabilities as well as the needs of constituencies served.

ISPS must ensure that staff members are knowledgeable of and trained in safety and emergency procedures for securing and vacating the facilities.

Part 14. ASSESSMENT and EVALUATION

International Student Programs and Services (ISPS) must establish systematic plans and processes to meet internal and external accountability expectations with regard to program as well as student learning and development outcomes. ISPS must conduct regular assessment and evaluations. Assessments must include qualitative and quantitative methodologies as appropriate, to determine whether and to what degree the stated mission, goals, and student learning and development outcomes are being met. The process must employ sufficient and sound measures to ensure comprehensiveness. Data collected must include responses from students and other affected constituencies.

ISPS must evaluate regularly how well they complement and enhance the institution's stated mission and educational effectiveness.

Results of these evaluations must be used in revising and improving programs and services, identifying needs and interests in shaping directions of program and service design, and recognizing staff performance.

General Standards revised in 2008;
ISPS content developed/revised in 1996 & 2008

The Role of Internship Programs
CAS Standards Contextual Statement

In the 1960s, with its social upheaval, a movement to make the college curriculum more relevant and to apply the knowledge of theoretical disciplines to solve societal problems gained considerable momentum. As higher education institutions revamped their curricula, they began to recognize that supervised learning experiences outside the classroom were relevant to the educational process and that ways could be found to evaluate these experiences, possibly for academic credit.

In the early 1970s, two professional associations, the Society for Field Experience and National Center for Public Service Internship Programs, were formed among those involved in college-based field experiences and those involved in policy issues and government-based projects, such as the Urban Corps. These organizations merged in 1978 to form the organization known today as the National Society for Experiential Education (NSEE). Other experiential education organizations include the Cooperative Education and Internship Association (CEIA), the Association for Experiential Education (AEE), NAFSA: The Association of International Educators, and the National Association of Colleges and Employers (NACE), among others. A goal of these organizations has been to advocate experiential and related forms of active or engaged learning, both within and outside the classroom or campus setting, and to establish appropriate standards and ethics in the profession.

As a result of the efforts of these organizations, as well as the demand by students and parents for a more career-oriented curriculum, internships have become an integral part of a college education. What distinguishes internships from other forms of active learning is that there is a degree of supervision and self-study that allows students to "learn by doing" and to reflect upon that learning in a way that achieves certain learning goals and objectives. Feedback for improvement and the development or refinement of learning goals is also essential. What distinguishes an intern from a volunteer is the deliberative form of learning that takes place. There must be a balance between learning and contributing, and the student, the student's institution, and the internship placement site must share in the responsibility to ensure that the balance is appropriate and that the learning is of sufficiently high quality to warrant the effort, which might include academic credit.

Major questions and concerns arise regarding how colleges and universities can provide an appropriate internship experience, given the various goals of the institution, the academic and student affairs divisions, and the student. For example, some institutions encourage internships but refuse to grant academic credit for them. Some have policies that restrict academic credit to internships only outside the major. Also, accreditation standards within a professional field may conflict with institutional policy. Some may prohibit students from receiving academic credit for internships that provide compensation, although this attitude is declining as quality placements increase. Then there are the variable standards as to what constitutes a credit-worthy internship (i.e.., how many hours equal how many credits) and concern for the liability of students and their institution should mistakes be made.

The kind of internship experience sanctioned by an institution may vary. Some emphasize a form of cooperative education in which compensation for professional work is a high expectation, although credit for the experience is not necessarily expected. Some may involve a heavily supervised semester or summer-long experience either for or not for academic credit, while others might utilize a form of externship, which is similar to short-term, field-based learning with minimal or limited interaction with an organization.

Setting standards for internship programs will establish for administrators, faculty, and staff a set of benchmarks that identify what a quality internship program on a college campus should be. But it is important that we distinguish between an academic internship within academic affairs and the co-curricular internship found in the student affairs division. The CAS Internship Program standards take into account the importance of establishing standards within each of these areas to meet student academic, career, and personal goals. It also assumes that there is sufficient communication between the two areas so that the appropriate expertise can be utilized across divisions and throughout the campus.

Of considerable significance is the intent of CAS to include the notion that an internship program is not the sole purview of a career center or off-campus programs office. Academic departments that grant credit for internships, have faculty designated to oversee internships, or have faculty members who accompany students on a short-term or long-term basis to locations off-campus, such as Washington or London, should be considered as having internship programs that are expected to meet these CAS standards.

While professionalism in experiential education has made

significant leaps in the past decade, the establishment of these standards is an important milestone within the field. For the first time, a major statement is made that defines an internship within the context of an academic institution of higher education. It emphasizes that careful thought, planning, administration, implementation, and feedback are important in the entire learning process and that sufficient resources should be available to accomplish the established goals of the learning experience. Also, this professionalism must exist within both the academic and the co-curricular areas of the institution.

With the proliferation of internships at the local, state/provincial, national and international levels, administrators and faculty have a special obligation not only to ensure the high quality of the learning environment for their students, but also to assess the risk management and safety of students in these settings. Both faculty and staff need to be sufficiently trained to appropriately oversee an internship, to recognize the warning signs, and to take appropriate action. Increasingly, institutions work with third party organizations to place, supervise, and evaluate students because these organizations have dedicated personnel who are expert in these areas. Yet, similar diligence must be paid to the evaluation of their performance as well.

Internships and other forms of experiential education have become much more accepted as part of the college experience. Many new faculty are often former interns who understand the value of an internship and understand the appropriate ways of measuring student performance. More agencies understand how to utilize interns and to give them substantive work and responsibilities. More financial assistance is available either through the institution or the placement site to help cover the student's costs. Technology is providing career centers, internship offices, or off-campus programs with the ability to match the interests of the student with an appropriate placement more efficiently and effectively. Also, the movement toward on-line portfolio systems allows more participation in the development and evaluation of the student by all those involved in the internship experience. Such advances will very likely lead to greater advances in assessment of student outcomes in internships and other forms of experiential learning.

References, Readings, and Resources

Chickering, A. W. (1977). *Experience and learning: An introduction to experiential learning.* Rochelle, NY: Change Magazine Press.

Inkster, R. P., & Ross, R. G. (1998) *The Internship as partnership: A handbook for businesses, nonprofits, and government agencies.* Raleigh, NC: National Society for Experiential Education.

Inkster, R. P., & Ross, R. G. (1995). *The Internship as partnership: A handbook for campus-based coordinators and advisors.* Raleigh, NC: National Society for Experiential Education.

Kendall, J. C., Duley, J. S., Little, T. C., Permaul, J. S., & Rubin, S. (1986). *Strengthening experiential education within your institution.* Raleigh, NC: National Society for Internships and Experiential Education.

Kiser, P. M. (2000). *Getting the most out of your internship: Learning from experience.* Belmont, CA: Wadsworth/Thomson Learning.

Kolb, D. A. (1984). *Experiential learning: Experience as the source of learning and development.* Upper Saddle River, N.J.: Prentice-Hall.

Stanton, T. and Ali, K. (1994). *The experienced hand: A student manual for making the most of an internship* (2nd ed.). New York: Caroll Press.

Sweitzer, H. F., and King, Mary A. (2004). *The successful internship: Transformation and empowerment in experiential learning.* Belmont, CA: Brooks Cole.

National Society for Experiential Education, 19 Mantua Road, Mt. Royal, NJ 08061; 856.423.3427; fax: 856.423.3420; http://www.nsee.org

Contributor:

Gene Alpert, The Washington Center, NSEE

Internship Programs
CAS Standards and Guidelines

Part 1. MISSION

The primary mission of Internship Programs (IP) is to engage students in planned, educationally-related work and learning experiences that integrate knowledge and theory with practical application and skill development in a professional setting.

IP must develop, disseminate, implement, and regularly review their mission. Mission statements must be consistent with the mission of the institution and with professional standards. IP in higher education must enhance overall educational experiences by incorporating student learning and development outcomes in their mission.

Part 2. PROGRAM

The formal education of students, consisting of the curriculum and the co-curriculum, must promote student learning and development outcomes that are purposeful and holistic and that prepare students for satisfying and productive lifestyles, work, and civic participation. The student learning and development outcome domains and their related dimensions are:

• knowledge acquisition, integration, construction, and application
  o Dimensions: understanding knowledge from a range of disciplines; connecting knowledge to other knowledge, ideas, and experiences; constructing knowledge; and relating knowledge to daily life

• cognitive complexity
  o Dimensions: critical thinking; reflective thinking; effective reasoning; and creativity

• intrapersonal development
  o Dimensions: realistic self-appraisal, self-understanding, and self-respect; identity development; commitment to ethics and integrity; and spiritual awareness

• interpersonal competence
  o Dimensions: meaningful relationships; interdependence; collaboration; and effective leadership

• humanitarianism and civic engagement
  o Dimensions: understanding and appreciation of cultural and human differences; social responsibility; global perspective; and sense of civic responsibility

• practical competence
  o Dimensions: pursuing goals; communicating effectively; technical competence; managing personal affairs; managing career development; demonstrating professionalism; maintaining health and wellness; and living a purposeful and satisfying life

[See *The Council for the Advancement of Standards Learning and Developmental Outcomes* statement for examples of outcomes related to these domains and dimensions.]

Consistent with the institutional mission, Internship Programs (IP) must identify relevant and desirable student learning and development outcomes from among the six domains and related dimensions. When creating opportunities for student learning and development, IP must explore possibilities for collaboration with faculty members and other colleagues.

IP must assess relevant and desirable student learning and development outcomes and provide evidence of their impact on student learning and development. IP must articulate how they contribute to or support students' learning and development in the domains not specifically assessed.

IP must be:
  ▪ integrated into the life of the institution
  ▪ intentional and coherent
  ▪ guided by theories and knowledge of learning and development
  ▪ reflective of developmental and demographic profiles of the student population
  ▪ responsive to needs of individuals, diverse and special populations, and relevant constituencies

Learning goals of IP must:
  ▪ be clear about the educational purpose and expected student learning outcomes of the internship experience
  ▪ encourage the learner to test assumptions and hypotheses about the outcomes of decisions and actions taken, then weigh the outcomes against past learning and future implications
  ▪ develop and document intentional goals and objectives for the internship experience and measure learning outcomes against these goals and objectives
  ▪ maintain intellectual rigor in the field experience

IP must:
  ▪ ensure that the participants enter the experience with sufficient foundation to support a successful experience
  ▪ engage students in appropriate and relevant internships that facilitate practical application of theory and knowledge
  ▪ provide the learner, the facilitator, and any organizational partners with important background information about each other and about the context and environment in which the experience will operate
  ▪ articulate the relationship of the internship experience to the expected learning outcomes
  ▪ determine criteria for internship sites and train

appropriate internship personnel to ensure productive and appropriate learning opportunities for students

- ensure that all parties engaged in the experience are included in the recognition of progress and accomplishment

When course credit is offered for an internship, the credit must primarily be for learning, not just for the practical work completed at the internship. Whether the internship is for credit or not, the focus must be on learning and educational objectives, not just on hours accrued at the site.

IP must offer a wide range of internship experiences appropriate for students at various developmental levels, abilities, and with various life circumstances.

Examples may include older students, commuter students, parents, part-time students, fully employed students, and students with disabilities.

IP must initiate collaborative relations among faculty and staff members within the institution for the design and implementation of internship experiences. They must also develop partnerships with external organizations to meet student learning and development outcomes and the organizations' needs.

Whether integrated into a course, completed as an independent study, or designed for co-curricular learning or personal development, internships should encourage practical application of knowledge and theory, development of skills and interests, and exploration of career options in a professional setting. Internships may be for pay or non-pay, for credit or non-credit, and for a variety of lengths or terms. IP experiences could include the following:

Discipline-specific course-based internships: These can be designed to achieve a variety of student learning outcomes relevant to the course and discipline within which the internship is based, including introducing students to career opportunities as a critical aspect of their college education and their chosen field of study, enabling students to learn what types of work within their chosen field of study best suit their interests, and helping students to understand the different career opportunities available to them both inside and outside their curriculum. These experiences should be part of the academic curriculum for credit.

Student-initiated internships: These internships can be designed to enable students to explore internship opportunities within or outside their course of study and their discipline, to apply knowledge learned in their academic program to practice in different situations and venues, and to gain exposure to a broader array of internship experiences than a course- or discipline-based internship might allow. These experiences, if approved in advance, should be considered for academic credit. These experiences could also add to co-curricular learning and personal development.

Short-term internships: These internship programs offer students the opportunity to explore career opportunities through internships without the longer term commitment required by

a quarter-term program, academic semester, or year. Typically these occur during week-long breaks or during the short sessions between fall and spring semesters and summer (i.e., January or May term). These experiences can be integrated into the academic curriculum or serve as a co-curricular experience, for credit or not-for-credit, in the student's discipline, or in a broader learning context.

Paid internships: Whether integrated into a course, completed as independent-study, or planned during the summer or semester breaks, these internships are designed to provide students with exposure to career opportunities within a paid employment environment. Structured within a real-world context, students are encouraged to apply theory and knowledge in the career setting while receiving financial compensation for their work and time.

Internship experiences must be described in a syllabus or plan.

The internship course syllabus or plan for academic or co-curricular experiences should describe:
- purpose of the internship
- desired learning and development outcomes of the internship for all participants
- assignments that link the internship to academic, career, or personal goals
- opportunities to reflect on one's personal reactions to internship experiences
- logistics (e.g., time required, transportation, materials required, access to services and resources, credit/non-credit, paid/unpaid, financial costs, and benefits)
- roles and responsibilities of students and site personnel
- risk management procedures
- supervision and accommodation requirements by institution personnel and internship site
- evaluation of the internship experience and assessment of the extent to which desired outcomes were achieved
- if for credit, course requirements, including criteria for grading

Part 3. LEADERSHIP

Because effective and ethical leadership is essential to the success of all organizations, Internship Program (IP) leaders with organizational authority for the programs and services must:
- **articulate a vision and mission for their programs and services**
- **set goals and objectives based on the needs of the population served and desired student learning and development outcomes**
- **advocate for their programs and services**
- **promote campus environments that provide meaningful opportunities for student learning, development, and integration**
- **identify and find means to address individual, organizational, or environmental conditions that foster or inhibit mission achievement**
- **advocate for representation in strategic planning**

- initiatives at appropriate divisional and institutional levels
- initiate collaborative interactions with stakeholders who have legitimate concerns and interests in the functional area
- apply effective practices to educational and administrative processes
- prescribe and model ethical behavior
- communicate effectively
- manage financial resources, including planning, allocation, monitoring, and analysis
- incorporate sustainability practices in the management and design of programs, services, and facilities
- manage human resource processes including recruitment, selection, development, supervision, performance planning, and evaluation
- empower professional, support, and student staff to accept leadership opportunities
- encourage and support scholarly contribution to the profession
- be informed about and integrate appropriate technologies into programs and services
- be knowledgeable about federal, state/provincial, and local laws relevant to the programs and services and ensure that staff members understand their responsibilities by receiving appropriate training
- develop and continuously improve programs and services in response to the changing needs of students and other populations served and the evolving institutional priorities
- recognize environmental conditions that may negatively influence the safety of staff and students and propose interventions that mitigate such conditions

Part 4. HUMAN RESOURCES

Internship Programs (IP) must be staffed adequately by individuals qualified to accomplish the mission and goals. Within institutional guidelines, IP must establish procedures for staff selection, training, and evaluation; set expectations for supervision; and provide appropriate professional development opportunities to improve the leadership ability, competence, and skills of all employees.

IP professional staff members must hold an earned graduate or professional degree in a field relevant to the position they hold or must possess an appropriate combination of educational credentials and related work experience.

To facilitate the process of identifying internship sites, professional development of staff and faculty members engaged in IP should include enhancing their ability to:

- identify the compatibility between site needs and student interests
- build relationship with business, organizations, institutions, and other career and professional settings
- establish and maintain collaborative relationships with academic and other units on campus

- understand career and workforce trends

To ensure goal achievement of the IP experience, the professional development of staff and faculty members engaged in IP should include:

Development of assessment skills:

- access previous evaluations of internship sites and make appropriate recommendations as to the learning value of the internship
- develop, implement, and evaluate internship and learning goals
- ensure the time commitment for the internship is appropriate
- ensure that the time spent at internships produces an appropriate balance between the objectives of the site and the learning objectives of the student
- match the unique needs of students and internship sites

Proper communication with students:

- prepare, mentor, and monitor students to fulfill internship requirements according to legal and risk management policies
- clarify the responsibilities of students, the institution, and internship sites

Enhancement of student learning:

- engage students in internship experiences to enhance student learning and exposure to career opportunities
- use active learning strategies that are effective in achieving identified learning outcomes
- engage students in structured opportunities for self-reflection and reflection on the internship experience
- sustain genuine and active commitment of students, the institution, and internship sites
- educate, train, and support students to apply learning from internship experiences to future endeavors

Management skills:

- foster participation by and with diverse populations
- develop fiscal and other resources for program support

Degree- or credential-seeking interns must be qualified by enrollment in an appropriate field of study and by relevant experience. These individuals must be trained and supervised adequately by professional staff members holding educational credentials and related work experience appropriate for supervision.

Student employees and volunteers must be carefully selected, trained, supervised, and evaluated. They must be educated on how and when to refer those in need of additional assistance to qualified staff members and must have access to a supervisor for assistance in making these judgments. Student employees and volunteers must be provided clear and precise job descriptions, pre-service training based on assessed needs, and continuing staff development.

Employees and volunteers must receive specific training on institutional policies and privacy laws regarding their access to student records and other sensitive institutional information (e.g., in the USA, Family Educational Rights and Privacy Act, FERPA, or equivalent privacy laws in other states/provinces or countries).

IP must have technical and support staff members adequate to accomplish their mission. All members of the staff must be technologically proficient and qualified to perform their job functions, be knowledgeable about ethical and legal uses of technology, and have access to training and resources to support the performance of their assigned responsibilities.

All members of the staff must receive training on policies and procedures related to the use of technology to store or access student records and institutional data.

IP must ensure that staff members are knowledgeable about and trained in emergency procedures, crisis response, and prevention efforts. Prevention efforts must address identification of threatening conduct or behavior of students, faculty members, staff, and others and must incorporate a system or procedures for responding, including but not limited to reporting them to the appropriate campus officials.

Salary levels and benefits for all staff members must be commensurate with those for comparable positions within the institution, in similar institutions, and in the relevant geographic area.

IP must maintain position descriptions for all staff members.

To create a diverse staff, IP must institute hiring and promotion practices that are fair, inclusive, proactive, and non-discriminatory.

IP must conduct regular performance planning and evaluation of staff members. IP must provide access to continuing and advanced education and professional development opportunities.

Part 5. ETHICS

Persons involved in the delivery of Internship Programs (IP) must adhere to the highest principles of ethical behavior. IP must review relevant professional ethical standards and develop or adopt and implement appropriate statements of ethical practice. IP must publish these statements and ensure their periodic review by relevant constituencies.

IP must orient new staff members to relevant ethical standards and statements of ethical practice.

IP staff members must ensure that privacy and confidentiality are maintained with respect to all communications and records to the extent that such records are protected under the law and appropriate statements of ethical practice. Information contained in students' education records must not be disclosed except as allowed by relevant laws and institutional policies. IP staff members must disclose to appropriate authorities information judged to be of an emergency nature, especially when the safety of the individual or others is involved, or when otherwise required by institutional policy or relevant law.

IP staff members must be aware of and comply with the provisions contained in the institution's policies pertaining to human subjects research and student rights and responsibilities, as well as those in other relevant institutional policies addressing ethical practices and confidentiality of research data concerning individuals.

IP staff members must recognize and avoid personal conflicts of interest or appearance thereof in the performance of their work.

IP staff members must strive to insure the fair, objective, and impartial treatment of all persons with whom they interact.

When handling institutional funds, IP staff members must ensure that such funds are managed in accordance with established and responsible accounting procedures and the fiscal policies or processes of the institution.

Promotional and descriptive information must be accurate and free of deception.

IP staff members must perform their duties within the limits of their training, expertise, and competence. When these limits are exceeded, individuals in need of further assistance must be referred to persons possessing appropriate qualifications.

All IP faculty and staff members responsible for supervising internship activities must monitor student performance and alter placements as needed.

IP staff members must use suitable means to confront and otherwise hold accountable other staff members who exhibit unethical behavior.

IP staff members must be knowledgeable about and practice ethical behavior in the use of technology.

Part 6. LEGAL RESPONSIBILITIES

Internship Programs (IP) staff members must be knowledgeable about and responsive to laws and regulations that relate to their respective responsibilities and that may pose legal obligations, limitations, or ramifications for the institution as a whole. As appropriate, staff members must inform users of programs and services, as well as officials, of legal obligations and limitations including constitutional, statutory, regulatory, and case law; mandatory laws and orders emanating from federal, state/provincial, and local governments; and the institution's policies.

IP staff and faculty members and internship site personnel engaged in internships must be knowledgeable about and responsive to laws and regulations that relate to their respective responsibilities.

IP must have written policies on all relevant operations, transactions, or tasks that may have legal implications.

IP staff members must neither participate in nor condone any form of harassment or activity that demeans persons or creates an intimidating, hostile, or offensive campus environment.

IP staff members must use reasonable and informed practices to limit the liability exposure of the institution and its officers, employees, and agents. IP staff members must be informed about institutional policies regarding risk management, personal liability, and related insurance coverage options and must be referred to external sources if coverage is not provided by the institution.

IP staff members must establish, review, and disseminate safety and emergency company procedures and policies for the work site and accompanying residential facility.

The institution must provide access to legal advice for IP staff members as needed to carry out assigned responsibilities.

The institution must inform IP staff and students in a timely and systematic fashion about extraordinary or changing legal obligations and potential liabilities.

Part 7. EQUITY and ACCESS

Internship Programs (IP) must be provided on a fair, equitable, and non-discriminatory basis in accordance with institutional policies and with all applicable state/provincial and federal statutes and regulations. IP must maintain an educational and work environment free from discrimination in accordance with law and institutional policy.

Discrimination must be avoided on the basis of age; cultural heritage; disability; ethnicity; gender identity and expression; nationality; political affiliation; race; religious affiliation; sex; sexual orientation; economic, marital, social, or veteran status; and any other bases included in local, state/provincial, or federal laws.

IP staff members must select sites that adhere to this non-discrimination standard.

Consistent with the mission and goals, IP must take action to remedy significant imbalances in student participation and staffing patterns.

IP must ensure physical and program access for persons with disabilities. IP must be responsive to the needs of all students and other populations served when establishing hours of operation and developing methods of delivering programs and services.

IP must recognize the needs of distance learning students by providing appropriate and accessible services and assisting them in identifying and gaining access to other appropriate services in their geographic region.

Part 8. DIVERSITY

Within the context of each institution's unique mission, diversity enriches the community and enhances the collegiate experience for all; therefore, Internship Programs (IP) must create and nurture environments that are welcoming to and bring together persons of diverse backgrounds.

IP must promote environments that are characterized by open and continuous communication that deepens understanding of one's own identity, culture, and heritage, as well as that of others. IP must recognize, honor, educate, and promote respect about commonalties and differences among people within their historical and cultural contexts.

IP must address the characteristics and needs of a diverse population when establishing and implementing policies and procedures.

Part 9. ORGANIZATION and MANAGEMENT

To promote student learning and development outcomes, Internship Programs (IP) must be structured purposefully and managed effectively to achieve stated goals. Evidence of appropriate structure must include current and accessible policies and procedures, written performance expectations for all employees, functional workflow graphics or organizational charts, and clearly stated program and service delivery expectations.

IP must monitor websites used for distributing information to ensure that the sites are current, accurate, appropriately referenced, and accessible.

Evidence of effective management must include use of comprehensive and accurate information for decisions, clear sources and channels of authority, effective communication practices, procedures for decision-making and conflict resolution, responses to changing conditions, systems of accountability and evaluation, and processes for recognition and reward. IP must align policies and procedures with those of the institution and provide channels within the organization for their regular review.

Part 10. CAMPUS and EXTERNAL RELATIONS

Internship Programs (IP) must reach out to relevant individuals, campus offices, and external agencies to:
- establish, maintain, and promote effective relations
- disseminate information about their own and other related programs and services
- coordinate and collaborate, where appropriate, in offering programs and services to meet the needs of students and promote their achievement of student learning and development outcomes

These agencies include government, private business, and nonprofit organizations at the local, national, or international level.

If there is more than one campus unit that facilitates internship experiences, those offices should share information and collaborate as appropriate.

IP should develop productive working relationships with a wide range of campus agencies.

IP must have procedures and guidelines consistent with

institutional policy for responding to threats, emergencies, and crisis situations. Systems and procedures must be in place to disseminate timely and accurate information to students and other members of the campus community during emergency situations.

IP must have procedures and guidelines consistent with institutional policy for communicating with the media.

IP must be concerned about issues of risk management and consult with appropriate campus offices and officials to insure proper procedures.

IP flourishes best when the institution as a whole is engaged as part of its surrounding community. IP should advocate for the institution to share its resources with its community and to develop a wide range of mutually beneficial campus-community partnerships. The "community" may include individuals and organizations beyond the immediate physical location of the campus and include state/provincial, national, and international relationships.

Part 11. FINANCIAL RESOURCES

Internship Programs (IP) must have adequate funding to accomplish their mission and goals. In establishing funding priorities and making significant changes, a comprehensive analysis, which includes relevant expenditures, external and internal resources, and impact on the campus community, must be conducted.

IP must demonstrate fiscal responsibility and cost effectiveness consistent with institutional protocols.

Part 12. TECHNOLOGY

Internship Programs (IP) must have adequate technology to support their mission. The technology and its use must comply with institutional policies and procedures and be evaluated for compliance with relevant federal, state/provincial, and local requirements.

IP must maintain policies and procedures that address the security and back up of data.

When technology is used to facilitate student learning and development, IP must select technology that reflects current best pedagogical practices.

Technology, as well as any workstations or computer labs maintained by the IP for student use, must be accessible and must meet established technology standards for delivery to persons with disabilities.

When IP provide student access to technology, they must provide:
- access to policies that are clear, easy to understand, and available to all students
- access to instruction or training on how to use the technology
- access to information on the legal and ethical implications of misuse as it pertains to intellectual

property, harassment, privacy, and social networks

Student violations of technology policies must follow established institutional student disciplinary procedures.

Students who experience negative emotional or psychological consequences from the use of technology must be referred to support services provided by the institution.

Part 13. FACILITIES and EQUIPMENT

Internship Programs (IP) must have adequate, accessible, suitably located facilities and equipment to support their mission and goals. If acquiring capital equipment as defined by the institution, IP must take into account expenses related to regular maintenance and life cycle costs. Facilities and equipment must be evaluated regularly, including consideration of sustainability, and be in compliance with relevant federal, state/provincial, and local requirements to provide for access, health, safety, and security.

IP staff members must have work space that is well-equipped, adequate in size, and designed to support their work and responsibilities. For conversations requiring privacy, staff members must have access to a private space.

IP staff members who share work space must have the ability to secure their work adequately.

The design of the facilities must guarantee the security of records and ensure the confidentiality of sensitive information.

The location and layout of the facilities must be sensitive to the special needs of persons with disabilities as well as the needs of constituencies served.

IP must ensure that staff members are knowledgeable of and trained in safety and emergency procedures for securing and vacating the facilities.

Part 14. ASSESSMENT and EVALUATION

Internship Programs (IP) must establish systematic plans and processes to meet internal and external accountability expectations with regard to program as well as student learning and development outcomes. IP must conduct regular assessment and evaluations. Assessments must include qualitative and quantitative methodologies as appropriate, to determine whether and to what degree the stated mission, goals, and student learning and development outcomes are being met. The process must employ sufficient and sound measures to ensure comprehensiveness. Data collected must include responses from students and other affected constituencies.

IP must evaluate regularly how well they complement and enhance the institution's stated mission and educational effectiveness.

Results of these evaluations must be used in revising and

improving programs and services, identifying needs and interests in shaping directions of program and service design, and recognizing staff performance.

IP must regularly evaluate, assess, and respond appropriately regarding the extent to which internship sites add to student learning.

General Standards revised in 2008;
IP standards developed in 2006

The Role of Learning Assistance Programs
CAS Standards Contextual Statement

Learning assistance programs facilitate student development and academic success by helping students develop appropriate strategies and behaviors to increase learning efficiency (Dansereau, 1985). Participation in learning assistance programs can also improve student retention (Beal, 1980; Ryan & Glenn, 2004) and provide the kinds of "rewarding interactions" that foster student intellectual and social growth (Tinto, 1987).

Although formal and informal learning assistance has been provided since the opening of the first U.S. colleges (Maxwell, 1996), the earliest "how to study" books for underprepared entering freshmen were not published until 1900. The reading clinics and study methods laboratories of the 1930s and 1940s and self-help programs, learning modules, and programmed instruction of the 1950s and 1960s formed part of the historical foundation for learning assistance programs (Arendale, 2004; Enright, 1975; Lissner, 1990; Sullivan, 1980). Modern learning assistance centers offer tutoring, course-based learning assistance, learning and study strategies, and reading, writing, and mathematics support (Christ, 1971). By the late 1970s, learning assistance centers incorporated educational technology, tutoring, and special services for the many new nontraditional students (Caverly, 1995; Christ, 1982); many centers now provide on-line tutoring.

Academic departments have long provided learning assistance services and developmental courses. At more selective colleges and universities, however, comprehensive learning centers, organized under the auspices of either academic affairs or student affairs, typically make services available to all students. In all of these programs, paraprofessional student employees—peer tutors, mentors, and instructors—may provide services; therefore one function of a learning assistance program is to train these student employees.

By the mid-1970s, learning assistance professionals had formed regional, national, and international organizations. One of these groups, Commission XVI: Learning Centers in Higher Education, was charged by its parent organization, the American College Personnel Association (ACPA), to participate in drafting CAS Standards and Guidelines for Learning Assistance Programs. After five years, the first LAP standards were completed for adoption in 1986—the first major document articulating shared concepts, beliefs, and practices for learning assistance practitioners and their programs.

CAS Standards provided the impetus for certification and professional development programs. In 1989, the College Reading and Learning Association (CRLA) initiated International Tutor Program Certification to ensure minimum standards for tutor training. Their *Tutor Training Handbook* provides a collection of examples of best practices that meet certification standards (Deese-Roberts, 2003). Nine years later CRLA also developed International Mentor Program Certification. The National Association for Developmental Education (NADE) created the *NADE Self-Evaluation Guides: Models for Assessing Learning Assistance / Developmental Education Programs* (Clark-Thayer, 1995). All three certification programs were endorsed by the American Council of Developmental Education Associations (ACDEA), now the Council of Learning Assistance and Developmental Education Associations (CLADEA), through which the organizations continue to examine and approve certifications in the field.

In the early 1990s, CRLA and NADE joined CAS and committed to active participation in the revision of the LAP Standards and Guidelines. Another collaboration in 2006-7 produced the latest revision, which represents professional consensus on the role and importance of learning assistance programs in higher education.

References

Arendale, D. R. (2004). Mainstreamed academic assistance and enrichment for all students: The historical origins of learning assistance centers. *Research for Educational Reform, 9*(4), 3-20.

Beal, P. E. (1980). Learning centers and retention. In O. T. Lenning & D. L. Wayman (Eds.), *New roles for learning assistance* (pp. 59-73). San Francisco: Jossey-Bass.

Caverly, D. (1995). Technology in learning centers: past, present, future. In S. Mioduski & G. Enright (Eds.), *Proceedings of the 15th and 16th Annual Institutes for Learning Assistance Professionals*, 15-34.

Christ, F. L. (1971). Systems for learning assistance: Learner, learning facilitators, and learning centers. *Fourth Annual Proceedings of the Western College Reading Association*, 32-41.

Christ, F. L. (1982). Computers in learning assistance centers and developmental education: Beginning to explore. *Journal of Developmental and Remedial Education* (Fall 1982), 10-13.

Clark-Thayer, S., Ed. (1995). *NADE Self-Evaluation Guides: Models for Assessing Learning Assistance/Developmental Education Programs.* Available from:

http://www.hhpublishing.com/_professional/nade_guides.html

Dansereau, D. F. (1985). Learning strategy research. In J. W. Segal, S. F. Chipman, & R. Glaser (Eds.), *Thinking and learning skills*. Hillsdale, NJ: Erlbaum.

Deese-Roberts, S., Ed. (2003). *CRLA Tutor Training Handbook* (rev. ed.). Available from: http://www.crla.net/TTH_orderform.pdf

Enright, G. (1975). College learning skills: Frontierland origins of the learning assistance. *Proceedings of the Eighth Annual Conference of the Western College Reading Association*, 81-92.

Lissner, L. S. (1990). The learning center from 1829 to the year 2000 and beyond. In R. M. Hashway (Ed.), *Handbook of Developmental Education* (pp. 128-154). New York: Praeger.

Maxwell, M. (1996). *Evaluating academic skills programs: A sourcebook* (3rd ed.). Kensington, MD: MM Associates.

Ryan, M. P., & Glenn, P. A. (2004). What do first-year students need most: Learning strategies instruction or academic socialization? *Journal of College Reading and Learning*, *34*(2), 4-28.

Sullivan, L. L. (1980). Growth and influence in the learning center movement. In K. V. Lauridsen (Ed.), *Examining the scope of learning centers* (pp. 1-8). San Francisco: Jossey-Bass.

Tinto, V. (1987). *Leaving college: Rethinking the causes and cures of student attrition*. Chicago: University of Chicago Press.

Resources

Casazza, M. E., & Silverman, S. L. (2000). *Learning and development: Making connections to enhance teaching*. San Francisco: Jossey-Bass.

Casazza, M. E., & Silverman, S. L. (1996). *Learning assistance and developmental education: A guide for effective practice*. San Francisco: Jossey-Bass.

Christ, F. L. (2002). Academic support. In J. Forest & K. Kinser (Eds.), *Higher education in the United States: An encyclopedia*. Santa Barbara, CA: ABC-CLIO.

Christ, F., Sheets, R., & Smith, K., Eds. (2000). *Starting a learning assistance center: Conversations with CRLA members who have been there and done that*. Clearwater, FL: H&H Publishing.

Kerstiens, G. (1995). A taxonomy of learning support services. In S. Mioduski and G. Enright (Eds.), *Proceedings of the 15th and 16th Annual Institutes For Learning Assistance Professionals*, 48.

Maxwell, M., Ed. (1994). *From access to success: A book of readings on college developmental education and learning assistance programs*. Clearwater, FL: H&H Publishing.

Maxwell M. (1997). *Improving student learning skills* (2nd ed.). Clearwater, FL: H&H Publishing.

New York College Learning Skills Association Ethics and Standards Committee (April 1994). *Statement of ethics and general guidelines for learning assistance programs*. New York: New York College Learning Skills Association.

Robert, E. R. & Thompson, G. (Spring 1994). Learning assistance and the success of underprepared students at Berkeley. *Journal of Developmental Education*, *17*(3), 4-15.

White, W. G., Jr. (2004). The physical environment of learning support centers. *The Learning Assistance Review*, *9*(1), 17-27.

Organizations, Websites, and Journals

Association of Colleges for Tutoring and Learning Assistance: www.actla.info

College Reading and Learning Association, www.crla.net: *Journal of College Reading and Learning*

Council of Learning Assistance and Developmental Education Associations: http://www.crla.net/CLADEA/index.htm LRNASST listserv archives: www.lists.ufl.edu/archives/lrnasst-l.html

LSCHE, Learning Support Centers in Higher Education web portal: http://www.pvc.maricopa.edu/~lsche

National Association for Developmental Education, www.nade.net: *NADE Digest* and *NADE Monograph Series*

National Center for Developmental Education, Appalachian State University, www.ncde.appstate.edu: *Journal of Developmental Education* and *Research in Developmental Education*

National College Learning Center Association, www.nclca.org: *The Learning Assistance Review*

New York College Learning Skills Association, www.nyclsa.org: *Research & Teaching in Developmental Education*

Contributors:

Karen S. Agee, University of Northern Iowa, CRLA
Frank L. Christ, University of Texas at Austin
Gladys Shaw, University of Texas at El Paso

Learning Assistance Programs
CAS Standards and Guidelines

Part 1. MISSION

The primary mission of Learning Assistance Programs (LAP) must be to provide students with resources and opportunities to improve their ability to learn and to achieve academic success.

LAP must develop, disseminate, implement, and regularly review their mission. Mission statements must be consistent with the mission of the institution and with professional standards. LAP in higher education must enhance overall educational experiences by incorporating student learning and development outcomes in their mission.

LAP must collaborate with faculty members, staff, and administrators in addressing the learning needs, academic performance, and retention of students.

Models of LAP vary, but must have the following goals:
- ensure that students are the central focus of the program
- assist students in achieving their personal potential for learning
- introduce students to the academic expectations of the institution, the faculty members, and the culture of higher education
- help students develop positive attitudes toward learning and confidence in their ability to learn
- foster students' personal responsibility and accountability for their own learning
- provide a variety of instructional approaches appropriate to the skill levels and learning styles of students
- assist students in applying newly learned skills and strategies to their academic work
- support the academic standards and requirements of the institution

Models of LAP should also share the following common goals:
- provide instruction and services that address the cognitive, affective, and socio-cultural dimensions of learning
- provide to faculty members, staff, and administrators, both services and resources that enhance and support student learning, instruction, and professional development

Part 2. PROGRAM

The formal education of students, consisting of the curriculum and the co-curriculum, must promote student learning and development outcomes that are purposeful and holistic and that prepare students for satisfying and productive lifestyles, work, and civic participation. The student learning and development outcome domains and their related dimensions are:

- knowledge acquisition, integration, construction, and application
  - Dimensions: understanding knowledge from a range of disciplines; connecting knowledge to other knowledge, ideas, and experiences; constructing knowledge; and relating knowledge to daily life
- cognitive complexity
  - Dimensions: critical thinking; reflective thinking; effective reasoning; and creativity
- intrapersonal development
  - Dimensions: realistic self-appraisal, self-understanding, and self-respect; identity development; commitment to ethics and integrity; and spiritual awareness
- interpersonal competence
  - Dimensions: meaningful relationships; interdependence; collaboration; and effective leadership
- humanitarianism and civic engagement
  - Dimensions: understanding and appreciation of cultural and human differences; social responsibility; global perspective; and sense of civic responsibility
- practical competence
  - Dimensions: pursuing goals; communicating effectively; technical competence; managing personal affairs; managing career development; demonstrating professionalism; maintaining health and wellness; and living a purposeful and satisfying life

[See *The Council for the Advancement of Standards Learning and Developmental Outcomes* statement for examples of outcomes related to these domains and dimensions.]

Consistent with the institutional mission, Learning Assistance Programs (LAP) must identify relevant and desirable student learning and development outcomes from among the six domains and related dimensions. When creating opportunities for student learning and development, LAP must explore possibilities for collaboration with faculty members and other colleagues.

LAP must assess relevant and desirable student learning and development outcomes and provide evidence of their impact on student learning and development. LAP must articulate how they contribute to or support students' learning and development in the domains not specifically assessed.

LAP must be:
- integrated into the life of the institution
- intentional and coherent
- guided by theories and knowledge of learning and development
- reflective of developmental and demographic profiles of the student population
- responsive to needs of individuals, diverse and special

populations, and relevant constituencies

The scope of programs and services must be determined by the needs of the student populations whom LAP are charged to serve.

LAP should serve all students at the institution. Individual LAP may serve specific populations such as culturally and ethnically diverse students, international and English-as-a-second-language students, student athletes, returning students, students with disabilities, and those provisionally admitted or on academic probation.

LAP should provide instruction and services for the development of reading, mathematics and quantitative reasoning, writing, critical thinking, problem-solving, technological literacy, scientific literacy, and learning strategies. Other programs may include subject-matter tutoring, course-based instructional programs such as Supplemental Instruction, time management programs, college success courses, first-year student seminars, and preparation for graduate and professional school admissions tests and for professional certification requirements.

In recognition of the fact that all students do not learn in the same manner, modes of delivering learning assistance programs should be diverse, including individual and group instruction and/or tutoring, cooperative learning, peer assisted learning, and accelerated learning. A variety of instructional media such as print, electronic, and skills laboratories should be incorporated. Instruction and programs may be delivered traditionally or via technology, either on or off site.

Formal and informal screening or diagnostic procedures must be conducted to identify the knowledge, skills, and motivation that students need to develop to achieve the level of proficiency prescribed or required by the institution, program, or instructor.

Assessment results must be shared with the student to formulate recommendations and a plan of instruction.

LAP should provide systematic feedback to students concerning their progress in reaching cognitive and affective goals; teach methods of self-regulation; and give students practice in applying and transferring skills and strategies learned through the LAP.

LAP professional staff must have access to institutional databases with student information relevant to its work.

LAP must promote, either directly or by referral, the cognitive and affective skills that influence learning, such as stress management, test anxiety reduction, assertiveness, time management, concentration, and motivation.

LAP must refer students to appropriate campus and community resources for assistance with personal problems, learning disabilities, financial difficulties, and other areas of need that may be outside the purview or beyond the expertise of the learning assistance program.

LAP must promote an understanding among campus community members of the learning needs of the student population.

Actions to promote this understanding may include:

- establishing advisory boards consisting of members from key segments of the campus community
- holding periodic informational meetings and consulting with staff, faculty members, and administrators
- participating in staff and faculty development and in-service programs on curriculum and instructional approaches that address the development of learning skills, attitudes and behaviors, and the assessment of student learning outcomes
- encouraging the use of learning assistance program resources, materials, instruction, and services as integral or supplemental classroom activities
- conducting in-class workshops that demonstrate the application of learning strategies to course content
- disseminating information that describes programs and services, hours of operation, and procedures for registering or scheduling appointments
- training and supervising paraprofessionals and pre-professionals to work in such capacities as tutors, peer mentors, and other group leaders, such as Supplemental Instruction (SI) leaders
- providing jobs, practica, courses, internships, mentoring, and assistantships for students interested in learning assistance and related careers
- collaborating with other community groups and educational institutions to provide college preparation assistance

Part 3. LEADERSHIP

Because effective and ethical leadership is essential to the success of all organizations, Learning Assistance Programs (LAP) leaders with organizational authority for the programs and services must:

- **articulate a vision and mission for their programs and services**
- **set goals and objectives based on the needs of the population served and desired student learning and development outcomes**
- **advocate for their programs and services**
- **promote campus environments that provide meaningful opportunities for student learning, development, and integration**
- **identify and find means to address individual, organizational, or environmental conditions that foster or inhibit mission achievement**
- **advocate for representation in strategic planning initiatives at appropriate divisional and institutional levels**
- **initiate collaborative interactions with stakeholders who have legitimate concerns and interests in the functional area**
- **apply effective practices to educational and administrative processes**
- **prescribe and model ethical behavior**
- **communicate effectively**
- **manage financial resources, including planning, allocation, monitoring, and analysis**

- incorporate sustainability practices in the management and design of programs, services, and facilities
- manage human resource processes including recruitment, selection, development, supervision, performance planning, and evaluation
- empower professional, support, and student staff to accept leadership opportunities
- encourage and support scholarly contribution to the profession
- be informed about and integrate appropriate technologies into programs and services
- be knowledgeable about federal, state/provincial, and local laws relevant to the programs and services and ensure that staff members understand their responsibilities by receiving appropriate training
- develop and continuously improve programs and services in response to the changing needs of students and other populations served and the evolving institutional priorities
- recognize environmental conditions that may negatively influence the safety of staff and students and propose interventions that mitigate such conditions

LAP leaders must be knowledgeable about issues, trends, theories, research, and methodologies related to student learning and retention.

LAP leaders should:
- participate in institutional planning, policy, procedural, and fiscal decisions that affect learning assistance for students
- seek opportunities for additional funding, resources, and facilities, as needed
- represent the learning assistance program on institutional committees
- collaborate with leaders of academic departments and support services in addressing the learning needs and retention of students
- be involved in research, publication, presentations, consultation, and activities of professional organizations
- communicate with professional colleagues in the learning assistance field and related professions
- promote and advertise their programs and services

Part 4. HUMAN RESOURCES

Learning Assistance Programs (LAP) must be staffed adequately by individuals qualified to accomplish the mission and goals. Within institutional guidelines, LAP must establish procedures for staff selection, training, and evaluation; set expectations for supervision; and provide appropriate professional development opportunities to improve the leadership ability, competence, and skills of all employees.

Staff and faculty who hold a joint appointment with LAP must be committed to the mission, philosophy, goals, and priorities of the program and must possess the necessary expertise for assigned responsibilities.

LAP professional staff members must hold an earned graduate or professional degree in a field relevant to the position they hold or must possess an appropriate combination of educational credentials and related work experience.

Relevant disciplines include English, reading, mathematics, student affairs professional preparation, student development, higher education, counseling, psychology, or education.

LAP professionals should be competent and experienced in:
- the content areas in which they teach, conduct labs, or provide assistance
- learning theory, instruction and assessment, and the theory and professional standards of practice for their areas of specialization and responsibility
- understanding the unique characteristics and needs of the populations they assist and teach
- demonstrating the ability to adjust pedagogical approaches according to the learning needs and styles of their students, the nature of the learning task, and the content of academic disciplines across the curriculum
- working with college students with different learning styles and abilities, including those with disabilities
- writing and communicating at a professional level
- working in culturally and academically diverse environments
- consulting, collaborating, and negotiating with staff, faculty members, and administrators of academic and student affairs units
- designing, implementing, and utilizing instructional strategies, materials, and technologies
- training, supervising, and mentoring paraprofessionals and pre-professionals
- identifying and establishing lines of communication for student referral to other institutional and student support units

Degree- or credential-seeking interns must be qualified by enrollment in an appropriate field of study and by relevant experience. These individuals must be trained and supervised adequately by professional staff members holding educational credentials and related work experience appropriate for supervision.

LAP professionals must be knowledgeable of the policies and procedures to be followed for internships and practica as required by students' academic departments.

Roles and responsibilities of LAP and those of the academic department should be clearly defined.

Student employees and volunteers must be carefully selected, trained, supervised, and evaluated. They must be educated on how and when to refer those in need of additional assistance to qualified staff members and must have access to a supervisor for assistance in making these judgments. Student employees and volunteers must be provided clear and precise job descriptions, pre-service training based on assessed needs, and continuing staff development.

Employees and volunteers must receive specific training on institutional policies and privacy laws regarding their access to student records and other sensitive institutional information (e.g., in the USA, Family Educational Rights and Privacy Act, FERPA, or equivalent privacy laws in other states/provinces or countries).

LAP must have technical and support staff members adequate to accomplish their mission. All members of the staff must be technologically proficient and qualified to perform their job functions, be knowledgeable about ethical and legal uses of technology, and have access to training and resources to support the performance of their assigned responsibilities.

Administrative and technical staff should be knowledgeable about changes in programs, services, policies, and procedures in order to expedite smooth and efficient assistance to students. Appropriate staff development opportunities should be available.

All members of the staff must receive training on policies and procedures related to the use of technology to store or access student records and institutional data.

LAP must ensure that staff members are knowledgeable about and trained in emergency procedures, crisis response, and prevention efforts. Prevention efforts must address identification of threatening conduct or behavior of students, faculty members, staff, and others and must incorporate a system or procedures for responding, including but not limited to reporting them to the appropriate campus officials.

Salary levels and benefits for all staff members must be commensurate with those for comparable positions within the institution, in similar institutions, and in the relevant geographic area.

LAP must maintain position descriptions for all staff members.

Faculty members assigned to LAP must be informed about the implications for tenure and promotion.

To create a diverse staff, LAP must institute hiring and promotion practices that are fair, inclusive, proactive, and non-discriminatory.

LAP must conduct regular performance planning and evaluation of staff members. LAP must provide access to continuing and advanced education and professional development opportunities.

Part 5. ETHICS

Persons involved in the delivery of Learning Assistance Programs (LAP) must adhere to the highest principles of ethical behavior. LAP must review relevant professional ethical standards and develop or adopt and implement appropriate statements of ethical practice. LAP must publish these statements and ensure their periodic review by relevant constituencies.

LAP must orient new staff members to relevant ethical standards and statements of ethical practice.

LAP staff members must ensure that privacy and confidentiality are maintained with respect to all communications and records to the extent that such records are protected under the law and appropriate statements of ethical practice. Information contained in students' education records must not be disclosed except as allowed by relevant laws and institutional policies. LAP staff members must disclose to appropriate authorities information judged to be of an emergency nature, especially when the safety of the individual or others is involved, or when otherwise required by institutional policy or relevant law.

Specific attention must be given to properly orienting and advising student staff about matters of confidentiality. Clear statements must be distributed and reviewed with student staff regarding what information is not appropriate for them to access or communicate.

LAP staff members must be aware of and comply with the provisions contained in the institution's policies pertaining to human subjects research and student rights and responsibilities, as well as those in other relevant institutional policies addressing ethical practices and confidentiality of research data concerning individuals.

LAP staff members must recognize and avoid personal conflicts of interest or appearance thereof in the performance of their work.

Information and training should be made available regarding institutional policies on conflict of interest.

LAP staff members must strive to insure the fair, objective, and impartial treatment of all persons with whom they interact.

When handling institutional funds, LAP staff members must ensure that such funds are managed in accordance with established and responsible accounting procedures and the fiscal policies or processes of the institution.

Promotional and descriptive information must be accurate and free of deception.

LAP staff members must perform their duties within the limits of their training, expertise, and competence. When these limits are exceeded, individuals in need of further assistance must be referred to persons possessing appropriate qualifications.

LAP staff members must use suitable means to confront and otherwise hold accountable other staff members who exhibit unethical behavior.

LAP staff members must be knowledgeable about and practice ethical behavior in the use of technology.

Because LAP staff work with students' academic coursework, they must be knowledgeable of policies related to academic integrity, plagiarism, student code of conduct, students' rights and responsibilities and other similar policies. All staff members must be cognizant of the implications of these policies.

Statements or claims made about outcomes that can be achieved from participating in learning assistance programs and services must be truthful and realistic.

LAP funds acquired through grants and other non-institutional resources must be managed according to the regulations and guidelines of the funding source and the institution.

Part 6. LEGAL RESPONSIBILITIES

Learning Assistance Programs (LAP) staff members must be knowledgeable about and responsive to laws and regulations that relate to their respective responsibilities and that may pose legal obligations, limitations, or ramifications for the institution as a whole. As appropriate, staff members must inform users of programs and services, as well as officials, of legal obligations and limitations including constitutional, statutory, regulatory, and case law; mandatory laws and orders emanating from federal, state/provincial, and local governments; and the institution's policies.

LAP must have written policies on all relevant operations, transactions, or tasks that may have legal implications.

LAP staff members must neither participate in nor condone any form of harassment or activity that demeans persons or creates an intimidating, hostile, or offensive campus environment.

LAP staff members must use reasonable and informed practices to limit the liability exposure of the institution and its officers, employees, and agents. LAP staff members must be informed about institutional policies regarding risk management, personal liability, and related insurance coverage options and must be referred to external sources if coverage is not provided by the institution.

The institution must provide access to legal advice for LAP staff members as needed to carry out assigned responsibilities.

The institution must inform LAP staff and students in a timely and systematic fashion about extraordinary or changing legal obligations and potential liabilities.

Staff development programs should be available to educate LAP staff of changing legal obligations.

Part 7. EQUITY and ACCESS

Learning Assistance Programs (LAP) must be provided on a fair, equitable, and non-discriminatory basis in accordance with institutional policies and with all applicable state/provincial and federal statutes and regulations. LAP must maintain an educational and work environment free from discrimination in accordance with law and institutional policy.

Discrimination must be avoided on the basis of age; cultural heritage; disability; ethnicity; gender identity and expression; nationality; political affiliation; race; religious affiliation; sex; sexual orientation; economic, marital, social, or veteran status; and any other bases included in local, state/provincial, or federal laws.

Consistent with the mission and goals, LAP must take action to remedy significant imbalances in student participation and staffing patterns.

LAP must ensure physical and program access for persons with disabilities. LAP must be responsive to the needs of all students and other populations served when establishing hours of operation and developing methods of delivering programs and services.

LAP must recognize the needs of distance learning students by providing appropriate and accessible services and assisting them in identifying and gaining access to other appropriate services in their geographic region.

Part 8. DIVERSITY

Within the context of each institution's unique mission, diversity enriches the community and enhances the collegiate experience for all; therefore, Learning Assistance Programs (LAP) must create and nurture environments that are welcoming to and bring together persons of diverse backgrounds.

LAP must promote environments that are characterized by open and continuous communication that deepens understanding of one's own identity, culture, and heritage, as well as that of others. LAP must recognize, honor, educate, and promote respect about commonalties and differences among people within their historical and cultural contexts.

LAP must address the characteristics and needs of a diverse population when establishing and implementing policies and procedures.

The program should facilitate student adjustment to the academic culture of the institution by orienting students to the practices, resources, responsibilities, and behaviors that contribute to academic success.

The instructional content, materials, and activities of learning assistance programs should provide opportunities to increase awareness and appreciation of the individual and cultural differences of students, staff, and faculty members.

Part 9. ORGANIZATION and MANAGEMENT

To promote student learning and development outcomes, Learning Assistance Programs (LAP) must be structured purposefully and managed effectively to achieve stated goals. Evidence of appropriate structure must include current and accessible policies and procedures, written performance expectations for all employees, functional workflow graphics or organizational charts, and clearly stated program and service delivery expectations.

LAP must monitor websites used for distributing information to ensure that the sites are current, accurate, appropriately referenced, and accessible.

Evidence of effective management must include use of comprehensive and accurate information for decisions, clear sources and channels of authority, effective communication practices, procedures for decision-making and conflict resolution, responses to changing conditions, systems of accountability and evaluation, and processes for recognition and reward. LAP must align policies and procedures with those of the institution and provide channels within the organization for their regular review.

The mission and goals of LAP, the needs and demographics of their clients, and their institutional role should determine where the unit is located in the organizational structure of the institution. Learning assistance programs are frequently organized as units in the academic affairs or the student affairs division.

Regardless of where LAP is positioned within the organization structure, it must communicate and collaborate with a network of key units across the institution to ensure coordination of related functions, programs, services, policies, and procedures, and to expedite student referrals.

LAP should have a broadly constituted advisory board to share information and make suggestions to strengthen the program.

LAP must provide written goals, objectives, and anticipated outcomes for each program and service.

Written procedures should exist for collecting, processing, and reporting student assessment and program data.

LAP must hold regularly scheduled meetings to share information; coordinate the planning, scheduling, and delivery of programs and services; identify and discuss potential and actual problems and concerns; and collaborate on making decisions and solving problems.

Part 10. CAMPUS and EXTERNAL RELATIONS

Learning Assistance Programs (LAP) must reach out to relevant individuals, campus offices, and external agencies to:
- **establish, maintain, and promote effective relations**
- **disseminate information about their own and other related programs and services**
- **coordinate and collaborate, where appropriate, in offering programs and services to meet the needs of students and promote their achievement of student learning and development outcomes**

LAP should:
- be integrated into the academic program of the institution
- establish communication with academic units and student services
- collaborate with appropriate academic departments and faculty members when providing course-based learning assistance
- encourage the exchange of ideas, knowledge, and expertise
- provide mutual consultation, as needed, on student cases
- expedite student referrals to and from the LAP
- collaborate on programs and services that efficiently and effectively address student needs
- have representation on institutional committees relevant to the mission and goals of the program such as committees on retention, orientation, basic skills, learning communities, first-year student seminars, probation review (e.g., academic, financial aid), academic standards and requirements, curriculum design, assessment and placement, and professional development
- solicit and use trained volunteers from the local community to contribute their skills and talents to the services of the learning assistance program, consistent with the LAP mission and goals and the institution's risk management policies
- provide training and consultation to community-based organizations, e.g., literacy associations, corporate training, and school-to-college transitions, initiatives, and programs

LAP must have procedures and guidelines consistent with institutional policy for responding to threats, emergencies, and crisis situations. Systems and procedures must be in place to disseminate timely and accurate information to students and other members of the campus community during emergency situations.

LAP must have procedures and guidelines consistent with institutional policy for communicating with the media.

Part 11. FINANCIAL RESOURCES

Learning Assistance Programs (LAP) must have adequate funding to accomplish their mission and goals. In establishing funding priorities and making significant changes, a comprehensive analysis, which includes relevant expenditures, external and internal resources, and impact on the campus community, must be conducted.

Adequate funds should be provided for the following budget categories: staff and student salaries, general office functions, student assessment and instructional activities, data management and program evaluation processes, staff training and professional development activities, instructional materials and media, and instructional and office technology.

LAP must demonstrate fiscal responsibility and cost effectiveness consistent with institutional protocols.

A financial analysis of costs and available resources must be completed before implementing new programs or changing existing ones. This analysis must include an assessment of the impact on students served prior to making significant changes

Opportunities for additional funding should be pursued; however, these sources should not be expected to supplant institutional funding.

Part 12. TECHNOLOGY

Learning Assistance Programs (LAP) must have adequate technology to support their mission. The technology and its use must comply with institutional policies and procedures and be evaluated for compliance with relevant federal, state/provincial, and local requirements.

LAP must maintain policies and procedures that address the security and back up of data.

Electronic systems for scheduling and record keeping must be secure.

Such systems should be integrated with institutional systems.

When technology is used to facilitate student learning and development, LAP must select technology that reflects current best pedagogical practices.

Technology, as well as any workstations or computer labs maintained by the LAP for student use, must be accessible and must meet established technology standards for delivery to persons with disabilities.

When LAP provide student access to technology, they must provide:

- access to policies that are clear, easy to understand, and available to all students
- access to instruction or training on how to use the technology
- access to information on the legal and ethical implications of misuse as it pertains to intellectual property, harassment, privacy, and social networks

Student violations of technology policies must follow established institutional student disciplinary procedures.

Students who experience negative emotional or psychological consequences from the use of technology must be referred to support services provided by the institution.

Part 13. FACILITIES and EQUIPMENT

Learning Assistance Programs (LAP) must have adequate, accessible, suitably located facilities and equipment to support their mission and goals. If acquiring capital equipment as defined by the institution, LAP must take into account expenses related to regular maintenance and life cycle costs. Facilities and equipment must be evaluated regularly, including consideration of sustainability, and be in compliance with relevant federal, state/provincial, and local requirements to provide for access, health, safety, and security.

LAP staff members must have work space that is well-equipped, adequate in size, and designed to support their work and responsibilities. For conversations requiring privacy, staff members must have access to a private space.

Facilities and equipment should support the instructional, service, and office functions of the learning assistance program. Facilities should include flexible space to accommodate different delivery modes and student needs. Consideration should be given to universal instructional design in creating classrooms, labs, resource rooms, media and computer centers, and group and one-to-one tutorial space to support instruction. Adequate space should be provided for quiet areas to support testing and other activities that require concentration.

LAP staff members who share work space must have the ability to secure their work adequately.

The design of the facilities must guarantee the security of records and ensure the confidentiality of sensitive information.

There must be adequate and secure storage for equipment, supplies, instructional and testing materials, and confidential records.

The location and layout of the facilities must be sensitive to the special needs of persons with disabilities as well as the needs of constituencies served.

LAP must ensure that staff members are knowledgeable of and trained in safety and emergency procedures for securing and vacating the facilities.

Environmental conditions such as appropriate acoustics, lighting, ventilation, heating, and air-conditioning should enhance the teaching/learning process.

Part 14. ASSESSMENT and EVALUATION

Learning Assistance Programs (LAP) must establish systematic plans and processes to meet internal and external accountability expectations with regard to program as well as student learning and development outcomes. LAP must conduct regular assessment and evaluations. Assessments must include qualitative and quantitative methodologies as appropriate, to determine whether and to what degree the stated mission, goals, and student learning and development outcomes are being met. The process must employ sufficient and sound measures to ensure comprehensiveness. Data collected must include responses from students and other affected constituencies.

Qualitative methods may include standard evaluation forms, questionnaires, interviews, focus groups, observations, or case studies, with input solicited from faculty members, staff, and students.

Quantitative measurements range from data on an individual student's performance to data on campus retention rates and success for various cohorts. Quantitative methods may include follow-up studies on students' grades in targeted courses, gain scores, grade point averages, graduation, re-enrollment, and retention figures. Program effectiveness may also be measured by comparing data of learning assistance program participants and non-participants. Quantitative program measures may include data on the size of the user population, numbers utilizing particular services and number of contact hours, sources of student referrals to the program, or numbers of students who may be on a waiting list or who have requested services not provided by the learning assistance program. Quantitative data should be collected within specific time periods as well as longitudinally to reveal trends.

LAP must evaluate regularly how well they complement and enhance the institution's stated mission and educational effectiveness.

Results of these evaluations must be used in revising and improving programs and services, identifying needs and interests in shaping directions of program and service design, and recognizing staff performance.

LAP should have the ability to collect and analyze data through its own resources as well as through access to appropriate data generated by the institution.

Periodic evaluations of LAP or services may be performed by on-campus experts and outside consultants. Evaluations should be disseminated to appropriate administrators and constituencies.

LAP should conduct periodic self-assessments, utilizing self-study processes endorsed by professional organizations. The assessments should examine the quality of services provided as well as the potential impact on student learning over time. Additionally, learning outcomes associated with LAP instructional courses should reflect what students learn or do better as a result of being exposed to course materials and instructional strategies.

Various means of individual assessment should be conducted for the purpose of identifying the learning needs of the students and guiding them to appropriate programs and services. Assessment results should be communicated to students confidentially, honestly, and sensitively. Students should be advised and directed to appropriate, alternative educational opportunities when there is reasonable cause to believe that students may not be able to meet requirements for academic success.

LAP should periodically review and revise its goals and services based on evaluation outcomes and based on changes in institutional goals, priorities, and plans. Data that reveal trends or changes in student demographics, characteristics, needs, and outcomes should be utilized for learning assistance program short- and long-term planning.

General Standards revised in 2008;
LAP content developed/revised in 1986, 1996, & 2007

The Role of Lesbian, Gay, Bisexual, Transgender Programs
CAS Standards Contextual Statement

History: It is no longer a matter of whether to provide services for lesbian, gay, bisexual, and transgender (LGBT) college students; rather, it is a matter of when. The talent, energy, and hope with which LGBT students are entering college must be acknowledged and encouraged (Sanlo, 1998). Some students are declaring their bisexual or homosexual orientations in high school, then knocking on institutional doors with expectations of being fully appreciated for who they are in their entirety—including their sexual orientations. Many more students enter college questioning their sexual identities, not yet ready to make pronouncements nor embrace labels, but they deserve the institution's demonstrated acceptance and attention.

When LGBT people refused to allow police to raid the Stonewall Bar in New York City on June 27, 1969, one more time, a stunning message was heard throughout the United States. In response to this singular event, which occurred on the heels of the civil rights movement of the 1960s, numerous Gay Liberation Front groups sprang up on college campuses everywhere, challenging both administration and faculty alike. Marcus (1993) documented the role and involvement of lesbian and gay college students and the importance of these challenges. Sexual orientation issues had finally made their way into the academy.

Public Policy: In early scientific theories, homosexuality was often described as a genetic defect, a mental disorder, or a learning disability. However, Evelyn Hooker's (1963) research found no significant differences in the psychological adjustment of homosexual men when compared to a comparable group of heterosexual men. On the basis of further research by others demonstrating similar findings, the American Psychiatric Association removed homosexuality as a diagnostic mental disorder in 1973. Two years later, the American Psychological Association took the same action and also issued a statement that its member mental health providers must actively stop discrimination against lesbians and gay men. Concurrently, the National Education Association added sexual orientation to its non-discrimination policy. To date, over 200 professional organizations, including the American Educational Research Association, NASPA, ACPA, the American Federation of Teachers, the American Counseling Association, and the National Association of Social Workers, have done the same. The revised standards of the National Council for the Accreditation of Teacher Education (NCATE) now require institutions to recruit and retain a culturally diverse faculty and student body, including individuals with diverse sexual orientations.

However, despite statements of non-discrimination by professional organizations and by institutions, everyday life has not changed dramatically for LGBT people. Given the historical context, many LGBT people still choose to remain invisible rather than face the consequences of campus intolerance and hostility (Sanlo, 1999).

The Consortium: The Consortium of Higher Education LGBT Resource Professionals (the Consortium) was officially founded in San Diego in 1997 to provide support for the professionals in this growing new arena in student affairs. Beyond membership support, the Consortium seeks to assist colleges and universities in developing equity in every respect for lesbian, gay, bisexual, and transgender students, faculty, staff, administrators, and alumni. The Consortium also focuses on developing curricula to enhance its professional goals, to promote improved campus climates, and to advocate for policy change, program development, and the establishment of campus LGBT offices and centers. The Consortium's website—www.lgbtcampus.org—offers valuable information relating specifically to higher education.

Recruitment, Retention, and Numbers of LGBT Students Unknown: Minimal data are currently available as to the number of LGBT students on college campuses. Several reasons exist to explain this fact (Eyermann & Sanlo, 2001). First, some surveys regarding sexual behavior rely on people to self-disclose same-sex interactions, thoughts, or feelings. It is unlikely that people will answer such questions honestly or at all if they do not explicitly trust the anonymity of the process. Second, some surveys rely on people to identify themselves through labels such as homosexual, lesbian, gay, or bisexual. While some LGBT people may use these labels, many others, especially LGBT people of color, may not. Either they have decided to not attach a label to their non-heterosexual identity; or they have not journeyed through the "coming-out" process sufficiently to yet identify with a label; or they use different terminology, all of which are the experiences of LGBT college students. Finally, while some people may have strong feelings of same-sex attraction, it is likely that they remain in heterosexual relationships or become non-sexual and never act on their feelings of such same-sex attraction (Eyermann & Sanlo, 2001).

Consequently, limited empirical data exist to identify numbers of LGBT students. Three factors figure into college data-gathering. First, while surveys may elicit opinions about homosexual issues, few institutions or national polls ask respondents to identify their sexual orientation. For example, neither the General Social Survey (GSS), which surveys the population at large, nor the Annual Freshman Survey conducted by the Higher Education Research Institute (HERI), elicit sexual orientation demographics.

Second, colleges and universities do not have sexual orientation or gender identity boxes on admission forms, and retention studies related to LGBT students have not yet been conducted. Therefore, when administrators wish to ascertain the number of LGBT students on campuses, there are few, if any, data bases available to provide such information. Consequently, they find themselves resorting to asking an openly gay student or staff member or simply projecting numbers from LGBT college chat rooms.

Third, student survey respondents may not use the labels used by researchers. Of the few campuses that do ask about sexual identity on campus surveys, most use the traditional terms previously noted. These labels may be offensive to some or too graphic a description for others, depending upon the stage of sexual awareness and development. Either of these opinions may prompt LGB students to falsely answer or to ignore such questions, and few surveys and campuses even consider transgender students in any context.

Violence: Like racism, sexism, and other ideologies of oppression, heterosexism - that only heterosexuality is normal–is manifested in social customs, institutions, and in attitudes and behaviors of individuals. Preserved through the routine operation of institutions, the maintenance of heterosexism is possible because it is in keeping with prevalent social norms. Higher education contributes to the maintenance of institutionalized heterosexism as evidenced by hate crimes directed toward LGBT students, faculty, and staff members (Evans & Rankin, 1998). Given that heterosexism's values underlie higher education, the work involved in proactively addressing violence against LGBT individuals and building communities that are inclusive and welcoming of LGBT persons is both controversial and demanding.

Schuh (1998) noted that campuses are "no longer safe havens for students, faculty, or staff. Violence is a community and societal problem that has found its way into institutions of higher education" (p. 347). Institutions must make concerted efforts to create campus climates where every student is safe and every faculty and staff member is secure in knowing that there will never be another incident such as the one involving Matthew Shepard at the University of Wyoming.

Services: More than 150 higher education institutions currently have full-time professionally staffed offices or centers that provide services for and about LGBT students, faculty, and staff (National Consortium website, accessed 2009). Other campuses have LGBT offices staffed by part-time graduate students, while some campuses with no actual LGBT office or center employ a person who is responsible for providing services to LGBT students (Sanlo, Rankin, & Schoenberg, 2002). Some such services include information and referral; advocacy; support/discussion groups; LGBT student organization advising; safe zones and ally projects; leadership programs; peer counseling; and Lavender Graduation celebrations (Sanlo, 2000).

References, Reading, and Resources

Evans, N., & Rankin, S. (1998). Heterosexism and campus violence: Assessment and intervention strategies. In A. M. Hoffman, J. H., Schuh, & R. H. Fenske (Eds.), *Violence on campus: Defining the problems, strategies for action* (169-186). Gaithersburg, MD: Aspen.

Eyermann, T., & Sanlo, R. (2002). Documenting their existence: Lesbian, gay, and bisexual students in the residence halls In R. Sanlo, S. Rankin, & R. Schoenberg (Eds.), *Our place on campus: Lesbian, gay, bisexual, and transgender services and programs in higher education* (pp.33-40). Westport, CT: Greenwood.

Hooker, E. (1963). Male homosexuality. In N. L. Farberow (Ed.), *Taboo topics* (44-55). New York: Atherton.

Marcus, E. (1993). *Making history: The struggle for gay and lesbian equal rights, 1945-1990: An oral history.* NY: HarperPerennial.

Sanlo, R. (2000). The LGBT campus resource center director: The new profession in student affairs. *NASPA Journal, 37,* 485-495.

Sanlo, R. (Ed.) (1998). *Working with lesbian, gay, bisexual, and transgender college students: A handbook for faculty and administrators.* Westport, CT: Greenwood.

Sanlo, R. (1999). *Unheard voices: The effects of silence on lesbian and gay educators.* Westport, CT: G Bergin & Garvey.

Sanlo, R., Rankin, S., & Schoenberg, R. (2002). *Our place on campus: Lesbian, gay, bisexual, and transgender services and programs in higher education.* Westport, CT: Greenwood.

Schuh, J. (1998). Conclusion. In A. M. Hoffman, J. H., Schuh, & R. H. Fenske (Eds.), *Violence on campus: Defining the problems, strategies for action* (347). Gaithersburg, MD: Aspen.

<u>**Contributor:**</u>
Ronni Sanlo, University of California at Los Angeles

Lesbian, Gay, Bisexual, Transgender Programs and Services
CAS Standards and Guidelines

Part 1. MISSION

Lesbian, Gay, Bisexual, Transgender (LGBT) programs and services must develop, disseminate, implement, and regularly review their mission. Mission statements must be consistent with the mission of the institution and with professional standards. LGBT programs and services in higher education must enhance overall educational experiences by incorporating student learning and development outcomes in their mission.

The scope and nature of the programs and services should be shaped by the mission of the institution.

The mission of LGBT programs and services must promote academic and personal growth and development of LGBT students, ensure unrestricted access to and full involvement in all aspects of the institution, and serve as a catalyst for the creation of a campus environment free from prejudice, bigotry, harassment, and violence and hospitable for all students.

To accomplish this mission, the goals of the program must be based on assessment of the needs of and campus climate for LGBT students. LGBT programs and services must select priorities among those needs and respond to the extent that resources permit.

To respond to the presence of LGBT students, some institutions create a separate unit. When this is the case, standards outlined here apply. Whether there is a separate unit for LGBT students or not, institutional units share responsibility for meeting the needs of LGBT students. Coordinated efforts to promote the elimination of prejudicial behaviors should be made by all functional areas.

LGBT programs and services should not be the only organized agency to meet the needs of LGBT students. All institutional units share responsibility for meeting the needs of LGBT students in their areas of responsibility. Coordinated efforts to promote the elimination of prejudicial behaviors should be made at every institution by all functional areas.

Part 2. PROGRAM

The formal education of students, consisting of the curriculum and the co-curriculum, must promote student learning and development outcomes that are purposeful and holistic and that prepare students for satisfying and productive lifestyles, work, and civic participation. The student learning and development outcome domains and their related dimensions are:

- knowledge acquisition, integration, construction, and application
    o Dimensions: understanding knowledge from a range of disciplines; connecting knowledge to other knowledge, ideas, and experiences; constructing knowledge; and relating knowledge to daily life

- cognitive complexity
    o Dimensions: critical thinking; reflective thinking; effective reasoning; and creativity

- intrapersonal development
    o Dimensions: realistic self-appraisal, self-understanding, and self-respect; identity development; commitment to ethics and integrity; and spiritual awareness

- interpersonal competence
    o Dimensions: meaningful relationships; interdependence; collaboration; and effective leadership

- humanitarianism and civic engagement
    o Dimensions: understanding and appreciation of cultural and human differences; social responsibility; global perspective; and sense of civic responsibility

- practical competence
    o Dimensions: pursuing goals; communicating effectively; technical competence; managing personal affairs; managing career development; demonstrating professionalism; maintaining health and wellness; and living a purposeful and satisfying life

[See *The Council for the Advancement of Standards Learning and Developmental Outcomes* statement for examples of outcomes related to these domains and dimensions.]

Consistent with the institutional mission, Lesbian, Gay, Bisexual, Transgender (LGBT) programs and services must identify relevant and desirable student learning and development outcomes from among the six domains and related dimensions. When creating opportunities for student learning and development, LGBT programs and services must explore possibilities for collaboration with faculty members and other colleagues.

LGBT programs and services must assess relevant and desirable student learning and development outcomes and provide evidence of their impact on student learning and development. LGBT programs and services must articulate how they contribute to or support students' learning and development in the domains not specifically assessed.

LGBT programs and services must be:
- integrated into the life of the institution
- intentional and coherent
- guided by theories and knowledge of learning and

development
- reflective of developmental and demographic profiles of the student population
- responsive to needs of individuals, diverse and special populations, and relevant constituencies

LGBT programs and services must:
- advocate for the creation of a campus climate that is free from harassment and violence
- identity environmental conditions that negatively influence student welfare
- advocate for solutions to be enacted that neutralize such condition
- work to create policies and procedures within the institution that promote and maintain a hospitable climate

LGBT programs and services must work to assure equitable access to and involvement in all educational programs.

Particular attention should be given to financial aid, athletic scholarships, and employment opportunities on campus.

LGBT programs and services must promote institutional understanding for the concerns of LGBT students, faculty, and staff, educating other campus programs and services to be responsive to the unique concerns of LGBT students.

These programs and services must include:
1. individual and group psychological counseling such as:
   1a. coming out support
   1b. services for victims and perpetrators of homophobia
   1c. services to address family issues
   1d. services to address same sex dating issues
   1e. services to address same sex domestic violence
   1f. support for victims and perpetrators of hate crimes
2. health services such as:
   2a. health forms with inclusive language
   2b. LGBT health issues brochures
   2c. safer sex information for same sex couples
3. career services such as:
   3a. resume development
   3b. information on LGBT friendly employers
   3c. employer mentoring programs for LGBT students
   3d. information on LGBT issues in the workplace
4. academic advising such as the support of students' educational choices

LGBT programs and services must provide educational opportunities that include:
- examination of the intersection of sexual orientation with race, class, gender, disability, and age

- promotion of self awareness, self-esteem, and self-confidence
- promotion of leadership experiences
- identification of and networking with role models and mentors
- support of students and their families in achieving academic success

LGBT programs and services must educate the campus community when decisions or policies may affect the achievement of LGBT students; publicize services, events, and issues of concern to LGBT students; and sponsor events that meet educational, personal, physical, and safety needs of LGBT students and their allies.

LGBT programs and services may:
- encourage awareness of off-campus networks and other support systems for LGBT students including affiliation with state and national organizations
- improve campus awareness of the complex identity issues inherent in the lives of LGBT students
- publicize the accomplishments of LBGT students, faculty members, and staff
- represent LGBT concerns and issues on campus-wide committees
- promote scholarship, research, and assessment on LGBT issues
- encourage campus-wide inclusion of LGBT students and avoidance of negative stereotyping in campus media

LGBT programs and services should maintain or have ready access to resources regarding LGBT issues.

LGBT programs and services must address the needs of all LGBT students regardless of their ethnicity, race, gender, religion, age, socioeconomic status, disability, and degree or enrollment status. In addition, LGBT programs and services must plan for and recognize the diversity among the LGBT student population.

LGBT programs and services should advocate for the human rights of LGBT persons.

Part 3. LEADERSHIP

Because effective and ethical leadership is essential to the success of all organizations, Lesbian, Gay, Bisexual, Transgender (LGBT) leaders with organizational authority for the programs and services must:
- articulate a vision and mission for their programs and services
- set goals and objectives based on the needs of the population served and desired student learning and development outcomes
- advocate for their programs and services
- promote campus environments that provide meaningful opportunities for student learning, development, and integration
- identify and find means to address individual,

organizational, or environmental conditions that foster or inhibit mission achievement

- advocate for representation in strategic planning initiatives at appropriate divisional and institutional levels
- initiate collaborative interactions with stakeholders who have legitimate concerns and interests in the functional area
- apply effective practices to educational and administrative processes
- prescribe and model ethical behavior
- communicate effectively
- manage financial resources, including planning, allocation, monitoring, and analysis
- incorporate sustainability practices in the management and design of programs, services, and facilities
- manage human resource processes including recruitment, selection, development, supervision, performance planning, and evaluation
- empower professional, support, and student staff to accept leadership opportunities
- encourage and support scholarly contribution to the profession
- be informed about and integrate appropriate technologies into programs and services
- be knowledgeable about federal, state/provincial, and local laws relevant to the programs and services and ensure that staff members understand their responsibilities by receiving appropriate training
- develop and continuously improve programs and services in response to the changing needs of students and other populations served and the evolving institutional priorities
- recognize environmental conditions that may negatively influence the safety of staff and students and propose interventions that mitigate such conditions

Part 4. HUMAN RESOURCES

Lesbian, Gay, Bisexual, Transgender (LGBT) programs and services must be staffed adequately by individuals qualified to accomplish the mission and goals. Within institutional guidelines, LGBT programs and services must establish procedures for staff selection, training, and evaluation; set expectations for supervision; and provide appropriate professional development opportunities to improve the leadership ability, competence, and skills of all employees.

Program leaders should possess the academic preparation, experience, abilities, professional interests, and competencies essential for the efficient operation of the office as charged, as well as the ability to identify additional areas of concern about LGBT students. Specific course work in organizational development, counseling, group dynamics, leadership development, human development, LGBT studies, multicultural education, women's studies, higher education, and research and assessment may be desirable.

LGBT professional staff members must hold an earned graduate or professional degree in a field relevant to the position they hold or must possess an appropriate combination of educational credentials and related work experience.

In addition to providing services, staff members should be provided time for advising and reporting, updating institutional information, research, faculty and staff contacts, staff meetings, training, supervision, personal and professional development, and consultation. Similarly, teaching, administration, research, and other responsibilities should be identified as relevant staff functions.

Staff members should have a combination of graduate course work, formal training (including gay/lesbian/bisexual/ transgender issues), and supervised experience.

Degree- or credential-seeking interns must be qualified by enrollment in an appropriate field of study and by relevant experience. These individuals must be trained and supervised adequately by professional staff members holding educational credentials and related work experience appropriate for supervision.

Student employees and volunteers must be carefully selected, trained, supervised, and evaluated. They must be educated on how and when to refer those in need of additional assistance to qualified staff members and must have access to a supervisor for assistance in making these judgments. Student employees and volunteers must be provided clear and precise job descriptions, pre-service training based on assessed needs, and continuing staff development.

Employees and volunteers must receive specific training on institutional policies and privacy laws regarding their access to student records and other sensitive institutional information (e.g., in the USA, Family Educational Rights and Privacy Act, FERPA, or equivalent privacy laws in other states/provinces or countries).

Student staff members should be provided with clear and precise job descriptions, pre-service training, and on-going staff development.

LGBT programs and services must have technical and support staff members adequate to accomplish their mission. All members of the staff must be technologically proficient and qualified to perform their job functions, be knowledgeable about ethical and legal uses of technology, and have access to training and resources to support the performance of their assigned responsibilities.

All members of the staff must receive training on policies and procedures related to the use of technology to store or access student records and institutional data.

LGBT programs and services must ensure that staff members are knowledgeable about and trained in emergency procedures, crisis response, and prevention efforts.

Prevention efforts must address identification of threatening conduct or behavior of students, faculty members, staff, and others and must incorporate a system or procedures for responding, including but not limited to reporting them to the appropriate campus officials.

Support staff should have a thorough knowledge of the institution and be able to perform office and administrative functions, including reception, information giving, problem identification, and referral. Special emphasis should be placed on skills in the areas of public relations, information dissemination, problem identification, and referral.

All LGBT program and services staff members must be responsive to and knowledgeable about LGBT issues.

Salary levels and benefits for all staff members must be commensurate with those for comparable positions within the institution, in similar institutions, and in the relevant geographic area.

LGBT programs and services must maintain position descriptions for all staff members.

To create a diverse staff, LGBT programs and services must institute hiring and promotion practices that are fair, inclusive, proactive, and non-discriminatory.

LGBT programs and services must conduct regular performance planning and evaluation of staff members. LGBT programs and services must provide access to continuing and advanced education and professional development opportunities.

Staff development is an essential activity. Additional credit courses, seminars, and access to current research are examples of professional development activities that could be made available. Additionally, staff members should participate in appropriate professional organizations and should have the budgetary support to do so. Staff members should be encouraged to participate in community activities related to the student population being served.

LGBT program and services staff members must ensure that the confidentiality of students' sexual orientation and gender identity are protected when appropriate.

The level of services must be established and reviewed regularly with regard to service demands, enrollment, user surveys, diversity of services offered, institutional resources, and other student services available on the campus and in the local community.

LGBT program and services staff must be comfortable and interested in working with gay, lesbian, bisexual, and transgender students.

Part 5. ETHICS

Persons involved in the delivery of Lesbian, Gay, Bisexual, Transgender (LGBT) programs and services must adhere to the highest principles of ethical behavior. LGBT programs and services must review relevant professional ethical standards and develop or adopt and implement appropriate statements of ethical practice. LGBT programs and services must publish these statements and ensure their periodic review by relevant constituencies.

LGBT programs and services must orient new staff members to relevant ethical standards and statements of ethical practice.

LGBT staff members must ensure that privacy and confidentiality are maintained with respect to all communications and records to the extent that such records are protected under the law and appropriate statements of ethical practice. Information contained in students' education records must not be disclosed except as allowed by relevant laws and institutional policies. LGBT staff members must disclose to appropriate authorities information judged to be of an emergency nature, especially when the safety of the individual or others is involved, or when otherwise required by institutional policy or relevant law.

LGBT programs and services staff members must ensure that the confidentiality of individuals' sexual orientation and gender identity are protected.

Information should be released only at the written request of a student who has full knowledge of the nature of the information that is being released and of the parties to whom it is being released. Instances of limited confidentiality should be clearly articulated. The decision to release information without consent should occur only after careful consideration and under the conditions described above.

LGBT programs and services staff members must be aware of and comply with the provisions contained in the institution's policies pertaining to human subjects research and student rights and responsibilities, as well as those in other relevant institutional policies addressing ethical practices and confidentiality of research data concerning individuals.

LGBT programs and services staff members must recognize and avoid personal conflicts of interest or appearance thereof in the performance of their work.

LGBT programs and services staff members must strive to insure the fair, objective, and impartial treatment of all persons with whom they interact.

When handling institutional funds, LGBT programs and services staff members must ensure that such funds are managed in accordance with established and responsible accounting procedures and the fiscal policies or processes of the institution.

Promotional and descriptive information must be accurate and free of deception.

LGBT programs and services staff members must perform their duties within the limits of their training, expertise, and competence. When these limits are exceeded, individuals in need of further assistance must be referred to persons possessing appropriate qualifications.

LGBT programs and services staff members must use suitable means to confront and otherwise hold accountable other staff members who exhibit unethical behavior.

LGBT programs and services staff members must be knowledgeable about and practice ethical behavior in the use of technology.

Part 6. LEGAL RESPONSIBILITIES

Lesbian, Gay, Bisexual, Transgender (LGBT) staff members must be knowledgeable about and responsive to laws and regulations that relate to their respective responsibilities and that may pose legal obligations, limitations, or ramifications for the institution as a whole. As appropriate, staff members must inform users of programs and services, as well as officials, of legal obligations and limitations including constitutional, statutory, regulatory, and case law; mandatory laws and orders emanating from federal, state/provincial, and local governments; and the institution's policies.

LGBT programs and services must have written policies on all relevant operations, transactions, or tasks that may have legal implications.

LGBT programs and services staff members must neither participate in nor condone any form of harassment or activity that demeans persons or creates an intimidating, hostile, or offensive campus environment.

LGBT programs and services staff members must use reasonable and informed practices to limit the liability exposure of the institution and its officers, employees, and agents. LGBT programs and services staff members must be informed about institutional policies regarding risk management, personal liability, and related insurance coverage options and must be referred to external sources if coverage is not provided by the institution.

The institution must provide access to legal advice for LGBT programs and services staff members as needed to carry out assigned responsibilities.

The institution must inform LGBT programs and services staff and students in a timely and systematic fashion about extraordinary or changing legal obligations and potential liabilities.

Part 7. EQUITY and ACCESS

Lesbian, Gay, Bisexual, Transgender (LGBT) programs and services must be provided on a fair, equitable, and non-

discriminatory basis in accordance with institutional policies and with all applicable state/provincial and federal statutes and regulations. LGBT programs and services must maintain an educational and work environment free from discrimination in accordance with law and institutional policy.

Discrimination must be avoided on the basis of age; cultural heritage; disability; ethnicity; gender identity and expression; nationality; political affiliation; race; religious affiliation; sex; sexual orientation; economic, marital, social, or veteran status; and any other bases included in local, state/provincial, or federal laws.

Consistent with the mission and goals, LGBT programs and services must take action to remedy significant imbalances in student participation and staffing patterns.

LGBT programs and services must ensure physical and program access for persons with disabilities. LGBT programs and services must be responsive to the needs of all students and other populations served when establishing hours of operation and developing methods of delivering programs and services.

LGBT programs and services must recognize the needs of distance learning students by providing appropriate and accessible services and assisting them in identifying and gaining access to other appropriate services in their geographic region.

Part 8. DIVERSITY

Within the context of each institution's unique mission, diversity enriches the community and enhances the collegiate experience for all; therefore, Lesbian, Gay, Bisexual, Transgender (LGBT) programs and services must create and nurture environments that are welcoming to and bring together persons of diverse backgrounds.

LGBT programs and services must promote environments that are characterized by open and continuous communication that deepens understanding of one's own identity, culture, and heritage, as well as that of others. LGBT programs and services must recognize, honor, educate, and promote respect about commonalties and differences among people within their historical and cultural contexts.

LGBT programs and services must address the characteristics and needs of a diverse population when establishing and implementing policies and procedures.

Part 9. ORGANIZATION and MANAGEMENT

To promote student learning and development outcomes, Lesbian, Gay, Bisexual, Transgender (LGBT) programs and services must be structured purposefully and managed effectively to achieve stated goals. Evidence of appropriate structure must include current and accessible policies and procedures, written performance expectations for all employees, functional workflow graphics or organizational charts, and clearly stated program and service delivery expectations.

LGBT programs and services must monitor websites used for distributing information to ensure that the sites are current, accurate, appropriately referenced, and accessible.

Evidence of effective management must include use of comprehensive and accurate information for decisions, clear sources and channels of authority, effective communication practices, procedures for decision-making and conflict resolution, responses to changing conditions, systems of accountability and evaluation, and processes for recognition and reward. LGBT programs and services must align policies and procedures with those of the institution and provide channels within the organization for their regular review.

LGBT programs and services should play a major role in implementing institutional programs developed in response to the assessed needs of LGBT students. Access to the policymakers of the institution should be readily available. The organization should be administered in a manner that permits the stated mission to be fulfilled. LGBT programs and services should be afforded the opportunity to organize in a manner that is efficient and best promotes equity concerns. Emphasis should be placed on achieving an organization in which services are not limited to a specific group of LGBT students (e.g. solely undergraduate students).

Part 10. CAMPUS and EXTERNAL RELATIONS

Lesbian, Gay, Bisexual, Transgender (LGBT) programs and services must reach out to relevant individuals, campus offices, and external agencies to:
- establish, maintain, and promote effective relations
- disseminate information about their own and other related programs and services
- coordinate and collaborate, where appropriate, in offering programs and services to meet the needs of students and promote their achievement of student learning and development outcomes

The success of the LGBT programs and services is dependent on the maintenance of good relationships with students, faculty, administrators, alumni, the community at large, contractors, and support agencies.

LGBT programs and services should collaborate with campus referral agencies for LGBT students (e.g., multicultural student affairs, women's centers, special academic support units, campus security, health centers, counseling centers, religious programs, and career services).

LGBT programs and services should establish relationships with a wide range of student groups (e.g., LGBT student association, student government association, fraternities and sororities) to promote visibility and to serve as a resource.

LGBT programs and services should foster relationships with academic units (especially in LGBT studies, ethnic studies, women's studies, higher education, and college student affairs) and with campus professionals (e.g., student activities, athletics, commuter affairs, and residential life.) Staff should be an integral part of appropriate campus networks to effectively participate in the establishment of institution-wide policy and practices, and to collaborate with other staff and faculty in providing services.

LGBT programs and services should establish effective relations with institutional legal counsel and legal staff of relevant professional organizations in order to effectively respond to pertinent legal issues and precedents, which underlie the delivery components.

Where adequate LGBT resources are not available on campus, LGBT programs and services should establish and maintain close working relationships with off-campus community LGBT counseling and support agencies.

An advisory board made up of students, faculty, staff, alumni, and community members may be established to advise, support, and guide the LGBT programs and services.

LGBT programs and services must have procedures and guidelines consistent with institutional policy for responding to threats, emergencies, and crisis situations. Systems and procedures must be in place to disseminate timely and accurate information to students and other members of the campus community during emergency situations.

LGBT programs and services must have procedures and guidelines consistent with institutional policy for communicating with the media.

Part 11. FINANCIAL RESOURCES

Lesbian, Gay, Bisexual, Transgender (LGBT) programs and services must have adequate funding to accomplish their mission and goals. In establishing funding priorities and making significant changes, a comprehensive analysis, which includes relevant expenditures, external and internal resources, and impact on the campus community, must be conducted.

LGBT programs and services must demonstrate fiscal responsibility and cost effectiveness consistent with institutional protocols.

Funding for LGBT programs and devices may come from a composite of institutional funds, grant money, student government funds, and government contracts.

Part 12. TECHNOLOGY

Lesbian, Gay, Bisexual, Transgender (LGBT) programs and services must have adequate technology to support their mission. The technology and its use must comply with institutional policies and procedures and be evaluated for compliance with relevant federal, state/provincial, and local requirements.

LGBT programs and services must maintain policies and procedures that address the security and back up of data.

When technology is used to facilitate student learning and development, LGBT programs and services must select technology that reflects current best pedagogical practices.

Technology, as well as any workstations or computer labs maintained by the LGBT programs and services for student use, must be accessible and must meet established technology standards for delivery to persons with disabilities.

When LGBT programs and services provide student access to technology, they must provide:
- access to policies that are clear, easy to understand, and available to all students
- access to instruction or training on how to use the technology
- access to information on the legal and ethical implications of misuse as it pertains to intellectual property, harassment, privacy, and social networks

Student violations of technology policies must follow established institutional student disciplinary procedures.

Students who experience negative emotional or psychological consequences from the use of technology must be referred to support services provided by the institution.

Part 13. FACILITIES and EQUIPMENT

Lesbian, Gay, Bisexual, Transgender (LGBT) programs and services must have adequate, accessible, suitably located facilities and equipment to support their mission and goals. If acquiring capital equipment as defined by the institution, LGBT programs and services must take into account expenses related to regular maintenance and life cycle costs. Facilities and equipment must be evaluated regularly, including consideration of sustainability, and be in compliance with relevant federal, state/provincial, and local requirements to provide for access, health, safety, and security.

LGBT programs and services staff members must have work space that is well-equipped, adequate in size, and designed to support their work and responsibilities. For conversations requiring privacy, staff members must have access to a private space.

LGBT programs and services staff members who share work space must have the ability to secure their work adequately.

The design of the facilities must guarantee the security of records and ensure the confidentiality of sensitive information.

The location and layout of the facilities must be sensitive to the special needs of persons with disabilities as well as the needs of constituencies served.

LGBT programs and services must ensure that staff members are knowledgeable of and trained in safety and emergency procedures for securing and vacating the facilities.

LGBT programs and services should maintain a physical and social environment that facilitates appropriate attention to safety factors. In addition it should provide confidential individual and group meeting space.

LGBT programs and services should have access to resources for research including access to private computer space.

Part 14. ASSESSMENT and EVALUATION

Lesbian, Gay, Bisexual, Transgender (LGBT) programs and services must establish systematic plans and processes to meet internal and external accountability expectations with regard to program as well as student learning and development outcomes. LGBT programs and services must conduct regular assessment and evaluations. Assessments must include qualitative and quantitative methodologies as appropriate, to determine whether and to what degree the stated mission, goals, and student learning and development outcomes are being met. The process must employ sufficient and sound measures to ensure comprehensiveness. Data collected must include responses from students and other affected constituencies.

LGBT programs and services must evaluate regularly how well they complement and enhance the institution's stated mission and educational effectiveness.

Results of these evaluations must be used in revising and improving programs and services, identifying needs and interests in shaping directions of program and service design, and recognizing staff performance.

Both internal and external on-going evaluations are encouraged as part of a thoughtful plan of continuous evaluation of the mission and goals of the LGBT programs and services. Periodic reports, statistically valid research, outside reviews, and studies exploring student needs and opinions should be utilized.

General Standards revised in 2008;
LGBT content developed/revised in 2000

The Role of Masters-Level Student Affairs Preparation Programs
CAS Standards Contextual Statement

Standards for the professional education of student affairs practitioners are of relatively recent vintage, having largely been established during the past several decades. In 1964 the Council of Student Personnel Associations in Higher Education (COSPA) drafted "A Proposal for Professional Preparation in College Student Personnel Work," which subsequently evolved into "Guidelines for Graduate Programs in the Preparation of Student Personnel Workers in Higher Education," dated March 5, 1967. The change in title from "proposal for" in the 1964 version to "guidelines for" in this fourth draft revision exemplifies the movement from a rather tentative statement of what professional preparation should entail to one asserting specific guidelines that should be followed in graduate education programs. A final statement, popularly recognized as the COSPA Report, was actually published some time after the dissolution of the Council (1975).

During this period, others concerned with the graduate education of counselors and other helping professionals were busy establishing counselor education standards and exploring the possibilities for accrediting graduate academic programs. A moving force in this effort was the Association of Counselor Educators and Supervisors (ACES), a division of the American Personnel and Guidance Association (APGA), now the American Counseling Association (ACA). In 1978, ACES published a set of professional standards to be used to accredit counseling and personnel services education programs. APGA had recognized ACES as its official counselor education accrediting body and moved to establish an inter-association committee to guide counselor education program accreditation activity and the review and revision of the ACES/APGA preparation standards. In response to this initiative, the American College Personnel Association (ACPA) established an ad hoc Preparation Standards Drafting Committee to create a set of standards designed to focus on the special concerns of student affairs graduate education. At its March 1979 meetings, the ACPA Executive Council adopted the committee's statement entitled "Standards for the Preparation of Counselors and College Student Affairs Specialists at the Master's Degree Level." ACPA then initiated a two-pronged effort in the area of professional standards. One was a collaborative effort with NASPA to establish a profession-wide program of standards creation and the other was a concerted effort to work under the then-APGA organizational umbrella to establish an agency for the accreditation of counseling and student affairs preparation programs. The former initiative

resulted in the creation of the Council for the Advancement of Standards in Higher Education (CAS) and the latter in the establishment of the Council for the Accreditation of Counseling and Other Related Educational Programs (CACREP), an academic program accrediting agency. Both the CAS and CACREP professional preparation standards reflected the influence of the ACPA standards for student affairs preparation.

The foregoing process was prelude to the *CAS Masters-Level Student Affairs Professional Preparation Program Standards and Guidelines*, which follow. A major value of graduate standards is that they provide criteria by which an academic program of professional preparation can judge its educational efforts. Whether used for accreditation or program development purposes, standards provide faculty, staff, administrators, and students alike a tool to measure a program's characteristics against a set of well-conceived criteria designed to ensure educational quality.

The CAS standards for student affairs graduate programs were revised in 2001 and offer standards and guidelines based on profession-wide inter-association collaboration. Topics addressed in the standards include the program's mission; recruitment and admission policies and procedures; curriculum policies; pedagogy; the curriculum; equal opportunity access and affirmative action; academic and student support; professional ethics and legal responsibilities; and program evaluation.

Curriculum standards are organized around Foundation Studies, Professional Studies, and Supervised Practice. Foundation Studies pertain to the historical and philosophical foundations of higher education and student affairs. This includes historical documents of the profession such as the *Learning Reconsidered I and II (2004, 2006)*, *Student Personnel Point of View* (ACE, 1937), *Return to the Academy* (Brown, 1972), the *Student Learning Imperative* (ACPA, 1996), *Principles of Good Practice* (Blimling & Whitt, 1999), *Powerful Partnerships* (Joint Task Force, 1998), and *Reasonable Expectations* (Kuh et al, 1994) among others. Professional Studies pertains to student development theory, student characteristics, the effects of college on students, individual and group interventions, the organization and administration of student affairs, and assessment, evaluation and research. Supervised Practice includes practica, internships, and externships under professionally supervised work conditions.

Two groups that exist to support and promote the preparation of professionals are the Commission of Professional Preparation of ACPA and NASPA's Faculty Fellows. The primary value of the CAS student affairs professional preparation standards is to assist in ensuring that an academic program is offering what the profession, through representative consensus, has deemed necessary to graduate prepared student affairs professionals.

References, Readings, and Resources

American College Personnel Association [ACPA]. Commission for Professional Preparation. ACPA National Office, One Dupont Circle, N.W., Suite 300. Washington, DC 20036-1110. (202) 835-2272; Fax (202) 296-3286. http://www.myacpa.org/comm/profprep/

American College Personnel Association (1996). The student learning imperative: Implications for student affairs. *Journal of College Student Development, 37,* 118-122.

American Council on Education (ACE) (1937). *The student personnel point of view* (Ser. 1, Vol. 1, No. 3,). Washington, DC: Author. [revised in 1949 and 1989].

Association of Counselor Educators and Supervisors (ACES). (1978). Standards for the preparation of counselors and other personnel services specialists at the master's degree level. Washington, DC: Author.

Blimling, G. S. & Whitt, E. J. (1999). *Good practice in student affairs.* San Francisco: Jossey-Bass.

Brown, R. D. (1972). Student development in tomorrow's higher education - A return to the academy. *Student Personnel Series, 16.* Washington, D.C.: American College Personnel Association.

Bryant, W. A., Winston, R. B. Jr., & Miller, T. K. (Eds.) (1991). *Using professional standards in student affairs,* No. 53. New Directions for Student Affairs. San Francisco: Jossey-Bass.

Cooper, D. L., Saunders, S. A., Winston, R. B., Jr., Hirt, J. B., Creamer, D. G., Janosik, S, M. (2002). *Learning through supervised practice in student affairs.* New York: Taylor Francis.

Council of Student Personnel Associations (COSPA). (1964). A proposal for professional preparation in college student personnel work. Unpublished manuscript, Indianapolis: Author.

Council of Student Personnel Associations (COSPA). (March, 1967). Guidelines for graduate programs in the preparation of student personnel workers in higher education. Unpublished manuscript, Washington, DC: Author.

Council of Student Personnel Associations (COSPA). (1975). Student development services in post-secondary education. *Journal of College Student Personnel, 16* (6), 524-528.

Evans, N., & Phelps Tobin, C. (1996). *State of the art of preparation and practice in student affairs: Another look.* Lanham, MD: University Press of America.

Joint Task Force of Student Learning. (1998). *Powerful partnerships: A shared responsibility for learning.* Washington, D. C. American Association for Higher Education.

Kuh, G. D. (1994). *Reasonable expectations: Renewing the educational compact between institutions and students.* Washington, D.C.: National Association of Student Personnel Administrators.

Langseth, M. & Plater, W. (Eds.). (2004). *Public work and the academy: An academic administrator's guide to civic engagement and service-learning.* Boston: Anker Publishing.

Magolda, P & Carnaghi, J. (Eds.). (2004). *Job one: Experiences of new professionals in student affairs.* New York: University Press of America.

National Association of Student Personnel Administrators (NASPA). (1987). *A perspective on student affairs: A statement issued on the 50th anniversary of the student personnel point of view.* Washington, DC: Author.

Whitt, E. J., Carnaghi, J. E., Matkin, J., Scalese-Love, P., & Nestor, D. (1990). Believing is seeing: Alternative perspectives on a statement of professional philosophy for student affairs. *NASPA Journal, 27* (3), 178-184.

Winston, R. B. Jr., Creamer, D. G., Miller, T. K., & Associates (2001). *The professional student affairs administrator: Educator, leader, and manager.* Philadelphia: Taylor and Francis.

Contributor:

Jan Arminio, Shippensburg University

Masters-Level Student Affairs Professional Preparation Programs

CAS Standards and Guidelines

Part 1. MISSION and OBJECTIVES

The mission of professional preparation programs shall be to prepare persons through graduate education for professional positions in student affairs in schools, colleges, and universities. Each program mission must be consistent with the mission of the institution offering the program.

Program missions should reflect a particular emphasis, such as administration, counseling, student learning and development, student cultures, or other appropriate emphases as long as the standards herein are met.

The program's mission may include providing in-service education, professional development, research, and consultation for student affairs professional staff members at the institution.

Each professional preparation program must publish a clear statement of mission and objectives prepared by the program faculty in consultation with collaborating student affairs professionals and relevant advisory committees. The statement must be readily available to current and prospective students and to appropriate faculty and staff members and agencies. It must be written to allow accurate assessment of student learning and program effectiveness. The statement must be reviewed periodically.

This review may be conducted with the assistance of current students and faculty, graduates of the program, student affairs professionals, and personnel in cooperating agencies.

The program faculty should consider recommendations of local, state/provincial, regional, and national legislative bodies and professional groups concerned with student affairs when developing, revising, and publishing the program's mission and objectives. The mission and objectives should reflect consideration of the current issues and needs of society, of higher education, and of the student populations served. Personnel in cooperating agencies and faculty members with primary assignments in other disciplines should be aware of and encouraged to support and work toward the achievement of the program's mission and stated objectives.

The mission and objectives should specify both mandatory and optional areas of study and should include a plan for assessing student progress throughout the program of study. The mission and objectives may address recruitment, selection, retention, employment recommendations, curriculum, instructional methods, research activities, administrative policies, governance, and program evaluation.

Part 2. RECRUITMENT and ADMISSION

Accurate descriptions of the graduate program, including the qualifications of its faculty and records of its students' persistence, degree completion, and subsequent study and employment, must be made readily available for review by both current and prospective students.

Students selected for admission to the program must meet the institution's criteria for admission to graduate study. Program faculty members must make admission decisions using written criteria that are disseminated to all faculty members and to prospective students.

Admissions materials must be clear about preferences for particular student status, such as full-time students, currently employed students, or students seeking learning opportunities by distance, and the manner in which such preferences may affect admissions decisions.

Students admitted to the program should have ample intellectual capacities, strong interpersonal skills, serious interest in the program, commitment to pursuing a career in student affairs, the potential to serve a wide range of students of varying developmental levels and backgrounds, and the capacity to be open to self-assessment and growth. Criteria known to predict success in the program for students of various backgrounds and characteristics should be used in their selection. Students from diverse backgrounds should be encouraged to apply.

Students from diverse backgrounds must be given equal opportunity for entry into the program.

Part 3. CURRICULUM POLICIES

The preparation program must specify in writing and distribute to prospective students its curriculum and graduation requirements. The program must conform to institutional policy and must be fully approved by the institution's administrative unit responsible for graduate programs. The institution must employ only faculty members with credentials that clearly reflect professional knowledge, ability, and skill to teach, advise, or supervise in the program.

Any revisions to the publicized program of studies must be published and distributed to students in a timely fashion. Course syllabi must be available that reflect purposes, teaching/learning methods, and outcome objectives.

All prerequisite studies and experiences should be identified clearly in course descriptions and syllabi.

The equivalent of two years full-time academic study must be required for the masters degree.

Ordinarily, to accomplish the goals of the curriculum as outlined later in this document, a program should include a total of 42-48 semester credit hours.

Programs must demonstrate that the full curriculum, as outlined in Part 5 of these standards and guidelines, is

covered and that graduates reflect relevant proficiency.

Because of the benefits of immersion-like educational experiences characterized by full-time study, full-time enrollment should be encouraged. However, to serve those students for whom full-time study is not possible, programs may provide opportunities for part-time study. Part-time enrollment will result in a program of more than two academic years of study.

Appropriate consideration and provisions for admission and curriculum decisions should be made for students with extensive student affairs experience.

Distance learning options may be used in the program.

There must be a sequence of basic to advanced studies. Any required associated learning experiences must be included in the required program of studies.

Associated learning experiences may include comprehensive examinations, degree candidacy, and research requirements.

Opportunity for students to develop understandings and skills beyond minimum program requirements must be provided through elective course options, supervised individual study, and/or enrichment opportunities.

Programs should encourage students to take advantage of special enrichment opportunities and education that encourages learning beyond the formal curriculum, such as experiences in student affairs organizations, professional associations and conferences, and outreach projects.

An essential feature of the preparation program must be to foster an appreciation of spirit of inquiry, in faculty members and students, as evidenced by active involvement in producing and using research, evaluation, and assessment information in student affairs.

Research, program evaluation, and assessment findings should be used frequently in instructional and supervised practical experience offerings. The study of methods of inquiry should be provided in context of elected program emphasis, such as administration, counseling, student learning and development, student cultures, or other program options.

Part 4. PEDAGOGY

Each program must indicate its pedagogical philosophy in the program literature. In addition, the individual faculty member must identify his or her pedagogical strategies. Faculty members must accommodate multiple student learning styles. Teaching approaches must be employed that lead to the accomplishment of course objectives, achievement of student learning outcomes, and are subject to evaluation by academic peers for the purpose of program improvement.

Such teaching approaches include active collaboration, service-learning, problem-based learning, experiential learning, and constructivist learning. Faculty members should elect to use multiple teaching strategies. Recognition of the student's role in learning

should play a significant role in choice of teaching approach.

Part 5. THE CURRICULUM

All programs of study must include 1) foundational studies, 2) professional studies, and 3) supervised practice. Foundational studies must include the study of the historical and philosophical foundations of higher education and student affairs. Professional studies must include (a) student development theory, (b) student characteristics and the effects of college on students, (c) individual and group interventions, (d) organization and administration of student affairs, and (e) assessment, evaluation, and research. Supervised practice must include practica and/or internships consisting of supervised work involving at least two distinct experiences.

Demonstration of minimum knowledge and skill in each area is required of all program graduates.

The curriculum described above represents areas of study and should not be interpreted as specific course titles. The precise nature of courses should be determined by a variety of factors, including institutional mission, policies and practices, faculty judgment, current issues, and student needs. It is important that appropriate courses be available within the institution or from another institution, but it is not necessary that all be provided directly within the department or college in which the program is located administratively. Although all areas of study must be incorporated into the academic program, the precise nature of study may vary by institution, program emphasis, and student preference. The requirements for demonstration of competence and minimum knowledge in each area should be established by the faculty and regularly reviewed to assure that students are learning the essentials that underlie successful student affairs practice. A formal comprehensive examination or other culminating assessment project designed to provide students the opportunity to exhibit their knowledge and competence toward the end of their programs of study is encouraged.

Programs of study may be designed to emphasize one or more distinctive perspectives on student affairs such as educational program design, implementation, and evaluation; individual and group counseling and advising; student learning and human development; and/or administration of student affairs in higher education. Such program designs should include the most essential forms of knowledge and groupings of skills and competencies needed by practicing professionals and should be fashioned consistent with basic curriculum requirements. The wide range of expertise and interest of program faculty members and other involved and qualified contributors to curriculum content should be taken into account when designing distinctive perspectives in programs of study.

Each program must specify the structure of its degree options including which courses are considered core, which are considered thematic, which are required, and which are elective.

A "core" course is one that is principal to the student affairs preparation program. Theme courses are those that center on a common content area (such as introduction to student development theory, the application of student development theory, and using student development theory for environmental assessment).

Programs may structure their curriculum according to their distinctive perspectives and the nature of their students insuring adequacy of knowledge in foundation, professional, and supervised experience studies.

Part 5a: Foundation Studies

This component of the curriculum must include study in the historical, philosophical, ethical, cultural, and research foundations of higher education that inform student affairs practice. The study of the history and philosophy of student affairs are essential components of this standard.

Graduates must be able to reference historical and current documents that state the philosophical foundations of the profession and to communicate their relevance to current student affairs practice.

Graduates must also be able to articulate the inherent values of the profession that are stipulated in these documents in a manner that indicates how these values guide practice.

These values may include educating the whole student, treating each student as a unique individual, offering seamless learning opportunities, and ensuring the basic rights of all students.

This standard encompasses studies in other disciplines that inform student affairs practice, such as cultural contexts of higher education; governance, public policy, and finance of higher education; the impact of environments on behavior, especially learning; and international education and global understanding. Studies in this area should emphasize the diverse character of higher education environments. The foundational studies curriculum component should be designed to enhance students' understanding of higher education systems and exhibit how student affairs programs are infused into the larger educational picture.

Graduates must be knowledgeable about and be able to apply a code of ethics or ethical principles sanctioned by a recognized professional organization that provides ethical guidance for their work.

Part 5b: Professional Studies

This component of the curriculum must include studies of basic knowledge for practice and all programs must encompass at least five related areas of study including (a) student development theory; (b) student characteristics and effects of college on students; (c) individual and group interventions; (d) organization and administration of student affairs; and (e) assessment, evaluation, and research.

Other areas of study, especially when used as enrichment or cognate experiences, are encouraged. Studies in disciplines such as sociology, psychology, political science, and ethnic studies, for example, may be helpful to students depending upon the particular program emphasis. Communication skills and using technology as a learning tool should be emphasized in all the professional studies areas listed above.

Part 5b.1: Student Development Theory

This component of the curriculum must include studies of student development theories and research relevant to student learning and personal development. There must be extensive examination of theoretical perspectives that describe students' growth in the areas of intellectual, moral, ego, psychosocial, career, and spiritual development; racial, cultural, ethnic, gender, and sexual identity; the intersection of multiple identities; and learning styles throughout the late adolescent and adult lifespan. Study of collegiate environments and how person-environment interactions affect student development is also required.

Graduates must be able to demonstrate the ability to use appropriate development theory to understand, support, and advocate for student learning and development by assessing learning and developmental needs and creating learning and developmental opportunities.

This component should include studies of and research about human development from late adolescence through the adult life span and models and processes for translating theory and research into practice. Studies should stress differential strengths and applications of student development theories relative to student age, gender, ethnicity, race, culture, sexual identity, disability, spirituality, national origin, socioeconomic status, and resident/commuter status. Studies should also include specialized theories of development particular to certain populations or groups.

Subpart 5b.2: Student Characteristics and Effects of College on Students

This component of the curriculum must include studies of student characteristics, how such attributes influence student educational and developmental needs, and effects of the college experience on student learning and development.

Graduates must be able to demonstrate knowledge of how student learning and learning opportunities are influenced by student characteristics and by collegiate environments so that graduates can design and evaluate learning experiences for students.

This area should include studies of the effects of college on students, satisfaction with the college experience, student involvement in college, and factors that correlate with student persistence and attrition. This curriculum component should include, but is not limited to, student characteristics such as age, gender, ethnicity, race, religion, sexual identity, academic ability and preparation, learning styles, socioeconomic status, national origin, immigrant status, disability, developmental status, cultural background and orientation, transfer status, and family situation. Also included should be the study of specific student populations such as resident, commuter, and distance learners, part-time and full-time students, student athletes, members of fraternities and sororities, adult learners, first generation students and international students.

Subpart 5b.3: Individual and Group Interventions

This component of the curriculum must include studies of techniques and methods of interviewing; helping skills; and assessing, designing, and implementing developmentally appropriate interventions with individuals and organizations.

Graduates must be able to demonstrate knowledge and skills necessary to design and evaluate effective educational interventions for individuals and groups. Graduates must be able to identify and appropriately refer persons who need additional resources.

This curriculum component should include opportunities for study, skill building, and strategies for the implementation of advising, counseling, disciplining, instructing, mediating, and facilitating to assist individuals and groups. The program of study should include substantial instruction in counseling and group dynamics. Students should be exposed to a variety of theoretical perspectives, provided opportunities to practice individual and group interventions, and receive extensive supervision and feedback. Intervention skills are complex and require periods of time to practice under supervised conditions.

In addition to exposure to intervention theory, programs of study should include instruction in individual and group techniques and practices for addressing personal crises as well as problem solving, self-examination, and growth needs. Further, studies should include problem analyses, intervention design, and subsequent evaluation. Studies should emphasize theory plus individual and group interventions that are appropriate for and applicable to diverse populations.

Subpart 5b.4: Organization and Administration of Student Affairs

This component of the curriculum must include studies of organizational, management, and leadership theory and practice; student affairs functions; legal issues in higher education; and professional issues, ethics, and standards of practice.

Graduates must be able to identify and apply leadership, organizational, and management practices that assist institutions in accomplishing their mission.

This curriculum component should include opportunities for the study of student affairs programs and services including but not limited those for which CAS has developed standards and guidelines such as admissions, financial aid, orientation, counseling, academic advising, residence life, judicial services, campus activities, commuter student programs, recreational sports, career services, fraternity and sorority advising, religious programs, service-learning, disability services, academic support

services, education opportunity programs, multicultural student affairs, international student affairs, and health services, among others. Studies of organizational culture, budgeting and finance, planning, technology as applied to organizations, and the selection, supervision, development, and evaluation of personnel should be included as well.

Subpart 5b.5: Assessment, Evaluation, and Research

This component of the curriculum must include the study of assessment, evaluation, and research. Studies must include both qualitative and quantitative research methodologies, measuring learning processes and outcomes, assessing environments and organizations, measuring program and environment effectiveness, and critiques of published studies.

Graduates must be able to critique a sound study or evaluation and be able to design, conduct, and report on a sound research study, assessment study, or program evaluation, grounded in the appropriate literature.

Graduates must be aware of research ethics and legal implications of research, including the necessity of adhering to a human subjects review.

This curriculum component should include studies of the assessment of student needs and developmental attributes, the assessment of educational environments that influence student learning, and the assessment of student outcomes of the educational experience particular to student affairs work. This curriculum component also should include studies of program evaluation models and processes suitable for use in making judgments about the value of a wide range of programs and services. Students should be introduced to methodologies and techniques of quantitative and qualitative research, plus the philosophical foundations, assumptions, methodologies, methods, and criteria of worthiness of both. Students should be familiar with prominent research in student affairs that has greatly influenced the profession.

Part 5c: Supervised Practice

A minimum of 300 hours of supervised practice, consisting of at least two distinct experiences, must be required. Students must gain exposure to both the breadth and depth of student affairs work. Students must gain experience in developmental work with individual students and groups of students in: program planning, implementation, or evaluation; staff training, advising, or supervision; and administration functions or processes.

Supervision must be provided on-site by competent professionals working in cooperation with qualified program faculty members. On-site supervisors must provide direct regular supervision and evaluation of students' experiences and comply with all ethical principles and standards of the ACPA - College Student Educators International, NASPA — Student Affairs Administrators in Higher Education, and other recognized professional associations.

Qualified student affairs professionals possessing appropriate student affairs education and experience should be invited to sponsor and supervise students for practicum and internship experiences. Typical qualifications include at least a master's degree in student affairs or a related area of professional study, several years of successful professional experience, and experience at that institution. Student affairs professionals serving as on-site supervisors and evaluators of students in training should be approved by the responsible faculty member as competent to accomplish this task.

Site supervisors must be approved in advance by program faculty. Program faculty must offer clear expectations of learning goals and supervision practices to site supervisors.

Supervised practice includes practica and internships consisting of supervised work completed for academic credit in student programs and services in higher education. The exposure of students to diverse settings and work with diverse clientele or populations should be encouraged.

Because individual supervision of students in practica and internships is labor intensive for faculty with this instructional responsibility, supervision must be limited to a small group to enable close regular supervision. Students must be supervised closely by faculty individually, in groups, or both.

When determining practicum and internship course loads, faculty members who provide direct practicum or internship supervision during any academic term should receive instructional credit for the equivalent of one academic course for each small group. Likewise, students enrolled in such internships should receive academic credit.

A graduate assistantship in programs and services in higher education, which provides both substantive experience and professional supervision, may be used in lieu of a practicum or internship. For this to be effective, faculty members responsible for assuring quality learning outcomes should work closely with graduate assistantship supervisors in students' assignment and evaluation processes. Appropriate consideration and provisions should be made for students with extensive experience in student affairs.

Preparation of students for practica and internships is required. Practica and internship experiences must be reserved for students who have successfully completed a sequence of courses pertaining to basic foundational knowledge of professional practice. This must include basic knowledge and skills in interpersonal communication, consultation, and referral skills. Students must comply with all ethical principles and standards of appropriate professional associations.

Preparation of students for supervised practice may be accomplished through special pre-practica seminars, laboratory experiences, and faculty tutorials as well as coursework.

Student membership in professional associations should be expected. Attendance at professional conferences, meetings, or other professional development opportunities should also be encouraged.

Part 6. EQUITY and ACCESS

A graduate program must adhere to the spirit and intent of equal opportunity in all activities. The program must encourage establishment of an ethical community in which diversity is viewed as an ethical obligation. The program must ensure that its services and facilities are programmatically and physically accessible. Programs that indicate in their admissions materials convenience and encouragement for working students must provide services, classes, and resources that respond to the needs of evening, part-time, and commuter students.

Discrimination must be avoided on the basis of age; cultural heritage; disability; ethnicity; gender identity and expression; nationality; political affiliation; race; religious affiliation; sex; sexual orientation; economic, marital, social, or veteran status; and any other bases included in local, state/provincial, or federal laws.

Graduate programs must be provided on a fair, equitable, and non-discriminatory basis in accordance with institutional policies and with all applicable state/provincial and federal statutes and regulations. Graduate programs must maintain an educational and work environment free from discrimination in accordance with law and institutional policy.

Consistent with the mission and goals, programs must take action to remedy significant imbalances in student participation and staffing patterns.

The program should recognize the important educational opportunities that diversity among its students and faculty brings to student affairs preparation. Therefore, programs should encourage the recognition of and adherence to the spirit of multiculturalism by all who are allied with the program's educational enterprise.

Part 7. ACADEMIC and STUDENT SUPPORT

Institutions must provide sufficient faculty and staff members, resource materials, advising, career services, student financial support, facilities, and funding resources for the program.

Outcome indicators to determine whether a program has adequate resources could include student retention.

Part 7a: Faculty and Staff Members
The institution must provide adequate faculty and support staff members for the various aspects of the student affairs graduate program.

The institution must provide an academic program coordinator who is qualified by preparation and experience to manage the program.

The program coordinator or administrative director should have responsibility for managing the program's day to day operations, convening the program faculty as required, developing curriculum, and generally administering the preparation program within the context of the academic unit to which it is assigned. This individual should be the person responsible for guiding faculty teaching assignments, establishing and maintaining connections with student affairs staff members who serve as practicum/internship site supervisors, guiding general program activities, and representing the program to external constituencies.

Faculty assignments must demonstrate a serious commitment to the preparation of student affairs professionals. Sufficient full-time core faculty members must be devoted to teaching and administering the program to graduate not only employable students but also students capable of designing, creating, and implementing learning opportunities. At least one faculty member must be designated full-time to the program.

Faculty members should be available according to a reasonable faculty-student ratio that permits quality teaching, advising, supervision, research, and professional service. A core faculty member is one who identifies principally with the preparation program. Primary teaching responsibility in the program is recognized when core faculty member's instructional responsibilities are dedicated half-time or greater to teaching the program's curriculum. Devoted full-time to the program is defined as a faculty member whose institutional responsibilities are fully dedicated to the program. Teaching loads should be established on the basis of institutional policy and faculty assignments for service, research, and supervision. A system within the program and the institution should exist for involving professional practitioners who are qualified to assist with faculty responsibilities. Collaboration between full-time faculty members and student affairs practitioners is recommended for the instruction, advisement, and practicum and internship supervision of students in the preparation program. Student affairs practitioners should be consulted in the design, implementation, and evaluation of the preparation program, particularly regarding practicum and internship requirements.

Faculty members must be skilled as teachers and knowledgeable about student affairs in general, plus current theory, research, and practice in areas appropriate to their teaching or supervision assignments. Faculty members must also have current knowledge and skills appropriate for designing, conducting, and evaluating learning experiences using multiple pedagogies.

Faculty must maintain regular office hours that are clearly listed on course syllabi and in other prominent locations.

Faculty must act in accordance with ethical principals and standards of good practice disseminated by recognized professional organizations.

The institution must provide opportunity and resources for the continuing professional development of program faculty members. To ensure that faculty members can devote adequate time to professional duties, the academic program must have sufficient clerical and technical support staff.

Technical support must be of sufficient quality and quantity to accomplish word processing, data management, scheduling, electronic instructional material development, and distance

learning. **Equipment sufficient for electronic communications and Internet use is essential.**

For more information on distance education standards refer to the CAS Standards and Guidelines for Distance Education.

Technical support should include regular training in software upgrades and new hardware developments, hardware and software repairs, virus protection, access to the web, on-line journals, courseware, and presentation software.

Classroom facilities should have the capacity to offer classes using eletronic technologies.

Adjunct and part-time faculty must be fully qualified and adequately trained to serve as teachers, advisors, and internship supervisors.

Adjuncts and part-time faculty should be provided with information about institutional policies and procedures, access to program resources and faculty, and feedback about their performance.

Part 7b: Resource Materials
Adequate resource materials must be provided to support the curriculum.

Resources may include career information; standardized tests and technical manuals; and materials for simulations, structured group experiences, human relations training, and data-based interventions for human and organization development. In addition, resources may include instruments and assessment tools that measure development and leadership from various theoretical points of view and materials that facilitate leadership, organizational design, management style, conflict management, and time management development. Resources should include software that allows for the analysis of qualitative and quantitative data.

Library resources must be provided for the program including current and historical books, periodicals, on-line journals, search mechanisms, and other media for the teaching and research aspects of the program. Library resources must be accessible to students and must be selected carefully, reviewed, and updated periodically by the program faculty.

The library resources should be available days, evenings, and weekends and should include adequate interlibrary loan services, ERIC and similar data sources, computerized search capabilities, and photocopy services.

Research support must be adequate for both program faculty and students.

Computing services, data collection and storage services, research design consultation services, and adequate equipment should be available in support of research activities of both students and faculty members. The program should provide students with individualized research project development and implementation.

Part 7c: Advising
Faculty members must provide high quality academic and professional advising.

Academic advising should be viewed as a continuous process of clarification and evaluation. High quality academic advising should include, but is not limited to, development of suitable educational plans; selection of appropriate courses and other educational experiences; clarification of professional and career goals; knowledge of and interpretation of institutional and program policies, procedures, and requirements; knowledge of course contents, sequences, and support resources; evaluation of student progress; referrals to and use of institutional and community support services; support for and evaluation of scholarly endeavors including research and assessment; and knowledge and interpretation of professional ethics and standards. Advisors should be readily available to students and should possess abilities to facilitate a student's career exploration, self-assessment, decision-making, and responsible behavior in interactions with others. Advisors should be able to interpret the scores of assessment tools used in the advising process. These might include the Graduate Record Examination, Myers-Briggs Type Indicator, and Learning Styles Inventory. The number of faculty advisees should be monitored and adjusted as necessary to ensure that faculty can give adequate attention to all advisees.

Part 7d: Career Services
The institution must provide professional career assistance, either by institutional career services or by the program faculty.

Students should be assisted in clarifying objectives and establishing goals; exploring the full range of career possibilities; preparing for the job search including presenting oneself effectively as a candidate for employment; and making the transition from graduate student to professional practitioner. Faculty members should collaborate with campus career service providers to develop an active program of assistance including acquiring job listings; the preparation of credentials such as recommending applications, correspondence, and resumes; development of employment interview skills; identification of appropriate job search networks including professional associations; selection of suitable positions; and communication of ethical obligations of those involved in the employment process. Ideally, these services should be available to graduates throughout their professional careers.

Part 7e: Student Financial Support
Information must be provided to students about the availability of graduate assistantships, fellowships, work-study, research funding, travel support, and other financial aid opportunities.

Graduate assistantships should be made available to students to provide both financial assistance and opportunities for supervised work experience.

Part 7f: Facilities and Funding Resources
The institution must provide facilities accessible to all students and a budget that ensures continuous operation of all aspects of the program.

A program office should be located in reasonable proximity to faculty offices, classrooms, and laboratory facilities. Adequate and appropriate space, equipment, and supplies should be provided for faculty members, staff members, and graduate assistants. There should be facilities for advising, counseling, and student development activities that are private, adequate in size, and properly equipped. Special facilities and equipment may include audio and video recording devices, one-way observation rooms, small group rooms, and computer labs. Adequate classroom, seminar, and laboratory facilities to meet program needs also should be available. Adequate office and technical equipment should be provided including access to e-mail and other relevant technological resources.

Part 8.
PROFESSIONAL ETHICS and LEGAL RESPONSIBILITIES

Faculty members must comply with institutional policies and ethical principles and standards of ACPA — College Student Educators International, NASPA — Student Affairs Administrators in Higher Education, American Association of University Professors, and the CAS functional area ethical standards. Faculty members must demonstrate the highest standards of ethical behavior and academic integrity in all forms of teaching, research, publication, and professional service and must instruct students in ethical practice and in the principles and standards of conduct of the profession.

Ethical expectations of graduate students must be disseminated in writing on a regular basis to all students.

Ethical principles and standards of all relevant professional organizations should be consulted and used as appropriate. An ethical climate should prevail throughout the preparation program wherein faculty members model appropriate ethical behavior at all times for students to experience, observe, and emulate. Faculty members should present various theoretical positions and encourage students to make comparisons and to develop personally meaningful theoretical positions. Faculty members are expected to ensure that educational experiences focusing on self-understanding and personal growth are voluntary or, if such experiences are program requirements, that reasonable effort is made to inform prospective students of them prior to admission to the program. Students should be held accountable for appropriate ethical behavior at all times with special attention paid to the ethics components of the various CAS functional area standards when students participate in related practicum and internship assignments.

Faculty members must strive to ensure the fair and impartial treatment of students and others.

Faculty members must maintain ethical relationships with students exemplifying respect and the ideals of pedagogy.

Faculty members must not teach, supervise, or advise any student with whom they have an intimate relationship. When a student enters an academic program having a pre-existing intimate relationship with a faculty member, both must notify a third party, such as a department chair, to monitor the pedagogical relationship and assign appropriate teaching, supervisory, and advising responsibilities.

Graduate program faculty members must evaluate annually

all students' progress and suitability for entry into the student affairs profession. Evaluation of students' ethical behaviors must be included. Faculty members must keep students informed about their progress toward successful program completion.

Through continual evaluation and appraisal of students, faculty members are expected to be aware of ethically problematic student behaviors, inadequate academic progress, and other behaviors or characteristics that may make a student unsuitable for the profession. Appropriate responses leading to remediation of the behaviors related to students' academic progress or professional suitability should be identified, monitored, evaluated, and shared with individual students as needed. Faculty members are expected in cases of significant problematic behaviors to communicate to the student the problems identified and the remediation required to avoid being terminated from the preparation program. After appropriate remediation has been proposed and evaluated, students who continue to be evaluated as being unsuitable for the profession, making poor academic progress, or having ethically problematic behaviors should be dismissed from the preparation program following appropriate due process procedures. If termination is enforced, faculty members are expected to explain to the student the grounds for the decision.

Faculty members must ensure that privacy is maintained with respect to all communication and records considered to be educational records unless written permission is given by the student or when the disclosure is allowable under the law and institution policy.

Faculty members must respond to requests for employment-related recommendations by students. When endorsement cannot be provided for a particular position, the student must be informed of the reason for non-endorsement.

Faculty members should base endorsements on knowledge of the student's competencies, skills, and personal characteristics.

Each candidate should be informed of procedures for endorsement, certification, registry, and licensure, if applicable.

Faculty members must inform all students of the institutional and program policies regarding graduate student liability.

Program policy should be established to ensure that all students are periodically informed of their liabilities and options for protection. Programs may wish to establish policies requiring students to hold membership in particular professional associations and to purchase liability insurance prior to entering into practica or internships.

Part 9. PROGRAM EVALUATION

Planned procedures for continuing evaluation of the program must be established and implemented, and the evaluation information must be used for appropriate program enhancements.

Criteria for program evaluation should include knowledge and competencies learned by students, employment rates of graduates,

professional contributions to the field made by graduates, and quality of faculty teaching, advising, and research. Evaluation of program effectiveness should reflect evidence obtained from former students; course evaluations; supervisors from institutions and agencies employing graduates of the program; personnel in state/provincial, regional, and national accrediting agencies during formal reviews; and clientele served by graduates.

Review of policies and procedures relating to recruitment, selection, retention, and career services should be included in program evaluations. The timing and regularity of evaluations should be determined in accordance with institutional policy. Generally, the length of time between comprehensive program evaluations by the program faculty should not exceed five years.

Preparation Program content developed/revised in 1979, 1986, & 1997

The Role of Multicultural Student Programs and Services
CAS Standards Contextual Statement

The expansion of the civil rights movement begun in the 1960s promoted increased access to students whose attendance in higher education had been highly under-represented, especially at predominately White institutions. Although some under-represented student enrollments have increased since the 1960s, enrollment that is representative of the national population, as well as the retention and degree completion of students of color, continues to be of considerable concern. For example, *The Chronicle of Higher Education* sited the report "A Matter of Degree" that "while 64% of fulltime students at four-year colleges graduate within six years, less than half of black students and less and half of Hispanic students do so in that period of time. The rates from low-income families are only slightly better" (Burd, 2004, p. A19). The report went on to state that the difference in graduation rates between Latino/a and White students is at "the average college" seven percentage points and 15% at a quarter of all four-year institutions.

A contributing factor in the disparity of retention rates has been the initial lack of readiness by institutions to serve expanded student populations. The establishment of Multicultural Student Programs and Services (MSPS) was initially created to respond to this lack of readiness, but more recently has developed to offer proactively programs and services that serve to create environments where all students can thrive. Although MSPS vary in structure and purpose from institution to institution, most advocate for the academic success of students. This often includes advocating for changing policies, practices, and attitudes of the campus and its students and employees that inhibit student confidence and success; offering mentoring and other community building opportunities including cultural support systems where students can feel comfortable rather than feeling that they have to assimilate into the dominant culture; implementing programs to educate the campus community about various cultures and to promote awareness of multicultural and social justice issues; ensuring access to academic support services including tutoring, special study skills training, supplemental instruction, referral to other learning assistance resources, distinctive orientation programs, academic advising, personal counseling, financial assistance counseling, career development, and graduate school advising; and offering an academic curricula where multicultural perspectives are embedded. On campuses where academic departments for ethnic, women, or queer studies exist, the MSPS sometimes coordinates services with these academic departments. Some MSPS organize services to address specific populations, while others seek to serve all under-represented and oppressed students collectively. Some have autonomous facilities that include programming, advising, classroom, and counseling space, whereas other MSPS are located in spaces under the management of other campus entities such as the campus union or housing and residence life.

Strong MSPS are essential to the retention and graduation rates of students as well as the multicultural education of the campus. Clearly, institutions exhibit their commitment to providing quality education for all their students through the level of support they provide to MSPS.

Many multicultural offices and centers have been established to serve under-represented students including students of color, women students, and LGBT students separately. These standards will focus on general programs and services for under-represented and oppressed students. For standards related to programs and services for other under-represented students see the CAS Standards for Lesbian, Gay, Bisexual, and Transgender Programs; Women Student Programs; and Disability Services.

References, Readings, and Resources

Burd, S. (June 4, 2004). Colleges permit too many needy students to drop out, says report on graduation rates. *The Chronicle of Higher Education*, A19.

Cox, T., Jr. (2001). *Creating the multicultural organization*. San Francisco: Jossey Bass, 2001.

Helms, J. E. (1992). *A race is a nice thing to have.* Topeka: Content Communications. [available through www.emicrotraining.com

Komives, S. R. & Woodard, Jr., D. B. (Eds.). (2003). *Student Services: A handbook for the profession* (4th ed.). San Francisco: Jossey-Bass.

McEwen, M. K., Kodoma, C. M., Alvarez, A., Lee, S., Liang, C. T. H. (2002). *Working with Asian college students.* San Francisco: Jossey Bass: New Directions for Student Services Series.

Pope, R. L., & Reynolds, A. L. (1997). Student affairs core competencies: Integrating multicultural awareness, knowledge, and skills. *Journal of College Student Development, 38,* 266-277.

Pope, R. L., Reynolds, A. L., & Mueller, J. A. (2004). *Multicultural competence in student affairs.* San Francisco: Jossey-Bass.

Talbot, D. (2003). Multiculturalism. In S. R. Komives & D. B. Woodard, Jr., (Eds.), *Student Services: A handbook for the profession* (4th ed.) (pp. 423-446). San Francisco: Jossey-Bass.

Tatum, B. D. (1999). Why *are all the Black kids sitting together in the cafeteria?: And other questions about race.* New York: Basic Books.

California Council of Cultural Centers in Higher Education: www.caccche.org

Contributor:
Jan Arminio, Shippensburg University

Multicultural Student Programs and Services
CAS Standards and Guidelines

Part 1. MISSION

Multicultural Student Programs and Services (MSPS) must promote academic and personal growth of traditionally underserved students, work with the entire campus to create an institutional and community climate of justice, promote access and equity in higher education, and offer programs that educate the campus about diversity.

MSPS must develop, disseminate, implement, and regularly review their mission. Mission statements must be consistent with the mission of the institution and with professional standards. MSPS in higher education must enhance overall educational experiences by incorporating student learning and development outcomes in their mission.

MSPS must assist the institution in developing shared goals and creating a sense of common community that serves all its constituents fairly and equitably and is marked by:
- access to academic, social, cultural, recreational, and other groups and activities
- opportunities for intentional interaction and engagement
- integration

MSPS must encourage the institution to hold units responsible for meeting the needs of traditionally underserved students in their area of responsibility; this includes under-represented or oppressed students, such as students of color; lesbian, gay, bisexual and transgender students; and students with disabilities.

Institutions may have more than one MSPS organization. Each of these MSPS organizations' missions may address the needs of a particular student group or groups. These missions should be complementary. If only one MSPS organization exists, the mission should address the needs of students of the many cultural and oppressed groups.

In addition, MSPS should encourage all units to include explicitly in their mission serving a wide range of underserved students fairly and equitably.

Part 2. PROGRAM

The formal education of students, consisting of the curriculum and the co-curriculum, must promote student learning and development outcomes that are purposeful and holistic and that prepare students for satisfying and productive lifestyles, work, and civic participation. The student learning and development outcome domains and their related dimensions are:

- knowledge acquisition, integration, construction, and application
    o Dimensions: understanding knowledge from a range of disciplines; connecting knowledge to other knowledge, ideas, and experiences; constructing knowledge; and relating knowledge to daily life

- cognitive complexity
    o Dimensions: critical thinking; reflective thinking; effective reasoning; and creativity

- intrapersonal development
    o Dimensions: realistic self-appraisal, self-understanding, and self-respect; identity development; commitment to ethics and integrity; and spiritual awareness

- interpersonal competence
    o Dimensions: meaningful relationships; interdependence; collaboration; and effective leadership

- humanitarianism and civic engagement
    o Dimensions: understanding and appreciation of cultural and human differences; social responsibility; global perspective; and sense of civic responsibility

- practical competence
    o Dimensions: pursuing goals; communicating effectively; technical competence; managing personal affairs; managing career development; demonstrating professionalism; maintaining health and wellness; and living a purposeful and satisfying life

[See *The Council for the Advancement of Standards Learning and Developmental Outcomes* statement for examples of outcomes related to these domains and dimensions.]

Consistent with the institutional mission, Multicultural Student Programs and Services (MSPS) must identify relevant and desirable student learning and development outcomes from among the six domains and related dimensions. When creating opportunities for student learning and development, MSPS must explore possibilities for collaboration with faculty members and other colleagues.

MSPS must assess relevant and desirable student learning and development outcomes and provide evidence of their impact on student learning and development. MSPS must articulate how they contribute to or support students' learning and development in the domains not specifically assessed.

MSPS must be:
- integrated into the life of the institution
- intentional and coherent
- guided by theories and knowledge of learning and development
- reflective of developmental and demographic profiles of the student population
- responsive to needs of individuals, diverse and special

populations, and relevant constituencies

MSPS must be based on models, approaches, or theories that address students across developmental levels.

MSPS must provide educational programs and services for all students that focus on awareness of cultural differences, cultural commonalties, privilege, and identity; self-assessment of cultural awareness and possible prejudices; and changing prejudicial, oppressive, and stereotypical attitudes or behavior.

MSPS may support other institutional functional areas such as recruitment, career services, academic advising, counseling, health services, and alumni relations.

MSPS must promote academic success of students by:
- **offering distinctive programs that introduce students to a community network and teach students how to negotiate processes within the institution (e. g., registration, academic advising, financial aid, housing, campus employment)**
- **assisting them to determine and assess their educational goals and academic skills**
- **providing support services that assist in achieving educational goals and attaining or refining academic skills**
- **informing students of educational opportunities, such as internships, special scholarship opportunities, study abroad programs, research, seminars, and conferences**
- **promoting intellectual, career, social, ethical, and social justice development**
- **networking with staff and faculty members**
- **connecting them to campus networks and groups and organizations.**

MSPS should act as a liaison for referrals and interventions with staff and faculty members and administrators on behalf of students when appropriate.

MSPS must promote personal growth of students by:
- **enhancing students' understanding of their own culture, heritage, and identities**
- **enhancing students' understanding of cultures, heritages, and identities other than their own**
- **providing opportunities for students to establish satisfying interpersonal relationships**
- **providing opportunities for interactions, exchange of ideas, and reflection**

MSPS must work to create an engaging climate for students by advocating for the following opportunities and encouraging students take advantage of them:
- **campus and community service including leadership opportunities**
- **practice in leadership including training, education, and development**
- **access to appropriate mentors and role models**
- **shared inter- and intra-social experiences**

MSPS must work to create a just campus climate by:
- **challenging tacit and overt prejudices or discrimination against students**
- **coordinating efforts to promote multicultural sensitivity and the elimination of prejudicial behaviors**
- **facilitating desired changes with the cooperation of other campus entities**
- **identifying and addressing impediments to the growth and development of full participation of students**

If institutional practices or policies have prejudicial effects, staff members must bring these facts to the attention of the proper authorities in the institution and work to change them.

MSPS must offer to the campus community programs that increase multicultural awareness, knowledge, and skills by:
- **promoting and enhancing the understanding of a variety of cultures and historical experiences**
- **promoting and enhancing the understanding of privilege, power, and prejudicial and stereotypical assumptions**
- **promoting and enhancing identity development**
- **teaching skills on how to combat racism, homophobia, sexism, and other forms of discrimination**
- **complementing the academic curricula**

MSPS must serve as a resource for multicultural training, education, and development.

Educational programs may be provided in collaboration with efforts by academic and student affairs units and other program support services. Staff members in MSPS should coordinate their efforts with academic and student affairs units and other support services. Various dimensions of students' cultures, such as history, philosophy, world view, literature, and various forms of communication and artistic expression, should be explored. Human relations programs should be designed to assist faculty members, staff members, and students in developing more tolerance, understanding, and ability to relate to others around issues of privilege; age; color; creed; cultural heritage; disability; ethnicity; gender identity; nationality; political affiliation; religious affiliation; sex; sexual orientation; or social, economic, marital, or veteran status.

Activities that attempt to promote students' development should be based upon assessments and should reflect unique dimensions of the multicultural student experience.

MSPS must assist students across the range of their experiences at the institution.

These areas may include:
- monitoring scholastic progress of groups and individual students and recommending strategies for improvement
- providing workshops, programs, retreats, and seminars on relevant topics and encouraging attendance at activities and services sponsored by other campus offices
- encouraging student attendance at conferences, meetings, and programs
- advising student organizations that advance the equality and

interests of specific groups (e. g., Black/African American students, Asian/Pacific Islander students, Latino/a students, Native students, LGBT students, and allies), editorial staffs of multicultural publications, fraternal groups, pre-professional clubs, and program councils

- providing assistance and advice in planning multicultural student celebrations (e.g., Black/African American History Month, Kwanzaa, Stonewall Anniversary, Day of Silence, Take Back the Night, Transgender Day of Remembrance)
- assisting multicultural student groups or individuals in identifying and gaining access, where appropriate, to institutional services such as printing, bulk mailing, and computer services
- providing a directory of multicultural faculty and staff members
- providing a directory of faculty and staff members who have agreed to provide mentoring and assistance
- publishing a newsletter, website, or other means of focusing on current events, leadership opportunities, and other relevant information

Part 3. LEADERSHIP

Because effective and ethical leadership is essential to the success of all organizations, Multicultural Student Programs and Services (MSPS) leaders with organizational authority for the programs and services must:

- **articulate a vision and mission for their programs and services**
- **set goals and objectives based on the needs of the population served and desired student learning and development outcomes**
- **advocate for their programs and services**
- **promote campus environments that provide meaningful opportunities for student learning, development, and integration**
- **identify and find means to address individual, organizational, or environmental conditions that foster or inhibit mission achievement**
- **advocate for representation in strategic planning initiatives at appropriate divisional and institutional levels**
- **initiate collaborative interactions with stakeholders who have legitimate concerns and interests in the functional area**
- **apply effective practices to educational and administrative processes**
- **prescribe and model ethical behavior**
- **communicate effectively**
- **manage financial resources, including planning, allocation, monitoring, and analysis**
- **incorporate sustainability practices in the management and design of programs, services, and facilities**
- **manage human resource processes including recruitment, selection, development, supervision, performance planning, and evaluation**
- **empower professional, support, and student staff to accept leadership opportunities**

- **encourage and support scholarly contribution to the profession**
- **be informed about and integrate appropriate technologies into programs and services**
- **be knowledgeable about federal, state/provincial, and local laws relevant to the programs and services and ensure that staff members understand their responsibilities by receiving appropriate training**
- **develop and continuously improve programs and services in response to the changing needs of students and other populations served and the evolving institutional priorities**
- **recognize environmental conditions that may negatively influence the safety of staff and students and propose interventions that mitigate such conditions**

MSPS leaders must base their work on models and approaches that are theory-based and data driven.

Part 4. HUMAN RESOURCES

Multicultural Student Programs and Services (MSPS) must be staffed adequately by individuals qualified to accomplish the mission and goals. Within institutional guidelines, MSPS must establish procedures for staff selection, training, and evaluation; set expectations for supervision; and provide appropriate professional development opportunities to improve the leadership ability, competence, and skills of all employees.

MSPS professional staff members must hold an earned graduate or professional degree in a field relevant to the position they hold or must possess an appropriate combination of educational credentials and related work experience.

MSPS professional staff members must possess the requisite multicultural knowledge, awareness, and skills.

MSPS professional staff should possess the awareness that cultural differences are valuable. MSPS professional staff should value the significance of their own cultural heritage and understand that of different cultures. They should have insight into the interpersonal process of how one's own behavior impacts others. They should be aware of when change is necessary for the realization of a positive and just campus.

MSPS professional staff must have knowledge about identity development and the intersections of various aspects of diversity (i.e., race and class, race and gender, race and sexual orientation) on identity development and the acculturation process. MSPS professional staff must know how various groups experience the campus and what institutional and societal barriers limit their access and their success. MSPS professional staff must know how culture affects verbal and non-verbal communication. Professional staff must be knowledgeable about research and practice in areas appropriate to their programming with students.

MSPS professional staff must be skilled in identifying cultural issues and assessing their impact. MSPS professional staff must be able to develop empathetic and trusting relationships with students. MSPS professional staff must recognize individual, cultural, and universal similarities. MSPS professional staff must be able to make culturally appropriate interventions to seek to optimize learning experiences for students. MSPS professional staff must demonstrate respect for cultural values.

The professional staff of MSPS should reflect the various student cultures involved in MSPS.

In addition to professional staff being knowledgeable in their areas of responsibility, they should be knowledgeable about career planning and development, health promotion, group facilitation, leadership training and development, workshop design, social-interpersonal development, individual and group counseling, and campus resources.

MSPS professional staff should complete specific coursework in organizational development, counseling theory and practice, identity development theory, group dynamics, leadership development, human development, and research and assessment.

MSPS professional staff must have a personal commitment to justice and social change.

Degree- or credential-seeking interns must be qualified by enrollment in an appropriate field of study and by relevant experience. These individuals must be trained and supervised adequately by professional staff members holding educational credentials and related work experience appropriate for supervision.

The use of graduate assistants and interns should be encouraged to expand staff abilities, provide peer role models, and give valuable pre-professional experience. Particular attention should be given to preparing all pre-professional assistants to be especially sensitive to cultural differences of focus populations.

Student employees and volunteers must be carefully selected, trained, supervised, and evaluated. They must be educated on how and when to refer those in need of additional assistance to qualified staff members and must have access to a supervisor for assistance in making these judgments. Student employees and volunteers must be provided clear and precise job descriptions, pre-service training based on assessed needs, and continuing staff development.

Student employees and volunteers from multicultural groups should be utilized.

Student employees must be assigned responsibilities that are within their scope of competence.

Training and activities for student employees could include retreats, leadership classes, and workshops.

Employees and volunteers must receive specific training on institutional policies and privacy laws regarding their access to student records and other sensitive institutional information (e.g., in the USA, Family Educational Rights and Privacy Act, FERPA, or equivalent privacy laws in other states/provinces or countries).

MSPS must have technical and support staff members adequate to accomplish their mission. All members of the staff must be technologically proficient and qualified to perform their job functions, be knowledgeable about ethical and legal uses of technology, and have access to training and resources to support the performance of their assigned responsibilities.

All members of the staff must receive training on policies and procedures related to the use of technology to store or access student records and institutional data.

MSPS must ensure that staff members are knowledgeable about and trained in emergency procedures, crisis response, and prevention efforts. Prevention efforts must address identification of threatening conduct or behavior of students, faculty members, staff, and others and must incorporate a system or procedures for responding, including but not limited to reporting them to the appropriate campus officials.

Salary levels and benefits for all staff members must be commensurate with those for comparable positions within the institution, in similar institutions, and in the relevant geographic area.

MSPS must maintain position descriptions for all staff members.

To create a diverse staff, MSPS must institute hiring and promotion practices that are fair, inclusive, proactive, and non-discriminatory.

MSPS must conduct regular performance planning and evaluation of staff members. MSPS must provide access to continuing and advanced education and professional development opportunities.

Part 5. ETHICS

Persons involved in the delivery of Multicultural Student Programs and Services must adhere to the highest principles of ethical behavior. MSPS must review relevant professional ethical standards and develop or adopt and implement appropriate statements of ethical practice. MSPS must publish these statements and ensure their periodic review by relevant constituencies.

MSPS must orient new staff members to relevant ethical standards and statements of ethical practice.

MSPS staff members must ensure that privacy and confidentiality are maintained with respect to all communications and records to the extent that such records are protected under the law and appropriate statements of ethical practice. Information contained in students' education records must not be disclosed except as allowed by relevant laws and institutional policies. MSPS staff members must disclose to appropriate authorities information judged to be of an emergency nature, especially when the safety of the individual or others is involved, or when otherwise required by institutional policy or relevant law.

MSPS staff members must be aware of and comply with the provisions contained in the institution's policies pertaining to human subjects research and student rights and responsibilities, as well as those in other relevant institutional policies addressing ethical practices and confidentiality of research data concerning individuals.

MSPS staff members must recognize and avoid personal conflicts of interest or appearance thereof in the performance of their work.

MSPS staff members must strive to insure the fair, objective, and impartial treatment of all persons with whom they interact.

When handling institutional funds, MSPS staff members must ensure that such funds are managed in accordance with established and responsible accounting procedures and the fiscal policies or processes of the institution.

Promotional and descriptive information must be accurate and free of deception.

MSPS staff members must perform their duties within the limits of their training, expertise, and competence. When these limits are exceeded, individuals in need of further assistance must be referred to persons possessing appropriate qualifications.

MSPS staff members must use suitable means to confront and otherwise hold accountable other staff members who exhibit unethical behavior.

MSPS staff members must be knowledgeable about and practice ethical behavior in the use of technology.

Part 6. LEGAL RESPONSIBILITIES

Multicultural Student Programs and Services (MSPS) staff members must be knowledgeable about and responsive to laws and regulations that relate to their respective responsibilities and that may pose legal obligations, limitations, or ramifications for the institution as a whole. As appropriate, staff members must inform users of programs and services, as well as officials, of legal obligations and limitations including constitutional, statutory, regulatory, and case law; mandatory laws and orders emanating from federal, state/provincial, and local governments; and the institution's policies.

MSPS must have written policies on all relevant operations, transactions, or tasks that may have legal implications.

MSPS staff members must neither participate in nor condone

any form of harassment or activity that demeans persons or creates an intimidating, hostile, or offensive campus environment.

MSPS staff members must use reasonable and informed practices to limit the liability exposure of the institution and its officers, employees, and agents. MSPS staff members must be informed about institutional policies regarding risk management, personal liability, and related insurance coverage options and must be referred to external sources if coverage is not provided by the institution.

The institution must provide access to legal advice for MSPS staff members as needed to carry out assigned responsibilities.

The institution must inform MSPS staff and students in a timely and systematic fashion about extraordinary or changing legal obligations and potential liabilities.

Part 7. EQUITY and ACCESS

Multicultural Student Programs and Services (MSPS) must be provided on a fair, equitable, and non-discriminatory basis in accordance with institutional policies and with all applicable state/provincial and federal statutes and regulations. MSPS must maintain an educational and work environment free from discrimination in accordance with law and institutional policy.

Discrimination must be avoided on the basis of age; cultural heritage; disability; ethnicity; gender identity and expression; nationality; political affiliation; race; religious affiliation; sex; sexual orientation; economic, marital, social, or veteran status; and any other bases included in local, state/provincial, or federal laws.

Consistent with the mission and goals, MSPS must take action to remedy significant imbalances in student participation and staffing patterns.

MSPS must ensure physical and program access for persons with disabilities. MSPS must be responsive to the needs of all students and other populations served when establishing hours of operation and developing methods of delivering programs and services.

MSPS must recognize the needs of distance learning students by providing appropriate and accessible services and assisting them in identifying and gaining access to other appropriate services in their geographic region.

Part 8. DIVERSITY

Within the context of each institution's unique mission, diversity enriches the community and enhances the collegiate experience for all; therefore, Multicultural Student Programs and Services (MSPS) must create and nurture environments that are welcoming to and bring together persons of diverse backgrounds.

MSPS must promote environments that are characterized by open and continuous communication that deepens understanding of one's own identity, culture, and heritage, as well as that of others. MSPS must recognize, honor, educate, and promote respect about commonalties and differences among people within their historical and cultural contexts.

MSPS must address the characteristics and needs of a diverse population when establishing and implementing policies and procedures.

Part 9. ORGANIZATION and MANAGEMENT

To promote student learning and development outcomes, Multicultural Student Programs and Services (MSPS) must be structured purposefully and managed effectively to achieve stated goals. Evidence of appropriate structure must include current and accessible policies and procedures, written performance expectations for all employees, functional workflow graphics or organizational charts, and clearly stated program and service delivery expectations.

MSPS must monitor websites used for distributing information to ensure that the sites are current, accurate, appropriately referenced, and accessible.

Evidence of effective management must include use of comprehensive and accurate information for decisions, clear sources and channels of authority, effective communication practices, procedures for decision-making and conflict resolution, responses to changing conditions, systems of accountability and evaluation, and processes for recognition and reward. MSPS must align policies and procedures with those of the institution and provide channels within the organization for their regular review.

MSPS must be located in an organizational structure that can best provide for effective programs and services for achievement of its mission.

Wherever located MSPS should collaborate and form close alliances with student affairs.

In response to assessed student needs, MSPS must play a principal role in creating and implementing institutional policies and programs.

Part 10. CAMPUS and EXTERNAL RELATIONS

Multicultural Student Programs and Services (MSPS) must reach out to relevant individuals, campus offices, and external agencies to:
- establish, maintain, and promote effective relations
- disseminate information about their own and other related programs and services
- coordinate and collaborate, where appropriate, in offering programs and services to meet the needs of students and promote their achievement of student learning and development outcomes

MSPS professional staff members must coordinate, or where appropriate, collaborate with staff and faculty members and other staff in providing services and programs to meet the needs of multicultural students.

MSPS must identify and address retention issues of underserved populations and advocate for the creation of welcoming surrounding community.

This could include MSPS involvement in community collaborations and coalitions that confront racism, sexism, and homophobia. Community services necessities should be available for all students.

MSPS must have procedures and guidelines consistent with institutional policy for responding to threats, emergencies, and crisis situations. Systems and procedures must be in place to disseminate timely and accurate information to students and other members of the campus community during emergency situations.

MSPS must have procedures and guidelines consistent with institutional policy for communicating with the media.

Part 11. FINANCIAL RESOURCES

Multicultural Student Programs and Services (MSPS) must have adequate funding to accomplish their mission and goals. In establishing funding priorities and making significant changes, a comprehensive analysis, which includes relevant expenditures, external and internal resources, and impact on the campus community, must be conducted.

MSPS must demonstrate fiscal responsibility and cost effectiveness consistent with institutional protocols.

As programs grow and student diversity increases, institutions should increase financial support.

Part 12. TECHNOLOGY

Multicultural Student Programs and Services (MSPS) must have adequate technology to support their mission. The technology and its use must comply with institutional policies and procedures and be evaluated for compliance with relevant federal, state/provincial, and local requirements.

MSPS must maintain policies and procedures that address the security and back up of data.

When technology is used to facilitate student learning and development, MSPS must select technology that reflects current best pedagogical practices.

Technology, as well as any workstations or computer labs maintained by the MSPS for student use, must be accessible and must meet established technology standards for delivery to persons with disabilities.

When MSPS provide student access to technology, they must provide:
- access to policies that are clear, easy to understand, and available to all students

- access to instruction or training on how to use the technology
- access to information on the legal and ethical implications of misuse as it pertains to intellectual property, harassment, privacy, and social networks.

Student violations of technology policies must follow established institutional student disciplinary procedures.

Students who experience negative emotional or psychological consequences from the use of technology must be referred to support services provided by the institution.

Part 13. FACILITIES and EQUIPMENT

Multicultural Student Programs and Services (MSPS) must have adequate, accessible, suitably located facilities and equipment to support their mission and goals. If acquiring capital equipment as defined by the institution, MSPS must take into account expenses related to regular maintenance and life cycle costs. Facilities and equipment must be evaluated regularly, including consideration of sustainability, and be in compliance with relevant federal, state/provincial, and local requirements to provide for access, health, safety, and security.

Adequate space should be provided for a resource library, private individual consultations, group workshops, and work areas for support staff. Many of the activities offered by MSPS require the same level of privacy as individual and group counseling.

Wherever it is located, MSPS should provide a safe haven for students. In addition, MSPS should provide a place for all students to learn to become more multi-culturally competent.

MSPS staff members must have work space that is well-equipped, adequate in size, and designed to support their work and responsibilities. For conversations requiring privacy, staff members must have access to a private space.

MSPS staff members who share work space must have the ability to secure their work adequately.

The design of the facilities must guarantee the security of records and ensure the confidentiality of sensitive information.

The location and layout of the facilities must be sensitive to the special needs of persons with disabilities as well as the needs of constituencies served.

MSPS must ensure that staff members are knowledgeable of and trained in safety and emergency procedures for securing and vacating the facilities.

Part 14. ASSESSMENT and EVALUATION

Multicultural Student Programs and Services (MSPS) must establish systematic plans and processes to meet internal and external accountability expectations with regard to program as well as student learning and development outcomes. MSPS must conduct regular assessment and evaluations. Assessments must include qualitative and quantitative methodologies as appropriate, to determine whether and to what degree the stated mission, goals, and student learning and development outcomes are being met. The process must employ sufficient and sound measures to ensure comprehensiveness. Data collected must include responses from students and other affected constituencies.

Assessments may involve many methods. Survey instruments, interviews, behavioral observations, or some combination of these methods may be appropriate in a given institution.

General evaluation of the multicultural student programs and services must be conducted on a regularly scheduled basis. MSPS must solicit evaluative data from current multicultural students.

MSPS should solicit evaluative and developmental data from alumni.

Assessments must be conducted in a manner to assure an effective response.

MSPS should consult with the population to be assessed on the nature of the assessment.

MSPS must evaluate regularly how well they complement and enhance the institution's stated mission and educational effectiveness.

Results of these evaluations must be used in revising and improving programs and services, identifying needs and interests in shaping directions of program and service design, and recognizing staff performance.

MSPS should assess the degree of congruence between students' educational goals and offerings of the institution and communicate the results of the assessment to appropriate decision makers.

General Standards revised in 2008;
MSPS (formerly Minority Student Programs) content developed/revised in 1986, 1997, & 2006

The Role of Orientation Programs
CAS Standards Contextual Statement

To understand current trends in orientation programs, it is helpful to view today's practice within an historical context. The history of orientation programs in the United States is virtually as old as the history of the country's higher education. Harvard College was the first to formalize a system by which experienced students assisted new students in their transition to the institution. In addition to a personalized support system, students also experienced certain rites of passage which, from today's perspective, would likely be considered hazing. While the system was somewhat flawed, it was the beginning of the formalization of orientation as a process that included support of students and their families as the transition to higher education began.

Later in the 19th century, Harvard institutionalized faculty-student contact by assigning faculty members educational and administrative responsibilities outside the classroom. One of these responsibilities was the orientation of new students. Soon other colleges also took an interest in the concerns specific to freshman students..

The National Orientation Directors Association (NODA) was chartered in 1976 and continues the tradition of orientation, retention, and transition professionals who have met annually for over 40 years. The Association is governed by a Board of Directors consisting of regional representatives and officers. Editors for the various NODA publications, regional coordinators, and other appointed positions work closely with the Board to plan and implement activities and services. National and regional networks address special interests such as nontraditional students, two-year and small colleges, Canadian colleges, multicultural affairs, and GLBT issues as well as transfer and parent services.

Today's orientation programs have responded to changing demographics by changing institutional agendas across the nation. Programs have evolved from simply providing individualized faculty attention to focusing on a multitude of important issues while responding to the needs of an increasingly diverse student and family population. Many programs rely extensively on highly trained and motivated peer groups (Orientation Leaders) in the achievement of the Orientation mission.

Today, most orientation programs seek to provide a clear and cogent introduction to an institution's academic community. Orientation is viewed by most as an important tool for continued student recruitment and retention. Most institutions include academic advising and registration for classes in their orientation programs as an impetus for active participation. Many institutions are implementing continuing orientation programs via a first-year experience course. Because of such changes, colleges and universities are taking steps to encourage student and parent attendance by formalizing and marketing orientation programs from a decidedly academic perspective, but which address many issues of wider interest and concern related to matriculation, student support services, and campus life. A growing trend has been the high level of attendance at orientation programs by parents and families; they often are very involved in the transition process, and in response, many institutions deliver parent orientation programs separate from the student.

One of the most important changes is that orientation is now viewed as a comprehensive process rather than as a minimal program. Examples include programs lasting from one day to a week in length, welcome weeks, and tradition camps. Colleges and universities nationally and internationally are developing wide-ranging orientation programs that truly address the transitional needs of diverse students and families.

What trends will guide future approaches to orientation programs? It is certain that recruitment and retention will continue to be major forces in the development of orientation programs. Likewise, attempts to foster an environment responsive to the individual needs of students and families will have a significant effect on orientation programming. Additionally, funding for orientation programs will continue as a matter of concern. Demographic changes in institutions of higher education and in society at large will require institutional and programmatic responses. Maintaining current orientation and transitional programs by simply reacting to change does little to address the interests of all constituents. New and creative programs and methodologies must be planned, implemented, and assessed if the personal and educational needs of new and transfer students and their families are to be met.

For orientation programs, research, assessment, and evaluation are vital and must include evidence of program impact on the achievement of student learning and development outcomes. The CAS Orientation Programs Standards and Guidelines that follow have utility for national and international institutions and provide criteria by which to evaluate the quality and appropriateness of orientation programs.

References, Readings, and Resources

Designing Successful Transitions: A Guide for Orienting Students to College Columbia, SC: University of South Carolina.

National Orientation Directors Association: www.nodaweb.org

National Orientation Directors Data Bank.
College Park, MD: University of Maryland at College Park.

National Orientation Directors Association Member Handbook
Minneapolis: University of Minnesota.

National Orientation Directors Association
The Orientation Review
Minneapolis: University of Minnesota

National Orientation Directors Association
Orientation Planning Manual
Flint, MI: University of Michigan-Flint

The Journal of College Orientation and Transition
DeKalb, IL: Northern Illinois University

Contributors:
Current edition:
Ralph Busby, Stephen F. Austin State University, NODA
Previous editions:
Ralph Busby, Stephen F. Austin State University, NODA
Gerry Strumpf, University of Maryland, NODA

Orientation Programs
CAS Standards and Guidelines

Part 1. MISSION

The mission of Orientation Programs (OP) must include facilitating the transition of new students into the institution; preparing students for the institution's educational opportunities and student responsibilities; initiating the integration of new students into the intellectual, cultural, and social climate of the institution; and supporting the parents, partners, guardians, and children of the new student.

OP must develop, disseminate, implement, and regularly review their mission. Mission statements must be consistent with the mission of the institution and with professional standards. OP in higher education must enhance overall educational experiences by incorporating student learning and development outcomes in their mission.

Part 2. PROGRAM

The formal education of students, consisting of the curriculum and the co-curriculum, must promote student learning and development outcomes that are purposeful and holistic and that prepare students for satisfying and productive lifestyles, work, and civic participation. The student learning and development outcome domains and their related dimensions are:

• knowledge acquisition, integration, construction, and application
  o Dimensions: understanding knowledge from a range of disciplines; connecting knowledge to other knowledge, ideas, and experiences; constructing knowledge; and relating knowledge to daily life

• cognitive complexity
  o Dimensions: critical thinking; reflective thinking; effective reasoning; and creativity

• intrapersonal development
  o Dimensions: realistic self-appraisal, self-understanding, and self-respect; identity development; commitment to ethics and integrity; and spiritual awareness

• interpersonal competence
  o Dimensions: meaningful relationships; interdependence; collaboration; and effective leadership

• humanitarianism and civic engagement
  o Dimensions: understanding and appreciation of cultural and human differences; social responsibility; global perspective; and sense of civic responsibility

• practical competence
  o Dimensions: pursuing goals; communicating effectively; technical competence; managing personal affairs; managing career development; demonstrating professionalism; maintaining health and wellness; and living a purposeful and satisfying life

[See *The Council for the Advancement of Standards Learning and Developmental Outcomes* statement for examples of outcomes related to these domains and dimensions.]

Consistent with the institutional mission, Orientation Programs (OP) must identify relevant and desirable student learning and development outcomes from among the six domains and related dimensions. When creating opportunities for student learning and development, OP must explore possibilities for collaboration with faculty members and other colleagues.

OP must assess relevant and desirable student learning and development outcomes and provide evidence of their impact on student learning and development. OP must articulate how they contribute to or support students' learning and development in the domains not specifically assessed.

OP must be:
  ▪ integrated into the life of the institution
  ▪ intentional and coherent
  ▪ guided by theories and knowledge of learning and development
  ▪ reflective of developmental and demographic profiles of the student population
  ▪ responsive to needs of individuals, diverse and special populations, and relevant constituencies

OP must aid students and their families (i.e., parents, guardians, partners and children) in understanding the nature and purpose of the institution, their membership in the academic community, and their relationship to the intellectual, cultural, and social climate of the institution.

OP should introduce students to the learning and development that will occur throughout the collegiate experience.

OP must continue as a process to address, as appropriate, transitional events, issues, and needs. The orientation process must include pre-enrollment, entry, and post-matriculation services and programs.

Components of OP may include credit and non-credit courses, seminars, adventure programs, service-learning, summer readings, learning communities, Freshmen Interest Groups (FIGs), web-based educational opportunities, comprehensive mailings, electronic communications, and campus visitations and may be administered through multiple institutional offices.

OP must:
  ▪ be based on stated goals and objectives
  ▪ be coordinated with the relevant programs and activities of other institutional units

- **be available to all students new to the institution, as well as to families**
  First-year, transfer, and entering graduate students, as well as their families, should be served as distinct populations with specific attention given to the needs of sub-groups such as students with disabilities, athletes, adult learners, under-prepared students, under-represented students, honor students, and international students.

- **assist new students as well as their families in understanding the purposes of higher education and the mission of the institution**
  New students should have a clear understanding of the overall purpose of higher education and how this general purpose translates to the institution they are attending. The roles, responsibilities, and expectations of students, faculty and staff members, and families should be included.

- **articulate the institution's expectations of students (e.g., scholarship, integrity, conduct, financial obligations, ethical use of technology) and provide information that clearly identifies relevant administrative policies and procedures and programs to enable students to make well-reasoned and well-informed choices**

- **provide new students with information and opportunities for academic and personal self-assessment**
  OP should assist students in the selection of appropriate courses and course levels, making use of relevant placement examinations, entrance examinations, and academic records.

- **use qualified faculty members, staff, or peer advisors to explain class scheduling, registration processes, and campus life**

- **provide new students, as well as their families, with information about laws and policies regarding educational records and other protected information**
  OP should emphasize the independence of students in accomplishing their goals while acknowledging their interdependence with their peers and families.

- **inform new students, as well as their families, about the availability of services and programs**

- **assist new students, as well as their families, in becoming familiar with the campus and local environment**
  OP for students and families should provide information about the physical layout of the campus, including the location and purposes of campus facilities, support services, co-curricular venues, and administrative offices. Information about personal health, safety, and security should also be included.

- **assist new students, as well as their families, in becoming familiar with the wide range of electronic and information resources available and expectations for their use**
  OP should provide information about technological resources used to conduct institutional business and scholarly work including information about student information systems, electronic databases, email, and online course software. Information about how to manage responsible and ethical use of institutional technological resources should also be presented.

- **provide time for students to become acquainted with**

their new environment

- **provide intentional opportunities for new students to interact with fellow new students as well as continuing students and faculty and staff members**
  OP should design and facilitate opportunities for new students to discuss their expectations and perceptions of the campus and to clarify their personal and educational goals.
  OP should design and facilitate opportunities for new students to meet their peers and begin forming new relationships.

OP must inform students about the history, traditions, and campus cultures to facilitate an identification with and integration into the institution.

Part 3. LEADERSHIP

Because effective and ethical leadership is essential to the success of all organizations, Orientation Program (OP) leaders with organizational authority for the programs and services must:

- **articulate a vision and mission for their programs and services**
- **set goals and objectives based on the needs of the population served and desired student learning and development outcomes**
- **advocate for their programs and services**
- **promote campus environments that provide meaningful opportunities for student learning, development, and integration**
- **identify and find means to address individual, organizational, or environmental conditions that foster or inhibit mission achievement**
- **advocate for representation in strategic planning initiatives at appropriate divisional and institutional levels**
- **initiate collaborative interactions with stakeholders who have legitimate concerns and interests in the functional area**
- **apply effective practices to educational and administrative processes**
- **prescribe and model ethical behavior**
- **communicate effectively**
- **manage financial resources, including planning, allocation, monitoring, and analysis**
- **incorporate sustainability practices in the management and design of programs, services, and facilities**
- **manage human resource processes including recruitment, selection, development, supervision, performance planning, and evaluation**
- **empower professional, support, and student staff to accept leadership opportunities**
- **encourage and support scholarly contribution to the profession**
- **be informed about and integrate appropriate technologies into programs and services**
- **be knowledgeable about federal, state/provincial, and local laws relevant to the programs and services**

and ensure that staff members understand their responsibilities by receiving appropriate training

- develop and continuously improve programs and services in response to the changing needs of students and other populations served and the evolving institutional priorities
- recognize environmental conditions that may negatively influence the safety of staff and students and propose interventions that mitigate such conditions

Part 4. HUMAN RESOURCES

Orientation Programs (OP) must be staffed adequately by individuals qualified to accomplish the mission and goals. Within institutional guidelines, OP must establish procedures for staff selection, training, and evaluation; set expectations for supervision; and provide appropriate professional development opportunities to improve the leadership ability, competence, and skills of all employees.

Faculty involvement in the development and delivery of OP is essential to its success. Faculty members should be included as part of the overall staffing.

OP professional staff members must hold an earned graduate or professional degree in a field relevant to the position they hold or must possess an appropriate combination of educational credentials and related work experience.

Degree- or credential-seeking interns must be qualified by enrollment in an appropriate field of study and by relevant experience. These individuals must be trained and supervised adequately by professional staff members holding educational credentials and related work experience appropriate for supervision.

Student employees and volunteers must be carefully selected, trained, supervised, and evaluated. They must be educated on how and when to refer those in need of additional assistance to qualified staff members and must have access to a supervisor for assistance in making these judgments. Student employees and volunteers must be provided clear and precise job descriptions, pre-service training based on assessed needs, and continuing staff development.

Student staff must be informed as to the limits of their authority, the expectation for appropriate role modeling, and their potential influence on new students.

Employees and volunteers must receive specific training on institutional policies and privacy laws regarding their access to student records and other sensitive institutional information (e.g., in the USA, Family Educational Rights and Privacy Act, FERPA, or equivalent privacy laws in other states/provinces or countries).

OP must have technical and support staff members adequate to accomplish their mission. All members of the staff must be technologically proficient and qualified to perform their job functions, be knowledgeable about ethical and legal uses of technology, and have access to training and resources to support the performance of their assigned responsibilities.

All members of the staff must receive training on policies and procedures related to the use of technology to store or access student records and institutional data.

OP must ensure that staff members are knowledgeable about and trained in emergency procedures, crisis response, and prevention efforts. Prevention efforts must address identification of threatening conduct or behavior of students, faculty members, staff, and others and must incorporate a system or procedures for responding, including but not limited to reporting them to the appropriate campus officials.

Salary levels and benefits for all staff members must be commensurate with those for comparable positions within the institution, in similar institutions, and in the relevant geographic area.

OP must maintain position descriptions for all staff members.

To create a diverse staff, OP must institute hiring and promotion practices that are fair, inclusive, proactive, and non-discriminatory.

OP must conduct regular performance planning and evaluation of staff members. OP must provide access to continuing and advanced education and professional development opportunities.

Part 5. ETHICS

Persons involved in the delivery of Orientation Programs (OP) must adhere to the highest principles of ethical behavior. OP must review relevant professional ethical standards and develop or adopt and implement appropriate statements of ethical practice. OP must publish these statements and ensure their periodic review by relevant constituencies.

OP must orient new staff members to relevant ethical standards and statements of ethical practice.

OP staff members must ensure that privacy and confidentiality are maintained with respect to all communications and records to the extent that such records are protected under the law and appropriate statements of ethical practice. Information contained in students' education records must not be disclosed except as allowed by relevant laws and institutional policies. OP staff members must disclose to appropriate authorities information judged to be of an emergency nature, especially when the safety of the individual or others is involved, or when otherwise required by institutional policy or relevant law.

OP staff members must be aware of and comply with the provisions contained in the institution's policies pertaining to human subjects research and student rights and responsibilities, as well as those in other relevant institutional policies addressing ethical practices and confidentiality of research data concerning individuals.

OP staff members must recognize and avoid personal conflicts of interest or appearance thereof in the performance of their work.

OP staff members must strive to insure the fair, objective, and impartial treatment of all persons with whom they interact.

When handling institutional funds, OP staff members must ensure that such funds are managed in accordance with established and responsible accounting procedures and the fiscal policies or processes of the institution.

Promotional and descriptive information must be accurate and free of deception.

OP staff members must perform their duties within the limits of their training, expertise, and competence. When these limits are exceeded, individuals in need of further assistance must be referred to persons possessing appropriate qualifications.

OP staff members must use suitable means to confront and otherwise hold accountable other staff members who exhibit unethical behavior.

OP staff members must be knowledgeable about and practice ethical behavior in the use of technology.

Part 6. LEGAL RESPONSIBILITIES

Orientation Program (OP) staff members must be knowledgeable about and responsive to laws and regulations that relate to their respective responsibilities and that may pose legal obligations, limitations, or ramifications for the institution as a whole. As appropriate, staff members must inform users of programs and services, as well as officials, of legal obligations and limitations including constitutional, statutory, regulatory, and case law; mandatory laws and orders emanating from federal, state/provincial, and local governments; and the institution's policies.

OP must have written policies on all relevant operations, transactions, or tasks that may have legal implications.

OP staff members must neither participate in nor condone any form of harassment or activity that demeans persons or creates an intimidating, hostile, or offensive campus environment.

OP staff members must use reasonable and informed practices to limit the liability exposure of the institution and its officers, employees, and agents. OP staff members must be informed about institutional policies regarding risk management, personal liability, and related insurance coverage options and must be referred to external sources if coverage is not provided by the institution.

The institution must provide access to legal advice for OP staff members as needed to carry out assigned responsibilities.

The institution must inform OP staff and students in a timely and systematic fashion about extraordinary or changing legal obligations and potential liabilities.

Part 7. EQUITY and ACCESS

Orientation Programs (OP) must be provided on a fair, equitable, and non-discriminatory basis in accordance with institutional policies and with all applicable state/provincial and federal statutes and regulations. (OP) must maintain an educational and work environment free from discrimination in accordance with law and institutional policy.

Discrimination must be avoided on the basis of age; cultural heritage; disability; ethnicity; gender identity and expression; nationality; political affiliation; race; religious affiliation; sex; sexual orientation; economic, marital, social, or veteran status; and any other bases included in local, state/provincial, or federal laws.

Consistent with the mission and goals, programs and services must take action to remedy significant imbalances in student participation and staffing patterns.

OP must ensure physical and program access for persons with disabilities. OP must be responsive to the needs of all students and other populations served when establishing hours of operation and developing methods of delivering programs and services.

OP must recognize the needs of distance learning students by providing appropriate and accessible services and assisting them in identifying and gaining access to other appropriate services in their geographic region.

Part 8. DIVERSITY

Within the context of each institution's unique mission, diversity enriches the community and enhances the collegiate experience for all; therefore, Orientation Programs (OP) must create and nurture environments that are welcoming to and bring together persons of diverse backgrounds.

OP must promote environments that are characterized by open and continuous communication that deepens understanding of one's own identity, culture, and heritage, as well as that of others. OP must recognize, honor, educate, and promote respect about commonalties and differences among people within their historical and cultural contexts.

OP must address the characteristics and needs of a diverse population when establishing and implementing policies and procedures.

Part 9. ORGANIZATION and MANAGEMENT

To promote student learning and development outcomes, Orientation Programs (OP) must be structured purposefully and managed effectively to achieve stated goals. Evidence of appropriate structure must include current and accessible policies and procedures, written performance expectations for all employees, functional workflow graphics or organizational charts, and clearly stated program and service delivery expectations.

OP must monitor websites used for distributing information to ensure that the sites are current, accurate, appropriately referenced, and accessible.

Evidence of effective management must include use of comprehensive and accurate information for decisions, clear sources and channels of authority, effective communication practices, procedures for decision-making and conflict resolution, responses to changing conditions, systems of accountability and evaluation, and processes for recognition and reward. OP must align policies and procedures with those of the institution and provide channels within the organization for their regular review.

All institutional offices involved in program delivery should be involved in the review of administrative policies and procedures.

Coordination of OP must occur even though a number of offices may be involved in the delivery of structured activities.

The size, nature, and complexity of the institution should guide the administrative scope and structure of OP.

Part 10. CAMPUS and EXTERNAL RELATIONS

Orientation Programs (OP) must reach out to relevant individuals, campus offices, and external agencies to:
- establish, maintain, and promote effective relations
- disseminate information about their own and other related programs and services
- coordinate and collaborate, where appropriate, in offering programs and services to meet the needs of students and promote their achievement of student learning and development outcomes

OP should be an institution-wide process that systematically involves student affairs, academic affairs, and other administrative units, such as public safety, physical plant, and the business office.

OP should establish policies and practices that address how the institution should interact with parents and families.

OP must have procedures and guidelines consistent with institutional policy for responding to threats, emergencies, and crisis situations. Systems and procedures must be in place to disseminate timely and accurate information to students and other members of the campus community during emergency situations.

OP must have procedures and guidelines consistent with institutional policy for communicating with the media.

Part 11. FINANCIAL RESOURCES

Orientation Programs (OP) must have adequate funding to accomplish their mission and goals. In establishing funding priorities and making significant changes, a comprehensive analysis, which includes relevant expenditures, external and internal resources, and impact on the campus community, must be conducted.

OP must demonstrate fiscal responsibility and cost effectiveness consistent with institutional protocols.

OP should be funded through institutional resources. In addition to institutional funding, other sources may be considered, including state appropriations, student fees, user fees, donations, contributions, concession and store sales, rentals, and dues.

Overnight programs may require students and their families to stay on campus. Recovering room and board costs directly from participants is an acceptable practice.

Resources, such as grants or loans, should be available to those students unable to afford the cost associated with orientation.

Part 12. TECHNOLOGY

Orientation Programs (OP) must have adequate technology to support their mission. The technology and its use must comply with institutional policies and procedures and be evaluated for compliance with relevant federal, state/provincial, and local requirements.

OP must maintain policies and procedures that address the security and back up of data.

When technology is used to facilitate student learning and development, OP must select technology that reflects current best pedagogical practices.

Technology, as well as any workstations or computer labs maintained by the OP for student use, must be accessible and must meet established technology standards for delivery to persons with disabilities.

When OP provide student access to technology, they must provide:
- access to policies that are clear, easy to understand, and available to all students
- access to instruction or training on how to use the technology
- access to information on the legal and ethical implications of misuse as it pertains to intellectual property, harassment, privacy, and social networks.

Student violations of technology policies must follow established institutional student disciplinary procedures.

Students who experience negative emotional or psychological consequences from the use of technology must be referred to support services provided by the institution.

Part 13. FACILITIES and EQUIPMENT

Orientation Programs (OP) must have adequate, accessible, suitably located facilities and equipment to support their mission and goals. If acquiring capital equipment as defined by the institution, OP must take into account expenses related to regular maintenance and life cycle costs. Facilities and equipment must be evaluated regularly, including consideration of sustainability, and be in compliance with relevant federal, state/provincial, and local requirements to provide for access, health, safety, and security.

OP staff members must have work space that is well-equipped, adequate in size, and designed to support their work and responsibilities. For conversations requiring privacy, staff members must have access to a private space.

OP staff members who share work space must have the ability to secure their work adequately.

The design of the facilities must guarantee the security of records and ensure the confidentiality of sensitive information.

The location and layout of the facilities must be sensitive to the special needs of persons with disabilities as well as the needs of constituencies served.

OP must ensure that staff members are knowledgeable of and trained in safety and emergency procedures for securing and vacating the facilities.

Cooperation from the campus community is necessary to provide appropriate facilities to implement orientation programs. Whenever possible, a single office location to house personnel and provide adequate workspace should be conveniently located and suitable for its high level of interaction with the public.

Part 14. ASSESSMENT and EVALUATION

Orientation Programs (OP) must establish systematic plans and processes to meet internal and external accountability expectations with regard to program as well as student learning and development outcomes. OP must conduct regular assessment and evaluations. Assessments must include qualitative and quantitative methodologies as appropriate, to determine whether and to what degree the stated mission, goals, and student learning and development outcomes are being met. The process must employ sufficient and sound measures to ensure comprehensiveness. Data collected must include responses from students and other affected constituencies.

OP must evaluate regularly how well they complement and enhance the institution's stated mission and educational effectiveness.

Results of these evaluations must be used in revising and improving programs and services, identifying needs and interests in shaping directions of program and service design, and recognizing staff performance.

Evaluation of student and institutional needs, goals, objectives, and the effectiveness of orientation programs should occur on a regular basis. A representative cross-section of appropriate people from the campus community should be involved in reviews of orientation programs.

General Standards revised in 2008;
OP content developed/revised in 1986, 1996, & 2005

The Role of Recreational Sports Programs
CAS Standards Contextual Statement

Recreational sports programs are viewed as essential components of higher education, supplementing the educational process through enhancement of students' physical, mental, and emotional development. Students who participate in recreational sports tend to develop positive self-images, awareness of strengths, increased tolerance and self-control, stronger social interaction skills, and maturity — all gleaned from recreational sports experiences. The field of recreational sports has grown into a dynamic, organized presence providing quality co-curricular opportunities for the majority of the student body.

The term "intramural" is derived from the Latin words "intra," meaning "within," and "muralis," meaning "walls." Intramurals began in U.S. colleges and universities during the 19th century as students developed leisure time sporting events. Throughout that century, intramural sports were almost exclusively the only form of athletic competition for college males. Originating from intramurals, interest in varsity athletics increased in popularity and institutions assumed responsibility for organizing athletic events.

Until late in the 1800s, intramural sports were perceived by most to be of little instructional or educational value. Near the end of the century, however, colleges and universities began to administer intramural sports for men. In 1913, the first professional staff members were employed to direct intramural programs. Intramurals continued to grow in strength and gain support, until by the 1950s there was a general realization by institutional leaders of the intrinsic educational value of sports participation. Programs expanded and additional facilities were constructed in response to student-led initiatives, and campus facilities were established exclusively for recreational sports activities.

Over time, intramural programs diversified and participation increased. The rise in popularity of aerobic exercise and a societal push toward greater gender equity, including implementation of Title IX of the Education Amendments of 1972, produced an influx of women into collegiate recreational sports, resulting in even higher levels of interest and participation. Consequently, the late 1980s witnessed a second period of rapid growth in programs and the advent of new and better campus facilities for physical activities.

The beginning of the 21st century found even greater expansion of collegiate recreational sports opportunities and facilities, reaching an estimated combined enrollment of 7.1 million students, with an estimated 5.3 million students considered heavy or regular users of established campus recreational sports programs and facilities (NIRSA, 2005). New construction of campus recreational sports facilities, and refurbishing of existing facilities, continues unabated and has helped to provide needed recreational sports services to students. The National Intramural Recreational Sports Association (NIRSA), reported that between 2005—2010, at least $3.17 billion will be spent in new construction and renovations for indoor campus recreational sports facilities at 333 NIRSA Member Institutions, at an average cost of $14.2 million. Total student enrollment for the reporting colleges and universities is 3.8 million (NIRSA, 2005).

Recreational sports programs experienced changing perceptions about their institutional roles and the standards appropriate for their administration as they evolved and expanded. At a majority of institutions, recreational sports programs are placed under the administrative auspices of a division of student affairs, though some programs may be found within a variety of other administrative structures, including athletic departments, physical education programs, and business units. NIRSA suggested that while organizational designs vary among institutions, the full realization for the contribution of recreational sports to any campus depends on institutional commitment to that endeavor. NIRSA (1996) delineated seven primary goals of recreational sports programs:

1. To provide participation in a variety of activities that satisfy the diverse needs of students, faculty, and staff members, and where appropriate, guests, alumni, and public participants can become involved.
2. To provide value to participants by helping individuals develop and maintain a positive self-image, stronger social interactive skills, enhanced physical fitness, and good mental health.
3. To enhance college and university student and faculty recruitment and retention initiatives.
4. To coordinate the use of campus recreation facilities in cooperation with other administrative units such as athletics, physical education, and student activities.
5. To provide extracurricular education opportunities through participation in recreational sports and the provision of relevant leadership positions.
6. To contribute positively to institutional relations through significant and high-quality recreational sports programming.
7. To cooperate with academic units, focusing on the development of recreational sports curricula and

accompanying laboratory experiences.

Recreational sports programming significantly impacts student life, development, and learning, as well as recruitment and retention. Hossler and Bean (1990) wrote that "recreational sports (i.e., informal leisure time, relaxation, games, intramurals) have been endorsed by institutions for their value in helping students maintain good physical health, enhancing their mental health by providing a respite from rigorous academic work, and teaching recreational skills with a carryover for leisure time exercise throughout life." NIRSA (2004) found that "participation in recreational sports programs is a key determinant of college satisfaction, success, recruitment and retention." The study also reported that at schools with established campus recreational sports departments, 75% of college students participate in recreational sports programs.

Through participation in recreational sports, students are encouraged to develop critical thinking skills, create new problem-solving strategies, hone decision-making skills, enhance creativity, and more effectively synthesize and integrate this information into all aspects of their lives. In this way, students both perform more effectively in an academic environment and flourish throughout all phases of the co-curricular experience.

References, Readings, and Resources

Hossler, D. and Bean, J. P., & Associates. (1990). *The strategic management of college enrollments*. San Francisco: Jossey-Bass.

Keeling, R. P. (Ed.). (2004). *Learning reconsidered: A campus-wide focus on the student experience*. Washington, DC: American College Personnel Association & National Association of Student Personnel Administrators.

Keeling, R. P. (Ed.). (2006). *Learning reconsidered 2*. Washington, DC: American College Personnel Association & National Association of Student Personnel Administrators.

Mull, R. F., Bayless, K. G., & Ross, C. M. (1987). *Recreational sports programming*. North Palm Beach, FL: The Athletic Institute.

National Center for Education Statistics. (October, 2003). *College/university enrollment as found in projections of education statistics to 2013*. Washington, DC: Author.

National Intramural-Recreational Sports Association. (1996). *General and specialty standards for collegiate recreational sports*. Champaign, IL: Human Kinetics.

National Intramural-Recreational Sports Association. (2004). *The value of recreational sports in higher education — Impact on student enrollment, success, and buying power*. Champaign, IL: Human Kinetics.

National Intramural-Recreational Sports Association. (2005). *Collegiate recreational sports facility construction report*. Champaign, IL: Human Kinetics.

National Intramural-Recreational Sports Association. *Recreational Sports Journal*. Champaign, IL: Human Kinetics.

National Intramural-Recreational Sports Association, NIRSA National Center, 4185 SW Research Way, Corvallis, OR 97333-1067. 541-766-8211; Fax 541-766-8284.
e-mail: nirsa@nirsa.org; website www.nirsa.org

Contributors:
Current edition: Kent J. Blumenthal, NIRSA
Previous editions: Dixie Bennett, Loyola University Chicago

Recreational Sports Programs
CAS Standards and Guidelines

Part 1. MISSION

The mission of Recreational Sports Programs (RSP) must be to enhance the mind, body, and spirit of students and other eligible individuals by providing programs, services, and facilities that are responsive to the physical, social, recreational, and lifelong educational needs of the campus community as they relate to health, fitness, and learning.

To accomplish this mission, RSP should:
- provide programs and services for participants that are conducive to the development of holistic health, particularly fitness and wellness
- provide comprehensive programs and services in a variety of program formats that reflect and promote the diversity of participant interests, needs, and ability levels
- provide participation, employment, and leadership opportunities designed to enhance learning, growth, and development
- provide participation, employment, and leadership opportunities designed to increase interaction and understanding among individuals from various backgrounds
- contribute to the public relations efforts of the institution, including the recruitment and retention of students, faculty members, and staff members
- facilitate service-learning opportunities for students
- work in collaboration with academic units to facilitate professional preparation opportunities for students
- provide programs, facilities, and equipment that are delivered in a safe, healthy, clean, accessible, and enjoyable environment
- ensure the effective administration, operation, and stewardship of all aspects of the RSP, working in collaboration with other services, programs, campus affiliates (e.g., faculty, staff, alumni, guests, families, general public), and academic units where appropriate

RSP must develop, disseminate, implement, and regularly review their mission. Mission statements must be consistent with the mission of the institution and with professional standards. RSP in higher education must enhance overall educational experiences by incorporating student learning and development outcomes in their mission.

Part 2. PROGRAM

The formal education of students, consisting of the curriculum and the co-curriculum, must promote student learning and development outcomes that are purposeful and holistic and that prepare students for satisfying and productive lifestyles, work, and civic participation. The student learning and development outcome domains and their related dimensions are:

- **knowledge acquisition, integration, construction, and application**
  - o Dimensions: understanding knowledge from a range of disciplines; connecting knowledge to other knowledge, ideas, and experiences; constructing knowledge; and relating knowledge to daily life

- **cognitive complexity**
  - o Dimensions: critical thinking; reflective thinking; effective reasoning; and creativity

- **intrapersonal development**
  - o Dimensions: realistic self-appraisal, self-understanding, and self-respect; identity development; commitment to ethics and integrity; and spiritual awareness

- **interpersonal competence**
  - o Dimensions: meaningful relationships; interdependence; collaboration; and effective leadership

- **humanitarianism and civic engagement**
  - o Dimensions: understanding and appreciation of cultural and human differences; social responsibility; global perspective; and sense of civic responsibility

- **practical competence**
  - o Dimensions: pursuing goals; communicating effectively; technical competence; managing personal affairs; managing career development; demonstrating professionalism; maintaining health and wellness; and living a purposeful and satisfying life

[See *The Council for the Advancement of Standards Learning and Developmental Outcomes* statement for examples of outcomes related to these domains and dimensions.]

Consistent with the institutional mission, Recreational Sports Programs (RSP) must identify relevant and desirable student learning and development outcomes from among the six domains and related dimensions. When creating opportunities for student learning and development, RSP must explore possibilities for collaboration with faculty members and other colleagues.

RSP must assess relevant and desirable student learning and development outcomes and provide evidence of their impact on student learning and development. RSP must articulate how they contribute to or support students' learning and development in the domains not specifically assessed.

RSP must be:
- integrated into the life of the institution
- intentional and coherent
- guided by theories and knowledge of learning and development
- reflective of developmental and demographic profiles of the student population
- responsive to needs of individuals, diverse and special populations, and relevant constituencies

RSP must reflect the needs and interests of students and other eligible users.

Valid indicators include needs assessment surveys, research findings, and documented best practices.

RSP, in collaboration with other campus units and community providers when appropriate, should design programs and services through participation, employment, volunteerism, and leadership opportunities to encourage, enhance, and highlight the value of learning outcomes.

RSP should utilize various program delivery formats including:
- informal - to provide for self-directed, individualized approach to participation. Specific times and facility locations should be reserved to provide a variety of self-directed individual or small group participation opportunities.
- intramural - to provide structured contests, challenges, meets, tournaments, and leagues for participants within the institution
- club - to provide opportunities for individuals to organize around a common interest. Opportunities should be available to students for a variety of interests within or beyond the institution.
- instructional - to provide individualized or group learning opportunities, knowledge, and skills through activity sessions, lessons, clinics, workshops, and various media
- extramural - to provide structured tournaments, contests, and meets between campus participants and other institutions

In addition to these program formats, the RSP may utilize specialized designations to describe programs or service delivery, including aquatics, fitness, wellness, outdoor, special events, special populations, and facilities.

Program planning and implementation process must be inclusive and include:
- **equitable participation for men and women, with opportunities to participate at various levels of ability and disability**
- **interpretation of institutional policies and procedures**
- **a variety of opportunities that reflect and address cultural diversity**
- **participant involvement in shaping program content and procedures**
- **co-recreational activity with opportunities to participate at various levels of ability and disability**

Program operational planning and implementation process must include:
- **participant safety through the use of rules, regulations, and facilities management**
- **effective risk management policies, procedures, and practices**
- **supervision of recreational sports activities and facilities**
- **facility coordination and scheduling**
- **consultation with groups and organizations for sport and fitness programming**

- **training of office and field staff**
- **conflict resolution management protocols**
- **procedures for the inventory, maintenance, and use and security of equipment**
- **recognition for participants, employees, and volunteers**
- **publicity, promotion, and media relations**
- **volunteerism in service delivery and leadership**
- **customer service practices**
- **promotion of socially responsible behaviors**

Part 3. LEADERSHIP

Because effective and ethical leadership is essential to the success of all organizations, Recreational Sports Programs (RSP) leaders with organizational authority for the programs and services must:
- **articulate a vision and mission for their programs and services**
- **set goals and objectives based on the needs of the population served and desired student learning and development outcomes**
- **advocate for their programs and services**
- **promote campus environments that provide meaningful opportunities for student learning, development, and integration**
- **identify and find means to address individual, organizational, or environmental conditions that foster or inhibit mission achievement**
- **advocate for representation in strategic planning initiatives at appropriate divisional and institutional levels**
- **initiate collaborative interactions with stakeholders who have legitimate concerns and interests in the functional area**
- **apply effective practices to educational and administrative processes**
- **prescribe and model ethical behavior**
- **communicate effectively**
- **manage financial resources, including planning, allocation, monitoring, and analysis**
- **incorporate sustainability practices in the management and design of programs, services, and facilities**
- **manage human resource processes including recruitment, selection, development, supervision, performance planning, and evaluation**
- **empower professional, support, and student staff to accept leadership opportunities**
- **encourage and support scholarly contribution to the profession**
- **be informed about and integrate appropriate technologies into programs and services**
- **be knowledgeable about federal, state/provincial, and local laws relevant to the programs and services and ensure that staff members understand their responsibilities by receiving appropriate training**
- **develop and continuously improve programs and services in response to the changing needs of students and**

other populations served and the evolving institutional priorities

- recognize environmental conditions that may negatively influence the safety of staff and students and propose interventions that mitigate such conditions.

RSP leaders also must...

- empower student staff and participants to build their own leadership skills
- value diversity through effective recruitment and retention of professional and student staff
- identify organization values and innovative opportunities
- establish risk management, technology, and marketing plans
- establish strategic, operational, and resource utilization plans
- manage facility resources
- advocate for financial and physical resources

RSP leaders must educate other institutional leaders about the significant differences in mission among intercollegiate athletics, physical education and recreation academic units, and the recreational sports programs.

Leaders should establish effective working relationships throughout their institution, with special emphasis on those units that impact, affect, or support the mission of the RSP. Leaders should actively seek opportunities for collaboration that may result in partnerships that benefit the institution as well as the RSP.

Part 4. HUMAN RESOURCES

Recreational Sports Programs (RSP) must be staffed adequately by individuals qualified to accomplish the mission and goals. Within institutional guidelines, RSP must establish procedures for staff selection, training, and evaluation; set expectations for supervision; and provide appropriate professional development opportunities to improve the leadership ability, competence, and skills of all employees.

RSP professional staff members must hold an earned graduate or professional degree in a field relevant to the position they hold or must possess an appropriate combination of educational credentials and related work experience.

Degree- or credential-seeking interns must be qualified by enrollment in an appropriate field of study and by relevant experience. These individuals must be trained and supervised adequately by professional staff members holding educational credentials and related work experience appropriate for supervision.

RSP should provide graduate assistant and/or internship opportunities to enhance professional preparation experiences. Desirable characteristics of interns and graduate assistants should include: knowledge of the principles and philosophy of recreational sports, demonstrated skills on leadership and communication, a well-developed sense of responsibility, sensitivity to individual differences,

academic success, enthusiasm for working with students, and an understanding of current issues facing students.

Student employees and volunteers must be carefully selected, trained, supervised, and evaluated. They must be educated on how and when to refer those in need of additional assistance to qualified staff members and must have access to a supervisor for assistance in making these judgments. Student employees and volunteers must be provided clear and precise job descriptions, pre-service training based on assessed needs, and continuing staff development.

RSP should develop mechanisms designed to recognize employees and volunteers. These efforts should recognize contributions, improvements, and involvement.

Employees and volunteers must receive specific training on institutional policies and privacy laws regarding their access to student records and other sensitive institutional information (e.g., in the USA, Family Educational Rights and Privacy Act, FERPA, or equivalent privacy laws in other states/provinces or countries).

RSP must have technical and support staff members adequate to accomplish their mission. All members of the staff must be technologically proficient and qualified to perform their job functions, be knowledgeable about ethical and legal uses of technology, and have access to training and resources to support the performance of their assigned responsibilities.

Technical and support staff includes those positions with an expertise in such areas as customer service, facility/equipment maintenance and operations, marketing, information technology, fundraising, research, and business services.

All members of the staff must receive training on policies and procedures related to the use of technology to store or access student records and institutional data.

RSP must ensure that staff members are knowledgeable about and trained in emergency procedures, crisis response, and prevention efforts. Prevention efforts must address identification of threatening conduct or behavior of students, faculty members, staff, and others and must incorporate a system or procedures for responding, including but not limited to reporting them to the appropriate campus officials.

Salary levels and benefits for all staff members must be commensurate with those for comparable positions within the institution, in similar institutions, and in the relevant geographic area.

National salary surveys should be consulted when evaluating salaries.

RSP must maintain position descriptions for all staff members.

To create a diverse staff, RSP must institute hiring and promotion practices that are fair, inclusive, proactive, and non-discriminatory.

RSP must conduct regular performance planning and evaluation of staff members. RSP must provide access to continuing and advanced education and professional development opportunities.

Part 5. ETHICS

Persons involved in the delivery of Recreational Sports Programs (RSP) must adhere to the highest principles of ethical behavior. RSP must review relevant professional ethical standards and develop or adopt and implement appropriate statements of ethical practice. RSP must publish these statements and ensure their periodic review by relevant constituencies.

Ethical standard statements utilized by relevant professional associations should be reviewed in the formulation of RSP ethical standards.

RSP must orient new staff members to relevant ethical standards and statements of ethical practice.

RSP staff members must ensure that privacy and confidentiality are maintained with respect to all communications and records to the extent that such records are protected under the law and appropriate statements of ethical practice. Information contained in students' education records must not be disclosed except as allowed by relevant laws and institutional policies. RSP staff members must disclose to appropriate authorities information judged to be of an emergency nature, especially when the safety of the individual or others is involved, or when otherwise required by institutional policy or relevant law.

RSP staff members must be aware of and comply with the provisions contained in the institution's policies pertaining to human subjects research and student rights and responsibilities, as well as those in other relevant institutional policies addressing ethical practices and confidentiality of research data concerning individuals.

RSP staff members must recognize and avoid personal conflicts of interest or appearance thereof in the performance of their work.

RSP staff members must strive to insure the fair, objective, and impartial treatment of all persons with whom they interact.

When handling institutional funds, RSP staff members must ensure that such funds are managed in accordance with established and responsible accounting procedures and the fiscal policies or processes of the institution.

Promotional and descriptive information must be accurate and free of deception.

RSP staff members must perform their duties within the limits of their training, expertise, and competence. When these limits are exceeded, individuals in need of further assistance must be referred to persons possessing appropriate qualifications.

RSP staff members must use suitable means to confront and otherwise hold accountable other staff members who exhibit unethical behavior.

RSP staff members must be knowledgeable about and practice ethical behavior in the use of technology.

Part 6. LEGAL RESPONSIBILITIES

Recreational Sports Programs (RSP) must be knowledgeable about and responsive to laws and regulations that relate to their respective responsibilities and that may pose legal obligations, limitations, or ramifications for the institution as a whole. As appropriate, staff members must inform users of programs and services, as well as officials, of legal obligations and limitations including constitutional, statutory, regulatory, and case law; mandatory laws and orders emanating from federal, state/provincial, and local governments; and the institution's policies.

To address and minimize the risks inherent in RSP, a comprehensive risk management plan must be implemented.

Development and implementation of a risk management plan should include: identification of appropriate certifications, training and development of personnel, development and implementation of emergency action and critical incident plans, accident care and documentation, participant waivers and consents, participant conduct policies, and the inspection, supervision, and care of facilities and equipment.

RSP must have written policies on all relevant operations, transactions, or tasks that may have legal implications.

RSP staff members must neither participate in nor condone any form of harassment or activity that demeans persons or creates an intimidating, hostile, or offensive campus environment.

RSP staff members must use reasonable and informed practices to limit the liability exposure of the institution and its officers, employees, and agents. RSP staff members must be informed about institutional policies regarding risk management, personal liability, and related insurance coverage options and must be referred to external sources if coverage is not provided by the institution.

The institution must provide access to legal advice for RSP staff members as needed to carry out assigned responsibilities.

Recreational sports professionals should understand legal responsibilities related to individual rights and liability including but not limited to due process, employment procedures, equal opportunity, civil rights and liberties, and liability of wrongful or negligent acts.

RSP should conduct a periodic audit of its policies and practices with university counsel and risk management officials.

The institution must inform RSP staff and students in a timely and systematic fashion about extraordinary or changing legal obligations and potential liabilities.

Part 7. EQUITY and ACCESS

Recreational Sports Programs (RSP) must be provided on a fair, equitable, and non-discriminatory basis in accordance with institutional policies and with all applicable state/provincial and federal statutes and regulations. RSP must maintain an educational and work environment free from discrimination in accordance with law and institutional policy.

Discrimination must be avoided on the basis of age; cultural heritage; disability; ethnicity; gender identity and expression; nationality; political affiliation; race; religious affiliation; sex; sexual orientation; economic, marital, social, or veteran status; and any other bases included in local, state/provincial, or federal laws.

Consistent with the mission and goals, RSP must take action to remedy significant imbalances in student participation and staffing patterns.

RSP must ensure physical and program access for persons with disabilities. RSP must be responsive to the needs of all students and other populations served when establishing hours of operation and developing methods of delivering programs and services.

RSP must adhere to applicable government standards and legal directives regarding access.

RSP must recognize the needs of distance learning students by providing appropriate and accessible services and assisting them in identifying and gaining access to other appropriate services in their geographic region.

RSP must define the eligible user population, with consideration given to such groups as undergraduate and graduate students, faculty members, staff, retirees, alumni, and the general public.

RSP should:
- consider the impact of fees and charges on access to programs and services
- participate in establishing institutional facility scheduling policies to support and encourage appropriate and equitable utilization of resources

Part 8. DIVERSITY

Within the context of each institution's unique mission, diversity enriches the community and enhances the collegiate experience for all; therefore, Recreational Sports Programs (RSP) must create and nurture environments that are welcoming to and bring together persons of diverse backgrounds.

RSP must promote environments that are characterized by open and continuous communication that deepens understanding of one's own identity, culture, and heritage, as well as that of others. RSP must recognize, honor, educate, and promote respect about commonalties and differences among people within their historical and cultural contexts.

RSP must address the characteristics and needs of a diverse population when establishing and implementing policies and procedures.

In support of diversity, RSP must:
- publish, post, and circulate a statement to articulate a commitment to diversity in programs, services, and staffing
- recruit, hire, and seek to retain a diverse professional and student staff
- include diversity education for its employees and volunteers
- reach out to diverse and under-represented populations through such means as surveys, assessments, focus groups, and campus organizations to identify needs and interests used in program design and delivery and in student employment practices

Part 9. ORGANIZATION and MANAGEMENT

To promote student learning and development outcomes, Recreational Sports Programs (RSP) must be structured purposefully and managed effectively to achieve stated goals. Evidence of appropriate structure must include current and accessible policies and procedures, written performance expectations for all employees, functional workflow graphics or organizational charts, and clearly stated program and service delivery expectations.

Members of the campus community should be involved in the selection, design, governance, and administration of programs and facilities. Students and other eligible users may be involved through participant, employee, and living unit committees, councils, and boards.

The organizational placement of recreational sports within the institution should ensure the accomplishment of the program's mission.

RSP must monitor websites used for distributing information to ensure that the sites are current, accurate, appropriately referenced, and accessible.

Evidence of effective management must include use of comprehensive and accurate information for decisions, clear sources and channels of authority, effective communication practices, procedures for decision-making and conflict resolution, responses to changing conditions, systems of accountability and evaluation, and processes for recognition and reward. RSP must align policies and procedures with those of the institution and provide channels within the organization for their regular review.

To fulfill its mission and goals effectively, RSP must maintain well-structured management functions, including planning, personnel, property and risk management, emergency response, purchasing, contract administration, marketing, financial control, and information systems.

A short and long range planning document that specifies goals, objectives, student learning outcomes, strategies, and timelines should be developed to provide direction for the program. This plan should be reviewed annually.

Purchasing and property management procedures should be designed to ensure value for money spent, security for equipment and supplies, and maintenance of property inventories.

Other areas for consideration in determining structure and management of the RSP should include:
- size, nature, and mission of the institution
- scope of recreational sports programs
- philosophy and method of service delivery
- financial resources
- availability and characteristics of facilities

Part 10. CAMPUS and EXTERNAL RELATIONS

Recreational Sports Programs (RSP) must reach out to relevant individuals, campus offices, and external agencies to:
- establish, maintain, and promote effective relations
- disseminate information about their own and other related programs and services
- coordinate and collaborate, where appropriate, in offering programs and services to meet the needs of students and promote their achievement of student learning and development outcomes

RSP must have procedures and guidelines consistent with institutional policy for responding to threats, emergencies, and crisis situations. Systems and procedures must be in place to disseminate timely and accurate information to students and other members of the campus community during emergency situations.

RSP must have procedures and guidelines consistent with institutional policy for communicating with the media.

RSP should establish advisory councils to facilitate communication and collaboration with other campus and community units to improve programs and services. Representatives should be solicited from a variety of units and should represent diverse users. This may include representatives from student organizations, student union, clinical health services, health promotion services, counseling services, campus information visitor services, career services, student government, faculty and staff governance councils, conference services, residence halls/apartments, cultural centers, fraternity and sorority affairs, academics, campus police/public safety, athletics, alumni affairs, financial affairs, and physical plant. Community organizations may include hospitals and recreation and fitness centers.

Part 11. FINANCIAL RESOURCES

Recreational Sports Programs (RSP) must have adequate

funding to accomplish their mission and goals. In establishing funding priorities and making significant changes, a comprehensive analysis, which includes relevant expenditures, external and internal resources, and impact on the campus community, must be conducted.

RSP must demonstrate fiscal responsibility and cost effectiveness consistent with institutional protocols.

Institutional funds for RSP should be allocated to ensure long term viability. Sources of income may include governmental appropriations, student fees (e.g., general, recreational, or health), user fees, donations, contributions, sponsorships, fines, entry fees, rentals, grants, contracts, dues, concessions, and retail sales.

If student funds from any source are dedicated to RSP, those funds should be designated for programs and services that directly benefit students, and the students should retain first priority for the use of facilities, programs, equipment, and services.

The budget process must include consideration of all expenses that are incurred in order to produce a quality RSP.

Expenses include but are not limited to programs and operations, human resource processes and labor costs, support area expenses (e.g., technology, facility support, member services, marketing, research and development), equipment replacement, capital improvement, administrative cost recovery, and reserve account allocations.

Expenditures should be based upon departmental and institutional goals and protocols, periodic needs assessments, and cost/benefit analysis.

All members of RSP staff should be accountable for financial and other resources.

Part 12. TECHNOLOGY

Recreational Sports Programs (RSP) must have adequate technology to support their mission. The technology and its use must comply with institutional policies and procedures and be evaluated for compliance with relevant federal, state/ provincial, and local requirements.

RSP must maintain policies and procedures that address the security and back up of data.

When technology is used to facilitate student learning and development, RSP must select technology that reflects current best pedagogical practices.

Technology, as well as any workstations or computer labs maintained by the RSP for student use, must be accessible and must meet established technology standards for delivery to persons with disabilities.

When RSP provide student access to technology, they must provide:
- access to policies that are clear, easy to understand, and available to all students
- access to instruction or training on how to use the

technology
- access to information on the legal and ethical implications of misuse as it pertains to intellectual property, harassment, privacy, and social networks.

Student violations of technology policies must follow established institutional student disciplinary procedures.

Students who experience negative emotional or psychological consequences from the use of technology must be referred to support services provided by the institution.

Part 13. FACILITIES and EQUIPMENT

Recreational Sports Programs (RSP) must have adequate, accessible, suitably located facilities and equipment to support their mission and goals. If acquiring capital equipment as defined by the institution, RSP must take into account expenses related to regular maintenance and life cycle costs. Facilities and equipment must be evaluated regularly, including consideration of sustainability, and be in compliance with relevant federal, state/provincial, and local requirements to provide for access, health, safety, and security.

RSP staff members must have work space that is well-equipped, adequate in size, and designed to support their work and responsibilities. For conversations requiring privacy, staff members must have access to a private space.

RSP staff members who share work space must have the ability to secure their work adequately.

The design of the facilities must guarantee the security of records and ensure the confidentiality of sensitive information.

The location and layout of the facilities must be sensitive to the special needs of persons with disabilities as well as the needs of constituencies served.

The institution must provide adequate indoor and outdoor facilities with a documented facility usage schedule that includes prioritized blocks of time for RSP to accommodate the needs and interests of the campus community. The use of the facilities must be coordinated to provide efficient and effective utilization.

The schedule should be disseminated to all user groups and reviewed periodically.

RSP must ensure that staff members are knowledgeable of and trained in safety and emergency procedures for securing and vacating the facilities.

Institutions should use available research and assessment data when assessing facility needs. Consideration should be given to sustainability and to a balance of facilities that support the program delivery formats of RSP. Examples of such facilities include swimming pools, strength and cardiovascular training facilities, multi-purpose activity spaces, multi-use fields, nature trails, group exercise and dance rooms, challenge adventure facilities, martial arts mat/studio rooms, personal training rooms, mind-body studios, health and wellness labs, skateboard and rollerblade venues, and racquet sport courts. Facilities should provide activity areas that are diverse as well as flexible and spaces for such support activities as offices, member services, repair rooms, locker/shower rooms, and storage.

Social space should be provided for users to encourage socialization and an inclusive environment. Examples of such facilities include lounges, lobbies, or food service areas.

Renovation, design, and development of facilities must adhere to established federal, state/provincial, and local laws.

RSP may also refer to separate standards and guidelines for specializations governed by professional organizations for the use of facilities.

Technology resources including software and hardware as well as resources for training should be available to support RSP.

RSP must provide equipment adequate to meet the needs of participants.

Institutions should use available research and other assessment data when assessing technology and equipment needs.

RSP must require personal protective equipment and safety devices as appropriate.

Processes must be established for determining needs, inspecting, cleaning, maintaining, repairing, and replacing equipment.

RSP must establish appropriate policies and procedures for responding to emergency situations, especially where RSP facilities, personnel, and resources could assist the institution.

Part 14. ASSESSMENT and EVALUATION

Recreational Sports Programs (RSP) must establish systematic plans and processes to meet internal and external accountability expectations with regard to program as well as student learning and development outcomes. RSP must conduct regular assessment and evaluations. Assessments must include qualitative and quantitative methodologies as appropriate, to determine whether and to what degree the stated mission, goals, and student learning and development outcomes are being met. The process must employ sufficient and sound measures to ensure comprehensiveness. Data collected must include responses from students and other affected constituencies.

Evaluation procedures should yield evidence relative to student/staff recruitment and retention, the achievement of program goals, scope of program offerings, responsiveness to expressed interests, program attendance and effectiveness, participant satisfaction, cost effectiveness, quality of facilities, equipment use and maintenance, staff performance, recruitment and retention, and data as a result of benchmarking against other programs.

Data sources should include student and other eligible users and nonusers. Data should include program evaluations and internal or external assessments and should be maintained in the office of the RSP administrator. They should be accessible to planners of subsequent programs.

RSP should pursue best practices and meaningful research to review and improve programs and services.

RSP must evaluate regularly how well they complement and enhance the institution's stated mission and educational effectiveness.

Results of these evaluations must be used in revising and improving programs and services, identifying needs and interests in shaping directions of program and service design, and recognizing staff performance.

General Standards revised in 2008;
RSP content developed/revised in 1986, 1996, & 2007

The Role of Registrar Programs and Services
CAS Standards Contextual Statement

The registrar, a critical position in any college or university, serves as the institution's gatekeeper for all academic processes, records, and data and has authority for interpreting legal and compliance issues (e.g., the U.S. Family Educational Rights and Privacy Act, Homeland Security, and the Student and Exchange Visitor Information System). Regardless of the campus governance or organization, the registrar's role is vital and central to managing campus enrollment and possesses primary responsibility for maintaining the security and integrity of the institution's academic records.

The role of registrar evolved from the position of "Bedel" in Europe, which appeared in the 12th century. As responsibilities evolved and the office changed, the term "registrar" emerged in the 15th century. Recognition of the registrar's integral role in American higher education was realized with the founding of Harvard. It was not until 1910, however, when fifteen registrars met in Detroit to discuss the need to share information and develop common practices. This meeting marked the birth of the American Association of Collegiate Registrars (AACR). The group expanded in 1949 to include admissions officers and changed its name to the American Association of Collegiate Registrars and Admissions Officers (AACRAO) (Quann, 1979). In subsequent years, AACR and AACRAO, along with more than 30 state and regional associations, have provided linkages among registrars, nationally and internationally, for the exchange of ideas and information that has led to a set of generally accepted policies and practices.

As the role of registrar progressed, it shifted from being essentially the number two leadership position at an institution, responsible for handling the many aspects of administration, to filling a more narrowly focused role, yet one essential to the life of institutions of higher learning. Presently, the registrar typically reports to the vice president for academic affairs or student affairs, is often associated with other enrollment management functional areas, and manages a staff that may exceed more than 100 individuals, depending on institution size. The registrar determines the organizational structure for the office; ensures the availability of adequate facilities, technology, equipment, supplies, and services; develops position descriptions and employs, trains, and supervises office staff; and oversees day-to-day activities.

The office of the registrar is an important point of contact for students on the college campus. Through the registrar's office, students obtain schedules of classes (including online and paper formats); register for courses; adjust schedules through drop/add/withdrawal procedures; obtain grade reports, letters of certification and transcripts; and receive diplomas and other academic records as needed. Therefore, accurate and efficient service to students and continuous quality improvement are major objectives for the registrar.

The registrar's office is also a primary point of contact for faculty members, academic advisors, and administrators for the scheduling of classes, and often for the assigning of classroom and laboratory space. While duties and responsibilities vary from institution to institution, the registrar is typically responsible for working with academic departments and faculty to determine which courses and sections are offered each term. In addition, the registrar is typically responsible for producing the course catalog, developing the schedule of classes, and implementing a scheduling process.

Other duties of registrars may include receiving and processing grades; producing class rosters, grade rosters, grade reports and transcripts; clearing students for graduation; preparing diplomas; and organizing graduation ceremonies. Additional essential roles for registrars are developing and implementing policies, procedures, services, and systems to facilitate student enrollment; maintaining student records; transferring records to other institutions; and managing the assignment of transfer credits. Finally, the registrar is often the individual responsible for assuring that requirements related to privacy laws are met throughout the institution.

Registrars are at the forefront of implementing new technologies on campus and ensure that administrative software systems reflect current technological developments and trends, balance integrity of and access to records, and appropriately anticipate administrator and user implications. While paper records may still be maintained, most student records are now stored electronically. Today, the registration process by which students select classes each term is typically conducted on-line, as are most of the registrar's services. With the increase of distance learning and international education, new challenges arise for monitoring the associated course offerings and records.

Given the changing nature of communication and dissemination of information (i.e., shifting emphasis from publications to website), and the increasing need for data both internal to the institution and external, the registrar possesses the primary academic responsibility for systems and information management for the campus. This includes providing leadership to ensure continuity of records in case of disaster.

The overarching role of the registrar is increasingly that of an educator, defining student needs through learning outcomes and identifying assessment strategies that involve innovative learning techniques including those provided through distance education. The registrar wears multiple hats and must juggle many roles on a daily basis, serving as collaborator, connector, initiator, and a prominent leader within the institution. The standards that follow, in addition to providing basic functional guidelines, are designed to assist the registrar to navigate and respond to the complexity of issues and ever-challenging assigned duties.

References, Readings, and Resources

American Association of Collegiate Registrars and Admissions Officers (AACRAO). (2008). http://www.aacrao.org.

Aucion, P., & Associates. (1996). *Academic record and transcript guide*. Washington, DC: American Association of Collegiate Registrars and Admissions Officers.

Black, J. (Ed.). (2001). *Strategic enrollment management revolution*. Annapolis Junction, MD: American Association of Collegiate Registrars and Admissions Officers.

Cramer, S. F. (2006). Student information systems implementations: A context for campus change. *College and University, 81*(2), 21—33.

Henderson, S. E. (1990). Competencies for admissions and records professionals: An AACRAO guide to entry & advancement in the profession. *College and University, 65*(3), 243-259.

Henderson, S. E. (2005). Refocusing enrollment management: Losing structure and finding the academic context. *College and University, 80*(3), 3—8.

Lonabocker, L., & Gwinn, D. (1996). *Breakthrough systems: Student access and registration*. Washington, DC: American Association of Collegiate Registrars and Admissions Officers.

Pugh, G. (2001). The registrar as an academic officer. *College and University, 77*(2), 29-34.

Quann, C. J., & Associates. (1979). *Admissions, academic records, and registrar services: A handbook, for policies and procedures*. San Francisco: Jossey-Bass.

Rainsberger, R. A., Baker, E. G., Hicks, D., Myers, B., Noe, J., & Weese, F. A. (2000). *The AACRAO 2001 FERPA guide: The family educational rights and privacy act*. AACRAO Professional Development & Education Series. Annapolis Junction, MD: American Association of Collegiate Registrars and Admissions Officers.

Sevigny, J. (2001). *The AACRAO international guide: A resource for international education professionals*. AACRAO Professional Development & Education Series. Annapolis Junction, MD: American Association of Collegiate Registrars and Admissions Officers.

Wager, J. J. (2005). Support services for the net generation: The Penn State approach. *College and University, 81*(1), 3—10.

Westman, C. (2005). *AACRAO's basic guide to enrollment management*. Washington, DC: American Association of Collegiate Registrars and Admissions Officers.

Contributors:

Current edition:
S. Regina Sargent, University of Georgia
Sheri King, University of Georgia - Griffin Campus
Karen D. Boyd, University of Georgia/Carnegie Mellon University
Previous editions:
Jan Arminio, Shippensburg University
Wayne Becraft, AACRAO

Registrar Programs and Services
CAS Standards and Guidelines

Part 1. MISSION

The mission of Registrar Programs and Services (RPS) is to maintain stewardship and integrity of student academic records and manage student and institutional academic policies. Therefore, RPS must:
- maintain student academic records in perpetuity
- collaborate with complementary services regarding enrollment management functions
- coordinate academic calendars and academic registration
- support academic advising activities
- interpret, implement, and ensure compliance with policies and procedures related to academic record-keeping
- provide accurate individual and aggregate data to internal and external constituencies

Such constituencies needing data may include but are not limited to offices of institutional research, assessment, or enrollment management; faculty members and administrators; accreditation or certification agencies; athletic associations with whom the institution holds membership; entities providing services for veterans or students with special needs; and provincial/state/federal government agencies, such as Homeland Security in the US.

RPS must develop, disseminate, implement, and regularly review their mission. Mission statements must be consistent with the mission of the institution and with professional standards. RPS in higher education must enhance overall educational experiences by incorporating student learning and development outcomes in their mission.

Part 2. PROGRAM

The formal education of students, consisting of the curriculum and the co-curriculum, must promote student learning and development outcomes that are purposeful and holistic and that prepare students for satisfying and productive lifestyles, work, and civic participation. The student learning and development outcome domains and their related dimensions are:

- knowledge acquisition, integration, construction, and application
  - Dimensions: understanding knowledge from a range of disciplines; connecting knowledge to other knowledge, ideas, and experiences; constructing knowledge; and relating knowledge to daily life

- cognitive complexity
  - Dimensions: critical thinking; reflective thinking; effective reasoning; and creativity

- intrapersonal development
  - Dimensions: realistic self-appraisal, self-understanding, and self-respect; identity development; commitment to ethics and integrity; and spiritual awareness

- interpersonal competence
  - Dimensions: meaningful relationships; interdependence; collaboration; and effective leadership

- humanitarianism and civic engagement
  - Dimensions: understanding and appreciation of cultural and human differences; social responsibility; global perspective; and sense of civic responsibility

- practical competence
  - Dimensions: pursuing goals; communicating effectively; technical competence; managing personal affairs; managing career development; demonstrating professionalism; maintaining health and wellness; and living a purposeful and satisfying life

[See *The Council for the Advancement of Standards Learning and Developmental Outcomes* statement for examples of outcomes related to these domains and dimensions.]

Consistent with the institutional mission, Registrar Programs and Services (RPS) must identify relevant and desirable student learning and development outcomes from among the six domains and related dimensions. When creating opportunities for student learning and development, RPS must explore possibilities for collaboration with faculty members and other colleagues.

RPS must assess relevant and desirable student learning and development outcomes and provide evidence of their impact on student learning and development. RPS must articulate how they contribute to or support students' learning and development in the domains not specifically assessed.

RPS must be:
- integrated into the life of the institution
- intentional and coherent
- guided by theories and knowledge of learning and development
- reflective of developmental and demographic profiles of the student population
- responsive to needs of individuals, diverse and special populations, and relevant constituencies

RPS must:
- treat students courteously with respect for them as individuals
- ensure that relevant policies and procedures, including record changes, are communicated effectively to students, faculty members, and other affected constituents

- **provide accurate information to all constituents**
- **provide timely service to all constituents**
- **ensure the accuracy and reliability of the data collected and distributed**
- **provide for the maintenance, upkeep, security, integrity, and proper dissemination of academic information**
- **develop and implement effective and secure processes for exchange of transcripts between institutions**
- **provide leadership on the implementation of cooperative academic programs, articulation agreements, and other programs involving academic credit**
- **ensures that cooperative agreements articulate the responsibility for student support and services and the appropriate student conduct policies**
- **develop a workable disaster recovery plan that will allow RPS to function in the event of catastrophic circumstances**
- **educate the institutional community with regard to the security and release of student data**

In support of the overall mission of the institution, and when responsibility is assigned, the mission of RPS must be to:
- **provide leadership for developing and maintaining the student record data base and archival files**
- **provide campus leadership for the application of information technology to academic processes, records, and information**
- **ensure that the security and confidentiality of student record data are maintained throughout the institution**
- **contribute to the enrollment management efforts of the institution**
- **provide a registration process for enrolling students in classes each term,** which may include the calculation of tuition and fees
- **verify student academic eligibility for graduation, honors, academic probation, or dismissal**
- **coordinate course schedules to provide information on courses and sections being offered in any given term with their day, time, location, and delivery formats**
- **coordinate the scheduling of appropriate space and resources for classes, including non-classroom-based courses**
- **manage the transfer of matriculating student records from admissions to RPS**
- **document approved transfer credit**
- **verify records for graduation for the preparation and distribution of diplomas**
- **provide information about courses, programs, policies, and procedures for the development of institutional publications, websites, and other educational materials**
- **provide information on academic regulations, policies, and procedures including appeals processes**
- **certify student enrollment status** (e.g., veterans services, rehabilitation services, student loans, insurance, athletic eligibility, residency status)
- **provide reports as required** (e.g., class rosters, grade rosters, grade reports, transcripts, committee needs)

- **provide appropriate institutional access to academic records and information**
- **prepare statistical reports** (as needed for institutional research, enrollment management, assessment, and other purposes, e.g., enrollment projections, retention, attrition, and graduation rates)

If responsibility for other student records, policies, procedures, or regulations is assigned to the RPS, those matters should be handled in accordance with the standards above.

RPS may also be responsible for the academic calendar, coordinate the arrangements for commencement, and provide administrative support to the faculty governance bodies.

RPS should develop appropriate policies and procedures for allowing students to be referenced by a preferred name.

Part 3. LEADERSHIP

Because effective and ethical leadership is essential to the success of all organizations, Registrar Programs and Services (RPS) leaders with organizational authority for the programs and services must:
- **articulate a vision and mission for their programs and services**
- **set goals and objectives based on the needs of the population served and desired student learning and development outcomes**
- **advocate for their programs and services**
- **promote campus environments that provide meaningful opportunities for student learning, development, and integration**
- **identify and find means to address individual, organizational, or environmental conditions that foster or inhibit mission achievement**
- **advocate for representation in strategic planning initiatives at appropriate divisional and institutional levels**
- **initiate collaborative interactions with stakeholders who have legitimate concerns and interests in the functional area**
- **apply effective practices to educational and administrative processes**
- **prescribe and model ethical behavior**
- **communicate effectively**
- **manage financial resources, including planning, allocation, monitoring, and analysis**
- **incorporate sustainability practices in the management and design of programs, services, and facilities**
- **manage human resource processes including recruitment, selection, development, supervision, performance planning, and evaluation**
- **empower professional, support, and student staff to accept leadership opportunities**
- **encourage and support scholarly contribution to the profession**
- **be informed about and integrate appropriate technologies**

into programs and services
- be knowledgeable about federal, state/provincial, and local laws relevant to the programs and services and ensure that staff members understand their responsibilities by receiving appropriate training
- develop and continuously improve programs and services in response to the changing needs of students and other populations served and the evolving institutional priorities
- recognize environmental conditions that may negatively influence the safety of staff and students and propose interventions that mitigate such conditions

RPS leaders must:
- ensure that newly adopted technologies meet standards of data integrity and accuracy
- be sensitive to the special needs of students such as part-time students, non-traditional students, students with disabilities, LGBT students, students of various ethnic and cultural groups, distance learners, students studying off campus, international students, and students who restrict information access under privacy laws
- be sensitive to the special needs of faculty members including those teaching abroad and those using distance learning or other alternative delivery systems

RPS leaders should have:
- the skill to motivate and inspire staff members to develop a team atmosphere
- fiscal management skills
- the ability to identify and apply relevant information technology
- strong communication, customer relationship, and service management skills

RPS leaders should:
- maintain awareness of changing technology and how it applies to RPS; communicate changes to others and educate them about rationale for adopting technologies
- assess decision-making and problem-solving models and select those most appropriate to the institutional milieu
- incorporate student input in decision-making, as appropriate
- serve as a catalyst in institution-wide partnerships due to the broad scope of RPS responsibilities
- demonstrate a philosophy of service to students and the institution
- maintain awareness of the changing ways people identify and how they name their identities to include references to race, ethnicity, gender identity, and sexual orientation
- provide leadership in institutional compliance with federal, state/provincial, and local regulations

Part 4. HUMAN RESOURCES

Registrar Programs and Services (RPS) must be staffed adequately by individuals qualified to accomplish the mission and goals. Within institutional guidelines, RPS must establish procedures for staff selection, training, and evaluation; set expectations for supervision; and provide appropriate professional development opportunities to improve the leadership ability, competence, and skills of all employees.

RPS professional staff members must hold an earned graduate or professional degree in a field relevant to the position they hold or must possess an appropriate combination of educational credentials and related work experience.

Degree- or credential-seeking interns must be qualified by enrollment in an appropriate field of study and by relevant experience. These individuals must be trained and supervised adequately by professional staff members holding educational credentials and related work experience appropriate for supervision.

Student employees and volunteers must be carefully selected, trained, supervised, and evaluated. They must be educated on how and when to refer those in need of additional assistance to qualified staff members and must have access to a supervisor for assistance in making these judgments. Student employees and volunteers must be provided clear and precise job descriptions, pre-service training based on assessed needs, and continuing staff development.

Employees and volunteers must receive specific training on institutional policies and privacy laws regarding their access to student records and other sensitive institutional information (e.g., in the USA, Family Educational Rights and Privacy Act, FERPA, or equivalent privacy laws in other states/provinces or countries.)

RPS must have technical and support staff members adequate to accomplish their mission. All members of the staff must be technologically proficient and qualified to perform their job functions, be knowledgeable about ethical and legal uses of technology, and have access to training and resources to support the performance of their assigned responsibilities.

All members of the staff must receive training on policies and procedures related to the use of technology to store or access student records and institutional data.

RPS must ensure that staff members are knowledgeable about and trained in emergency procedures, crisis response, and prevention efforts. Prevention efforts must address identification of threatening conduct or behavior of students, faculty members, staff, and others and must incorporate a system or procedures for responding, including but not limited to reporting them to the appropriate campus officials.

Salary levels and benefits for all staff members must be commensurate with those for comparable positions within the institution, in similar institutions, and in the relevant geographic area.

RPS must maintain position descriptions for all staff members.

To create a diverse staff, RPS must institute hiring and promotion practices that are fair, inclusive, proactive, and non-discriminatory.

RPS must conduct regular performance planning and evaluation of staff members. RPS must provide access to continuing and advanced education and professional development opportunities.

Specific titles and reporting structures will vary based on institutional mission, goals, and objectives. RPS should report to a senior officer in academic affairs, student affairs, or enrollment management.

On-going training and staff development should be designed to enhance and broaden understanding of roles and responsibilities within the office and the institution. The support staff should be skilled in interpersonal communications, public relations, knowledge of campus resources, dissemination of information, and the handling of complex and detailed activities. Development for the support staff should include adequate initial training to be able to represent the institution in their office function in a competent, professional, and educational manner.

Part 5. ETHICS

Persons involved in the delivery of Registrar Programs and Services (RPS) must adhere to the highest principles of ethical behavior. RPS must review relevant professional ethical standards and develop or adopt and implement appropriate statements of ethical practice. RPS must publish these statements and ensure their periodic review by relevant constituencies.

RPS must orient new staff members to relevant ethical standards and statements of ethical practice.

RPS staff members must ensure that privacy and confidentiality are maintained with respect to all communications and records to the extent that such records are protected under the law and appropriate statements of ethical practice. Information contained in students' education records must not be disclosed except as allowed by relevant laws and institutional policies. RPS staff members must disclose to appropriate authorities information judged to be of an emergency nature, especially when the safety of the individual or others is involved, or when otherwise required by institutional policy or relevant law.

RPS offices must develop appropriate protocols regarding such disclosure of information and must ensure that all staff members, including students, are trained to understand and follow department policies.

Basic principles of privacy and confidentiality must govern both electronic and paper communications and records. RPS must ensure that the institution has a written policy and published statement regarding confidentiality of records and procedures for access, release, and challenge of educational records, and that the means for enforcement are clearly delineated.

RPS staff members must be aware of and comply with the provisions contained in the institution's policies pertaining to human subjects research and student rights and responsibilities, as well as those in other relevant institutional policies addressing ethical practices and confidentiality of research data concerning individuals.

RPS staff members must recognize and avoid personal conflicts of interest or appearance thereof in the performance of their work.

RPS staff members must strive to insure the fair, objective, and impartial treatment of all persons with whom they interact.

When handling institutional funds, RPS staff members must ensure that such funds are managed in accordance with established and responsible accounting procedures and the fiscal policies or processes of the institution.

Promotional and descriptive information must be accurate and free of deception.

RPS staff members must perform their duties within the limits of their training, expertise, and competence. When these limits are exceeded, individuals in need of further assistance must be referred to persons possessing appropriate qualifications.

RPS staff members must use suitable means to confront and otherwise hold accountable other staff members who exhibit unethical behavior.

RPS staff members must be knowledgeable about and practice ethical behavior in the use of technology.

Part 6. LEGAL RESPONSIBILITIES

Registrar Programs and Services (RPS) staff members must be knowledgeable about and responsive to laws and regulations that relate to their respective responsibilities and that may pose legal obligations, limitations, or ramifications for the institution as a whole. As appropriate, staff members must inform users of programs and services, as well as officials, of legal obligations and limitations including constitutional, statutory, regulatory, and case law; mandatory laws and orders emanating from federal, state/provincial, and local governments; and the institution's policies.

RPS must have written policies on all relevant operations, transactions, or tasks that may have legal implications.

RPS staff members must neither participate in nor condone any form of harassment or activity that demeans persons or creates an intimidating, hostile, or offensive campus environment.

RPS staff members must use reasonable and informed practices to limit the liability exposure of the institution and its officers, employees, and agents. Staff members must be informed about institutional policies regarding risk management, personal liability, and related insurance coverage options and must be referred to external sources if coverage is not provided by the institution.

The institution must provide access to legal advice for RPS staff members as needed to carry out assigned responsibilities.

The institution must inform RPS staff and students in a timely and systematic fashion about extraordinary or changing legal obligations and potential liabilities.

RPS must provide leadership in the development of institutional policies related to educational information and appropriate legal issues, especially privacy laws. RPS must ensure that the institution has written policies on all RPS transactions which may have legal implications.

Relevant areas include: privacy laws (e.g., Family Educational Rights and Privacy Act (FERPA) in the USA); affirmative action policies; certification of academic transcript information; academic and disciplinary sanctions and dismissals; parental access to records; refund policies; fraudulent records; name changes; gender transitioning; record-keeping practices; facility scheduling policies; access to student information systems; residency status determination; student enrollment status; policies on applicant and student criminal or judicial history; requests for information from government or law enforcement agencies (e.g., in the USA, those related to Homeland Security or the Solomon Amendment); security procedures; social security number usage; court orders; and subpoenas. RPS leaders should meet with the institution's legal counsel regularly to review all relevant documents for clarity and to determine that current regulations are being followed.

RPS must have procedures to keep staff members informed of all requirements related to the maintenance of academic records. RPS must ensure that procedures and forms used to implement regulations must be developed and regularly reviewed to assure fulfillment of institutional requirements.

RPS staff should meet with the institution's legal counsel periodically to review all relevant documents for clarity and to determine that current regulations are being followed. Some of the relevant areas that should be reviewed include affirmative action policies; certification of academic transcript information; academic and disciplinary sanctions and dismissals; parental access to records; privacy laws; refund policies; fraudulent records; name changes; gender transitioning; record-keeping practices; facility scheduling policies; access to student information systems; residency status determination; student enrollment status; policies on applicant and student criminal or judicial history; requests for information from government or law enforcement agencies (e.g., those related to Homeland Security or the Solomon Amendment in the USA); security procedures; social security number usage; court orders; and subpoenas.

Part 7. EQUITY and ACCESS

Registrar Programs and Services (RPS) must be provided on a fair, equitable, and non-discriminatory basis in accordance with institutional policies and with all applicable state/ provincial and federal statutes and regulations. RPS must maintain an educational and work environment free from discrimination in accordance with law and institutional policy.

Discrimination must be avoided on the basis of age; cultural heritage; disability; ethnicity; gender identity and expression; nationality; political affiliation; race; religious affiliation; sex; sexual orientation; economic, marital, social, or veteran status; and any other bases included in local, state/provincial, or federal laws.

Consistent with the mission and goals, RPS must take action to remedy significant imbalances in student participation and staffing patterns.

RPS must ensure physical and program access for persons with disabilities. RPS must be responsive to the needs of all students and other populations served when establishing hours of operation and developing methods of delivering programs and services.

RPS must recognize the needs of distance learning students by providing appropriate and accessible services and assisting them in identifying and gaining access to other appropriate services in their geographic region.

Part 8. DIVERSITY

Within the context of each institution's unique mission, diversity enriches the community and enhances the collegiate experience for all; therefore, RPS must create and nurture environments that are welcoming to and bring together persons of diverse backgrounds.

RPS must promote environments that are characterized by open and continuous communication that deepens understanding of one's own identity, culture, and heritage, as well as that of others. RPS must recognize, honor, educate, and promote respect about commonalties and differences among people within their historical and cultural contexts.

RPS must address the characteristics and needs of a diverse population when establishing and implementing policies and procedures.

Part 9. ORGANIZATION and MANAGEMENT

To promote student learning and development outcomes, Registrar Programs and Services (RPS) must be structured purposefully and managed effectively to achieve stated goals. Evidence of appropriate structure must include current and accessible policies and procedures, written performance expectations for all employees, functional workflow graphics or organizational charts, and clearly stated program and service delivery expectations.

RPS must monitor websites used for distributing information to ensure that the sites are current, accurate, appropriately referenced, and accessible.

Evidence of effective management must include use of comprehensive and accurate information for decisions, clear sources and channels of authority, effective communication practices, procedures for decision-making and conflict resolution, responses to changing conditions, systems of accountability and evaluation, and processes for recognition and reward. RPS must align policies and procedures with those of the institution and provide channels within the organization for their regular review.

RPS must identify and be responsive to external constraints and requirements that impact unit operation (e.g., implications of local, state/provincial, and federal regulations, governing body policies, union agreements, accreditation, professional associations, athletic conference requirements).

RPS should:
- develop an organizational chart that identifies cooperative interrelationships with other institutional units and those outside the institution (e.g., institutions with cooperative programs or agreements, study abroad partnerships)
- coordinate programs and services with other institutional personnel, offices, functions, and activities
- collaborate with other enrollment management offices
- establish clear and concise criteria for decision-making and define primary responsibility when more than one unit is involved

Part 10. CAMPUS and EXTERNAL RELATIONS

Registrar Programs and Services (RPS) must reach out to relevant individuals, campus offices, and external agencies to:
- establish, maintain, and promote effective relations
- disseminate information about their own and other related programs and services
- coordinate and collaborate, where appropriate, in offering programs and services to meet the needs of students and promote their achievement of student learning and development outcomes

Relevant constituencies include administrators, faculty members, students, alumni, and the public, as well as other institutions with which there are articulation agreements, cooperative programs, or transfer of students.

RPS must have procedures and guidelines consistent with institutional policy for responding to threats, emergencies, and crisis situations. Systems and procedures must be in place to disseminate timely and accurate information to students and other members of the campus community during emergency situations.

RPS must have procedures and guidelines consistent with institutional policy for communicating with the media.

RPS must provide leadership to the institution to set standards regarding interpretation of policy and appropriate dissemination of information.

Part 11. FINANCIAL RESOURCES

Registrar Programs and Services (RPS) must have adequate funding to accomplish their mission and goals. In establishing funding priorities and making significant changes, a comprehensive analysis, which includes relevant expenditures, external and internal resources, and impact on the campus community, must be conducted.

RPS must demonstrate fiscal responsibility and cost effectiveness consistent with institutional protocols.

RPS leaders must comply with the institution's financial policies that could affect the budget, with required accounting reports that track expenditures, and with policies governing unused funds.

Expenses specific to RPS responsibilities may include purchase and maintenance of customized software systems, adequate security of electronic and hard-copy data, and appropriate back-up systems for all data.

Part 12. TECHNOLOGY

Registrar Programs and Services (RPS) must have adequate technology to support their mission. The technology and its use must comply with institutional policies and procedures and be evaluated for compliance with relevant federal, state/provincial, and local requirements.

RPS must maintain policies and procedures that address the security and back up of data.

When technology is used to facilitate student learning and development, RPS must select technology that reflects current best pedagogical practices.

Technology, as well as any workstations or computer labs maintained by the RPS for student use, must be accessible and must meet established technology standards for delivery to persons with disabilities.

When RPS provide student access to technology, they must provide:
- access to policies that are clear, easy to understand, and available to all students
- access to instruction or training on how to use the technology
- access to information on the legal and ethical implications of misuse as it pertains to intellectual property, harassment, privacy, and social networks

Student violations of technology policies must follow established institutional student disciplinary procedures.

Students who experience negative emotional or psychological consequences from the use of technology must be referred to support services provided by the institution.

When RPS is responsible for determining facilities usage outside the immediate office, policies and procedures must be developed and disseminated with respect to the assignment of such space.

Backup copies of important documentation such as transcripts, the student data base, and the processes for accessing the back-ups must be stored off site in the event of a natural disaster or damage to the records.

RPS should provide to other offices and departments appropriate access to store or retrieve data on students they serve.

Part 13. FACILITIES and EQUIPMENT

Registrar Programs and Services (RPS) must have adequate, accessible, suitably located facilities and equipment to support their mission and goals. If acquiring capital equipment as defined by the institution, RPS must take into account expenses related to regular maintenance and life cycle costs. Facilities and equipment must be evaluated regularly, including consideration of sustainability, and be in compliance with relevant federal, state/provincial, and local requirements to provide for access, health, safety, and security.

RPS staff members must have work space that is well-equipped, adequate in size, and designed to support their work and responsibilities. For conversations requiring privacy, staff members must have access to a private space.

RPS staff members who share work space must have the ability to secure their work adequately.

The design of the facilities must guarantee the security of records and ensure the confidentiality of sensitive information.

The location and layout of the facilities must be sensitive to the special needs of persons with disabilities as well as the needs of constituencies served.

RPS must ensure that staff members are knowledgeable of and trained in safety and emergency procedures for securing and vacating the facilities.

Part 14. ASSESSMENT and EVALUATION

Registrar Programs and Services (RPS) must establish systematic plans and processes to meet internal and external accountability expectations with regard to program as well as student learning and development outcomes. RPS must conduct regular assessment and evaluations. Assessments must include qualitative and quantitative methodologies as appropriate, to determine whether and to what degree the stated mission, goals, and student learning and development outcomes are being met. The process must employ sufficient and sound measures to ensure comprehensiveness. Data collected must include responses from students and other affected constituencies.

RPS must evaluate regularly how well they complement and enhance the institution's stated mission and educational effectiveness.

Results of these evaluations must be used in revising and improving programs and services, identifying needs and interests in shaping directions of program and service design, and recognizing staff performance.

Student input should be incorporated into program improvement planning and policy development.

General Standards revised in 2008;
RPS content developed/revised in 1995 & 2008

The Role of Service-Learning Programs
CAS Standards Contextual Statement

Service-learning enables colleges and universities to meet their goals for student learning and development while making unique contributions to addressing community, national, and global needs. Both college students and the communities they serve stand to reap substantial benefits from engaging in service-learning.   Among frequently cited benefits to student participants are developing the habit of critical reflection; deepening comprehension of course content; integrating theory with practice; increasing understanding of the issues underlying social problems; strengthening sense of social responsibility; enhancing cognitive, personal, and spiritual development; heightening understanding of human difference and commonality; and sharpening abilities to solve problems creatively and to work collaboratively. Community benefits include new energy and assistance to broaden delivery of existing services or to begin new ones; fresh approaches to solving problems; access to resources; and opportunities to participate in teaching and learning. Through improved town-gown relationships, colleges and universities also gain additional new learning settings for students and new opportunities for faculty to orient research and teaching to meet human and community needs.

For the purpose of the *CAS Standards for Service-Learning Programs*, service-learning is defined as follows: "Service-learning is a form of experiential education in which students engage in activities that address human and community needs together with structured opportunities intentionally designed to promote student learning and development." The hyphen in service-learning is critical in that it symbolizes the symbiotic relationship between the service and the learning. The term community in the definition of service-learning refers to local neighborhoods, the state, the nation, and the world community. Service-learning enables all participants to define their needs and interests (Jacoby, 1996).

Reflection and reciprocity are fundamental concepts of service-learning. As a form of experiential education, service-learning is based on the pedagogical principle that learning and development do not necessarily occur as a result of experience itself. Rather, they occur as a result of reflection intentionally designed to foster learning and development. Service-learning programs emphasize various types of learning goals, including intellectual, civic, ethical, moral, cross-cultural, and spiritual. Programs may highlight different combinations of these goals. Service-learning programs are also explicitly structured to promote learning about the larger social issues behind the needs to which the service is responding. This learning includes a deeper understanding of the historical, sociological, cultural, economic, and political contexts of the needs or issues being addressed. Reflection can take many forms: individual and group, oral and written, directly related to discipline-based course material or not.

The other essential concept of service-learning is reciprocity between the server and the person or group being served. Service-learning avoids placing students into community settings based solely on desired student-learning outcomes and providing services that do not meet actual needs or that perpetuate a state of need, rather than seeking and addressing the causes of need. Through reciprocity, students develop a greater sense of belonging and responsibility as members of a larger community. Service-learning thus stands in contrast to the traditional, one-way approach to service in which one person or group has resources that they share with a person or group that they assume lacks resources. Reciprocity also eschews the concept of service that is based on the idea that a more competent person comes to the aid of a less competent person. Service-learning encourages students to do things *with* others rather than *for* them. Everyone should expect to learn and change in the process.

Although service-learning that is embedded in the curriculum provides opportunities for faculty to enhance students' learning by integrating course content with practical experience in a structured manner intended to meet course objectives, powerful opportunities for student learning and development also occur outside the academic program. Student affairs professionals can and do involve students in co-curricular service-learning programs that contribute to their learning and development. While service-learning that is connected to faculty research and community involvement can lead to more broad-based and long-term community enhancement, shorter-term service projects also make considerable contributions to communities in both direct and indirect ways. Even one-time experiences that address community needs and that are designed to achieve specific student learning and development outcomes can appropriately be called service-learning.

References, Readings, and Resources

Campus Compact: www.compact.org.

Eyler, J., & Giles, D. (1999). *Where's the learning in service-learning?* San Francisco: Jossey-Bass.

Howard, J. (Ed.). (Summer 2001). *Service-learning course design workbook*. Ann Arbor, MI: University of Michigan.

Jacoby, B. (Ed). (2003). *Building partnerships for service-learning*. San Francisco: Jossey-Bass.

Jacoby, B. (Ed.). (1996). *Service-learning in higher education: Concepts and practices.* San Francisco: Jossey-Bass.

Kendall, J. (Ed.). (1990). *Combining service and learning: A resource book for community and public service,* Vol. 1. Raleigh, NC.: National Society for Experiential Education.

Michigan Journal of Community Service Learning: www.umich.edu/~ocsl/MJCSL.

National Service-Learning Clearinghouse: www.servicelearning.org.

Porter Honnet, E., & Poulsen, S. J. (1989). *Principles of good practice for combining service and learning.* Racine, WI.: Johnson Foundation.

Contributor:
Barbara Jacoby, University of Maryland, NCCP

- emphasize SL outcomes
- help campuses meet the outcomes

- prof. development to do programs

- diversity as means to support NCC goals?

- help institutions assess, and evaluate how SLP + CEP enhance the institution's mission, educational effectiveness, student learning + satisfaction

Service-Learning Programs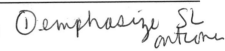
CAS Standards and Guidelines

Part 1. MISSION

The primary mission of Service-Learning Programs (S-LP) is to engage students in experiences that address human and community needs together with structured opportunities for reflection intentionally designed to promote student learning and development.

S-LP must develop, disseminate, implement, and regularly review their mission. Mission statements must be consistent with the mission of the institution and with professional standards. S-LP in higher education must enhance overall educational experiences by incorporating student learning and development outcomes in their mission.

Part 2. PROGRAM

The formal education of students, consisting of the curriculum and the co-curriculum, must promote student learning and development outcomes that are purposeful and holistic and that prepare students for satisfying and productive lifestyles, work, and civic participation. The student learning and development outcome domains and their related dimensions are:

- knowledge acquisition, integration, construction, and application
  - o Dimensions: understanding knowledge from a range of disciplines; connecting knowledge to other knowledge, ideas, and experiences; constructing knowledge; and relating knowledge to daily life

- cognitive complexity
  - o Dimensions: critical thinking; reflective thinking; effective reasoning; and creativity

- intrapersonal development
  - o Dimensions: realistic self-appraisal, self-understanding, and self-respect; identity development; commitment to ethics and integrity; and spiritual awareness

- interpersonal competence
  - o Dimensions: meaningful relationships; interdependence; collaboration; and effective leadership

- humanitarianism and civic engagement
  - o Dimensions: understanding and appreciation of cultural and human differences; social responsibility; global perspective; and sense of civic responsibility

- practical competence
  - o Dimensions: pursuing goals; communicating effectively; technical competence; managing personal affairs; managing career development; demonstrating professionalism; maintaining health and wellness; and living a purposeful and satisfying life

[See *The Council for the Advancement of Standards Learning and Developmental Outcomes* statement for examples of outcomes related to these domains and dimensions.]

Consistent with the institutional mission, Service-Learning Programs (S-LP) must identify relevant and desirable student learning and development outcomes from among the six domains and related dimensions. When creating opportunities for student learning and development, S-LP must explore possibilities for collaboration with faculty members and other colleagues.

S-LP must assess relevant and desirable student learning and development outcomes and provide evidence of their impact on student learning and development. S-LP must articulate how they contribute to or support students' learning and development in the domains not specifically assessed.

S-LP must be:
- integrated into the life of the institution
- intentional and coherent
- guided by theories and knowledge of learning and development
- reflective of developmental and demographic profiles of the student population
- responsive to needs of individuals, diverse and special populations, and relevant constituencies

Service-Learning Programs (S-LP) must be integrated into and enhance both the academic curriculum and co-curricular programs.

S-LP must:
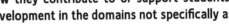
- allow all participants to define their needs and interests
- engage students in responsible and purposeful actions to meet community-defined needs
- enable students to understand needs in the context of community assets
- articulate clear service and learning goals for everyone involved, including students, faculty and staff members, community agency personnel, and those being served
- ensure intellectual rigor
- establish criteria for selecting community service sites to ensure productive learning opportunities for everyone involved
- educate students regarding the philosophy of service and learning, the particular community service site, the work they will do, and the people they will be serving in the community
- establish and implement risk management procedures to protect students, the institution, and the community agencies
- offer alternatives to ensure that students are not required to participate in service that violates a religious

or moral belief
- **engage students in reflection designed to enable them to deepen their understanding of themselves, the community, and the complexity of social problems and potential solutions**
- **educate students to differentiate between perpetuating dependence and building capacity within the community**
- **establish mechanisms to assess service and learning outcomes for students and communities**
- **provide on-going professional development and support to faculty and staff members**

When course credit is offered for service-learning, the credit must be for learning, not only for service. Whether service-learning is for academic credit or not, the focus must be on learning and educational objectives, not on hours served.

S-LP must offer a wide range of curricular and co-curricular service-learning experiences appropriate for students at all developmental levels and with a variety of lifestyles and abilities.

Examples may include older students, commuter students, students who are parents, part-time students, fully employed students, and students with disabilities.

S-LP must initiate and maintain collaborative relations among faculty members and departments within the institution for the design and implementation of service-learning experiences. They must also develop partnerships with community-based organizations to meet organizations' service needs and to achieve student learning and development outcomes.

Service-learning experiences should include:
- *One-time and short-term experiences.* These can be designed to achieve a variety of student learning outcomes, including introducing students to service-learning as a critical aspect of their college education, enabling students to learn what types of service best suit their interests, familiarizing students with the community in which the institution is located, and understanding the approaches different agencies take to address community problems. These experiences can be co-curricular or part of the academic curriculum, such as first-year seminars.

- *Discipline-based service-learning courses.* Such courses can be designed to enable students to deepen their understanding of course content, apply knowledge to practice, and test theory through practical application. These courses can be designed for students at all levels. Service-learning internships and capstone courses can provide opportunities for students to consider how disciplinary knowledge can be applied in a socially responsible manner in professional settings.

- *Community-based research.* Whether integrated into a course or done on an independent-study basis, students engage in community-based research work with faculty and community partners to design, conduct, analyze, and report research results to serve community purposes.

- *Intensive service-learning experiences.* Service-learning experiences can immerse students intensively in an unfamiliar setting or culture, whether domestically or abroad. They can engage in dialogue and problem solving with the people most affected by the issues and develop a sense of solidarity with people whose lives and perspectives differ from their own. These experiences vary in length from a one-week alternative break to a semester or a year.

The service-learning course syllabus or plan for co-curricular experiences should describe:
- needs that the service will address
- desired outcomes of the service and learning for all participants
- assignments that link service and academic content
- opportunities to reflect on one's personal reactions to service and learning experiences
- logistics (e.g., time required, transportation, materials required)
- nature of the service work
- roles and responsibilities of students and community members
- risk management procedures
- evaluation of the service and learning experiences and assessment of the degree to which desired outcomes were achieved

S-LP should foster student leadership through service-learning experiences and should encourage student-initiated and student-led service and learning.

Part 3. LEADERSHIP

Because effective and ethical leadership is essential to the success of all organizations, Service-Learning Programs (S-LP) leaders with organizational authority for the programs and services must:
- **articulate a vision and mission for their programs and services**
- **set goals and objectives based on the needs of the population served and desired student learning and development outcomes**
- **advocate for their programs and services**
- **promote campus environments that provide meaningful opportunities for student learning, development, and integration**
- **identify and find means to address individual, organizational, or environmental conditions that foster or inhibit mission achievement**
- **advocate for representation in strategic planning initiatives at appropriate divisional and institutional levels**
- **initiate collaborative interactions with stakeholders who have legitimate concerns and interests in the functional area**
- **apply effective practices to educational and administrative processes**
- **prescribe and model ethical behavior**
- **communicate effectively**

- manage financial resources, including planning, allocation, monitoring, and analysis
- incorporate sustainability practices in the management and design of programs, services, and facilities
- manage human resource processes including recruitment, selection, development, supervision, performance planning, and evaluation
- empower professional, support, and student staff to accept leadership opportunities
- encourage and support scholarly contribution to the profession
- be informed about and integrate appropriate technologies into programs and services
- be knowledgeable about federal, state/provincial, and local laws relevant to the programs and services and ensure that staff members understand their responsibilities by receiving appropriate training
- develop and continuously improve programs and services in response to the changing needs of students and other populations served and the evolving institutional priorities
- recognize environmental conditions that may negatively influence the safety of staff and students and propose interventions that mitigate such conditions

Part 4. HUMAN RESOURCES

Service-Learning Programs (S-LP) must be staffed adequately by individuals qualified to accomplish the mission and goals. Within institutional guidelines, S-LP must establish procedures for staff selection, training, and evaluation; set expectations for supervision; and provide appropriate professional development opportunities to improve the leadership ability, competence, and skills of all employees.

S-LP professional staff members must hold an earned graduate or professional degree in a field relevant to the position they hold or must possess an appropriate combination of educational credentials and related work experience.

Professional development of staff and faculty members engaged in service-learning programs should address how to:
- build relationships with community agencies
- establish and maintain collaborative relationships with campus units
- engage students in community action for the common good
- prepare, mentor, and monitor students to deliver services according to legal and risk management policies
- use learning strategies that are effective in achieving learning outcomes
- engage students in structured opportunities for reflection
- develop, implement, and evaluate service and learning goals
- facilitate the process of identifying student and community needs and interests
- clarify the responsibilities of students, the institution, and agencies
- match the unique needs of agencies and students

- sustain genuine and active commitment of students, the institution, and agencies
- educate, train, and support students to facilitate service-learning experiences for their peers
- ensure that the time commitments for service and learning are balanced and appropriate
- foster participation by and with diverse populations
- develop fiscal and other resources for program support

Faculty and staff members who integrate service-learning into their courses should receive institutional support (e.g., reduced course load, mini-grants, or teaching assistants.)

SL-P staff should provide professional development for community partners regarding how to work effectively with students, faculty members, and staff in higher education institutions.

Degree- or credential-seeking interns must be qualified by enrollment in an appropriate field of study and by relevant experience. These individuals must be trained and supervised adequately by professional staff members holding educational credentials and related work experience appropriate for supervision.

Student employees and volunteers must be carefully selected, trained, supervised, and evaluated. They must be educated on how and when to refer those in need of additional assistance to qualified staff members and must have access to a supervisor for assistance in making these judgments. Student employees and volunteers must be provided clear and precise job descriptions, pre-service training based on assessed needs, and continuing staff development.

Employees and volunteers must receive specific training on institutional policies and privacy laws regarding their access to student records and other sensitive institutional information (e.g., in the USA, Family Educational Rights and Privacy Act, FERPA, or equivalent privacy laws in other states/provinces or countries).

S-LP must have technical and support staff members adequate to accomplish their mission. All members of the staff must be technologically proficient and qualified to perform their job functions, be knowledgeable about ethical and legal uses of technology, and have access to training and resources to support the performance of their assigned responsibilities.

All members of the staff must receive training on policies and procedures related to the use of technology to store or access student records and institutional data.

S-LP must ensure that staff members are knowledgeable about and trained in emergency procedures, crisis response, and prevention efforts. Prevention efforts must address identification of threatening conduct or behavior of students, faculty members, staff, and others and must incorporate a system or procedures for responding, including but not limited to reporting them to the appropriate campus officials.

Salary levels and benefits for all staff members must be

commensurate with those for comparable positions within the institution, in similar institutions, and in the relevant geographic area.

S-LP must maintain position descriptions for all staff members.

To create a diverse staff, S-LP must institute hiring and promotion practices that are fair, inclusive, proactive, and non-discriminatory.

S-LP must conduct regular performance planning and evaluation of staff members. S-LP must provide access to continuing and advanced education and professional development opportunities.

Part 5. ETHICS

Persons involved in the delivery of Service-Learning Programs (S-LP) must adhere to the highest principles of ethical behavior. S-LP must review relevant professional ethical standards and develop or adopt and implement appropriate statements of ethical practice. S-LP must publish these statements and ensure their periodic review by relevant constituencies.

The faculty members, staff, and students involved in service-learning must be held to the same ethical standards as the SL-P staff members.

S-LP must orient new staff members to relevant ethical standards and statements of ethical practice.

S-LP staff members must ensure that privacy and confidentiality are maintained with respect to all communications and records to the extent that such records are protected under the law and appropriate statements of ethical practice. Information contained in students' education records must not be disclosed except as allowed by relevant laws and institutional policies. S-LP staff members must disclose to appropriate authorities information judged to be of an emergency nature, especially when the safety of the individual or others is involved, or when otherwise required by institutional policy or relevant law.

S-LP staff members must be aware of and comply with the provisions contained in the institution's policies pertaining to human subjects research and student rights and responsibilities, as well as those in other relevant institutional policies addressing ethical practices and confidentiality of research data concerning individuals.

S-LP staff members must recognize and avoid personal conflicts of interest or appearance thereof in the performance of their work.

S-LP staff members must strive to insure the fair, objective, and impartial treatment of all persons with whom they interact.

When handling institutional funds, S-LP staff members must ensure that such funds are managed in accordance with established and responsible accounting procedures and the fiscal policies or processes of the institution.

Promotional and descriptive information must be accurate and free of deception.

S-LP staff members must perform their duties within the limits of their training, expertise, and competence. When these limits are exceeded, individuals in need of further assistance must be referred to persons possessing appropriate qualifications.

All faculty and staff members responsible for supervising service-learning activities must monitor student performance based on training expertise and competence and alter placements as needed.

S-LP staff members must use suitable means to confront and otherwise hold accountable other staff members who exhibit unethical behavior.

S-LP staff members must be knowledgeable about and practice ethical behavior in the use of technology.

Part 6. LEGAL RESPONSIBILITIES

All faculty and staff members engaged in Service-Learning Programs (S-LP) must be knowledgeable about and responsive to laws and regulations that relate to their respective responsibilities and that may pose legal obligations, limitations, or ramifications for the institution as a whole. As appropriate, S-LP staff members must inform users of programs and services, as well as officials, of legal obligations and limitations including constitutional, statutory, regulatory, and case law; mandatory laws and orders emanating from federal, state/provincial, and local governments; and the institution's policies.

S-LP must have written policies on all relevant operations, transactions, or tasks that may have legal implications.

All faculty and staff members engaged in service-learning must neither participate in nor condone any form of harassment or activity that demeans persons or creates an intimidating, hostile, or offensive campus environment.

S-LP staff members must use reasonable and informed practices to limit the liability exposure of the institution and its officers, employees, and agents. All faculty and staff members engaged in service-learning must be informed about institutional policies regarding risk management, personal liability, and related insurance coverage options and must be referred to external sources if coverage is not provided by the institution.

The institution must provide access to legal advice for all faculty and staff members engaged in service-learning as needed to carry out assigned responsibilities.

The institution must inform all faculty and staff members and students engaged in service-learning in a timely and systematic fashion about extraordinary or changing legal obligations and potential liabilities.

Part 7. EQUITY and ACCESS

Service-Learning Programs (S-LP) must be provided on a fair, equitable, and non-discriminatory basis in accordance with institutional policies and with all applicable state/provincial and federal statutes and regulations. S-LP must maintain an educational and work environment free from discrimination in accordance with law and institutional policy.

Discrimination must be avoided on the basis of age; cultural heritage; disability; ethnicity; gender identity and expression; nationality; political affiliation; race; religious affiliation; sex; sexual orientation; economic, marital, social, or veteran status; and any other bases included in local, state/provincial, or federal laws.

Consistent with the mission and goals, S-LP must take action to remedy significant imbalances in student participation and staffing patterns.

S-LP must ensure physical and program access for persons with disabilities. S-LP must be responsive to the needs of all students and other populations served when establishing hours of operation and developing methods of delivering programs and services.

S-LP must recognize the needs of distance learning students by providing appropriate and accessible services and assisting them in identifying and gaining access to other appropriate services in their geographic region.

Part 8. DIVERSITY

Within the context of each institution's unique mission, diversity enriches the community and enhances the collegiate experience for all; therefore, Service-Learning Programs (S-LP) must create and nurture environments that are welcoming to and bring together persons of diverse backgrounds.

S-LP must promote environments that are characterized by open and continuous communication that deepens understanding of one's own identity, culture, and heritage, as well as that of others. S-LP must recognize, honor, educate, and promote respect about commonalties and differences among people within their historical and cultural contexts.

S-LP must address the characteristics and needs of a diverse population when establishing and implementing policies and procedures.

Part 9. ORGANIZATION and MANAGEMENT

To promote student learning and development outcomes, Service-Learning Programs (S-LP) must be structured purposefully and managed effectively to achieve stated goals. Evidence of appropriate structure must include current and accessible policies and procedures, written performance expectations for all employees, functional workflow graphics or organizational charts, and clearly stated program and service delivery expectations.

S-LP must monitor websites used for distributing information to ensure that the sites are current, accurate, appropriately referenced, and accessible.

Evidence of effective management must include use of comprehensive and accurate information for decisions, clear sources and channels of authority, effective communication practices, procedures for decision-making and conflict resolution, responses to changing conditions, systems of accountability and evaluation, and processes for recognition and reward. S-LP must align policies and procedures with those of the institution and provide channels within the organization for their regular review.

Part 10. CAMPUS and EXTERNAL RELATIONS

Service-Learning Programs (S-LP) must reach out to relevant individuals, campus offices, and external agencies to:
- establish, maintain, and promote effective relations
- disseminate information about their own and other related programs and services
- coordinate and collaborate, where appropriate, in offering programs and services to meet the needs of students and promote their achievement of student learning and development outcomes

If there is more than one campus unit that facilitates community service and service-learning experiences, those offices should share information and collaborate as appropriate.

S-LP should develop productive working relationships with a wide range of campus agencies, including risk management, transportation, health services, academic departments and colleges, leadership programs, orientation, student activities, and institutional relationships and development.

Service-learning flourishes best when the institution as a whole is engaged as a responsible citizen in its surrounding communities. S-LP professionals should advocate for the institution to share its resources with its community and to develop a wide range of mutually beneficial campus-community partnerships.

S-LP must have procedures and guidelines consistent with institutional policy for responding to threats, emergencies, and crisis situations. Systems and procedures must be in place to disseminate timely and accurate information to students and other members of the campus community during emergency situations.

S-LP must have procedures and guidelines consistent with institutional policy for communicating with the media.

Part 11. FINANCIAL RESOURCES

Service-Learning Programs (S-LP) must have adequate funding to accomplish their mission and goals. In establishing funding priorities and making significant changes, a comprehensive analysis, which includes relevant expenditures, external and internal resources, and impact on the campus community, must be conducted.

S-LP must demonstrate fiscal responsibility and cost effectiveness consistent with institutional protocols.

Part 12. TECHNOLOGY

Service-Learning Programs (S-LP) must have adequate technology to support their mission. The technology and its use must comply with institutional policies and procedures and be evaluated for compliance with relevant federal, state/provincial, and local requirements.

S-LP must maintain policies and procedures that address the security and back up of data.

When technology is used to facilitate student learning and development, S-LP must select technology that reflects current best pedagogical practices.

Technology, as well as any workstations or computer labs maintained by the programs and services for student use, must be accessible and must meet established technology standards for delivery to persons with disabilities.

When S-LP provide student access to technology, they must provide:
- access to policies that are clear, easy to understand, and available to all students
- access to instruction or training on how to use the technology
- access to information on the legal and ethical implications of misuse as it pertains to intellectual property, harassment, privacy, and social networks

Student violations of technology policies must follow established institutional student disciplinary procedures.

Students who experience negative emotional or psychological consequences from the use of technology must be referred to support services provided by the institution.

Part 13. FACILITIES and EQUIPMENT

Service-Learning Programs (S-LP) must have adequate, accessible, suitably located facilities and equipment to support their mission and goals. If acquiring capital equipment as defined by the institution, S-LP must take into account expenses related to regular maintenance and life cycle costs. Facilities and equipment must be evaluated regularly, including consideration of sustainability, and be in compliance with relevant federal, state/provincial, and local requirements to provide for access, health, safety, and security.

S-LP staff members must have work space that is well-equipped, adequate in size, and designed to support their work and responsibilities. For conversations requiring privacy, staff members must have access to a private space.

S-LP staff members who share work space must have the ability to secure their work adequately.

The design of the facilities must guarantee the security of records and ensure the confidentiality of sensitive information.

The location and layout of the facilities must be sensitive to the special needs of persons with disabilities as well as the needs of constituencies served.

S-LP must ensure that staff members are knowledgeable of and trained in safety and emergency procedures for securing and vacating the facilities.

Part 14. ASSESSMENT and EVALUATION

Service-Learning Programs (S-LP) must establish systematic plans and processes to meet internal and external accountability expectations with regard to program as well as student learning and development outcomes. S-LP must conduct regular assessment and evaluations. Assessments must include qualitative and quantitative methodologies as appropriate, to determine whether and to what degree the stated mission, goals, and student learning and development outcomes are being met. The process must employ sufficient and sound measures to ensure comprehensiveness. Data collected must include responses from students and other affected constituencies.

S-LP must evaluate regularly how well they complement and enhance the institution's stated mission and educational effectiveness.

Results of these evaluations must be used in revising and improving programs and services, identifying needs and interests in shaping directions of program and service design, and recognizing staff performance.

General Standards revised in 2008;
S-LP content developed in 2005

The Role of Student Conduct Programs
CAS Standards Contextual Statement

Throughout the history of American higher education, colleges have struggled with how to respond to student misconduct. In his letter to Thomas Cooper on November 2, 1822, Thomas Jefferson described the problem of student discipline as "a breaker ahead" which he was not sure that American higher education could weather. In recent years, issues related to student discipline including sexual assault, use and abuse of alcohol and other drugs, and campus safety have come to the forefront.

Traditionally, the U.S. courts viewed the administration of student discipline as an internal institutional matter and did not become actively involved in the process through judicial rulings. However, this position changed in 1961, with the landmark case of *Dixon v. Alabama State Board of Education*, 294 F.2d 150 (5th Cir. 1961), the first of an ever-growing modern body of case law related to the administration of student discipline. The courts have held under the 14th Amendment to the U.S. Constitution that public colleges and universities must afford basic due process rights to students accused of violating student conduct codes. However, it is important to note that the rights of due process described in this body of case law differ significantly from those observed in the criminal court system. The limitations placed upon private institutions are substantially less prescriptive. Although the Constitutional rights afforded to students at public institutions are not generally applicable to private institutions, several authors, including Kaplin and Lee (1995), Stoner and Cerminara (1990), and Stoner and Lowery (2004) have encouraged private institutions to bear in mind the restrictions placed upon public institutions and accord their students the same general rights and protections.

In the early American colleges and universities, student discipline was primarily the responsibility of the faculty. As the positions of dean of men and women were established and the field of student affairs evolved, the responsibility for the administration of student discipline shifted. Barry and Wolf (1957) observed, "Despite all of their later disclaimers, most deans of men seem to have been appointed primarily to act as disciplinarians" (p.14). Only in the past twenty-five years has student discipline emerged as a distinct functional area within student affairs. Prior to that time, the responsibility for student discipline was one of a number of duties which fell to an individual or office such as the dean of men or the dean of women and later the dean of students.

In the early 1970s, the American College Personnel Association established Commission XV, Campus Judicial Affairs and Legal Issues, to meet the needs of this emerging profession. In 1988, the Association for Student Judicial Affairs (ASJA) was founded to facilitate the integration of student development concepts with principles of student conduct practice in post-secondary education and to promote, encourage, and support student development professionals responsible for judicial affairs. Reflecting the evolution of the profession, ASJA changed its name in 2008 to the Association for Student Conduct Administration — ASCA.

Over the past fifteen years, the practice of student judicial affairs in the U.S. has been profoundly affected by the passage of federal legislation. While the Family Educational Rights and Privacy Act of 1974 (FERPA) had implications for judicial affairs, the legislation passed more recently has differed significantly in that it directly targeted aspects of the campus student conduct system. For example, the amendments to the Student Right-to-Know and Campus Security Act included in the Higher Education Amendments of 1998 require colleges and universities to include statistics for liquor law violations, drug law, and weapons law violations addressed through the student conduct system. The Higher Education Amendments of 1998 also amended FERPA to allow the release for the final results of a campus disciplinary proceeding when a student is found responsible of a crime of violence or nonforcible sexual offense and to allow parental notification when the institution determined that a student under the age of 21 had violated alcohol or drug policies. In the years between the reauthorization, several pieces of legislation impacting student conduct programs were being introduced into Congress annually as well. This increased governmental involvement demands that student conduct professionals remain knowledgeable about legislative developments and actively work to address legislative proposals which would have a negative impact on the fundamental educational mission of the student conduct system.

The Association for Student Conduct Administration established three principles for the administration of student conduct programs, reflecting current thinking in this area:
- The development and enforcement of standards of conduct for students is an educational endeavor which fosters students' personal and social development; students must assume a significant role in developing and enforcing such regulations in order that they might be better prepared for the responsibilities of citizenship.

- Standards of conduct form the basis for behavioral expectations in the academic community; the enforcement of such standards must protect the rights, health, and safety of members of that community in order that they may pursue their educational goals without undue interference.
- Integrity, wisdom, and empathy are among the characteristics most important to the administration of student conduct standards; officials who have such responsibilities must exercise them impartially and fairly.

The primary role of student conduct administrators is that of educator. The maintenance and enhancement of the ethical climate on campus and the promotion of academic integrity are the primary purposes for enforcing standards of student conduct (ASJA, 1993). , The student conduct programs standards and guidelines that follow represent the fundamental criteria by which programs can assess their quality and effectiveness.

References, Readings, and Resources

ACPA — College Student Educators International - Commission for Student Conduct and Legal Issues. One Dupont Circle Suite 300 Washington, DC 20036; (202) 835-2272. Web page: http://www.myacpa.org/comm/judicial/

Association for Student Conduct Administration: P.O. Box 2237, College Station, TX 77841-2237; 979-845-5262; Web page: http://asja.tamu.edu/

Association for Student Judicial Affairs. (1993). *Ethical principles and standards of conduct: Preamble.* Retrieved May 20, 2009, from http://www.theasca.org/en/cms/?60

Dannells, M. (1997). *From discipline to development: Rethinking student conduct in higher education.* ASHE-ERIC Higher Education Report Vol. 25, No. 2. Washington, DC: The George Washington University, Graduate School of Education and Human Development.

Dixon v. Alabama State Board of Education, 294 F.2d 150 (5th Cir. 1961).

Hoekema, D. A. (1994). *Campus rules and moral community: In place of in loco parentis.* Lanham, MD: Rowman & Littlefield.

Kaplin, W. A., & Lee, B. (1995). *The law of higher education* (3rd ed.). San Francisco: Jossey-Bass.

Letter from Thomas Jefferson to Thomas Cooper (Nov. 2, 1822), in *Thomas Jefferson: Writings 1463, 1465* (M. Patterson, ed., The Library of America) (1984).

Mercer, W. L. (Ed.). (1996). *Critical issues in judicial affairs: Current trends in practice.* San Francisco: Jossey-Bass.

Paterson, G. P., & Kibler, W. L. (Eds.). (1999). *The administration of student discipline: Student, organizational, and community issues.* Asheville, NC: College Administration Publications.

Stoner, E. N., II, & Cerminara, K. L. (1990). Harnessing the "spirit of insubordination": A model student disciplinary code. *Journal of College and University Law, 17,* 89-121.

Stoner, E. N., II, & Lowery, J. W. (2004). Navigating past the "spirit of insubordination": A twenty-first century model student conduct code with a model hearing script. *Journal of College and University Law, 31,* 1-77.

Contributors:

John Wesley Lowrey, Indiana University of Pennsylvania, ASCA
John Zacker, University of Maryland, ASCA.

Student Conduct Programs
CAS Standards and Guidelines

Part 1. MISSION

Student Conduct Programs (SCP) develop and enforce standards of conduct, an educational endeavor to foster students' and learning development.

SCP must develop, disseminate, implement, and regularly review their mission. Mission statements must be consistent with the mission of the institution and with professional standards. SCP in higher education must enhance overall educational experiences by incorporating student learning and development outcomes in their mission.

The goals of SCP must address the institution's needs to:
- develop, disseminate, interpret, and enforce campus policies and procedures
- protect rights of students in the administration of the student conduct program
- respond to student behavioral problems in a fair and reasonable manner
- facilitate and encourage respect for and involvement in campus governance
- provide learning experiences for students who are found to be responsible for conduct which is determined to be in violation of institutional standards or who participate in the operations of the student conduct system
- initiate and encourage educational activities that serve to reduce violations of campus regulations

SCP should support appropriate individual and group behavior as well as serve the campus community by reducing disruption and harm. The programs should be conducted in ways that will serve to foster the ethical development and personal integrity of students and the promotion of an environment that is consistent with the overall educational goals of the institution.

Part 2. PROGRAM

The formal education of students, consisting of the curriculum and the co-curriculum, must promote student learning and development outcomes that are purposeful and holistic and that prepare students for satisfying and productive lifestyles, work, and civic participation. The student learning and development outcome domains and their related dimensions are:

- knowledge acquisition, integration, construction, and application
  o Dimensions: understanding knowledge from a range of disciplines; connecting knowledge to other knowledge, ideas, and experiences; constructing knowledge; and relating knowledge to daily life

- cognitive complexity
  o Dimensions: critical thinking; reflective thinking; effective reasoning; and creativity

- intrapersonal development
  o Dimensions: realistic self-appraisal, self-understanding, and self-respect; identity development; commitment to ethics and integrity; and spiritual awareness

- interpersonal competence
  o Dimensions: meaningful relationships; interdependence; collaboration; and effective leadership

- humanitarianism and civic engagement
  o Dimensions: understanding and appreciation of cultural and human differences; social responsibility; global perspective; and sense of civic responsibility

- practical competence
  o Dimensions: pursuing goals; communicating effectively; technical competence; managing personal affairs; managing career development; demonstrating professionalism; maintaining health and wellness; and living a purposeful and satisfying life

[See *The Council for the Advancement of Standards Learning and Developmental Outcomes* statement for examples of outcomes related to these domains and dimensions.]

Consistent with the institutional mission, SCP must identify relevant and desirable student learning and development outcomes from among the six domains and related dimensions. When creating opportunities for student learning and development, SCP must explore possibilities for collaboration with faculty members and other colleagues.

SCP must assess relevant and desirable student learning and development outcomes and provide evidence of their impact on student learning and development. SCP must articulate how they contribute to or support students' learning and development in the domains not specifically assessed.

SCP must be:
- integrated into the life of the institution
- intentional and coherent
- guided by theories and knowledge of learning and development
- reflective of developmental and demographic profiles of the student population
- responsive to needs of individuals, diverse and special populations, and relevant constituencies

SCP must establish the following within the context of its mission and purpose:

1. Authority
A written statement describing the authority, philosophy, jurisdiction, and procedures of the student conduct programs must be developed and disseminated to all members of the

campus community.

This statement should address (a) how student academic or non-academic misconduct is within the program's jurisdiction, (b) which campus policies and regulations are enforced by these programs, (c) sanctions that may be imposed, (d) a clear description of the relationship between student conduct programs and both campus and external law enforcement agencies, including guidelines regarding when law enforcement authorities will be called in, (e) authority under the policy to address misconduct which occurs off campus including education abroad, and (f) information regarding the impact, if any, of decisions by the criminal courts on the outcome of corresponding student conduct proceedings.

2. Components

The institution's policies regarding the administration of student discipline must be clearly described in writing. Elements to be addressed in this policy must include prohibited conduct; sanctions; boards and administrators with roles in the adjudication of student misconduct; procedures for the investigation and adjudication of allegations of student misconduct; appeal procedures (if provided); procedures for interim suspension (if provided); and policies regarding student disciplinary records.

Generally, the student conduct system should involve significant roles for students in the adjudication of allegations of misconduct; however, membership on boards need not be limited to students. The system should allow sufficient time for an investigation of all allegations prior to a hearing, while responding to complaints in a timely fashion.

Procedures and processes must be designed to provide for substantive and procedural due process at public institutions of higher education and fundamental fairness at private institutions of higher education.

SCP should provide students with ample opportunity to receive advice about the process, a general time frame for resolution, and a delineation of individual responsibilities in the process.

Institutional disciplinary action against individual students or recognized student organizations must be administered in the context of a coordinated set of regulations and processes in order to ensure fair and reasonable outcomes and the equitable treatment of students and groups. Allegations of improper behavior originating from both instructional and non-instructional components of the institution must be encompassed in a comprehensive student conduct system for students.

Different procedures may be used to address the various forms of misconduct.

The institution must be clear about which board or individual has jurisdiction over specific conduct regulations.

Students should be assisted in understanding the sources and lines of authority.

The sanctions imposed as a result of institutional disciplinary

action must be educationally and developmentally appropriate.

SCP must follow up on cases, including enforcement of sanctions, assessing the developmental processes that have been affected, and ensuring that students are directed to appropriate services for assistance.

The institution must be clear about how it defines student status and the jurisdiction of the system to include whether students can be held responsible for behavior that takes place off campus or between academic sessions.

SCP should maintain written records to serve as referral materials, to document precedents, to provide source material for identifying recurring problems, or to use for appeals.

The institution must clearly state the conduct regulations that apply to student organizations, the procedures that will be followed in the hearing of cases related to student organizations, and the guidelines used to determine if actions of individual members or small groups within an organization constitute action by the organization.

3. Information to Campus Community
The institution must publish information about the SCP.

Publications should contain (a) campus policies, such as those concerning legal representation, the protection of privacy of student disciplinary records, and the destruction of disciplinary records; (b) campus procedures, such as filing a disciplinary action, gathering information, conducting a hearing, and notifying a student of the hearing or appeal board's decision; (c) the composition, authority, and jurisdiction of all student conduct bodies; (d) the types of advice and assistance that the complainant and others can receive about the process; (e) the types of disciplinary sanctions, including interim suspension procedures; and (f) a general explanation of how and when non-campus law enforcement officials are used.

Publications must be distributed through methods that will reach all students.

Dissemination methods may include electronic media; the institutional catalog; the orientation program; the student handbook; and admissions, registration, and billing materials.

Published information should include not only descriptions about how the system works, but also the results of the system. By publishing the outcomes of student conduct cases in a manner which protects the privacy of those involved, the institution demonstrates that the system does work and encourages an open discussion of issues related to student conduct.

4. Hearing Authority
In addition to a hearing officer, SCP must include a hearing or appellate board, composed of representatives of the campus community, that is responsible for carrying out student conduct functions delegated by the administration.

Roles and functions of student conduct board members may include (a) reviewing disciplinary referrals and claims; (b) interpreting misconduct allegations and identifying specific charges to be brought against the student(s); (c) conducting preliminary hearings and gathering information pertinent to the charges; (d) advising students on their rights and responsibilities; (e) engaging in substantive discussions with students about relevant ethical issues; (f) scheduling, coordinating, and conducting hearings; (g) reviewing decisions from other hearing bodies, when applicable; (h) notifying the accused in writing about relevant decisions and the board's rationale for such; (i) maintaining accurate written records of the entire proceeding; (j) referring information to an appeal board when applicable; (k) following up on sanctions to ensure they have been implemented; (l) following up with students who have been sanctioned to ensure awareness of available counseling services; (m) establishing and implementing a procedure for maintenance and destruction of disciplinary records; and (n) assessing student conduct procedures, policies, and outcomes.

A student conduct officer may be assigned responsibility for training student conduct board members, scheduling and facilitating evaluations, and informing faculty members, administration, and staff about legal and disciplinary matters.

Student conduct board members should participate on campus government committees associated with student conduct, except when a conflict of interest will result. Student conduct board members may also be involved in the outreach efforts of the SCP.

5. Training of Student Conduct Board Members
Initial and in-service training of all hearing board members must be provided.

In order for student conduct board members to fulfill their roles and functions, initial training should include (a) an overview of all judicial policies and procedures; (b) an explanation of the operation of the judicial process at all levels including authority and jurisdiction; (c) an overview of the institution's philosophy on student conduct and its role in this process; (d) roles and functions of all student conduct bodies and their members; (e) review of constitutional and other relevant legal individual and institutional rights and responsibilities; (f) an explanation of sanctions; (g) an explanation of pertinent ethics, including particularly the importance of privacy of student disciplinary records and addressing bias and conflict of interest in the student conduct process; (h) a description of available personal counseling programs and referral resources; (i) an outline of conditions and interactions which may involve external enforcement officials, attorneys, witnesses, parents of accused students, and the media; and (j) an overview of developmental and interpersonal issues likely to arise among college students.

In-service training should include participation in relevant and on-going workshops, seminars, and conferences. A library containing current resources about the student conduct system should be maintained and be accessible to student conduct board members.

Part 3. LEADERSHIP
Because effective and ethical leadership is essential to the success of all organizations, Student Conduct Programs (SCP) leaders with organizational authority for the programs

and services must:
- **articulate a vision and mission for their programs and services**
- **set goals and objectives based on the needs of the population served and desired student learning and development outcomes**
- **advocate for their programs and services**
- **promote campus environments that provide meaningful opportunities for student learning, development, and integration**
- **identify and find means to address individual, organizational, or environmental conditions that foster or inhibit mission achievement**
- **advocate for representation in strategic planning initiatives at appropriate divisional and institutional levels**
- **initiate collaborative interactions with stakeholders who have legitimate concerns and interests in the functional area**
- **apply effective practices to educational and administrative processes**
- **prescribe and model ethical behavior**
- **communicate effectively**
- **manage financial resources, including planning, allocation, monitoring, and analysis**
- **incorporate sustainability practices in the management and design of programs, services, and facilities**
- **manage human resource processes including recruitment, selection, development, supervision, performance planning, and evaluation**
- **empower professional, support, and student staff to accept leadership opportunities**
- **encourage and support scholarly contribution to the profession**
- **be informed about and integrate appropriate technologies into programs and services**
- **be knowledgeable about federal, state/provincial, and local laws relevant to the programs and services and ensure that staff members understand their responsibilities by receiving appropriate training**
- **develop and continuously improve programs and services in response to the changing needs of students and other populations served and the evolving institutional priorities**
- **recognize environmental conditions that may negatively influence the safety of staff and students and propose interventions that mitigate such conditions.**

Part 4. HUMAN RESOURCES
Student Conduct Programs (SCP) must be staffed adequately by individuals qualified to accomplish the mission and goals. Within institutional guidelines, SCP must establish procedures for staff selection, training, and evaluation; set expectations for supervision; and provide appropriate professional development opportunities to improve the leadership ability, competence, and skills of all employees.

SCP professional staff members must hold an earned graduate or professional degree in a field relevant to the position they hold or must possess an appropriate combination of educational credentials and related work experience.

Degree- or credential-seeking interns must be qualified by enrollment in an appropriate field of study and by relevant experience. These individuals must be trained and supervised adequately by professional staff members holding educational credentials and related work experience appropriate for supervision.

Student employees and volunteers must be carefully selected, trained, supervised, and evaluated. They must be educated on how and when to refer those in need of additional assistance to qualified staff members and must have access to a supervisor for assistance in making these judgments. Student employees and volunteers must be provided clear and precise job descriptions, pre-service training based on assessed needs, and continuing staff development.

Students from graduate academic programs, particularly in areas such as counseling, student development, higher education administration, law, or criminology, may assist the student conduct programs through practica, internships, and assistantships.

Students who participate on conduct boards may be awarded academic credit for proper supervision. Clear objectives and assignments should be outlined to ensure that a student's grade for this participation is in no way influenced by his/her decisions on a particular case.

Employees and volunteers must receive specific training on institutional policies and privacy laws regarding their access to student records and other sensitive institutional information (e.g., in the USA, Family Educational Rights and Privacy Act, FERPA, or equivalent privacy laws in other states/provinces or countries.)

SCP must have technical and support staff members adequate to accomplish their mission. All members of the staff must be technologically proficient and qualified to perform their job functions, be knowledgeable about ethical and legal uses of technology, and have access to training and resources to support the performance of their assigned responsibilities.

All members of the staff must receive training on policies and procedures related to the use of technology to store or access student records and institutional data.

SCP must ensure that staff members are knowledgeable about and trained in emergency procedures, crisis response, and prevention efforts. Prevention efforts must address identification of threatening conduct or behavior of students, faculty members, staff, and others and must incorporate a system or procedures for responding, including but not limited to reporting them to the appropriate campus officials.

Salary levels and benefits for all staff members must be commensurate with those for comparable positions within the institution, in similar institutions, and in the relevant geographic area.

SCP must maintain position descriptions for all staff members.

To create a diverse staff, SCP must institute hiring and promotion practices that are fair, inclusive, proactive, and non-discriminatory.

SCP must conduct regular performance planning and evaluation of staff members. SCP must provide access to continuing and advanced education and professional development opportunities.

A qualified member of the campus community must be designated as the person responsible for student conduct programs.

The designee should have an educational background in the behavioral sciences (e.g., college student affairs, psychology, sociology, student development including moral and ethical development, higher education administration, counseling, law, criminology, or criminal justice).

The designee and any other professional staff member in the student conduct programs should possess (a) a clear understanding of the legal requirements for substantive and procedural due process; (b) legal knowledge sufficient to confer with attorneys involved in student disciplinary proceedings and other aspects of the student conduct services system; (c) a general interest in and commitment to the welfare and development of students who participate on boards or who are involved in cases; (d) demonstrated skills in working with decision-making processes and conflict resolution; (e) teaching and consulting skills appropriate for the education, advising, and coordination of hearing bodies; (f) the ability to communicate and interact with students regardless of race, sex, disability, sexual orientation, and other personal characteristics; (g) understanding of the requirements relative to confidentiality and security of student conduct programs files; and (h) the ability to create an atmosphere where students feel free to ask questions and obtain assistance.

Part 5. ETHICS

Persons involved in the delivery of Student Conduct Programs (SCP) must adhere to the highest principles of ethical behavior. SCP must review relevant professional ethical standards and develop or adopt and implement appropriate statements of ethical practice. SCP must publish these statements and ensure their periodic review by relevant constituencies.

SCP must orient new staff members to relevant ethical standards and statements of ethical practice.

SCP staff members must ensure that privacy and confidentiality are maintained with respect to all communications and records to the extent that such records are protected under the law and appropriate statements of ethical practice. Information contained in students' education records must not be disclosed except as allowed by relevant laws and institutional policies. SCP staff members must disclose to appropriate authorities information judged to be of an emergency nature, especially when the safety of the individual or others is involved, or when otherwise required by institutional policy or relevant law.

SCP staff members must be aware of and comply with the provisions contained in the institution's policies pertaining to human subjects research and student rights and responsibilities, as well as those in other relevant institutional policies addressing ethical practices and confidentiality of research data concerning individuals.

SCP staff members must recognize and avoid personal conflicts of interest or appearance thereof in the performance of their work.

SCP staff members must strive to insure the fair, objective, and impartial treatment of all persons with whom they interact.

When handling institutional funds, SCP staff members must ensure that such funds are managed in accordance with established and responsible accounting procedures and the fiscal policies or processes of the institution.

Promotional and descriptive information must be accurate and free of deception.

SCP staff members must perform their duties within the limits of their training, expertise, and competence. When these limits are exceeded, individuals in need of further assistance must be referred to persons possessing appropriate qualifications.

SCP staff members must use suitable means to confront and otherwise hold accountable other staff members who exhibit unethical behavior.

SCP staff members must be knowledgeable about and practice ethical behavior in the use of technology.

Part 6. LEGAL RESPONSIBILITIES

Student Conduct Programs (SCP) staff members must be knowledgeable about and responsive to laws and regulations that relate to their respective responsibilities and that may pose legal obligations, limitations, or ramifications for the institution as a whole. As appropriate, staff members must inform users of programs and services, as well as officials, of legal obligations and limitations including constitutional, statutory, regulatory, and case law; mandatory laws and orders emanating from federal, state/provincial, and local governments; and the institution's policies.

SCP must have written policies on all relevant operations, transactions, or tasks that may have legal implications.

SCP staff members must neither participate in nor condone any form of harassment or activity that demeans persons or creates an intimidating, hostile, or offensive campus environment.

SCP staff members must use reasonable and informed practices to limit the liability exposure of the institution and its officers, employees, and agents. SCP staff members must be informed about institutional policies regarding risk management, personal liability, and related insurance coverage options and must be referred to external sources if coverage is not provided by the institution.

The institution must provide access to legal advice for SCP staff members as needed to carry out assigned responsibilities.

The institution must inform SCP staff and students in a timely and systematic fashion about extraordinary or changing legal obligations and potential liabilities.

Appropriate policies and practices to ensure compliance with regulations should include notification to all constituencies of their rights and responsibilities under the student conduct system, a written description, accurate record keeping of all aspects of the student conduct proceedings, and regular reviews of the student conduct policies and practices.

Part 7. EQUITY and ACCESS

Student Conduct Programs (SCP) must be provided on a fair, equitable, and non-discriminatory basis in accordance with institutional policies and with all applicable state/provincial and federal statutes and regulations. SCP must maintain an educational and work environment free from discrimination in accordance with law and institutional policy.

Discrimination must be avoided on the basis of age; cultural heritage; disability; ethnicity; gender identity and expression; nationality; political affiliation; race; religious affiliation; sex; sexual orientation; economic, marital, social, or veteran status; and any other bases included in local, state/provincial, or federal laws.

Consistent with the mission and goals, SCP must take action to remedy significant imbalances in student participation and staffing patterns.

SCP must ensure physical and program access for persons with disabilities. SCP must be responsive to the needs of all students and other populations served when establishing hours of operation and developing methods of delivering programs and services.

SCP must recognize the needs of distance learning students by providing appropriate and accessible services and assisting them in identifying and gaining access to other appropriate services in their geographic region.

Part 8. DIVERSITY

Within the context of each institution's unique mission, diversity enriches the community and enhances the collegiate experience for all; therefore, Student Conduct Programs (SCP) must create and nurture environments that are welcoming to and bring together persons of diverse backgrounds.

SCP must promote environments that are characterized by open and continuous communication that deepens understanding of one's own identity, culture, and heritage, as well as that of others. SCP must recognize, honor, educate, and promote respect about commonalties and differences among people within their historical and cultural contexts.

SCP must address the characteristics and needs of a diverse population when establishing and implementing policies and procedures.

Part 9. ORGANIZATION and MANAGEMENT

To promote student learning and development outcomes, Student Conduct Programs (SCP) must be structured purposefully and managed effectively to achieve stated goals. Evidence of appropriate structure must include current and accessible policies and procedures, written performance expectations for all employees, functional workflow graphics or organizational charts, and clearly stated program and service delivery expectations.

SCP must monitor websites used for distributing information to ensure that the sites are current, accurate, appropriately referenced, and accessible.

Evidence of effective management must include use of comprehensive and accurate information for decisions, clear sources and channels of authority, effective communication practices, procedures for decision-making and conflict resolution, responses to changing conditions, systems of accountability and evaluation, and processes for recognition and reward. SCP must align policies and procedures with those of the institution and provide channels within the organization for their regular review.

Part 10. CAMPUS and EXTERNAL RELATIONS

Student Conduct Programs (SCP) must reach out to relevant individuals, campus offices, and external agencies to:
- establish, maintain, and promote effective relations
- disseminate information about their own and other related programs and services
- coordinate and collaborate, where appropriate, in offering programs and services to meet the needs of students and promote their achievement of student learning and development outcomes

SCP must have procedures and guidelines consistent with institutional policy for responding to threats, emergencies, and crisis situations. Systems and procedures must be in place to disseminate timely and accurate information to students and other members of the campus community during emergency situations.

SCP must have procedures and guidelines consistent with institutional policy for communicating with the media.

Representatives of the student conduct system should meet regularly with pertinent campus constituencies (e.g., student government, student development offices, staff, faculty members, academic administrators, public safety, legal counsel) to exchange information concerning their respective operations and to identify ways to work together to prevent behavioral problems and to correct existing ones. Such collaborative efforts might include educational programs and joint publications.

Representatives should also meet periodically with relevant external agencies(e.g., local police, district attorneys, service providers) to ensure understanding about the student conduct programs as well as to address student behavior problems in an effective manner.

Part 11. FINANCIAL RESOURCES

Student Conduct Programs (SCP) must have adequate funding to accomplish their mission and goals. In establishing funding priorities and making significant changes, a comprehensive analysis, which includes relevant expenditures, external and internal resources, and impact on the campus community, must be conducted.

SCP must demonstrate fiscal responsibility and cost effectiveness consistent with institutional protocols.

Part 12. TECHNOLOGY

Student Conduct Programs (SCP) must have adequate technology to support their mission. The technology and its use must comply with institutional policies and procedures and be evaluated for compliance with relevant federal, state/provincial, and local requirements.

SCP must maintain policies and procedures that address the security and back up of data.

When technology is used to facilitate student learning and development, SCP must select technology that reflects current best pedagogical practices.

Technology, as well as any workstations or computer labs maintained by the SCP for student use, must be accessible and must meet established technology standards for delivery to persons with disabilities.

When SCP provide student access to technology, they must provide:
- access to policies that are clear, easy to understand, and available to all students
- access to instruction or training on how to use the technology
- access to information on the legal and ethical implications of misuse as it pertains to intellectual property, harassment, privacy, and social networks.

Student violations of technology policies must follow established institutional student disciplinary procedures.

Students who experience negative emotional or psychological consequences from the use of technology must be referred to support services provided by the institution.

Part 13. FACILITIES and EQUIPMENT

Student Conduct Programs (SCP) must have adequate, accessible, suitably located facilities and equipment to support their mission and goals. If acquiring capital equipment as defined by the institution, SCP must take into account expenses related to regular maintenance and life cycle costs. Facilities and equipment must be evaluated regularly, including consideration of sustainability, and be in compliance with relevant federal, state/provincial, and local requirements to provide for access, health, safety, and security.

SCP staff members must have work space that is well-equipped, adequate in size, and designed to support their work and responsibilities. For conversations requiring privacy, staff members must have access to a private space.

SCP staff members who share work space must have the ability to secure their work adequately.

The design of the facilities must guarantee the security of records and ensure the confidentiality of sensitive information.

The location and layout of the facilities must be sensitive to the special needs of persons with disabilities as well as the needs of constituencies served.

SCP must ensure that staff members are knowledgeable of and trained in safety and emergency procedures for securing and vacating the facilities.

SCP must have access to facilities of sufficient size and arrangement to ensure privacy of records, meetings, and interviews.

The facilities should include a private office where individual consultations and pre-hearing conferences with those involved in disciplinary actions may be held, hearing room facilities, a meeting room for small groups, a library or resource area, and a secure location for student disciplinary records. The facilities should also be designed to promote the personal safety of the individuals involved in the SCP (e.g., multiple methods of egress, panic buttons).

Part 14. ASSESSMENT and EVALUATION

Student Conduct Programs (SCP) must establish systematic plans and processes to meet internal and external accountability expectations with regard to program as well as student learning and development outcomes. SCP must conduct regular assessment and evaluations. Assessments must include qualitative and quantitative methodologies as appropriate, to determine whether and to what degree the stated mission, goals, and student learning and development outcomes are being met. The process must employ sufficient and sound measures to ensure comprehensiveness. Data collected must include responses from students and other affected constituencies.

SCP must evaluate regularly how well they complement and enhance the institution's stated mission and educational effectiveness.

Results of these evaluations must be used in revising and improving programs and services, identifying needs and interests in shaping directions of program and service design, and recognizing staff performance.

Evaluation of SCP should include:
- performance evaluations of all staff members by their supervisors
- periodic performance evaluations of individual hearing boards
- on-going evaluation of training programs and publications
- periodic review of applicable state/provincial and federal laws and current case law to ensure compliance

Assessment and evaluation activities may include:
- whether student conduct boards accurately follow the institution's procedural guidelines
- general impressions of the student conduct system according to students, faculty members, staff members, and the community
- developmental effects on students and student conduct board members
- annual trends in case load, rates of recidivism, types of offenses, and efficacy of sanctions
- effects of programming designed to prevent behavioral problems
- unique aspects of special function or special population student conduct boards (e.g., student organization, residence hall boards)

General Standards revised in 2008;
SCP content (formerly Judicial Programs and Services) developed/revised in 1986, 1996, & 2005

The Role of Student Leadership Programs
CAS Standards Contextual Statement

Many college mission statements contain commitments to develop citizen leaders or prepare students for professional and community responsibilities in a global context. Throughout the history of higher education, however, leadership development has primarily been targeted toward students holding leadership positions, such as student government officials, officers in fraternities and sororities, and resident assistants. Consequently, only a handful of students had a genuine opportunity for focused experience in leadership development.

During the 1970s, many colleges refocused efforts on leadership development when events such as the Watergate scandal caused institutions to ponder how they taught ethics, leadership, and social responsibility. Subsequent initiatives such as the women's and African-American civil rights movements and adult reentry programs increased access to college. New forms of campus shared governance, coupled with a focus on intentional student development, led to new forms of leadership development through programs such as assertiveness training, emerging leaders' retreats, and leadership targeted toward special populations.

By the 1970s, professional associations were becoming increasingly interested in broad-based leadership efforts. Several associations, including the American College Personnel Association (ACPA), National Association of Student Personnel Administrators (NASPA), National Association for Campus Activities (NACA), and National Association for Women in Education (NAWE), expanded projects and initiatives with a leadership focus. Burns' seminal book, *Leadership* (1978), brought new energy with its discussion of transformational leadership grounded in values and moral purpose. Thinking about leadership expanded in the 1980s and 1990s to include such perspectives as cultural influences, service learning, social change, and spirituality. Leadership educators focused on developing leadership models with applicability to the college context. Two such models, the Social Change Model of Leadership (SCM) (HERI, 1996), and the Relational Leadership Model (Komives, Lucas, & McMahon, 1996) have been widely adopted.

This shift to colleges developing not just better, but more leaders, has resulted in leadership education efforts directed toward the entire student body. Because students experience leadership in many different settings–in and out of the classroom, on and off campus–virtually every student engages in some type of activity that involves the practice

of leadership. Regardless of differences in academic discipline, organizational affiliation, cultural background, or geographical location, students must be better prepared to serve as citizen-leaders in a global community. The role of student affairs professionals in this arena is to help students understand their experiences and to facilitate their learning, so that they become effective contributors to their communities. Comprehensive leadership programs should be based on an active learning pedagogy where learning is situated in students' experiences, where students are validated as knowers, and where there is mutually constructed meaning (Baxter Magolda, 1999).

The Inter-Association Leadership Project brought student affairs leadership educators together in the mid-1980s to create and sustain a leadership agenda. By the end of the decade, higher education's commitment to leadership was clear with over 600 campuses teaching leadership courses; creating special leadership centers such as the Jepson School of Leadership Studies at the University of Richmond and the McDonough Leadership Center at Marietta College; and establishing special programs, including the National LeaderShape Institute. In 1992 the National Clearinghouse for Leadership Programs (NCLP) was established at the University of Maryland, and a co-sponsored series of symposia encouraged leadership educators to identify a leadership agenda for the new millennium. Projects funded by the Kellogg, Pew, and Lilly Foundations; FIPSE; and the federal Eisenhower Leadership grant program have also focused broad-based attention on leadership development. By late 1990s, there were over 800 college leadership programs. The new International Leadership Association (ILA) was established in 1999 to bring a global lens to leadership education. Other leadership institutes serve the leadership educator professional; for example, NCLP and the NACA host the annual summer leadership educators' symposium, and NCLP in partnership with NASPA and ACPA now hosts the Leadership Educators Institute, a bi-annual program for entry and mid-level leadership educators.

The *CAS Student Leadership Program Standards and Guidelines* can be used to help professionals provide comprehensive leadership programs and enhance students' learning opportunities. Leadership for positional leaders will still occur within specific functional areas such as student activities and residence life; campuses that seek to develop a comprehensive leadership program will recognize the need to make intentional leadership development opportunities available to all students through coordinated campus-wide efforts. Recent research has identified a Leadership Identity Development model (Komives, Owen, Longerbeam, Mainella, & Osteen, 2005) that can guide intentional practice. Further, a 2006 national Multi-Institutional Study of Leadership has established normative data using the SCM (see www.nclp. umd.edu).

Leadership is an inherently relational process of working with others to accomplish a goal or to promote change. Most leadership programs seek to empower students to enhance their self efficacy as leaders and understand how they can make a difference, whether as positional leaders or active participants in a group or community process. Leadership development involves self-awareness and understanding of others, values and diverse perspectives, organizations, and change. Leadership also requires competence in establishing purpose, working collaboratively, and managing conflict. Institutions can initiate opportunities to study leadership and to experience a range of leadership-related activities designed to intentionally promote desired outcomes of student leadership learning.

References, Readings, and Resources

Astin, H., & Astin, A., (Eds.). (2000). *Leadership reconsidered: Engaging higher education in social change.* Battle Creek, MI: W.K. Kellogg Foundation.

Baxter Magolda, M. B. (1999). *Creating contexts for learning and self-authorship: Constructive-developmental pedagogy.* Nashville, TN: Vanderbilt University Press.

Boatman, S. (1987). *Student leadership development: Approaches, methods, and models.* Columbia, SC: National Association for Campus Activities.

Boatman, S. (1992). *Supporting student leadership: Selections from the student development series.* Columbia, SC: National Association for Campus Activities.

Brungardt, C. (1996). The making of leaders: A review of the research in leadership development and education. *Journal of Leadership Studies, 3*(3), 81-95.

HERI (1996). *A social change model of leadership development: Guidebook version III.* Los Angeles: University of California Los Angeles Higher Education Research Institute. *(Available from National Clearinghouse for Leadership Programs).*

Komives, S. R., Lucas, N., & McMahon, T. (1998). *Exploring leadership.* San Francisco: Jossey-Bass.

Komives, S. R., Owen, J. E., Longerbeam, S., Mainella, F. C., & Osteen, L. (2005). Developing a leadership identity: A grounded theory. *Journal of College Student Development, 46,* 593-611.

Komives, S. R., Dugan, J., Owen, J. E., Slack, C. & Wagner, W. (Eds). (2006). *Handbook for student leadership programs.* College Park, MD: National Clearinghouse for Leadership Programs.

Murray, J. I. (1994). *Training for student leaders.* Dubuque, IA: Kendall/Hunt.

Roberts, D. C. (1981). *Student leadership programs in higher education.* Carbondale, IL: American College Personnel Association.

Rogers, J. L. (2003). Leadership. In S. Komives & D. B. Woodard (Eds.), *Student services: A handbook for the profession* (4th ed.)(pp. 447-465). San Francisco: Jossey-Bass.

Zimmerman-Oster, K., & Burkhardt, J. C. (1999). *Leadership in the making: Impact and insights from leadership development programs in U. S. colleges and universities.* Battle Creek, MI: W. K. Kellogg Foundation.

Center for Creative Leadership, One Leadership Place, P.O. Box 26300, Greensboro, NC 27438-6300. (910) 288-7210. Publisher of periodic sourcebooks.

Concepts & connections: A newsletter for leadership educators. The National Clearinghouse for Leadership Programs, 1135 Stamp Student Union, University of Maryland at College Park, College Park, MD 20742-4631. (301) 314-7174

Journal of Leadership Studies. Baker College of Flint, 1050 W. Bristol Rd., Flint, MI 48507-9987. (313) 766-4105

Leadership Quarterly. JAI Press, 55 Old Post Road, # 2, P.O. Box 1678, Greenwich, CT 06836-1678. (203) 661-7602

Contributors:

Jan Arminio, Shippensburg University, NACA
Susan Komives, University of Maryland, ACPA
Julie Owen, George Mason University, NCLP
Craig Slack, University of Maryland, NCLP

Student Leadership Programs
CAS Standards and Guidelines

Part 1. MISSION

The mission of Student Leadership Programs (SLP) must be to prepare students to engage in the process of leadership. To accomplish this mission, the program must:
- be grounded in the belief that leadership can be learned
- be based upon clearly stated principles, values, and assumptions
- use multiple leadership theories, models, and approaches
- provide students with opportunities to develop and enhance a personal philosophy of leadership that includes understanding of self, others, and community, and acceptance of responsibilities inherent in community membership
- promote intentional student involvement and learning in varied leadership experiences
- acknowledge effective leadership behaviors and processes
- be inclusive and accessible, by encouraging and seeking out underrepresented populations

SLP must develop, disseminate, implement, and regularly review their mission. Mission statements must be consistent with the mission of the institution and with professional standards. SLP must enhance overall educational experiences by incorporating student learning and development outcomes in their mission.

Student leadership development must be an integral part of the institution's educational mission.

The SLP mission should be developed in collaboration with appropriate and multiple constituents interested in leadership development.

SLP should seek an institution-wide commitment that transcends the boundaries of the units specifically charged with program delivery.

SLP must advocate for student involvement in institutional governance.

Part 2. PROGRAM

The formal education of students, consisting of the curriculum and the co-curriculum, must promote student learning and development outcomes that are purposeful and holistic and that prepare students for satisfying and productive lifestyles, work, and civic participation. The student learning and development outcome domains and their related dimensions are:

- knowledge acquisition, integration, construction, and application
  - Dimensions: understanding knowledge from a range of disciplines; connecting knowledge to other knowledge, ideas, and experiences; constructing knowledge; and relating knowledge to daily life

- cognitive complexity
  - Dimensions: critical thinking; reflective thinking; effective reasoning; and creativity

- intrapersonal development
  - Dimensions: realistic self-appraisal, self-understanding, and self-respect; identity development; commitment to ethics and integrity; and spiritual awareness

- interpersonal competence
  - Dimensions: meaningful relationships; interdependence; collaboration; and effective leadership

- humanitarianism and civic engagement
  - Dimensions: understanding and appreciation of cultural and human differences; social responsibility; global perspective; and sense of civic responsibility

- practical competence
  - Dimensions: pursuing goals; communicating effectively; technical competence; managing personal affairs; managing career development; demonstrating professionalism; maintaining health and wellness; and living a purposeful and satisfying life

[See *The Council for the Advancement of Standards Learning and Developmental Outcomes* statement for examples of outcomes related to these domains and dimensions.]

Consistent with the institutional mission, Student Leadership Programs (SLP) must identify relevant and desirable student learning and development outcomes from among the six domains and related dimensions. When creating opportunities for student learning and development, programs and services must explore possibilities for collaboration with faculty members and other colleagues.

SLP must assess relevant and desirable student learning and development outcomes and provide evidence of their impact on student learning and development. SLP must articulate how they contribute to or support students' learning and development in the domains not specifically assessed.

SLP and services must be:
- integrated into the life of the institution
- intentional and coherent
- guided by theories and knowledge of learning and development
- reflective of developmental and demographic profiles of the student population
- responsive to needs of individuals, diverse and special populations, and relevant constituencies

SLP must be comprehensive in nature and provide opportunities for students to develop leadership knowledge and skills. SLP staff must design learning environments reflective of the institutional mission, organizational context, learning goals, and intended audience. Programs must have clear theoretical foundations and be based upon well-defined principles, values, and assumptions. Programs must facilitate students' self-awareness, their capacity for collaboration, and their ability to engage within multiple contexts while understanding diverse perspectives.

Key components of SLP must include the following: (1) opportunities for students to develop the competencies required for effective leadership; (2) multiple delivery formats, strategies, and contexts; and (3) collaboration with campus and community partners. These components are described in more detail below.

1) **SLP must provide opportunities for students to develop the competencies required for effective leadership.**

   SLP must advance student competencies in the categories of a) foundations of leadership, b) personal development, c) interpersonal development, and d) the development of groups, organizations, and systems.

   Suggested content for each of these categories follows:

   a) Foundations of leadership should include:
   - historical perspectives on leaders, leadership, and leadership development
   - established and evolving theoretical, conceptual, and philosophical frameworks of leadership
   - the distinction between management and leadership
   - diverse approaches to leadership including positional (leadership-follower dynamics) and non-positional (collaborative-process models)
   - theories and strategies of change
   - the integrative and interdisciplinary nature of leadership
   - cross-cultural and global approaches to leadership

   b) Personal development should include:
   - an awareness and understanding of various leadership styles and approaches
   - exploration of a personal leadership philosophy, including personal values exploration, leadership identity development, and reflective practice
   - connection of leadership to social identities and other dimensions of human development, such as psychosocial, cognitive, moral, and spiritual development
   - leadership skill development, including accessing and critiquing sources of information, ethical reasoning and decision making, oral and written communication skills, critical thinking and problem-solving, cultural competence, goal setting and visioning, motivation, creativity, and risk-taking

   c) Interpersonal development should include:
   - movement from dependent or independent to interdependent relationships
   - development of self-efficacy for leadership

   - recognition of the influences on leadership of multiple aspects of identity, such as race, gender identity and expression, sexual orientation, class, disability, nationality, religion, and ethnicity

   d) Development of groups, organizations, and systems should include the following three competencies:

   Group competencies:
   - team building
   - developing trust
   - group roles, group dynamics, and group development
   - group problem-solving, conflict management, and decision-making
   - shared leadership and collaboration

   Organizational competencies:
   - organizational planning, communication, and development
   - organizational culture, values, and principles
   - organizational politics and political systems
   - organizational lifecycles, sustainability, and stewardship
   - methods of assessing and evaluating organizational effectiveness

   Systems competencies:
   - understanding and critiquing of systems and human behavior within systems including functional and dysfunctional practices
   - coalition-building and other methods of systemic change
   - civic and community engagement
   - leadership across diverse organizations, environments, and contexts

2) **SLP must provide multiple delivery formats, strategies, and contexts. SLP must be intentionally designed to meet the developmental needs of participants across diverse contexts. SLP programs must be based on principles of active learning.**

   Examples of delivery formats include retreats, conferences, credit-bearing courses, workshops, internships, panel discussions, case studies, films, lectures, simulations, mentor programs, adventure training, assessment tools, portfolios, and participation in local, regional, and national associations. Consideration should be given to on-line delivery methods.

   SLP should provide strategies that may include training, education, and development. SLP *training* refers to activities designed to improve individual performance within specific roles; *education* consists of activities designed to provide improve the overall leadership knowledge of an individual; and *development* involves activities and environments that encourage growth and increasing complexity.

   SLP should provide strategies that involve programs and services that are *open* to all students, *targeted* to a specific group of students, and aimed at students with *positional* leadership roles.

   SLP should include multiple *contexts* for leadership development, such as diverse academic and career fields, campus organizations and committees, employment and internship settings, community involvement and service-learning, family, international settings, and social and religious organizations.

3) SLP must collaborate with campus and community partners

SLP must involve a diverse range of partners in the planning, delivery, and assessment of programs and services.

This group may include faculty members, students, staff members, group advisors, community members, and on- and off-campus organizations.

SLP should consider collaborating with a broad range of campus departments, community groups, schools, and businesses to increase awareness of leadership programs, fiscal and human resources, and access to additional sources of leadership expertise.

Part 3. LEADERSHIP

Because effective and ethical leadership is essential to the success of all organizations, leaders with organizational authority for Student Leadership Programs (SLP) must:
- articulate a vision and mission for their programs and services
- set goals and objectives based on the needs of the population served and desired student learning and development outcomes
- advocate for their programs and services
- promote campus environments that provide meaningful opportunities for student learning, development, and integration
- identify and find means to address individual, organizational, or environmental conditions that foster or inhibit mission achievement
- advocate for representation in strategic planning initiatives at appropriate divisional and institutional levels
- initiate collaborative interactions with stakeholders who have legitimate concerns and interests in the functional area
- apply effective practices to educational and administrative processes
- prescribe and model ethical behavior
- communicate effectively
- manage financial resources, including planning, allocation, monitoring, and analysis
- incorporate sustainability practices in the management and design of programs, services, and facilities
- manage human resource processes including recruitment, selection, development, supervision, performance planning, and evaluation
- empower professional, support, and student staff to accept leadership opportunities
- encourage and support scholarly contribution to the

profession
- be informed about and integrate appropriate technologies into programs and services
- be knowledgeable about federal, state/provincial, and local laws relevant to the programs and services and ensure that staff members understand their responsibilities by receiving appropriate training
- develop and continuously improve programs and services in response to the changing needs of students and other populations served and the evolving institutional priorities
- recognize environmental conditions that may negatively influence the safety of staff and students and propose interventions that mitigate such conditions

An individual or team should be designated with responsibility for the coordination of the leadership program, including allocation and maintenance of resources and creating leadership opportunities.

Part 4. HUMAN RESOURCES

Student Leadership Programs (SLP) must be staffed adequately by individuals qualified to accomplish the mission and goals. Within institutional guidelines, programs and services must establish procedures for staff selection, training, and evaluation; set expectations for supervision; and provide appropriate professional development opportunities to improve the leadership ability, competence, and skills of all employees.

SLP professional staff members must hold an earned graduate or professional degree in a field relevant to the position they hold or must possess an appropriate combination of educational credentials and related work experience.

Professional staff or faculty involved in leadership programs should possess:
- knowledge of the history of and current trends in leadership theories, models, and philosophies
- an understanding of the contextual nature of leadership
- knowledge of organizational development, group dynamics, strategies for change, and principles of community
- knowledge of how social identities and dimensions of diversity influence leadership
- experience in leadership development
- the ability to work with diverse range of students
- the ability to create, implement and evaluate student learning as a result of leadership programs
- the ability to effectively organize learning opportunities that are consistent with students' stages of development
- the ability to use reflection in helping students understand leadership concepts
- the ability to develop and assess student learning outcomes

Degree- or credential-seeking interns must be qualified by enrollment in an appropriate field of study and by relevant experience. These individuals must be trained and supervised adequately by professional staff members holding educational credentials and related work experience appropriate for supervision.

Student employees and volunteers must be carefully selected, trained, supervised, and evaluated. They must be educated on how and when to refer those in need of additional assistance to qualified staff members and have access to a supervisor for assistance in making these judgments. Student employees and volunteers must be provided clear and precise job descriptions, pre-service training based on assessed needs, and continuing staff development.

SLP employees and volunteers must receive specific training on institutional policies and privacy laws regarding their access to student records and other sensitive institutional information (e.g., in the USA, Family Educational Rights and Privacy Act, FERPA, or equivalent privacy laws in other states, provinces, or countries.).

SLP must have technical and support staff members adequate to accomplish their mission. All members of the SLP staff must be technologically proficient and qualified to perform their job functions, be knowledgeable about ethical and legal uses of technology, and have access to training and resources to support the performance of their assigned responsibilities.

All members of the SLP staff must receive training on policies and procedures related to the use of technology to store or access student records and institutional data.

SLP must ensure that staff members are knowledgeable about and trained in emergency procedures, crisis response, and prevention efforts. Prevention efforts must address identification of threatening conduct or behavior of students, faculty members, staff, and others and incorporate a system or procedures for responding, including but not limited to reporting them to the appropriate campus officials.

Salary levels and benefits for all SLP staff members must be commensurate with those for comparable positions within the institution, in similar institutions, and in the relevant geographic area.

SLP must maintain position descriptions for all staff members.

To create a diverse staff, SLP must institute hiring and promotion practices that are fair, inclusive, proactive, and non-discriminatory.

SLP must conduct regular performance planning and evaluation of staff members. Programs and services must provide access to continuing and advanced education and professional development opportunities.

SLP staff serving as leadership educators must be knowledgeable about learning theories and their implications for student development, program design, and assessment.

Program staff should engage in continuous discovery and understanding of student leadership models, research, theories, and definitions through on-going study and professional development activities.

Part 5. ETHICS

Persons involved in the delivery of Student Leadership Programs (SLP) must adhere to the highest principles of ethical behavior. SLP must review relevant professional ethical standards and develop or adopt and implement appropriate statements of ethical practice. SLP must publish these statements and ensure their periodic review by relevant constituencies.

SLP must orient new staff members to relevant ethical standards and statements of ethical practice.

SLP staff members must ensure that privacy and confidentiality are maintained with respect to all communications and records to the extent that such records are protected under the law and appropriate statements of ethical practice. Information contained in students' education records must not be disclosed except as allowed by relevant laws and institutional policies. SLP staff members must disclose to appropriate authorities information judged to be of an emergency nature, especially when the safety of the individual or others is involved, or when otherwise required by institutional policy or relevant law.

SLP staff members must be aware of and comply with the provisions contained in the institution's policies pertaining to human subjects research, student rights and responsibilities, as well as those in other relevant institutional policies addressing ethical practices and confidentiality of research data concerning individuals.

SLP staff members must recognize and avoid personal conflicts of interest or appearance thereof in the performance of their work.

SLP staff members must strive to insure the fair, objective, and impartial treatment of all persons with whom they interact.

When handling institutional funds, SLP staff members must be fiscally responsible and ensure that such funds are managed in accordance with established and responsible accounting procedures and the fiscal policies or processes of the institution.

Promotional and descriptive information must be accurate and free of deception.

SLP staff members must perform their duties within the limits of their training, expertise, and competence. When these limits are exceeded, individuals in need of further assistance must be referred to persons possessing appropriate qualifications.

SLP staff members must use suitable means to confront and otherwise hold accountable other staff members who exhibit unethical behavior.

SLP staff members must be knowledgeable about and practice ethical behavior in the use of technology.

SLP staff members must ensure that facilitators have appropriate training, experience, and credentials. Expertise and certification, where appropriate, are essential in the administration and interpretation of personality, developmental, and leadership assessment instruments.

Part 6. LEGAL RESPONSIBILITIES

Student Leadership Programs (SLP) staff members must be knowledgeable about and responsive to laws and regulations that relate to their respective responsibilities and that may pose legal obligations, limitations, or ramifications for the institution as a whole. As appropriate, SLP staff members must inform users of programs and services, as well as officials, of legal obligations and limitations including constitutional, statutory, regulatory, and case law; mandatory laws and orders emanating from federal, state/provincial, and local governments; and the institution's policies.

SLP must have written policies on all relevant operations, transactions, or tasks that may have legal implications.

SLP staff members must neither participate in nor condone any form of harassment or activity that demeans persons or creates an intimidating, hostile, or offensive campus environment.

SLP staff members must use reasonable and informed practices to limit the liability exposure of the institution and its officers, employees, and agents. SLP staff members must be informed about institutional policies regarding risk management, personal liability, and related insurance coverage options and must be referred to external sources if coverage is not provided by the institution.

The institution must provide access to legal advice for SLP staff members as needed to carry out assigned responsibilities.

The institution must inform SLP staff and students in a timely and systematic fashion about extraordinary or changing legal obligations and potential liabilities.

Permission to use copyrighted materials and instruments must be obtained by purchasing the materials from legally compliant sources, or by seeking alternative permission from the publisher or owner. Written references to copyrighted materials and instruments in writing must include appropriate citation.

Part 7. EQUITY and ACCESS

Student Leadership Programs (SLP) must be provided on a fair, equitable, and non-discriminatory basis in accordance with institutional policies and with all applicable state/provincial and federal statutes and regulations. SLP must maintain an educational and work environment free from discrimination in accordance with law and institutional policy.

Discrimination must be avoided on the basis of age; cultural heritage; disability; ethnicity; gender identity and expression; nationality; political affiliation; race; religious affiliation; sex; sexual orientation; economic, marital, social, or veteran status; and any other bases included in local, state/provincial, or federal laws.

Consistent with the mission and goals, SLP must take action to remedy significant imbalances in student participation and staffing patterns.

SLP must ensure physical and program access for persons with disabilities. SLP must be responsive to the needs of all students and other populations served when establishing hours of operation and developing methods of delivering programs and services.

SLP must recognize the needs of distance learning students by providing appropriate and accessible services and assisting them in identifying and gaining access to other appropriate services in their geographic region.

Part 8. DIVERSITY

Within the context of each institution's unique mission, diversity enriches the community and enhances the collegiate experience for all; therefore, Student Leadership Programs (SLP) must create and nurture environments that are welcoming to and bring together persons of diverse backgrounds.

SLP must promote environments that are characterized by open and continuous communication that deepens understanding of one's own identity, culture, and heritage, as well as that of others. SLP must recognize, honor, educate, and promote respect about commonalties and differences among people within their historical and cultural contexts.

SLP must provide students with the opportunity to:
- recognize the influences of aspects of social identity on personal and organizational leadership
- examine social identities, multiple identities, and other aspects of development and how they influence experiences in different contexts
- develop multicultural awareness, knowledge, and skills

SLP must address the characteristics and needs of a diverse population when establishing and implementing policies and procedures.

Part 9. ORGANIZATION and MANAGEMENT

To promote student learning and development outcomes, Student Leadership Programs (SLP) must be structured purposefully and managed effectively to achieve stated goals. Evidence of appropriate structure must include current and accessible policies and procedures, written performance expectations for all employees, functional workflow graphics or organizational charts, and clearly stated program and service delivery expectations.

SLP must monitor websites used for distributing information to ensure that the sites are current, accurate, appropriately referenced, and accessible.

Evidence of effective management must include use of comprehensive and accurate information for decisions; clear sources and channels of authority; effective communication practices; procedures for decision-making and conflict resolution; responses to changing conditions; systems of accountability and evaluation; and processes for recognition and reward. SLP must align policies and procedures with those of the institution and provide channels within the organization for their regular review.

SLP are organized in a variety of offices and departments in student and academic affairs, and in other administrative areas. An advisory group with representatives from the involved areas and other relevant campus and community partners should be established for the purpose of communication and consultation.

Part 10. CAMPUS and EXTERNAL RELATIONS

Student Leadership Programs (SLP) must reach out to relevant individuals, campus offices, and external agencies to:
- establish, maintain, and promote effective relations
- disseminate information about their own and other related programs and services
- coordinate and collaborate, where appropriate, in offering programs and services to meet the needs of students and promote their achievement of student learning and development outcomes
- seek additional staff and financial resources when appropriate

SLP must have procedures and guidelines consistent with institutional policy for responding to threats, emergencies, and crisis situations. Systems and procedures must be in place to disseminate timely and accurate information to students and other members of the campus community during emergency situations.

SLP must have procedures and guidelines consistent with institutional policy for communicating with the media.

Part 11. FINANCIAL RESOURCES

Student Leadership Programs (SLP) must have adequate funding to accomplish their mission and goals. In establishing funding priorities and making significant changes, a comprehensive analysis, which includes relevant expenditures, external and internal resources, and impact on the campus community, must be conducted.

SLP must demonstrate fiscal responsibility and cost effectiveness consistent with institutional protocols.

Funding for SLP may come from a variety of sources, including institutional funds, grants, student fees, fees for services, individual donors, academic departments, course fees, and government contracts. Where possible, institutional funding should be allocated regularly and consistently for the operation of leadership programs.

Part 12. TECHNOLOGY

Student Leadership Programs (SLP) must have adequate technology to support their mission. The technology and its use must comply with institutional policies and procedures and be evaluated for compliance with relevant federal, state/provincial, and local requirements.

SLP must maintain policies and procedures that address the security and back up of data.

When technology is used to facilitate student learning and development, SLP must select technology that reflects current best pedagogical practices.

Technology, as well as any workstations or computer labs maintained by the SLP for student use, must be accessible and must meet established technology standards for delivery to persons with disabilities.

When SLP provide student access to technology, SLP must provide:
- access to policies that are clear, easy to understand, and available to all students
- access to instruction or training on how to use the technology
- access to information on the legal and ethical implications of misuse as it pertains to intellectual property, harassment, privacy, and social networks

Student violations of technology policies must follow established institutional student disciplinary procedures.

Students who experience negative emotional or psychological consequences from the use of technology must be referred to support services provided by the institution.

Part 13. FACILITIES and EQUIPMENT

Student Leadership Programs (SLP) must have adequate, accessible, suitably located facilities and equipment to support their mission and goals. If acquiring capital equipment as defined by the institution, SLP must take into account expenses related to regular maintenance and life cycle costs. Facilities and equipment must be evaluated regularly, including consideration of sustainability, and be in compliance with relevant federal, state/provincial, and local requirements to provide for access, health, safety, and security.

SLP offices and programming space should be conveniently located on campus and designed to facilitate maximum interaction among students, faculty members, and staff.

SLP staff members must have work space that is well-equipped, adequate in size, and designed to support their work and responsibilities. For conversations requiring privacy, staff members must have access to a private space.

SLP staff members who share work space must have the ability to secure their work adequately.

The design of the facilities must guarantee the security of records and ensure the confidentiality of sensitive information.

The location and layout of the facilities must be sensitive to the special needs of persons with disabilities as well as the needs of constituencies served.

SLP must ensure that staff members are knowledgeable of and trained in safety and emergency procedures for securing and vacating the facilities.

Part 14. ASSESSMENT and EVALUATION

Student Leadership Programs (SLP) must establish systematic plans and processes to meet internal and external accountability expectations with regard to program as well as student learning and development outcomes. SLP must conduct regular assessment and evaluations. Assessments must include qualitative and quantitative methodologies as appropriate, to determine whether and to what degree the stated mission, goals, and student learning and development outcomes are being met. The process must employ sufficient and sound measures to ensure comprehensiveness. Data collected must include responses from students, SLP staff, and other affected constituencies.

SLP must evaluate regularly how well they complement and enhance the institution's stated mission and educational effectiveness.

Results of these evaluations must be used in revising and improving programs and services, identifying needs and interests in shaping directions of program and service design, securing additional resources, and recognizing staff performance.

Assessment efforts should include:
- student needs
- student satisfaction
- student learning outcomes
- overall program evaluation

Assessment efforts should be linked to strategic planning efforts including the articulation of a clear program mission, vision, and values; theoretical orientation; and short- and long-term goals.

General Standards revised in 2008;
SLP content developed/revised in 1996 & 2009

The Role of TRIO and Other Educational Opportunity Programs
CAS Standards Contextual Statement

Students from low-income and first-generation (i.e., neither parent has a baccalaureate degree) backgrounds historically have had limited access to higher education. Realizing that the ideal of American higher education includes opportunities for all students, federal and state legislation has been enacted to mitigate some of the inequities to access. Since the 1960s, a variety of educational opportunity programs have been developed at the state and federal levels to increase access, persistence, and success in higher education for students from disadvantaged backgrounds. And, beginning in the 1990s, foundation, corporate and non-profit groups began funding scholarship and pre-college support programs focused on these populations.

The TRIO Programs are federally funded educational opportunity programs designed to motivate and support students from disadvantaged backgrounds to attend and persist in post-secondary education. TRIO includes five programs working with students who are from low-income families and are first-generation. TRIO programs serve students from middle school through postsecondary. In addition, TRIO's professional development component provides training opportunities TRIO staff.

The TRIO programs are authorized under the U. S. Higher Education Act of 1965, Title IV, Part A, Subpart 2. FEDERAL TRIO PROGRAMS, recently reauthorized by the Higher Education Opportunity Act, August 2008. Programs are administered by the U. S. Department of Education, Office of Postsecondary Education (OPE). TRIO projects are funded through competitive grant applications. In 2008, there were 2,886 TRIO projects hosted by over 1,100 higher education institutions and community agencies and annually serving over 844,889 pre-college and postsecondary students.

The initial TRIO programs included Upward Bound, which emerged from the Economic Opportunity Act of 1964 as part of President Johnson's War on Poverty; Talent Search, created in 1965 as part of the Higher Education Act; and Student Support Services, in 1968. The term "TRIO" referred to these original federal programs. The Higher Education Amendments of 1972 added Educational Opportunity Centers, and the 1986 Amendments authorized the Ronald E. McNair Post-baccalaureate Achievement Program. The Department of Education established the Upward Bound Math/Science Program as a subset to Upward Bound in 1990.

TRIO Program Descriptions

- Educational Opportunity Centers (EOC) provide counseling and information about college admissions and financial aid with the goal of increasing the number of adult participants who enroll in post-secondary education. Services include advising; counseling; provision of information about educational opportunities and financial assistance; help with completing applications for college admissions; testing, and financial aid; coordination with educational institutions and community partnerships; and provision of referrals, tutoring, and mentoring.

- The Ronald E. McNair Post-baccalaureate Achievement program prepares undergraduates to enter doctoral studies. The goal of McNair is to increase graduate degree attainment by students from low-income, first-generation, and designated under-represented groups. Services include faculty mentoring; scholarly activities to prepare students for doctoral study; summer research internships; tutoring; counseling; assistance with securing graduate program admission and financial aid; preparation for GRE exams; and other activities that enhance successful entry to and persistence in doctoral programs.

- The Student Support Services (SSS) program provides academic support for participants, including students with disabilities, to motivate students to complete post-secondary education with the goal of increasing participant college retention and graduation rates, and facilitating two-year college student transition to four year institutions. Activities include basic skills instruction and tutoring; academic, financial, career and personal counseling; assistance with graduate school admission; mentoring; special services for students with limited English proficiency, or are homeless or aged out of foster care systems; cultural activities; and academic accommodations for students with disabilities.

- The Talent Search program identifies, motivates, and assists participants to complete high school and enter and persist in higher education. Talent Search also serves high school dropouts by encouraging them to reenter the educational system. The goal is to increase the number of youth from disadvantaged backgrounds who complete high school and enroll in post-secondary education. Talent Search serves sixth to twelfth grade students with academic, financial, career, and personal counseling; tutoring; information about post-secondary education and college visits; completing college admissions and financial aid applications; preparation for college entrance exams; mentoring; and family involvement activities.

- Upward Bound is an intensive college preparatory project designed to provide high school participants with encouragement and skills to complete high school and earn a post-secondary degree. Upward Bound provides instruction and enrichment activities throughout the calendar year, including summer academic programs at college campuses. Other services include study skills; academic, financial, and personal counseling; tutoring; cultural and social activities; college visits, assistance with college entrance and financial aid applications; and preparation for college entrance exams. The Veterans Upward Bound program serves military veterans who are preparing to enter post-secondary education. The Upward Bound Math Science programs focus on strengthening math and science skills and encouraging students to pursue post-secondary degrees in math and science through intensive summer math and science experiences, computer instruction, and research activities.

Gaining Early Awareness and Readiness for Undergraduate Programs (Gear Up) is also reauthorized through the Higher Education Opportunity Act, 2008, and is administered by the U. S. Department of Education OPE. This discretionary grant program is designed to increase the number of low-income students who are prepared to enter and succeed in postsecondary education. GEAR UP provides six-year grants to states and partnerships for pre-college preparation services to high-poverty middle and high schools. GEAR UP projects serve entire cohorts of students beginning with the seventh grade, following cohorts through high school. GEAR UP funds also provide college scholarships to low-income students. GEAR UP funds both state and partnership grants. In 2008, there were 41 state grants serving 437,320 students and 156 partnership grants serving 301,648 students.

Some states support educational opportunity programs designed to increase access to higher education for lower income, first-generation, and/or underrepresented students. An example is the New Jersey Educational Opportunity Fund created in 1968 "to ensure meaningful access to higher education for those who come from backgrounds of economic and educational disadvantage. The Fund assists low-income New Jersey residents who are capable and motivated but lack adequate preparation for college study." The NJEOF provides supplemental financial aid and campus-based outreach and support services at 28 public and 13 independent New Jersey institutions.

In addition to federal and state educational opportunity programs, numerous foundation, corporate and non-profit organizations fund scholarship and/or pre-college access and preparation programs. Examples of these include the Lumina Foundation, the I Have a Dream Foundation, Daniels Fund Scholars, Gates Millennium Scholars, National College Access Network programs such as the Ohio College Access Network, Jack Kent Cooke Foundation Scholars, and the Denver Scholarship Foundation, an example of a PromiseNet organization—a place-based community program located across the U.S. and providing the promise of a scholarship and a network of services to increase college access and success among low-income students and contributing to community economic development by providing access to postsecondary education.

The Council for Opportunity in Education is the professional association representing over 8,000 TRIO and Gear Up personnel. COE sponsors professional development activities including national conferences, symposia; workshops and publications; TRIO and access research through the Pell Institute for the Study of Opportunity in Higher Education; advocates for TRIO programs and students; and acts as liaison to the US Department of Education. COE provided leadership with CAS in recognizing a need for, and developing the first set of TRIO and Other EOP Standards and Guidelines in 1999, and promotes their use for TRIO and other EOP programs.

Other professional associations representing educational opportunity programs include the National College Access Network and the Educational Opportunity Fund Association of New Jersey.

References, Readings, and Resources

Council for Opportunity in Education, 1025 Vermont Avenue, N.W. Suite 900, Washington, DC 20005. (202) 347-7430. www.coenet.us

National College Access Network. http://www.collegeaccess.org/

Pathways to College Network. www.pathwaystocollege.net

Pell Institute for the Study of Opportunity in Higher Education. www.pellinstitute.org

U. S. Department of Education Office of Postsecondary Education Gear Up.
http://www.ed.gov/gearup

U. S. Department of Education Office of Postsecondary Education TRIO Programs.
http://www.ed.gov/about/offices/list/ope/trio/index.htmlprograms/gearup/index.html

Wolanin, T. (April, 1997). The history of TRIO: Three decades of success and counting. NCEOA Journal, pp. 2-4.

<u>Contributor:</u>
Andrea Reeve, Colorado State University, COE

TRIO and Other Educational Opportunity Programs
CAS Standards and Guidelines

Part 1. MISSION

The mission of TRIO and Other Educational Opportunity Programs (TOEOP) is to encourage and assist people who are traditionally under-represented in postsecondary education because of income, family educational background, disability, or other relevant federal, state/provincial, or institutional criteria, in the preparation for, entry to, and completion of a postsecondary degree.

- To accomplish this mission, TOEOP must:
- serve as advocates for access to higher education
- address the developmental needs of the individuals served
- provide services to assist individuals in developing and achieving educational goals
- assist individuals in acquiring the necessary skills, knowledge, and attributes to enter and complete a postsecondary education
- provide an environment that recognizes the diversity of backgrounds and learning styles of the individuals served
- develop collaborative relationships with institutions, organizations, schools, parents and families, and communities to promote an environment conducive to the completion of a postsecondary degree

TOEOP must develop, disseminate, implement, and regularly review their mission. Mission statements must be consistent with the mission of the institution and with professional standards. TOEOP in higher education must enhance overall educational experiences by incorporating student learning and development outcomes in their mission.

TOEOP mission statements must be consistent with the mission and goals of the relevant federal, state/provincial, or other external grant or funding agency.

Part 2. PROGRAM

The formal education of students, consisting of the curriculum and the co-curriculum, must promote student learning and development outcomes that are purposeful and holistic and that prepare students for satisfying and productive lifestyles, work, and civic participation. The student learning and development outcome domains and their related dimensions are:

- knowledge acquisition, integration, construction, and application
  - o Dimensions: understanding knowledge from a range of disciplines; connecting knowledge to other knowledge, ideas, and experiences; constructing knowledge; and relating knowledge to daily life

- cognitive complexity
  - o Dimensions: critical thinking; reflective thinking; effective reasoning; and creativity

- intrapersonal development
  - o Dimensions: realistic self-appraisal, self-understanding, and self-respect; identity development; commitment to ethics and integrity; and spiritual awareness

- interpersonal competence
  - o Dimensions: meaningful relationships; interdependence; collaboration; and effective leadership

- humanitarianism and civic engagement
  - o Dimensions: understanding and appreciation of cultural and human differences; social responsibility; global perspective; and sense of civic responsibility

- practical competence
  - o Dimensions: pursuing goals; communicating effectively; technical competence; managing personal affairs; managing career development; demonstrating professionalism; maintaining health and wellness; and living a purposeful and satisfying life

[See The Council for the Advancement of Standards Learning and Developmental Outcomes statement for examples of outcomes related to these domains and dimensions.]

Consistent with the institutional mission, TRIO and Other Educational Opportunity Programs (TOEOP) must identify relevant and desirable student learning and development outcomes from among the six domains and related dimensions. When creating opportunities for student learning and development, TOEOP must explore possibilities for collaboration with faculty members and other colleagues.

TOEOP must assess relevant and desirable student learning and development outcomes and provide evidence of their impact on student learning and development. TOEOP must articulate how they contribute to or support student learning and development in the domains not specifically assessed.

TOEOP should write student learning and development outcomes in at least two student learning and development outcome domains specific to their programs.

TOEOP must provide activities that support the matriculation, achievement, persistence, success, and graduation of their students, as relevant to the mission of their specific program.

TOEOP must be:
- integrated into the life of the institution
- intentional and coherent
- guided by theories and knowledge of learning and development

- reflective of developmental and demographic profiles of the student population
- responsive to needs of individuals, diverse and special populations, and relevant constituencies

TOEOP must address their specific learning objectives and the allowable activities of each program.

Programs, services, and activities for students involved in specific TOEOP should be relevant to the demographic profile of individuals served. Programs, services, and activities should provide or ensure access to academic support services such as academic instruction; tutoring; English as a Second Language (ESL) activities; collaborative learning opportunities; Supplemental Instruction; development of oral and written communication skills; assessment of academic needs, skills, and individual plans to provide appropriate interventions; monitoring of academic progress; preparation for proficiency and entrance exams; academic advising; opportunities for national and international study exchange; research internships; and opportunities to present and publish program reports or research.

TOEOP should implement unique programming as well as utilize and coordinate with programming at their institutions, agencies, schools, or communities.

Part 3. LEADERSHIP

Because effective and ethical leadership is essential to the success of all organizations, TRIO and Other Educational Opportunity Program (TOEOP) leaders with organizational authority for the programs and services must:
- articulate a vision and mission for their programs and services
- set goals and objectives based on the needs of the population served and desired student learning and development outcomes
- advocate for their programs and services
- promote campus environments that provide meaningful opportunities for student learning, development, and integration
- identify and find means to address individual, organizational, or environmental conditions that foster or inhibit mission achievement
- advocate for representation in strategic planning initiatives at appropriate divisional and institutional levels
- initiate collaborative interactions with stakeholders who have legitimate concerns and interests in the functional area
- apply effective practices to educational and administrative processes
- prescribe and model ethical behavior
- communicate effectively
- manage financial resources, including planning, allocation, monitoring, and analysis
- incorporate sustainability practices in the management and design of programs, services, and facilities
- manage human resource processes including recruitment,

selection, development, supervision, performance planning, and evaluation
- empower professional, support, and student staff to accept leadership opportunities
- encourage and support scholarly contribution to the profession
- be informed about and integrate appropriate technologies into programs and services
- be knowledgeable about federal, state/provincial, and local laws relevant to the programs and services and ensure that staff members understand their responsibilities by receiving appropriate training
- develop and continuously improve programs and services in response to the changing needs of students and other populations served and the evolving institutional priorities
- recognize environmental conditions that may negatively influence the safety of staff and students and propose interventions that mitigate such conditions

TOEOP leaders must be knowledgeable about issues, trends, theories, research, and methodologies related to student learning and retention, especially with regard to populations served by their programs.

TOEOP leaders should:
- participate in institutional or organizational planning, policy, procedural, and fiscal decisions that affect program and student goal achievement
- seek opportunities for additional funding, resources, and facilities, as needed
- represent the TOEOP on institutional or organizational committees
- promote community environments, where relevant to the program, services, or activities, that result in multiple opportunities for student learning and development
- collaborate with leaders of other programs to address learning needs and persistence of program participants
- educate others within the institution and community about the characteristics, challenges, and persistence of populations served by their programs

TOEOP leaders must collect, understand, and use data to make program decisions as well as to communicate to constituents about the relevance of the program within the context of the institution's or organization's mission, goals, and objectives.

TOEOP leaders should cultivate relationships with colleagues in their own and related professional disciplines. TOEOP leaders should be involved in research, publication, presentations, consultation, and participation in professional development opportunities.

Part 4. HUMAN RESOURCES

TRIO and Other Educational Opportunity Programs (TOEOP) must be staffed adequately by individuals qualified to accomplish the mission and goals. Within institutional guidelines, TOEOP services must establish procedures for staff selection, training, and evaluation; set expectations for supervision; and provide appropriate professional development opportunities to improve the leadership ability, competence, and skills of all employees.

TOEOP professional staff members must hold an earned graduate or professional degree in a field relevant to the position they hold or must possess an appropriate combination of educational credentials and related work experience.

Degree- or credential-seeking interns must be qualified by enrollment in an appropriate field of study and by relevant experience. These individuals must be trained and supervised adequately by professional staff members holding educational credentials and related work experience appropriate for supervision.

Student employees and volunteers must be carefully selected, trained, supervised, and evaluated. They must be educated on how and when to refer those in need of additional assistance to qualified staff members and have access to a supervisor for assistance in making these judgments. Student employees and volunteers must be provided clear and precise job descriptions, pre-service training based on assessed needs, and continuing staff development.

TOEOP should hire student employees and volunteers from groups traditionally under-represented in higher education.

Employees and volunteers must receive specific training on institutional policies and privacy laws regarding their access to student records and other sensitive institutional information (e.g., in the USA, Family Educational Rights and Privacy Act, FERPA, or equivalent privacy laws in other states/provinces or countries).

TOEOP must have technical and support staff members adequate to accomplish their mission. All members of the staff must be technologically proficient and qualified to perform their job functions, be knowledgeable about ethical and legal uses of technology, and have access to training and resources to support the performance of their assigned responsibilities.

All members of the staff must receive training on policies and procedures related to the use of technology to store or access student records and institutional data.

TOEOP must ensure that staff members are knowledgeable about and trained in emergency procedures, crisis response, and prevention efforts. Prevention efforts must address identification of threatening conduct or behavior of students, faculty members, staff, and others and must incorporate a system or procedures for responding, including but not limited to reporting them to the appropriate campus officials.

Salary levels and benefits for all staff members must be commensurate with those for comparable positions within the institution, in similar institutions, and in the relevant geographic area.

TOEOP must maintain position descriptions for all staff members.

To create a diverse staff, TOEOP must institute hiring and promotion practices that are fair, inclusive, proactive, and non-discriminatory.

Hiring and promotion practices must ensure diverse staffing profiles.

The size, scope, and role of the program staff depend on the mission of TOEOP and the populations served. Staffing should be based on the needs of the students or participants and the resources available. TOEOP should employ a diverse staff to provide readily identifiable role models for students and to enrich the learning community. When possible, the staff should reflect the characteristics of the population being served.

TOEOP must conduct regular performance planning and evaluation of staff members. TOEOP must provide access to continuing and advanced education and professional development opportunities.

TOEOP professionals must possess a combination of knowledge and experience applicable to their work with individuals who are traditionally under-represented in postsecondary education.

TOEOP professional staff members should possess:
- effective oral and written communication skills
- an understanding of the culture, heritage, social context (e.g., socioeconomic standing, rural vs. urban) and learning styles of the persons served by the program
- leadership, management, organizational, and human relations skills
- ability to work effectively with individuals of diverse backgrounds and ages
- openness to new ideas coupled with flexibility and willingness to change

TOEOP should provide continuing professional development opportunities for staff such as in-service training programs, TRIO professional training seminars, participation in professional conferences, workshops, mentoring, job shadowing, or other continuing education activities.

TOEOP staff should contribute to the knowledge and practice of the profession through presentations, research, or publications.

Part 5. ETHICS

Persons involved in the delivery of TRIO and Other Educational Opportunity Programs (TOEOP) must adhere to the highest principles of ethical behavior. TOEOP must review relevant professional ethical standards and develop or adopt and implement appropriate statements of ethical practice. TOEOP must publish these statements and ensure their periodic review by relevant constituencies.

TOEOP must orient new staff members to relevant ethical standards and statements of ethical practice.

TOEOP staff members must ensure that privacy and confidentiality are maintained with respect to all communications and records to the extent that such records are protected under the law and appropriate statements of ethical practice. Information contained in students' education records must not be disclosed except as allowed by relevant laws and institutional policies. TOEOP staff members must disclose to appropriate authorities information judged to be of an emergency nature, especially when the safety of the individual or others is involved, or when otherwise required by institutional policy or relevant law.

TOEOP staff members must be aware of and comply with the provisions contained in the institution's policies pertaining to human subjects research and student rights and responsibilities, as well as those in other relevant institutional policies addressing ethical practices and confidentiality of research data concerning individuals.

TOEOP staff members must recognize and avoid personal conflicts of interest or appearance thereof in the performance of their work.

TOEOP staff members must strive to insure the fair, objective, and impartial treatment of all persons with whom they interact.

When handling institutional funds, TOEOP staff members must ensure that such funds are managed in accordance with established and responsible accounting procedures and the fiscal policies or processes of the institution.

Promotional and descriptive information must be accurate and free of deception.

TOEOP staff members must perform their duties within the limits of their training, expertise, and competence. When these limits are exceeded, individuals in need of further assistance must be referred to persons possessing appropriate qualifications.

TOEOP staff members must use suitable means to confront and otherwise hold accountable other staff members who exhibit unethical behavior.

TOEOP staff members must be knowledgeable about and practice ethical behavior in the use of technology.

Part 6. LEGAL RESPONSIBILITIES

TRIO and Other Educational Opportunity Program (TOEOP) staff members must be knowledgeable about and responsive to laws and regulations that relate to their respective responsibilities and that may pose legal obligations, limitations, or ramifications for the institution as a whole. As appropriate, staff members must inform users of programs and services, as well as officials, of legal obligations and limitations including constitutional, statutory, regulatory,

and case law; mandatory laws and orders emanating from federal, state/provincial, and local governments; and the institution's policies.

TOEOP sponsored by community-based agencies or organizations must also adhere to their comparable standards.

TOEOP must have written policies on all relevant operations, transactions, or tasks that may have legal implications.

TOEOP staff members must neither participate in nor condone any form of harassment or activity that demeans persons or creates an intimidating, hostile, or offensive campus environment.

TOEOP staff members must use reasonable and informed practices to limit the liability exposure of the institution and its officers, employees, and agents. TOEOP staff members must be informed about institutional policies regarding risk management, personal liability, and related insurance coverage options and must be referred to external sources if coverage is not provided by the institution.

The institution must provide access to legal advice for TOEOP staff members as needed to carry out assigned responsibilities.

The institution must inform TOEOP staff and students in a timely and systematic fashion about extraordinary or changing legal obligations and potential liabilities.

Part 7. EQUITY and ACCESS

TRIO and Other Educational Opportunity Programs (TOEOP) must be provided on a fair, equitable, and non-discriminatory basis in accordance with institutional policies and with all applicable state/provincial and federal statutes and regulations. TOEOP must maintain an educational and work environment free from discrimination in accordance with law and institutional policy.

TOEOP must adhere to eligibility criteria set by funding sources.

Discrimination must be avoided on the basis of age; cultural heritage; disability; ethnicity; gender identity and expression; nationality; political affiliation; race; religious affiliation; sex; sexual orientation; economic, marital, social, or veteran status; and any other bases included in local, state/provincial, or federal laws.

Consistent with the mission and goals, TOEOP must take action to remedy significant imbalances in student participation and staffing patterns.

TOEOP must ensure physical and program access for persons with disabilities. TOEOP must be responsive to the needs of all students and other populations served when establishing hours of operation and developing methods of delivering programs and services.

TOEOP must recognize the needs of distance learning students by providing appropriate and accessible services and assisting them in identifying and gaining access to other appropriate services in their geographic region.

Part 8. DIVERSITY

Within the context of each institution's unique mission, diversity enriches the community and enhances the collegiate experience for all; therefore, TRIO and Other Educational Opportunity Programs (TOEOP) must create and nurture environments that are welcoming to and bring together persons of diverse backgrounds.

TOEOP must promote environments that are characterized by open and continuous communication that deepens understanding of one's own identity, culture, and heritage, as well as that of others. TOEO must recognize, honor, educate, and promote respect about commonalties and differences among people within their historical and cultural contexts.

TOEOP must address the characteristics and needs of a diverse population when establishing and implementing policies and procedures.

Part 9. ORGANIZATION and MANAGEMENT

To promote student learning and development outcomes, TRIO and Other Educational Opportunity Programs (TOEOP) must be structured purposefully and managed effectively to achieve stated goals. Evidence of appropriate structure must include current and accessible policies and procedures, written performance expectations for all employees, functional workflow graphics or organizational charts, and clearly stated program and service delivery expectations.

TOEOP must monitor websites used for distributing information to ensure that the sites are current, accurate, appropriately referenced, and accessible.

Evidence of effective management must include use of comprehensive and accurate information for decisions; clear sources and channels of authority; effective communication practices; procedures for decision-making and conflict resolution; responses to changing conditions; systems of accountability and evaluation; and processes for recognition and reward. TOEOP must align policies and procedures with those of the institution and provide channels within the organization for their regular review.

TOEOP must be placed in the institution's organizational structure to ensure visibility, promote cooperative interaction with appropriate campus or community entities, and enlist the support of senior administrators.

Part 10. CAMPUS and EXTERNAL RELATIONS

TRIO and Other Educational Opportunity Programs (TOEOP) must reach out to relevant individuals, campus offices, and external agencies to:

- establish, maintain, and promote effective relations
- disseminate information about their own and other related programs and services
- coordinate and collaborate, where appropriate, in offering programs and services to meet the needs of students and promote their achievement of student learning and development outcomes

TOEOP must seek collaborative relations with program area schools, community organizations, government agencies, and students' families.

TOEOP must have procedures and guidelines consistent with institutional policy for responding to threats, emergencies, and crisis situations. Systems and procedures must be in place to disseminate timely and accurate information to students and other members of the campus community during emergency situations.

TOEOP must have procedures and guidelines consistent with institutional policy for communicating with the media.

TOEOP must include a public relations component to regularly inform the institution, communities, agencies, and schools about their missions, services, and outcomes.

Part 11. FINANCIAL RESOURCES

TRIO and Other Educational Opportunity Programs (TOEOP) must have adequate funding to accomplish their mission and goals. In establishing funding priorities and making significant changes, a comprehensive analysis, which includes relevant expenditures, external and internal resources, and impact on the campus community, must be conducted.

TOEOP must know and adhere to state/provincial, federal, or agency fiscal regulations governing their funding.

TOEOP must demonstrate fiscal responsibility and cost effectiveness consistent with institutional protocols.

Opportunities for additional funding should be pursued; however, these sources should not be expected to supplant current funding.

TOEOP should negotiate with their institutions to provide additional funding to support areas underfunded by their grants.

Part 12. TECHNOLOGY

TRIO and Other Educational Opportunity Programs (TOEOP) must have adequate technology to support their mission. The technology and its use must comply with institutional policies and procedures and be evaluated for compliance with relevant federal, state/provincial, and local requirements.

TOEOP must maintain policies and procedures that address the security and back up of data.

When technology is used to facilitate student learning and development, TOEOP must select technology that reflects current best pedagogical practices.

Technology, as well as any workstations or computer labs maintained by the TOEOP for student use, must be accessible and must meet established technology standards for delivery to persons with disabilities.

When TOEOP provide student access to technology, they must provide:

- access to policies that are clear, easy to understand, and available to all students
- access to instruction or training on how to use the technology
- access to information on the legal and ethical implications of misuse as it pertains to intellectual property, harassment, privacy, and social networks

TOEOP must promote alternate access to information in formats accessible for participants and their families, especially when technology is not available to them.

TOEOP should advocate for and facilitate access to technology for program participants and their families. Technology should be employed to promote TOEOP, to provide academic and other student services, to assist participants with career exploration and the processes related to postsecondary transitions (e.g., admissions, financial aid, course registration, housing), and to communicate with students including those at outreach locations. Programs should intentionally model for their students the use of technology.

Student violations of technology policies must follow established institutional student disciplinary procedures.

Students who experience negative emotional or psychological consequences from the use of technology must be referred to support services provided by the institution.

Part 13. FACILITIES and EQUIPMENT

TRIO and Other Educational Opportunity Programs (TOEOP) must have adequate, accessible, suitably located facilities and equipment to support their mission and goals. If acquiring capital equipment as defined by the institution, TOEOP must take into account expenses related to regular maintenance and life cycle costs. Facilities and equipment must be evaluated regularly, including consideration of sustainability, and be in compliance with relevant federal, state/provincial, and local requirements to provide for access, health, safety, and security.

TOEOP facilities must be physically located to promote visibility of the programs and to ensure coordination with other campus or organizational programs and services.

TOEOP staff members must have work space that is well-equipped, adequate in size, and designed to support their work and responsibilities. For conversations requiring privacy, staff members must have access to a private space.

TOEOP staff members who share work space must have the ability to secure their work adequately.

The design of the facilities must guarantee the security of records and ensure the confidentiality of sensitive information.

The location and layout of the facilities must be sensitive to the special needs of persons with disabilities as well as the needs of constituencies served.

TOEOP must ensure that staff members are knowledgeable of and trained in safety and emergency procedures for securing and vacating the facilities.

Part 14. ASSESSMENT and EVALUATION

TRIO and Other Educational Opportunity Programs (TOEOP) must establish systematic plans and processes to meet internal and external accountability expectations with regard to program as well as student learning and development outcomes. TOEOP must conduct regular assessment and evaluations. Assessments must include qualitative and quantitative methodologies as appropriate, to determine whether and to what degree the stated mission, goals, and student learning and development outcomes are being met. The process must employ sufficient and sound measures to ensure comprehensiveness. Data collected must include responses from students and other affected constituencies.

Assessments, evaluations, and annual program performance reports must be conducted in accordance with conditions required by applicable sponsoring agreements.

TOEOP must evaluate regularly how well they complement and enhance the institution's stated mission and educational effectiveness.

Results of these evaluations must be used in revising and improving programs and services, identifying needs and interests in shaping directions of program and service design, and recognizing staff performance.

Assessments, evaluations, or annual evaluation reports should be made available, when appropriate, to the program's various stakeholders, such as relevant campus offices, external agencies, area schools, community organizations, and program advisory committees and boards.

General Standards revised in 2008;
TOEOP content developed/revised in 1999 & 2008

The Role of Undergraduate Research Programs
CAS Standards Contextual Statement

Colleges and universities have long recognized the value of student scholarship as the culminating hallmark of an engaged and successful undergraduate career. Research experiences and creative practice projects–conducted in collaboration with and/or under the mentorship of concerned and dedicated faculty–have the potential to be transformative, moving our undergraduates to deeper understanding of and engagement with the world around them. Undergraduate research and creative practice also provide an important measure of cumulative student learning (AAC&U, 2007).

This position of the Association of American Colleges and Universities crystallizes the value of undergraduate research programs. All too often these activities are loosely connected to the overall academic program and are implemented as boutique opportunities. The CAS undergraduate research program standards are designed to integrate undergraduate research across the institution and implement a vision of undergraduate education that offers students the opportunity to emphasize their identities as learners and scholars.

Although the origins of the undergraduate research concept are not clear, it is likely that credit for this phenomenon of American higher education resides in the undergraduate liberal arts college. In 1958 the U.S. was awakened to deficiencies in science education by the launching of Sputnik by the USSR. In the early 1960s the National Science Foundation created its Undergraduate Research Program to encourage faculty-student science research. Credit needs to be given to two organizations that have been instrumental in promoting undergraduate research.

The Council on Undergraduate Research (CUR), founded in 1978, is a national organization of individual and institutional members representing over 900 colleges and universities. CUR and its affiliated colleges, universities, and individuals share a focus on providing undergraduate research opportunities for faculty and students at predominantly undergraduate institutions. CUR believes that faculty members enhance their teaching and contribution to society by remaining active in research and by involving undergraduates in research. CUR's leadership works with agencies and foundations to enhance research opportunities for faculty and students. CUR provides support for faculty development (www.cur.org).

The National Conferences on Undergraduate Research (NCUR), established in 1987, is dedicated to promoting undergraduate research, scholarship, and creative activity in all fields of study by sponsoring an annual conference for students. Unlike meetings of academic professional organizations, this gathering of young scholars welcomes presenters from all institutions of higher learning and from all corners of the academic curriculum. Through this annual conference, NCUR creates a unique environment for the celebration and promotion of undergraduate student achievement, provides models of exemplary research and scholarship, and helps to improve the state of undergraduate education (www.ncur.org).

The National Collegiate Honors Council (NCHC) has contributed to the undergraduate research movement through its influence on honors programs and colleges. Although there is not a standard requirement for research projects and theses, most programs offer that track for interested students.

There is a rich tradition of highly developed college and university undergraduate research programs, awards and grants, symposia, workshops, research presentations, poster sessions, and journals (print and on-line). Student organizations, particularly honor societies, also offer regional and national conferences that feature oral reports, poster sessions, and awards. Mercyhurst College maintains a directory of undergraduate journals and conferences (www.upd.mercyhurst.edu). About 30 institutions have formed the Undergraduate Research Community for the Human Sciences (URC) that seeks to develop a dynamic and pervasive culture of the human sciences for developing the next generation of scholars (www.kon.org/urc/undergraduate_research.html). All of these initiatives advance undergraduate learning and development.

The undergraduate research standards and guidelines provide a basis for institutional self-assessment and program development. In addition, because a comprehensive assessment of student outcomes has not had a high priority in undergraduate research, the student learning and development outcomes can be instrumental in raising the bar for assessment.

Reference

AAC&U. (2007). The student as scholar: Undergraduate research and creative practice. www.aacu.org.

Contributor:
Dorothy Mitstifer, ACHS

Undergraduate Research Programs
CAS Standards and Guidelines

Part 1. MISSION

The primary mission of Undergraduate Research Programs (URP) is to engage students in investigative and creative activity to experience firsthand the processes of scholarly exploration and discovery. Undergraduate research is an inquiry or investigation conducted by an undergraduate student to examine, create, and share new knowledge in the context of disciplinary and interdisciplinary traditions.

URP must develop, disseminate, implement, and regularly review their mission. Mission statements must be consistent with the mission of the institution and with professional standards. URP in higher education must enhance overall educational experiences by incorporating student learning and development outcomes in their mission.

Part 2. PROGRAM

The formal education of students, consisting of the curriculum and the co-curriculum, must promote student learning and development outcomes that are purposeful and holistic and that prepare students for satisfying and productive lifestyles, work, and civic participation. The student learning and development outcome domains and their related dimensions are:

• knowledge acquisition, integration, construction, and application
   o Dimensions: understanding knowledge from a range of disciplines; connecting knowledge to other knowledge, ideas, and experiences; constructing knowledge; and relating knowledge to daily life

• cognitive complexity
   o Dimensions: critical thinking; reflective thinking; effective reasoning; and creativity

• intrapersonal development
   o Dimensions: realistic self-appraisal, self-understanding, and self-respect; identity development; commitment to ethics and integrity; and spiritual awareness

• interpersonal competence
   o Dimensions: meaningful relationships; interdependence; collaboration; and effective leadership

• humanitarianism and civic engagement
   o Dimensions: understanding and appreciation of cultural and human differences; social responsibility; global perspective; and sense of civic responsibility

• practical competence
   o Dimensions: pursuing goals; communicating effectively; technical competence; managing personal affairs; managing career development; demonstrating

professionalism; maintaining health and wellness; and living a purposeful and satisfying life

[See *The Council for the Advancement of Standards Learning and Developmental Outcomes* statement for examples of outcomes related to these domains and dimensions.]

Consistent with the institutional mission, Undergraduate Research Programs (URP) must identify relevant and desirable student learning and development outcomes from among the six domains and related dimensions. When creating opportunities for student learning and development, URP must explore possibilities for collaboration with faculty members and other colleagues.

URP must assess relevant and desirable student learning and development outcomes and provide evidence of their impact on student learning and development. URP must articulate how they contribute to or support students' learning and development in the domains not specifically assessed.

URP must be:
▪ integrated into the life of the institution
▪ intentional and coherent
▪ guided by theories and knowledge of learning and development
▪ reflective of developmental and demographic profiles of the student population
▪ responsive to needs of individuals, diverse and special populations, and relevant constituencies

URP must:
▪ create an active learning environment supportive of scholarship and research
▪ integrate research activities with professional and liberal education
▪ create an infrastructure to recognize and reward research excellence and successful completion of research
▪ create a collegial climate in which to conduct research
▪ allow students to define their interests within the context of the research activity
▪ promote intellectual rigor and student intellectual growth and development
▪ require an appropriate report of the student's completed work
▪ provide opportunities for research dissemination

URP must encourage research that is commensurate with practice in the disciplines and enables students to recognize work that is original, current, and significant.

URP must establish mechanisms for individual or small-group mentoring on a regular basis that is based on the intellectual readiness of students. Mentoring must address research design; appropriate forms of data collection, verification, and analysis; information retrieval; oversight of research on human subjects; and appropriate forms of written and oral scholarly communication.

URP must ensure that students are made aware that disciplines and publications have specific authorship policies and ethical standards and are provided resources to identify those relevant to their research.

URP should provide opportunities for undergraduate students to present their research to peers, faculty members, professionals, and appropriate others and to participate in undergraduate and disciplinary research conferences. These may include institutional, local, regional, national, and international meetings.

URP should offer opportunities for academic credit for research activity where applicable.

URP should offer a range of research experiences appropriate for students at various developmental levels, abilities, and with various life circumstances.

Because a particular research activity may not be appropriate for every student, a range of options should be provided so that all students may find appropriate opportunities. Examples of such opportunities may include first-year experiences, living-learning programs, honors programs, graduation requirements, general education courses, major requirements, capstone courses, and community-based research. These illustrative examples are not mutually exclusive. An undergraduate research activity may involve two or more of these. Activities may be initiated by students, faculty members, programs, or institutions.

Part 3. LEADERSHIP

Because effective and ethical leadership is essential to the success of all organizations, Undergraduate Research Programs (URP) leaders with organizational authority for the programs and services must:

- articulate a vision and mission for their programs and services
- set goals and objectives based on the needs of the population served and desired student learning and development outcomes
- advocate for their programs and services
- promote campus environments that provide meaningful opportunities for student learning, development, and integration
- identify and find means to address individual, organizational, or environmental conditions that foster or inhibit mission achievement
- advocate for representation in strategic planning initiatives at appropriate divisional and institutional levels
- initiate collaborative interactions with stakeholders who have legitimate concerns and interests in the functional area
- apply effective practices to educational and administrative processes
- prescribe and model ethical behavior

- communicate effectively
- manage financial resources, including planning, allocation, monitoring, and analysis
- incorporate sustainability practices in the management and design of programs, services, and facilities
- manage human resource processes including recruitment, selection, development, supervision, performance planning, and evaluation
- empower professional, support, and student staff to accept leadership opportunities
- encourage and support scholarly contribution to the profession
- be informed about and integrate appropriate technologies into programs and services
- be knowledgeable about federal, state/provincial, and local laws relevant to the programs and services and ensure that staff members understand their responsibilities by receiving appropriate training
- develop and continuously improve programs and services in response to the changing needs of students and other populations served and the evolving institutional priorities
- recognize environmental conditions that may negatively influence the safety of staff and students and propose interventions that mitigate such conditions.

URP leaders must promote a research environment that recognizes and respects all aspects of diversity. This includes research topics and the recruitment, access, and full participation of diverse students in research activity.

Part 4. HUMAN RESOURCES

Undergraduate Research Programs (URP) must be staffed adequately by individuals qualified to accomplish the mission and goals. Within institutional guidelines, URP must establish procedures for staff selection, training, and evaluation; set expectations for supervision; and provide appropriate professional development opportunities to improve the leadership ability, competence, and skills of all employees.

URP should offer training for individuals who mentor undergraduate researchers about research policies and procedures, URP goals and opportunities, and the diversity of student learning styles.

URP professional staff members must hold an earned graduate or professional degree in a field relevant to the position they hold or must possess an appropriate combination of educational credentials and related work experience.

The professional development of staff and faculty members engaged in URP should address:
- identification of the compatibility between research activities and student interests
- establishment and maintenance of relationships with academic and other units on campus
- development, implementation, and assessment of learning goals
- preparation, mentoring, and monitoring of students involved in

research experiences
- use of active learning strategies
- education and support of students to apply learning from research experiences to future endeavors

Degree- or credential-seeking interns must be qualified by enrollment in an appropriate field of study and by relevant experience. These individuals must be trained and supervised adequately by professional staff members holding educational credentials and related work experience appropriate for supervision.

Student employees and volunteers must be carefully selected, trained, supervised, and evaluated. They must be educated on how and when to refer those in need of additional assistance to qualified staff members and must have access to a supervisor for assistance in making these judgments. Student employees and volunteers must be provided clear and precise job descriptions, pre-service training based on assessed needs, and continuing staff development.

Employees and volunteers must receive specific training on institutional policies and privacy laws regarding their access to student records and other sensitive institutional information (e.g., in the USA, Family Educational Rights and Privacy Act, FERPA, or equivalent privacy laws in other states/provinces or countries).

URP must have technical and support staff members adequate to accomplish their mission. All members of the staff must be technologically proficient and qualified to perform their job functions, be knowledgeable about ethical and legal uses of technology, and have access to training and resources to support the performance of their assigned responsibilities.

All members of the staff must receive training on policies and procedures related to the use of technology to store or access student records and institutional data.

URP must ensure that staff members are knowledgeable about and trained in emergency procedures, crisis response, and prevention efforts. Prevention efforts must address identification of threatening conduct or behavior of students, faculty members, staff, and others and must incorporate a system or procedures for responding, including but not limited to reporting them to the appropriate campus officials.

Salary levels and benefits for all staff members must be commensurate with those for comparable positions within the institution, in similar institutions, and in the relevant geographic area.

URP must maintain position descriptions for all staff members.

To create a diverse staff, URP must institute hiring and promotion practices that are fair, inclusive, proactive, and non-discriminatory.

URP must conduct regular performance planning and evaluation of staff members. URP must provide access to continuing and advanced education and professional development opportunities.

Part 5. ETHICS

Persons involved in the delivery of Undergraduate Research Programs (URP) must adhere to the highest principles of ethical behavior. URP must review relevant professional ethical standards and develop or adopt and implement appropriate statements of ethical practice. URP must publish these statements and ensure their periodic review by relevant constituencies.

URP must orient new staff members to relevant ethical standards and statements of ethical practice.

URP staff members must ensure that privacy and confidentiality are maintained with respect to all communications and records to the extent that such records are protected under the law and appropriate statements of ethical practice. Information contained in students' education records must not be disclosed except as allowed by relevant laws and institutional policies. URP staff members must disclose to appropriate authorities information judged to be of an emergency nature, especially when the safety of the individual or others is involved, or when otherwise required by institutional policy or relevant law.

URP staff members must be aware of and comply with the provisions contained in the institution's policies pertaining to human subjects research and student rights and responsibilities, as well as those in other relevant institutional policies addressing ethical practices and confidentiality of research data concerning individuals.

These policies and procedures must guard against potential physical and psychological harm to human subjects of research.

URP staff members must recognize and avoid personal conflicts of interest or appearance thereof in the performance of their work.

URP staff members must strive to insure the fair, objective, and impartial treatment of all persons with whom they interact.

When handling institutional funds, URP staff members must ensure that such funds are managed in accordance with established and responsible accounting procedures and the fiscal policies or processes of the institution.

Promotional and descriptive information must be accurate and free of deception.

URP staff members must perform their duties within the limits of their training, expertise, and competence. When these limits are exceeded, individuals in need of further assistance must be referred to persons possessing appropriate qualifications.

URP staff members must use suitable means to confront and otherwise hold accountable other staff members who exhibit unethical behavior.

URP staff members must be knowledgeable about and practice ethical behavior in the use of technology.

URP staff members must acknowledge authorship based on disciplinary guidelines and practices.

Part 6. LEGAL RESPONSIBILITIES

Undergraduate Research Programs (URP) staff members must be knowledgeable about and responsive to laws and regulations that relate to their respective responsibilities and that may pose legal obligations, limitations, or ramifications for the institution as a whole. As appropriate, staff members must inform users of programs and services, as well as officials, of legal obligations and limitations including constitutional, statutory, regulatory, and case law; mandatory laws and orders emanating from federal, state/provincial, and local governments; and the institution's policies.

URP must have written policies on all relevant operations, transactions, or tasks that may have legal implications.

URP staff members must neither participate in nor condone any form of harassment or activity that demeans persons or creates an intimidating, hostile, or offensive campus environment.

URP staff members must use reasonable and informed practices to limit the liability exposure of the institution and its officers, employees, and agents. URP staff members must be informed about institutional policies regarding risk management, personal liability, and related insurance coverage options and must be referred to external sources if coverage is not provided by the institution.

The institution must provide access to legal advice for URP staff members as needed to carry out assigned responsibilities.

The institution must inform URP staff and students in a timely and systematic fashion about extraordinary or changing legal obligations and potential liabilities.

Part 7. EQUITY and ACCESS

Undergraduate Research Programs (URP) must be provided on a fair, equitable, and non-discriminatory basis in accordance with institutional policies and with all applicable state/provincial and federal statutes and regulations. URP must maintain an educational and work environment free from discrimination in accordance with law and institutional policy.

Discrimination must be avoided on the basis of age; cultural heritage; disability; ethnicity; gender identity and expression; nationality; political affiliation; race; religious affiliation; sex; sexual orientation; economic, marital, social, or veteran status; and any other bases included in local, state/provincial, or federal laws.

Consistent with the mission and goals, URP must take action to remedy significant imbalances in student participation and staffing patterns.

URP must ensure physical and program access for persons with disabilities. URP must be responsive to the needs of all students and other populations served when establishing hours of operation and developing methods of delivering programs and services.

URP must recognize the needs of distance learning students by providing appropriate and accessible services and assisting them in identifying and gaining access to other appropriate services in their geographic region.

Part 8. DIVERSITY

Within the context of each institution's unique mission, diversity enriches the community and enhances the collegiate experience for all; therefore, Undergraduate Research Programs (URP) must create and nurture environments that are welcoming to and bring together persons of diverse backgrounds.

URP must promote environments that are characterized by open and continuous communication that deepens understanding of one's own identity, culture, and heritage, as well as that of others. URP must recognize, honor, educate, and promote respect about commonalties and differences among people within their historical and cultural contexts.

URP must address the characteristics and needs of a diverse population when establishing and implementing policies and procedures.

Part 9. ORGANIZATION and MANAGEMENT

To promote student learning and development outcomes, Undergraduate Research Programs (URP) must be structured purposefully and managed effectively to achieve stated goals. Evidence of appropriate structure must include current and accessible policies and procedures, written performance expectations for all employees, functional workflow graphics or organizational charts, and clearly stated program and service delivery expectations.

URP must monitor websites used for distributing information to ensure that the sites are current, accurate, appropriately referenced, and accessible.

Evidence of effective management must include use of comprehensive and accurate information for decisions, clear sources and channels of authority, effective communication practices, procedures for decision-making and conflict resolution, responses to changing conditions, systems of accountability and evaluation, and processes for recognition and reward. URP must align policies and procedures with those of the institution and provide channels within the organization for their regular review.

Part 10. CAMPUS and EXTERNAL RELATIONS

Undergraduate Research Programs (URP) must reach out to relevant individuals, campus offices, and external agencies to:
- establish, maintain, and promote effective relations
- disseminate information about their own and other related programs and services
- coordinate and collaborate, where appropriate, in offering programs and services to meet the needs of students and promote their achievement of student learning and development outcomes

URP must have procedures and guidelines consistent with institutional policy for responding to threats, emergencies, and crisis situations. Systems and procedures must be in place to disseminate timely and accurate information to students and other members of the campus community during emergency situations.

URP must have procedures and guidelines consistent with institutional policy for communicating with the media.

Part 11. FINANCIAL RESOURCES

Undergraduate Research Programs (URP) must have adequate funding to accomplish their mission and goals. In establishing funding priorities and making significant changes, a comprehensive analysis, which includes relevant expenditures, external and internal resources, and impact on the campus community, must be conducted.

URP should seek funding to increase undergraduate research activities that involve a wide range of students and disciplines.

URP must demonstrate fiscal responsibility and cost effectiveness consistent with institutional protocols.

Part 12. TECHNOLOGY

Undergraduate Research Programs (URP) must have adequate technology to support their mission. The technology and its use must comply with institutional policies and procedures and be evaluated for compliance with relevant federal, state/provincial, and local requirements.

URP must maintain policies and procedures that address the security and back up of data.

When technology is used to facilitate student learning and development, URP must select technology that reflects current best pedagogical practices.

Technology, as well as any workstations or computer labs maintained by the URP for student use, must be accessible and must meet established technology standards for delivery to persons with disabilities.

When URP provide student access to technology, they must provide:
- access to policies that are clear, easy to understand, and available to all students
- access to instruction or training on how to use the technology
- access to information on the legal and ethical implications of misuse as it pertains to intellectual property, harassment, privacy, and social networks.

Student violations of technology policies must follow established institutional student disciplinary procedures.

Students who experience negative emotional or psychological consequences from the use of technology must be referred to support services provided by the institution.

Part 13. FACILITIES and EQUIPMENT

Undergraduate Research Programs (URP) must have adequate, accessible, suitably located facilities and equipment to support their mission and goals. If acquiring capital equipment as defined by the institution, URP must take into account expenses related to regular maintenance and life cycle costs. Facilities and equipment must be evaluated regularly, including consideration of sustainability, and be in compliance with relevant federal, state/provincial, and local requirements to provide for access, health, safety, and security.

URP staff members must have work space that is well-equipped, adequate in size, and designed to support their work and responsibilities. For conversations requiring privacy, staff members must have access to a private space.

URP staff members who share work space must have the ability to secure their work adequately.

The design of the facilities must guarantee the security of records and ensure the confidentiality of sensitive information.

The location and layout of the facilities must be sensitive to the special needs of persons with disabilities as well as the needs of constituencies served.

URP must ensure that staff members are knowledgeable of and trained in safety and emergency procedures for securing and vacating the facilities.

Part 14. ASSESSMENT and EVALUATION

Undergraduate Research Programs (URP) must establish systematic plans and processes to meet internal and external accountability expectations with regard to program as well as student learning and development outcomes. URP must conduct regular assessment and evaluations. Assessments must include qualitative and quantitative methodologies as appropriate, to determine whether and to what degree the stated mission, goals, and student learning and development outcomes are being met. The process must employ sufficient and sound measures to ensure comprehensiveness. Data collected must include responses from students and other affected constituencies.

URP must evaluate regularly how well they complement and enhance the institution's stated mission and educational effectiveness.

Results of these evaluations must be used in revising and improving programs and services, identifying needs and interests in shaping directions of program and service design, and recognizing staff performance.

General Standards revised in 2008;
URP content developed in 2007

The Role of Women Student Programs and Services
CAS Standards Contextual Statement

History

Women Student Programs and Services (WSPS) refers to campus offices that support and advance women and seek to redress gender inequity, including women's centers, offices for women, and other units. In 2009, there are over 490 WSPS housed within colleges and universities across the U.S., including at public and private institutions, 2-year and 4-year schools, historically black colleges and universities, tribal institutions, and Hispanic-serving institutions. While the first women's center was established in 1960 at the University of Minnesota, women's centers have been created and dissolved in a fluid way since, reflecting the changing resources, priorities, politics, and needs of institutions.

WSPS were established on campuses as a result of concerns about gender equity raised by students, administrators, faculty, and staff. Informed by the women's and civil rights movements, WSPS were developed to respond to individual and institutional needs to support women in achieving their educational goals, encouraging them to think more broadly about fields of study and leadership positions, and advancing women in higher education. Reporting lines for Women Student Programs and Services differ between institutions, with some WSPS embedded in the missions and services of divisions of student affairs, and others with reporting lines reflecting different institutional organizational structures.

Important Tenets

WSPS have varied missions that express the unique cultures and goals of the institutions within which they reside. Most WSPS include in their mission the need to address equity, including institutional change; education, including equal access, affordability, recruitment, retention, and professional development; support and advocacy; personal safety; and developing community (Davie, 2002; Kunkel, 2002). Some WSPS provide services to students only, while others also provide services to faculty and staff, alumnae, and community members (Davie). For many Women Student Programs and Services, supporting the success of women-identified students involves working with individuals of all gender identities to raise awareness about and contribute to cultural change relating to gender issues more broadly, addressing concerns that affect all members of a campus community and beyond.

The unique experiences of women-identified college and university students require that WSPS — regardless of their reporting structures — engage with every element of campus life, including collaborating with all sectors of student affairs, health and mental health services, residence life and housing services, law enforcement, athletics, academic and co-curricular units, and student organizations. Ultimately, WSPS are dedicated to advancing knowledge of sex and gender roles and equity issues both on campus and in society so that all people can reach their full potential. WSPS are informed by academic disciplines and professions such as gender and women's studies; sexuality studies; African American and critical race studies; cultural and ethnic studies; student affairs and higher education administration; student and public health; social work; and continuing and adult education.

Current Issues

When WSPS were first founded, they tended to focus on questions of access; that is, assisting women in gaining entrance into academic institutions. Given that for the past 40 years the majority of students in higher education have been women (Allen, Dean, & Bracken, 2008), the focus has changed to supporting access for specific subsets of women who remain underrepresented in higher education, fostering the full integration of women students once they are on campus, and continuing to advocate for equity and change in the seemingly intractable area of traditional sex and gender roles. Many WSPS have assumed leadership roles on their campuses, conducting campus climate assessments and advocating for policy change at the institutional level. WSPS prioritize forming collaborations to accelerate institutional changes so that campus climates reflect sensitive and inclusive policies. WSPS demonstrate success in reaching traditionally underserved and underrepresented populations, including students of color, LGBTQ students, students with disabilities, immigrant students, and international students.

WSPS operate in the context of historical roots in social justice, community activism, and social change efforts, as well as student development theory and administrative leadership practice. Acknowledging the immense potential of higher education to improve the lives of people of all gender identities, WSPS translate the richness of feminist and womanist community organization- and movement-based work to college and university settings, demonstrating the relevance of women to all aspects of higher education. Through support, advocacy, and education, WSPS address sexual assault, sexual harassment, gender discrimination, sexism, and other barriers to student academic achievement that disproportionally impact women student success. With a commitment to the continuous examination of power, privilege, and the intersection of gender with other forms of difference, WSPS seek to support and advocate for the positive educational experiences of all members of college and university communities while simultaneously maintaining a specific focus on gender and women. With increasingly limited resources, WSPS, like other functional areas, are creatively responding to increased demand for services through collaboration and the use of technology. In light of women comprising the majority of students enrolled in colleges and universities in the U.S., obtaining and sustaining funding and resources sufficient to fully actualize the missions of Women Student Programs and Services remains one of the most significant challenges facing WSPS.

These standards have been updated over time to reflect the changing focus and missions of women's centers and WSPS offices.

References, Readings, and Resources

Allen, J. K., Dean, D. R., & Bracken, S. J. (2008). *Most college students are women: Implications for teaching, learning, and policy.* Sterling, VA: Stylus.

Davie, S. L. (Ed.). (2002). *University and college women's centers: A journey toward equity.* Westport, CT: Greenwood Press.

College and University Professional Association for Human Resources (CUPA-HR)
http://www.cupahr.org/surveys/
CUPA-HR conducts an Annual Administrative Compensation Survey that includes the categories "Director, Women's Center" and "Associate/Assistant Director, Women's Center." Executive summaries of annual survey results can be downloaded for free.

National Council for Research on Women (NCRW)
http://www.ncrw.org/
The National Council for Research on Women is a network of more than 100 leading U.S. research, advocacy, and policy centers with a growing global reach. The Council harnesses the resources of its network to ensure fully informed debate, policies, and practices to build a more inclusive and equitable world for women and girls.

National Women's Studies Association Women's Centers Committee
http://www.nwsa.org/centers/index.php
Women's centers have representation on the NWSA Governing Council as a standing committee. This is more than a symbolic recognition of the important role that women's centers play in feminist education. NWSA recognizes that "women's studies" is broader than what happens in the classroom and that women's centers are the chief co-curricular feminist educators. Campus-based women's centers have a long history of working together with women's studies to transform the curriculum, the campus environment, and society at large. The NWSA Women's Centers Committee (WCC) provides a

forum for women's center directors, staff and others to share information, ideas, challenges, successes and support. The WCC sponsors an annual pre-conference as well as sessions during the NWSA annual conference. Current WCC projects include: *Handbook for Women's Centers,* Intersectionality Working Group, Women's Centers Database, and others.

NWSA Women's Centers Resources (must be an NWSA member to access)
http://www.nwsa.org/centers/resources.php

Women in Student Affairs Knowledge Community (WISA), National Association of Student Personnel Administrators (NASPA).
http://www.naspa.org/kc/wisa/default.cfm
The purpose of the WISA Knowledge Community is to give voice to the needs of women in student affairs and to provide professional development opportunities through both regional and national activities designed to address gender equity and prompt personal growth. WISA initiatives work to center the experiences of marginalized people and focuses on the intersections of race, class, sexuality, disability and gender identity with gender and sex. WISA provides a home for student affairs professionals who work in women's and gender centers or with gender-related concerns on college campuses, creating networking opportunities for those professionals.

WRAC-L: The Women's Resource and Action Centers List
http://www.dartmouth.edu/~cwg/wracl.html
WRAC-L is a forum for discussion about and sharing of resources regarding issues of significance to women's centers. The list is open to the staff and affiliates of women's centers, whether community-based or associated with schools, colleges or universities.

Scholarly Literature

Bengiveno, T.A. (1996). Campus based women's centers: An analysis of the development and survival of a student-run center in the struggle for gender equity in higher education (Ph.D. dissertation, University of Hawai'i, 1996). Retrieved November 6, 2007, from ProQuest Digital Dissertations database. (Publication No. AAT 9700507).

Bertelson, J. (1975). *Women's centers: Where are they?* Washington, D.C.: Project on the Status and Education of Women.

Girard, K.L., Sorce, P.A., & Sweeney, J.L. (1980, January 1). *Increasing the effectiveness of women's programs on college campuses: A summary of the activities and accomplishments of the National Women's Centers Training Project.* (ERIC Document Reproduction Service No. ED235721). Retrieved November 18, 2007, from ERIC database.

Gould, J. S. (1989). *Women's centers as agents of change.* In C. S. Pearson, D. L. Shavlik, & J. G. Touchton (Eds.), Educating the majority: Women challenge tradition in higher education. New York: American Council on Education & Macmillan.

Kasper, B. (2004b). Campus-based women's centers: A review of problems and practices. *Affilia, 19*(2), 185-198.

Keller, M. J., & Rogers, J. L. (1983). The awareness, impressions, and use of a campus women's center by traditional and nontraditional women students. *Journal of College Student Personnel, 24,* 550-556.

Kunkel, C.A. (1994) Women's needs on campus: How universities meet them. *Initiatives, 56,* 15-28.

National Association of Women Deans, Administrators, and Counselors (NAWDAC) (1988, Summer) (Eds.). *Initiatives* (Vol. 51) [Special issue: Women's centers]. Washington, D.C.: Author.

National Women's Studies Association (2005, Fall). Women's Centers at Work. *NWSAction, 17*(1).

Parker, J., & Freedman, J. (1999). Women's centers/women's studies programs: Collaborating for feminist activism. *Women's Studies Quarterly, 27,* 114-121.

Phillips, C.W. (1978). A national needs analysis of campus-based women's centers: Implications for higher education. Retrieved November 6, 2007, from ProQuest Digital Dissertations database. (Publication No. AAT 7818039).

Stineman F.C. (1984). Women's centers in public higher education: Evolving structure and function (retention, comparable worth, managerial style, feminism). Retrieved November 6, 2007, from ProQuest Digital Dissertations database. (Publication No. AAT 8511085).

Zaytoun Byrne, K. (2000). The role of campus-based women's centers. *Feminist Teacher, 13*(1), 48-60.

Contributors:

Current Edition:
Chimi Boyd, North Carolina Central University
Janine Cavicchia, Western Illinois University
Peg Lonnquist, University of Minnesota
Rebecca Morrow, Idaho State University
Claire Robbins, University of Maryland, NWSA
Cathy Seasholes, University of Wisconsin - Milwaukee
Jennifer Wies, Xavier University

Previous Editions:
Brenda Bethman, Texas A&M University
Ellen Plummer, Virginia Tech
Beth Rietveld, Oregon State University

Women Student Programs and Services
CAS Standards and Guidelines

Part 1. MISSION

The purpose of Women Student Programs and Services (WSPS) is to promote a supportive, equitable, and safe environment for women.

WSPS must develop, disseminate, implement, and regularly review their mission. Mission statements must be consistent with the mission of the institution and with professional standards. WSPS in higher education must enhance overall educational experiences by incorporating student learning and development outcomes in their mission.

The mission is accomplished by:
- empowering students to create a campus culture that values all women and their diverse identities and experiences
- providing, coordinating, or participating in comprehensive sexual violence risk reduction programs and services for survivors of sexual violence
- educating all students on the ways in which gender is constructed and shapes social structures and individual experiences
- assessing the climate for women and advocating for the diverse needs of women
- providing information and referrals about issues that disproportionately affect women, such as sexual harassment, relationship violence, rape, and disordered eating
- sponsoring speakers, performers, events, and activities that address gender issues
- creating opportunities for women's voices to be heard

Part 2. PROGRAM

The formal education of students, consisting of the curriculum and the co-curriculum, must promote student learning and development outcomes that are purposeful and holistic and that prepare students for satisfying and productive lifestyles, work, and civic participation. The student learning and development outcome domains and their related dimensions are:

- knowledge acquisition, integration, construction, and application
  - o Dimensions: understanding knowledge from a range of disciplines; connecting knowledge to other knowledge, ideas, and experiences; constructing knowledge; and relating knowledge to daily life

- cognitive complexity
  - o Dimensions: critical thinking; reflective thinking; effective reasoning; and creativity

- intrapersonal development

  - o Dimensions: realistic self-appraisal, self-understanding, and self-respect; identity development; commitment to ethics and integrity; and spiritual awareness

- interpersonal competence
  - o Dimensions: meaningful relationships; interdependence; collaboration; and effective leadership

- humanitarianism and civic engagement
  - o Dimensions: understanding and appreciation of cultural and human differences; social responsibility; global perspective; and sense of civic responsibility

- practical competence
  - o Dimensions: pursuing goals; communicating effectively; technical competence; managing personal affairs; managing career development; demonstrating professionalism; maintaining health and wellness; and living a purposeful and satisfying life

[See The Council for the Advancement of Standards Learning and Developmental Outcomes statement for examples of outcomes related to these domains and dimensions.]

Consistent with the institutional mission, Women Student Programs and Services (WSPS) must identify relevant and desirable student learning and development outcomes from among the six domains and related dimensions. When creating opportunities for student learning and development, WSPS must explore possibilities for collaboration with faculty members and other colleagues.

WSPS must assess relevant and desirable student learning and development outcomes and provide evidence of their impact on student learning and development. WSPS must articulate how they contribute to or support students' learning and development in the domains not specifically assessed.

WSPS must be:
- integrated into the life of the institution
- intentional and coherent
- guided by theories and knowledge of learning and development
- reflective of developmental and demographic profiles of the student population
- responsive to needs of individuals, diverse and special populations, and relevant constituencies

WSPS staff must address the needs of undergraduate and graduate women students by incorporating the dimensions of ethnicity, race, religion, ability, sexual orientation, age, socioeconomic status, and other aspects of identity through programs and services. WSPS must promote unrestricted access for full involvement of women in all aspects of the collegiate experience.

WSPS must provide programs and services that address institutional environment, social justice, campus support services, networking opportunities, and other educational issues of significance to women.

WSPS may address issues of equity for staff members, faculty members, and women in the surrounding community.

To address the institutional environment, WSPS must:
- advocate for a campus culture that eliminates barriers, prejudice, and bigotry, and creates a hospitable climate for all women
- assess and monitor the campus climate for women in areas of sexual harassment and sexual violence, and collaborate with on- and off-campus partners to create institutional policies, education, and programs to work toward the elimination of violence against women
- advocate for assessment of the campus environment for the presence of gender bias in areas including but not limited to employment, educational opportunities, and classroom climate
- advocate for the elimination of institutional policies and practices that result in an inequitable impact on women as students or employees
- promote awareness in ways in which gender bias intersects with racism, classism, and homophobia
- serve as a resource in helping campus constituencies identify and create equitable practices

WSPS must advance social justice through opportunities for involvement in global, national, state/provincial, and local action initiatives related to improving women's lives.

WSPS should provide models of non-hierarchical and collaborative leadership.

WSPS should provide social activism opportunities that allow for the integration of theory with practice.

WSPS must address the provision of campus support services including:
- advocacy, resources, and referrals related to sexual assault, sexual harassment, cyber-harassment, stalking, and relationship violence
- academic support that addresses concerns such as flexible scheduling, the environment for women students in traditionally male-dominated disciplines, and gender equity in the classroom
- resources and referrals for prevention, counseling, medical services, healthcare, disordered eating, physical and mental health, and equitable access to wellness, fitness, and health services
- resources and referrals for under-represented or under-served communities
- the need for adequate, accessible, affordable, and flexible child and family care

WSPS must facilitate networking opportunities that:
- create support systems and communication networks for women students

- identify role models by recognizing and celebrating the accomplishments of women on and off campus
- encourage liaisons between global, national, state/provincial, and local women's organizations and campus-based women student programs and services

WSPS must provide educational programs that promote awareness of the way in which gender is constructed and shapes social structures and individual experiences. WSPS must offer experiential opportunities that explore oppression, privilege, and racism to increase students' understanding of the intersections of sexism with racism, classism, homophobia, and other forms of oppression.

WSPS should support the promotion of scholarship and research on women and gender in collaboration with a women studies program, if available, as well as with other departments.

Educational programs should focus on women's physical and mental health, personal safety, sexual assault and relationship violence, healthy relationships, leadership, spirituality, current events, and global issues.

WSPS should provide service-learning and internship opportunities.

WSPS should advocate curricular change to include women's issues and contribution to society.

Part 3. LEADERSHIP

Because effective and ethical leadership is essential to the success of all organizations, Women Student Programs and Services (WSPS) leaders with organizational authority for the programs and services must:
- articulate a vision and mission for their programs and services
- set goals and objectives based on the needs of the population served and desired student learning and development outcomes
- advocate for their programs and services
- promote campus environments that provide meaningful opportunities for student learning, development, and integration
- identify and find means to address individual, organizational, or environmental conditions that foster or inhibit mission achievement
- advocate for representation in strategic planning initiatives at appropriate divisional and institutional levels
- initiate collaborative interactions with stakeholders who have legitimate concerns and interests in the functional area
- apply effective practices to educational and administrative processes
- prescribe and model ethical behavior
- communicate effectively
- manage financial resources, including planning, allocation, monitoring, and analysis
- incorporate sustainability practices in the management

and design of programs, services, and facilities
- manage human resource processes including recruitment, selection, development, supervision, performance planning, and evaluation
- empower professional, support, and student staff to accept leadership opportunities
- encourage and support scholarly contribution to the profession
- be informed about and integrate appropriate technologies into programs and services
- be knowledgeable about federal, state/provincial, and local laws relevant to the programs and services and ensure that staff members understand their responsibilities by receiving appropriate training
- develop and continuously improve programs and services in response to the changing needs of students and other populations served and the evolving institutional priorities
- recognize environmental conditions that may negatively influence the safety of staff and students and propose interventions that mitigate such conditions

Part 4. HUMAN RESOURCES

Women Student Programs and Services (WSPS) must be staffed adequately by individuals qualified to accomplish the mission and goals. Within institutional guidelines, WSPS must establish procedures for staff selection, training, and evaluation; set expectations for supervision; and provide appropriate professional development opportunities to improve the leadership ability, competence, and skills of all employees.

WSPS should be staffed by persons with the credentials and ability to forge gender equity on campus to promote the integrity of the unit.

Staff positions must be classified and compensated on a level commensurate with equivalent positions in other units.

WSPS professional staff members must hold an earned graduate or professional degree in a field relevant to the position they hold or must possess an appropriate combination of educational credentials and related work experience.

The leadership must have knowledge of and preferably experience with gender issues and their impact on learning and development.

The professional staff should possess the academic preparation, experience, professional interests, and competencies essential for the efficient operation of the office as charged, as well as the ability to identify additional areas of concern for women. Staff members should have coursework in women's studies or demonstrated experience in advocacy on women's issues. Specific coursework may include organization development, counseling theory and practice, group dynamics, leadership development, human development, and research and evaluation.

Professional staff should demonstrate a commitment to improving women's lives and a respect for the diversity of women's identities and experiences.

Professional staff should: (a) develop and implement programs and services; (b) conduct assessment, research, and evaluation; (c) advocate for the improvement of the quality of life for women as students, faculty members, and staff members; and (d) participate in institutional policy and governance efforts to ensure that policies and practices take into account the unique experiences of women.

Degree- or credential-seeking interns must be qualified by enrollment in an appropriate field of study and by relevant experience. These individuals must be trained and supervised adequately by professional staff members holding educational credentials and related work experience appropriate for supervision.

Student employees and volunteers must be carefully selected, trained, supervised, and evaluated. They must be educated on how and when to refer those in need of additional assistance to qualified staff members and must have access to a supervisor for assistance in making these judgments. Student employees and volunteers must be provided clear and precise job descriptions, pre-service training based on assessed needs, and continuing staff development.

WSPS should provide student staff with training and development that fosters an understanding of gender, race, class, sexual orientation, religion, ability, and other identity formations. Wherever possible, efforts should be made to ensure that student staff reflects the diversity of women students.

Employees and volunteers must receive specific training on institutional policies and privacy laws regarding their access to student records and other sensitive institutional information (e.g., in the USA, Family Educational Rights and Privacy Act, FERPA, or equivalent privacy laws in other states/provinces or countries).

WSPS must have technical and support staff members adequate to accomplish their mission. All members of the staff must be technologically proficient and qualified to perform their job functions, be knowledgeable about ethical and legal uses of technology, and have access to training and resources to support the performance of their assigned responsibilities.

Technical and support staff should be sufficient to perform office and administrative functions, including welcoming, sharing resources, problem identification, and referral. In the selection and training of technical and support staff members, special emphasis should be placed on skills in the areas of crisis response and management, public relations, information dissemination, problem identification, and referral. A thorough knowledge of the institution, its various offices, and relevant community resources is important.

All members of the staff must receive training on policies and procedures related to the use of technology to store or access student records and institutional data.

WSPS must ensure that staff members are knowledgeable about and trained in emergency procedures, crisis response, and prevention efforts. Prevention efforts must address identification of threatening conduct or behavior of students, faculty members, staff, and others and must incorporate a system or procedures for responding, including but not limited to reporting them to the appropriate campus officials.

Salary levels and benefits for all staff members must be commensurate with those for comparable positions within the institution, in similar institutions, and in the relevant geographic area.

WSPS must maintain position descriptions for all staff members.

To create a diverse staff, WSPS must institute hiring and promotion practices that are fair, inclusive, proactive, and non-discriminatory.

WSPS must conduct regular performance planning and evaluation of staff members. WSPS must provide access to continuing and advanced education and professional development opportunities.

To remain current and effective in understanding and addressing needs of women students, staff members should be encouraged to enroll in credit courses and seminars and be given access to published research, opinion, and relevant other media.

Part 5. ETHICS

Persons involved in the delivery of Women Student Programs and Services (WSPS) must adhere to the highest principles of ethical behavior. WSPS must review relevant professional ethical standards and develop or adopt and implement appropriate statements of ethical practice. WSPS must publish these statements and ensure their periodic review by relevant constituencies.

WSPS must orient new staff members to relevant ethical standards and statements of ethical practice.

WSPS staff members must ensure that privacy and confidentiality are maintained with respect to all communications and records to the extent that such records are protected under the law and appropriate statements of ethical practice. Information contained in students' education records must not be disclosed except as allowed by relevant laws and institutional policies. WSPS staff members must disclose to appropriate authorities information judged to be of an emergency nature, especially when the safety of the individual or others is involved, or when otherwise required by institutional policy or relevant law.

WSPS staff members must be aware of and comply with the provisions contained in the institution's policies pertaining to human subjects research and student rights and responsibilities, as well as those in other relevant institutional policies addressing ethical practices and confidentiality of

research data concerning individuals.

WSPS staff members must recognize and avoid personal conflicts of interest or appearance thereof in the performance of their work.

WSPS staff members must strive to insure the fair, objective, and impartial treatment of all persons with whom they interact.

When handling institutional funds, WSPS staff members must ensure that such funds are managed in accordance with established and responsible accounting procedures and the fiscal policies or processes of the institution.

Promotional and descriptive information must be accurate and free of deception.

WSPS staff members must perform their duties within the limits of their training, expertise, and competence. When these limits are exceeded, individuals in need of further assistance must be referred to persons possessing appropriate qualifications.

WSPS staff members must use suitable means to confront and otherwise hold accountable other staff members who exhibit unethical behavior.

WSPS staff members must be knowledgeable about and practice ethical behavior in the use of technology.

Part 6. LEGAL RESPONSIBILITIES

Women Student Programs and Services (WSPS) staff members must be knowledgeable about and responsive to laws and regulations that relate to their respective responsibilities and that may pose legal obligations, limitations, or ramifications for the institution as a whole. As appropriate, staff members must inform users of programs and services, as well as officials, of legal obligations and limitations including constitutional, statutory, regulatory, and case law; mandatory laws and orders emanating from federal, state/provincial, and local governments; and the institution's policies.

WSPS must have written policies on all relevant operations, transactions, or tasks that may have legal implications.

WSPS staff members must neither participate in nor condone any form of harassment or activity that demeans persons or creates an intimidating, hostile, or offensive campus environment.

WSPS staff members must use reasonable and informed practices to limit the liability exposure of the institution and its officers, employees, and agents. Staff members must be informed about institutional policies regarding risk management, personal liability, and related insurance coverage options and must be referred to external sources if coverage is not provided by the institution.

The institution must provide access to legal advice for

WSPS staff members as needed to carry out assigned responsibilities.

The institution must inform WSPS staff and students in a timely and systematic fashion about extraordinary or changing legal obligations and potential liabilities.

WSPS should serve as a resource to individuals and the institution on legal issues, institutional policy, state/provincial and federal laws related to FERPA or Canadian Freedom Of Information and Protection of Privacy (FOIPP), the Clery Act (the Campus Security Act), sexual harassment and discrimination, Title IX, and the rights and responsibilities associated with confidentiality.

Part 7. EQUITY and ACCESS

Women Students Programs and Services (WSPS) must be provided on a fair, equitable, and non-discriminatory basis in accordance with institutional policies and with all applicable state/provincial and federal statutes and regulations. WSPS must maintain an educational and work environment free from discrimination in accordance with law and institutional policy.

Discrimination must be avoided on the basis of age; cultural heritage; disability; ethnicity; gender identity and expression; nationality; political affiliation; race; religious affiliation; sex; sexual orientation; economic, marital, social, or veteran status; and any other bases included in local, state/provincial, or federal laws.

Consistent with the mission and goals, WSPS must take action to remedy significant imbalances in student participation and staffing patterns.

WSPS must ensure physical and program access for persons with disabilities. WSPS must be responsive to the needs of all students and other populations served when establishing hours of operation and developing methods of delivering programs and services.

WSPS must recognize the needs of distance learning students by providing appropriate and accessible services and assisting them in identifying and gaining access to other appropriate services in their geographic region.

Part 8. DIVERSITY

Within the context of each institution's unique mission, diversity enriches the community and enhances the collegiate experience for all; therefore, Women Student Programs and Services (WSPS) must create and nurture environments that are welcoming to and bring together persons of diverse backgrounds.

WSPS must promote environments that are characterized by open and continuous communication that deepens understanding of one's own identity, culture, and heritage, as well as that of others. WSPS must recognize, honor, educate, and promote respect about commonalties and differences among people within their historical and cultural contexts.

WSPS must address the characteristics and needs of a diverse population when establishing and implementing policies and procedures.

WSPS should be intentional about addressing race, ethnicity, class, sex, religion, sexual orientation, ability, and other aspects of identity in WSPS educational programs and services as well as in institutional policies and practices.

Part 9. ORGANIZATION and MANAGEMENT

To promote student learning and development outcomes, Women Student Programs and Services (WSPS) must be structured purposefully and managed effectively to achieve stated goals. Evidence of appropriate structure must include current and accessible policies and procedures, written performance expectations for all employees, functional workflow graphics or organizational charts, and clearly stated program and service delivery expectations.

WSPS must monitor websites used for distributing information to ensure that the sites are current, accurate, appropriately referenced, and accessible.

Evidence of effective management must include use of comprehensive and accurate information for decisions, clear sources and channels of authority, effective communication practices, procedures for decision-making and conflict resolution, responses to changing conditions, systems of accountability and evaluation, and processes for recognition and reward. WSPS must align policies and procedures with those of the institution and provide channels within the organization for their regular review.

In response to the assessed needs of women students, WSPS must play a principal role in creating and implementing institutional policies and programs developed.

In the case of student-run women's programs, student leaders should have access to policy and decision makers of the institution.

Emphasis should be placed on achieving an organizational placement so that activities of WSPS are not limited to a specific group of women students (e.g., solely undergraduate women) or specific service (e.g., solely counseling services).

WSPS should function as an autonomous unit rather than be housed as a component of other units on campus.

Individual units should be afforded the opportunity to organize in a manner that is efficient and best promotes equity.

Part 10. CAMPUS and EXTERNAL RELATIONS

Women Student Programs and Services (WSPS) must reach out to relevant individuals, campus offices, and external agencies to:
- establish, maintain, and promote effective relations
- disseminate information about their own and other

related programs and services

- coordinate and collaborate, where appropriate, in offering programs and services to meet the needs of students and promote their achievement of student learning and development outcomes

WSPS should maintain good working relationships with agencies such as counseling, financial aid, clinical health services, health promotion services, career services, recreational sports, athletics, residential life, multicultural affairs, and public safety. WSPS should maintain a high degree of visibility with academic units through direct promotion and delivery of services, involvement with co-curricular programs, and staff efforts to increase understanding of the needs of women students.

Program staff should be an integral part of appropriate campus networks to participate effectively in the establishment of institution-wide policy and practices and to collaborate effectively with other staff and faculty members in providing services.

WSPS should build effective partnerships with the community to articulate common concerns and share resources.

WSPS must have procedures and guidelines consistent with institutional policy for responding to threats, emergencies, and crisis situations. Systems and procedures must be in place to disseminate timely and accurate information to students and other members of the campus community during emergency situations.

WSPS must have procedures and guidelines consistent with institutional policy for communicating with the media.

Part 11. FINANCIAL RESOURCES

Women Student Programs and Services (WSPS) must have adequate funding to accomplish their mission and goals. In establishing funding priorities and making significant changes, a comprehensive analysis, which includes relevant expenditures, external and internal resources, and impact on the campus community, must be conducted.

WSPS must demonstrate fiscal responsibility and cost effectiveness consistent with institutional protocols.

Although initial funding for WSPS may come from a combination of institutional funds, grant money, student government funds, fees for services, and government contracts, permanent institutional funding should be allocated for the continuing operation of WSPS.

Part 12. TECHNOLOGY

Women Student Programs and Services (WSPS) must have adequate technology to support their mission. The technology and its use must comply with institutional policies and procedures and be evaluated for compliance with relevant federal, state/provincial, and local requirements.

WSPS must maintain policies and procedures that address the security and back up of data.

When technology is used to facilitate student learning and development, WSPS must select technology that reflects current best pedagogical practices.

Technology, as well as any workstations or computer labs maintained by the WSPS for student use, must be accessible and must meet established technology standards for delivery to persons with disabilities.

When WSPS provide student access to technology, they must provide:
- access to policies that are clear, easy to understand, and available to all students
- access to instruction or training on how to use the technology
- access to information on the legal and ethical implications of misuse as it pertains to intellectual property, harassment, privacy, and social networks.

Student violations of technology policies must follow established institutional student disciplinary procedures.

Students who experience negative emotional or psychological consequences from the use of technology must be referred to support services provided by the institution.

Technology and equipment must be updated regularly. In addition, support for technology must be provided to WSPS.

Part 13. FACILITIES and EQUIPMENT

Women Student Programs and Services (WSPS) must have adequate, accessible, suitably located facilities and equipment to support their mission and goals. If acquiring capital equipment as defined by the institution, WSPS must take into account expenses related to regular maintenance and life cycle costs. Facilities and equipment must be evaluated regularly, including consideration of sustainability, and be in compliance with relevant federal, state/provincial, and local requirements to provide for access, health, safety, and security.

WSPS staff members must have work space that is well-equipped, adequate in size, and designed to support their work and responsibilities. For conversations requiring privacy, staff members must have access to a private space.

WSPS staff members who share work space must have the ability to secure their work adequately.

The design of the facilities must guarantee the security of records and ensure the confidentiality of sensitive information.

The location and layout of the facilities must be sensitive to the special needs of persons with disabilities as well as the needs of constituencies served.

Facilities may be located in prominent, visible areas to visually demonstrate the institution's commitment to WSPS. Facilities should include private meeting areas and welcoming communal space. Facilities should be staffed beyond traditional business hours to ensure access for non-traditional students and other community members.

WSPS must ensure that staff members are knowledgeable of and trained in safety and emergency procedures for securing and vacating the facilities.

Part 14. ASSESSMENT and EVALUATION

Women Student Programs and Services (WSPS) must establish systematic plans and processes to meet internal and external accountability expectations with regard to program as well as student learning and development outcomes. WSPS must conduct regular assessment and evaluations. Assessments must include qualitative and quantitative methodologies as appropriate, to determine whether and to what degree the stated mission, goals, and student learning and development outcomes are being met. The process must employ sufficient and sound measures to ensure comprehensiveness. Data collected must include responses from students and other affected constituencies.

A comprehensive evaluation of the on-going program should be carried out in accordance with the general practice of program review for other units of the institution. To assist staff in planning and program formation, WSPS should establish an on-going evaluation process..

WSPS must evaluate regularly how well they complement and enhance the institution's stated mission and educational effectiveness.

Results of these evaluations must be used in revising and improving programs and services, identifying needs and interests in shaping directions of program and service design, and recognizing staff performance.

WSPS should inform constituencies and the institution of the results of assessment and evaluation. WSPS should engage the institution in climate-related research that addresses issues that might have a disparate effect on women.

General Standards revised in 2008;
WSPS content developed/revised in 1992, 1997, & 2005

Appendix A
CAS Member Associations - June 2009

Association	Member Since
ACPA: College Student Educators International (ACPA)	1979
American Association for Employment in Education (AAEE)	1979
American College Counseling Association (ACCA)	1993
American College Health Association (ACHA)	1995
Association for Student Conduct Administration (ASCA, formerly ASJA)	1990
Association of College and University Housing Officers-International (ACUHO-I)	1979
Association of College Honor Societies (ACHS)	2004
Association of College Unions International (ACUI)	1979
Association of Collegiate Conference and Events Directors-International (ACCED-I)	1999
Association of Fraternity/Sorority Advisors (AFA)	1981
Association on Higher Education and Disability (AHEAD)	1981
Canadian Association of College and University Student Services (CACUSS)	1994
College Information and Visitor Services Association (CIVSA)	1998
College Reading and Learning Association (CRLA)	1993
Cooperative Education and Internship Association (CEIA)	2009
Council for Opportunity in Education (COE)	1994
NAFSA: Association of International Educators (NAFSA)	1989
NASPA: Student Affairs Administrators in Higher Education (NASPA)	1979
National Academic Advising Association (NACADA)	1981
National Association for Campus Activities (NACA)	1979
National Association of College Auxiliary Services (NACAS)	1998
National Association of College and University Food Services (NACUFS)	2004
National Association of Colleges and Employers (NACE)	1979
National Association of College Stores (NACS)	2005
National Association of Developmental Educators (NADE)	1992
National Association of Student Affairs Professionals (NASAP)	2004
National Association of Student Financial Aid Administrators (NASFAA)	1991
National Clearinghouse for Commuter Programs (NCCP)	1980
National Clearinghouse for Leadership Programs (NCLP)	2004
National Consortium of Higher Education LGBT Resource Professionals (Consortium)	1999
National Council on Student Development (NCSD)	1979
National Intramural-Recreational Sports Association (NIRSA)	1981
National Orientation Directors Association (NODA)	1979
National Society for Experiential Education (NSEE)	2004
National Women's Studies Association (NWSA)	2006
The Network - Addressing Collegiate Alcohol and Other Drug Issues (The Network)	1999
Southern Association for College Student Affairs (SACSA)	1982

Appendix B
Protocol for Developing New CAS Standards and Guidelines

The CAS Board of Directors will move to create new Standards and Guidelines for functional areas as needed. The standards creation protocol is based on a broad based and inclusive process. It encompasses an internal-external-internal drafting procedure that is outlined below.

1. **Identify** the Functional Area: The CAS Board of Directors identifies and defines the functional area for which a CAS standard is to be written. Functional areas for which standards are developed may be proposed by any professional entity or group of concerned professional practitioners. If other standards created by one or more organizations currently exist outside of CAS, CAS will identify its source and seek its sponsoring agency's cooperation on developing CAS standards and guidelines for that functional area. The CAS Board of Directors must agree by majority vote to sponsor development of a new professional standard.

2. **Charging** a Drafting Committee for New Standards Creation: When the CAS Board determines that a new CAS Functional Area Standard needs to be developed; a Drafting Committee of three to five CAS Directors (or Alternate Directors) will be formed to guide the development process. At least one person on the committee must be or have been especially connected with the functional area about which the standard is to be written. The chair cannot be a representative of a professional association that has significant interest in the standard. The Committee is encouraged to use every available method of electronic communication, including the conference call service, to facilitate the process of soliciting and receiving input and feedback.

3. **Initial Draft**: If a professional association connected with the standard area is a member of CAS, that association is asked to write a rough draft of standards. If that professional association is not a member of CAS, the association would be asked to join provided they meet the membership requirement and/or be included in the drafting of the standards and guidelines. If they decide not to join, CAS will continue to move forward with the draft. This rough draft is forwarded to the Drafting Committee that uses it to create a first draft in the CAS standards and guideline format. The CAS General Standards and any other existing standards will be used as the foundation for any newly developed functional area standard.

4. **Soliciting Internal** Expert Review and Comment: The Drafting Committee then identifies all CAS member associations that have a significant interest in the functional area for which standards are being developed. The first draft will be sent to CAS Directors of identified organizations and asked to provide timely and substantive recommendations of the first draft of proposed standards. One month return time should be allowed for response. The Drafting Committee then creates a second draft based on feedback from CAS Directors. The second draft is posted on the CAS Management site. A minimum of two months should be allowed for the writing of the second draft.

5. **Soliciting External** Expert Review and Comment: Next, the Drafting Committee identifies expert professionals of both CAS member associations and non CAS member associations for their personal review of the second draft. Such experts could include chairs of ACPA commissions (www.acpa.nche.edu) and NASPA Knowledge Communities (www.naspa.org). It is recommended to consider soliciting feedback from practitioners through an on-line professional list, organizational web pages, and the data base of users collected from purchasers of CAS materials. A CAS designee, such as the graduate assistant, may be appointed to assist the drafting committee in contacting experts in the field and in soliciting their feedback. Also, CAS Directors should be consulted for names of those currently filling positions with interest in standards under review. It would be the goal to receive feedback from at least 5 experts from the field within six weeks.

6. **Incorporation** of comments into a second draft document: The Drafting Committee will evaluate all substantive recommendations, provide its own well-considered ideas to the standards development process, and prepare a third draft of the functional area standards and guidelines. This draft should be prepared within 6 months after initiation of the process.

7. **Submission** to the a member of the Executive Committee through the Editor: The proposed revisions to the standards are then forwarded to the CAS Executive Committee for review at least two weeks before their scheduled meeting.

8. **Executive Committee Review and Approval:** The Drafting Committee chairperson and/or functional area expert who participated on the Drafting Committee will present the draft to the Executive Committee in person or by phone conference as needed. The CAS Executive Committee reviews the draft and formulates a penultimate draft for consideration by the CAS Board of Directors. The CAS Executive Committee votes to send the standards and guidelines to the full Board of Directors. This is sent to the Directors no later than 30 days before a board meeting.

9. **Full CAS Board of Directors Review and Approval:** The CAS Board of Directors reviews the document and votes to adopt the standards and guidelines.

10. **Publication:** The newly developed standards, upon adoption by the Board, are then put into the CAS *Self Assessment Guide* format by the Executive Committee for distribution to the profession at large. Upon completion, the Standards and Guidelines will be published in the Book of Standards along with the appropriate contextual statement.

Appendix B – continued
Protocol for Revising Existing CAS Standards and Guidelines

The CAS Board of Directors will systematically review approximately six or more CAS Functional Area Standards and Guidelines per year on a projected five year staggered basis. The standards review protocol is based on a broad based and inclusive process. It encompasses an internal-external-internal drafting procedure that is outlined below. Member associations with interest in the functional area(s) under review will be called upon to help assess the need for revision. Members associations may also request consideration for a revision.

It is up to the CAS Director and sponsoring association to collect literature and documentation during a substantive revision of the existing standards.

1. **Review** Team: When it becomes necessary to consider standards for revision a review team consisting of an executive committee member and an expert from the field will be appointed. This team will study the current standards to determine if a substantial revision is necessary or whether an editorial revision will be adequate. Editorial revisions would include: a) basic word and punctuation corrections, b) altering phrases for purposes of clarity, c) updating required changes in general standards, d) presentation/format changes, and e) non-substantive word changes. The review team will make a recommendation to the executive committee.

   If the executive committee concurs that an editorial revision is sufficient, then the revision committee will consist of those two members. Contacting other experts in the field would not be necessary. The revised standards would subsequently need to be reviewed by the executive committee, and then would be a send for full board approval at a regular meeting or through email. This should take place within three months of initiating the review process.

2. **Charging** a Revision Committee for Substantial Standards Revision: The president will appoint and charge a Revision Committee, when the review team recommends to the Executive Committee that a CAS Functional Area Standard requires substantial revision. The charge will include: the members of the Revision Committee, a copy of this protocol, the anticipated timeline for completion of the process, an electronic copy of the current standard, suggested known experts in the field to include during the comment period and the availability of staff support to assist in the process. The composition of the committee will consist of a chair, to guide the revision process, and at least two other CAS Directors or Alternate Directors. The chair cannot be a representative of a professional association that has significant interest in the standard. However, at least one person on the committee must be connected with the functional area. Members of the revision committee who represent professional associations with significant interest in the standard should play a considerable role in ensuring that the revised standards demonstrate contemporary quality practices. The Committee is encouraged to use every available method of electronic communication, including the conference call service, to facilitate the process of soliciting and receiving input and feedback.

3. **Initial Draft**: The Revision Committee members make an initial revisions of the standards and create a draft revised standard. This should be completed within 2 months after initiating the revision charge.

4. **Soliciting Internal** Expert Review and Comment: The Revision Committee will poll all CAS member associations to establish which associations have a significant interest in the functional area standards are under consideration for revision. A notice of revision should be sent to organizations, while sending draft document to specific individuals. The Chair should also follow up with experts to ensure a timely response. Members of the revision committee who represent professional associations with significant interest in the standards should be charged with identifying such colleagues, for example the Chairs and members of ACPA Commissions (www.acpa.nche.edu) and NASPA Knowledge Communities (www.naspa.org).

5. **Soliciting External** Expert Review and Comment: The Chair of the Revision Committee should contact any professional organization that is not CAS members which might have a significant interest in the standards under revision. It is recommended soliciting feedback from practitioners through an on-line professional list, organizational web pages, and the data base of users collected from purchasers of CAS materials. Also, CAS Directors should be consulted for names of those currently serving positions related to the functional area standards under revision. Review and comment from at least ten external or internal experts from the field is suggested.

6. **Incorporation** of comments into a second draft document: A CAS designee sends the revised first draft to the identified experts. From the feedback of expert practitioners the Revision Committee prepares a second draft of the revised functional area standards and guidelines. This should take place within six months of initiating the revision process.

7. **Submission** to the a member of the Executive Committee through the Editor: The proposed revisions to the standards are then forwarded to the CAS Executive Committee for review at least two weeks before their scheduled meeting.

8. **Executive Committee Review and Approval**: The Drafting Committee chairperson and/or functional area expert who participated on the Drafting Committee will present the draft to the Executive Committee in person or by phone conference as needed. The CAS Executive Committee reviews the draft and formulates a penultimate draft for consideration by the CAS Board of Directors. The CAS Executive Committee votes to send the standards and guidelines to the full Board of Directors. This is sent to the Directors no later than 30 days before a board meeting.

9. **Full CAS Board of Directors Review and Approval**: The CAS Board of Directors reviews the document and votes to adopt the standards and guidelines.

10. **Publication**: The newly revised standards, upon adoption by the Board, are then put into the CAS *Self Assessment Guide* format for distribution to the profession at large. Upon completion, the Standards and Guidelines will be published in the Book of Standards along with the appropriate contextual statement.

Appendix C
Glossary of Terms

accreditation. A voluntary process conducted by peers through non-governmental agencies for purposes of improving educational quality and assuring the public that programs and services meet established standards. In higher education, accreditation is divided into two types - institutional and specialized. Although both are designed to assure fundamental levels of quality, the former focuses on the institution as a whole while the latter focuses on academic pre-professional or specialty professional programs such as law, business, psychology, and education; or services such as counseling centers within the institution. Although the CAS Standards have utility for accreditation self-study, CAS is not an accrediting body.

affirmative action. Policies and/or programs designed to redress historic injustices committed against racial minorities and other specified groups by making special efforts to provide members of these groups with access to educational and employment opportunities. This may apply to students as well as to faculty and staff members. Legality varies by state in the U.S.

best practice. A level of professional conduct or practice identified as being necessary for college and university personnel to exhibit in their daily work for the host program or service to be judged satisfactory, sufficient and of acceptable quality. CAS Standards and Guidelines represent best practice.

CAS. The Council for the Advancement of Standards in Higher Education. A consortium of professional associations concerned with the development and promulgation of professional standards and guidelines for student support programs and services in institutions of higher learning. The CAS Board of Directors is composed of representatives from member associations and meets semiannually in the spring and fall. Prior to 1992, the consortium's name was the Council for the Advancement of Standards for Student Services/Development Programs.

CAS Blue Book. The informal name of the publication entitled *CAS Professional Standards for Higher Education* (previous editions were "*The CAS Book of Professional Standards for Higher Education*") that presents the CAS standards and guidelines. The first iteration of the CAS standards was published in 1986. Revised editions were published in 1997, 1999, 2001, 2003, 2006, and the current 2009 edition. CAS policy calls for an updated revision to be published regularly.

CAS Board of Directors. A body of representatives from professional higher education associations in the U.S. and Canada that have joined the CAS consortium, pay annual dues, and keep their memberships informed about CAS standards and related initiatives. Each member association may designate two official representatives (Director and Alternate) to act on its behalf at CAS Board meetings; each association has one vote on the Council.

CAS consortium. An alliance of professional U.S. and Canadian higher education associations established in 1979 to develop and promulgate professional standards that guide and enhance the quality of student life, learning, and development through support programs and to educate practitioners in this regard.

CAS Executive Committee. A body of elected CAS officers, including president, secretary, treasurer, members at large, and others elected at the discretion of the Board of Directors. This body meets periodically to deal with CAS governance issues and to review penultimate standard statements prior to final review and adoption by the Board of Directors.

CAS Internet URL. http://www.cas.edu The CAS web site at which various CAS initiatives and resources are described, publications may be ordered, and links to CAS member associations are listed.

CAS member association. One of the higher education professional associations that has joined the CAS consortium and is committed to the development and promulgation of professional standards for college student learning and development support services.

CAS preparation program standards. A set of professional standards developed and promulgated for purposes of providing student affairs administration master's level programs with criteria to guide the professional education and preparation of entry-level practitioners in student affairs.

CAS Public Director. An individual appointed to the CAS Board of Directors to represent the public at large. CAS by-laws call for the appointment of public directors who do not represent a specific functional area or professional association.

CAS Standards and Guidelines. Published criteria and related statements designed to provide college and university support service providers with established measures against which to evaluate programs and services. A standard uses the auxiliary verbs "must" and "shall," while a guideline uses the verbs "should" and "may." Standards are essentials, guidelines are not.

certification. Official recognition by a governmental or professional body attesting that an individual practitioner meets established standards or criteria. Criteria usually include formal academic preparation in prescribed content areas and a period of supervised practice, and may also include a systematic evaluation (that is, standardized test) of the practitioner's knowledge.

compliance. Adherence to a standard of practice or preparation. Compliance with the CAS standards implies that an institution or program meets or exceeds the fundamental essential criteria established for a given functional area program and service or for an academic student affairs administration preparation program.

FALDOs. Frameworks for Assessing Learning and Development Outcomes. A companion publication to the CAS Professional Standards for Higher Education, the "FALDOs" are designed to assist practitioners in designing and implementing assessment of outcomes. Based on a set of outcome domains which are reflected in Part 2, Program, of each functional area standard, the FALDOs include a theoretical description of the learning outcome domain (e. g., leadership development, social responsibility, career choices), assessment examples, list of possible instruments, and additional resources. The FALDOs are published in both book and CD format.

functional area standard. A statement that presents criteria describing the fundamental essential expectations of practice agreed upon by the profession at large for a given institutional function. Standards are presented in **bold** type and use auxiliary verbs "**must**" and "**shall**." Currently there are 40 sets of CAS functional area standards (see Table of Contents).

general standards. Statements presenting criteria that represent the most fundamental essential expectations agreed on by the profession at large for all higher education support programs and services. The general standards are contained within every set of functional area standards; they apply to every area. These "boilerplate" criteria are presented in **bold** type and use the auxiliary verbs "**must**" and "**shall**" as do all CAS standards. The most recent revision of the General Standards, including significant revision of the section on learning and development outcomes and addition of a separate section on technology, was adopted in 2008.

guideline. A statement that clarifies or amplifies professional standards. Although not required for acceptable practice, a guideline is designed to provide institutions with suggestions and illustrations that can assist in establishing programs and services that more fully address the needs of students than those mandated by a standard. Guidelines may be thought of as providing guidance in ways to exceed fundamental requirements, to approach excellence, or to function at a more optimal level. CAS Guidelines use the auxiliary verbs "should" and "may."

learning and development outcomes. Change occurring in students as a direct result of their interaction with an educational institution and its programs and services. Part 2 of the CAS standards identifies six learning and development outcome domains that students should accomplish as a result of their higher education experiences. A number of dimensions of the outcome domains are also included to guide assessing the outcomes, as well as a chart providing examples of outcomes statements.

in-service (or inservice) education. Educational skill-building activities provided by an institution to staff members within the context of their work responsibilities. A form of staff development designed to strengthen the ability of practitioners to carry out their duties more effectively.

licensure. Official recognition, usually by a government entity, that authorizes practice in the public arena. A license is usually granted only upon the presentation of compelling evidence that the individual is well qualified to practice in a given profession. Granting of a professional license typically authorizes holders to announce their qualifications to provide selected services to the public and attach professional titles to their names. Insurance companies often require individuals to be licensed to qualify for third-party payments.

paraprofessional. An individual who has received an adequate level of training and supervision to work in support of professional practitioners, their offices, and programs. Paraprofessionals may be students, staff members, or volunteers who have not undertaken formal or graduate level professional preparation or earned credentials to function as a professional practitioner.

personal development. Closely related to student development, this term refers to the processes associated with human maturation, especially those concerned with evolving psychosocial, morale, relational, and self-concept changes that influence an individual's quality of life.

pre-professional. An individual who is in the process of obtaining professional education that will qualify her or him for professional practice (e.g., graduate student, intern).

program. Refers to one of two types: (a) organizational, a departmental level administrative unit or sub-unit; (b) activity, an institutional support service such as an invited lecture, a workshop, a social event, or a series of organized presentations over time (e.g., a "lunch and learn" program).

quality assurance. The *raison d'tre* for the CAS standards and virtually all types of credentialing activities devised to assure the public that educational institutions, programs, and services and those providing them exhibit high levels of competence leading to excellence. Quality assurance initiatives are intended to ensure that those accessing available programs and services will truly benefit from them.

registry. An official record of the names and qualifications of individuals who meet pre-established criteria to function as professional practitioners. The names of professionally licensed and/or certified practitioners are typically listed in a registry. In some instances a professional "register" may be maintained for purposes of providing individuals, institutions, and organizations with the names of those who meet an established level of competence for employment or other activity such as consulting or lecturing. A registry may also be used to identify those judged to possess relevant knowledge or skill outside the context of licensure.

Self-Assessment Guide (SAG). An operational version of the CAS Standards and Guidelines designed to provide users with an assessment tool that can be used for self-study or self-assessment purposes. A SAG is available for each functional area for which a CAS standard exists.

self-study. An internal process by which institutions and programs evaluate their quality and effectiveness in reference to established criteria such as the CAS standards. This process, often used for institutional and specialty accreditation purposes, results in a formal report presenting the findings of the internal evaluation implemented by institutional employees. For accreditation purposes, this report is then validated by a visiting, external committee of peers from comparable institutions or programs. CAS SAGs have great utility for this purpose.

self-regulation. The recommended process by which the CAS Standards and Guidelines can best be used to evaluate and assess institutional support programs and services. This approach calls for institutions and programs to establish, maintain, and enhance the quality of their offerings and environments by using the standards to evaluate themselves. From the CAS perspective, each institution and its programs can and should seek to identify and regulate its own best practices rather than relying on external agencies to do so.

staff development. Refers to the programs, workshops, conferences, and other training related activities offered by institutions, professional associations, and corporate agencies for purposes of increasing effectiveness in accomplishing work responsibilities of staff members.

standard. A statement framed within the context of a professional arena designed to provide practitioners with criteria against which to judge the quality of the programs and services offered. A standard reflects an essential level of practice that, when met, represents quality performance. CAS standards use auxiliary verbs "**must**" and "**shall**" presented in **bold** print.

student development. Refers to those learning outcomes that occur as a result of students being exposed to higher education environments designed to enhance academic, intellectual, psychosocial, psychomotor, moral, and, for some institutions, spiritual development. This concept is based on applying human development theories within the context of higher education. In some instances, the term has also been applied to administrative units (e.g., center for student development).

student learning and development. Refers to the outcomes students realize when exposed to new experiences, concepts, information, and ideas; the knowledge and understanding gleaned from interactions with higher education learning environments. Learning means acquiring knowledge and applying it to life, appreciating human differences, and approaching an integrated sense of self.

Appendix D
FAQ: Frequently Asked Questions about CAS and Its Initiatives

1. Why does CAS write standards?

One criterion for the existence of a profession is the existence of professional standards to guide and judge practice. Without standards there would be few if any criteria established that institutions and their programs and services could use to judge their quality. CAS was established to develop and promulgate the standards necessary to achieve educational excellence.

2. How many CAS Standards and Guidelines are currently in place? Where can I find the list?

As of July 2009, CAS had developed 39 sets of functional area standards and guidelines and one set of student affairs master's level preparation standards. They are listed in the Table of Contents of CAS Professional Standards for Higher Education and on the CAS website at www.cas.edu.

3. Why does CAS call them "functional areas" instead of using a more common term?

The areas for which CAS publishes standards represent functions on campuses; in some cases, these are commonly organized in departments or offices (e.g., housing and residential life, counseling), but in other cases, the function may be distributed across multiple offices or only one part of a department's total scope (e.g., assessment services, internships). The term "functional area" is used as an inclusive term to encompass the wide range of functions on campus.

4. What is the difference between a CAS standard and a CAS guideline?

A CAS standard, which is printed in **BOLD** type, is considered to be essential to successful professional practice and uses the auxiliary verbs "**must**" and "**shall**." Compliance with the CAS standards indicates that a program meets essential criteria as described in each standard statement and that there is tangible evidence available to support that fact. A CAS guideline, printed in light-face type, is a statement that clarifies or amplifies a CAS standard. Although not required for achieving compliance, CAS guidelines are designed to offer suggestions and illustrations that can assist programs and services to more fully address the learning and development needs of students. CAS guidelines use the auxiliary verbs "should" and "may."

5. Are institutions in jeopardy if they fail to meet the CAS Standards and Guidelines?

CAS Standards are provided primarily for institutions to use within the context of a "self-regulation" process. That is, although compliance with the standards evidences "good practice" that is recognized profession-wide, there are no external sanctions for non-compliance. However, institutions that do not meet the CAS standards will likely discover that their programs and services fail to function effectively or to meet the needs of their students. Further, institutions that evidence compliance with the CAS standards are virtually assured of receiving "high grades" from regional or specialized accrediting bodies.

6. What utility do the CAS Standards and Guidelines have for practitioners?

The CAS standards are multi-purpose in nature. They can be used to study and evaluate institutional divisions of student affairs and the various functional student support areas common across institutions. Likewise, they can be used for professional development purposes to ensure that staff members comprehend their roles and functions and develop the level of knowledge and skill essential for good practice. Also, the CAS standards can be used to guide the development of new or enhanced functional areas designed to provide students with additional learning and development opportunities.

7. Where will I find the CAS Standards and Guidelines?

CAS publishes two versions of its standards, one in text format and another in workbook format. *CAS Professional Standards for Higher Education* (2009, sometimes known as the "CAS Blue Book") provides an introduction to CAS, its mission, initiatives, and the principles upon which it was founded. Individual functional area standards accompanied by introductory contextual statements are included, along with the *CAS Learning and Development Outcomes*, the *CAS Characteristics of Individual Excellence*, and the *CAS Statement of Shared Ethical Principles*. In addition, for use in programmatic self-studies, there is a CAS Self-Assessment Guide (SAG) for each set of standards. These assessment workbooks include the standards and guidelines along with a series of "criterion measure" statements used to judge the level of program compliance with the standard. The CAS SAGs are available electronically via the CAS web site and also in CD-ROM format.

8. How can I obtain the CAS publications and what are their costs?

All available CAS publications, along with current costs and payment options, are listed on the CAS internet web site, www.cas.edu; they may also be purchased from the CAS national office, One Dupont Circle, NW, Suite 300, Washington, DC 20036-1188.   Current publications include the *CAS Professional Standards* and the SAGs, and packaged sets are available. The FALDOs are available at press time; however, stock is limited.

9. Where will I find information about using the CAS Standards and Guidelines?

An outline of how to put the CAS standards to work is included in the Blue Book, and each functional area SAG has an introductory section that describes how to apply the SAG for self-study purposes. The SAG CD also contains a PowerPoint presentation and E-learning course to help train users. PowerPoint presentations are also available on the CAS website.

10. Can a partial program self-study using less than a full functional area standard be implemented?

Each CAS standard is organized into 14 parts. These individual program components can be used on stand-alone bases for program self-studies or for program development purposes. That is, a partial self-study using selected components may be desirable for some programs to consider. Likewise, each component has utility for staff development purposes. One recommended training approach is to hold a series of training sessions in which individual parts are examined in detail. It should be understood, however, that a full program assessment cannot be accomplished using less than the complete functional area standard, and a functional area cannot be considered to be in compliance with CAS standards if all the component parts are not evaluated.

11. How long does a typical division or individual program self-study take to complete?

The time required to complete the self-study process varies greatly with size and complexity of institutions and programs. In most instances, it will take from 6 to 9 months to complete a comprehensive division or campus-wide self-study, while a single administrative unit functional area program self-study may well be completed in approximately 3 months. One of the major time-consuming factors of any self-study is the data collection process in which documentary evidence is obtained and organized into a usable format. More time will be required if the documentary evidence has not already been collected and analyzed.

12. Does CAS offer certification or accreditation?

CAS does not function as a certification or accreditation agency. Rather, CAS encourages institutions and their functional area programs to follow a "self-regulation" approach wherein program evaluation self-studies are implemented for internal assessment purposes.

13. Do the CAS Standards have utility for regional or other accreditation purposes?

Institutions undergoing accreditation self-studies will find the CAS standards most useful. Because CAS functional area standards are invariably more comprehensive than regional accreditation criteria, a self-study using the CAS standards will provide ample documentation that can be used as evidence of compliance with accreditation criteria.

14. How does one become a member of CAS?

Because CAS is a consortium of professional organizations, there are no individual memberships available. The CAS Board of Directors is composed of representatives from member organizations, and each member association has one vote on CAS business. Organizational membership information is available from the CAS national office.

15. Does CAS have a presence at national association meetings?

Because CAS is a consortium of professional associations, each member association is responsible for providing its membership with information about the nature and availability of CAS standards. Most member associations include CAS- related presentations at their conventions. Several CAS officers and directors are available upon request to provide CAS workshops or programs sponsored by professional organizations. CAS-oriented programs have been offered at numerous national and international conferences in recent years.

16. Does CAS provide institutional staff training programs and workshops?

The CAS national office can provide information about CAS officers and board members who are well qualified to provide staff development training workshops and programs for institutions, or to consult about use of the CAS materials.

17. How often are CAS functional area standards and guidelines revised?

CAS policy calls for every functional area standard to be reviewed periodically on a 5-year basis for purposes of determining whether a revision is needed. Individuals or organizations who believe a given standard is in need of revision are invited to contact CAS to make such recommendations.

18. My association has already written professional standards. What can CAS provide that we don't already have?

Several professional associations have established standards for their constituent members, some of which are quite comparable to CAS standards. In general, CAS standards are designed to be used in every type and size of higher educational institution and were created for this broad user base. A primary benefit of the CAS standards is the fact that CAS represents a profession-wide effort to develop, promulgate, and encourage use of its professional standards. Consequently, the professional credibility of the CAS Standards and Guidelines tends to exceed those proffered by a single organization. If an institution or division uses the CAS standards to study more than one functional area, use of CAS ensures that the areas to be examined and the criteria will be consistent across areas.

19. How are CAS projects funded?

CAS membership dues have been maintained at a low annual fee since the Council's inception in 1979. Consequently, CAS has come to rely upon sale of professional publications as its primary source of funding. As a non-profit organization, CAS can accept tax-exempt contributions from individuals as well as grants from philanthropic foundations.

20. Who uses the CAS Standards and how are they typically put to use?

This important question has been studied through a comprehensive, CAS sponsored nation-wide research project. Results, including publication citation, are included in Part I of the CAS Blue Book. A bibliography of articles is also available on the website.

21. Why use CAS standards to evaluate my program rather than using another process (e.g., benchmarks)?

The CAS standards were developed and adopted by knowledgeable representatives from a wide range of higher education organizations. They represent a profession-wide perspective about what constitutes good practice.

22. What is the appropriate citation format for referencing the CAS Professional Standards in Higher Education?

APA format citation for the Blue Book (subsections should follow the citation format for chapters in a book): Council for the Advancement of Standards in Higher Education. (2009). *CAS professional standards for higher education* (7th ed.). Washington, DC: Author.

Appendix E
CAS Publications Ordering and Website Information

Current publications include:

CAS Professional Standards for Higher Education (7th ed.), 2009

The 7th edition of CAS Professional Standards includes background information on the CAS approach, functional area contextual statements, functional area standards and guidelines, and related information to assist users in applying the CAS standards. New standards in this edition include Auxiliary Services, Adult Learner Programs, Graduate and Professional Student Programs, Dining Services, and Undergraduate Research Programs. Standards updated since the previous edition include Assessment Services, Campus Activities, International Student Programs, TRIO and Other Educational Opportunity Programs, Registrar Programs and Services, Recreational Sports, Student Leadership Programs, College Unions, and Learning Assistance Programs. Every functional area standard has been updated to reflect the recently revised General Standards, including the newly developed Student Learning and Development Outcomes and a new section addressing technology. The book also includes the *CAS Statement of Shared Ethical Principles* and *CAS Characteristics of Individual Excellence*.

CAS Self-Assessment Guides — interactive CD (version 4.0)

The 2009 release of the Self-Assessment Guides CD contains 39 sets of functional area self-assessment guides, functional area contextual statements, PowerPoint presentation, and E-learning course for conducting assessments.

Frameworks for Assessing Learning and Development Outcomes, 2006 (FALDOS Book/CD)

The FALDOs are complete with a theoretical description of the learning outcome domain, assessment examples, list of possible instruments, and additional resources. Limited availability; domains reflect structure of *CAS Professional Standards* (2006), which has been revised for the current edition. Below is a list of learning domains included:

- Career Choices
- Effective Communication
- Appreciating Diversity
- Personal and Educational Goals
- Healthy Behavior
- Independence
- Intellectual Growth
- Leadership Development

- Satisfying and Productive Lifestyles
- Meaningful Interpersonal Relationships
- Realistic Self-Appraisal
- Enhanced Self-Esteem
- Social Responsibility
- Spiritual Awareness
- Clarified Values
- Leadership Development

Packaged sets, quantity discounts, international shipping, and expedited shipping are available.

All CAS publications are available for purchase via the CAS website, www.cas.edu, or by contacting CAS:

> CAS
> One Dupont Circle, NW
> Suite 300
> Washington, DC 20036-1188
>
> Phone orders: (202) 862-1400; Fax: (202) 296-3286

For additional CAS information:

CAS website — www.cas.edu

Contact Phyllis Mable, Executive Director, PhyllisMable@aol.com; (202) 862-1400